Solidarity Economy

AF795479

Solidarity economy-based alternative spaces result from an interface among structural factors, institutional regimes and forms of collective action that mobilise narratives of change, collective identities and non-capitalist economic practices.

This book analyses how solidarity economy initiatives develop alternative spatialities as counterpower to mainstream economy. Based on case studies in Europe, Latin America, Africa and Asia, it elaborates on how different scales of solidarity economy-based alternative spaces result from an interface among structural factors, institutional regimes and forms of collective action that mobilise narratives of change, collective identities and non-capitalist economic practices.

Ana Margarida Esteves is Integrated Researcher at the Centro de Estudos Internacionais (CEI-IUL) and Guest Assistant Professor at the Department of Political Economy/ECSH, School of Social Sciences, Instituto Universitário de Lisboa (ISCTE-IUL) in Lisbon, Portugal.

Thomas Henfrey is Senior Research Fellow at the Schumacher Institute for Sustainable Systems in Bristol (UK) and Research Collaborator at the Centre for Ecology, Evolution and Environmental Change (Ce3C) in the Faculty of Sciences at Lisbon University, Portugal.

Luciane Lucas dos Santos is Associate Researcher at the Centre for Social Studies (CES), University of Coimbra (Portugal). She is Lecturer and Curricular Unit Coordinator in the Ph.D. Programme "Human Rights in Contemporary Societies" (a joint endeavour of CES and the Institute for Interdisciplinary Research – IIIUC). She also co-coordinates the Study Group on Solidarity Economy (ECOSOL-CES).

Leonardo Leal is Senior Lecturer at the Federal University of Alagoas (UFAL) in the State of Alagoas, Brazil. He is Director of the Center for Research and Outreach Activities Solidarity Economy Technological Incubator (ITES/UFAL).

Routledge Studies in Social Enterprise & Social Innovation
Series Editors: Jacques Defourny, Lars Hulgård, and Rocío Nogales

Social enterprises seek to combine an entrepreneurial spirit and behaviour with a primacy of social or societal aims. To various extents, their production of goods or services generates market income which they usually combine with other types of resources. A social innovation consists of the implementation of a new idea or initiative to change society in a fairer and more sustainable direction.

Routledge Studies in Social Enterprise & Social Innovation seeks to examine and promote these increasingly important research themes. It particularly looks at participatory governance and social innovation dynamics in social enterprises and more widely in partnerships involving third sector and civil society organizations, conventional businesses and public authorities. In such perspective, this series aims at publishing both breakthrough contributions exploring the new frontiers of the field as well as books defining the state of the art and paving the way to advance the field.

Social Enterprise in Central and Eastern Europe
Theory, Models and Practice
Edited by Jacques Defourny and Marthe Nyssens

Social Enterprise, Health and Wellbeing
Theory, Methods and Practice
Edited by Michael J. Roy and Jane Farmer

Solidarity Economy
Alternative Spaces, Power and Politics
Edited by Ana Margarida Esteves, Thomas Henfrey, Luciane Lucas dos Santos and Leonardo Leal

For more information about this series, please visit: www.routledge.com/Routledge-Studies-in-Social-Enterprise – Social-Innovation/book-series/RSESI

Solidarity Economy

Alternative Spaces, Power and Politics

Edited by Ana Margarida Esteves, Thomas Henfrey, Luciane Lucas dos Santos and Leonardo Leal

Routledge
Taylor & Francis Group
NEW YORK AND LONDON

First published 2024
by Routledge
605 Third Avenue, New York, NY 10158

and by Routledge
4 Park Square, Milton Park, Abingdon, Oxon, OX14 4RN

Routledge is an imprint of the Taylor & Francis Group, an informa business

ISBN: 978-1-032-30706-0 (hbk)
ISBN: 978-1-032-30709-1 (pbk)
ISBN: 978-1-003-30634-4 (ebk)

DOI: 10.4324/9781003306344

Typeset in Times New Roman
by Apex CoVantage, LLC

Contents

Contributors

Rogério Roque Amaro is Associate Professor at the Department of Political Economy/ECSH – School of Social Sciences, Instituto Universitário de Lisboa – ISCTE-IUL in Lisbon, Portugal.

Swati Banerjee is Professor at the Tata Institute of Social Sciences (TISS) in Mumbai, India.

Beatriz Caitana is Researcher at Centre for Social Studies (CES) in Coimbra, Portugal, and member of the scientific coordination of the H2020 URBiNAT Project.

Gaël Carrero Gros is a Ph.D. Student at the Universidad Autónoma de Madrid (UAM) in Madrid, Spain.

Dinesh Chand is a Post-Doctoral Research Associate at the Tata Institute of Social Sciences (TISS), in Mumbai, India.

Donatella Della Porta is Dean of the Faculty of Political and Social Sciences, Director of the Ph.D. program in Political Science and Sociology and Director of the Center on Social Movement Studies (Cosmos) at the Scuola Normale Superiore in Florence, Italy.

Ana Margarida Esteves is Integrated Researcher at the Centro de Estudos Internacionais (CEI-IUL) and Guest Assistant Professor at the Department of Political Economy/ECSH, School of Social Sciences, Instituto Universitário de Lisboa (ISCTE-IUL) in Lisbon, Portugal.

Philippe Eynaud is Professor in the IAE at Sorbonne Business School, Université Paris I, Panthéon Sorbonne in Paris, France.

Miguel Arturo Fajardo Rojas is Director of the Centre for Studies on Solidarity Economy and Professor at the University Foundation of San Gil (UniSangil) in San Gil, Colombia.

Noriko Hataya is Professor and Dean of the Faculty of Foreign Studies, Department of Hispanic Studies at Sophia University in Tokyo, Japan.

Henrik Hauggaard-Nielsen is Professor at the Department of People and Technology (IMT) at Roskilde University, Roskilde, Denmark.

Thomas Henfrey is Senior Research Fellow at the Schumacher Institute for Sustainable Systems in Bristol (UK) and Research Collaborator at the Centre for Ecology, Evolution and Environmental Change (Ce3C) in the Faculty of Sciences at Lisbon University, Portugal.

Lars Hulgård is Professor at the Department of People and Technology (IMT) at Roskilde University, Roskilde, Denmark.

Jean-Louis Laville is Professor at the Conservatoire National des Arts et Métiers in Paris, France.

Leonardo Leal is Senior Lecturer at the Federal University of Alagoas (UFAL) in Maceió, Brazil, and Director of the Center for Research and Outreach Activities on Solidarity Economy and of the Solidarity Economy Technological Incubator (ITES/UFAL).

Luciane Lucas dos Santos is Associate Researcher at the Centre for Social Studies (CES), University of Coimbra, and Lecturer at the PhD Programme "Human Rights in Contemporary Societies" (CES/IIIUC).

Bárbara Marques Ferreira is Researcher at the Instituto Superior de Economia e Gestão (ISEG) in Lisbon University, Lisbon, Portugal.

Ruth Muñoz is Researcher and Associate Professor at National University of General Sarmiento (UNGS) in Buenos Aires, Argentina.

Sara Sama Acedo is Lecturer and Researcher in the Social and Cultural Anthropology Department at the Universidad Nacional de Educación a Distancia (UNED) in Madrid, Spain.

Jesús Sanz Abad is a Professor in the Social Anthropology Department at the Universidad Complutense de Madrid (UCM) in Madrid, Spain.

Abdul Shaban is Professor at the Tata Institute of Social Sciences (TISS) in Mumbai, India.

Dražen Šimleša is Research Associate at the Institute of Social Science Ivo Pilar, Zagreb, Croatia.

Milena Tasheva-Petrova is Associate Professor at the University of Architecture, Civil Engineering and Geodesy (UACEG) in Sofia, Bulgaria.

Anna Umantseva is Ph.D. Fellow at the Department of People and Technology (IMT), Roskilde University, Roskilde, Denmark.

Nathalie Vallet is Professor at the Faculty of Design Sciences, University of Antwerp (UA), Belgium.

Foreword

No sectors or spheres in contemporary societies can escape the risk of colonisation, appropriation, marketisation and alienation. The benefits of a plant growing somewhere in the world become a patent and a property in the hands of a global pharmaceutical, although the ways of the plant have been known for centuries in the communities where it grows. From being just another element in the local ecosystem, or even in the *Sumak kawsay* – a source of well-being for all parts of the community – the plant becomes a commodity on the basis of molecular analysis, scientific declarations of its effects and a calculation of price, before being sold back in boxes to the people of its origin. Neither states nor societies have had the capacity to avoid such senseless transactions. Whereas the skill of farming in previous times was linked to a certain place and based upon an interaction, if not even a dialogue and collaboration, with soil and seasons, successful farmers today are investors in agricultural industries. As such, they need skills in reading the market and skills in believing in the miracles offered by modern time's wizards. The farmer needs investor skills when absorbing the highlights of global agricultural markets provided by Rabobank, a major European bank, in an almost poetic style: "Supply is expected to be tight in Q1, with consumption facing uncertainty. . . . The US herd is at an inflection point . . . but growth slow in Mexico and Canada" and in "Europe pork production is set to tighten further in 2023, with few exceptions. Pig carcass prices remains *[sic]* supported by tight supply and high input costs." When having decided between investing in the US herd or the European carcasses, or in the strong production growth in South East Asia, the farmer may enjoy an evening in the company of farming tech wizard Agreena offering "the world's first product that can tokenize soil carbon certificates and move Euros on blockchain." By providing climate certificates to farmers engaging in carbon capture and selling them to a corporate world looking for investment in compensation strategies, the magicians offer all stakeholders to join the regenerative agriculture trend that "actually turns soils into carbon sinks." By the end of the day, and before being able to sleep, given the challenges in comprehending the short journey that took him from an interaction with the soil to becoming a player on the global market, the farmer may need a pill whose impact was once known to his ancestors.

Not even solidarity economy is immune to becoming a vehicle for exploitation and alienation. There are reasons to be alert when the vocabularies of solidarity, sustainability and regeneration become tools and strategies offered by symbolic entrepreneurs whose success does not depend on the actual implementation of their promises, but on their ability to marketise the symbols they have created. The values of solidarity are spoken by corporate sustainability managers who, according to Aílton Krenak of the Krenak People in Brazil, "have become the *sacerdotes* of a new planetary order, self-righteously preaching something their employers, by the very nature, can't practise."

This book provides a much-needed framework for reinforcing solidarity economy as a space different from a neoliberal sustainability agenda. Through rigorous scholarship, the authors document how solidarity economy, when linked to counterhegemonic initiatives across the globe, may be a space for socio-ecological resilience and internal democracy. It documents how small-scale as well as large-scale practices of solidarity economy are mediated by multiple intersectionalities of caste, class, race and gender which can be applied to initiatives aimed at breaking free from binary frameworks of state–market, human–nature, etc. The vision of a global movement of solidarity economy is presented with theoretical and empirical evidence ranging from new types of cooperatives, community-led economic initiatives (CLIs), community-managed microfinance, regenerative farming practices, community entrepreneurship and transition initiatives linked to climate justice, as well as many more, proving the claim that another economy is possible.

Lars Hulgård

Preface

The closing decades of the 20th Century are often regarded as the end of the utopian age, marked by a retreat of the protest movements and counterculture evident during the decades immediately following World War II; the fall of the Soviet Union and an apparent victory of capitalism; representative democracy and the self-interested individual. The early years of the 21st Century, marked by growing geopolitical tensions, political polarisation and market volatility, led to a myriad of defensive measures, aimed at preventing the dissolution of the prevailing hegemony.

Still, a careful observation of the social world is enough to identify a variety of divergent practices and organisational forms that do not fit the neoclassical canon of "market economy" or "enterprise." They coexist side by side with market capitalism, creating alternative economic spatialities whose porous borders often intertwine with the mainstream, facilitating synergies and the hybridisation of practices. It is difficult not to wonder what makes it possible for these alternatives to emerge, sustain themselves and interact productively with incumbent economic and institutional regimes, without being absorbed by them. This wondering led to a long journey of questioning, auspicious encounters and collaborative research, of which this book is an output.

The process leading to this book started with an earlier postdoctoral project funded by the Portuguese Fundação para a Ciência e Tecnologia (grant number SFRH/BPD/94495/2013). It posed the core question of this book at the most grassroots level by comparing an ecovillage (*Tamera*, located in Portugal), an integral cooperative (*Cooperativa Integral Catalana*, in Catalonia) and an alternative commercialisation scheme (*Esperança/Cooesperança*, Brazil). The outputs of this project steered towards further research, analysing the role of translocal networks and movements in diffusing frames and practices, as well as in mediating between local initiatives and political institutions at different scales of governance. They also inspired the organisation of a series of annual international conferences, entitled "Social and Solidarity Economy and the Commons," bringing together researchers, activists and policymakers in these fields, whose first two editions took place at ISCTE – *Instituto Universitário de Lisboa* – in November of 2018 and 2019.

The exchanges taking place at these conferences added a wider variety of case studies and perspectives to the previous research outputs. This additional material showcased, on the one hand, a variety of counter-hegemonic epistemologies, ontologies and worldviews supporting alternative economic practices and organisational forms. On the other hand, there was evidence of a growing convergence of practices and interests among translocal networks promoting alternative economies.

A core outcome of the first two editions of the "Social and Solidarity Economy and Commons" conference is EuroREGEN – Transnational networks for regenerative development in Europe: a comparative perspective on grassroots mobilisation and policy advocacy – also funded by the Portuguese Fundação para a Ciência e Tecnologia (grant number PTDC/SOC-SOC/2061/2020). EuroREGEN is a collaboration between ISCTE, where I, the Principal Investigator, am a Research Fellow at the Centre for International Studies (CEI-IUL) and the *Centro de Estudos Sociais* (CES) at Coimbra University, where Luciane Lucas dos Santos is a Research Fellow. The team also includes, as Co-PI, Maria Fernandes-Jesus, a Research Fellow at CIS-ISCTE – Centre for Psychological Research and Social Intervention – and Lecturer at the School of Education, Language and Psychology at York St. John's University. It also counts on the input of Thomas Henfrey, a Research Fellow at the Schumacher Institute and long-time Research Collaborator with the Centre for Ecology, Evolution and Environmental Change in the Lisbon University Science Faculty, and of Donatella della Porta, from the *Scuola Normale Superiore* in Florence, as consultants. The current book, while contributing to EuroREGEN, extends its reach by bringing a variety of voices from the Global South, both as contributors and in the editorial team. Co-editor Leonardo Prates Leal is Director of ITES/UFAL – the Solidarity Economy Incubator at the Federal University of Alagoas in Brazil and Lecturer in Public Administration at the same institution.

The book gathers together a variety of case studies from different parts of the world, analysed from the standpoint of different intellectual traditions and political cultures. It dives into the contexts in which these initiatives are embedded to identify drivers of strategic choice in terms of practices, organisational forms and economic and political linkages, both within and across different fields and scales of activity. The goal is to contribute to the development of an analytic framework aimed at understanding how alternative economic spatialities result from the way initiatives, as well as networks, constitute themselves as forms of collective action and counterpower, therefore creating social value opportunities through multi-stakeholder and multi-level institutional settings.

This book would not have been possible if it was not for the generosity and dedication of all the contributors, who dedicated much time, energy and other resources to writing their chapters. Our gratitude extends equally to the series editors of Routledge Studies in Social Enterprise and Social Innovation – Jacques Defourny, Lars Hulgård and Rocio Nogales – for their generous support and guidance. A special note of thanks goes to the coordination team and members, past and present, of ECOLISE – the European Network for Community-led Initiatives on Climate Change and Sustainability – and in addition to Flor Avelino, now at Utrecht University, for introducing us to the research on Transformative Social Innovation carried out by DRIFT (the Dutch Research Institute for Transitions) and its partners.

Ana Margarida Esteves
Lisbon, March 2023

Introduction

Solidarity economy – an ecology of worldviews, identities and behaviours

Ana Margarida Esteves

A "pluriverse" of community-led economic initiatives

The social, economic and environmental externalities of globalisation have provoked, as a constructive response, a proliferation of community-led economic initiatives (CLIs) that prioritise the creation of social value and the reproduction of life over the production and accumulation of financial and material capital (e.g. Lockyer & Veteto, 2013; Laville, 2016; de Angelis, 2017; Hillenkamp & Lucas dos Santos, 2019). Although often small in scale, low in resources and sparsely networked (Miller, 2007), these initiatives are vehicles for strategies for protecting or rebuilding the fabric of social life and local biotas in the face of the destructive impacts of market pressures (Block, 2008). Their practices and social impacts often prefigure many of the intended outcomes of national and transnational environmental and social programmes, such as the United Nations' Sustainable Development Goals (SDGs), at the same time as they challenge their premises (Henfrey *et al.*, 2022). Existing evidence indicates that

> CLIs are already contributing, at local scale, to almost all of the SDGs, and achieving particular success in bringing different goals into synergy. However, these achievements are based on ethics, guiding philosophies, issue framings, practical goals and ways of organising that differ significantly from those behind the formulation and delivery of the SDGs.
>
> (Henfrey *et al.*, 2022: 211)

In contexts of perceived scarcity or marginalisation, projects such as worker and producer cooperatives, mutual aid organisations and alternative commercialisation/consumption networks represent ways of mobilising endogenous resources to meet basic needs in an autonomous fashion. In contexts where such concerns are less central, initiatives such as consumer cooperatives, social currencies, ecovillages and other intentional communities represent ways of building a "counterculture" to mainstream market economy (Miller, 2007). Despite

DOI: 10.4324/9781003306344-1

significant differences in the contexts in which these projects emerge, as well as in the interests and goals of those who pursue them, the initiatives generated share many operative values. They promote economic practices based on forms of solidarity that are neither contractual nor utilitarian (Laville & Eynaud, 2019), such as reciprocity, redistribution and householding, among actors who recognise each other as sharing similar interests and goals (Lucas dos Santos & Banerjee, 2019). They combine cooperative or social ownership of means of production with market mechanisms, promoting self-management and autonomy from centralised authorities (Gibson-Graham, 2006, 2008; Santos, 2006; Ould Ahmed, 2015).

To Forno and Graziano (2014), the proliferation of these initiatives is a result of the inadequacy of public institutions in mediating new claims to expand rights and better redistribute public goods. For critics of modernity as a technocratic project, aimed at ordering reality by means of linear thought and expert knowledge, it manifests a "pluriverse" of non-hegemonic epistemologies, outside those ordering the world system according to "rational principles from the perspective of a male Eurocentric consciousness" (Mignolo & Escobar, 2010: 36–37), which are centred on the interdependencies (including those of organic and affective nature) underlying human culture (Federici, 2010). Such epistemologies underlie collaborative and place-based approaches to relating with other species and natural elements, as well as with spirituality, hereby understood as the meaning-making dimension of the symbolic realm in its dimensions of ritual, myth and tradition (Anderson, 2014). They promote ontologies that configure worldviews and social relations, as well as relationships with the non-human world, in favour of tendentially collaborative and place-based approaches that support different forms and scales of commoning and community-building (Federici, 2010). These initiatives represent non-capitalist forms of economic activity and organisation, which have been marginalised in relation to theory and policy by the dominant neoclassical paradigm (Gibson-Graham, 1996; Eynaud *et al*., 2019). Such marginalisation results from a colonisation of the economic imaginary by a Eurocentric, heteropatriarchal approach, which assumes that only behaviours aimed at maximising individual gain are considered worthy of being taken seriously (Quijano, 2007; Machado de Oliveira, 2021).

Institutionalising alternative economic spatialities

The concept of solidarity economy is used in reference to emerging grassroots movements that aim to redefine the economic space by organising such counterhegemonic initiatives and practices in webs of mutual recognition and support, based on self-management and internal democracy. The goal of these movements is to improve the socio-ecological resilience of communities and territories via the institutionalisation of commoning as a practice, as well as the re-territorialisation of economic activity, by promoting the visibility and sustainability of such initiatives and practices (Avelino & Wittmayer, 2019; Eynaud *et al.*, 2019, Kothari *et al.*, 2019). Therefore, the designation of solidarity economy can be applied to a multiplicity of initiatives, from workers' and producers' cooperatives to community-managed microfinance, commercialisation and alternative currency schemes, as well as ecovillages and transition initiatives, among others (Esteves, 2022).

Central to the promotion of the plural economic space envisioned by solidarity economy is the development of parallel economic spatialities, made of "autonomous and intermediary public spaces" (Laville & Eynaud, 2019: 60) where "socio-ethical and counter-cultural practices" are experimented with, enacted and coordinated (Fois, 2019: 108). These spaces are "micro-public spheres" (Keane, 1998) where economic activity is pursued as a form of prefigurative politics based on the construction and performance of non-capitalist identities and forms of relating with humans, nature and the material world, as well as engaging the state in transforming structural power relations. These spaces are based on "democratic solidarity" (Ould Ahmed, 2015) that challenges and transforms social relations, both within their organisational boundaries and in the public domain (Laville, 2016; Avelino & Wittmayer, 2019; Laville & Eynaud, 2019; Lucas dos Santos & Banerjee, 2019). For Ould Ahmed (2015), "democratic solidarity" is co-constructed by actors who enter freely into non-competitive, self-managed modes of economic action, aimed at empowering excluded and/or disadvantaged groups, by prioritising non-economic concerns related to social justice, environmental sustainability and welfare. Therefore, besides being spaces of economic activity, these "autonomous and intermediary public spaces" are sites of construction of what Escoffier (2018) calls "mobilizational citizenship" through the processes of "production of belonging" inherent to the local identities of struggles "updated and reformed through processes of micromobilization" (Escoffier, 2018: 775).

Literature in the field explores various forms of "autonomous and intermediary public spaces" of solidarity economy that exist (Gibson-Graham, 2006, 2008; Mendell, 2009). There is a wide focus on the role of such spaces in the construction of circuits of value that re-territorialise economic activity, as well as the reproduction of the material resources, norms and rules necessary for the development of solidarity economy-based livelihoods (e.g. Poteete & Ostrom, 2010; Lietaer *et al.*, 2012; Ould Ahmed, 2015; Laville, 2016; de Angelis, 2017; Rigo & França Filho, 2017). However, the field lacks a solid view of how such spaces of solidarity economy are shaped by forms of collective action that re-signify, re-localise and regulate economic behaviour while challenging the practices and institutional structures of market societies.

Two major European research projects – TRANSformative Social Innovation Theory (TRANSIT)[1] and Accelerating and Rescaling Transitions to Sustainability (ARTS)[2] – proposed foundations for a mid-range theory of "Transformative Social Innovation". This supports a theoretical bridging between solidarity economy and collective action by suggesting conditions under which social innovations can scale up or out, as well as challenge, alter or replace dominant institutions in a specific socio-material context (Pel *et al.*, 2020). A central condition is embeddedness in constellations of actors, such as local communities, grassroots initiatives and government/civil society alliances, which empowers these initiatives vis-à-vis incumbent institutional regimes and power structures and, in addition, facilitate access to decision-makers and gatekeepers of key resources (Avelino *et al.*, 2019; Pel *et al.*, 2020). Translocal networks play a central role in promoting such embeddedness and empowerment, connecting actors by sharing ideas, resources, organisational forms and practices across local contexts (Loorbach *et al.*, 2020). They are also central in cultivating the political legitimacy of CLIs, namely by demonstrating their potential contributions to the realisation of national and international environmental and social agendas (Penha-Lopes & Henfrey, 2019; Henfrey *et al.*, 2022). This implies balancing respect for conventional norms and forms of political engagement with criticising, confronting and enacting alternatives to key tenets of contemporary market economies (D'Alisa *et al.*, 2013; Henfrey & Penha-Lopes, 2018).

Drivers of solidarity economy as counterpower

EuroREGEN – Transnational networks for regenerative development in Europe: a comparative perspective on grassroots mobilisation and policy advocacy[3] is a research project that builds upon the findings of TRANSIT and ARTS by identifying epistemological, institutional and structural drivers that shape: 1) meaning-making processes underlying agenda-setting and multi-scalar governance within solidarity economy networks and 2) strategic choices in terms of coalition-building with other networks and movements, and linkages with public institutions at different scales of policy-making. Identifying these drivers supports the analysis of how constraints and opportunities posed by the discursive and social structures in which CLIs are embedded affect their ability to leverage influence. This analysis also helps identify mechanisms through which CLIs circumvent constraints and exert leverage upon opportunities to build counterpower.

The present collection lays the foundation for the institutional analysis aimed at by EuroREGEN by analysing how alternative economic spatialities, within and beyond Europe, result from the way initiatives, as well as networks, constitute themselves as forms of collective action and counterpower, therefore creating opportunities to generate social value through multi-stakeholder and multi-level institutional formations. It identifies drivers of strategic choice in terms of practices, organisational forms and economic and political linkages, both within and across different fields and scales of activity. Such drivers are rooted in epistemological understandings of: 1) the social and ecological crises, to which solidarity economy initiatives are a constructive response; 2) agency, namely that of individuals and communities, the state at its different levels of governance and of non-human subjects, specifically nature and technology and 3) the types of relationships, within and across different types of agents, that promote the goals of solidarity economy. Such drivers inform strategies of adaptive hybridisation of practices, aimed at dealing with constraints posed by the institutional environment, as well as power relations that structure the different scales of political economy in which solidarity economy initiatives are embedded.

This book thus adds to pre-existing scholarship an understanding of how alternative economic spatialities, based on solidarity economy initiatives and practices, result as much from institutional regimes and power relations as they do from forms of collective action that mobilise narratives of change and collective identities that connect them with wider political projects. This understanding is based on case study analyses from diverse geographical origins, developed according to a range of methodologies including ethnography, action research and extended single and comparative case study analysis. As Sanz Abad, Sama Acedo and Carrero Gros point out in Chapter 9, and Eynaud and Laville also imply (Chapter 1), the processual, relational and situated approach underlying these methodologies enables the identification of the deeper debates, tensions, opportunities and constraints that frame solidarity economy initiatives and networks, as well as the multiple dimensions of their transformational goals and potential.

Epistemological drivers: culture, memory and framing of crises

Epistemology plays a central role in constituting the practices, organisational forms and power dynamics that structure both hegemonic and counter-hegemonic economic systems (Gibson-Graham, 2011; Esteves, 2016, 2019). In Chapter 3, Henfrey claims that capitalism, its hegemonic position in the world economy and its effects on people and planet are symptoms of an epistemological and ontological crisis that constrains the collective human capacity to develop alternative worldviews, identities and behaviours. Following Bateson (1979), Henfrey frames solidarity economy as an "ecology of mind", encompassing a range of epistemologies and ontologies that reflect, as well as help constitute, local peculiarities of place. These support the defence of uncolonised spaces, or rebuilding the fabric of social or natural life, from the impact of capitalist social (re)production, either through collective acts of resistance and renewal or the deliberate creation of alternative economies. For Santos (2018), recognising such diverse epistemologies and ontologies is a matter of cognitive justice, as it implies recognising conceptions of being an agency, which do not fit the European Enlightenment construction of the self-interested, heteropatriarchal human individual. This construction's false claim of universality, spread around the world through capitalism, colonialism and patriarchy, drew an abyssal line that relegated alternative ontologies into silence and epistemic invisibility.

According to Eynaud and Laville (Chapter 1), these alternative epistemologies/ontologies support the development of solidarity economy through a range of "processes of association, cooperation and communication", rooted in everyday life, which "constantly emerge, transversally to institutionalised spheres of experience and activity" (p. 14). These processes constitute innovative forms of everyday politics that have the potential to transform "spatiotemporal, symbolic and institutional environments" within the state, the market and the lifeworld (p. 14). Central to the transformative potential of such processes is the capacity to mobilise everyday culture, as well as historical memory, to conceive diverse organisational forms and practices from the local to the translocal scales. Epistemic diversity, rooted in the social and ecological realities of place, is thus regarded as key for solidarity economy initiatives and networks to resist isomorphic pressures from the capitalist system. Based on two case studies in Central and Eastern Europe, Šimleša (Chapter 6) argues that such rootedness can even contribute to circumventing institutional obstacles to solidarity economy posed by ideological misrepresentations of history by allowing grassroots initiatives to take inspiration and guidance from place-based interpretations of their rich national histories of cooperatives and mutual aid associations.

Epistemological drivers: conceptions of agency

Understanding translocal solidarity economy spatialities implies analysing how counter-hegemonic social worlds are formed at the local level, namely through epistemologies, as well as the practices they inform, which expand conceptions of agency beyond the idea of the self-interested individual maximising personal gain and into technology, the natural world and the symbolic realm (Federici, 2010; Gibson-Graham, 2011; Latour, 2014). Della Porta, in Chapter 2, explores the diverse framings and practices of the commons developed by social movements opposing neoliberalism in recent decades as sources of counter-hegemonic knowledge, which support the development of solidarity economy alternatives, at times with support from institutional allies. Esteves, in Chapter 4, applies the extended case study method to the comparative analysis of how an ecovillage in Portugal, an integral cooperative in Catalonia and an alternative commercialisation network in Brazil constitute themselves as incubators of political innovations. The analysis focuses on how their specific epistemologies of the social and environmental crisis, as well as ontologies of transformative agency (including that of non-human agents), 1) re-signify the spaces in which they operate, as well as the activities that take place therein, leading to distinct alternative economic spatialities; 2) produce practices, relationships and interactions with wider publics, which maximise their autonomy in relation to capitalism's isomorphic pressures through a process that De Angelis (2017) refers to as boundary commoning. Umantseva, Hulgård and Hauggaard-Nielsen, in Chapter 7, analyse how place-based epistemologies, developed within micro socio-spatial contexts, contribute to understanding nature as an agent, introducing concepts of reciprocity and social value that include relationships among humans and other beings. This supports regenerative and bioregional approaches to socio-ecological transition that require solutions beyond the local scale. Two chapters explore subaltern identities and spaces emerging from micro socio-spatial contexts of social inequality and grassroots solidarity as drivers of transformative social innovation through the medium of solidarity economy. Lucas dos Santos, in Chapter 5, discusses the social inequalities experienced by minority women in Europe, with particular attention to Afro-European women, and explores the potential of solidarity economy practices, emerging from the strategies of mutual help and social resilience in their communities to contribute to the promotion of strategies of urban regeneration more attuned with spatial democracy and representational justice. Banerjee, Shaban and Chand, in Chapter 8, apply a similar frame of analysis to a case study in a rural context, exploring how multiple dimensions of discrimination experienced by marginalised farmers in India, including those of caste, class, race and gender, impact their practices of grassroots solidarity and collectivisation.

Responding to structural and institutional constraints: hybridisation of practices

Solidarity economy initiatives and networks face institutional and structural obstacles that often tend to render them invisible or relegate them to a niche position in the wider economic system (Eynaud *et al.*, 2019; Esteves, 2021). In Chapter 9, Abad, Acedo and Gros, based on three case studies in Spain, argue that to be economically sustainable and interact productively with public institutions in a capitalist system, solidarity economy initiatives respond to such obstacles by developing practices that combine transformative elements with traits from incumbent institutional regimes. This results not only from their interactions with the market and public institutions, but also from the need to balance ideological coherence (usually of a relatively small militant social base) with reaching out to broader publics. Muñoz (Chapter 12), based on fieldwork in the municipalities of the Conurbano Bonaerense (Argentina), advances the concept of interstitial transformation. The chapter claims that the hybridisation of practices by solidarity economy initiatives is made possible by their embeddedness in social spaces that are not colonised by capitalist social (re)production. That supports symbiotic transformation in which solidarity economy initiatives not only adapt to incumbent institutional regimes, but also influence official power structures and processes to advance progressive policies. Fajardo Rojas and Hataya (Chapter 10) explore the role of popular education in Colombia, namely of pedagogies inspired by liberation theology and Freirean methods, in the development of spaces that are relatively autonomous from capitalist social (re)production, by supporting non-hegemonic interpretations of changing socio-economic contexts, both at the local scale and beyond.

Several chapters explore municipal-level politics as a laboratory of co-construction of innovations, involving public bureaucracy and grassroots initiatives, which legitimise previously invisible economic practices and support marginalised actors and territories through the promotion of solidarity economy ecosystems. Leal, analysing a Community Development Bank in Brazil (Chapter 11), argues that the practices of self-management and collective governance promoted by solidarity finance support marginalised territories not only by providing a safeguard against financial exclusion, but also by encouraging the participation of members in municipal-level decision-making processes. Amaro and Ferreira (Chapter 13) and Caitana, Tasheva-Petrova and Vallet (Chapter 14) analyse solidarity economy initiatives as drivers of policy innovation at the municipal level, promoting innovative models and practices of Shared and Participatory Local Governance in Lisbon, Portugal and Sofia, Bulgaria.

Methodological considerations and directions for future research

Understanding the alternative economic spatialities envisioned by solidarity economy requires a methodology that integrates institutions, market dynamics and the materiality of temporally and spatially situated practices in an understanding of economic behaviour as the result of "imaginative cultural translations of actual human encounters with consciousness and the cosmos" (Kripal, 2022: 1). This implies an approach that is:

a) **Hermeneutic**, assuming that every economic practice was created by humans for specific purposes that are temporally and spatially contextualised, based on evolving understandings of reality that are intersubjectively constructed around abyssal lines that favour some aspects, while marginalising others (Santos, 2018; Kripal, 2022);
b) **Comparative**, understanding economic practices as spatially and temporally situated phenomena, with no particular variations privileged as sources of a grand narrative on agency and exchange (Kripal, 2022);
c) **Transdisciplinary**, mobilising the social and natural sciences, as well as the humanities, to think critically and holistically about the economy as a dimension of a wider conceptual framework for understanding social (re)production.

Approaching solidarity economy as a "pluriverse" of collaborative and place-based practices implies a conception of agency that extends beyond that of the self-interested, heteropatriarchal human individual, promoted by the European Enlightenment. This means taking into account how place-based concepts of being and intersubjectivity are constituted, including the boundaries between self and other, and how they temporally evolve and change through practice and intersubjective reflection. This is necessary so as to understand the social construction and attribution of: 1) the capacity for engaging, in a self-determined manner, in exchanges among humans, as well as with the natural world, technology, institutions, structures of power and the symbolic realm; 2) the personal capabilities and resources that are engaged in such exchanges and 3) boundaries between the sphere of social production and that of social reproduction.

This constructivist and hermeneutic positioning is essential for understanding the processes of resignification of economic activity, beyond that of capitalist orthodoxy, which underlie the ways in which solidarity economy initiatives understand their position in the structural and institutional contexts in which they are embedded, as well as the opportunities and obstacles they contain. Such methodological positioning is also essential to understand how these initiatives engage in "boundary commoning", namely by strategically reaching out to public and private actors, with the purpose of establishing alliances or impacting institutional regimes at different scales of governance, temporality and spatiality.

Notes

1. www.transitsocialinnovation.eu/
2. https://drift.eur.nl/projects/arts/
3. https://ciencia.iscte-iul.pt/projects/redes-transnacionais-para-o-desenvolvimento-regenerativo-na-europa-uma-perspetiva-comparada-sobre/1536

References

Anderson, E. N. (2014). *Caring for Place: Ecology, Ideology and Emotion in Traditional Landscape Management*. Walnut Creek, CA: Left Coast Press.

Avelino, F., Dumitru, A., Cipolla, C., Kunze, I. and Wittmayer, J. (2019). "Translocal empowerment in transformative social innovation networks," *European Planning Studies*, 8, pp. 1–23. https://doi.org/10.1080/09654313.2019.1578339

Avelino, F. and Wittmayer, J. M. (2019). "The transformative potential of plural social enterprise: A multi-actor perspective," in Eynaud, P., Laville, J. L., Lucas dos Santos, L., Banerjee, S., Avelino, F. and Hulgard, L. (eds.) *Theory of Social Enterprise and Pluralism: Social Movements, Solidarity Economy and the Global South*. New York: Routledge, pp. 193–222.

Bateson, G. (1979). *Mind and Nature: A Necessary Unity*. New York: Dutton.

Block, F. (2008). "Polanyi's double movement and the reconstruction of critical theory," *Revue Interventions Economiques*, 38. https://doi.org/10.4000/interventionseconomiques.274

D'Alisa, G., Demaria, F. and Cattaneo, C. (2013). "Civil and uncivil actors for a degrowth society," *Journal of Civil Society*, 9(2), pp. 212–224. https://doi.org/10.1080/17448689.2013.788935

De Angelis, M. (2017). *Omnia Sunt Communia: On the Commons and Transformation to Postcapitalism*. London: Zed Books.

Escoffier, E. (2018). "Mobilisational citizenship: Sustainable collective action in underprivileged urban Chile," *Citizenship Studies*, 22(7), pp. 769–790.

Esteves, A. M. (2016). "Radical environmentalism and 'commoning': Synergies between ecosystem regeneration and social governance at Tamera ecovillage, Portugal," *Antipode*, 49(2), pp. 357–366. https://doi.org/10.1111/anti.12278

Esteves, A. M. (2019). "Constructing solidarity economy-based livelihoods," *Museum International*, 71(1–2), pp. 132–139. https://doi.org/10.1080/13500775.2019.1638069

Esteves, A. M. (2021). "'All watched over by machines of loving grace'? Information technology, in-person relationships and normative regulation in an 'integral cooperative'," *Community Development Journal*, 57(4), pp. 655–672. https://doi.org/10.1093/cdj/bsab019

Esteves, A. M. (2022). "Processes of normative regulation in spaces of 'solidarity economy'": A comparative case study analysis," *International Journal of Sociology and Social Policy*, 42(7/8), pp. 624–639. https://doi.org/10.1108/IJSSP-12-2020-0540

Eynaud, P., Laville, J. L., Lucas dos Santos, L., Banerjee, S., Avelino, F. and Hulgard, L. (eds.) (2019). *Theory of Social Enterprise and Pluralism: Social Movements, Solidarity Economy and the Global South*. New York: Routledge.

Federici, S. (2010). *Re-Enchanting the World: Feminism and the Politics of the Commons*. Oakland, CA: PM Press.

Fois, F. (2019). "Enacting experimental alternative spaces," *Antipode*, 51(1), pp. 107–128. https://doi.org/10.1111/anti.12414

Forno, F. and Graziano, P. (2014). "Sustainable community movement organisations," *Journal of Consumer Culture*, 14(2), pp. 139–157. https://doi.org/10.1177/1469540514526225

Gibson-Graham, J. K. (1996). *The End of Capitalism (As We Knew It): A Feminist Critique of Political Economy*. Oxford: Blackwell.

Gibson-Graham, J. K. (2006). *A Postcapitalist Politics*. Minneapolis: University of Minnesota Press.

Gibson-Graham, J. K. (2008). "Diverse economies: Performative practices for 'other worlds'," *Progress in Human Geography*, 32(5), pp. 613–632. https://doi.org/10.1177/0309132508090821

Gibson-Graham, J. K. (2011). "A feminist project of belonging for the Anthropocene," *Gender, Place and Culture*, 18(1), pp. 1–21. https://doi.org/10.1080/0966369X.2011.535295

Henfrey, T., Feola, G., Penha-Lopes, G., Sekulova, F. and Esteves, A. M. (2022). "Rethinking the sustainable development goals: Learning with and from community-led initiatives," *Sustainable Development*, 31(1), pp. 211–222. https://doi.org/10.1002/sd.2384

Henfrey, T. and Penha-Lopes, G. (2018). "Policy and community-led action on sustainability and climate change: Paradox and possibility in the interstices," *Environmental Innovation and Societal Transitions*, 29, pp. 52–54. http://dx.doi.org/10.1016/j.eist.2018.05.002

Hillenkamp, I. and Lucas dos Santos, L. (2019). "The domestic domain within a postcolonial, feminist reading of social enterprise: Towards a substantive, gender-based concept of solidarity enterprise," in Eynaud, P., Laville, J. L., Lucas dos Santos, L., Banerjee, S., Avelino, F. and Hulgard, L. (eds.) *Theory of Social Enterprise and Pluralism: Social Movements, Solidarity Economy and the Global South*. New York: Routledge, pp. 90–115.

Keane, J. (1998). *Democracy and Civil Society*. London: Verso.

Kothari, A., Salleh, A., Escobar, A., Demaria, F. and Acosta, A. (eds.) (2019). *Pluriverse: A Post-Development Dictionary*. New Delhi: Tulika Books.

Kripal, J. J. (2022). *The Superhumanities: Historical Precedents, Moral Objections, New Realities*. Chicago: University of Chicago Press.

Latour, B. (2014). "Agency at the time of the Anthropocene," *New Literary History*, 45(1), pp. 1–18. https://doi.org/10.1353/nlh.2014.0003

Laville, J. L. (2016). *A Economia Social e Solidária: Práticas, Teorias e Debates*. Coimbra: Almedina.

Laville, J. L. and Eynaud, P. (2019). "Rethinking social enterprise through philanthropic and democratic solidarities," in Eynaud, P., Laville, J. L., Lucas dos Santos, L., Banerjee, S., Avelino, F. and Hulgard, L. (eds.) *Theory of Social Enterprise and Pluralism: Social Movements, Solidarity Economy and the Global South*. New York: Routledge, pp. 18–43.

Lietaer, B., Arnsperger, C., Goerner, S. and Brunnhuber, S. (2012). *Money and Sustainability: The Missing Link*. Axminster, Devon: Triarchy Press.

Lockyer, J. and Veteto, J. R. (2013). "Environmental anthropology engaging Ecotopia: An introduction," in Lockyer, J. and Veteto, J. R. (eds.) *Environmental Anthropology Engaging Ecotopia: Bioregionalism, Permaculture, and Ecovillages*. New York: Berghahn Books, pp. 1–31.

Loorbach, D., Wittmayer, J., Avelino, F., von Wirth, T. and Frantzeskaki, N. (2020). "Transformative innovation and translocal diffusion," *Environmental Innovation and Societal Transitions*, 35, pp. 251–260. https://doi.org/10.1016/j.eist.2020.01.009

Lucas dos Santos, L. and Banerjee, S. (2019). "Social enterprise: Is it possible to decolonise this concept?," in Eynaud, P., Laville, J. L., Lucas dos Santos, L., Banerjee, S., Avelino, F. and Hulgard, L. (eds.) *Theory of Social Enterprise and Pluralism: Social Movements, Solidarity Economy and the Global South*. New York: Routledge, pp. 3–17.

Machado de Oliveira, V. (2021). *Hospicing Modernity: Facing Humanity's Wrongs and the Implications for Social Activism*. Berkeley: North Atlantic Books.

Mendell, M. (2009). "Financing the social economy in Quebec," *Makingwaves*, 20(3), pp. 46–50.

Mignolo, W. and Escobar, A. (eds.) (2010). *Globalization and the Decolonial Option*. New York: Routledge.

Miller, M. (2007). "'Other economies are possible!' building a solidarity economy," *Grassroots Economic Organizing*. Online at https://geo.coop/node/35 (accessed March 29th 2023)

Ould Ahmed, P. (2015). "What does 'solidarity economy' mean? Contours and feasibility of a theoretical and political project," *Business Ethics: A European Review*, 24, pp. 425–435. https://doi.org/10.1111/beer.12063

Pel, B., Wittmayer, J., Dorland, J. and Jørgensen, M. S. (2020). "Unpacking the social innovation ecosystem: An empirically grounded typology of empowering network constellations," *Innovation: The European Journal of Social Science Research*, 33(3), pp. 311–336. https://doi.org/10.1080/13511610.2019.1705147

Penha-Lopes, G. and Henfrey, T. (2019). *Reshaping the Future: How Local Communities Are Catalysing Social, Economic and Ecological Transformation in Europe. The First Status Report on Community-Led Action on Sustainability and Climate Change in Europe*. Brussels: ECOLISE.

Poteete, J. and Ostrom, E. (2010). *Working Together: Collective Action, the Commons, and Multiple Methods in Practice*. Princeton, NJ: Princeton University Press.

Quijano, A. (2007). "Coloniality and modernity/rationality," *Cultural Studies*, 21(2), pp. 168–178. https://doi.org/10.1080/09502380601164353

Rigo, A. S. and França Filho, G. C. (2017). "O paradoxo das Palmas: Análise do (des) uso da moeda social no 'bairro da economia solidária'," *Cadernos EBAPE.BR.*, 15(1), pp. 169–193. https://doi.org/10.1590/1679-395141258

Santos, B. S. (2006). *A Gramática do Tempo: para uma nova cultura política*. Porto: Afrontamento.

Santos, B. S. (2018). "Stay baroque: Boaventura de Sousa Santos on postabyssal thinking," *Artforum*, Print Summer 2018. Online at www.artforum.com/print/201806/boaventura-de-sousa-santos-on-postabyssal-thinking-75522 (accessed March 29th 2023).

1 A shared epistemological framework for the solidarity economy and the commons

Philippe Eynaud and Jean-Louis Laville

1.1 Introduction

The main problem faced by the solidarity economy and the commons is epistemological. In this chapter, we first examine the limits of dominant sociologies and explain why the epistemologies of the South provide another relation between science and action. Then, we summarise through the history of thought how solidarity economy and commons theories come from a gradually constructed heterodox economic sociology. By bridging the solidarity economy and the commons, we open new avenues for a shared epistemological framework. Our proposition is based on an analysis of the history of thought to underline the important conceptual and practical potential of a transversal approach to the fields of the solidarity economy and the commons. We argue for an approach to institutional change through the instituted/instituting dyad. Thus, alternative experiences at the confluence of the solidarity economy and the commons have to be approached as fields where new practices and pedagogies are emerging. It invites us to focus the study of solidarity economy initiatives and the commons on processes of association, cooperation and communication, which are intended to produce significant transformations within institutions.

The purpose of this chapter is threefold. It aims to highlight the significant conceptual and practical potential of a transversal approach to the fields of the solidarity economy and the commons. This implies moving away from an overly vague reference to the solidarity economy and the commons, which have taken on very different meanings, and to problematise the solidarity economy and the commons by identifying the different conceptions that have succeeded one another as well as points of convergence that pre-existed these different conceptions (Eynaud & Laville, 2021). This leads us to show that what characterises the solidarity economy, like the commons, is that it approaches the institution through the instituted/instituting dyad and logically, as a result, puts institutional change at the heart of the analysis (Laville & Sainsaulieu, 2018). This leads us also to emphasise the role of alternative practices, epistemologies and pedagogies that constitute what has been called as everyday politics (Martiskainen

DOI: 10.4324/9781003306344-2

et al., 2018) or incubators of political innovations (Esteves, 2022, this volume). It then remains to see and understand how collective actions are processes of association, cooperation and communication that constantly emerge, transversally to institutionalised spheres of experience and activity, and how they transform their spatiotemporal, symbolic and institutional environments.

After initiating the chapter by explaining the inadequacy of social sciences in search of certainty (Dewey, 1929), we then turn to the importance of escaping the debate focused on market–state dualism. This binary reasoning is beginning to be exhausted. The commons and solidarity economy stimulate the debate by making visible a third pole constituted by society itself. The evolution of the debate then raises the possibility of a shared epistemological framework.

1.2 Going beyond conventional social sciences

The shared character of the solidarity economy and the commons offers the opportunity to opt for the same epistemological approach. It creates a distance and a need to move away from an overarching sociology such as the critical sociology and the traditional science of organisations. It is interesting to note that, although in many ways opposed, these two well-known visions of sociology share a common invalidation of experiential knowledge. Therefore, we suggest opening epistemological avenues with the epistemologies of the South.

1.2.1 The limits of critical sociology

In traditional critical sociology as exemplified by Bourdieu (1987, 2012), the agent believes he is exercising his freedom, but, in reality, he participates in the reproduction of the social order by being governed by the expression in the situation of his *habitus*.[1] He is thus a prisoner of false representations and of the *doxa*.[2] The task of the scholar is thus to fight the obviousness of common sense. The researcher must practise asceticism through self-analysis to flush out all the lures conveyed by ordinary language. Sociology liberates by dispelling the illusion of freedom. There is therefore nothing to learn from the agent; in contrast, it is advisable to denounce all of the agent's misleading assertions and to replace them with a perception enlightened by theory. It is therefore impossible to defend the idea of knowledge other than academic knowledge, which is, moreover, unfalsifiable, since any disagreement is referred to as a resistance to the unveiling of the truth. As Rancière (2003) says, Bourdieusian analysis is the radical critique of a radically unchangeable situation. Emancipation is inaccessible to ordinary citizens, who can claim it only through the saving mediation of the sociologist. This self-confident macrosociology has long influenced social work studies, reducing every observation to structural effects. It still manifests itself in a post-Bourdieusian sociology of work, which relates the whole of the associative world to an operation of state disengagement.

Starting from a strong assertion that it is crucial to analyse, Bourdieusian sociology converts its own insights into an ultimate truth that it alone would be able to detect. This claim to a monopoly of exact interpretation is proving to be obsolete. The realisation of a participative research, not on the associative actors but with them, shows that the latter do not wait for 'scholars' to enunciate the threats to which they are subjected. Aware of the instrumentalisations in progress and their consequences for the future, they examine them precisely. Moreover, the dialogue between actors and researchers stimulates a diversity of approaches and methods that are evaluated throughout the process (cf. Amaro & Ferreira, this volume). This is why this interaction ends up uncovering problems and questions that an overly narrow, and above all uniformly applied, analytical grid misses. The dogmatic sociology of work fails to approach the field of associations. It pits public services against associations, whereas a better knowledge of neoliberalism highlights the importance of developing complementarities between public and associative responsibilities to deconstruct the forms of substitution and to intensify resistance to the excesses of capitalism.

1.2.2 The limits of the usual science of organisations

The sociology of organisations exemplified by Crozier and Friedberg (1980), insisting on the singularity of local situations, took the opposite view to Bourdieu by advocating a microsociology based on the notion of a concrete system of action, a structured human grouping that coordinates the actions of its participants by means of relatively stable game mechanisms and that maintains its structure, i.e., the stability of these games and the relationships between them, by means of regulation mechanisms that constitute other games. For this microsociology, in any organisation, power is the daily and inescapable mechanism that mediates the exchanges, ensuring the coexistence of relatively autonomous actors, with margins of freedom and control of a zone of uncertainty allowing them to implement strategies.

If Bourdieu was inspired by Bachelard, Crozier and Friedberg proposed a sociology influenced by economics, in which the driving force of human behaviour is self-interest. It is striking to note how much these very different sociologies converge towards a quest for certainty and how much, for this reason, they are part of this classical epistemology where theory overhangs society and must not mix with its practical agitations but rather reveal its hidden rules. If they have been so seductive, it is because they avoid any discussion with the "observed." The agent conforms to his habitus, and the actor follows his strategy. The studies are therefore carried out on their subjects, not with them. The two sociologies may start from contradictory hypotheses, but they share a common suspicion of the uninitiated. It is always the theory that authorises the apprehension of practices. It is important to be clear: these sociologies that devalue the judgments of the actors are incompatible with the consideration of pragmatic knowledge. We must therefore choose a sociology that belongs to another epistemology.

1.2.3 From instituting praxis to the epistemologies of the South

The project of another epistemology is synthesised by the epistemologies of the South, referring to many authors from decolonial studies (Dussel, 1992; Quijano, 1998) as well as promoters of a new science of organisations (Guerreiro Ramos, 1981). These epistemologies do not refer to a South perceived as a geographical entity (Sousa Santos, 2014). Certainly, the populations that have been most affected by inequalities and discriminations due to capitalism and colonialism live in the Southern Hemisphere. However, the South also exists in the North, just as there is a North in Southern countries represented by oligarchies that benefit from the dominant order (Laville *et al.*, 2019). The epistemologies of the South converge with some pragmatist analyses such as that of Latour, who has consistently reminded us of the extent to which we "moderns" have gone in the wrong direction by separating nature and culture (Latour, 2012). Stengers (1997) is also annoyed by the condescension with which science has been able to treat non-modern knowledge – in other words, knowledge from the South.

If pragmatism and the epistemologies of the South go in the same direction, the latter go a step further because they draw on a diversity of experiences by including the voices that have been silenced (França Filho *et al.*, 2022; Lucas dos Santos, this volume). Sousa Santos *(op. cit.)*, the author who has most worked with the epistemologies of the South, particularly insists on the consequences of the rupture inherent in modernity. The social sciences have become part of the science of moderns, which has the ambition of destroying so-called "prejudices." Supposed holders of legitimate knowledge construct the notions of common sense and profane language to group together false knowledge and thus invalidate the latter. Their monoculture of knowledge rejects the representations of those actors whose knowledge it characterises as profane ignorance. The epistemologies of the South uncover in the construction of science the springs of domination, even within the emancipatory pretensions of the social sciences (Rojas & Hataya, this volume; Banerjee, Shaban & Shand, this volume; Munoz, this volume). The latter have attributed to themselves the production of knowledge. They have contributed to the process of making invisible whole sections of the world and the various forms of knowledge that emerge from it. This *coup de force* is translated, among other things, by the imposition of universal conceptions of time and space. The commons and the solidarity economy offer an opportunity to apply the principles of the epistemologies of the South by rehabilitating citizen participation and the articulation of different knowledges in order to stimulate intercultural dialogues and to take into account the diversity of the world, far from global uniformity and commodification.

1.3 For a combined approach to the solidarity economy and the commons

If it is necessary to go beyond conventional social sciences approaches, it is also relevant to go beyond orthodox economic frameworks. In this section, we examine how there has been a parallel evolution in the respective theories of the solidarity economy and the commons. We argue that these two theories are complementary rather than separate and that they can be approached through three perspectives: third sector, social economy and solidarity economy.

1.3.1 Common pool resources and the third sector

The standard approach makes the market the central principle of the economy but stipulates that conditions are necessary for it to play such a role (Arrow, 1951). Private goods are rivalrous (use by one agent prevents use by others) and excludable (it is possible to prevent some agents from using the good), which is the case for a large number of goods (such as food, clothing, cars, parking). When a good proves to be non-rivalrous and non-excludable, such as broadcasting or national defence, it may be considered a public good and provided by the state. When a good is excludable and non-rivalrous, it is approached as corporate property (for example, movie theatres, private parks, cable TV). Using the same grid, Ostrom (1990) proposes to define *common pool resources (CPL)* as non-excludable goods, (access to the resource cannot be denied to some potential users as is the case for fisheries or forests) and rivalrous goods (actors compete over a limited resource).

Table 1.1 Theoretical and epistemological characteristics of the commons and social and solidarity economy

Theoretical characteristics of the two approaches / *Epistemological framework*	*Conceptions of the commons*	*Conceptions of the economy*
Orthodox conception of the economy	Common pool resources	Third sector
Conception of a non-capitalist organisation	Common property regimes	Social economy
Plural conception of economy and democracy	New commons	Solidarity economy

Contrary to previous analyses, which concluded that common pool resources were necessarily neglected, Ostrom and Ostrom (1977) establish that they can be appropriately managed through the self-organisation of the people concerned and outside the market and the state. According to the same logic, third-sector, non-profit organisations are recognised as having a place in situations where there are information asymmetries (Powell, 1987). Thus, in services with a strong relational dimension, such as childcare or home help, the provider benefits from a position of strength relative to the applicant. In this configuration, the service provider may be tempted to offer a lower-quality service or to increase its price without the payer being able to control it, as the young child cannot testify to the course of his or her day or the elderly person does not have the means to verify the exact content of what is done. Thus, it is possible to limit opportunism on the part of the service provider, which is constrained by its nonprofit nature. In the same way, minorities whose needs are not recognised or addressed by the public authorities can organise an association to satisfy them.

The concepts of common pool resources and the third sector both thus open up economic thinking to other perspectives, beyond those of market and state, which is decisive (also see Della Porta, this volume). Their conceptualisation is nonetheless part of orthodox economics, which implies several limitations. The market maintains a dominant position. The commons and the third sector retain a residual dimension; they are valid only for particular goods. Categorisation of goods and services suggests that they have intrinsic qualities that allow them to be categorised. They may differ according to the nature of the goods and services, but the premise of strategic and instrumental rationality is not called into question.

1.3.2 Common property regimes and the social economy

These features of orthodox economics, which situate observed realities as marginal phenomena, are questioned thanks to an alternative theorisation that places more emphasis on the question of property through the ideas of common property regimes and the social economy. Ostrom, with Schlager, had the innovation of breaking down property, which orthodox economics regards as complementary to the market in economics, into a *bundle of rights* (Schlager & Ostrom, 1992). Instead of adhering to the all-encompassing conventional notion of property, they show how it covers several types of rights that can be distinguished analytically and concern various aspects of the resource, namely, access to the resource, appropriation of its products, its management, the determination of access rights and their transfer. This characterisation distances itself from orthodoxy by recognising the existence of actions not strictly guided by self-interest and efficiency, and allowing them to contribute to the formation of values.

In parallel, Vienney (1994) defines the social economy beyond the third sector as a set of non-capitalist organisations (associations, cooperatives, mutual societies, etc.). Although not all are non-profit, they share the need to limit the generation and retention of profits and the power of shareholders. They also have statutes that are based on several characteristics: equality in voting regardless of capital held (one person one vote), constitution of a sustainable collective asset and services to members or the community *(ibid.)*.

However, the important progress made through the study of forms of ownership leads to an approach focused on organisations and approaches these organisations above all through their legal particularities. Questions remain unanswered about the concrete internal functioning of organisations, which cannot be reduced to statutory particularities. Statutes are necessary to establish a difference with respect to capitalist corporations, but they are not sufficient to guarantee democratic functioning. The recurrent tendencies towards trivialisation that the entities concerned are experiencing also lead us to address the issue of links between their internal rules and external rules emanating from the broader institutional framework in which they place their action.

1.3.3 New commons and solidarity economy

By specifying why open-source software can be seen as commons, Hess and Ostrom (2007) introduce discussion of the knowledge commons. Subsequently, other commons are identified, including cultural, health, neighbourhood, global, urban and infrastructure (Bollier, 2002; Bollier & Helfrich, 2012), which Hess (2008) proposes grouping under the generic term of "new commons." From then on, it becomes possible to free ourselves from the constraint that the commons apply only to certain types of goods and services.

Commons can be a way of approaching activities that seek responses to accelerated commodification and privatisation, including by promoting new epistemological categories of knowledge (cf. Fajardo Rojas & Hataya, this volume; Henfrey, this volume). In addition to common property regimes, this logic involves detailing the modalities of governance, the latter understood not in its neoliberal sense but as the forms of self-government put in place by collectives (Eynaud & Laville, 2021; Leal, this volume). Knowledge of the mechanisms of agreement, experimentation, creation, evaluation and modification of practical rules becomes essential. It also is crucial to think about the articulation of internal and external rules, hence the concept of polycentric governance (Ostrom, 2010), which designates a regulation process that respects the diversity of action processes at multiple levels of scale.

In addition, starting from the necessity of not limiting itself to the theme of collective property, the theory of the solidarity economy (Laville, 2022) insists, for its part, on two points. The first refers to the object of production. Its aspects of social utility and social innovation establish a link between the content of the project and the mode of organisation and between the collective benefits generated and the democratic functioning adopted. The solidarity economy reaffirms a political dimension to social movements initiatives, arguing that the formal equality guaranteed by the statutes is to be extended 1) by deliberative instances internally, 2) by participation in external debates and 3) by exerting pressure for institutional change. By denying the economist fallacy, which confuses the modern economy with the market, Polanyi (2011) posits that the economy requires the mobilisation of a plurality of principles. Through this broadening of the approach, the possibility of a conceptual pluralism is expressed (Eynaud *et al.*, 2019).

The new commons and the solidarity economy thus challenge the separation between the economic and political spheres (also see Della Porta, this volume). Commons, on the one hand, and the social and solidarity economy, on the other, are two anchor points for understanding reality beyond the state–market dualism. They have been defined in the course of dialogues between action and research. With the new commons and the solidarity economy, the convergence is strengthened around a plea for institutional diversity (Ostrom, 2005), which is as indispensable as biodiversity. It is an imaginary of renewed social change that is thus unfolding, more sensitive to transitions and alternatives than to sudden ruptures.

1.4 Approaching the institution through the instituted/instituting dyad

On the one hand, the instituted is the institution as it is given to social actors. On the other hand, the instituting praxis is a conscious activity of institution-making, of self-production of a collective subject (Dardot & Laval, 2014). This subject performs "both the activity that establishes a new system of rules and the activity that seeks to constantly revive this establishment to avoid the instituting getting bogged down in the instituted" (*ibid.*: 446). In this sense, the management of society by itself becomes the engine of institutionalisation, of "the permanent reinvention of the institution by which the group that created it can counteract its inertia" (*ibid.*).

By crossing the solidarity economy and commons fields, we open conceptual perspectives to renew the instituted/instituting dyad. In the vocabulary of neo-institutionalist sociology (Powell & Di Maggio, 1991), institutional isomorphism – that is coercive or mimetic pressures that force an entity to resemble the dominant models in the field in which it finds itself – was first privileged. After that, a stream of research was opened with literature emphasising institutional work and the ability to transform the institutional conditions in which it is placed. As many examples point out, solidarity economy and commons initiatives appear as everyday politics and are the fruit of an "instituting praxis" (Castoriadis, 2014) that manifests itself through logics crystallising common action around rules consistent with shared references, whether it is mutual aid among peers, social movement or multilateral discussion bringing together several categories of members.

These institutional logics stabilise relationships and provide reference points. Once established, they can sometimes spread more widely if they manage to influence institutions. However, this is never simple. For example the initially almost informal mutualist practices of the working class in the 19th Century experienced many ups and downs before being taken over by public action to establish norms and resume their use (Laville, 2022). They were first legalised on the condition that they were sponsored and therefore subject to elite control. Despite this normalisation, they then served as a model for developing a new form of redistributive public action. Despite their initial capture by philanthropy, a new institution was born from these local innovations, generalising social protection, with the corresponding difficulty of maintaining the power of the members and not merely slipping into the state orbit.

Today, as in the past, the negative discrimination from public authorities suffered by many citizen initiatives could encourage a one-sided reading of institutionalisation. Nevertheless, the instituting does not always dissolve into the institute. The latter can be subjected to deconstruction or modified by a joint reconstruction emanating from both citizens and public officials. This deconstruction is implemented in order to undermine the authority of incumbent institutions: when anti-nuclear activists reveal the state lies that the Chernobyl cloud did not pass through France; when legal appeals are filed against existing rules, such as those of farmers and gardeners attacking Monsanto because they have been poisoned by toxic products in the exercise of their profession; or when illegal activities are launched to then demand their regularisation, such as actions of civil disobedience and anti-advertising collectives.

1.4.1 The plurality of instituting initiatives

There are numerous and eloquent institutional initiatives. Experiences feel the need to structure themselves to influence negotiations around public spaces of proximity and thus testify to the institutional work done in their field.

First, we share a few examples from France. After having deserted a situation of pseudo-participation offered by the public authorities, the Association for the Maintenance of Peasant Agriculture "Les jardins de Cérès" in France (Zimmer, 2015) relaunched its dialogue with the public authorities on a different basis – this time an inter-associative one. Aides, an association fighting AIDS, conducted research on screening carried out by non-healthcare workers and non-physicians. The methods thus devised were then disseminated and financed by health insurance (Andréo, 2015). The Mouvement des Régies (Coqblin & Laville, 2023), representing 130 *régies*, is based on the involvement of the inhabitants as a lever to conceive, in consultation with local authorities and social landlords, adequate forms of upkeep and maintenance contributing to improving the daily life of the residents and providing them with work.

To these cases also can be added the early childhood care centres involving parental participation that are at the origin of institutional inflexions. The parents' involvement fostered a shift from a hygienic conception of child care to another, more focused on the awakening and socialisation of young children. This change led finally to the creation of a new profession, educator of young children, which reflects this shift. The process traced by Lévesque (2015) in the same field for Quebec, from 1968 to 2014, highlights three stages: self-institutionalisation on the margins for the first ten years, a difficult partial institutionalisation resulting from small steps forward for 15 years, and finally a "full" institutionalisation in the sense that it leads to a new model of public service by associations, reconciling freedom of choice and equality of access, which nevertheless remain threatened by neoliberal-oriented governments.

In Spain, the end of the Indignados movement does not mean that their uprising has failed (Rivas *et al.*, 2011). The collective voice that had challenged the ruling class fell silent, but the movement was prolonged by the amplification of local citizens' initiatives (Nez, 2022), sealing electoral agreements, which were victorious in several municipalities (Barcelona, Madrid, Zaragoza, Valencia, etc.). For the most part, these composite majorities have not lasted more than one term, but the limitations encountered cannot justify a simple denunciation. Again, a more detailed analysis is needed to discern the links between the "domestication" of social mobilisations and the "enslavement" of institutions (Neveu, 2011), the results of which depend on the previous implantation of citizen networks, as the differences between Barcelona and Madrid show (also see Esteves, this volume, cf. Sanz, Cama & Carrero, this volume).

The trajectory of Italian social solidarity cooperatives also is worth following. Born to gather around commons at the local level with reference to the Italian constitution, they initially brought together several categories of members (users, employees, volunteers, etc.) and were legalised only several years later. If, over time, many of them have lost their roots, others have seized this asset to carry out original collective actions to open up isolated areas or even to fight against the mafia, thanks to collaborations with the local authorities (Bucolo, 2021). By focusing on these actions, we defuse culturalist approaches that attribute to Sicilians an "amoral familialism" *(ibid.)* that blocks their way to economic development. However, this is not an exceptional context. In all parts of the world, from the Brazilian favelas to the French suburbs, unemployment and exclusion force inhabitants to revive solidarities in order to get by (Esteves; Lucas dos Santos; Banerjee, Shaban & Chand; Fajardo Rojas & Hataya; Muñoz; Amaro & Ferreira, all this volume). Either they rely on identity-based tensions or philanthropic intervention that maintains client-like networks, or they weave new links among citizens, communities and local businesses that come together around a territorialised project of emancipation from tutelage. It is because they have facilitated such empowerment processes, led by local populations, that the status of social cooperatives has risen in various countries.

1.4.2 The instituting relations among solidarity economy, commons and public authorities

The analysis of the relationships among solidarity experiences, commons and public actors raises a question originally posed by Habermas: does society develop, through autonomous public spaces, impulses vital enough to allow conflicts to be transported from the periphery of the political system into its very heart? (Habermas, 2011). Here, there are two opposing positions. One argues that any rapprochement with the dominant institutional framework entails an adoption of its norms and codes; the association is thus mired in either a subjugated marginality or an increased instrumentality. The other response does not accept this. In contrast, it stresses that any movement can give itself an objective of institutional change. We described the aforementioned examples (Section 1.4.1) as subject to sector-specific regulation. We will now mention other examples aiming for "new institutionality" at other levels and undertaking action on the ground in the form of everyday politics:

- At the local level, representative examples occur in municipalities where associative groups become co-responsible for a new generation of public services. Thus, in the Barcelona neighbourhood of *Nou Barris*, the *Ateneo Popular* was born, a structure emblematic of the opposition to Francoism since it was located in a former factory illegally occupied by the neighbourhood's residents during the dictatorship (Juan, 2018). It then became a pole of resistance to the commodification of urban space, offering cultural activities that were both varied and accessible. It claims affiliation with the anarchist and socialist *Ateneos Populares*, which closely articulated workers' associationism and culture in the 19th and 20th centuries in Spain. Like them, the *Ateneo* de *Nou Barris* includes users in five commissions that organise its activities (communication, art, management, programming, training). In this place, negative and constructive criticisms intertwine, as do emancipatory and emancipated practices. It is a relay of popular efforts to build renewed public action, in non-complacent dialogue with the municipality, reinforced by trainings, artistic workshops and organisation of big parties and meetings (also see Šimleša, this volume).
- At the national level, eminent cases of co-construction have been documented in Bolivia and Ecuador with the adoption of new constitutions in 2008, as well as new public policies in countries like Argentina (Muñoz, this volume), Brazil, Bulgaria (Caitana, Tasheva-Petrova & Vallet, this volume), Canada and Quebec, Chile and France.

These examples show that it is possible to build successful cooperation between commons and public authorities in the long run by adopting a plural conception of economy and democracy. They also posit that it is probably slightly short-sighted to treat popular mobilisations and the formal institutional sphere as if they were clearly distinct and disjointed universes. In the friction between the two, there are zones of transformation. If we no longer concentrate only on the reproduction of the institution, as traditional critical sociology does, processes of institutionalisation can then be placed at the centre of the scientific work of description.

1.5 Conclusion

Engagement in processes of institutionalisation is facilitated by the fact that autonomous public spaces can be formed by heterogeneous groups, some of which are focused on opposition and others more concerned with concrete action. If we continue with the example of the Ateneo Popular, those who take part in them then gain confidence in the recognition that comes from what they have created: a circus show or a theatrical performance here, a self-managed restaurant service there, which is appreciated by the neighbourhood.

The people involved in the associative mechanisms mentioned throughout this chapter do not display a desire for alternative autarky confined to the local, simply because they know how to draw upon a long history of association that provides them with a lexicon for thinking and acting together. They do not allow themselves to be caught up in the communitarian mirage of a parallel society and often face the institutional challenge of democracy on a global scale. In short, they bet on the reinstitution of society by itself, as Castoriadis would have said, not only without turning a blind eye to the phenomena of capture that affect all instituting work (Scinfolex, 2017) but also without giving credence to the idea of resigned impotence.

Finally, the important thing is not to distinguish between what is critical and what is institutional but to distinguish between who sets the standards and who must follow them, and how the result is a "hybrid" between the positions of individuals, collectives or institutions with more and with less power. Rules can be constructed within collectives by their own members. If we stick to a society that restricts everyone to a specific role, then institutionalisation is devoid of stakes. There is no point in acting if everything is decided in advance by meta-actors such as society and capitalism, or if micro-actors guided by self-interest determine social relations. It is this determinism that must be abandoned. The negative criticism of an "already instituted" social is no longer enough. We must follow the actors themselves in their institutional work, not just condemn the violence that existing institutions do to them. We must combine negative and constructive criticism with the recognition of emancipatory processes that already exist. Emerging realities therefore have to be analysed from an epistemological point of view, different from usual social and economic frameworks.

Notes

1. His way of being, his general appearance, his disposition of mind.
2. A set of shared opinions, common meaning, prejudices.

References

Andréo, C. (2015). "L'association avec et contre les pouvoirs publics," in Laville, J.-L. and Salmon, A. (dir.) *Associations et action publique*. Paris: Desclée de Brouwer, pp. 221–236.

Arrow, K. J. (1951). *Social Choice and Individual Values*. London: John Wiley and Son.

Bollier, D. (2002). "Reclaiming the commons," *Boston review*. Online at www.bostonreview.net/forum/david-bollier-reclaiming-commons/ (accessed March 29th 2023).

Bollier, D. and Helfrich, S. (2012). *The Wealth of Commons: A World beyond Market and State*. Amherst, MA: Levellers Press.

Bourdieu, P. (1987). *Distinction: A Social Critique of the Judgment of Taste*. Cambridge, MA: Harvard University Press.

Bourdieu, P. (2012). *The Key Concepts*. London and New York: Routledge.

Bucolo, E. (2021). *Antimafia, une histoire de solidarité*. Lormont: Le Bord de l'eau.

Castoriadis, C. (2014). *Commun, essai sur la révolution au 21e Siècle*. Paris: La Découverte.

Coqblin, A. and Laville, J.-L. (2023). *Les Régies de Quartier et de Territoire. Entre démarche citoyenne et pratique instituante*. Toulouse: Érès.

Crozier, M. and Friedberg, E. (1980). *Actors and Systems: The Politics of Collective Action*. Chicago: University of Chicago Press.

Dardot, P. and Laval, C. (2014). *Common. Essai sur la révolution au XXIe siècle*. Paris: La Découverte.

Dewey, J. (1929). *The Quest for Certainty*. New-York: Milton Balch and Co.

Dussel, E. (1992). *1492 el encubrimiento del otro. Hacia el origen del mito de la modernidad*. Bogotá: Plural Editores.

Esteves, A. M. (2022). "Processes of normative regulation in spaces of 'solidarity economy': A comparative case study analysis," *International Journal of Sociology and Social Policy*, 42(7/8), pp. 624–639.

Eynaud, P. and Laville, J. L. (2021). "How governance studies can be enriched by the commons framework: Towards a cross-fertilization agenda of research," in Donnelly-Cox, G., Meyer, M. and Wijkström, F. (eds.) *Research Handbook on Nonprofit Governance*. Cheltenham: Edward Elgar, pp. 220–234.

Eynaud, P., Laville, J. L., Dos Santos, L. L., Banerjee, S., Hulgard, H. and Avelino, F. (2019). *Theory of Social Enterprise and Pluralism: Social Movements, Solidarity Economy, and Global South*. Oxford: Routledge.

França Filho, G. C., Magnelli, A. and Eynaud, P. (2022). "Bridging the social and ecological transition: A development through democratic solidarity," in Baikady, R., Nadesan, V., Przeperski, J., Islam, M. R., Sajid, S. M. and Jianguo, G. (eds.) *The Palgrave Handbook of Global Social Change*. Basingstoke: Palgrave Macmillan, pp. 1–22.

Guerreiro Ramos, A. (1981). *The New Science of Organization: A Reconceptualization of the Wealth of Nation*. Toronto: University of Toronto Press.

Habermas, J. (2011). *The Discourse Theory on Law and Democracy*. Stanford University Press, Stanford Law Books, Stanford.

Hess, C. (2008). "Mapping the New Commons," *12th Biennial Conference of the International Association for the Study of the Commons,* University of Gloucester, Cheltenham, 14–18 July.

Hess, C. and Ostrom, E. (2007). *Understanding Knowledge as a Commons: From Theory to Practice*. Cambridge, MA and London: MIT Press.

Juan, M. (2018). *Les espaces publics autonomes, entre démocratie participative et économie solidaire*. Paris: Conservatoire national des arts et métiers.

Latour, B. (2012). *We Have Never Been Modern*. Cambridge, MA: Harvard University Press.

Laville, J. L. (2022). *The Social and Solidarity Economy*. Minneapolis: University of Minnesota press.

Laville, J. L., França Filho, G. C., Eynaud, P. and Dos Santos, L. L. (2019). "Social enterprise as a tension field: A historical and theoretical contribution based on the sociology of absences and emergences," in Gaiger, L. I., Nyssens, M. and Wanderley, F. (eds.) *Social Enterprise in Latin America Theory, Models and Practice*. Abingdon, UK: Routledge, pp. 262–285.

Laville, J. L. and Sainsaulieu, R. (2018). *L'association: Sociologie et économie* Série: Pluriel Éditions Fayard.

Lévesque, B. (2015). "Un nouveau modèle de service public par les associations: la garde de la petite enfance au Québec," in Laville, J. L and Salmon, A. (eds.) *Associations et action publique*. Paris: Desclée de Brouwer, pp. 461–502.

Martiskainen, M., Heiskanen, E. and Speciale, G. (2018). "Community energy initiatives to alleviate fuel poverty: The material politics of energy cafés," *Local Environment*, 23(1), pp. 20–35.

Neveu, C. (2011). "Démocratie participative et mouvements sociaux: entre domestication et ensauvagement?," *Participations*, 1, pp. 186–208.

Nez, H. (2022). *Démocratie réelle. L'héritage des indignés espagnols*. Paris: Editions du Croquant.

Ostrom, E. (1990). *Governing the Commons: The Evolution of Institutions for Collective Action*. Cambridge: Cambridge University Press.

Ostrom, E. (2005). *Understanding Institutional Diversity*. Princeton and Oxford: Princeton University Press.

Ostrom, E. (2010). "Beyond markets and states: Polycentric governance of complex economic systems," *American Economic Review*, 100(3), pp. 641–672.

Ostrom, E. and Ostrom, V. (1977). "Public goods and public choices," in Savas, E. S. (ed.) *Alternatives for Delivering Public Services: Toward Improved Performance*. Boulder: Westview Press, pp. 7–49.

Polanyi, K. (2011). *La subsistance de l'homme: La place de l'homme dans l'histoire et la société*. Paris: Flammarion.

Powell, W. W. (ed.) (1987). *The Nonprofit Sector. A Research Handbook*. New-Haven: Yale University Press.

Powell, W. W. and Di Maggio, P. J. (eds.) (1991). *The New Institutionalism in Organizational Analysis*. Chicago: Chicago University Press.

Quijano, A. (1998). *Modenidad, identitidad y utopia en America latina*. Lima: Sociedad y politica ediciones.

Rancière, J. (2003). *Éthique de la sociologie: Les Scènes du peuple*. Paris: Horlieu.

Rivas, O., Gallego, P., Gándara, F. and Álvarez, K. (2011). *Nosotros, los indignados: Las voces comprometidas del #15-M*. Barcelona: Ediciones Destino.

Schlager, E. and Ostrom, E. (1992). "Property-rights regimes and natural resources: A conceptual analysis," *Land Economics*, 68(3), pp. 249–262.

Scinfolex. (2017). "Le Comité invisible et les Communs: pourrons-nous encore être 'amis'?," Online at https://scinfolex.com/2017/08/31/le-comite-invisible-et-les-communs-pourrons-nous-encore-etre-amis/ (accessed February 17th 2022).

Sousa Santos, B. (2014). *The Epistemologies of the South; Justice against Epistemicide*. London: Routledge.

Stengers, I. (1997). *Cosmopolitiques, tome 7. Pour en finir avec la tolérance*. Paris: Editions La Découverte.

Vienney, C. (1994). *L'économie sociale*. Paris: La Découverte.

Zimmer, M. (2015). "Le débordement associatif face au cadrage de la participation: l'AMAP des Jardins de Cérès," in Laville, J. L and Salmon, A. (eds.) *Associations et action publique*. Paris: Desclée de Brouwer.

2 Framing and building the commons

Social movements and solidarity economy

Donatella Della Porta

2.1 Framing and practising the commons: an introduction

The chapter sheds light on the contributions by contemporary movements to the solidarity economy by locating it within social movement studies. It focuses in particular upon the key concept of commons, which is increasingly used in the field of social movement studies to describe initiatives of solidarity and participative management of goods and services. While social movement studies have rarely addressed solidarity economy, they have often dealt with closely interrelated concepts and phenomena. Social movements have often been considered as agents of alternative knowledge and innovation (della Porta & Diani, 2020: chapter 8). They have innovated various types of institutions through the development of prefigurative practices (Della Porta, 2020a). As for the definition of solidarity economy (Esteves, 2020, 2021), a co-productive relationship between the commons and social movements has been identified as "commons are produced within, through and because of social movements, while at the same time becoming the basis new social movements can sparkle from" (Varvarousis *et al.*, 2021: 294). The concept of commons and commons' practices have built upon these experiences, and developed especially in the framework of the anti-austerity protests, which were also considered as a sort of commons. It was especially in the *acampadas* that the prefiguration of possible futures emerged (Della Porta, 2015, 2020b), so paving the way for experimentation with alternative relations with society, politics and the market once the mobilisation in the streets declined.

From the theoretical point of view, the chapter aims at locating the debate around the commons within different streams of research that have, from different perspectives, looked at the relations between social movements and the economy. From the empirical point of view, it will look, first, at the framing of the commons as it emerged from within the global justice movement and was developed during the Italian referendum against privatisation of water supplies. Second, it will review research about the spreading of commons in Southern Europe, from within and as a spin-off of anti-austerity protests. Special attention

DOI: 10.4324/9781003306344-3

will be paid to struggles against privatisation of the provision of public goods, as well as the practices of the commons in the development of critical mutualism (e.g. self-managed clinics) and new cooperatives. In this context, solidarity economy acquires relevance as a set of practices that promote a transition to a commons-based economy which developed from within progressive social movements and spread cross-nationally.

2.2 Social movements as sites for innovation

While movements have been studied mainly as contentious actors, fighting in the streets to resist or promote political change, social movement studies have also pointed to their innovative capacity in terms of nurturing and spreading ideas through the prefiguration of different visions of politics, the market and society in general. Under the label of the commons, we, in fact, find both, a reflection of prefigurative politics within alternative spaces, which is at the core of research on solidarity economy, as well as empirically overlapping objects of analysis such as cooperatives, transition initiatives and intentional communities such as ecovillages. Also particularly relevant for this field of research is the consideration of the role of the commons as alternative spaces that serve as containers of practices, epistemologies and pedagogies that constitute what has been called everyday politics (Martiskainen *et al.*, 2018). Also in the case of the commons, prefiguration is moreover considered to be a method to achieve a goal, which could be a commons-based economy.

The important role of social movements, not only as agents of contentious politics in the street but also as actors capable of developing new knowledge through the prefiguration of different relations, is relevant for the specific form of innovation represented by initiatives within solidarity economy, including those focusing on the construction of commons. At the very origins of research on social movements as forms of collective behaviour, symbolic interactionists close to the so-called "Chicago School" stressed that collective phenomena do not simply reflect social crises. Rather, especially in moments of intense social change, they produce new norms and new solidarities that function as drivers of change, especially in value systems. (e.g. Turner & Killian, 1987). Scholars have acknowledged the positive epistemic contribution that movements can give to democracies (Bohman, 2006). In particular, the recent systemic turn in deliberative democracy sees movements as significant innovators and positive contributors to society-wide deliberation (Parkinson & Mansbridge, 2012).

Also, more recent social science literature has considered social movements as "learning sites" (Welton, 1993), capable of building knowledge through discursive processes that consist of the "talks and conversations – the speech acts – and written communications of movement members that occur in the context of, or in relation to, movement activities" (Benford & Snow, 2000: 623). Related to prefigurative activities, which are so important for solidarity economy, research on knowledge-practices within social movements singled out a broad range of them going

> from things we are more classically trained to define as knowledge, such as practices that engage and run parallel to the knowledge of scientists or policy experts, to micro-political and cultural interventions that have more to do with "know-how" or the "cognitive praxis that informs all social activity" and which vie with the most basic social institutions that teach us how to be in the world.
>
> (Casas-Cortés *et al.*, 2008)

Within alternative spaces, activists build knowledge by:

> 1) engaging in co-producing, challenging, and transforming expert scientific discourses; 2) creating critical subjects whose embodied discourse produces new notions of democracy; and 3) generating reflexive conjunctural theories and analyses that go against more dogmatic and orthodox approaches to social change, and as such contribute to ethical ways of knowing.
>
> (Casas-Cortés *et al.*, 2008)

The knowledge produced by progressive social movements is organised in view of social transformation. Practices of knowledge are both formal and informal, going from the development of concepts and theories to the generation of collective identities (Casas-Cortés *et al.*, 2008). Social movement knowledge is in fact situated rather than universal, committed rather than detached and focused on changes at the roots of the system rather than on the symptoms (Mayo, 1999). In social movements, as in particular in social movement initiatives focusing on solidarity economy, much knowledge emerges in action: the seed banks in the peasant movement come from such knowledge practices.

Thus, from the forum of the global justice movement to the squares of the anti-austerity protests, knowledge practices develop in particular within the construction of prefigurative spaces. During the anti-austerity global cycles of protests, the concept of the commons has been used to refer to the building of autonomous spaces. The commons "imply a plurality of people (a community) sharing resources and governing them and their own relations and (re)production processes through horizontal doing in common, commoning" (De Angelis, 2017: 29). With reference to social movements, commoning has been defined as "the social practices performed by commoners to manage and reclaim the commons" (Varvarousis *et al.*, 2021: 293). The definition has included practices such as Sustainable Community Organisations, Alternative Action Organisations or Alternative Forms of Resilience, characterising as focusing on alternative forms of consumption and (re)production rather than at street protests (Forno & Graziano, 2014). Commons are thus presented as "social systems in which resources are shared by a community of users/producers (commoners), who also define the modes of use and production, distribution and circulation of these resources through democratic and horizontal forms of governance (commoning)" (Varvarousis *et al.*, 2021: 297; on commoning, see also Esteves, 2017). Also defined as direct social action (Bosi & Zamponi, 2019), the experiences of the commons build upon long-lasting traditions in labour movements and, later, other social movements from feminism to environmentalism, for example in the cooperatives and mutual help experiences that bridged prefigurative with instrumental aims. As is the case in theorisation of the solidarity economy, a commons-based economy can be only achieved through the development of an alternative spatiality constituted by alternative spaces (along with supply chains connecting these spaces) where production, commercialisation and consumption are re-signified.

Grassroots initiatives of the type usually addressed through concepts such as the commons have been defined as

> networks of activists and organisations generating novel bottom-up solutions for sustainable development; solutions that respond to the local situation and the interests and the values of the community involved. . . . [They] operate in civil society arenas and involve committed activists experimenting with social innovations as well as using greener technologies.
>
> (Seyfang & Smith, 2007: 585)

They include cooperatives, voluntary associations, informal community groups and social enterprises that follow a double logic of catering for social needs while also meeting normative concerns (Seyfang & Smith, 2007). It has been noted that many such initiatives respond

> to both the social need for creating accessible spaces for social inclusion and socialisation, and the ideological motivation of 'de-commodifying' the provision and consumption of food, and empowering citizens. In this sense, ideological critique of mainstream food industry and the need to tackle urban poverty and social exclusion are both underlying triggering factors for the emergence of grassroots innovations. The production of food, its provision and consumption become thus goals to be pursued collectively rather than individually.
>
> (Monticelli & della Porta, 2019)

The commons have been defined as material (lands, livestock, etc.) or immaterial (knowledge, culture, etc.) things that communities possess and share in common (Gudeman, 2001: 27–28). So,

> From recuperated factories and cooperatives to social solidarity structures, the twofold character of the commons, meaning its use value and the plurality

> of subjects claiming its ownership, is constituted within and through an ecology of social practices and interactions that at the same time sustain and reproduce the two former elements.
>
> (Roussos & Malamidis, 2021: 366)

The commons are therefore based upon principles of cooperation and responsibility, to each other and to nature (Federici, 2018: 110). As noted, commoning involves an "instituting praxis" as a collectivity establishes a common, thereby basing production and reproduction upon principles of equality, horizontality and self-organisation (Dardot & Laval, 2019; Linebaugh, 2008).

While performing these activities, commoners develop forms of social relations and (re)produce values, affects and meanings, such as solidarity, mutual aid, reciprocity and care (De Angelis, 2017). Thus, the concept of commoning addresses interconnections between natural, social and cultural resources and a community on the one hand, and the multiple relations that are created among commoners through their plural interactions and active participation in the workings and everyday life of the community on the other. In this respect,

> social change is addressed in the active engagement with the experiment of self-governance and the collective social conditions within which commoners relate to one another in the here and now. Street politics have been complemented with the emergence and diffusion of numerous solidarity structures, actively providing informal welfare services to the affected population.
>
> (Roussos & Malamidis, 2021: 368)

As Bosi and Zamponi noted, in defining the twin concepts of direct social action,

> Through the reterritorialization of collective processes, direct social action proceeds towards the rapprochement between the individual and the community, production and consumption; citizens and institutions; users and management that the demands of neoliberal development have upset. In doing so, it aims to create aggregative processes, a sense of belonging, trust, relationships, sociality oriented towards the common good and social well-being. People who have lost the traditional references of parties, trade unions, associations or movements, find a community action in a popular gym, in an improvised garrison to bring food and blankets to migrants excluded from the reception system, and establish, within these contexts, bonds of belonging.
>
> (Bosi & Zamponi, 2019: 25)

2.3 Framing the commons: the water referendum in Italy

The very concept of the commons has been developed during social movement campaigns as related to participative forms of management of particularly important goods. Especially relevant for the definition of the commons was the campaign undertaken in Italy in 2011 in relation to a referendum, called from below, against the privatisation of water supply. The referendum, held in June 2011, was a great success for the organisers: not only did 50% of the electorate turn out to vote, ensuring a quorum, but also 95% of the voters voted against water privatisation. Furthermore, the referendum advanced public debate, first on water as a common pool good, and subsequently on the importance of participatory practices in the management of public goods that merit special attention.

The abrogative referendum had been called by a coalition of social movement organisations, mostly active also in anti-austerity protests (Della Porta *et al.*, 2016), which had collected 1.4 million signatures, about three times the number required by Italian law to initiate a citizen-induced referendum. Started by the core organisations of the Italian Forum of Water Movements, the campaign lasted 18 months during which water rights were to become a core icon not only against privatisation in general, but also for citizens' participation, as captured in the slogan "*Si scrive acqua, si legge democrazia*" ("It is written water, it is read democracy"). The experience of the social forum interacted with that of the anti-austerity protests in terms of the normative stress upon broad participation, managed through consensual methods.

Within the campaign against privatisation of water supplies, the framing of the commons was linked to the claims for universal rights and solidarity that had been at the core of the global justice movements (Mazzoni & Cicognani, 2013; Mazzoni *et al.*, 2015; Petrella, 2001). The commons were defined as

> those goods – natural resources like water, air, parks, basic social services . . . – that are functional to the promotion of fundamental human rights and the free development of peoples. . . . The law should therefore guarantee direct, collective and universal enjoyment of these goods, taking into account also future generations' needs.
>
> (Fantini, 2012: 35)

Water was thus framed as a common good, locating it beyond an individualistic conception of human rights. In general, the commons are considered as resources that require special (and especially strong) legal protection, which should be stronger than that already provided for public goods (Quarta & Ferrando, 2015: 270). Given the non-competing and non-exclusive nature of resources such as water, and their role in producing utilities that are necessary for the fulfilment of fundamental human rights, special legal protection was called for in order to guarantee their sustainable and intergenerational preservation. The conceptualisation of the commons thus allowed for overcoming a dualism between the private and the public, stressing the rights of a community to have access to and benefit from water supplies (Quarta & Ferrando, 2015: 271).

Part of the conceptualisation of the commons points to the need for active and direct involvement of the local population through decentralised and participatory management in order to produce social accountability and harmonious relationships with the entire ecosystem (Fantini, 2012: 31–32). Given their universal value, the commons must be kept "*extra commercium*" and put under diffused ownership and widespread responsibility to protect them, as

> any individual, for the sole fact of having an interest in or a contact with the resource, becomes responsible for the way in which it is managed, and holder of a right of action against any form of *mala gestio*, independently from the fact that the good is under public or private management.
>
> (Quarta & Ferrando, 2015: 271, emphasis in original)

Resonant with the UNESCO concept of a "Common Heritage of Mankind," the reference to water as a "common good (or shared resource) of humankind" pointed at a cosmopolitan vision of a global community. The management and delivery of such goods must include local communities and cooperatives of water users, as well as customary governance (Fantini, 2012: 39) through the preservation of community ties. As one activist put it, "this is actually the reason, sense of community, and the fact of being able to handle things in common and dealing with them together" (Mazzoni & Cicognani, 2013: 321). Because "private management also hinders the ability of citizens to make their voices heard" (Mazzoni & Cicognani, 2013: 320), this activist presents participatory democracy oriented to the common good as an alternative to privatisation and to neoliberal capitalism more generally (Cernison, 2014: 83).

Direct participation of citizens is promoted, both against privatisation and against centralised and top-down forms of public management. As one activist put it:

> [C]ommons is everything we share, gifts of nature and creations of society that belong to all of us equally, and should be maintained for future generations. These are goods that escape the idea of exclusive use and build social bonds. These goods must not allow discrimination in access to them according to individual wealth, but reintroduce the element of equality, as well as a relationship of care – rather than one of domination or subjection – between humanity and the rest of nature of which it is a part.
>
> (Fattori, 2013: 384–385)

In this vision, the commoners

> are all the members of a community or loosely connected group of people who steward and care for the shared goods, adopting a form of self-government

> based on their capability to give themselves rules (and incentives and sanctions to make them be respected) called commoning.
>
> (Fattori, 2013: 385)

Commoning implies an open, participatory, and inclusive form of decision making (Fattori, 2013: 385), and *commonification* refers then to self-government by citizens. Commoning is thus presented as the social and organisational dimension of the commons (De Angelis, 2017). The concept of the commons continues, in fact, to be a central reference for contemporary social movements, inspiring other progressive campaigns. The idea of a participatory form of democracy in the running of public services challenges the neoliberal capitalist tendency to commodify new areas by extending the market logic of profits (Bieler, 2015).

2.4 Building the commons: the aftermath of anti-austerity protests

If the global justice movement contributed to the framing of the commons, anti-austerity protests, especially in Southern Europe, have been seen as producing commons, both during the *acampadas* and as a spin-off of those protests. The cases of Spain, Greece and Italy can be taken as illustrations of the development of practices of the commons both during and after the peaks of the mobilisation.

The commons were in fact defined to be extremely resonant with the participatory and deliberative conceptions of democracy that had been practised in the camps. It has been noted that "the end of square mobilisations was followed by the proliferation of self-organised ventures at neighbourhood level, covering needs related to social (re)production such as solidarity clinics, community gardens and workers' cooperatives" (Varvarousis *et al.*, 2021: 293). The multiplication of the commons happened through the transplantation of some commons created during the protests, the implementation of commons that had only been thought of during the occupation and the proliferation of commons developed following the decentralisation of the protests (Varvarousis *et al.*, 2021).

As social outcomes of mobilisation, the commons include various social infrastructures that affect the collective organisation of everyday social life in various spheres of social production and reproduction, among them being care, education, food, housing and finance (Varvarousis *et al.*, 2021). They are presented as everyday resistance against the dispossession and enclosure imposed by neoliberalism, empowering citizens against austerity through experimentation with alternative modes of economic relations (*ibid*). Research on the commons as an organisational legacy of the anti-austerity protests is especially widespread not only on the Greek and Spanish cases, where those protests were stronger, but also on Italy, within a historical tradition of cooperative and solidarity economy.

In Greece, grassroots social innovations analysed under the label of the commons include time banks and community gardens (Dalakoglou & Vradis, 2011), collective kitchens and open markets without middlemen (Vaiou & Kalandides, 2016), social clinics providing free primary healthcare services (Kotronaki & Christou, 2019), the rehabilitated factory of Vio.Me. (Malamidis, 2020) and the K136 initiative against the privatisation of Thessaloniki's water company (Velegrakis & Frezouli, 2016). As many as 70% of the organisations practising some form of solidarity economy in the country have been created since the protests in 2011 (Varvarousis *et al.*, 2021). A short summary of the commons that have emerged from the anti-austerity protests in Athens mentions self-managed social clinics and pharmacies, workers' cooperatives, urban occupations, time banks, alternative currencies and solidarity exchange networks, urban gardens, farmer/consumer cooperatives, farmers' markets, art/publishing collectives and an occupied factory (Varvarousis *et al.*, 2021). It has been noted that:

> This "explosion" indicates that a horizontal solidarity and commoning network inherited partly from the square mobilisations was established as a resilience system to cope with the crisis and the dismantling of the welfare state. Social clinics, for instance, aim to provide healthcare to those excluded from the public health system; some also struggle against austerity by attempting to develop an alternative healthcare model. . . . Likewise, solidarity hubs mainly active at the neighbourhood level, are involved in the distribution of food, clothing, and free lessons. . . . Direct producer-to-consumer networks also flourished after 2011.
>
> (Varvarousis *et al.*, 2021: 302)

Similarly in Spain, social movement organisations that played key roles in the protests were the basis of various experiments with the practice of the commons. Self-managed cooperatives emerged in the area of housing with the PAH (Plataforma de Afectados por la Hipoteca), a network organising, among other things, squatting of vacant apartments (García-Lamarca, 2017). The *Marea Blanca* and *Marea Verde* mobilisations in the health and education sectors, respectively, are similar forms of practical political intervention on the basis of principles of direct democracy and self-management (Lois-González & Piñeira-Mantiñán, 2015). In another major site of anti-austerity protests, the city of Barcelona, as many as 4,700 solidarity economy initiatives have been counted, with 860 cooperatives and 260 communities (listing about 500,000 members and 100,000 volunteers) (Fernàndez & Miró, 2016). The emerging commons include time banks, social centres, free canteens for the disadvantaged, food banks, barter markets organised by neighbourhood assemblies, community gardens, anti-eviction networks and agro-ecological producer-to-consumer groups (Varvarousis *et al.*, 20217).

Also in Italy, where protests in the street were less widespread than in Greece and Spain, anti-austerity protests inspired various initiatives in direct social action, in which the principle of providing economic alternatives to capitalism was central. Building upon and innovating within a long-lasting tradition, commons' practices through ethical financing, groups for alternative production and consumption, microcredit, squatting for housing, sharing economy, and alternative agricultural practices have developed following the financial crisis. As in Spain, in Italy, alternative food networks and solidarity purchasing groups have spread, with more than 1,000 solidarity purchasing groups with as many as 150,000 participants now in existence (Grasseni, 2014). Moreover, alternative local markets, day-care centres, social centres, forms of mutual aid and the self-managed factories of RiMaflow and Officine Zero are all among the social outcomes of the anti-austerity wave of protests (Forno & Graziano, 2019; Bosi & Zamponi, 2015; Di Feliciantonio, 2017; Roussos & Malamidis, 2021). In particular, recovered factories have this way been brought into operation:

> Usually they arise from a specific action of workers who, in the face of the bankruptcy of the company or its transfer, mobilize by occupying the factory, trying to defend their workplace. Occupation of the workplace is not a novelty in itself, in the twentieth century workers have used this practice numerous times. But for an occupation to turn into a recovered factory it requires two other important steps. At a later stage, the mobilization of workers is not limited to protesting local and national management and institutions, but takes the initiative to restart the production cycle by self-managing production, or "working without bosses". In a third moment, the recovered factories open their space to cultural, educational and service initiatives by shifting their center of gravity towards the local communities in which they are inserted, aiming to create local society. The recovered factories that tend to stand out most from the experience of the workers buyout (the companies bought by the workers) aim at a reconstruction of horizontal social relations in the workplace, thus adopting mechanisms of direct democracy and collective taking charge of decisions and responsibilities.
>
> (Bosi & Zamponi, 2019: 99)

Beyond Europe, the emergence of solidarity grassroots initiatives also often coincides with periods of increased contention (Roussos & Malamidis, 2021), as was the case with the growth of alternative economic formations during the global justice movements in Latin America (Miller, 2005: 2; De França Filho *et al.*, 2012). It has in fact been noted that "commoning and solidarity initiatives share similar ethical and political values with social movements, such as solidarity, ecological thinking, collective and individual autonomy, local rootedness, and global interconnection" (Roussos & Malamidis, 2021: 363). Therefore, the need to strengthen the linkages between social movements and commoning and solidarity economy initiatives has been stressed, and particularly the need to integrate economic alternatives into social movements, and vice versa (Roussos & Malamidis, 2021).

From the organisational point of view, the commons have been characterised by a participatory model that resonates with the one promoted during the anti-austerity protests. So, it has been observed,

> The "grammar of the commons" which distinguishes commons from other types of social outcomes hence includes common management, horizontality and direct participation of all members in decision-making. Utilizing the concept of commons enables linking these contemporary experiences with the tradition of self-organization systems including the management of common resources.
>
> (Varvarousis *et al.*, 2021: 297)

The emerging commons, therefore,

> aim to enact different social relations, economic organisations and institutions at the local level, create networked alternatives at multiple scales, and mobilize a vision of organizing everyday life collectively based on democratic self-management. . . . Firstly, these commons not only hold inclusiveness and openness as foundational principles, but often also engage proactively with the wider neighbourhood and city, which turns them into spaces of resistance from which to launch counter austerity politics. . . . Secondly, the open and active engagement in the cities′ politics implies a (re)politicization of groups previously not active politically. . . . The commoning practices that proliferate in the squares' aftermath are political in opening up spaces for enacting direct democracy and performing novel ways of being and acting in common. They are political spaces where disagreement and conflict are recognized and negotiated, and where everyone appropriates voice and performs the capacity to govern, i.e. acts politically. In this sense, the political potential of these practices lies in their staging of alternative ways of being and acting in common, and materializing claims of equality, solidarity and freedom, as long as they remain open to new voices to be heard and new concerns to appear as common concerns.
>
> (Varvarousis *et al.*, 2021: 305)

From the point of view of the action repertoires, different practices are blended in the commons with production not only of services but also of alternative relations, mixing instrumental aims with prefiguration of possible alternatives that are also highly relevant for solidarity economy. Signalling the interplay of the repertoires of co-ownership, co-production and co-management of resources and spaces, the concept of commoning has focused attention on the social practices that communities adopt in the production and reproduction of the commons. Thus,

> a focus on the social practices developed by collective kitchens or grassroots food networks can help us to draw out the implications of alternative values and ethics

> in transforming the production and distribution of food. Similarly, in exploring the alternative educational practices that have been generated by various solidarity projects, we can provide nuanced understandings of education as a good or resource collectively produced and governed by the particular communities.
>
> (Roussos & Malamidis, 2021: 370; see also Pechtelidis & Kioupkiolis, 2020)

The grassroots practices of healthcare provisioning by participants in social clinics allowed them to "provide open and equal access to primary healthcare services without discriminations, incorporating in this way the aspects of community management and sharing in healthcare provision" (Roussos & Malamidis, 2021: 371).

2.5 Some conclusions

In conclusion, this chapter has aimed to show the theoretical relevance of bridging social movement studies with research on solidarity economy and at the same time the importance of social movements as incubators of innovative practices as well as of solidarity economy as a form through which social movement practices thrive and develop even after protests in the street subside. In particular, the chapter looked at the framing and practices of the commons as a form of solidarity economy that has grown from within the experiences of the global justice movement as well as anti-austerity protests. The idea of the commons as based on forms of production and reproduction alternative to capitalist ones emerges within social movements that oppose neoliberal commodification of spaces and services and develops in the practices put forward by social movement activists, at times with support by institutional allies (Della Porta, 2020a). Prefigured in the squares, initiatives based on the concept of the commons, as goods deserving special protection, build actual practices aiming at inventing forms of participatory management. As we have seen based on the examples of the referendum against the privatisation of water supply in Italy and the initiatives built in the aftermath of anti-austerity protests in areas of production and reproduction, social movements contribute to the frames and the practices of commoning. In doing this, they build upon and innovate forms of solidarity economy, which have been developed during previous waves of protests. While social movement studies have often focused on street protests, they have however expanded their interest well beyond the most visible forms of political contention, engaging more and more in research on practices of knowledge building and prefiguration of alternatives, that at times penetrated political and economic institutions. Recent research on the commons testifies for the importance of a growing dialogue between social movement studies and research on solidarity economy in order to understand the creative potential of social movements and help address the challenges involved in inventing alternative practices.

References

Benford, R. D. and. Snow, D. A. (2000). "Framing processes and social movements: An overview and assessment," *Annual Review of Sociology*, 26, pp. 611–639.

Bieler, A. (2015). "'Sic Vos Non Vobis' (For you, but not yours): The struggle for public water in Italy," *Monthly Review: An Independent Socialist Magazine*, 67(5). Online at http://monthlyreview.org/2015/10/01/sic-vos-non-vobis-for-you-but-not-yours/ (accessed March 29th 2023).

Bohman, J. (2006). "Deliberative democracy and the epistemic benefits of diversity," *Episteme*, 3, pp. 175–191.

Bosi, L. and Zamponi, L. (2015). "Direct social actions and economic crises: The relationship between forms of action and socio-economic context in Italy," *Partecipazione e conflitto* 8(2), pp. 367–391.

Bosi, L. and Zamponi, L. (2019). *Resistere alla crisi*. Bologna: Il Mulino.

Casas-Cortés, M. I., Osterweil, M. and Powell, D. E. (2008). "Blurring boundaries: Recognizing knowledge-practices in the study of social movements," *Anthropological Quarterly*, 81(1), pp. 17–58.

Cernison, M. (2014). *Online communication spheres in social movements campaigns: The Italian referendum on water*. Ph.D. Dissertation, European University Institute.

Dalakoglou, D. and Vradis, A. (2011). "Spatial legacies of December and the right to the city," in Dalakoglou, K. and Vradis, A. (eds.) *Revolt and Crisis in Greece: Between a Present Yet to Pass and a Future Still to Come*. Oakland, CA: AK Press, pp. 77–88.

Dardot, P. and Laval, C. (2019). *Common: On revolution in the 21st century*. London: Bloomsbury.

De Angelis, M. (2017). *Omnia Sunt Communia: On the Commons and the Transformation to Postcapitalism*. London: Zed Books.

De França Filho, G. C., Júnior, J. T. S. and Rigo, A. S. (2012). "Solidarity finance through community development banks as a strategy for reshaping local economies: Lessons from Banco Palmas," Revista de Administração, 47(3), pp. 500–515.

Della Porta, D. (2015). *Social Movements in Times of Austerity*. Cambridge: Polity.

Della Porta, D. (2020a). *How Social Movements Can Save Democracy*. Cambridge: Polity.

Della Porta, D. (2020b). "Protests as critical junctures: Some reflections towards a momentous approach to social movements," *Social Movement Studies*, 19(5–6), pp. 556–575.

Della Porta, D., Andretta, M., Fernandes, T., O'Connor, F., Romanos, E. and Vogiatzoglou, M. (2016). *Late Neoliberalism and Its Discontents in the Economic Crisis: Comparing Social Movements in the European Periphery*. Basingstoke: Palgrave Macmillan.

Della Porta, D. and Diani, M. (2020). *Social Movements: An Introduction*. 3rd edition. Oxford: Blackwell.

Di Feliciantonio, C. (2017). "Spaces of the expelled as spaces of the urban commons? Analysing the re-emergence of squatting initiatives in Rome," *International Journal of Urban and Regional Research*, 41(5), pp. 708–725.

Esteves, A. M. (2017). "Radical environmentalism and 'commoning': Synergies between ecosystem regeneration and social governance at Tamera ecovillage, Portugal," *Antipode*, 49(2), pp. 357–376.

Esteves, A. M. (2020). "Solidarity economy markets as mobilizational commons": Resignifying the market through the lens of cooperation," *Community Development Journal*, 56(2), pp. 470–486.

Esteves, A. M. (2021). "Processes of normative regulation in spaces of 'solidarity economy': A comparative case study analysis," *International Journal of Sociology and Social Policy*, 42(7/8), pp. 624–639.
Fantini, E. (2012). "Water as human right and commons: Themes and practices in the Italian water movement," *Pace diritti umani*, 2, pp. 15–40.
Fattori, T. (2013). "From the water commons movement to the commonification of the public realm," *South Atlantic Quarterly*, 112(2), pp. 377–387.
Federici, S. (2018). *Re-Enchanting the World: Feminism and the Politics of the Commons*. Oakland, CA: PM Press.
Fernàndez, A. and Miró, I. (2016). *L'economia social i solidària a Barcelona*. Barcelona: Comissionat d'Economia Cooperativa, Social i Solidaria & Ajuntament de Barcelona.
Forno, F. and Graziano, P. (2014). "Sustainable community movement organisations," *Journal of Consumer Culture*, 14(2), pp. 139–157.
Forno, F. and Graziano, P. (2019). "From global to glocal: Sustainable community movement organisations (SCMOs) in times of crisis." *European Societies*, 21(5), pp. 729–752.
García-Lamarca, M. (2017). "From occupying plazas to recuperating housing: Insurgent practices in Spain," *International Journal of Urban and Regional Research*, 41(1), pp. 37–53.
Grasseni, C. (2014). "Food activism in Italy as an anthropology of direct democracy," *Anthropological Journal of European Cultures*, 23(1), pp. 77–98.
Gudeman, S. (2001). *The Anthropology of Economy: Community, Market, and Culture*. Malden, MA: Blackwell.
Kotronaki, L. and Christou, S. (2019). "(De-) politicization trajectories in an anti-austerity contentious cycle. social clinics-pharmacies solidarity structures in Greece," *Partecipazione e Conflitto*, 12(2), pp. 325–352.
Linebaugh, P. (2008). *The Magna Carta Manifesto: Liberties and Commons for All*. Berkeley: University of California Press.
Lois-González, R. and Piñeira-Mantiñán, M. J. (2015). "The revival of urban social and neighbourhood movements in Spain: A geographical characterization," *DIE ERDE: Journal of the Geographical Society of Berlin*, 146(2–3), pp. 127–138.
Malamidis, H. (2020). *Social Movements and Solidarity Structures in Crisis-Ridden Greece*. Amsterdam: Amsterdam University Press.
Martiskainen, M., Heiskanen, E. and Speciale, G. (2018). "Community energy initiatives to alleviate fuel poverty: The material politics of energy cafés," *Local Environment*, 23(1), pp. 20–35.
Mayo, P. (1999). *Gramsci, Freire and Adult Education: Possibilities for Transformative Action*. London: Zed Books.
Mazzoni, D. and Cicognani, E. (2013). "Water as a commons: An exploratory study on the motives for collective action among Italian water movement activists," *Journal of Community & Applied Social Psychology*, 23(4), pp. 314–330.
Mazzoni, D., van Zomeren, M. and Cicognami, E. (2015). "The motivating role of perceived right violation and efficacy beliefs in identification with the Italian water movement," *Political Psychology*, 36(3), pp. 315–330.
Miller, E. (2005). *Solidarity Economics: Building Other Economies from the Bottom-Up and the Inside-Out*. Greene, ME: JED Collective.

Monticelli, L. and della Porta, D. (2019). "The successes of political consumerism as a social movement," in Boström, M., Micheletti, M. and Oosterveer, P. (eds.) *The Oxford Handbook of Political Consumerism*. Oxford: Oxford University Press, pp. 772–792.

Parkinson, J. and Mansbridge, J. (eds.) (2012). *Deliberative Systems*. New York: Cambridge University Press.

Pechtelidis, Y. and Kioupkiolis, A. (2020). "Education as commons, children as commoners: The case study of the little tree community," *Democracy and Education*, 28(1), pp. 2–11.

Petrella, R. (2001). *The Water Manifesto: Arguments for a World Water Contract*. London: Zed Books.

Quarta, A. and Ferrando, T. (2015). "Italian property outlaws: From the theory of the commons to the praxis of occupation," *Global Jurist*, 15(3), pp. 261–290.

Roussos, C. and Malamidis, H. (2021). "Social movements and the commons," *Mobilization: An International Quarterly*, 26(3), pp. 359–379.

Seyfang, G. and Smith, A. (2007). "Grassroots innovations for sustainable development: Towards a new research and policy agenda," *Environmental Politics*, 16(4), pp. 584–603.

Turner, R. and Killian, L. (1987) [1974, 1957]. *Collective Behavior*. Englewood Cliffs, NJ: Prentice Hall.

Vaiou, D. and Kalandides, A. (2016). "Practices of collective action and solidarity: Reconfigurations of the public space in crisis-ridden Athens, Greece," *Journal of Housing and the Built Environment*, 31(3), pp. 457–470.

Varvarousis, A., Asara, V. and Akbulut, B. (2021). "Commons: A social outcome of the movement of the squares," *Social Movement Studies*, 20(3), pp. 292–311.

Velegrakis, G. and Frezouli, E. (2016). *Environmental Conflicts and Social Movements: Twelve Case Studies from Greece*. Athens: Harokopio University.

Welton, M. (1993). "Social revolutionary learning: The new social movements as learning sites," *Adult Education Quarterly*, 43(3), pp. 152–164.

3 Solidarity economy as ecology of mind

Autopoiesis, enchantment and the commons

Thomas Henfrey

3.1 Introduction

This chapter examines solidarity economy as an ecology of mind (Bateson, 1979): as diverse epistemologies/ontologies reflecting (and themselves constitutive of) local peculiarities of place (cf. Maffi, 2001; Pretty, 2002). In doing so, it frames capitalism as, fundamentally, an epistemological and ontological crisis: an ongoing depletion of the collective human capacity to understand the world in different ways and to express those understandings through distinctive ways of being in the world (cf. Scott, 1990; Escobar, 2018; Federici, 2019). In such a framing, the destruction of social, ecological, cultural and biocultural diversity is an inevitable consequence of this epistemic depletion, and self-reinforcing because it undermines capacities to imagine and enact alternatives (Guattari, 2000 [1989]). Solidarity economy is thus portrayed as consisting of deliberate collective acts of epistemic resistance and renewal: the defence of economically autonomous space and the deliberate creation of alternatives within the spheres of production and exchange (Leyshon *et al.*, 2003). This takes place when people self-organise to create livelihoods that are *autopoietic* or, in other words, that are self-generative of the cultural, social and natural relationships on which they themselves depend for their own reproduction.

The following sections explore the epistemic foundations of autopoiesis in solidarity economy initiatives, both theoretically and through examination of empirical cases. Section 3.2 builds on Laville and Eynaud's exploration of solidarity economy as commons in Chapter 1, emphasising how the properties of autopoiesis and sympoiesis – self-generative and mutually generative capacities – arise in ecologically contextualised commons. Section 3.3 explores the epistemological foundations of autopoiesis, arguing that autopoietic forms of organisation entail composite epistemologies that combine multiple different ways of understanding the world. Section 3.4 describes how epistemic innovation of this type opens up new counter-hegemonic possibilities for political action. Section 3.5 examines how such possibilities are illustrated by the various case studies presented in other chapters in this volume. In conclusion, Section 3.6 argues for

DOI: 10.4324/9781003306344-4

closer attention to the epistemic dimensions of solidarity economy, in particular the role of counter-hegemonic epistemologies in the autopoietic organisation and sympoietic inter-relating of solidarity economy initiatives.

3.2 Commons and autopoiesis

The concept of *autopoiesis* originally arose in biology and refers to the self-sustaining capacity of living systems: their ability to regenerate and reproduce, on a continuous basis, their own constitutive structures and processes (Maturana & Valera, 1980: 78–79). Autopoiesis is different from material self-sufficiency – all living systems rely on ongoing interchanges of matter and energy with their environment – and more specifically refers to a living system's inherent capacity for structural self-generation. Although the concept refers to a system's self-organising properties, it also has social implications: when distinct autopoietic systems interact, they typically do so in ways that support each other's autopoiesis, a wider quality that Donna Haraway (2016) has termed *sympoiesis*.[1]

Autopoiesis has become an important concept in the study of commons through the concept of *commons ecologies* (De Angelis, 2017). For our present purposes, we can understand this to refer to commons that, whether through functional necessity or deliberate design, are autopoietic in their internal organisation, and hence in sympoietic interrelationship with adjacent ecological and social–ecological systems. Commons are, simply put, economic formations in which rights and responsibilities are allocated according to dynamic agreements among co-users as to appropriate behaviour, rather than market logic or government prescription. Although nothing logically compels commons to be autopoietically organised, in practice, the functional requirement to sustain productivity while maintaining or enhancing the resource base means this is in fact the case in most traditional commons (Berkes, 1989; Berkes & Folke, 1998). An aspiration for sustainability, implying autopoietic forms of organisation, is also often a deliberate choice in the design of new commons founded as explicit alternatives to capitalism (Henfrey & Kenrick, 2017; Bollier & Helfrich, 2019). When solidarity economy initiatives combine explicit ethical commitments to sustainability with more typical concerns with social justice and equity, they are often organised as commons ecologies (Esteves *et al.*, 2021). The concept of autopoiesis can thus aid understanding of whether, how and under what conditions solidarity economy can most effectively fulfil such aspirations.

Although highly important, the introduction of autopoiesis into commons theory by de Angelis is conceptually flawed, derived not from living systems theory but from Luhmann's secondary treatment, which conceptually delineates an economic system from the ecological and social contexts required for its reproduction and thus describes systems that are *allopoietic* rather than autopoietic (see Varela *et al.*, 1974). Allopoietic systems lack the self-generative quality of living systems and can reproduce their own structures only by undermining autopoiesis in adjacent systems. This is, of course, an inherent feature of capitalist economic formations, whose reproduction relies on constant extraction of value from workers, consumers and sources of raw materials and ecological services.

The predominance of capitalism as a form of economic organisation means that all commons exist in some form of dynamic interrelationship with capitalist organisations, for which De Angelis (2017) has introduced the term *boundary commoning*. Depending on circumstances, the consequences of this boundary commoning may be *allopoietic*, when the effect is to undermine the autopoietic capacity of the commons through externalisation of capitalism's associated environmental and social damage, or *heteropoietic* when the effect on the commons is neutral or stabilising. In contrast, as an autopoietic system, a commons ecology is not reliant on externalisation: either integrating the social and ecological conditions for its reproduction within its own boundaries or in relationships of boundary commoning that are *sympoietic* (Haraway, 2016) – in other words – that enhance the autopoietic capacity of the other commons with which it interacts (also cf. Sharma, 2015).

My central argument in this chapter is that this life-enhancing quality is a vital ingredient of solidarity economy's potential to be an alternative and antidote to capitalism's inherently predatory relationship with living systems and processes. Fulfilling this potential requires solidarity economy initiatives to be autopoietic in their own organisation, and sympoietic in their interrelationships. This, I believe, is possible only under certain epistemic conditions, as the following section explores.

3.3 Autopoiesis and enchantment

Several parallel strands of theorisation imply that, in human systems, autopoiesis is closely related to prevailing epistemologies. Writing from a post-development perspective, Kuecker (2017) identifies *enchantment* as a distinctive quality of indigenous lifeways that retain a sense of sacred relationship with nature and the cosmos, which meaningful alternatives to capitalism must aspire to recover. Similarly, Federici (2019) sees *re-enchantment* as a crucial, if not always explicit, ingredient of feminist approaches to commoning that emphasise the centrality of reproductive work. This observation is consistent with an understanding that the basic biological roots of humanity lie in participation in gynocentric social formations dedicated to love and care, which is therefore an essential condition for the full autopoietic flourishing of a human being (Maturana Romesin & Verden-Zoller, 2008). Philosopher Andreas Weber's concept of aliveness (or enlivenment) extends this observation to the more-than-human world, transcending nature–culture dualisms through its emphasis on dynamic inter-relatedness and mutual transformations of interacting subjectivities (Weber, 2019).

All these perspectives, among many others, share the insight that, as living beings, humans are active participants in the mutual unfolding of the entire community of life and flourish when they live in patterns of interrelationships, with both each other and with other species, that reflect and enable this. An integrating framework through which to explore this in more depth, and in relation to the specific case of solidarity economy, comes from Anglo-American scholar Gregory Bateson's work on the unity of mind and nature (Bateson, 1979). Working at the interface of Anthropology and Psychology, Bateson's key observation was that of *ecology of mind*, a common organisational pattern shared by the material structures of living systems and the epistemological structures of human thought. Epistemic complexity, consisting of the ability to shift among different epistemological frames of reference as the situation demands, is a necessary condition for navigating the complex and unpredictable social, social-ecological and other dynamics encountered in the living material world (Bateson, 1972, 1979; Bateson & Bateson, 1987).

In order to apply Bateson's ecology of mind to the concerns of this chapter, I here combine it with the more specific account of epistemic complexity found in the work of social theorist Jean Gebser (1983). Gebser's major work consisted of a broad hermeneutic analysis of the evolution of European thought and cultural expression through a series of successively predominant epistemological structures. The *magic structure* experiences the world in directly empirical terms (or through the intermediation of symbols that are directly representative of whatever they signify) and underlies an epistemology of immediate cause-and-effect.[2] The *mythical structure* is normatively-oriented, understanding the world through laws, rules, cycles and other regular patterns in space and time, whether perceived or culturally constructed. The *mental structure* is analytical in character, marked by predominantly hypothetico-deductive ways of understanding the world. Although the cross-cultural relevance of these structures has neither been examined nor demonstrated, we can for the sake of argument make provisional use of them as descriptions of specific epistemological frames of reference within Bateson's ecology of mind. This allows them to become analytical categories for examining the occurrence, nature and consequences of autopoiesis and sympoiesis in solidarity economy initiatives.

According to Gebser, each structure can be expressed in both beneficent and deficient forms, which I here identify as being, respectively, autopoietic and allopoietic in character. While beneficent expressions of any structure are mutually enlivening, deficient forms become self-referential, limiting diversity of expression both within the structure concerned and in others. Gebser considered his own time and place (mid-20th-Century Western Europe) to be characterised by the dominance of *ratio*, a deficient and increasingly dysfunctional involution of the mental structure. Alongside this, he described the accelerating emergence of the *integral structure*, which combines the faculties of the magic, mythical and mental structures in a dynamic form of interplay known as *systasis*.

Although Gebser apparently saw the integral structure as an antidote to the dominance of ratio, history since his time has shown that, in the capitalist world, it is emerging in a predominantly deficient form, expressed in *Empire*, capitalism's epistemologically pervasive post-modern form (Hardt & Negri, 2004). This flaw in Gebser's model reflects an underlying Eurocentrism: in common with all such attempts to construct a grand historical narrative, Gebser errs in treating the successive dominance of one structure and its subsequent replacement by another as universal, rather than a distinctive, contingent and indeed partial feature of European history (Johnson, 2019).

In contrast, in societies free from the hegemonic influences of highly centralising institutions, the magic, mythical and mental structures co-exist, in beneficent forms and endless variety of culturally specific expressions, as complementary subjective and intersubjective faculties (Henfrey, 2018). The resulting continuous movement among empirical (magic), normative (mythical structure) and analytical (mental structure) ways of understanding and decision-making is the systasis that Gebser identified as characteristic of the beneficent expression of the integral structure. It is also the fundamental and most important feature of Bateson's ecology of mind: the ability to shift epistemological frame of reference whenever the one currently employed becomes unsuited to the situation at hand. In such a situation, the mutual contextualisation of mental, mythical and magical structures creates feedbacks in the social–ecological system that maintain the ecological impacts of resource use within the system's limits of sustainability and resilience (Henfrey, 2018). Extrapolating from these findings, I suggest that the capacity for systasis is a necessary precondition for autopoiesis in any human organisation.

In this framing, we can define enchantment as an epistemic condition: culturally and functionally appropriate expression of the magic and mythical structures, along with their systatic interrelationship with each other and with the mental structure. Indigenous expressions of the magic structure include diverse epistemologies and ontologies of nature, many of which encode or enable ecologically adaptive resource-use strategies (e.g. Ellen & Fukui, 1996). Articulations of the mythical structure include the diverse beliefs, norms and customs that organise the social and spatial organisation of resource use in ecologically adaptive ways, which Anderson (1996) refers to as "Ecologies of the Heart." They are also the epistemic foundation of the traditional commons that support resilience and sustainability in the ecological relationships of many self-organised peoples (Berkes, 1989; Berkes & Folke, 1998). Expression of the mental structure occurs in the routine application of hypothetico-deductive forms of analytical reasoning, with methodological parallels with formal scientific inquiry and generating congruent information (Tulkin & Konner, 1973; Henfrey, 2020). The systatic combination of all three as a dynamic ecology of mind is a necessary basis for ecological sustainability (Henfrey, 2018, and cf. Toledo, 1992; Berkes, 2000) and hence a precondition for autopoiesis.

Re-enchantment, then, can be understood as the deliberate renewal of the magic and mythical structures, as a direct challenge to the epistemic dominance of ratio. New expressions of the magic structure documented in counter-hegemonic social movements include diverse forms of ritual action and counter-cultural expression among road protestors and other environmental activists involved in direct action in 1990s' Britain (McKay, 1996). Moving from protest to the creation of alternatives, permaculture[3] expresses the mythical structure through the use of models and metaphors derived from understandings of living systems as the basis for organising social processes (Taylor Aiken, 2017). The permaculture movement also finds new beneficent expressions of the mental structure in its ongoing self-constitution through collective learning processes, which thus acquire an autopoietic character (Henfrey, 2017). Simultaneous epistemological innovation in all three of the magic, mythical and mental structures allows engagement with incumbent political regimes, which are centralised in the mental structure, to take on a systatic character, thus mitigating risks of co-optation and establishing relationships that tend to be autopoietic rather than allopoietic (Henfrey & Ford, 2018; Henfrey & Penha-Lopes, 2018; also see Muñoz, this volume; Amaro & Ferreira, this volume; Caitana, Tasheva-Petrova & Vallet, this volume).

In summary and review, from Gregory Bateson's ecology of mind, we derive the insight that navigating the complex and unpredictable dynamics of social and social–ecological systems requires individual and collective access to multiple, distinct and complementary epistemological faculties (Bateson, 1972, 1979; Bateson & Bateson, 1987). A putative map of such a composite epistemology is found in Gebser's (1983) identification of the magic, mythical and mental structures, and their mutually contextualising interplay in the integral structure, a phenomenon known as systasis. My own previous research suggests that systasis is a necessary condition for sustainability and resilience in indigenous resource use (Henfrey, 2018). Enchantment thus refers to local and culturally specific expressions of the magic and mythical structures in ways that are functionally and culturally appropriate to local social and ecological contexts. Re-enchantment – the renewal of the magic and mythical structures, and their bringing into systatic relationship with the mental structure – is thus a vital precondition for autopoiesis and sympoiesis in any sociocultural formation.

3.4 (Re)-enchantment as political ecology of mind

In the terms introduced in the previous section, my central argument in this chapter is that re-enchantment, on the one hand, and the creation through solidarity economy of autopoietic commons linked in sympoietic interrelationships of boundary commoning, on the other, are mutually interdependent, to the degree that they can be understood as a single process. In the terms of Gebser's theory, re-enchantment amounts to liberation from the epistemological dominance of both ratio (a deficient expression of the mental structure) and what Hardt and Negri (2004) term Empire (which I here characterise as a deficient form of the integral structure). Achieving this requires reconstitution of both the magic structure (i.e. the faculty for participatory forms of epistemology) and the mythical structure (the faculty for normative forms of epistemology), in ways not prescriptively constrained by the structurally prevalent form of either the mental or integral structure. This, in turns, allows escape from the hegemony of both ratio and Empire, the reconstitution of the mental structure in a beneficent form and the coming into systasis of the magic, mythical and mental structures as a beneficent expression of the integral structure.

Opening this volume, Laville and Eynaud (Chapter 1) highlight an important distinction between the instituted and instituting. Ratio, the deficient form of the mental structure, is instituted in the culturally and historically specific form of neoliberal capitalism, which ideologically and materially reduces all that is of natural, social and cultural value to marketed, or potentially marketable, goods and services. This also amounts to an epistemic colonisation by ratio of the mythical and magical structures, whose expressions are limited to that which serves the commodification processes required by capitalism for its continuing, allopoietic functioning. Instituting is thus an act of rebellion against neoliberal hegemony on the part of solidarity economy actors seeking either to remain or to relocate themselves apart from ratio – spatially, socially and epistemologically – by operating within commons as autopoietic economic organisations.

A bridge from institutionalisation to epistemology can be found in James Scott's distinction between *techne* – the instrumentalising and highly technocratic way in which High Modern Capitalism understands and acts upon the world – and *metis*, the diverse vernacular, culturally distinctive, locally contextualised ways of knowing that underpin all ways of life that retain any form of material or political autonomy from the state (Scott, 1998). In the terminology employed here, techne is an expression of ratio while metis is by nature systatic, and in fact a characteristic feature of autopoietic commons. This distinction remains pertinent despite the increasing shift from territorialised states to deterritorialised Empire as the predominant vehicle of capitalist hegemony (Hardt & Negri, 2004) and the accompanying, as yet partial, supersession of techne as its supporting epistemology. The construction and mobilisation of counterpower – Scott's (1985) "Weapons of the Weak" – therefore begin with (re-)enchantment: autonomous and locally distinct counter-hegemonic expression of the magic and mythical structures. As della Porta describes (Chapter 2), social movements provide a necessary basis for the socialisation of the resulting epistemological innovations and their mobilisation through collective action.

3.5 Instituting epistemic transformations through solidarity economy

My key proposal here, then, is that processes of instituting involve bringing the magic and mythical structures into systatic relationship with the mental structure, as the epistemic foundation for creating new commons that are autopoietic in nature. If this is indeed the case, solidarity economy initiatives should reveal, particularly in their social and cultural dimensions, counter-hegemonic expressions of the magic and mythical structures – what I am referring to as re-enchantment – that in turn free the mental structure from the domination of ratio and enable forms of rationality that are not ideologically constrained by capitalism. The empirical studies in other chapters in this volume reveal multiple facets of such processes.

Several chapters point to the importance of marginalisation, whether spatial, social, economic or any combination of these. As well as a potential hardship, marginalisation is often a key correlate of enchantment, which requires a large measure of freedom from the influence of techne, ratio and Empire. Accordingly, Esteves (Chapter 4) describes how economic marginalisation among the Brazilian urban poor has obliged the adoption of autonomous, self-organised economic strategies based on small-scale agricultural production and crafts. Institutionalisation of these strategies and associated practices through the Esperança/Cooesperança movement embodies values of cooperation, horizontality and solidarity, socialised through participation in their markets, which are only secondarily sites of commercialisation. Commerce thus also becomes a strategy to support middle-class consumers to consume in ways better aligned with their own politics, perhaps cultivating conditions for a wider, more immanent epistemic challenge to the neoliberal values they have inevitability internalised.

Similar insights arise from Fajardo Rojas and Hataya's account of mestizo and Afro-descendant peoples in geographically isolated territories at Colombia's resource frontiers (Chapter 10). Both groups rely for survival on a high degree of social and cultural self-determination, founded on highly precarious strategies for economic autonomy. Introduction by ecclesiastical activists of organising strategies founded in solidarity economy principles, modified through their encounter with local sociocultural realities, has enabled new hybrid pathways of instituting. The result is the emergence of more resilient livelihood strategies based on community enterprise, along with grassroots institutions able to confront threats to livelihoods and survival on several fronts, including engagement with national environmental policy.

The two cases show a common pattern. Immediate individual and household responses to economic conditions take the form of survival strategies epistemically rooted in the magic structure. Strategic organisation based on shared expressions of the mythical structure complements this, instituting a support framework rooted in values of solidarity, cooperation and mutual aid. This collective mobilisation permits creative and locally contextualised expressions of the mental structure. The material manifestations of these autochthonous, systatic epistemologies and their accompanying ontologies are autopoietic economic structures engaged in forms of boundary commoning that are latently sympoietic –

and therefore potentially transformative of allopoietic systems with which they come into contact.

Both cases are also notable for the important support provided by social activists of the Catholic Church. Like all organised religions, this can be considered to institute a deficient form of the mythical structure with strong hegemonic tendencies. Epistemic resistance again originates in the magic structure, in this case in the form of individual striving to emulate the embodied divinity of the Christ figure. Moral guidance and community support derive from the principles of liberation theology, a direct challenge to the centralisation, elitism and dogmatism of the instituted mythical structure. This in turn allows an instituting of the mental structure via grassroots mobilisations of counter-power via solidarity economy. Here, we see a parallel pattern of epistemic resistance moving from the magic through the mythical to the mental structure.

In a similar vein, Banerjee, Shaban and Chand (Chapter 8) describe how small-scale agriculturalists subject to multidimensional inequity are improving their conditions via provision of microcredit. Again, initial organisation around shared conditions and identity (magic structure), supported by collective organisation for mutual support (mythical structure), leads to tangible improvements in economic conditions and status (mental structure). Structural barriers to sympoietic effects are in this case particularly powerful, being located in deficient, allopoietic institutionalisations of both the mythical and mental structures.

Marginalised populations within the instituted's realm of direct spatial control encounter parallel situations of allopoietic relationship with dominant socio-economic systems. Lucas dos Santos (Chapter 5) describes how Afro-European women experience multiple dimensions of marginalisation and discrimination, direct and indirect, resulting in lived experiences of exclusion, poverty and insecurity. In common with others among capitalism's human surplus, valued, if at all, only as cheap source of productive and reproductive labour, self-emancipation is systatic in nature. Individual and household-scale responses to the material challenges of everyday existence, including food, housing, employment, education and childcare, are supported through networking and collective action among women united by gender, class, economic circumstances, employment and motherhood. This is another example of the trajectory in epistemic drivers of action from magic to mythical structures and allows instituting of the mental structure in community enterprises such as solidarity groceries, repair shops and mothers' co-ops. Engagement of solidarity economy movements in such action is relatively weak, and explicit attention to the particular needs of minority women scarce. This is a marked shortcoming of solidarity economy initiatives and movements in Europe, reflecting continued, if partial, epistemic colonisation by ratio and consequent limitations in their autopoietic and sympoietic capacities.

Western European solidarity economy initiatives arising as direct challenges to the instituted follow a different trajectory towards autopoietic ways of being and sympoietic forms of interaction. Another case study presented by Esteves (Chapter 4) describes how for Cooperativa Integral in Catalonia, cooperative organisation is a key tool in counter-hegemonic strategies that enable alternative forms of entrepreneurship and commerce, liberated from neoliberal capitalism's epistemic domination in ways that perhaps reflect Catalonia's mixed current and historical relationships with the Spanish State. In this and other cases, the legal form of the cooperative plays a role parallel to that of the 'institutional shells' (Alcorn & Toledo, 1998) that provide space for indigenous societies to operate as commons within the legislative framework of the nation state, allowing emergence of a virtuous circle in which different structures mutually enable each other's autonomous expression and instituting. Instituting the mental structure on the basis of cooperative principles is both an outcome and enabler of expression of the mythical structure as a normative field conducive to the collaborative, mutually supportive forms of economic action through which the magic structure is instituted. The resulting systasis enables autopoietic self-organisation of individual solidarity enterprises and local and regional networks based on sympoietic forms of boundary commoning.

Other case studies show how, through the normative commitments and solidarity-oriented ways of being that characterise cooperative enterprise, the mythical and magic structures contextually regulate processes of boundary commoning through which cooperatives engage with the instituted via the mental structure. Sanz Abad, Sama Acedo and Carrero Gros (Chapter 9) describe the common dilemmas consequently experienced by several cooperative enterprises and community projects in Spain. Both the Agresta Cooperative and Fiare Ethical Bank encountered opportunities to expand their reach through new products and markets, at the cost of possible compromise of their commitment to cooperative principles. Madrid's urban community gardens experienced similar tensions between their core values and wider public acceptability, along with the prospect of municipal support. Resolving such dilemmas in practice is by no means ever simple. Our portrayal of systasis and autopoiesis as interdependent properties of living systems points to a possible orienting question: that of whether the proposed resolution enhances the quality of enchantment, as a lived experience of being in the world. In other words, does the interplay of mental and mythical structure bring about a deeper sense of enlivenment, as felt and expressed through the magical structure? Umantseva, Hulgård and Hauggaard-Nielsen (Chapter 7) hint at an answer in their account of how practitioners of regenerative agriculture in Denmark and Portugal describe their emerging consciousness of relationship with the soil and agroecosystem. Activities in Tamera's Healing Biotope described by Esteves (Chapter 4) seek to embed such consciousness in everyday experience and to institute it more widely through new systems for provision of food, water and energy at bioregional scale.

Šimleša (Chapter 6) describes a contrasting situation in case studies from Central and Eastern Europe, where free-market capitalism has become instituted only in the past few decades, and solidarity economy suffers unfortunate perceived associations with the economic institutions of former authoritarian state powers. Both the Jodzak Neighbourhood and Fair & Bio Coffee Roasters Cooperative operate in often-uneasy relationships of boundary commoning with the institutions of the newly liberalised state. Gaps in state capacity for effective provision for community governance and social care – reflecting an institutionalisation of the mental structure less pronounced than in established liberal democracies, and hence in some respects less deficient – create opportunities for solidarity economy initiatives to engage with the instituted through multiple structures simultaneously, a systatic form of boundary commoning that enhances the autopoietic and sympoietic potential of both parties.

A mature and more fully systatic form of instituting is evident in Leal's (Chapter 11) account of Ilhamar Bank in Bahia, Brazil, a solidarity finance initiative that operates as an autopoietic community commons. The magic structure is evident in the support of everyday subsistence and livelihood practices through the provision of microcredit, the mythical structure through a set of rules governing access to financial services agreed and enforced by the community and the mental structure in the resulting multi-level structure for democratic governance. Supporting and strengthening local livelihoods, Banco Ilhamar self-sustains its own internal organisation and promotes sympoietic forms of boundary commoning through its involvement in networks of solidarity finance initiatives. Its Concha social currency acts as a form of institutional shell, allowing input of financial capital from the national economy, but not its extraction by conversion back to Reals. This allows boundary commoning, such as acceptance of outside investment, that is by default heteropoetic rather than allopoietic in character.

The potential for instituting solidarity economy initiatives to stimulate latent autopoietic potential in the instituted is most evident in the case studies of collaboration between solidarity economy initiatives and networks and local government. Amaro and Ferreira (Chapter 13) provide a detailed account of self-organisation of community groups in Lisbon neighbourhoods dominated by marginalised social groups, as a new form of urban commons. As well as creating the social potential for effective solidarity economy interventions, these community groups have created a new model of Shared and Participatory Local Governance (SPLG) that provides the basis for an increasing volume and ambition of interactions with municipal government departments. SPLG's key features of being locally rooted, participatory and shared, with respective emphasis in the magic, mythical and mental structures, make it systatic in character and able to stimulate forms of relationship and collective action conducive to autopoietic development of the communities involved. For the municipal authorities, the ongoing complex challenge of delivering essential services to all parts of a large and highly heterogeneous city makes virtualism – the mischaracterisation of real communities as their representation in abstract models (Miller, 2001, 2003), which in my view is a reliable social correlate of *ratio* – a practical impossibility. Boundary commoning with community groups that tend towards systasis and autopoiesis is therefore a pragmatically sound strategy, one that also enhances the heteropoietic and potentially autopoietic tendencies of local government itself.

Illustrating this last point, Muñoz (Chapter 12) describes how municipalities in the Conurbano Bonaerense, one of Argentina's largest urban agglomerations, have introduced a raft of municipal-level policies to support social solidarity economy. The result has been to free the popular economy (that of workers dependent for material survival on wage labour) from the prescriptive economic rationality that characterises the private capitalist and state economies. This unlocking of the autopoietic potential of the popular economy reflects its emphasis on the reproduction of life – via systasis – rather than that of capital (an expression of ratio). The institutional shell provided by this legislative support has also offered a level of protection from the allopoietic effects of a marked neoliberal shift in national government policy.

Finally, Caitana, Tasheva-Petrova and Vallet (Chapter 14) describe another example of boundary commoning between solidarity economy and municipal policy in Sofia's Healthy Corridor. Here, solidarity economy enters into relationships of mutual enlivenment with an integrated development of Nature-Based Solutions (NBS). The autopoietic character and sympoietic potential here are clear: solidarity economy providing a challenge to the observed affinity of much NBS-related discourse with neoliberal assumptions concerning urban planning (Kotsila *et al.*, 2021). Detailed longitudinal investigation of the types of boundary commoning in which solidarity economy initiatives in the Healthy Corridor are engaged would undoubtedly be a rich source of insights into the potential, and pitfalls, that such a combination poses for the expression of systasis and emergence of sympoietic relationships on a city-wide scale.

3.6 Towards a sacred political ecology of solidarity economy and commons

The analyses presented in this chapter are necessarily brief and somewhat conjectural, even in some respects speculative. Any conclusions drawn at this point would at best be tentative. They do, however, demonstrate the need for closer and more sustained attention to the epistemic dimensions of solidarity economy, processes of boundary commoning among solidarity economy initiatives and with other community initiatives and instituted state and capitalist organisations, and the consequences for the autopoietic character of social–ecological economic systems, both objectively and through the subjective experience of enchantment among people within them.

In conclusion, solidarity economy initiatives and movements instituting through the creation of new economic commons notably differ from the instituted in both their epistemological foundations and systemic impacts. The ecological, social and cultural impoverishment that capitalism requires for its continued, allopoietic, operation, ultimately reflects its overreliance on a single structure, in Gebser's terms, or way of knowing. Challenges to capitalism and the creation of new alternatives rely on resisting such hegemonic influences and asserting or restoring systasis via beneficent expressions of the integral structure as an autopoietic ecology of mind.

In this framing, we can view commons as strategies for collective organisation without reliance on centralising institutions rooted in a single epistemological structure, and solidarity economy as building on the economic, social and cultural freedoms that this entails. The resulting systasis is the basis of a lived experience of enchantment, providing an epistemological foundation for autopoietic forms of economic organisation. Autopoiesis, and the possibility of sympoiesis it enables, are, in turn, a necessary functional basis for solidarity economy initiatives to achieve their moral as well as material aims: to enable livelihoods that are enlivening in all respects, promoting sustainability, human welfare and equity and so enhancing the biological, ecological, social and cultural richness of all the living systems with which they are in interrelationship.

Notes

1. In fact, Haraway sees sympoiesis as an alternative to autopoiesis, more adequately emphasising the relational character and functional interdependence of living systems (Haraway, 2016: 58). I prefer to consider them as complementary concepts, both of which are useful here.
2. Following Abram (1996), the associated ontology is one we might refer to as participatory, in other words one of direct sensory engagement with the world.
3. An international movement for the conscious design of human systems that fulfil three overlapping ethics of sustainability, social justice and equity, inspired by and seeking co-creative collaboration with natural systems (for further information, see, for example, Henfrey & Penha-Lopes, 2015).

References

Abram, D. (1996). *The Spell of the Sensuous. Perception and Language in a More-Than-Human World.* New York: Vintage Books.

Alcorn, J. B. and Toledo, V. M. (1998). "Resilient resource management in Mexico's forest ecosystems: The contribution of resource rights," in Berkes, F. and Folke, C. (eds.) *Linking Social and Ecological Systems: Management Practices and Social Mechanisms for Building Resilience.* Cambridge: Cambridge University Press, pp. 216–249.

Anderson, E. N. (1996). *Ecologies of the Heart: Emotions, Belief, and the Environment.* Cambridge: Cambridge University Press.

Bateson, G. (1972). *Steps to an Ecology of Mind.* Chicago: University of Chicago Press.

Bateson, G. (1979). *Mind and Nature: A Necessary Unity*. New York: Dutton.
Bateson, G. and Bateson, C. (1987). *Angels Fear: Towards an Epistemology of the Sacred*. New York: Bantam.
Berkes, F. (ed.) (1989). *Common Property Resources: Ecology and Community-Based Sustainable Management*. London: Belhaven Press.
Berkes, F. (2008). *Sacred Ecology*. 2nd edition. New York: Routledge.
Berkes, F. and Folke, C. (1998). *Linking Social and Ecological Systems: Management Practices and Social Mechanisms for Building Resilience*. Cambridge: Cambridge University Press.
Bollier. D. and Helfrich, S. (2019). *Free, Fair and Alive: The Insurgent Power of the Commons*. Gabriola Island: New Society Publishers.
De Angelis, M. (2017). *Omnia Sunt Communia*. London: Zed Books.
Ellen, R. F. and Fukui, K. (eds.) (1996). *Redefining Nature: Ecology, Culture and Domestication*. Oxford: Berg.
Escobar, A. (2018). *Designs for the Pluriverse*. Durham and London: Duke University Press.
Esteves, A. M., Genus, A., Henfrey, T., Penha-Lopes, G. and East, M. (2021). "Sustainable entrepreneurship and the sustainable development goals: Community-led initiatives, the social solidarity economy and commons ecologies," *Business Strategy and the Environment*, 30(3), pp. 1423–1435. https://doi.org/10.1002/bse.2706
Federici, S. (2019). *Re-Enchanting the World: Feminism and the Politics of the Commons*. Oakland: PM Press.
Gebser, J. (1983) [1949/1953]. *The Ever-Present Origin*. Translated by Noel Barstad. Athens, OH: Ohio University Press.
Guattari, F. (2000) [1989]. *The Three Ecologies*. Translated by I. Pindar and P. Sutton. London: The Athlone Press.
Haraway, D. J. (2016). *Staying with the Trouble: Making Kin in the Cthulucene*. Durham and London: Duke University Press.
Hardt, M. and Negri, A. (2004). *Empire*. Cambridge, MA: Harvard University Press.
Henfrey, T. (2017). "Grassroots education for sustainability as ecology of mind: The head, hands and heart of societal transformation," in Winn, J. and Hall, R. (eds.) *Mass Intellectuality and Democratic Leadership in Higher Education*. London: Bloomsbury, pp. 171–185. http://dx.doi.org/10.5040/9781474267618.ch-013
Henfrey, T. (2018). *Edges, fringes, frontiers: Integral ecology, indigenous knowledge and sustainability in Guyana*. New York: Berghahn Books. https://doi.org/10.2307/j.ctvw04jcb
Henfrey, T. (2020). "Relationships between scientific ecology and knowledge of primate ecology of Wapishana subsistence hunters in Guyana," in Urbani, B. and Lizarralde, M. (eds.) *Neotropical Ethnoprimatology: Indigenous Peoples' Perceptions of and Interactions with Nonhuman Primates*, Springer Nature Switzerland AG (Ethnobiology Series), pp. 263–282. https://doi.org/10.1007/978-3-030-27504-4_12
Henfrey, T. and Ford, L. (2018). "Permacultures of transformation: Steps to a cultural ecology of environmental action," *Journal of Political Ecology*, 25, pp. 104–119. http://dx.doi.org/10.2458/V25i1.22758
Henfrey, T. and Kenrick, J. (2017). "Climate, commons and hope: The transition movement in global perspective," in Henfrey, T., Maschkowski, G. and Penha-Lopes, G. (eds.) *Resilience, Community Action and Societal Transformation*. East Meon: Permanent Publications, pp. 161–190. Online at http://www.transitionresearchnetwork.org/uploads/1/2/7/3/12737251/4.2_climate_commons_and_hope.pdf

Henfrey, T. and Penha-Lopes, G. (2015). *Permaculture and Climate Change Adaptation: Inspiring Social, Ecological, Economic and Cultural Responses*. East Meon: Permanent Publications.

Henfrey, T. and Penha-Lopes, G. (2018). "Policy and community-led action on sustainability and climate change: Paradox and possibility in the interstices," *Environmental Innovation and Societal Transitions*, 29, pp. 52–54. http://dx.doi.org/10.1016/j.eist.2018.05.002

Johnson, J. (2019). *Seeing through the World: Jean Gebser and Integral Consciousness*. Seattle: Revelore.

Kuecker, G. (2017). "Enchanting transition: A post-colonial perspective," in Henfrey, T., Maschkowski, G. and Penha-Lopes, G. (eds.) *Resilience, Community Action and Societal Transformation*. East Meon: Permanent Publications, pp. 193–210. Online at http://www.transitionresearchnetwork.org/uploads/1/2/7/3/12737251/4.3_enchanting_transition.pdf

Kotsila, P., Anguelovski, I., Baró, F., Langemeyer, J., Sekulova, F. and Connolly, J. (2021). "Nature-based solutions as discursive tools and contested practices in urban nature's neoliberalisation processes," *Environment and Planning E: Nature and Space*, 4(2), pp. 252–274. https://doi.org/10.1177/2514848620901437

Leyshon, A., Williams, C. C. and Lee, R. (2003). *Alternative Economic Spaces*. London: Sage Publications.

Maffi, L. (ed.) (2001). *On Biocultural Diversity: Linking Language, Knowledge and the Environment*. Washington, DC: Smithsonian Institute.

Maturana, H. R. and Valera, F. J. (1980). *Autopoiesis and Cognition: The Realization of the Living*. Dordrecht: D. Reidel Publishing Company.

Maturana Romesin, H. and Verden-Zoller, G. (2008). *The Origin of Humanness in the Biology of Love*. Exeter: Imprint Academic.

McKay, G. (1996). *Senseless Acts of Beauty: Cultures of Resistance since the Sixties*. London: Verso.

Miller, D. (2001). "A theory of virtualism," in Carrier, J. G. and Miller, D. (eds.) *Virtualism: A New Political Economy*. Oxford: Berg, pp. 195–205.

Miller, D. (2003). "The virtual moment," *Journal of the Royal Anthropological Institute*, 9(1), 57–75.

Pretty, J. (2002). *Agri-Culture: Reconnecting People, Land and Nature*. London: Earthscan.

Scott, J. (1985). *Weapons of the Weak: Everyday Forms of Peasant Resistance*. New Haven: Yale University Press.

Scott, J. (1990). *Domination and the Arts of Resistance: Hidden Transcripts*. New Haven: Yale University Press.

Scott, J. (1998). *Seeing Like a State: Why Certain Schemes to Improve the Human Condition Have Failed*. New Haven: Yale University Press.

Sharma, K. (2015). *Interdependence: Biology and Beyond*. New York: Fordham University Press.

Taylor Aiken, G. (2017). "Permaculture and the social design of nature," *Geografiska Annaler: Series B, Human Geography*, 99(2), pp. 172–191. https://doi.org/10.1080/04353684.2017.1315906

Toledo, V. M. (1992). "What is ethnoecology? Origins, scope and implications of a rising discipline," *Etnoecológica*, 1, pp. 5–21.

Tulkin, S. R. and Konner, M. J. (1973). "Alternative conceptions of intellectual functioning," *Human Development*, 16, pp. 33–52.

Varela, F. G., Maturana, H. R. and Uribe, R. (1974). "Autopoiesis: The organization of living systems, its characterization and a model," *Biosystems*, 5(4), pp. 187–196. https://doi.org/10.1016/0303-2647(74)90031-8

Weber, A. (2019). *Enlivenment: Towards a Poetics for the Anthropocene*. Cambridge, MA: MIT Press.

4 Building counterpower

A comparative case study analysis of "boundary commoning" by solidarity economy initiatives[1]

Ana Margarida Esteves

4.1 Introduction

This chapter uses a comparative case study analysis to explore how different approaches to collective action promoting solidarity economy, resulting in distinct strategies of building counterpower, materialise as specific alternative economic spatialities.[2] It employs the concept of "boundary commoning" (De Angelis, 2017) to examine the practices, relationships and interactions that solidarity economy initiatives (SEIs) establish with wider publics, with the purpose of maximising their autonomy in relation to capitalism's isomorphic pressures. The analysis is based on comparison of three SEIs, each following different strategies of collective action towards solidarity economy:

a) *Tamera – Healing Biotope I*, founded in 1995 in southwestern Alentejo, southern Portugal, has been gradually developing as what it describes as a "testfield" for what aspires to be a replicable model for commons-based regenerative human settlement based on solidarity economy practices, nested within a regional-level strategy for water, energy and food autonomy.

b) *Esperança/Cooesperança* is a grassroots commercialisation network that became a template for public policies for solidarity economy introduced throughout Brazil, since the 1990s, at the regional, state and national levels. Founded in 1987 in the municipality of Santa Maria, in the Brazilian state of Rio Grande do Sul, *Esperança/Cooesperança* was inspired by grassroots education methodologies that supported the waves of mobilisation that led to the democratic transition of the late 1980s and the Pink Tide of the 2000s (Souza, 2006; Sarria Icaza & Freitas, 2009).

c) *Cooperativa Integral Catalana* (CIC), founded by an assembly of activists in Catalonia in 2010, is the template for the "integral cooperatives" that were founded throughout Europe in the 2010s to provide an expanding "precariat" with livelihood alternatives outside the wage economy (Dafermos, 2017). CIC mobilises online peer-to-peer platforms and alternative currencies to develop an autonomous, self-managed infrastructure for provision of essential services in areas such as housing, nutrition, health and education.

DOI: 10.4324/9781003306344-5

Data were collected during three, four-month fieldwork visits, one to each case study site, between 2015 and 2017. Fieldwork included:

- Archival research of documents related to the everyday management of each fieldwork site, as well as communication with institutional partners and the wider public;
- Participant observation: of everyday life in Tamera (including daily community meetings, monthly regional markets and scheduled public educational events), of weekly activities at *Esperança/Cooesperança*'s permanent marketspace *Centro de Referência Dom Ivo Lorscheider* (CRDIL) and of everyday activities at the social centres and *rebosts* (commercialisation and assembly venues) of CIC in Barcelona, Tarragona and Olot;
- In-depth interviews: twenty-four in Tamera (with community members and partner projects in the region), 33 in *Esperança/Cooesperança* (with producers, project managers, consumers and political allies in social movements and the state) and 25 in CIC (with producers, consumers and political allies in social movements).

4.2 "Micro-public spheres" of alternative practices and collective action

Solidarity economy envisions full institutional acknowledgment of practices that are neither contractual nor simply utilitarian (Laville & Eynaud, 2019: 61), such as those based on reciprocity, redistribution and householding (Lucas dos Santos & Banerjee, 2019). The goal is to foster economic democracy, as well as to promote the economic and ecological resilience of territories, by re-localising economic activity and supporting self-organised grassroots action for collective organisation of management, production and consumption, based on shared management towards production and consumption (Hillenkamp & Lucas dos Santos, 2019; Lucas dos Santos & Banerjee, 2019). Central to this goal is the development of parallel economic spaces for enaction and coordination of "socio-ethical and counter-cultural practices" (Fois, 2019: 108). In addition these spaces are what Keane (1998) calls "micro-public spheres," in which economic activity is a form of prefigurative politics. This refers to processes of "production of belonging" (Escoffier, 2018: 775) that aim to challenge the practices and institutional structures of market societies (Gibson-Graham, 2008; Mendell, 2009).

Research on such micro-public spheres shows them to be diverse in both form and activities. The following exploratory and non-exhaustive classification attempts to capture this diversity:

(1) *Educational models and living laboratories of sustainability*, focusing on indirectly influencing public institutions through diffusion of knowledge

and technologies relating to specific organisational models, practices and behaviours (Lockyer & Veteto, 2013: 19; also Avelino & Kunze, 2009; Fernandes-Jesus *et al.*, 2017; Esteves, 2022b);

(2) "*Alternative institutions*" (Cox, 1983) that engage social movements and grassroots organisations in a "war of position" striving for direct influence on policy making and regulatory environments (Laville, 2016; Laville & Eynaud, 2019);
(3) *Autonomist institutionalities* aimed at de-linking livelihoods from states and capitalist markets through the construction of parallel institutional apparatus (Duran, 2009; Dafermos, 2017).

Much literature focuses on the role of these micro-public spheres in the construction of circuits of value that re-territorialise supply chains and reproduction of the material resources, norms and rules that support solidarity economy-based livelihoods (e.g. Poteete & Ostrom, 2010; Lietaer *et al.*, 2012; Ould Ahmed, 2015; Laville, 2016; De Angelis, 2017; Rigo & França Filho, 2017). A key emerging trend considers how such spaces are shaped by practices and relationships through which SEIs interact with actors in the capitalist market and public institutions, with the purpose of maximising their ability to self-manage and self-reproduce while minimising the impact of capitalism's isomorphic pressures. De Angelis, in his study of transitions to postcapitalism, defines such process as "boundary commoning," since it "opens the boundaries" (of SEIs) and builds linkages that "could reshape existing institutions from the ground up" (De Angelis, 2017: 24). The following section explores, through a comparative case study analysis, how the three categories of micro-public spheres described earlier translate into different forms of boundary commoning.

4.3 Forms of "boundary commoning"

4.3.1 Tamera: cultural and technical mediation

According to Tamera's online[3] and printed[4] communication materials, this project, like other leading ecovillages, aims to impact society by being an educational model and living laboratory of sustainability. Tamera's prestige as a source of ecological best practices is the basis of a form of boundary commoning that can be viewed as cultural and technical mediation. It involves promoting contact and cross-fertilisation among different cultural, ecological, socio-economic and institutional realities: that of Tamera's own premises and that of the surrounding Alentejo region. In addition, Tamera's estate hosts a transient and international public of paying guests, students, trainees, philanthropic supporters and political activists, who are thus socialised into processes of resourcing and reproduction of frames and technologies produced within the ecovillage. This process of cultural and technical mediation involves four main sets of activities: education and training, diffusion of knowledge and technology, relocalisation of supply chains, and cultural rapprochement with local communities and their institutions (Esteves, 2017).

At the time of fieldwork, about 60% of Tamera's budget came from revenue from its educational programmes. These include the Ecology Practice or Practical Work in Ecology in which participants engage in at least one month of theoretical and experiential learning on ecological design and intentional community-building, under the supervision of community members, in Tamera's gardens and agroforestry project. Although it was not possible to obtain quantitative data on the nationality of participants in Tamera's educational programmes, my anecdotal impression, based on daily interactions during fieldwork, was that most visitors were university-educated, middle to upper-middle class individuals who came from Germany, Austria and Switzerland, followed by North America and Israel. Tamera's guest office confirmed this had been the case for more than a decade. The few Portuguese visitors were either higher education students or middle-class professionals, mostly from the metropolitan areas of Lisbon, Porto and Coimbra. The predominance of visitors with relatively high levels of economic and educational capital, namely nationals of core industrialised countries and urban Portuguese, most likely resulted from the fee structure at the time.[5]

At the core of Tamera's model of sustainability is the re-localisation of food production, distribution and consumption to regional level. The goal is to regulate the production, exchange and consumption of food, within the ecovillage and in the wider Southwest Alentejo region, according to regional production cycles by planting, purchasing, processing and eating only seasonal produce cultivated within the region. With this goal in mind, Tamera has become a key player in the regional food economy of southwestern Alentejo: as a source of technical knowledge for producers in the region,[6] as a consumer and as a promoter of commercial exchanges. In this role, Tamera organises regular public markets and fairs on its premises, to which it invites organic and biodynamic producers in the region. It also provides training and consulting services on organic agriculture, regenerative landscape management and water conservation to agricultural producers in the region. Being a major bulk buyer of organic produce in an impoverished and sparsely populated region gives Tamera leverage power to influence production choices among neighbouring farmers.

Tamera's positive impacts upon the regional economy, through attracting international visitors and as a source of agro-ecological knowledge for producers in the region, also promoted a prefigurative dynamic that acquired enough political power to influence public institutions in its favour (Esteves, 2017). This includes working with the local government (the council of Tamera's home municipality of Odemira) to develop an innovative regulatory framework for natural resource management in the region, known as PIER *(Plano de Intervenção em Espaço Rural)*. The purpose is to incorporate land use and sustainable construction techniques developed in Tamera into the political discourse and regulatory framework of the region. The terms of reference, approved in March 2015, also awarded Tamera a permanent public certification as a research and development centre authorised to use its premises for tourism and hosting events by other organisations for a fee, as well as to commercialise agricultural products and renewable energy technologies.

The collaboration with public authorities was largely facilitated by a process of cultural *rapprochement* with the population in the region, as well as the Portuguese public in general (Esteves, 2017). Portuguese-born and Portuguese-speaking Tamera residents played a central role in this process by translating Tamera's webpage into Portuguese and establishing linkages with journalists, documentary filmmakers, academic researchers and political activists in Portugal. Portuguese residents of neighbouring villages who had lived and worked in German-speaking Europe also played key roles in this process of cultural *rapprochement* by sharing insider knowledge on cultural norms and institutional processes, offering Portuguese language skills and providing meeting spaces that allowed socialisation, dialogue and exchange with locals.

4.3.2 Esperança/Cooesperança: re-signifying the market

Esperança/Cooesperança is part of a wider grassroots political project of working-class empowerment and emancipation through self-management (Esteves, 2020). Among its core goals is to fight the economic deprivation and political marginalisation among subsistence farmers caused by export-oriented economic policies favouring mass-scale, export-oriented manufacture and agribusiness. It is rooted in the movement of *Basic Ecclesial Communities*,[7] which emerged in the 1960s to promote grassroots subsistence and resistance to political repression (also see Fajardo Rojas & Hataya, this volume). In 1984, the regional office of *Cáritas Brasileira*[8] in Rio Grande do Sul launched *Banco da Esperança*, a microcredit system aimed at promoting economic self-determination and healthier livelihoods for the rural and urban poor by organising them into small producers' cooperatives designated *Projetos Alternativos Comunitários* (PACs) (Bertucci & Silva, 2003). The goal was to promote income generation among the urban poor by scaling up subsistence agriculture and cottage industries (Sarria Icaza & Freitas, 2009: 8–11). The launch of *Esperança/Cooesperança* in 1987 aimed to aggregate the PACs system by "aggregating all small community-based economic projects into a big project that would support them with technical assistance, as well as promote their organisational development as socially transformative experiences" (Sarria Icaza & Freitas, 2009: 43).

This project is a leading example of an "alternative institution" engaging with a web of peasant and labour movements, NGOs and grassroots initiatives, with the purpose of promoting a class-based, emancipatory political project (Laville & Eynaud, 2019). It gives participants access to a marketplace where their products are commercialised through a process that regulates lateral relationships among otherwise competing producers according to norms of cooperation and mutual help (Esteves, 2020). The central marketplace of *Esperança/Cooesperança*, known as *Centro de Referência Dom Ivo Lorscheider* (CRDIL), became the container of an outward movement of mobilisation of a translocal cohort of activists and visitors through the organisation of political workshops, gatherings and protest activities.

The weekly fairs taking place at CRDIL are spaces not only of commercialisation, but also of socialisation of both producers and consumers into the norms and practices of solidarity economy. CRDIL functions as a container for a Freirean "culture circle" where participants co-create strategies for economic self-determination through a problem-based learning model based on the See/Judge/Act[9] methodology used by *Ação Católica Brasileira*,[10] the Catholic Action branch in Brazil, to develop, within the network of *Basic Ecclesial Communities*, organisations of social intervention known as *Pastorais Sociais*[11] (Souza, 2006).

CRDIL thus became a space of experimentation, enactment and coordination of cooperative economic practices from a popular perspective. Such activities promote encounters between the wider public and otherwise socially and spatially segregated socio-economic realities. These include urban poor such as *catadores* (recyclable waste collectors), manufacturing workers in the industrial periphery of the city who were left unemployed by the collapse of local industries during the 1980s, *colonos* living in the rural belts of Santa Maria and neighbouring municipalities, indigenous and *quilombola* afro-descendent communities and settlements of the Landless Workers' Movement (*Movimento dos Trabalhadores Rurais Sem Terra*, or MST).

The activities taking place at CRDIL promote boundary commoning through a process of re-signification of market relations with three dimensions: (1) promotion of lateral interactions among producers based on reciprocity and cooperation; (2) engagement of wider publics through resignification of the products on offer and reframing of their consumption as a political act; (3) framing activities taking place at CRDIL as part of a wider process of social transformation through engagement with social movements and public institutions.

This methodology of social intervention regulates lateral interactions among participating producers, the public and social movements. To sell at CRDIL, producers need to operate within *grupos de produção*, each containing at least three family units with shared accounting and fiscal identity. The purpose is to promote economies of scale in production through incentives for cooperation among producers, such as sharing spaces of production and commercialisation, collective purchases and shared book-keeping. This process also includes a clientele composed mainly of left-leaning middle-class consumers predisposed to favour environmental and social concerns over instrumental motivations when making purchasing choices. This happens through the resignification of the products on offer and the framing of their consumption as a political act through both publicity material and hosting of political events during markets, most notably by MST and the *Movimento dos Pequenos Agricultores* (MPA). In addition, *Esperança/Cooesperança* aims to attract and educate wider sections of the public, as well as public and regulatory authorities, by emphasising the health benefits of the organic and artisanal practices of agriculture, livestock farming and food processing employed by participating producers.

The methodology followed by *Esperança/Cooesperança* also promotes local and translocal alliances that increase the project's political capital and resilience vis-à-vis the state and the judicial apparatus. These processes happen informally during project meetings and assemblies in which participants are encouraged to exchange skills, technology and management strategies. It also happens formally during training on cooperative management and agroecology offered to activists of MST and MPA by *Cáritas* and the *Pastorais Sociais*. These movements have a visible presence at weekly markets at CRDIL, including vending areas decorated with their flags and other symbols. The marketplace also hosts organisational gatherings and performative events of national and international social movements. This includes the first World Fair and World Forum of Solidarity Economy, which took place on 22–24 January 2010.

Esperança/Cooesperança also partners with the *Comissão Pastoral da Terra* (CPT) in the movement for agrarian reform. The partnership includes supporting the MST and MPA by hosting a native seed bank at CRDIL, as well as facilitating exchange of agroecological know-how between activists in these movements and other subsistence farmers in the region. Similar interactions take place with groups of *catadores* (collectors) of recyclable waste. *Esperança/Cooesperança* complements the organisational and technical support given by *Cáritas* to its regional network of associations by providing training and support in business and product development, along with vending spaces at weekly and thematic fairs for commercialisation of products made from recycled waste.

The network of grassroots leaders socialised by *Ação Católica* and the *Pastorais Sociais*, who entered electoral politics and high levels of public administration through the *Partido dos Trabalhadores* (PT) after the democratic transition in Brazil, granted institutional recognition to solidarity economy in the form of policy programmes at national, state and municipal levels nationwide. However, political influence of this kind is limited by two factors: the impact of electoral rotation on government agendas and budgets and the fact that the processes of micro-mobilisation carried out in CRDIL reach out mainly to producers, consumers and institutional partners connected with progressive Catholic circles. Fieldwork evidence indicates that efforts to reach out to public officials beyond these circles had limited effect. Further research is necessary to assess the extent to which *Esperança/Cooesperança* is able to compete with actors in the wider market, namely by attracting both consumers and public-sector and third-sector actors who do not share the same values and political orientation as project participants and managers.

4.3.3 *Cooperativa Integral Catalana: blended networked infrastructures for autonomist governance*

CIC is a prominent example of an SEI based on the development of an autonomist institutionality aimed at de-linking solidarity economy from the state and from capitalist markets (Dafermos, 2017). It uses a system of nested physical and virtual assembly spaces to promote a form of boundary commoning on the basis of the setting up of a web of *blended networked material and governance infrastructures for autonomist governance*. The goal of this structure is to emancipate the economy from capitalism and place it in the hands of grassroots self-organising groups (Duran, 2009). This has come about through the appropriation of cybernetic discourse and technology by SEIs and the setting up of autonomist institutionalities in the form of open cooperatives (Esteves, 2022a). Such cooperatives represent a synthesis of the governance models and practices of the solidarity economy with commons-based peer production (CBPP). Benkler (2006) defines CBPP as a logic of collaboration among networks of people, mediated using peer-to-peer online platforms, who freely organise around a common goal using shared resources. Such logic is exercised by "stable communities of individuals interacting on a regular basis and knowing each other" (Papadimitropoulos, 2018: 14) through membership-based cooperative governance structures aimed at shaping a community that produces, manages and/or consumes common-pool resources.

The strategy followed by CIC is to de-link the satisfaction of participants' basic needs, such as food and housing, from the state and the capitalist market (Dafermos, 2017). Registering CIC as a cooperative was part of a strategy of "economic disobedience" based on institutional hacking of the regulatory tools of the state and the capitalist market, with the goal of promoting the gradual withdrawal of its members from their structures (Esteves, 2022a). There are three forms of membership in the CIC: (1) as a "self-employed member" or "productive project," who produces independently as an individual or a small group and pays a monthly fee to the financial commons of the cooperative; (2) as a participant in a "collective unit of production" or co-housing community, which can take the form of a cooperative or association and (3) as a consumer who exchanges Euros for the basket of alternative currencies used in the cooperative in order to purchase goods and services from self-employed members, productive projects and units of production. Besides buying and selling products, members can obtain additional income and resources by selling goods or services within the mainstream economy without having to pay the taxes required by the Spanish law for microentrepreneurs and self-employed workers. Instead, they can pay a financial contribution to the cooperative, which is managed as a common-pool resource.

At the core of this process is the development of an online financial system that allows money to be produced, circulated interest-free, and managed collectively as a common good by assemblies of users. This happens through a concentric system of financial and exchange mechanisms, which connects and transfers resources between nodes in the cooperative as well as between members. The financial mechanism consists of a basket of local alternative currencies, which has been developed by bioregional groups of exchange and self-organisation known as *ecoxarxas*.[12] A core rule for the constitution of an *ecoxarxa* is the availability of a physical space, known as *rebost*, used for storage and commercialisation of goods produced by CIC members and for assembly meetings. Rebosts are also spaces of socialisation where lateral interactions among participants are coordinated to promote practices of effective communication, internal trust and reciprocity. In addition, they are sites of political mobilisation, hosting a range of gatherings, educational and training offerings and performative events by both members and like-minded non-members, which frame the CIC as part of a transnational anti-capitalist movement.

The earlier *ecoxarxas*, such as that of Montseny and Olot, are predominantly rural and peri-rural networks that preceded the creation of the CIC, dating back to the mid-1990s. Both the earlier *ecoxarxas* and those created after CIC was founded were integrated into its governance as part of four wider "bioregions" (northern, eastern and western regions of Catalonia, plus Barcelona). Each *ecoxarxa* acts as a regional node of the cooperative, with its own assembly and local currency.

The currencies developed by each *ecoxarxa* are connected through Integral Community Exchange System (IntegralCES),[13] an open-source online platform featuring social currencies managed by SEIs. This platform makes each community-level platform interoperable and convertible into its local currency equivalent through the ECO, the CIC's common currency, which is equivalent to the Euro in value. It also publicises offers of goods and services and congregates requests from individual members of the cooperative and affiliated projects. Complementing IntegralCES is *Central de Abastaçiment Catalana* (CAC),[14] an online system that coordinates collection of products from providers along with transportation and delivery to the rebost collection points across Catalonia, which may be social centres, assembly spaces, co-housing or co-working projects. In turn, IntegralCES and CAC are complemented by the use of online messaging apps for rapid decision-making on everyday aspects of management of the CIC. In-person assemblies, taking place at the physical premises of *ecoxarxas*, are used for decision-making on structural and strategic issues.

At the time of fieldwork, CIC operated three overlapping banking and credit mechanisms that connected participants and initiatives throughout Catalonia and abroad. *Cooperativa de Autofinançament Social en Xarxa* (CASX),[15] an interest-free deposit and credit system for production projects developed by individual members' collectives or assemblies, made the possibility of having a bank account and receiving loans available (in Euro or ECO) even to those members who did not have a tax identification number (NIF) or were refused credit in the mainstream banking system. *CoopFunding*[16] complements and expands the functions of CASX by serving as a platform for crowdfunding by, and for, SEIs around the world. The Bank of the Commons,[17] created by an international network of free software/free culture projects led by the team that created the CIC, plays a complementary role by connecting production projects within Catalonia and across the world. It uses FairCoin,[18] a cryptocurrency based on green blockchain technology and offering guarantees of equivalence in Euros and ECOs, to implement decentralised financial structures for commons and cooperative productive initiatives.

The core goal of FairCoin is to interconnect participants by simplifying their exchanges through decentralised technologies and a payment system without interest or middlemen. The Bank of the Commons is managed through English language open online assemblies via Telegram as well as through the in-person assemblies of FairCoop. It also counts on the technical support of the CIC's administrative structure. The goal is not only to promote decentralised financial structures for the development of a livelihood outside the realm of the state and the capitalist market but also to extend these goals beyond Catalonia.

4.4 Conclusions

This exploratory comparative analysis sheds light on how different forms of micro-public spheres of solidarity economy practices and collective action result in distinct forms of boundary commoning. The enactment of different approaches to collective action regulates the promotion of transparency, trust and reciprocity among actors, as well as re-territorialisation of their economic behaviour and establishment of linkages with external entities, through processes of experimentation, enactment and coordination of alternative practices within micro-public spheres. This leads to different strategies for impacting society.

Tamera is an *educational model* and *living laboratory of sustainability* that promotes a form of boundary commoning on the basis of *cultural and technical mediation*. This process has three dimensions: education and training, knowledge and technology diffusion for the purpose of relocalising supply chains and cultural *rapprochement* with local communities and their institutions. One of its core manifestations is the construction of a regional-level network of production, exchange and consumption of organic agricultural produce.

Esperança/Cooesperança promotes boundary commoning by *resignifying market relations*. It emerged organically from organised grassroots resistance to authoritarianism and economic exclusion in southern Brazil in the mid-1980s. Its weekly and yearly thematic markets aim to promote material and organisational incentives for the development of class consciousness and solidarity among marginalised communities, as well as engagement of wider society and the state in their emancipation. The main pillars of this strategy are creating a regional network of cooperation among subsistence producers and influencing public institutions and the wider public on their behalf. The project promotes trust-building and cooperation through the inclusion of subsistence producers in formal associations and application of methods from the *Base Ecclesial Communities, Ação Católica* and *Pastorais Sociais*.

Cooperativa Integral Catalana promotes an *autonomist institutionality*, based on *blended networked infrastructures for autonomist governance*, that aims to de-link solidarity economy from the state and the capitalist market. It does this through the application of online peer-to-peer platforms and social currencies to the re-localisation of production, exchange and consumption. This promotes synergies between online and physical spaces of exchange and decision-making, enabling transparency in decision-making and relationships of trust and reciprocity among regional nodes of actors.

These case studies challenge scholarship to expand its understanding of the nature of the alternative economic spatialities created by solidarity economy initiatives, as well as the practices that constitute solidarity economy as a field.

In order to fully understand how solidarity economy initiatives build counterpower, it is necessary to look beyond how they construct circuits of value that re-territorialise supply chains and reproduce material resources. The spaces of production and commercialisation that constitute such supply chains are also containers of everyday symbolic, performative and affective practices that sustain and signify forms of transaction based on reciprocity, redistribution and/or householding and are in turn reproduced by them. Analysing such practices is fundamental to understanding how they constitute a form of micro-politics, which produces non-hegemonic identities, political projects and forms of mobilisation with emancipatory goals.

Notes

1. The author would like to gratefully acknowledge the financial assistance of the Portuguese Fundação para a Ciência e a Tecnologia (Bolsa SFRH/BPD/94495/2013), which enabled her affiliation to the Centro de Estudos Internacionais ISCTE-IUL (UID/CPO/03122/2013) and allowed her to conduct the research required for this chapter.
2. Based on Laville and Eynaud (2019), one can define such alternative economic spatialities as spaces of economic activity (production, commercialisation, consumption) that exist in parallel to those of the capitalist economy.
3. Webpage of Tamera, with direct links to documents about the project: www.tamera.org/about/
4. Webpage of Verlag Meiga, Tamera's publishing company: https://verlag-meiga.org/
5. In 2015, participants in Practical Work in Ecology paid €20 per day to participate in the programme (€15 for Portuguese participants). Despite the national discount, the programme remained unaffordable for most of the population. According to data published by Instituto Nacional de Estatística (National Institute of Statistics), in 2013, about 20% of the Portuguese population lived on less than €411 a month. Only 4% of people aged 35 or lower earned more than €900 a month.
6. www.transicaoportugal.net/iniciativas-de-transicao/portugal/sao-luis/

7. A term introduced in the 1968 meeting of the Latin American Council of Bishops in Medellin, Colombia, to refer to small grassroots groups, present in both rural and urban areas, that organised agricultural, industrial and informal workers into self-organised groups that met to reflect upon Christian scripture and apply their reflections to the analysis of their socioeconomic context.
8. *Cáritas Brasileira* was founded in 1956 as an organism of the *Conferência Nacional dos Bispos do Brasil* (CNBB). It organises national and international campaigns to promote the economic and political empowerment of marginalised communities. One of its founders was Bishop Hélder Câmara, a liberation theologian and leading figure of the movement of *Basic Ecclesial Communities* in Brazil.
9. An inductive method, developed by Belgian Cardinal Joseph Cardijn (1882–1967), to support reflection and strategising at the grassroots level by Catholic Action groups.
10. Part of Catholic Action, an international movement founded in the 1920s by the hierarchy of the Catholic Church to train lay members for evangelisation. The Brazilian branch was founded in 1935 by Cardinal Sebastião Leme da Silveira Cintra.
11. Organisations created by the hierarchy of the Brazilian Catholic Church to coordinate interventions in specific social groups, such as peasants, children and youth, homeless people and industrial workers.
12. https://cooperativa.cat/xarxa-territorial-2/ecoxarxes/
13. www.integralces.net
14. https://commonstransition.org/the-catalan-integral-cooperative-an-organizational-study-of-a-post-capitalist-cooperative/#section17
15. https://cooperativa.cat/apoya-a-casx-desde-la-cic/
16. https://coopfunding.net
17. https://bankofthecommons.coop/about-us/
18. https://faircoin.world

References

Avelino, F. and Kunze, I. (2009). "Exploring the transition potential of the ecovillage movement," *European Conference on Sustainability Transitions: Dynamics and Governance of Transitions to Sustainability*, Amsterdam, June 4–5, 2009.

Benkler, Y. (2006). *The Wealth of Networks: How Social Production Transforms Markets and Freedom*. New Haven and London: Yale University Press.

Bertucci, A. and Silva, R. M. A. (2003). *20 Anos de Economia Popular solidária: trajetória da Cáritas Brasileira dos PACs à EPS*. Brasília: Cáritas Brasileira.

Cox, R. (1983). "Gramsci, hegemony and international relations: An essay in method," *Millennium: Journal of International Studies*, 12(2), pp. 162–175. https://doi.org/10.1177/03058298830120020701

Dafermos, G. (2017). "The Catalan integral cooperative: An organizational study of a postcapitalist cooperative," P2P Foundation and Robin Hood Coop, online at https://commonstransition.org/the-catalan-integral-cooperative-an-organizational-study-of-a-post-capitalist-cooperative/ (accessed March 29th 2023).

De Angelis, M. (2017). *Omnia Sunt Communia: On the Commons and Transformation to Postcapitalism*. London: Zed Books.

Duran, E. (2009). *Abolim la Banca: Testimoni d'um Activista Que há Desafiat el Poder*. Barcelona: Eres.

Escoffier, E. (2018). "Mobilisational citizenship: Sustainable collective action in underprivileged urban Chile," *Citizenship Studies*, 22(7), pp. 769–790. https://doi.org/10.1080/13621025.2018.1508412

Esteves, A. M. (2017). "'Commoning' at the borderland: Ecovillage development, socio-economic segregation and institutional mediation in southwestern Alentejo, Portugal," *Journal of Political Ecology*, 24(1), pp. 968–991. https://doi.org/10.2458/v24i1.20978

Esteves, A. M. (2020). "Solidarity economy markets as 'mobilizational commons': Re-signifying the market through the lens of cooperation," *Community Development Journal*, 56(3), pp. 470–486. https://doi.org/10.1093/cdj/bsaa008

Esteves, A. M. (2022a). "'All watched over by machines of loving grace'? Information technology, in-person relationships and normative regulation in an 'integral cooperative'," *Community Development Journal*, 57(4), pp. 655–672. https://doi.org/10.1093/cdj/bsab019

Esteves, A. M. (2022b). "Processes of normative regulation in spaces of 'solidarity economy': A comparative case study analysis," *International Journal of Sociology and Social Policy*, 4(7/8), pp. 624–639. https://doi.org/10.1108/IJSSP-12-2020-0540

Fernandes-Jesus, M., Carvalho, A., Fernandes, L. and Bento, S. (2017). "Community engagement in the transition movement: Views and practices in Portuguese initiatives," *Local Environment*, 22(12), pp. 1546–1562. https://doi.org/10.1080/13549839.2017.1379477

Fois, F. (2019). "Enacting experimental alternative spaces," *Antipode*, 51(1), pp. 107–128. https://doi.org/10.1111/anti.12414

Gibson-Graham, J. K. (2008). "Diverse economies: Performative practices for 'other worlds'," *Progress in Human Geography*, 32(5), pp. 613–632. https://doi.org/10.1177/0309132508090821

Hillenkamp, I. and Lucas dos Santos, L. (2019). "The domestic domain within a postcolonial, feminist reading of social enterprise: Towards a substantive, gender-based concept of solidarity enterprise," in Eynaud, P., Laville, J. L., Lucas dos Santos, L., Banerjee, S., Avelino, F. and Hulgard, L. (eds.) *Theory of Social Enterprise and Pluralism: Social Movements, Solidarity Economy and the Global South*. New York: Routledge, pp. 90–115.

Keane, J. (1998). *Democracy and Civil Society*. London: Verso.

Laville, J. L. (2016). *A Economia Social e Solidária: Práticas, Teorias e Debates*. Coimbra: Almedina.

Laville, J. L. and Eynaud, P. (2019). "Rethinking social enterprise through philanthropic and democratic solidarities," in Eynaud, P., Laville, J. L., Lucas dos Santos, L., Banerjee, S., Avelino, F. and Hulgard, L. (eds.) *Theory of Social Enterprise and Pluralism: Social Movements, Solidarity Economy and the Global South*. New York: Routledge, pp. 18–43.

Lietaer, B., Arnsperger, C., Goerner, S and Bruhuber, S. (2012). *Money and sustainability: The missing link*. Axminster, Devon: Triarchy Press.

Lockyer, J. and Veteto, J. R. (2013). "Environmental anthropology engaging Ecotopia: An introduction," in Lockyer, J. and Veteto, J. R. (eds.) *Environmental Anthropology Engaging Ecotopia*. Bioregionalism, Permaculture, and Ecovillages, New York: Berghahn Books, pp. 1–31.

Lucas dos Santos, L. and Banerjee, S. (2019). "Social enterprise: Is it possible to decolonise this concept?," in Eynaud, P., Laville, J. L., Lucas dos Santos, L., Banerjee, S., Avelino, F. and Hulgard, L. (eds.) *Theory of Social Enterprise and Pluralism: Social Movements, Solidarity Economy and the Global South*. New York: Routledge, pp. 3–17.

Mendell, M. (2009). "Financing the social economy in Quebec," *Makingwaves*, 20(3), pp. 46–50.

Ould Ahmed, P. (2015). "What does 'solidarity economy' mean? Contours and feasibility of a theoretical and political project," *Business Ethics: A European Review*, 24, pp. 425–435. https://doi.org/10.1111/beer.12063

Papadimitropoulos, V. (2018). "Commons-based peer production in the work of Yochai Benkler," *TripleC*, 16 (2), 835–856. https://doi.org/10.31269/triplec.v16i2.1009

Poteete, J. and Ostrom, E. (2010). *Working Together: Collective Action, the Commons, and Multiple Methods in Practice*. Princeton, NJ: Princeton University Press.

Rigo, A. S. and França Filho, G. C. (2017). "O paradoxo das Palmas: Analise do (des) uso da moeda social no 'bairro da economia solidaria'," *Cadernos EBAPE.BR.*, 15(1), pp. 169–193. https://doi.org/10.1590/1679-395141258

Sarria Icaza, A. M. and Freitas, M. R. (2009). *O Projeto Esperança/Cooesperança e a construção da Economia Solidária no Brasil: Relato de Uma experiência*. Porto Alegre: Cáritas Brasileira.

Souza, N. (2006). "Ação Católica, Militância Leiga no Brasil – Méritos e Limites," *Revista de Cultura Teológica*, 55, pp. 39–59. https://doi.org/10.19176/rct.v0i55.15033

5 Urban regeneration and minority women

Can solidarity economy contribute to environmental and social justice within the urban space?[1]

Luciane Lucas dos Santos

5.1 Introduction

This chapter reflects upon the arrangements of community economy (Gibson-Graham, 2006) and their contribution to reinforce not only the individuals' sense of belonging in urban spaces but also their agency as part of a collectivity. Employing feminist intersectional lenses with regard to the right to the city, I argue that a socially fair perspective on urban regeneration needs to pay attention to three issues: (1) the extent to which the unequal distribution of environmental burdens exacerbates material constraints experienced by some groups, particularly black women; (2) the connection between the concept of spatial democracy and attention to heterogeneous community aesthetics within the city – homogenisation of landscapes being a way of erasing these marks and (3) the possibility for solidarity economy (henceforth SE) arrangements to become a vector of community agency for marginalised groups who fight for spatial democracy.

This chapter particularly aims to debate this third issue, considering gender and race as social markers of unequal environmental burden in the production of urban space. This is thus a text that intertwines SE, intersectional fights for spatial democracy and representational justice in urban regeneration.

The chapter has four sections. The first debates the very concepts of urban planning, regeneration and landscape production from which we depart, in the sense that landscaping in itself may or may not be a way to build the right to the city. It depends on the prevalent meanings that the landscape design provides; it also depends on its capacity to communicate plurality or predominance of a particular view of the city. It means that it is not enough to provide access for those who have been excluded or gated, although access should be taken as the tip of the iceberg, that is the visible material consequence of a broadened system of exclusion.

As such, the very aesthetic sense brought to the scene in a regeneration project should depart from the heterogeneity of European societies in contrast to

DOI: 10.4324/9781003306344-6

the prevalent social imaginary of homogeneity between and within European countries. As reminded by Name and Moassab (2020: 337, my translation), the "landscape is not a mere fact: it is as much a feature of nature as a subject of culture." From this statement, we retain that decisions on landscape production, as well as the way such decisions are taken, are as important within a regenerative urban plan as concerns with having more inclusive spaces.

The second section is devoted to a discussion of the connection between minority women and the production of space. Once committed to social and environmental justice, urban planning (as well as its recently reclaimed regenerative role) should challenge prevailing senses of gender roles in public space, which have undermined women's full enjoyment of the city, whether it be in terms of urban mobility, safeness or suitability for specific needs they might have. A socially oriented urban planning should also challenge the way hegemonic views have neglected the heterogeneity of women and the different constraints they might face in urban spaces – as immigrants, low-income workers, Roma women, Afro-Europeans, Muslim women, transgender women and non-sheltered homeless women, to name but a few. It is important to debate the underrepresentation of minority bodies in European urban planning and landscape production.

The third section presents the role that the SE might play within urban projects with regard to environmental and social justice (henceforth ESJ). How might ESJ goals be connected with active citizenship through the SE? How might the SE contribute to a more plural sense of urban planning? And how can active citizenship be related to the idea of more resilient communities?

The fourth and final section focuses on how SE arrangements on collective care can refresh our views on public uses of space, also helping to challenge minority women's underrepresentation in urban planning. The underlying idea of this section is to demonstrate that community-based initiatives run by black and other minority women in European contexts can contribute to bridging the gap between needs for environmental and social justice and gender/ethnic-sensitive approaches on landscape designing.

My central argument can be summarised as follows: urban regeneration – either in environmental terms or as an issue of social inclusion – cannot succeed without challenging the hierarchical sense that underlies the production of space. SE may be a way to challenge this hierarchy by contesting prevalent uses of public spaces and evoking new social practices in urban contexts. Urban regeneration needs to effectively invest in what the Art Historian Sara Lewis (2020: 23) has called "representational justice." By this, she particularly refers to the visual representation of black people through "images of black life"[2] not only in the Arts but also in Architecture.

Although this chapter focuses on black women, representational justice is an issue that ought to be given to all groups that have been transformed into minorities within European contexts – Roma people, migrants, Muslim women and communities, homeless people and others. Although SE arrangements themselves do not guarantee spatial democracy, they bring to the scene the relevance of the collective dimension and its capacity for agency as they strengthen the sense of belonging and social ties in the neighbourhood. SE contributes to raising the awareness of city dwellers' rights, thus recognising a political dimension of spatial democracy.

The idea of representational justice calls for the diversity and heterogeneity of European societies through plural views on aesthetics and ethics in everyday life. In this sense, urban and landscaping planning should pursue visual and spatial justice (Soja, 2009) rather than mere inclusive spaces. A more horizontal approach between the State and civil society is also needed so that we can effectively tackle structural inequalities embodied in the production of space. SE, I argue, might play a pivotal role in this call for representational justice in urban spaces.

5.2 Urban planning communicates hierarchies no matter how inclusive it may appear

What could architecture and urban planning be if they were closer to the heterogeneity of people they are expected to serve? This question is intrinsically connected with other thorny issues. How can we move beyond outdated but not yet achieved goals on inclusion/integration? How can we deepen the debate on a socially oriented urban planning without sneakily reaffirming mottoes and asymmetries of power? How can we move from a discourse on bashful tolerance on otherness towards a well-balanced, fair distribution of opportunities and burdens?

Moassab (2020: 9), a Brazilian architect, has distinguished herself for debating the need for decolonising Architecture. Grounded in Sergio Ferro's work, she reminds us that, in Latin America, the use of concrete is itself a consequence of responses to trade unions (due to the fact that using concrete allows a reduction in the number of workers in the building sites) rather than a choice of the most suitable building material. As she remarks, concrete does not require bricklayers and carpenters. Besides revealing that some solutions might not result from a technical choice but instead from vested interests, her work demonstrates how a field of knowledge – in this case, Architecture – might veil relevant ancestral building technologies such as riverside stilt houses, indigenous huts and fishing village cottages. She calls for our attention, for example, to Andean peoples' knowledge of anti-seismic structures, stressing how the potential of ancestral building technologies has been otherwise neglected. Likewise, she highlights the need for critical engagement with a set of neglected burning issues. Her analysis of construction sites in Brazil compares them to the new galley-ships, given the overrepresentation of black workers in the building sector and their unbearable work conditions.

What do these reflections have to do with our discussion if we are not talking about Latin America? First and foremost because assuming specific building technologies as the best for everyone everywhere is a misapprehension. The contexts in which these beliefs are grounded and the way they might bias social perception and approval are under no circumstance irrelevant. Likewise, suggesting alternative economic arrangements without questioning the surrounding environment in which they appear is not enough. It is necessary to interrogate the processes supporting the materiality that surrounds us. A political economy of materiality is needed, in such a way to debate how the dependency of some social groups might be built and fed by ill-considered decisions grounded on universalised assumptions. The choice of concrete as a building material is just one of them. We should interrogate more and more the fields of knowledge on which we have grounded our policies and projects, promoting a kind of postcolonial archaeology of knowledges – architecture, economics, history, engineering, landscape designing and so on.

An architecture and urban planning closer to the heterogeneity of social groups should (1) recognise not only the relevance but also the invisibility of some popular knowledges, (2) question the usual patterns of the buildings provided to the poor and (3) challenge the gauge of what is considered as appropriate (in terms, for example, of gender roles associated with public/private spaces or of what we have understood as inclusiveness). The social and popular commitment of Architecture and Urban Planning should, thus, not be limited to fighting against the real estate speculation and the consequent gentrification and privatisation of space or to forging tailored and cheaper solutions for groups that have faced exclusion in public space. It is more than that. In this age of diversity and migration flows all over the world, concerns with environmental and social justice will require from us, instead of ready-made solutions, the proper recognition of other rationalities in residential construction, in the organisation of space and in the handling of locally available and scant resources. As remarked by Name and Moassab (2020: 342), there are four important roles to be considered by landscape architects and landscape designers concerned with social and environmental justice:

> First: demanding public policies for the expansion of leisure spaces and environmental amelioration in racially or socially segregated territories. Second: incorporating, in their projects, forms of sociability of these groups, re-signifying typologies and uses. Third: understanding that, in segregated areas, the production of free public spaces enables the expression of marginalised cultures in other spaces, expanding the possibilities of political agency . . . Finally: having the project design aligned with an ecology of landscapes, agroecology (as socially and ecologically fair

> form of family farming) and landscape infrastructure (such as retention of slopes, capture and micro-drainage of rainwater, etc.), with a view to environmental regeneration and integration between distribution of ecosystem functions and risk management. . . Landscaping thus becomes a vehicle for the right to the city, in terms of social inclusion and environmental equity.
>
> (Name and Moassab, 2020: 342, my translation)

These concerns are particularly relevant when it comes to call upon the State to make reparations for androcentric bias in the prevalent meanings of construction and landscape design. A fairer urban planning thus implies: (1) technical preparation for a wide-ranging perception of urban space in which heterogenous female points of view are properly recognised and (2) ongoing evaluation of the ways space has been employed, occupied and socially appropriated by different groups (Name & Moassab, 2020). Since vested interests are likely to mould the perception of what is worthy of consideration (Arantes, 1998; Name & Moassab, 2020), urban and environmental regeneration policies need to fight for representational justice. In other words, inclusive projects that do not challenge these vested interests in landscape design are just scratching the surface and should be treated as such. The next section will discuss this contradiction in urban projects pointing out their gender bias in the intersection with other social markers.

Before moving forward, it is worth noting that SE might be an accomplice in this idea of decolonising architecture and urban planning, since it is engaged with representational justice (Lewis, 2020). Architecture, in turn, might inspire SE to think of economic and cultural arrangements connected with the right to the city – as can be seen, for example, in the idea of edible landscape design (Name, 2020; also see Caitana, Tasheva-Petrova & Vallet, this volume). This partnership could indeed bring to the table many issues regarding social and environmental justice.

In line with the prior four goals proposed by Name and Moassab (2020), SE can reinforce communities' autonomy and self-esteem by democratising the use of leisure spaces, stimulating communities' knowledges through economic and cultural arrangements and/or reinforcing promising sociabilities. With regard to a fairer production of the space, SE can foster a collective, self-managed perspective to environment regeneration schemes and, of no less importance, popular strategies for risk mitigation. The proper recognition of communities' knowledges – including building techniques, such as the case of river populations' floating homes to deal with flood season conditions (Cunha & Moassab, 2020) – is an example of a point of intersection between SE and decolonial architecture. At the crossroads of these fields, there is also a gender-sensitive approach, which the next section refers to in more details.

5.3 Gender, intersectionality and unequal production of space

In the debate on the right to the city, it is worth questioning the ways through which the public sphere has been gendered and created material constraints for minority women. I will start from the usual material constraints experienced by black women, particularly Afro-European women, in European countries. Discussing these constraints requires an understanding of previous asymmetries affecting the conditions of belonging, moving and self-provision of well-being (Lewis, 2013; CIJ, 2019).

Afro-European women embody disadvantaged conditions due to their over-representation in low-paid jobs and/or night shifts. In the latter case, they are further adversely affected by the lack of public transport. In contrast, public transport is noted by women in general as being of great importance to allow their participation in education and employment (EIGE, 2019). This means that low-income black women are likely to be even more affected by this shortcoming in European countries.

Afro-European women have also had to deal with housing segregation (FRA, 2019),[3] which imposes constraints upon their employability. Moreover, these women are likely to be seen as immigrant bodies, regardless of their place of birth – a situation that could be aggravated by European statistical vagueness on ethnic data (Escafré-Dublet & Simon, 2012). Additional disadvantage results from the way black women are discriminated against by educational systems, credit institutions, social welfare states, public services and potential employers, which happens in multiple contexts (Mutari *et al.*, 2002; Constance-Huggins, 2011; Lewis, 2013). However, despite the specificity of the context, there seems to be a common root: the mismatch of social location[4] between decision makers and final recipients, with influence not only on the attitudes and judgements by the former but also on concrete material consequences by the latter. As notably recalled by Anderson (2020), situatedness has impacted on "knowers' assessment of which claims are significant or important."[5]

Here we arrive at the direct connection between inequality, mobility and the use of public space. It is of great importance to debate the veiled racialisation of space, meaning different ways that minority groups experience the space and constitute their spatiality and mobility within the city. It is not possible for us to discuss challenging perspectives in urban planning without considering the everyday material constraints many minority women face regarding spatial segregation, lack of public transport, lack of proper street lighting, distance from important public facilities and lack of public day nurseries for their children, to name but a few.

If the usual victims of violence and harassment in public spaces are women, black women have dealt with higher levels of harassment,[6] not only because racialised bodies are hyper-sexualised but also because these women face precarious safety conditions in moving around the city. Minority women, including black women, have witnessed this mismatch between their needs in terms of mobility or use of public space and urban planning as it is – gendered, ethnically-underrepresented and produced according to middle-class lifestyles.

Building a city "for all" through an urban planning concerned with social and economic justice thus requires reflecting upon how impoverishment, shortage of public facilities and racial segregation have been intertwined. While it is true that all of us will be affected by big issues – such as climate change, disease outbreaks, water crises, rising global food prices or the growth of the far-right and its politics of fear – it is also true that their material effects are inequitably distributed. Black and poor people, along with Roma people and migrants in a (non-recognised) heterogeneous Europe, are the ones who have been gated in devalued areas with higher levels of toxic waste, industrial pollution and occurrence of landfills (CEPL & HEAL, 2006; Equinox, 2021). They are also the ones who have faced disproportionate impact of the COVID-19 pandemic in many countries (FRA, 2020). Moreover, they have also been neglected with regard to public policies. It is thus important both to take an attentive look at the usual unequal distribution of the burden of growth and to foster more resilient communities.

Grounded on a perspective of horizontal solidarity, SE has been attached to environmental issues in Europe, discussing themes such as transition currencies, short supply circuits and community gardening, among others. However, regardless of this welcome proximity between SE arrangements and the concerns of environmental activists, the impact of solidarity economy upon the resilience of minority groups in Europe has been notably slight.

Herein lies a gap to be closed. Despite the relevance of discussing impacts of consumption practices and ecological footprint, the debate on how environmental justice can be achieved by the poor and less visible minorities is urgently required. It is important to look at environmental issues from the perspectives of social and representational justice. In this sense, a political alliance between SE and urban regeneration projects should be in line with the idea of promoting fairer conditions of living and making use of the public space for people who have been gated in devalued areas without proper access to public facilities (cf. Šimleša, this volume; Amaro & Ferreira, this volume). Regenerative projects that overlook underlying inequalities and the way they have determined the use of space (e.g. minority women being disadvantaged due to spatial segregation and processes of ghettoisation) will remain superficial as an approach to issues of social exclusion in Europe.

I argue that this proximity between SE and urban planning needs to be enhanced in European countries, where internal inequalities have been neglected or assumed to be simply a matter of poverty rather than reflecting structural issues. Besides, SE's capacity for increasing citizen participation in public issues and its concern with social and economic justice could constitute an asset towards fairer urban planning and landscape design processes. In other words, providing public decision-making processes in urban planning with higher levels of citizen participation and plurality of perspectives represents challenging consolidated vested interests. In doing so, SE might contribute to diversifying the use and occupation of space, also guaranteeing its social appropriation by marginalised groups.

5.4 How can solidarity economy contribute towards fairer uses of space and community resilience?

SE has been a disputed issue over time, being conceptualised in different ways over time (Coraggio, 1994; Singer, 2002; Laville, 2010; Hespanha & Lucas dos Santos, 2016; Amaro, 2006; Esteves *et al.*, 2021).[7] For the purpose of this chapter, SE should be understood as a set of collective economic arrangements devoted to production, consumption, savings, distribution and trading activities, in urban or rural areas, grounded on the following principles: horizontal solidarity (meaning proper distribution of opportunities and assets), shared management (collective decision-making processes) and cooperation among citizens/workers/neighbours (Hespanha & Lucas dos Santos, 2016). Valuing popular knowledge and technologies, SE has emphasised the agency of the individuals who are formally or informally organised in these economic arrangements.

Within the European context, solidarity initiatives have been increasingly closer to environmental concerns (Avelino & Kunze, 2009; Esteves *et al.*, 2021; Hespanha, 2022; Moreira & Morell, 2020). Being a fast-growing and theoretically consistent approach, this perspective connecting SE and sustainability issues has been grounded in the dialogue between two main concepts: grassroots initiatives (or community-led arrangements) and commons (Ostrom, 1990). Since this perspective has primarily analysed ecovillages, agroecological food networks and transition movement, mostly constituted of middle-class activists, it is worth recalling that solidarity economy in Europe might otherwise assume a more popular and informal design, also referring to a set of informal peasant practices of mutual help and community spaces in rural areas (community ovens, threshing floors, community wash-houses and community lands, latter being known as "baldios"). For some authors (Hespanha & Lucas dos Santos, 2016; Hespanha, 2022), these practices should be considered as part of the SE legacy in Europe, not only because they encompass horizontal forms of solidarity, shared management of the commons and cooperation among neighbours but also because they gave rise to fruitful and collective dynamics in the urban spaces (edible gardens, community kitchens, community gardening, community repair shops, community-based revolving savings).[8] Due to its capacity of strengthening social ties and evoking a fair division of the resources, SE may play a pivotal role, I argue, for the achievement of both socio-environmental justice (Velicu & Barca, 2020) and political awareness.

In general terms, environmental injustice might be understood as the situation in which

> ethnic minorities, communities of lower socio-economic status, the least educated and otherwise marginalised segments of society disproportionately: 1) suffer from exposure to environmental hazards . . ., and/or 2) are denied environmental benefits such as water, sewage treatment facilities, sanitation, and access to natural resources.
>
> (CEPL & HEAL, 2006: 9)

Environmental justice thus implies an effective concern with the minorities' conditions of voicing dissent and building up their own resistance.

Against the grain, and captured by an institutionalised third-party mediation on social shortcomings, the agency of poor and disadvantaged communities remains a delayed political project in Europe. A misplaced perception fuels the prevalent discourse that internal inequalities are more concerned with poverty rather than with other forms of discrimination. As a result, we have had, among other misinterpretations, the colour-blindness effect (Escafré-Dublet & Simon, 2012) and the social exclusion due to migrant origin (EUMC, 2005).

The politics of resistance which Hossein (2014) refers to seems to be the most streamlined process for minorities to deal with social ills such as colour blindness, disincentivisation of critical and horizontal forms of participation and neglect of basic needs and rights. Calling the attention to women-led informal banks in Caribbean "as a counter-movement because they are localised, community-driven and share financial resources . . . in an equitable manner in contrast to conventional financial systems," she denounces the exclusion of poor racialised women from credit access and emphasises the political dimension of giving the community "a way to safe safely" (2014: 86, 92).

In the specific field of urban planning, the political agency might be boosted or disregarded, independently of a regeneration agenda. A promising way for the European SE movement to foster the citizens' political agency instead of the hierarchical relationship between institutions and aid recipients is to be aligned with popular interests in fairer housing and urban regeneration policies. In practical terms, it means, for example, to support. Likewise, it represents the achievement of underlying goals other than economic ones, such as the refinement of participative democracy processes, the fostering of the sense of belonging and the representation of subaltern aesthetic perspectives in landscape design.

SE can thus play a key role in forging active citizenship by raising subalternised groups' participation in the decisions associated with urban regeneration projects. Participatory budgeting and popular assemblies can be gateways to popular engagement. It is, however, worth considering that the ongoing devaluation of minorities' perspectives has impacted over time their conditions of voicing points of view. It means that regeneration projects interested in forging effective participation should take into account that time is a valuable asset, since confidence and balanced conditions for minorities to voice their views are to be built up (cf. Amaro & Ferreira, this volume).

SE can also boost popular economic arrangements committed to enhancing conviviality and sharing resources. Edible gardens are a good example, especially if their social role of feeding people is properly taken into account –not seen, as such, as an outside assistance but as a collective action towards neighbourhood resilience. Likewise, community kitchens/ovens in the neighbourhood and community gardening constitute ways of gathering people, valuing collective activity and making them less dependent on market fluctuations.

SE also has a word to say regarding homeless people and the way they have been set apart from the debate on public spaces. Different from the usual policy of social surveillance of their bodies and wandering behaviour, SE has aimed to bring these "left behind" people into the conviviality. Collective arrangements of production and exchange fairs with social currencies involving homeless people (Šimleša *et al.*, 2015; Lucas dos Santos, 2018) have proven to be a successful solution for their recognition as legitimate town-dwellers and the recovery of their power of choice. Homeless people's collective work towards producing recycled goods through recyclable waste and rubbish is a kind of economic arrangement to be stimulated (Lucas dos Santos, 2018) – autonomy and power of choice being fostered instead of a charitable approach.

With regard to minority women in general and Afro-European women in particular – to whom this chapter primarily refers – I argue that they should be among the groups to be better portrayed in the framings employed in public policies and urban planning, since they are among the most affected by a one-size-fits-all approach (EUMC, 2005; FRA, 2019). Under no circumstances should community-led initiatives be used as an excuse for States to reduce their commitments to equity in public service infrastructure. However, public bodies should support and stimulate these arrangements as a way to foster communities' resilience, given the Gordian knots on the suitability requirements of some policies and their corresponding limited coverage.

In the face of the precariousness and uncertainty experienced by minority women in many different European countries, some community-led initiatives help them manage day-to-day difficulties, such as childcare during work shifts, purchase of basic foodstuff when earnings are about to run out or everyday dilemmas associated with a vicious circle of in-work poverty. Mutual help, reciprocity and community forms of redistribution and care not only strengthen social bonds in the territories but also transform individual scarcity and eventual surplus into a kind of collective storeroom, guaranteeing more consistent provisioning for low-income families. A set of solidarity initiatives, directly associated or not with landscape design and urban planning, might contribute to reducing these women's vulnerability in a gender-biased urban space, making a different use of public spaces. They can benefit, for example, from time banks and solidarity fairs in open areas by exchanging knowledges and surpluses to enhance their own provisioning (Lucas dos Santos, 2018, 2019; Cunha *et al.*, 2011; Guimarães *et al.*, 2019). Edible and community-led urban gardens could also be boosted in landscape design, as a resource for family food provisioning in the neighbourhood.

Although gender-sensitive spatial solutions concerning issues such as public transport and safe spaces for leisure, health activities and women's grassroots organising are to be boosted, socio-environmental justice requires institutions, local authorities, technical bodies and mediators to challenge the decision-making processes that have fed housing segregation, lack of public facilities in some areas and the deterioration of public transport, to name but a few. It is expected that these bodies reduce the impacts of such shortcomings on minority women's opportunities in education and employment. SE is likely to reduce the material impact of some gaps through community-led economic initiatives (CLIs) on issues such as care, food production, water supply, housing and savings. For this reason, SE arrangements should be taken into consideration within spatial planning.

5.5 Afro-European women and the perspective of collective care in public space: solidarity economy, mutual help and community resilience

Solidarity groceries, community repair shops and mothers' co-ops can be of help for minority women to tackle situations of in-work poverty. Solidarity groceries, for example, can constitute a way of putting different people in solidarity contact, reinforcing social cohesion in the neighbourhood (Cunha *et al.*, 2011; Guimarães *et al.*, 2019). In these arrangements, there are those who provide the grocery with fruits and vegetables from rural areas and those who are in charge of supplying it with non-perishable goods, less likely to be obtained in the absence of money.[9] Both groups will be given the corresponding value of what they brought to the shop in social currency, so that they can purchase what they are in need of subsequently. Social currency, however, is a matter of choice. Resulting from cooperatives or collectives of workers (such as the Glut Food Coop, a majority-women run vegetarian grocery store in the United States) or from non-profit association-led projects (such as Comunitas in Portugal or the Epicentre in France), solidarity groceries have contributed to the provisioning of low-income families in a way different from a charitable scheme. In the particular case of Lyon, Epicentre connects other associations such as the "Croc'éthic" short supply chain grocer, the group of solidarity groceries in the region of Auvergne-Rhône-Alpes (GESRA), and the Rhône's food bank.

In the field of care, a growing number of diversified experiences have resulted from formal and informal alliances among women, some of them from minority groups: parent-led nurseries, single mothers' co-housing,[10] mothers' co-ops, self-managed schools, working single mothers' support organisations and community mothering in the neighbourhood. Although the existing literature on initiatives such as these is still lacking, some references that analyse initiatives of sharing economy, peer-led parenting programmes and collective mothering (Edwards, 2000; Lietaert, 2010; Day *et al.*, 2012; Tummers, 2016; Bresson & Labit, 2020; Caballero *et al.*, 2019) provide hints on how useful the collaborative designs might be for low-income single mothers in the absence of the State.

These women-led initiatives have proven to be a popular and creative solution that is within the reach of low-income mothers. Cooperatives or informal parent-led daycare spaces could help working mothers rotate responsibilities for their children's care and guarantee their self-esteem associated with their own background. Sankofa Co-op, in Washington (the United States), for example, has demonstrated how homeschooling projects might have an additional political dimension, constituting an "empowering space for children whose culture is otherwise being gentrified," namely, African and African-American children.[11] Grounded on a different approach, the Council of Single Mothers and their Children – a community organisation in Victoria, Australia – has supported working single-mothers with essential information about "affordable housing, income security, family law, child support, family violence . . ., flexible employment and study,"[12] having advocacy and mutual help as two of its main pillars. In the long run, initiatives such as these promote different ways of thinking about the space, its planning and a gender-sensitive approach applied to the imagination of what a city should contain to address its heterogeneity of subjects.

Last but not least, groups of mothers in rotation of the collective care of children have constituted another way of dealing with their lack of time and resources. Black single mothers have called our attention to a collective perspective of care in which supporting networks might play a pivotal role in child-rearing. This community mothering – that is, the idea of community "othermothers" co-existing with the "bloodmothers" in the neighbourhood – seems to communicate three concerns: (1) preparing children for autonomy and resistance to oppression; (2) supporting bloodmothers who can be overwhelmed by their duties as single-mothers; (3) promoting a "nurturing Black value-structure" (Hale, 1980 *apud* Edwards, 2000: 88).

Learning from this perspective of community mothering, SE can be a kind of seedbed for collective experiences of care in Europe, given the scarce coverage of minority women's needs. Although parent-led nurseries are already a common solution in countries such as France, the UK and Canada, it is worth recalling that parent co-ops in Europe have been usually created and run by middle-class parents. However, if the black community mothering experience was valued, boosted and appropriately supported by public bodies in black communities and other disadvantaged groups, minority women could be less affected in their employment and education opportunities. Although the

State should guarantee equal access of parents to childcare, the gap regarding minorities' rights is so well-established that minority women have been doubly discriminated against. Once the Afro-European women's right to choose is guaranteed, it is noteworthy that collective care – of children, disabled people and the elderly – is to be valued and stimulated as a way of fostering the resilience of neighbourhoods. In doing so, urban planning would also benefit from gender- and ethnic-sensitive approaches by contributing not only to enhancing ethnic representation in the city but also to fostering plural views on the ethics of care.

What is at stake is the following set of questions: how can minority women – and black women among them – be relieved from the material constraints associated with asymmetric perspectives of public space? How can community-led initiatives be fostered towards child-rearing to enhance community resilience and social justice? How can environmental programmes become relevant to effectively promoting environmental and social justice, going beyond the middle classes in European countries? How can public bodies stimulate this process, relinquishing their usual control over the experiences in favour of more resilient communities?

5.6 Conclusions

Solidarity economy can be successfully paired with emancipatory perspectives in urban planning, urban regeneration and landscaping design, contributing to healthier and fairer cities. However, this outcome entails a deeper meaning of environmental justice, in which the hierarchical sense of inclusion is to be challenged. Landscape design and urban regeneration projects, once grounded in environmental and social concerns, should thus evince and defy the way in which the production of public spaces has been gendered and asymmetrically constituted.

Solidarity economy can boost communities' resilience through arrangements connecting the economic, political and social dimensions in different territories. In this sense, it can promote social bonds in the neighbourhood as well as the mitigation of material constraints experienced by minorities. This chapter aimed to demonstrate that a strategic alliance between solidarity economy and urban regeneration is possible, being forged in a fine-tuned comprehension regarding the value of people's knowledges and their capacity for self-organisation. Focused on minority women in general – and, in particular, on the situation of precariousness and underrepresentation of Afro-European women – I argue that a possible next revolution in the European solidarity economy movement might refer to its capacity for not only unveiling the intersectional roots of inequality, but also valuing minority women's self-organising capacity to develop (a non-neoliberal) resilience, as well as autonomy and power of choice.

Notes

1. The chapter was written as a scientific contribution to the URBiNAT Project as an Advisory Board member. URBiNAT – Healthy Corridors as drivers of social housing neighbourhoods for the co-creation of social, environmental and marketable NBS – is a project financed by the European Commission H2020, Smart and Sustainable Cities programme, under the grant agreement No. 776783.
2. Sarah Lewis Reflects on Vision and Justice. Gallery View Gallery. Words. Cultured Magazine. May 7, 2019. Available at: www.culturedmag.com/article/2019/05/06/sarah-lewis
3. This information refers to research published by FRA in 2018 regarding racism and poor housing and jobs in European countries and the situation of black women and men not being analysed separately. Through a large-scale survey with almost 6,000 African-descent people in 12 European Union Member States, the report "Second European Union Minorities and Discrimination Survey – Being Black in the EU," whose summary was published in 2019, evinced the urgency for an intersectional approach in different social affairs.
4. Social location is a key concept in Feminist Epistemology. According to Anderson (2020), "individuals' social locations consist of their ascribed social identities (gender, race, sexual orientation, caste, class, kinship status, trans/cis etc.) and social relations, roles, and role-given interests, which are affected by these identities." See https://plato.stanford.edu/entries/feminism-epistemology/#SituKnow, section 1, social situation.
5. See https://plato.stanford.edu/entries/feminism-epistemology/#SituKnow, section 1, situated knowledge in general.
6. In the United States, a 2019 study demonstrated that women of colour are more likely to be targeted as victims of sexual harassment than white women. Being more vulnerable in the workplace, women of colour are less likely to report the harassment. See www.independent.co.uk/news/world/americas/black-women-sexual-harassment-abuse-work-study-a8997296.html. In the UK, a study by Girlguiding (2021) demonstrated that girls of colour are more often confronted with sexual harassment in public (street harassment and intimidation) rather than white girls). See www.girlguiding.org.uk/globalassets/docs-and-resources/research-and-campaigns/girlguiding-research-briefing_girls-experiences-of-sexual-harassment_june2021.pdf
7. This is not an extensive list but illustrates a set of relevant approaches.
8. An ever-changing typology of Solidarity Economy in Portugal, which could be extended to some European countries, is proposed by the Study Group on Solidarity Economy of the Centre for Social Studies (Ecosol-CES). More details on this conceptual approach and typology can be found in Hespanha and Lucas dos Santos (2016: 44).
9. Epicentre (https://letsfoodideas.com/en/initiative/promouvoir-la-solidarite-grace-a-une-epicerie/), Glut Food Coop (https://glut.org/about/), Comunitas (https://mercearíacomunitas.wordpress.com/).
10. See https://commune.house/en/living-at-commune/#choose, www.theguardian.com/lifeandstyle/2018/sep/29/it-was-like-a-marriage-only-better-the-single-mothers-who-moved-in-together, www.bbc.com/worklife/article/20190827-the-single-mums-who-live-together-on-mommunes
11. www.sankofahomeschool.org/getting-started
12. www.csmc.org.au/about/

References

Amaro, R. R. (2006). "A Economia Solidária da Macaronésia: um novo conceito," *Revista de Economia Solidária*, 1, pp. 11–30.

Anderson, E. (2020). "Feminist epistemology and philosophy of science," in Zalta, E. N. (ed.) *The Stanford Encyclopedia of Philosophy*. Entry. Online at https://plato.stanford.edu/archives/spr2020/entries/feminism-epistemology/ (accessed April 19th, 2023).

Arantes, O. B. (1998). *Urbanismo em fim de linha e outros estudos sobre o colapso da modernização arquitetônica*. São Paulo: EdUSP.

Avelino, F. and Kunze, I. (2009). *Exploring the transition potential of the ecovillage movement*. Online at https://iriskunze.files.wordpress.com/2015/06/transition-potential-ecovillages-avelino-kunze-2009.pdf (accessed April 19th, 2023).

Bresson, S. and Labit, A. (2020). "How does collaborative housing address the issue of social inclusion? A French perspective," *Housing, Theory and Society*, 37(1), pp. 118–138.

Caballero, C., Martínez-Vu, Y., Pérez-Torres, J., Téllez, M. and Vega, C. (eds.) (2019). *The Chicana M(Other)Work Anthology*. Tucson: University of Arizona Press.

Center for Environmental Policy and Law (CEPL) and The Health and Environment Alliance (HEAL). (2006). *Making the Case for Environmental Justice in Central & Eastern Europe*. Online at www.env-health.org/IMG/pdf/ceu_teljes_pdf.pdf (accessed April 19th, 2023).

Centre for Intersectional Justice (CIJ). (2019). *Intersectional Discrimination in Europe: Relevance, Challenges and Ways Forward*. Report commissioned by the European Network against Racism (ENAR). Online at www.enar-eu.org/wp-content/uploads/intersectionality-report-final-3.pdf (accessed April 19th, 2023).

Constance-Huggins, M. (2011). "A review of the racial biases of social welfare policies," *Journal of Human Behavior in the Social Environment*, 21(8), pp. 871–887.

Coraggio, J. L. (1994). *Economía Urbana: la perspectiva popular*. Quito: Instituto Fronesis.

Cunha, G. and Moassab, A. (2020). "Decolonizando o ensino de estruturas em arquitetura: uma proposta a partir da experiência na Unila," in Moassab, A. and Name, L. (eds.) *Por um ensino insurgente em arquitetura e urbanismo*. Foz do Iguaçu: EdUnila, pp. 270–290.

Cunha, T., Moura, T., Silvestre, S. and Silva, S. (2011). "Pirilampa: A mercearia solidária da Granja do Ulmeiro," in Cunha, T. and Santos, C. (eds.) *Elas no Sul e no Norte*. Granja do Ulmeiro: AJP, pp. 130–140.

Day, C., Michelson, D., Thomson, S., Penney, C. and Draper, L. (2012). "Innovations in practice: Empowering parents, empowering communities: A pilot evaluation of a peer-led parenting programme," *Child and Adolescent Mental Health*, 17(1), pp. 52–57.

Edwards, A. (2000). "Community mothering: The relationship between mothering and the community work of black women," *Journal of the Motherhood Initiative for Research and Community Involvement*, 2(2), pp. 87–100.

EIGE. (2019). "Gender equality index 2019," *Work-Life Balance*. Online at https://eige.europa.eu/publications/gender-equality-index-2019-report/transport-and-public-infrastructure (accessed April 19th, 2023).

Equinox Initiative for Racial Justice (Equinox). (2021). *Towards Climate Justice*. Report. Online at www.equinox-eu.com/wp-content/uploads/2021/06/Towards-Climate-Justice-Equinox.pdf (accessed April 15th, 2023).

Escafré-Dublet, A. and Simon, P. (2012). "Ethnic statistics in Europe: The paradox of colour-blindness," in Triandafyllidou, A., Modood, T. and Meer, N. (eds.) *European Multiculturalisms: Cultural, Religious and Ethnic Challenges*. Edinburgh: Edinburgh University Press, pp. 213–237.

Esteves, A. M., Genus, A., Henfrey, T., Penha-Lopes, G. and East, M. (2021). "Sustainable entrepreneurship and the sustainable development goals: Community-led initiatives, the social solidarity economy and commons ecologies," *Business Strategy and the Environment*, 30(3), pp. 1423–1435.

European Monitoring Centre on Racism and Xenophobia (EUMC). (2005). *Migrants, Minorities and Housing: Exclusion, Discrimination and Anti-Discrimination in 15 Member States of the European Union*. Report. Online at https://fra.europa.eu/sites/default/files/fra_uploads/188-CS-Housing-en.pdf (Accessed November 4th, 2021)

European Union Agency for Fundamental Rights (FRA). (2019). *Second European Union Minorities and Discrimination Survey: Being Black in the EU*. Summary. Online at https://fra.europa.eu/sites/default/files/fra_uploads/fra-2019-being-black-in-the-eu-summary_en.pdf (accessed April 10th, 2023).

Gibson-Graham, J-K. (2006). *A Postcapitalist Politics*. Minneapolis: University of Minnesota Press.

Girlguiding (2021). *Research Briefing: It Happens All the Time: Girls' and Young Women's Experiences of Sexual Harassment*. Online at www.girlguiding.org.uk/globalassets/docs-and-resources/research-and-campaigns/girlguiding-research-briefing_girls-experiences-of-sexual-harassment_june2021.pdf (accessed April 10th, 2023).

Guimarães, I., Coelho. S. and Soares, C. (2019). "Portuguese local currencies: The recent cases of Fundão and Covilhã," in Coelho, S. and Marcelo, G. (eds.) *Ética, Economia e Sociedade*. Porto: Universidade Católica Editora, pp. 324–342.

Hale, J. (1980). "The Black Woman and Childrearing," in Rodgers-Rose, L. F. (ed.) *The Black Woman*. Beverley Hills, CA: Sage Publications, pp. 79-88.

Hespanha, P. (2022). "El desafío de los nuevos usos de las tierras comunales en Portugal," in Urtasun, A. A., Castell-Cogollos, R. and Llopis-Goig, R. (eds.) *La sociedad colaborativa. Los impactos de la acción colectiva en la sociedad contemporânea*. Madrid: Centro de Investigaciones Sociológicas, pp. 189–210.

Hespanha, P. and Lucas dos Santos, L. (2016). "O nome e a coisa. Sobre a invisibilidade e a ausência de reconhecimento institucional da Economia Solidária em Portugal," *Revista de Economia Solidária*, 9, pp. 22–68.

Hossein, C. (2014). "The politics of resistance: Informal banks in the Caribbean," *The Review of Black Political Economy*, 41(1), pp. 85–100.

Laville, J-L. (2010). *L'économie sociale et solidaire. Pratiques, théories, débats*. Paris: Éditions du Seuil.

Lewis, G. (2013). "Unsafe travel: Experiencing intersectionality and feminist displacements," *Signs: Journal of Women in Culture and Society*, 38(4), p. 880.

Lewis, S. (2020). "Groundwork: Race and aesthetics in the era of stand your ground law," *Art Journal*, 79(4), pp. 92–113.

Lietaert, M. (2010). "Cohousing's relevance to degrowth theories," *Journal of Cleaner Production*, 18(6), pp. 576–580.

Lucas dos Santos, L. (2018). "Under the flyover: Homeless people, power of choice and the practice of autonomy through an exchange fair," *Conjunctions: Transdisciplinary Journal of Cultural Participation*, 5(1), pp. 3–22. Online at https://sciendo.com/pdf/10.7146/tjcp.v5i1.105293 (accessed April 19th, 2023).

Lucas dos Santos, L. (2019). "Broadening the economic imagery through European complementary currencies: Citizen-driven economic initiatives and community autonomy as key concepts," in Coelho, S. and Marcelo, G. (eds.) *Ética, Economia e Sociedade*. Porto: Universidade Católica Editora, pp. 343–364.

Moassab, A. (2020). "De que lado a arquitetura está? Reflexões sobre ensino, tecnologia, classe e relações raciais," *Revista Projetar: Projeto e Percepção do Ambiente*, 5(1), pp. 8–19.

Moreira, S. and Morell, M. F. (2020). "Food networks as urban commons: Case study of a Portuguese 'prosumers' group," *Ecological Economics*, 177, 106777.

Mutari, E., Power, M. and Figart, D. (2002). "Neither mothers nor breadwinners: African-American women's exclusion from US minimum wage policies, 1912–1938," *Feminist Economics*, 8(2), pp. 37–61.

Name, L. (2020). "Paisagens para a América Latina e o Caribe famintos: paisagismo comestível com base nos direitos humanos e voltado à justiça alimentar," in Moassab, A. and Name, L. (eds.) *Por um ensino insurgente em arquitetura e urbanismo*. Foz do Iguaçu: EdUnila, pp. 349–365.

Name, L. and Moassab, A. (2020). "Por um ensino de paisagismo crítico e emancipatório na América Latina: um debate sobre tipos e paisagens dominantes e subalternos," in Moassab, A. and Name, L. (eds.) *Por um ensino insurgente em arquitetura e urbanismo*. Foz do Iguaçu: EdUnila, pp. 336–344.

Ostrom, E. (1990). *Governing the Commons: The Evolution of Institutions for Collective Action*. New York: Cambridge University Press.

Šimleša, D., Puđak, J., Majetić, F. and Bušljeta Tonković, A. (2015). "Solidarity economy in Croatia: The case study of city split." Online at www.bib.irb.hr/793845 (accessed April 10th, 2023).

Singer, P. (2002). *Introdução à Economia Solidária*. São Paulo: Fundação Perseu Abramo.

Soja, E. W. (2009). *The City and Spatial Justice*. Online at www.jssj.org/wp-content/uploads/2012/12/JSSJ1-1en4.pdf (accessed April 19th, 2023).

Tummers, L. (ed.) (2016). *The Re-Emergence of Co-Housing in Europe*. Abingdon: Routledge.

Velicu, I. and Barca, S. (2020). "The just transition and its work of inequality," *Sustainability: Science, Practice and Policy*, 16(1), pp. 263–273.

6 Social and solidarity economy in Central/Eastern Europe – case studies from Poland and Czech Republic

Dražen Šimleša

6.1 Introduction

The turbulent political and social history of Central and Eastern Europe (CEE) has significantly shaped its social and solidarity economy (SSE) sector. We can follow this impact from the earliest development of social economy in the mid-19th Century, when almost all countries in the region were under a single ruling monarchy, to more recent history as separate states, some oriented towards western democracy and others ruled by communist regimes.

Neither part of the region is particularly noted as a hotspot for SSE, for different reasons. Countries oriented towards western democracy have maintained quite active roles for the state and other public authorities, with SSE actors emerging into civil life mostly within the last two decades. On the other hand, in many formerly communist countries, the SSE sector began from scratch in the 1990s, having first been controlled from above in the immediate post-WW2 period, later viewed as an obsolete leftover of the old regime. This is an example of what Giulia Galera calls "negative cultural memories" (Borzaga & Spear, 2004: 22) and is somewhat tragic considering the situation in the early 20th Century, before the establishment of non-democratic regimes, marked by strong networks of active cooperatives with high levels of knowledge and expertise. For example it is estimated that in pre-WW2 Poland, one-fifth of all adults belonged to an organisation in the cooperative sector (Ciepielewska-Kowalik, 2020, 2021), most of them in the fields of production and agriculture, commerce and grocery, and trade and banking. In the Czech Republic, there were over 9,000 active public and humanitarian organisations (Dohnalová *et al.*, 2021) and 16,670 registered cooperatives in diverse spheres: from credit, agricultural, housing, energy, consumer and producer cooperatives to student organisations, sport clubs, associations of national minorities and many more (Fraňková, 2019: 16).

This chapter examines the autonomous and intermediary spaces that are supporting solidarity economy-based practices in Eastern European countries where, until a few years ago, misrepresentations and ideological misinterpretations of history had made the association with SSE almost embarrassing. It addresses a

DOI: 10.4324/9781003306344-7

need to explore, in this context, where, when and with what kind of actors SSE livelihood practices are happening, along with their social impact in local communities. It does this through the analysis of two case studies: Jazdów, a self-managed neighbourhood in Warsaw (Poland), and Fair & Bio Coffee Roasters Cooperative in Prague (Czech Republic).

Based on these two case studies, and expanding the scope of analysis to Central and Eastern Europe as a whole, it then examines the extent to which these initiatives take their inspiration and guidance from their rich national histories of cooperatives and mutual aid associations, and to what extent they are completely new phenomena influenced and encouraged by their contemporary western counterparts. To understand the development of SSE in the region, there is a need to consider, on the one hand, to what degree we can find unique and specific approaches to solidarity economy livelihoods, and on the other if the adoption of universal strategies and steps is creating local variations of a global movement.

6.2 Social and solidarity economy in Central and Eastern Europe: the regional situation

Central and Eastern European countries that until the 1990s were part of the so-called Eastern Bloc and had employed a centralised and authoritarian approach to political economy have a common heritage. This is also evident in relation to their experiences with SSE, which, despite differences in their operational approach to the concept, show many similarities (Šimleša *et al.*, 2015):

- Acceptance by the early 1990s of neoliberal agendas that labelled cooperatives and SSE as remnants of former communist regimes
- Even when the SSE sector became established, it did so in piecemeal fashion, heavily dependent on the EU funds
- Low levels of the general trust and solidarity on which the SSE sector relies
- Limited entrepreneurial know-how and skills among SSE actors
- Difficulties in deriving adequate financial incomes from the market

This situation was exacerbated by a lack of any legislative or institutional framework for the sector, the absence of clear definitions and labels for SSE actors or enterprises, insufficient data and an inadequate base of SSE actors (Borzaga *et al.*, 2008). The 2020 European Commission report on social enterprises and their ecosystems in Europe categorised EU countries in terms of their degree of acceptance of the social enterprise concept. Of 13 countries in the category "Politically and legally accepted but narrow understanding (work integration) – weak self-recognition", only 2 were not from the CEE region (Borzaga *et al.*, 2020).

In addition, the analysis of the regional situation in the report *Social Enterprise in Central and Eastern Europe: theory, models and practices* emphasised the prevalence of the 'transition myth', leading to a dependence on neoliberal agendas and free-market doctrine and ignorance concerning good practices from the historically large and dynamic SSE and cooperative sectors (Defourny & Nyssens, 2021). This led to a self-reinforcing cycle of increased individualism and declining levels of trust, further undermining the sociocultural conditions necessary for the development of SSE.

The discouraging situation concerning the development of SSE in the CEE region makes it all the more important to highlight those actors in the region who are promoting and practising alternative spatialities based on the values and methods of SSE (Laville & Eynaud, 2019: 60). They are doing this despite the lack of any institutional framework oriented towards strengthening the SSE sector, and without the relative mainstream social and economic acceptance that SSE enjoys in some other parts of Europe. They are more like good practice cases to inform possible forthcoming transitions to stronger national and regional SSE sectors and to inspire new actors in the field: a parallel to the mainstream economic agenda, acting in line with SSE values as spaces for the transformation of the economic system from one that blindly prioritises private profit and GDP growth, to one that puts people and planet at its core (RIPESS, 2015).

Our two case studies also share this experience of going against the flow because of their promotion and practice of cooperation, solidarity, participation and bottom-up approaches. Similar to the situation described in the Nadezhda district in Sofia, Bulgaria (Caitana, Tasheva-Petrova & Vallet, this volume), this pressure was relieved as a result of EU policies in the SSE sector and the lack of state capacity to address the needs of many vulnerable and marginalised groups. At the EU level, space was opened up, while at national level, space was left empty, allowing the entry of SSE actors, along with many others engaged in citizen mobilisation.

6.2.1 Case Study 1: Jazdów self-managed neighbourhood (Poland)

Jazdów is a unique initiative, whose innovative co-management structure and practices make it a case study in solidarity-based livelihood of interest beyond the CEE region. It is a small neighbourhood, home to 29 organisations and informal groups occupying several houses and practising a form of active democracy known as "community management for urban spaces". Of 96 wood-finished houses built following the Second World War, 26 that remain today form the main part of the community. The houses are used for both living and working and are surrounded by gardens and apiaries that provide a common space for recreation, gatherings and cultural events.

The place has a long, interesting and rich history, documented in sources such as *Toward the Urban Revolution* by Monika Milewska (2019) and the project website at https://jazdow.pl/en/. A crucial moment from the recent past was in 2011, when local officials decided to destroy the whole area and replace it with something more in keeping, in their view, with the numerous embassies and national parliament building in the close vicinity. Environmental and urban commons activists joined forces to oppose the proposed development, raising awareness locally by organising an event as part of the annual Europe-wide Night of Museums and inviting everyone interested to visit the houses. Two years later, 30 associations collaborated over a period of several months to organise numerous social, educational and cultural activities within the Open Jazdów festival as a showcase to Warsaw citizens of the potential and importance of the place. This ongoing advocacy and activism secured approval from city officials for Jazdów residents and supporters to continue with cultural events. Subsequently, a campaign mounted through the city council resolution on public consultations collected enough signatures to initiate a public discussion process about the future of the site. In 2015, city authorities accepted the key finding of the consultation process: the need for the continuation of the Jazdów community. The same year, the group Open Jazdów – A Partnership For The Jazdów Settlement – was set up, with the support of the BORIS Association (Office for Support of Social Initiatives), and the foundations for co-management of this private–public area were in place. Open Jazdów organised a 2016 conference whose title, "Community-powered Urban Commons", clearly expressed the ideological position of the Jazdów neighbourhood. This takes into account five dimensions: decision-making structure, regulation, funding, spatial design and sustainability.

At the site itself, 6 houses are still occupied by their original (pre-2011) inhabitants, while another 18 are used by various associations and citizen initiatives. The other two houses are abandoned and not currently in use (one house is not usable because of fire damage incurred several years ago, but still standing and in need of renovation). Near the site are a private kindergarten and primary school, a refuge for homeless women and an old hospital that provides mental health services. Socially, the space combines private living and collective activities, all integrated in a commons-based management regime. This is supported by a democratic decision-making system in which all participants meet publicly at open monthly meetings, where all important topics are discussed and decisions made.

Jazdów is connecting solidarity economy and mutual aid with an inclusive and participatory decision-making structure, covering site-wide design, including its sustainability aspects, while also ensuring financial stability, recognition of legal rights and compliance with regulatory conditions. It is a place that supports diverse activities: while one group of participants experimented with *Wymiennik* (Exchanger) – an online system for the exchange of goods and services using its own *Alterka* currency – others meet in the community garden *Hoe and Sun*, run on cooperative principles and where participants share their time, work, revenues and responsibilities. Other facilities include a co-working place for architects, designers and others from creative industries; a meeting point for the Polish Extinction Rebellion group and *Solatorium*, an indoor garden where sufferers of Seasonal Affective Disorder can gather and socialise on cold, dark winter nights.

The importance of Jazdów for the city's social and cultural life can be demonstrated in numbers. For example, in 2017, the Open Jazdów Partnership organised 1,400 events, attended by more than 36,000 people (Milewska, 2019), while in 2019, over 3,800 events received close to 70,000 visitors (Partnerstwo Otwarty Jazdów, 2019). For this reason, Jazdów is now widely considered to be the largest cultural and educational site in Poland and one of the main laboratories for urban social action and co-management of urban space (Górz & Zielińska, 2018; Zielińska & Wilczyńska, 2019). This is a good example of what Escoffier calls "mobilizational citizenship" (Esteves, 2021: 4), where local citizens set up a space for the "production of belonging " and for self-definition of their autonomous political life.

One Jazdów neighbourhood participant has stated that

> building a community is also crucial to form lasting bonds between members of an endeavour to ensure the commitment that is needed for developing an economic model that is based on people's needs and a common good as a substitute or complement for mainstream economy based on monetary gains. (Mejor, 2020: 20)

The basis of this community is a combination of Right to the City activism, SSE practice, spaces run as commons, democratic management, social and cultural life and provision of domestic living space.

Of course, such a complex system, within a wider policy environment that is not always favourable, faces many challenges. Of 29 organisations and informal groups that use Jazdów Estate facilities and spaces, only 8 are active in the Union of Associations of the Open Jazdów Partnership, which since 2018 has acted as an intermediary between the Jazdów community and city government. An interview with a close supporter of Jazdów revealed occasional tensions between residents who want a more quiet and peaceful living environment and associations based onsite who favour more lively cultural and social activities. Such a large and challenging operation needs a substantial body of engaged people, and some of the most active members have experienced burnout. COVID-19 and the associated lockdown caused the suspension of many activities, important not only for the provision of services and communication with Warsaw citizens, but also for financial sustainability. The city, in its role as landlord, offered a 15% discount on building rents. The partnership initiated a crowdfunding campaign to ameliorate the financial impacts, but this reached only 25% of its target.

Relationships with city authorities are mixed, with periods of good understanding of Jazdów's commons-based values and democratic principles alternating with phases of ignorance, pressure on community organisational structures and processes, and ill-conceived proposals for infrastructural improvements that take insufficient account of the sustainability and needs of the Jazdów neighbourhood. Navigating this requires a balance between self-management as a practical laboratory with the requisite internal structures and processes on the one hand and, on the other hand, a co-management approach characterised by openness to communication, coordination and cooperation with city institutions and officials. This co-management system is a success to the degree that the city government cannot easily act contrary to the wishes and needs of Jazdów residents and users. A downside is that it often obliges Jazdów to wait for city officials to acknowledge its importance to the city. It is a slow process, but brings many long-term benefits and has already proved its ability to sustain direction and momentum in the face of obstacles and challenges. The partnership's ultimate goal is

> to create a new tool for participation, within which part of the responsibility for urban space will be transferred to the community. Such a tool would not only allow for changes in public space thanks to micro-projects but would also guarantee its strategic development.
>
> (Górz & Zielińska, 2018: 50)

6.2.2 Case Study 2 – Fair & Bio Coffee Roasters (Czech Republic)

Fair & Bio Družstvo (Cooperative) was set up in 2011 as a cooperative. Two years later, it founded Fair & Bio Coffee Roasters (Fair & Bio Pražírna, F&BCR) to run a fair trade organic coffee roastery in the small town of Kostelec nad Labem (some 30 km from Prague). As is very common in the CEE region, the story starts with an activist not-for-profit association working on economic solidarity and democratisation, which at some point decided to create an entity to act as a formal vehicle for its work. In this case, the association is Ecumenical Academy (Ekumenická Akademie – EA) who, alongside their work on social and solidarity economy, are among the pioneers of fair trade in the Czech Republic. Since 2004, they have promoted and advocated for SSE through political education programmes, campaigning and advocating for global justice. As they themselves state in an interview conducted for this chapter, "We used fair trade as a pedagogical tool to understand the economic system and its alternatives".

After years of activism and advocacy work, EA ran two projects financed through EU grants in 2011 and, as a side project, founded the F&BCR in 2013. Translating their political rhetoric into workable practice raised numerous challenges: organised as a cooperative – not a popular style of business – employing vulnerable people and aiming to achieve market sustainability, all while labelling themselves as an SSE enterprise and reliant on a financially uncompetitive product. Several years after its foundation, the business was still not economically viable, relying on direct financial support from the surrounding SSE ecosystem, including several interest-free loans from members. Since 2018, however, the F&BCR cooperative has operated fully within the market, without relying on any grants beyond the usual state support for businesses that employ people with disabilities.

F&BCR is by definition a WISE (Work Integration Social Enterprise): of 12 employees, 75% are mentally or physically handicapped. They provide their employees with more than just paid work and a friendly working environment: increased self-esteem and the opportunity to live more meaningful lives. In going beyond being a good employer for marginalised people, they have much in common with Italian style social cooperatives or SSE enterprises in the European context (Borzaga *et al.*, 2014). They are not only providing people in need with good jobs, they are also integrating them into their local and global community, while at the same time attaching their work to the bountiful history of the SSE movement in their country through cooperative experience.

In their own words, F&BCR are the continuation of 170+ years of cooperative history in the Czech Republic (Fraňková, 2019: 16) with "transparent and collective decision-making as well as promoting social cohesion and creating space for active individuals". The main product is, in addition, part of the global fair trade and sustainability movements: all coffee is organically produced and has a fair trade certificate. They work with producers who are themselves nurturing cooperative values and principles, ensuring that the solidarity economy in the Czech Republic supports the well-being of local communities in the countries from which they import coffee beans. They proudly state how from time to time they host the partner cooperatives who form part of their social and solidarity supply chain. With this approach – caring less for labels and more for direct contact with producers, sharing common values and principles and elevating democratic practices – they are in line with the third wave of fair trade actors, according to Benjamin Huybrechts' (2012) classification.

F&BCR's affiliation to the global SSE movement takes them beyond national borders. They have benefitted from the transfer of experience and know-how from cooperative partners in Germany and Austria and are a member of Solidarity Economy Europe (RIPESS Europe), a continental chapter of the global network for social and solidarity economy. F&BCR are not seeking to be slightly better than a capitalist company: they are fully dedicated to the original fair trade principles and are a member of the Decent Company Movement Association and Union of Czech and Moravian Manufacturing Cooperatives. Additionally, they actively promote and support fair trade in their city and country by organising fair trade fairs, food sovereignty forums and SSE conferences.

Following the tests of their resilience and market endurance during their first years of existence, the COVID-19 crisis brought a new challenge. Before the pandemic, F&BCR's main customers were bars, restaurants, offices and the events sector, all of whom made regular orders of the larger zero waste barrels. When lockdown brought many parts of the economy to a halt, F&BCR needed to draw even more deeply upon their adaptive capacity. At the same time, further challenges arose through restrictions on the maximum number of people allowed to collaborate in person in cooperative manufacture, along with problems with global supplies of coffee and packaging. Adaptation strategies included reorienting production towards smaller packages for individual consumers, training in online marketing and opening an eShop and increased social media presence to connect with potential customers. They managed to avoid shutting down roasting operations throughout the entire pandemic period, unlike many small businesses in their vicinity.

Today, F&BCR's founding organisation EA runs a fair trade shop in the city of Prague, selling many blends of coffee of its own manufacture along with other fair trade products from all over the world. This way, they increase their visibility to the public and presence in progressive movements in the local community.

F&BCR thus combine activity in fair trade, cooperative values and principles, solidarity economy and employment of marginalised and vulnerable people, along with collaboration with other movements in the country, region and wider world that are pioneering deep and transformative transitions towards more sustainable, solidarity-focused and resilient societies. The combination of so many elements is not typical in the CE region, which makes F&BCR an instructive case study in both regional and global terms. F&BCR can be identified with the social model of cooperatives since they are not only taking care of their members, and through their outward-looking way of working, they are "promoting the general interest of the community or they can tailor the economic system's democratisation" as well (Borzaga & Spear, 2004: 20). This is also why F&BCR can be labelled an SSE enterprise and more specifically as an Italian-style social cooperative whose model is characterised by pursuing cooperative members' interests in ways aligned with the interests of the surrounding community and other groups in their ecosystem (Defourny & Nyssens, 2021). They are also a multi-stakeholder cooperative (Abell, 2014; Ciepielewska-Kowalik, 2020): besides employees, members come from the local community, other SSE actors and other interested groups, a total of 25 members for the whole cooperative. Their work covers three important dimensions of social, environmental and economic: the social through the creation of jobs for disadvantaged people and their integration into social life, the environmental by making organic coffee a source of cooperative revenue and mutual support throughout the supply chain and the economic through fair trade business and, nowadays, financial sustainability.

6.3 Discussion and conclusions

The two case studies of SSE in the CEE region are quite different in many specific respects; each has its own unique trajectory and everyday existence. However, they also share several common points that illuminate the general experience of creating and running alternative economic spaces in this part of the world. Fair & Bio Coffee Roasters and Jazdów neighbourhood share their bottom-up approach, and both emerged from activist movements. Neither is a self-sufficient autarchic island; both are integrated within local networks of potentially transformative movements for social–ecological and economic resilience. Both are creating and practising counterpower to dominant economic and political narratives, but in a constructive way that embraces openness to dialogue. In Erik Olin Wright's (2010) categorisation of transformative possibilities, both cases closely fit that of interstitial transformation: they work within their own autonomous space, which is not colonised by capitalist social (re)production, and are willing to present themselves as alternatives. However, they are also not completely closed to pursuing symbiotic transformation, which is open to influencing official power structures and processes to advance progressive policies. Fair & Bio Coffee Roasters leverage official support as employers of disadvantaged groups and actively promote fair trade as necessary to support their everyday business. Jazdów neighbourhood, with its open partnership and co-management model, is always in tension between running its own development model and influencing city official representatives and the way politics influence culture, social life, commons, well-being and sustainability. This way, the two initiatives are advancing the frontiers of genuine and participatory democracy – what is referred to as "democratic solidarity", a political and social life co-constructed by actors who enter freely into non-competitive, self-managed modes of economic action, aimed at empowering excluded and/or disadvantaged groups, by prioritising non-economic concerns related to social justice, environmental sustainability and welfare (Ould, 2015).

As already stated,

> A crucial element of a solidarity economy approach is to recognise the ways that conventional economics has described reality so as to make invisible a whole host of practices, initiatives, human relationships and motivations, and thus to limit our abilities to imagine economic alternatives. Acknowledging this, and working to make these other forms of economic life visible and valued, opens up the terrain upon which solidarity economy organising does its work.
>
> (Miller, 2010: 3)

Fair & Bio Coffee Roasters and Jazdów neighbourhood are doing exactly that – initiating collective action and citizen mobilisation for non-capitalist economic activities, for distributing public and common goods openly and fairly and for improving social life and well-being. Through collective action and citizen mobilisation, every participant gets a chance to elevate their "Nested-I" (Bollier & Helfrich, 2019), an identity that is created through relationships and not as the mythical isolated individual that defines *Homo economicus* in the neoliberal capitalist narrative. They are transforming their communities by shifting the focus from isolation and fear, market pressures and corporatisation to a connected and strengthened social fabric, associational life and the engagement of citizens (Block, 2008).

Their stories are even more striking because their SSE practice takes place in institutional and legislative environments that are not always supportive or friendly. As noted at the beginning of the chapter, it is not easy to develop alternative economic concepts in countries that lack "awareness and understanding of the concept of the social economy, social enterprises, and other related concepts, in society, in public debate, and academia" and where "the main support for the social economy (both financial and awareness raising) comes from EU programmes and initiatives" (Chavez & Manzón, 2019: 19). The impact of EU policies and funds was also noticed in other places (Defourny & Nyssens, 2021).

With this in mind, we can now try to answer the question of whether these two cases are nationally and/or regionally specific variations of SSE approaches, or if they reflect universal strategies for solidarity and a fairer and more sustainable world. My conclusion is that they are both: a locally unique approach to perpetuating a long-standing cooperative tradition that was suppressed because of political shortcomings and economic ideology in the case of F&BCR, and a very special version of protecting commons and promoting democratisation through co-management of private–public spaces in the case of Jazdów. It is what authors such as Jean Louis Laville, Isabelle Hillenkamp and Luciane Lucas dos Santos labelled as "promotion of economic and ecological resilience of territories through the re-territorialization of economic activity, supported by participatory politics" (Esteves, 2021: 2). On the other hand, they are very much aligned with global movements for social and solidarity economy and revitalising the commons, connected and cooperating with similar initiatives in Europe and elsewhere, and making that collaboration a strong feature of their political identity.

When we analyse their co-management models and community-based approaches, we can see how they are rooted in solidarity economy principles and values. They are practising economic democracy based on reciprocity, redistribution and householding (Lucas dos Santos & Banerjee, 2019). In any discussion of social and solidarity economy, it can never be overstated how "solidarity" is much more than a concept. First, it is a framework for designing and implementing strategies that strengthen the resilience of communities, regions and societies. Second, it elevates the idea of advancing the common good collaboratively rather than going it alone. Third, solidarity is a vital motivational resource and a renewable one. It is a resource that we need from each other in order to sustain the efforts that transition will require (Lewis, 2017: 10). The two case studies from the CCE region presented here are excellent illustrations of how SSE is an active and evolving expression of solidarity in all these respects.

References

Abell, H. (2014). *Workers Cooperative: Pathways to Scale*. Online at https://project-equity.org/wp-content/uploads/2017/02/Worker-Cooperatives-Pathways-to-Scale.pdf (accessed November 4th, 2022).

Block, P. (2008). *Community: The Structure of Belonging*. San Francisco: Berrett-Koehler Publishers.

Bollier, D. and Helfrich, S. (2019). *Free, Fair, and Alive: The Insurgent Power of the Commons*. Gabriola Island: New Society Publishers.

Borzaga, C., Bodini, R., Carini, C., Depedri, S., Galera, G. and Salvatori, G. (2014). *Europe in Transition: The Role of Social Cooperatives and Social Enterprises* (Euricse Working Papers No. 69|14). http://dx.doi.org/10.2139/ssrn.2436456

Borzaga, C., Galera, G., Franchini, B., Chiomento, S., Nogales, R. and Carini, C. (2020). *Social Enterprises and Their Ecosystems in Europe: Comparative Synthesis Report*. Luxembourg: Publications Office of the European Union. Online at https://ec.europa.eu/social/main.jsp?catId=738&langId=en&pubId=8274 (accessed November 4th, 2022).

Borzaga, C., Galera, G. and Nogales, R. (2008). *Social Enterprise: A New Model for Poverty Reduction and Employment Generation: An Examination of the Concept and Practice in Europe and the Commonwealth of Independent States*. UNDP. Online at https://emes.net/publications/books/social-enterprise-a-new-model-for-poverty-reduction-and-employment-generation/ (accessed November 4th, 2022).

Borzaga, C. and Spear, R. (eds.) (2004). *Trends and Challenges for Co-Operatives and Social Enterprises in Developed and Transition Countries*. Trento: Edizioni31.

Chavez, R. and Manzón, J. L. (2019). *Recent Evolutions of the Social Economy in the European Union*. Online at https://base.socioeco.org/docs/wp2019-02en.pdf (accessed November 4th, 2022).

Ciepielewska-Kowalik, A. (2020). *Social Enterprises and Their Ecosystems in Europe: Updated Country Report: Poland*. Luxembourg: Publications Office of the European Union.

Ciepielewska-Kowalik, A. (2021). "Social enterprise in Poland: Institutional and historical context," in Jacques Defourny and Marthe Nyssens (eds.) *Social Enterprise in Central and Eastern Europe: Theory, Models and Practice*. New York: Routledge, pp. 138–152.

Defourny, J. and Nyssens, M. (eds.) (2021). *Social Enterprise in Central and Eastern Europe: Theory, Models and Practice*. New York: Routledge.

Dohnalová, M., Guri, D., Hrabětová, J., Legnerová, K. and Šlechtová, V. (2021). "Social enterprise in the Czech Republic: Heritage and new developments," in Defourny, J. and Nyssens, M. (eds.) *Social Enterprise in Central and Eastern Europe: Theory, Models and Practice*. New York: Routledge, pp. 56–71.

Esteves, A. M. (2021). "Processes of normative regulation in spaces of 'solidarity economy': A comparative case study analysis," *International Journal of Sociology and Social Policy*, 42(7/8), pp. 624–639. https://doi.org/10.1108/IJSSP-12-2020-0540

Fraňková, E. (2019). *Social Enterprises and Their Ecosystems in Europe: Updated Country Report: Czech Republic*. Luxembourg: Publications Office of the European Union.

Górz, A. and Zielińska, E. (2018). "A village in the center of town," *Magazyn Miasta, Cities Magazine*, 2, pp. 46–53. Online at www.sharedcities.eu/wp-content/uploads/2018/07/MagazynMiasta_CitiesMagazine_2-2018_WhatDoWeShareInPostCommunistCities.pdf (accessed November 4th, 2022).

Huybrechts, B. (2012). *Fair Trade Organizations and Social Enterprise: Social Innovation through Hybrid Organization Models*. London: Routledge.

Laville, J. L. and Eynaud, P. (2019). "A cross-disciplinary and international perspective about social enterprise," in Eynaud, P., Laville, J. L., Lucas dos Santos, L., Banerjee, S., Avelino, F. and Hulgard, L. (eds.) *Theory of Social Enterprise and Pluralism: Social Movements, Solidarity Economy and the Global South*. New York: Routledge, pp. 44–66.

Lewis, M. T. (2017). *Navigating System Transition in a Volatile Century*. Online at https://thenextsystem.org/sites/default/files/2017-08/MichaelLewis.pdf (accessed November 4th, 2022).

Lucas dos Santos, L. and Banerjee, S. (2019). "Social enterprise: Is it possible to decolonise this concept?," in Eynaud, P., Laville, J. L., Lucas dos Santos, L., Banerjee, S., Avelino, F. and Hulgard, L. (eds.) *Theory of Social Enterprise and Pluralism: Social Movements, Solidarity Economy and the Global South*. New York: Routledge, pp. 3–17.

Mejor, W. (2020). "Community building," in *Building Up Social Solidarity Economy*, pp. 20–29. Online at https://base.socioeco.org/docs/busse_05_en.pdf (accessed November 4th, 2022).

Milewska, M. (2019). *Towards the Urban Revolution: Open Jazdów Partnership for Jazdów Settlement, A Grassroots Initiative That Transformed the Historical Housing Estate into Socially and Culturally Active Space Co-Managed by the Residents of Warsaw*. Dissertation, Goldsmiths, University of London.

Miller, E. (2010). "Solidarity economy: Key concepts and issues," in Kawano, E., Masterson, T. and Teller-Ellsberg, J. (eds.) *Solidarity Economy I: Building Alternatives for People and Planet*. Amherst, MA: Center for Popular Economics, pp. 25–41.

Ould, A. P. (2015). "What does 'solidarity economy' mean? Contours and feasibility of a theoretical and political project," *Business Ethics: A European Review*, 24(4), pp. 425–435.

Partnerstwo Otwarty Jazdów. (2019). *Raporty 2019 Sprawozdanie Merytoryczne*. Online at https://jazdow.pl/raporty/(accessed November 4th, 2022).

RIPESS. (2015). *Global Vision for a Social Solidarity Economy: Convergences and Differences in Concepts, Definitions and Frameworks*. Online at www.ripess.org/ripess-releases-its-global-vision-of-sse/?lang=en (accessed November 4th, 2022).

Šimleša, D., Puđak, J., Majetić, F. and Bušljeta Tonković, A. (2015). *Across the Borders: Social Economy in Europe*. Zagreb: Institute of Social Sciences Ivo Pilar.

Wright, E. O. (2010). *Envisioning Real Utopias*. London: Verso.

Zielińska, E. and Wilczyńska, A. (2019). "Urban autonomies as laboratories for co-governance: Case study of Open Jazdów in Warsaw (part 1)," *Trzeci Sektor*, 45. https://doi.org/10.26368/17332265-045-1-2019-1

7 A passion for soil

Solidarity economy and regenerative agriculture[1]

Anna Umantseva[2], *Lars Hulgård and Henrik Hauggaard-Nielsen*

7.1 Introduction

The Anthropocene Epoch underlines that human activities as the root cause of environmental, social and governance (ESG) challenges and that sustaining may not be enough to offset related crises (Olsson *et al.*, 2017; Beacham, 2018). Given the agricultural sector's significant roles in environmental degradation, the need for transition to more sustainable farming systems is evident. Agriculture, Forestry, and Other Land Use (AFOLU) is responsible for about a quarter of global anthropogenic greenhouse gas emissions, mainly due to deforestation and agricultural emissions from livestock, soil and nutrient management (Smith *et al.*, 2014). This situation is characterised by technological lock-in based on an agrochemical and mechanisation paradigm supported by public policies, along with market dynamics that promote centralisation and specialisation (Magrini *et al.*, 2016). Therefore, to achieve the necessary societal transitions, the agricultural sectors must deliver climate adaptation and mitigation at much higher levels, while also promoting economic, environmental and social co-benefits. There are already initiatives mobilising people engaged in new production and consumption practices that could be strengthened if they had the organisational and financial capacity to compete with conventional enterprises.

The emerging trend of regenerative agriculture (RA) aims at improving soil and landscapes rather than merely reducing rates of degradation (Rhodes, 2017). More consumers are pushing organisations and individuals to adopt RA practices. This "regenerative turn" demonstrates transitions "from historical notions of mastery and extraction towards renewed attentiveness and human engagement" and, besides attention to soil and biodiversity, incorporates experimentation with "cooperative and economic structures beyond extractivism" (Egmose *et al.*, 2021: 4).

The growing body of research on RA from an agronomic perspective tends to focus on evaluating benefits for soil health, biodiversity and carbon sequestration (Al-Kaisi & Lal, 2020). However, following Duncan *et al.* (2020: 4), thinking of RA beyond its benefits to soil fertility, as one element of a broader concept

DOI: 10.4324/9781003306344-8

of "regenerative food systems", requires changes not only in the way how we interact with nature, but also how economic and institutional dimensions frame the possibilities and constraints for these changing human–nature relations. In this sense, RA is not only a set of agronomic techniques for soil regeneration and biodiversity enhancement. It is, arguably more importantly, a political movement that envisions changes in agri-economies.

In this chapter, we discuss how the dialogue between RA and agricultural spaces of solidarity economy can frame directions for transformation of agri-economies towards non-extractivist practices. Social and solidarity economy (SSE) in the domain of agri-food production exists in various forms, such as agricultural cooperatives, solidarity purchase groups and community-supported agriculture initiatives. Following Rossi and Brunori (2010), these alternative spaces challenge predominant food production practices by aiming to replace specialisation and competition with solidarity, embeddedness and diversity. Although often existing at the margins, agricultural SSE spaces spark processes transformative of predominant agri-food structures, because their commitment to ecologically sound production, protection of local resources and collaborative organisational forms can be seen as a political act among farmers (Blättel-Mink *et al.*, 2017; Hvitsand, 2016). Accordingly, we explore the role solidarity economy spaces play in RA trends, complementing a growing body of research more focused on individual farms and farmers (Giller *et al.*, 2021; Gosnell *et al.*, 2019). Through analysis of two case studies that contain elements of SSE and RA practice, we will trace synergies between regenerative trends in farming and the agricultural solidarity economy movement and also look at how they complement each other, creating alternative spaces of "more-than-human" economies.

7.1.1 ***Regenerative agriculture***

The concept of "regenerative" action has been entering sustainability discussions due to the growing need of not only to go beyond the idea of reducing harm, but rather to create positive change. Following Mehmood *et al.* (2020: 462), regenerative action contains "a radical and disruptive mindset shift among citizens" to address current ESG crises, which require "approaches which actively repair the environmental, social and economic damages", surpassing the idea of solely sustaining (*ibid*: 462).

RA combines farm production with nature conservation, fundamentally challenging the current food production paradigm (LaCanne & Lundgren, 2018). RA can be defined as practices aimed at promoting soil health by restoring soil organic carbon to overcome soil degradation for sustained human existence on Earth (Rhodes, 2017; Sherwood & Uphoff, 2000). That means improving soil health in ways that are also beneficial in terms of human health, food safety, biodiversity, environmental protection and resource-use efficiency (El Mujtar *et al.*, 2019). Examples of management techniques useful for improving soil health include application of organic materials like animal manure and household waste, incorporation of crop residues into the soil, curtailment of pesticide use, reducing soil tillage (conservation agriculture), changing from only annual crops to diversified rotations including perennials and shaping landscape with spatial agroforestry designs (LaCanne & Lundgren, 2018).

The blooming discussion about a regenerative turn in agriculture not only highlights its capacity to provide high-quality food and potential for economic benefits because of cost savings resulting from low-input strategies (Al-Kaisi & Lal, 2020; LaCanne & Lundgren, 2018). It also emphasises a shift towards thinking in terms of human–nature relations, where the restoration of ecosystems is a goal in itself, alongside the production of nutritious food (Rhodes, 2017).

Another example of a management strategy for improved soil health is giving up the practice of ploughing (Lal *et al.*, 2007) following the principles of Conservation Agriculture (CA): 1) reduced or zero tillage, 2) permanent plant cover and 3) a varied crop rotation. Although Europe is behind other countries in adoption of CA, about 20% of the total agricultural area is now practising reduced tillage because of knowledge sharing by pioneering farmers and the need to reduce production costs. Following an experience exchange group of CA farmers across three years showed how the farmers' professional (and private) interactions play a vital role in their rediscovery of the interrelations between agriculture and nature (Hansen *et al.*, 2020). These farmers explained their deep interests in the soil as a living organism and that nutrient application (fertilisation) is not only done in order to optimise final harvest levels but also to satisfy the needs of the soil microbiome. In the same paper, one farmer is quoted as saying that "*When the soil isn't touched, the weed seeds perish by simply lying on the ground; it is much more than you would think, so much more. Trials have shown that for years. Only nobody takes it seriously*" (Hansen *et al.*, 2020: 1024). The use of a plough to battle with weeds (nature), a common concern for farmers, is suddenly not relevant anymore.

7.1.2 Solidarity economy in the agri-food sector

Following Laville (2010), SSE has economic and political dimensions. Alternative spaces of SSE serve as containers of practices, epistemologies and pedagogies that constitute what has been called "everyday politics" (Martiskainen *et al.*, 2018). They generate active citizenship and emphasise the importance of citizen engagement in decision-making processes *(ibid)*. In the agricultural domain, cooperatives have often been an organisational form that supports many SSE values. In the case study locations in Denmark and Portugal, rural cooperatives historically had important roles in shaping agricultural production and rural livelihoods, values, rules and norms.

In Denmark, farmers' and workers' cooperatives have a long history. Following Hulgård and Bisballe (2004), the first cooperative period starts in the middle of the 19th Century with the workers' and farmers' cooperative movements as two distinct and influential actors. The farmers' cooperative movement was linked to the Danish priest and educator Nicolaj Frederik Severin Grundtvig (1783–1872). Moreover, the Danish cooperative movement was closely associated with a peasant political movement unified around the farmers' party (Venstre, The Liberal Party of Denmark), and with rural cultural movements, for instance the free church, free school and folk high school movements (Chloupkova *et al.*, 2003). However, the farmers' cooperative movement, besides serving the economic interests of farmers, also served their cultural, educational and political interests, since it was directly linked to a social movement with major influences on the making of modern Danish society: Grundtvigism and the Danish Folk High Schools Movement (*Højskolebevægelsen*). Even today, more than 130 years after his death, Grundtvig, who was also a poet, a bishop, politician, educational rebel, philosopher and member of the Danish constitutional assembly, is still an influential actor in Danish politics. Currently, co-operatives are among Denmark's largest enterprises, with a collective turnover of nearly 10% of the country's GDP (Danish Agriculture & Food Council, 2014).

The history of cooperatives in Portugal is more uneven. From the late 18th Century, cooperatives in Portugal, aiming both to protect workers' rights and improve quality of production, on the one hand, and promote the social role of civil society, on the other hand, were thriving. During the dictatorship between 1926 and 1974, the state imposed strict control over the cooperative movement, encouraging the formation of agricultural producers' cooperatives as an authoritarian tool rather than in support of collaborative spirit (Freire & Pereira, 2017). This state control of cooperatives generated mistrust towards cooperative structures among the population. Nevertheless, after the fall of the dictatorship in 1974, cooperatives regained autonomy and began to rebuild their identity (Cruz, 2013). For example housing cooperatives aimed at providing affordable housing in a democratic and non-speculative manner became an important civil society platform (*ibid.*).

More recent forms of agri-food solidarity economy spaces, such as community-supported agriculture farms and solidarity purchase groups, often involving farmers and consumers, form a part of a large alternative food movement that counters industrialised agriculture (Hvitsand, 2016). With an emphasis on active citizenship in food production, their objectives are to provide safe, locally produced food with a focus on "actively defining the agenda" of local food production (*ibid.*: 348). These spaces, which exist both in Portugal and in Denmark (Moreira, 2022; Torjusen *et al.*, 2008), often engage with practices of environmental care and animal welfare (Beacham, 2018).

7.2 Methodology

Research was conducted from June 2019 to December 2020 on two case studies: a collective farm in Zealand, Denmark, and a users' cooperative in Central

Alentejo, Portugal. The countries and regions were selected as a part of a bigger research project on social innovations in European rural areas. The two cases are comparable in view of their SSE-based organisational structures and agricultural dimension with elements of RA. At the same time, they are different in size, agricultural techniques (largely resulting from differences in climate – Mediterranean and Northern European) and their levels of consumer engagement.

Methods of data collection included semi-structured interviews and participant observation. The cases were selected based on: (1) their engagement in RA and (2) activities that fall under the umbrella concept of SSE.

We applied a research strategy of theory-building through case studies (Eisenhardt & Graebner, 2007) using situational analysis (Clarke, 2003) to explore analytically relevant "human and nonhuman, material and symbolic/discursive elements" and relations among them to capture diverse practices and experiences that intersect in the cases (*ibid.*: 561). Through ethnography, we intended to zoom into the practices of the organisations by participating in everyday work and leisure, including farming, lunch breaks and meetings, to capture and situate the unfolding interdependencies, tensions and negotiations between practices of RA and SSE spaces. Interviews with diverse actors such as farmers, volunteers and consumers allowed the analysis of a variety of narratives, experiences and perceptions of the phenomenon.

We will analyse the cases along two main themes: (1) multi-stakeholder cooperation in SSE spaces and its economic and political implications for RA practices and (2) dialogues between SSE spaces and RA, with a focus on diversity of narratives and opinions.

7.3 Case study descriptions: users' cooperative and collective farm

7.3.1 Collective farm (Denmark)

The collective farm was started in 2000 with both social and environmental aims through a collective purchase of a 30 HA farm by 500 shareholder-consumers. In its initial stages, the project attracted many supporters, who agreed to finance the land collectively and to support farmers by directly buying produce. The farmers were paid wages financed through vegetable sales. Originally, the farmers were responsible for the whole process, from production to delivery. Later, shareholders formed into working groups of volunteers responsible for areas such as packaging, delivery, accounting and communication with customers.

7.3.2 Users' cooperative (Portugal)

The farm has a long history dating back to the 1800s, including many changes in ownership and management. The most recent such change, in 2015, was to the users' cooperative format, with workers and consumers as members. The transition from private ownership is partial, as the land (500 HA) is still under the private ownership of the farmer. The cooperative is a multi-sector enterprise that undertakes different activities, including consumption, production and eco-tourism. Members are required to purchase four shares in a section of the cooperative in order to join.

7.3.3 Agricultural transitions

Both cases, on different temporal and spatial scales, have gone through several similar transitions between stages, which can be characterised as: (1) transition from intensive monocrop production to organic farming and (2) eventually integrating regenerative thinking in their agricultural practices with a focus on nature restoration. In both national contexts, the projects were initially pioneers of organic farming and are now pioneers as regenerative producers. The transitions we can observe in the history of these two farming projects thus reflect different waves of resistance against industrial large-scale farming.

The cooperative in Portugal has been through many agricultural and organisational transitions during its history. First, from around 1993, when the land was returned to family ownership after a long period of land nationalisation in Portugal, the farm started a transition from an industrial agriculture model towards the agroecosystem known as *montado*.[3] Under nationalisation, the farm was managed as an intensive monocrop farming system dominated by three products – cork, lamb and wheat. The first step following its return to family ownership was to introduce organic production in both meat and vegetable farming, with black turkey produced at the farm becoming the first nationally certified organic meat in 1998. In 2001, certified organic production was applied to the entire farm, also adding processing infrastructures such as an olive oil mill and bakery. Nowadays, besides the diverse organic production, the most ambitious project is the creation of an agroforestry system. Parts of the land are undergoing reforestation, with the aim of regenerating soil for further integration of crops and animals into the system:

> "Outside the greenhouses, we do agroforestry systems. We have trees in the same lines as where we have vegetables and, in that way, we are different from conventional agriculture. The sun is covered, and we also do not use tractors.
>
> [Team leader of vegetable production]

Similarly, the collective farm project in Denmark started with an ambition to turn a monocrop farm into a space where farmers could produce organically without the pressure of being a competitive agri-food business – through the direct support of consumers. In 2017, an agreement was made with a young farmer, who started producing vegetables using regenerative techniques, with the help of interns and volunteers. Many of the techniques used by the farmer were aimed at soil regeneration and the cultivation of organic matter. For example, the farmer used mushroom compost to fertilise the soil and, in addition, was experimenting with combining use of compost with production of green manure – growing a fertility-enhancing crop and leaving it to decompose, then planting vegetables that benefit from improved soil moisture and nutrient content. The intention was to become completely nutrient self-sufficient without ploughing and tilling the soil, and only working the top layer. Soil, furthermore, became an affective element, and the care dedicated to its regeneration was perceived as joyful: "*I got interested in soil, and vegetable and fruits, and foods in general. From there it kind of just went into soil. Soil is the passion now, you can say*" [farmer].

7.4 Analysis

7.4.1 Multi-stakeholder engagement – towards sharing responsibility, joy and risks of food production

Leviten-Reid and Fairbairn (2011) and Ajates Gonzalez (2017) observe that agri-food SSE initiatives currently tend to be multi-stakeholder in nature, including producers, consumers and other actors (e.g. restaurants) rather than one type of member, such as farmers. Ajates Gonzalez (2017: 288) concludes that multi-stakeholder cooperatives in the domain of food and farming often tend to go beyond the approach of solely benefitting the members and strive for creating a joint space between "open economy and the cooperative movements that brings about a series of more-than-economic benefits to members, wider society and the environment". The inclusion of multiple stakeholders thus creates a more relational way of running the agri-food sector, where both producers and consumers need to adapt their buying and producing habits to more socially just and environmentally beneficial habits. Agri-food multi-stakeholder SSE spaces include a diverse spectrum of organisations, with a variety of ownership models and degrees of stakeholder involvement. They can range from privately owned producer farms that integrate community-supported agriculture (CSA), where consumers commit to buying seasonal produce, to consumer-owned farms where the customers own and take a central role in governance of the farm (Howard, 2010). A rarer type of multi-stakeholder agri-food coops comprises entities where membership is extended beyond producers and consumers to include other actors, for example workers involved in distribution *(ibid.)*.

In the case of the collective farm, multi-stakeholder involvement comes from consumers taking vital roles in production processes. In the collective farm project, consumers, first, collectively purchase the land, with the objective of allowing farmers to have a debt- and speculation-free environment for organic farming. Second, consumer-volunteers actively partake in running the business: working groups of volunteers include the packaging group, delivery group and people volunteering for accounting and communication with customers. This structure creates a favourable environment for the farmers, who have the direct support of consumer-volunteers.

In the case of the users' cooperative, the community-supported agriculture model reflects its vision of multi-stakeholder engagement. The programme implies a several-month commitment from customers, including their participation in decision-making about prices and selection of produce through CSA meetings, and the concept of an "open farm" where customers can observe the production processes and understand how prices are set. A farm manager explained that the CSA vision is related to ambitions of changing relations between consumers and producers and making the consumer more embedded into the production system: "*The idea is to be independent of the market and find the right cost for the given product – people share the risk with the agriculture. So it makes no sense that the consumer is separate from the producer*".

Based on conversations with the owner and participation in the farm tours he gives to visitors, his vision can be described as largely inspired by what he calls "*communitarian agriculture*", the system where people are highly dependent on their natural environment:

> "[A] system not based on farming and pastoralism, where plants and animals are used solely for the benefit of people and are deprived of their functions in the ecosystem, but based on complex mosaic of relations with nature where trees, plants, and animals have functions other than serving humans.
>
> [Farm owner]

Thus, he intends to realise this vision through a multi-stakeholder cooperative involving participatory decision-making and create an agroforestry system for multiple users: "*an insect is a user, people who work here, people who buy products*" [farm owner].

How does multi-stakeholder engagement create synergies with RA thinking? Following Krzywoszynska (2019), it is crucial to recognise that care for soil in agri-food production is an indispensable part of sustaining life, along with producing food for people. Krzywoszynska, hence, suggests that responding to the needs of the soil biota requires extending the responsibility of care from people working with land to the broader range of actors and processes *(ibid.)*. In both case studies, multi-stakeholder engagement is a strategy for sharing the pressures and risks of food production among multiple actors. This can allow the farmer to integrate processes and considerations in farming practices, such as soil regeneration, which are difficult to integrate if the farmer needs to comply with market pressures. In RA, care for soil requires time and attentiveness, which goes against an economic logic based on extractive exploitation of nature (Gosnell *et al.*, 2019). Hence, multi-stakeholder engagement can be conducive to allowing farmers to practise non-extractivist relations with nature. The idea of multi-stakeholder engagement in food production, as exemplified by the two case studies, is to allow the farmer to transition from exhaustion of nature for profit generation to a possibility of developing caring and reciprocal human–nature relations.

7.4.2 Dialogue between regenerative farming and SSE spaces

We see strong synergies between agricultural spaces of SSE and regenerative agri-food production, reflected in thinking of economy/spaces of production beyond profit generation and market pressure that exploits both nature and people. Both case study SSE projects were started because of mutual agreement among activists/participants that monocultural, industrialised, market-driven production was damaging to farmers and not beneficial to the locality, which motivated the creation of multi-stakeholder solidarity spaces. In turn, regenerative farmers, who joined the projects later, are passionate about doing farming differently, with soil and ecosystem restoration as the main priority – a process that is also incompatible with purely profit-driven production. Therefore, spaces of SSE become a fruitful ground for regenerative farmers. SSE spaces as spaces of everyday politics resonate with practitioners of RA in search of alternative ways to farm in which care (for people or for nature) can become a part of their work.

However, the question arises, can SSE spaces be a long-term companion of RA transitions? Interviews with various actors in the case studies demonstrate that these spaces are not homogenous and tension-free but reflect a multiplicity of voices. We identified two main points: 1) the need of farmers to have a greater focus on the entrepreneurial dimensions of production and 2) the complexity of decision-making.

In the case of the collective farm, the young farmers collaborating with the project insist that changes must be implemented on the farm in order for it to play a role in sustainability transitions. They argue for the improvement of business strategies, social media, equipment and infrastructures – in other words, for a more entrepreneurial approach to running the farm, which could help to advance the development of RA:

> Even though it is not as such a business, it is still a business, and you have to run it as a business. We have sales going on, because there are expenses in having a farm. What I saw when I came was a very ineffective way of running a business. I couldn't work with that, because it would affect the way that I was growing and selling my vegetables.
>
> [Farmer]

Similarly, one of the cooperative participants, a volunteer who manages an experimental syntropic[4] plot with an intention to "*produce our food in a way that actually benefits the place*", mentioned that although the farm is a role model of regenerative ideas in Portugal, many ideas are yet to be implemented: "*They don't have the time and economy to do this well. So, this is one of the reasons why I believe that so far it hasn't really gone forward here. Which I really hope that with more time and patience we can bring it forward*". In the future, he wants to step away from the community-supported agriculture model used by the cooperative and instead focus on bulk production and sale of a single cash crop. When asked if such production might contradict the farm's principles in relation to biodiversity, the farmer, strongly inspired by ideas of regenerating ecosystems through imitating natural processes in food production, answered: "*But that's the interesting thing – how can we plant jalapeños to create a forest?*" His ambition is to produce a cash crop, combining the lines with trees and other plants, such as beans and sunflowers, to create a multi-level system for soil fertility and water retention. While recognising that the cooperative farm is an important and unique space in Portugal for re-embedding farming into social textures of rurality, he notes that for advancing his vision of production, he would need more focus on agronomic aspects, thus simplifying the community aspect of sales:

> I don't really want to do this [CSA] because of a lot of small pieces of work, I really want to have cash crops and have someone who can take them in a large quantity, like a wholesaler. I can produce, for example, jalapeños, and I sell it to a company, and they make sauce from it?
>
> [Farmer-volunteer]

The farmer from the collective farm similarly points to a certain rigidity of the project due to the complex decision-making and how it might be a challenge for the development of thriving regenerative farming practice: "*It takes a long time to make decisions here, and it is hard to say exactly why, but one of the reasons is because there are many people with opinions, strong opinions*".

Through these observations, we can see dialogues and productive tensions around the diverse potential forms of economic and social organisation of RA. In both cases, we see that young regenerative farmers often seek to modify their practices in order to accommodate RA, sometimes even pushing in a direction of less involvement of consumers and other stakeholders and more towards entrepreneurial action or bulk sales. From a profit-maximising point of view that attributes most economic decisions and strategies to rational calculations on the part of *Homo economicus* (Phillips, 2019), we could conclude that these farmers simply want to make a better living for themselves by optimising their sales. A wish to turn a socially and ecologically sustainable farming enterprise into a financially sustainable one to provide dignified livelihoods, is, of course, entirely valid. Nevertheless, their struggle to be integrated into mainstream agricultural markets suggests that the mindset of RA is in essence incompatible with that of competition-driven extractivism, because the practice of RA is grounded in relations of reciprocity, notwithstanding its formal economic organisational pattern. Hence, we can observe that regenerative farmers passionate about soil restoration and doing agriculture differently are drawn to solidarity spaces, while at the same time they envision changes to achieve economic sustainability and sustain production at a commercial level.

7.5 Discussion: solidarity economy and regenerative farming: transitions to a "more-than-human" economy?

On the one hand, we can consider SSE spaces as a manifestation of SSE principles of plurality (Laville, 2014), where market exchange is balanced with reciprocity-based economic activity in order to resist the processes of "commodification of social life" (*ibid:* 111). However, the passion for soil and nature restoration in the case study projects adds another layer to the plural economy perspective – solidarity with more-than-human nature, thus challenging the anthropocentric vision of the plural economy and suggesting that relationships of more-than-human reciprocity also have a role in shaping the practices of social and economic organisation in agricultural spaces.

Miller (2020: 407) suggests a need to rethink economy as processes by which collectivities negotiate "the multiple biosocial and geosocial dimensions of life in common amidst a mesh of planetary interdependence". This vision of "more-than-human economy" implies aiming to reconsider economy as processes not only beyond capitalist relations, but also beyond human-centric needs – where the work of nature is treated as an active agent in the plural economic space. Hence, the dialogue between SSE spaces and RA suggests that for non-extractivist practices, there is a need not only to rethink the predominance of industrialised agri-economies, but also to introduce epistemological notions of more-than-human care into SSE spaces. Hence, agri-food SSE initiatives can not only become spaces of re-embedding the social in economic spaces, but also become spaces of reconsidering epistemologies of human mastery over nature.

RA practices go beyond food production as a market-driven process, framed in relation to the pursuit of profit. In addition, we can observe that RA practices go beyond the SSE aims of social well-being and cooperation and the question of producing food for the benefit of people. It adds the question of how we can produce food with the central issue of nature's well-being in mind.

7.6 Conclusion

The chapter interconnects two related but often decoupled lines of social innovation in rural and agricultural domain: rural SSE spaces and RA.

Following Laville (2010), who points to the economic and political dimensions of SSE, these dimensions provide nurturing environments for innovative practices of RA. The economic dimension – reciprocity among multiple actors aimed at sharing risks and relieving farming of market pressures – allows farmers to integrate practices of soil and ecosystem regeneration, which would be challenging for them to do if they entered the mainstream agri-food system. Furthermore, the political dimension of SSE spaces makes them platforms of active citizenship where ideas and practices of resistance and resilience become mobilised (Esteves *et al.*, 2021). These spaces become a productive ground for diverse actors collectively to generate ideas and practices of farming systems for the well-being of people and nature. Hence, SSE structures become a cradle for innovative agricultural practices that aim at respectful, non-extractive relations with nature.

Notes

1. Research was supported by funding from the Horizon 2020 research and innovation programme under Marie Sklodowska-Curie Grant Agreement No. 721999.
2. Corresponding author.
3. An extensive multifunctional system that combines low-density and heterogeneous tree cover with livestock grazing and crop production, typical in the Mediterranean Basin (Pinto-Correia & Godinho, 2013).
4. A successional form of agroforestry, aiming to improve soil water and temperature resilience (Damant & Villela, 2018).

References

Ajates Gonzalez, R. (2017). "Going back to go forwards? From multi-stakeholder cooperatives to open cooperatives in food and farming," *Journal of Rural Studies*, 53, pp. 278–290.

Al-Kaisi, M. and Lal, R. (2020). "Aligning science and policy of regenerative agriculture," *Soil Science Society of America Journal*, 84(6), pp. 1808–1820.

Beacham, J. (2018). "Organising food differently: Towards a more-than-human ethics of care for the Anthropocene," *Organization*, 25(4), pp. 533–549.

Blättel-Mink, B., Boddenberg, M., Gunkel, L., Schmitz, S. and Vaessen, F. (2017). "Beyond the market: New practices of supply in times of crisis: The example community-supported agriculture," *International Journal of Consumer Studies*, 41(4), pp. 415–421.

Chloupkova, J., Svendsen, G. and Svendsen, G. T. (2003). "Building and destroying social capital: The case of cooperative movements in Denmark and Poland," *Agriculture and Human Values*, 20(3), pp. 241–252.

Clarke, A. E. (2003). "Situational analyses : Grounded theory mapping after the postmodern turn," *Symbolic Interaction*, 26(4), pp. 553–576.

Cruz[RefCheck12] , M. (2013). "Housing cooperatives in Portugal: Shifts in the understanding of quality for the housing sector," *Proceedings of the ENHR 2013 Conference 'Overcoming the Crisis: Integrating the Urban Environment'*, Tarragon, Spain pp. 1–16.

Damant[RefCheck13] . G. and Villela, F. (2018). "Can agroforestry improve soil water and temperature dynamics in agriculture? A case study with syntropic farming in Bahia, Brazil," *4th European Agroforestry Conference: Agroforestry as Sustainable Land Use*, University of Santiago de Compostela, Lugo, Spain pp. 161–164.

Danish Agriculture and Food Council. (2014). *Facts and Figures about Danish Agriculture and Food 2014*. Copenhagen: Danish Agriculture and Food Council.

Duncan, J., Carolan, M. and Wiskerke, J. (2020). "Regenerating food systems: A social-ecological approach," in Duncan, J., Carolan, M. and Wiskerke, J. (eds.) *Routledge Handbook of Sustainable and Regenerative Food Systems*. London: Routledge, pp. 1–11.

Egmose, J., Gaarsmand Jacobsen, S., Hauggaard-Nielsen, H. and Hulgård, L. (2021). "The regenerative turn: On the re-emergence of reciprocity embedded in living ecologies," *Globalizations*, pp. 2–6.

Eisenhardt, K. and Graebner, M. (2007). "Theory building from cases : Opportunities and challenges," *The Academy of Management Journal*, 50(1), pp. 25–32.

El Mujtar, V., Muñoz, N., McCormick, B. P., Pulleman, M. and Tittonell, P. (2019). "Role and management of soil biodiversity for food security and nutrition; where do we stand?," *Global Food Security*, 20, pp. 132–144.

Esteves, A. M., Genus, A., Henfrey, T., Penha-Lopes, G. and East, M. (2021). "Sustainable entrepreneurship and the sustainable development goals: Community-led initiatives, the social solidarity economy and commons ecologies," *Business Strategy and the Environment*, 30(3), pp. 1423–1435.

Freire, D. and Pereira, J. D. (2017). "Consumer co-operatives in Portugal: Debates and experiences from the nineteenth to the twentieth century," in Hilson, M., Neunsinger, S. and Patmore, G. (eds.) *A Global History of Consumer Co-Operation since 1850*. Leiden: Brill, pp. 296–325.

Giller, K., Hijbeek, R., Andersson, J. and Sumberg, J. (2021). "Regenerative agriculture: An agronomic perspective," *Outlook on Agriculture*, 50(1), pp. 13–25.

Gosnell, H., Gill, N. and Voyer, M. (2019). "Transformational adaptation on the farm: Processes of change and persistence in transitions to 'climate-smart' regenerative agriculture," *Global Environmental Change*, 59, pp. 1–13.

Hansen, E., Egmose, J., Lund, S. and Hauggaard-Nielsen, H. (2020). "The role of experience exchange groups in farmers' practice transitions: The case of reduced tillage in Danish conventional farming," *Agroecology and Sustainable Food Systems*, 44(8), pp. 1012–1032.

Howard, J. (2010). "Solidarity food cooperatives?," *Affinities: A Journal of Radical Theory, Culture, and Action*, 4(1), pp. 151–154.

Hulgård, L. and Bisballe, T. (2004). *Work Integration Social Enterprises in Denmark* (EMES Working Paper No. 04/08).

Hvitsand, C. (2016). "Community supported agriculture (CSA) as a transformational act: Distinct values and multiple motivations among farmers and consumers," *Agroecology and Sustainable Food Systems*, 40(4), pp. 333–351.

Krzywoszynska, A. (2019). "Caring for soil life in the Anthropocene: The role of attentiveness in more-than-human ethics," *Transactions of the Institute of British Geographers*, 44, pp. 661–675.

LaCanne, C. and Lundgren, J. (2018). "Regenerative agriculture: Merging farming and natural resource conservation profitably," *PeerJ*, pp. 1–13.

Lal, R., Reicosky, D. and Hanson, J. (2007). "Evolution of the plow over 10,000 years and the rationale for no-till farming," *Soil and Tillage Research*, 93(1), pp. 1–12.

Laville, J. (2010). "Solidarity economy," in Anheier, H. and Toepler, S.(eds.) *International Encyclopedia of Civil Society*. New York, NY: Springer, pp. 1464–1470.

Laville, J. (2014). "The social and solidarity economy: A theoretical and plural framework," in Defourny, J., Hulgård, L. and Pestoff, V. (eds.) *Social Enterprise and the Third Sector:*

Changing European Landscapes in a Comparative Perspective. Abingdon: Routledge, pp. 118–129.

Leviten-Reid, C. and Fairbairn, B. (2011). "Multi-stakeholder governance in cooperative organizations: Toward a new framework for research?," *Canadian Journal of Non-profit and Social Economy Research*, 2(2), pp. 25–36.

Magrini, M., Anton, M., Cholez, C., Corre-Hellou, G., Duc, G., Jeuffroy, M. J., Pelzer, E., Voisin, A. and Walrand, S. (2016). "Why are grain-legumes rarely present in cropping systems despite their environmental and nutritional benefits? Analyzing lock-in in the French agrifood system," *Ecological Economics*, 126, pp. 152–162.

Martiskainen, M., Heiskanen, E. and Speciale, G. (2018). "Community energy initiatives to alleviate fuel poverty : The material politics of energy cafés," *Local Environment*, 23(1), pp. 20–35.

Mehmood, A., Marsden, T., Taherzadeh, A., Axinte, L. and Rebelo, C. (2020). "Transformative roles of people and places: Learning, experiencing, and regenerative action through social innovation," *Sustainability Science*, 15(2), pp. 455–466.

Miller, E. (2020). "More-than-human agency : From the human economy to ecological livelihood," in Gibson-Graham, J. K. and Dombroski, K. (eds.) *The Handbook of Diverse Economies*, Cheltenham: Edward Elgar, pp. 402–410.

Moreira, S. (2022). "Communication for food commons: A comparative analysis of community supported agriculture in Portugal," *Comunicación y Sociedad*, pp. 1–31.

Olsson, P., Moore, M., Westley, F. and McCarthy, D. (2017). "The concept of the Anthropocene as a game-changer: A new context for social innovation and transformations to sustainability," *Ecology and Society*, 22(2).

Phillips, M. (2019). "'Daring to care': Challenging corporate environmentalism," *Journal of Business Ethics*, 156(4), pp. 1151–1164.

Pinto-Correia, T. and Godinho, S. (2013). "Changing agriculture: Changing landscapes: What is going on in the high valued montado," in Dionisio Ortiz, M., Arnalte Alegre, E. V. and Moragues Faus, A. M. (eds.) *Agriculture in Mediterranean Europe: Between Old and New Paradigms*. Bingley: Emerald Group Publishing Limited, pp. 75–90.

Rhodes, C. (2017). "The imperative for regenerative agriculture," *Science Progress*, 100(1), pp. 80–129.

Rossi, A. and Brunori, G. (2010). "Drivers of transformation in the agro-food system: GAS as co-production of alternative food networks," *Proceedings of 9th European IFSA Symposium*, Vienna, pp. 1913–1931.

Sherwood, S. and Uphoff, N. (2000). "Soil health: Research, practice and policy for a more regenerative agriculture," *Applied Soil Ecology*, 15(1), pp. 85–97.

Smith, P., Bustamante, M., Ahammad, H., Clark, H., Dong, H., Elsiddig, E. A., Haberl, H., Harper, R., House, J., Jafari, M., Masera, O., Mbow, C., Ravindranath, N. H., Rice, C. W., Robledo Abad, C., Romanovskaya, A., Sperling, F. and Tubiello, F. (2014). "Agriculture, forestry and other land use (AFOLU)," in Edenhofer, O., Pichs-Madruga, R., Sokona, Y., et al. (eds.) *Climate Change 2014: Mitigation of Climate Change*. Cambridge and New York: Cambridge University Press, pp. 811–892.

Torjusen, H., Lieblein, G. and Vittersø, G. (2008). "Learning, communicating and eating in local food-systems: The case of organic box schemes in Denmark and Norway," *Local Environment*, 13(3), pp. 219–234.

8 Exploring the interface of societal inequities and grassroots solidarities as drivers and spaces of social innovation in India

Swati Banerjee, Abdul Shaban and Dinesh Chand

8.1 Introduction

Banerjee (2018) explores the context of multidimensional poverty and inequity in South Asia with a specific focus on India and argues that it is both a social need and a driver for the emergence of grassroots collectives and solidarities of marginalised groups and communities. Further, Banerjee and Shaban (2019) outline how processes of social change are inherently complex and interlinked with micro socio-spatial contexts and the diverse and plural realities of everyday subjectivities of people within such contexts. Such diversity and dynamism within lifeworlds are further mediated by multiple intersectionalities of caste, class, race, gender, among others, which anchor the daily experiences of actors and their participation in social innovation pathways. Naveed (2021) reiterates how such complex contexts and constellations of mutually reinforcing social structures lead to differential access and participation. This is also true for participation in grassroots solidarities and social innovations, which are located within such intersectional contexts and structures, leading to struggles, conflicts, tensions, competition, cooperation and co-creation. This chapter unpacks such nuanced interfaces among intersectional societal inequities and grassroots solidarities of marginalised actors to explore the drivers, spaces and pathways of social innovation.

This chapter explores the process of social innovation by focusing on the case of a community-based collective of marginalised farmers in India. This is explored through two key perspectives: (1) the micro socio-spatial context of inequity and social needs that drives social innovation and (2) processes of collectivisation of marginalised actors for social innovation and social change. Through a reconsidered understanding of social context and grassroots solidarities, the chapter aims to reframe the narrative of social innovation and unfold the potential, contradictions, challenges and ways forward.

This argument proceeds as follows. Section 8.2 discusses the overall context of inequity in India and grassroots solidarities as drivers and spaces for social change. Section 8.3 describes a case study on grassroots solidarity and

DOI: 10.4324/9781003306344-9

collectivisation of marginal farmers in India. Section 8.4 discusses the findings, arguing that social innovation is necessary not just for economic development but also to overcome entrenched inequalities that currently limit the scope and potential scale of involvement in social enterprise on the part of people from marginal groups. Finally, the chapter concludes with a proposal for a future research agenda for social innovation.

8.2 The context of inequity and grassroots solidarities as drivers for social innovation

Among the world's 50 Least Developed Countries (LDCs), 9 are in Asia (UNCTAD, 2022). Of the eight South Asian countries, five have been categorised as LDCs (Raghuram, 2008: 35). This makes South Asia an important region to understand the broad context of inequity and marginalisation and also the processes of social innovation that emerge to address this context. Kabadurmus (2021) explains that there are many challenges that South Asian countries face, including lack of human capital (Khilji, 2012) and financial capital (Shaban, 2022; World Bank, 2017), stringent labour regulations (Acharya *et al.*, 2013), political instability (Tushnet & Khosla, 2015), inadequate infrastructure (Andrés *et al.*, 2014; Jha & Arao, 2018; Rasul, 2016), corruption (Borooah, 2016; Daoud, 2015), inequality (Huynh & Nguyen, 2019; Kumar Mishra *et al.*, 2019) and conflicts within and between some countries (Goldstone, 2001; Khan, 2019).

South Asia is home to a large measure of multidimensional poverty and a low share of global income. It provides shelter to 20% of the global population, with a combined 1.3% of global income (Hall, 2019; Yadav & Iqbal, 2021). The individuals who are deprived in more than one area, such as education, health, living standards or employment, are considered as multidimensionally poor (Deyshappriya, 2018; Yadav & Iqbal, 2021). Thus, this context of multidimensional poverty and inequity prevents them from accessing assets and having free agency.

India, a country in South Asia, is diverse and reflects multidimensional poverty and inequity. In 2011, literacy rates were only about 66% among Scheduled Castes[1] (SCs) and 59% among Scheduled Tribes[2] (STs) (Census of India, 2011a), while multidimensional poverty was as high as 50% among STs and 33% among SCs (Tiwari & Mishra, 2019). In common with other South Asian countries, there are large numbers of actors living in multidimensional social inequalities resulting from caste, gender, religion and economic class (Banerjee *et al.*, 2021b). In this situation, societal inequities emerge due to unequal distribution of resources, structural inequity, gender-based norms and their practices, religious extremism and class-based vested interests in liberal economic policies and markets. In the web of social relationships based on inequity, unequal relationships become manifest, leading to disparities and challenges. Intersectional inequities – of caste, gender, ethnicity, etc. – further multiply the challenges, necessitating pathways that are inclusive.

Having discussed the context of inequity, it is significant to explore the possibility and processes of social innovation. Banerjee *et al.* (2021a) underline that social innovation occurs in complex networks and spaces. South Asia as a region is increasingly gaining importance in the international geopolitical sphere (Banerjee *et al.*, 2021b). Within its diversity, multidimensional forms of poverty emerge as a common characteristic and key concern in the region (Banerjee, 2018). Many researchers have argued that innovation can occur in emerging contexts despite the challenges (Kabadurmus, 2021; Agarwal *et al.*, 2018; Khan, 2016; Radjou *et al.*, 2012), which include lack of resources, inadequate infrastructure, inequity and poor quality of institutions (Kabadurmus, 2021).

Banerjee (2018) suggests that innovations in South Asia and specifically India can be broadly categorised into four major types: 1) grassroots innovation/community-led innovation, 2) design innovation, 3) societal innovation and 4) structural innovation. Structural innovation particularly focuses on changing the overall innovation environment in order to address larger structural inequities and exclusion, for example gender, caste and race divisions. Simultaneously, social innovation has become important for overcoming barriers to lasting and sustainable economic growth. Social innovations can help challenge structural and non-structural inequities, promoting a more favourable environment marked by higher levels of social solidarity, which in turn can pave the way for raising and sustaining the rate of economic growth. Social innovation also partly addresses rising demands for alternative models of economic growth that enhance rather than damage human relationships and well-being (Urama & Acheampong, 2013).

8.3 Grassroots solidarities and processes of social innovation and social change

In South Asia and India, marginalities mediate the everyday lifeworld of the community, and of actors within these communities, due to various structural inequities. Banerjee and Shaban (2019) further mention that grassroots innovation primarily focuses on processes of intervention in addressing social, economic and political problems at the local level through people's participation and community-led solutions. Smith *et al.* (2016) further conceptualise grassroots innovation as a community-driven social innovation that aims to develop local and sustainable solutions by collectivising and mobilising networks of community groups and organisations. Solidarity is best conceived as a set of established norms that together enhance the ability of groups to produce collective good (Lindenber, 2014). Saari and Pessi (2014) provide a model of solidarity where value, resources and institutions are significant components of the process of solidarity. Grassroots solidarity and community-based collaboration, therefore, open up spaces for pooling resources and collectivising to address socio-economic inequities.

One of the success stories in poverty reduction over the past 30 years in India has been the collectivisation of women at the grassroots level and the development of micro-finance institutions (MFIs) that provide small (a few hundred rupees) uncollateralised loans ('micro-credit') to poor entrepreneurs to start up micro-enterprises. The loan repayment rate among MFIs is exceptionally high (usually greater than 90%), especially when loans are made to women rather than men.

The Self-Employed Women's Association (SEWA) in India was founded in 1971 and registered in 1972 as a trade union movement for women in the informal sector, which was an unrecognised and neglected part of the economy. In India, the informal sector employs approximately 90% of the total workforce. Approximately 663,632 members are from the agriculture sector (SEWA, 2020). SEWA aims to address financial and social inequity in society by collectivising women to confront structural and intersectional challenges.

8.3.1 Addressing agricultural distress and promoting livelihood security through collectivisation of small and marginal farmers in Osmanabad district, India, under a government programme: 'Baliraja Chetana Abhiyan'

'*Baliraja Chetana Abhiyan,*' a programme to collectivise small and marginal farmers, was initiated in Osmanabad district, Maharashtra, India, in response to rising farmer suicides in the region. A study was conducted by Tata Institute of Social Sciences, Tuljapur Campus, through immersive community engagement and action research to understand innovative processes, including the context of inequity as social problem and driver, processes of collectivisation and solidarity, and the social value emerging from these processes. The case study given next is based on the report of this study (Shaban & Das, 2018) and the authors' experiences of working in this region.

The context of inequity in Osmanabad district, Maharashtra, India

Osmanabad district in Maharashtra, India, suffers from a high level of socio-economic underdevelopment. The population in the district is largely dependent on agriculture and related activities. According to the 2011 national census (Census of India, 2011b), 38.4% of workers are engaged in cultivation, while 38.7% are agricultural labourers. This indicates very high economic and livelihood vulnerability in the district for a large proportion of the population. The district is largely dependent on rainfall for agriculture. Furthermore, declining ground and surface water resources and increasing variability in rainfall are further increasing livelihood insecurity in the district. Frequent failure of rains has created enormous indebtedness and distress among farmers, even driving some farmers to suicide. In addition, landholdings are very small, as indicated by the fact that only about 2.7% of farmers in the district come under the large farmer category. The respective proportions of marginal, small and medium-sized farmers are 29.47%, 40.76% and 20.81%. The extent and depth of poverty in the district are also high, forcing people to emigrate in search of livelihoods. Available data show that in 2004–05, the rate of poverty in the district was 58.8%, up from 50.8% in 1993–94 (Government of Maharashtra, 2014).

Farmers' distress in Osmanabad district and 'Baliraja Chetana Abhiyan' as a community-based innovative initiative

From 2011 to 2017, the total number of farmer suicides in the district was 597. There were about 332,000 farmers in the district. An analysis of 316,381 farmers showed that about 70% of them were in the marginal, small and medium categories, that is with less than four hectares of land. Furthermore, 82% of farmers only have unirrigated land, while a further 9% have less than 1 hectare of irrigated land. This shows the high dependency of agriculture in the district upon rainfall. Due to frequent crop failures, there is enormous distress among farmers, and about 68% of farmers have resorted to loans from various sources. To counter farmers' distress, avoid suicides and promote meaningful development in the district, '*Baliraja Chetana Abhiyan*' was introduced in 2015 and implemented in 2016. This programme was primarily implemented by mobilising and collectivising small and marginal farmers for livelihood promotion through various micro-enterprises. It involved multiple activities, including facilitating farmers to deal with drought by focusing on alternative livelihoods, accessing loans, cutting out intermediate traders of agricultural products and providing farmers with direct access to markets.

Processes of collectivisation of marginal farmers for livelihood promotion activities

Various collectives of marginal farmers were formed in the villages of Osmanabad District under the *Baliraja Chetana Abhiyan* programme. *Sitarambaba Shetkari Gat* was a collective formed of 15 farmers, 10 of them with less than 2 hectares of land each. The primary occupation of all members was agriculture. The group also included members from marginalised and excluded caste groups. This group came together to start a goat-rearing microenterprise. Another collective, *Om Raje Shetkari Gat*, was a group of 13 marginal farmers, including 4 farmers with less than 2 hectares of land each and 4 woman farmers. The group established a dairy microenterprise: members started working together in the dairy and divided the income among themselves. Another collective, *Shri Tulja Bhawani Shetkari Gat*, was a group of 17 marginal and distressed farmers, all with less than 2 hectares of land. The group not only started a dairy microenterprise, but also lent money to other farmers' collectives who required it for emergencies like hospitalisation expenses. The group is getting positive outcomes from the venture: the economic conditions of members have improved.

The collective *Krishi Samrat Organic Farming Shetkari Gat*, consisting of 21 marginal farmers with less than 2 hectares of land, many from socially excluded and marginalised caste groups, came together to start sericulture (cultivation of silkworms), which was supported by the district agriculture department. *Bhairunath Shetkari Gat*, a group of 20 marginal farmers, 16 of them with less than 2 hectares of land and belonging to marginalised groups, started organic farming, supported by the Agricultural Department. The *Shetkari Gat* collective, a group of 11 members, all having less than 2 hectares of land and belonging to marginalised groups, started a dairy microenterprise. The group also provides monetary loans to both members and non-members, at a 1% monthly interest rate. Common reasons for borrowing include illness, marriage and agricultural and livestock costs.

The *Krushi Mitra Shetkari Gat* collective is a group of 16 marginal farmers, each with less than 2 hectares of land. This group is unique in terms of caste combination, including members from seven different castes: one member each from *Dhangar* (NT[3]/DNT[4]), *Mali* (OBC[5]), *Wani*[6] (general category) and *Sutar* (OBC), three from *Vanjari* (NT/DNT), three from *Mahar* (SC[7]) and the remaining six members from *Maratha* (general category). All members have agriculture as their primary occupation, including dairy, which they further expand collectively.

Krushi Sakhi Mandal is an all-woman farmers' collective of 11 marginal woman farmers. Two members are landless, while the others each have less than 2 hectares of land. The group started a goat-rearing microenterprise and also lends money at a 2% monthly interest rate to needy villagers in their vicinity. Some women in the group also work as cooks under the mid-day meal scheme for children in a local primary school. Another collective, *Bhawani Shankar Agro Producer Company* of Barul Village, was established in April 2015 and registered under the Companies Act of 2013 with the Ministry of Corporate Affairs (registration implies that the registered entity follows the accounting system laid down by the Act and adheres strictly to relevant by-laws). This farmer producer company is led by 10 youths of the village. The company has seven male and three female members, each with less than 2 hectares of land. Not only have the board members experienced improvements in their economic situations, but many other villagers have also been employed in their enterprise.

The initiatives of the communities aforementioned show significant possibilities for collectivisation among marginal populations, which can unfold possibilities to exploit the potential of the market and 'collective' for social and economic development. Collectivisation helps to generate social value through an inclusive approach, which can be further strengthened, as we discuss in the following section.

8.4 Discussion

The micro-contexts and dynamics of solidarities and collectivisation of people at the grassroots are located within the inherent heterogeneity of groups and communities and the power hierarchies of caste, class, ethnicity, race, gender and intersectionalities that operate within them. Crenshaw (1991) argues that a unidimensional understanding of identities doesn't adequately account for the disadvantages and oppression faced by marginalised groups and communities. Intersectionality, therefore, becomes an important analytical perspective that plays out in the everyday struggles and lives of people, which the discourse on social innovation needs to understand more deeply. This is also revealed in the case of farmers' collectivisation under *Baliraja Chetana Abhiyan*, an innovative farmer-centred programme focusing on promoting solidarity among marginal farmers so that they can collectively overcome economic distress.

It has been revealed that the marginalised communities have very limited space to begin and negotiate for funding for social enterprises, leading to farmers' distress on the one hand and, on the other hand, also acting as a driver of social innovation. Figure 8.1, based on data from 75 enterprises started in Osmanabad during 2015–18 under Baliraja Chetna Abhiyan, shows that: (1) a large number of social enterprises have little or no involvement of SC, ST and DNT, which together constitute 20% of the total population of the district (Census of India, 2011b); (2) only a few social enterprises have a higher share of members from these marginalised sectors of the population and (3) the current total value of enterprises with higher proportions of members from such groups is also moderate: between INR 0.3 and 0.6 million.

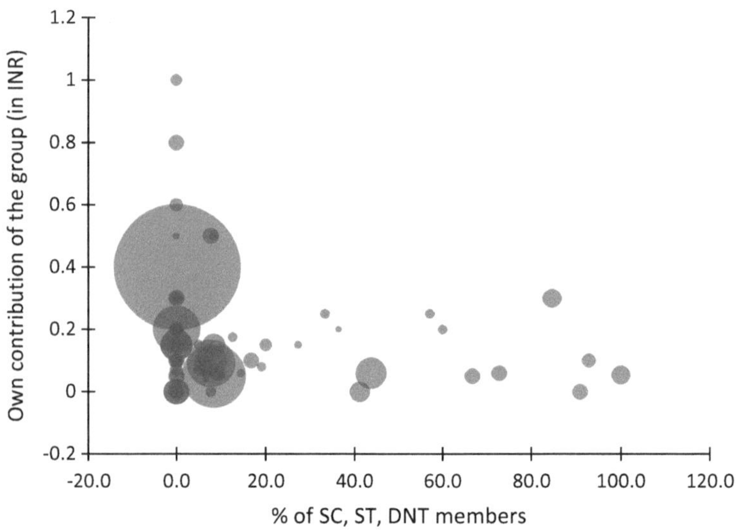

Figure 8.1 The relationship between the share of marginalised section members, own contribution in investment and total worth of social enterprises in Osmanabad district under Baliraja Chetna Abhiyan.

Source: Based on data from Shaban and Das (2018)

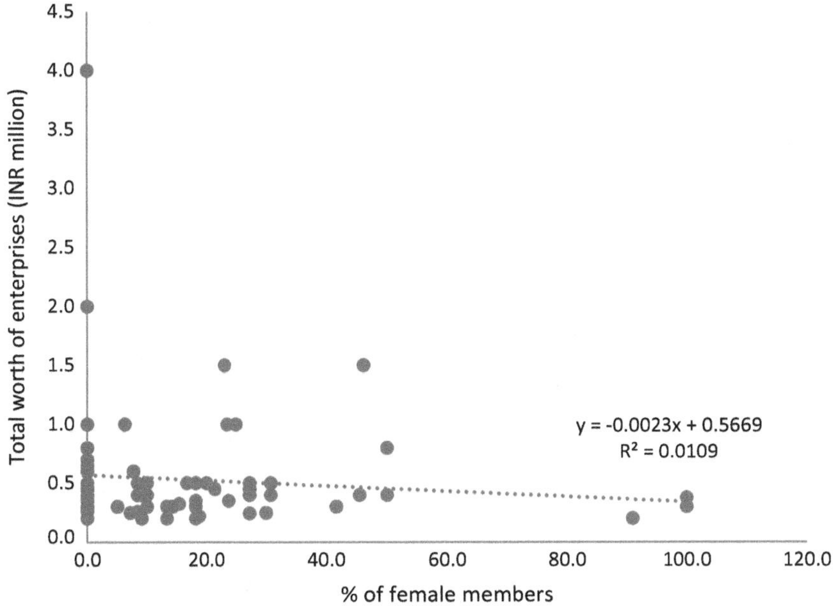

Figure 8.2 Relationship between the proportion of woman members in enterprises and total value of the social enterprises under Baliraja Chetana Abhiyan, Osmanabad district, India

Source: Based on data from Shaban and Das (2018)

The societal context of inequity not only reflects factors such as caste and ethnicity, which are strong determinants of socio-economic status, the intersection with gender is also very sharp. Figure 8.2 shows that the proportion of women in social enterprises is also quite low. The average total value of enterprises declines as the proportion of women among the members increases; most woman-owned social enterprises are tiny.

Taken together, Figures 8.1 and 8.2 show that not only do marginalised groups in India still have limited possibilities to start and own a social enterprise, but that, in addition, the small numbers of such enterprises that they own are very tiny in terms of their economic value. Social innovation thus has a huge role to play, not only in economic development but also in addressing unequal power structures in order to bring about transformative social change.

8.5 Conclusion

This chapter is an attempt to highlight the contextual realities affecting processes of collectivisation and innovation, and how social inequities mediate and drive social innovation. Cornwall (1998) reiterates the importance of intersectionality, asserting that the complexity of difference among different groups, among different groups of women and men, and other intersectionalities, needs to be grasped within the specific contexts and cultural settings. Such understanding is often lacking within mainstream discourses on social innovation. Different actors are affected differently by development interventions, including innovation and enterprise development. Simultaneously, such embeddedness also determines their participation in innovation processes and the formation of new actor networks for everyday negotiations and mobilisation within these contexts. Howaldt and Hochgerner (2019: 19) thus state,

> [W]hat distinguishes social innovations from other manifestations of social change is that they are driven by certain actors in an intentionally targeted manner with the goal of better satisfying or answering needs and problems than is possible on the basis of established practices.

The case study analysis of Baliraja Chetana Abhiyan presented here thus emphasises the importance of understanding challenges and centring processes of grassroots collectivisation for addressing inequities experienced by marginalised groups and communities, especially within South Asia and specifically the Indian context.

The Baliraja Chetana Abhiyan case also highlights the potential and relevance of grassroots and community-led collectives and their approaches to innovation for transformative social change. Banerjee and Shaban (2022) articulate how enterprises, especially grassroots enterprises, are not only drivers of innovation by collectives of local people within a micro socio-spatial context, but also help in understanding people's intersectional lived experiences and therefore have potential for epistemic inclusion of marginalised groups and communities. Furthermore, Banerjee and Shaban (2019) highlight the potential of marginalised people's collectives in challenging the dominant idea of 'individual entrepreneurs,' especially within a context of poverty and deprivation where both the financial and risk-taking capacities of an individual are lower. They further add that such collective processes simultaneously allow for the pooling of risks and expansion of collective agency for coping with and adapting to neoliberal markets and inequitable societal contexts.

The key research questions that emerge from this chapter help reframe the narrative of social innovation for framing a future research agenda and include: (1) How does a local context of inequity become a driver of social innovation? (2) What are the processes of grassroots collective solidarities emerging from such contexts? Exploration of these questions will provide alternative narratives and perspectives to understand the interrelationships between grassroots solidarities and spaces for social innovation and social change.

In conclusion, we emphasise the relevance of collectives and solidarities in reimagining alternatives to renew action and to undertake social innovation for social change. The focus is therefore on change that creates possibilities, enables agency of marginalised people and leads to transformative social change that attempts to address structural inequities.

Notes

1. SCs are the most disadvantaged socio-economic caste groups in India, often known as Dalits. They are listed in Article 341 of the Indian Constitution.
2. STs are tribal communities of India. They are listed in Article 342 of the Indian Constitution. They are also one of the most disadvantaged groups in India.
3. People who regularly moved from place to place for practising traditional livelihoods are referred to as nomadic communities (NT). In India, there are three main types of nomadic communities – hunter/gatherers, pastoralists and traditional entertaining communities.
4. The term 'De-Notified Tribes' (DNT) stands for all those communities which were once notified under the Criminal Tribes Acts, enforced by the British regime between 1871 and 1947.
5. 'Other Backward Classes.'
6. The Wani community falls in the general category among the four – SC, ST, OBC and General.
7. Mahars are the lower caste group from Maharashtra.

References

Acharya, V. V., Baghai, R. P. and Subramanian, K. V. (2013). "Labor laws and innovation," *The Journal of Law and Economics*, 56(4), pp. 997–1037.

Agarwal, N., Brem, A. and Grottke, M. (2018). "Towards a higher socio-economic impact through shared understanding of product requirements in emerging markets: The case of the Indian healthcare innovations," *Technological Forecasting and Social Change*, 135, pp. 91–98.

Andrés, L., Biller, D. and Dappe, M. H. (2014). "Infrastructure gap in South Asia: Infrastructure needs, prioritization, and financing," *The World Bank*. Online at https://documents1.worldbank.org/curated/en/504061468307152462/pdf/WPS7032.pdf

Banerjee, S. (2018). "Social innovation in South Asia," in Howaldt, J., Kaletka, C., Schroder, A. and Zirngiebl, M. (eds.) *Atlas of Social Innovation: New Practices for a Better Future*. Dortmund: Sozialforschungsstelle, TU Dortmund University, pp. 157–160.

Banerjee, S., Carney, S. and Hulgård, L. (eds.) (2021a). *People Centered Social Innovation: Global Perspectives on an Emerging Paradigm*. New York: Routledge.

Banerjee, S., Lucas dos Santos, L. L. and Hulgård, L. (2021b). "Intersectional knowledge as rural social innovation," *Journal of Rural Studies*. https://doi.org/10.1016/j.jrurstud.2021.04.007. 99 (2023) pp. 252–261.

Banerjee, S. and Shaban, A. (2019). "Reimagining the social enterprise through grassroots social innovations in India," in Eynaud, P., Laville, J. L., Lucas de Santos, L., Banerjee, S., Hulgard, L. and Avelino, F. (eds.) *Theory of Social Enterprise and Pluralism*. New York: Routledge, pp. 116–129.

Banerjee, S. and Shaban, A. (2022). "Unpacking epistemic diversities in grassroots social innovation and enterprises in India: A critical agenda for re-centering people," in

Howaldt, J., Kaletka, C. and Schroder, A. (eds.) *A Research Agenda for Social Innovation*. Cheltenham: Edward Elgar, pp. 133–148.

Borooah, V. K. (2016). "Deconstructing corruption: A study of cash for favours in rural India," *Journal of South Asian Development*, 11(1), pp. 1–37.

Census of India (2011a). *Census Tables*. Online at https://censusindia.gov.in/census.website/data/census-tables (accessed February 15th 2023).

Census of India (2011b). *Osmanabad District Population, Caste, Religion Data (Maharashtra)*. Online at www.censusindia.co.in/district/osmanabad-district-maharashtra-525 (accessed February 15th 2023).

Cornwall, J. R. (1998). "The entrepreneur as a building block for community," *Journal of Developmental Entrepreneurship*, 3, pp. 141–148.

Crenshaw, K. (1991). "Mapping the margins: Intersectionality, identity politics, and violence against women of color," *Stanford Law Review*, *43*(6), pp. 1241–1299. https://doi.org/10.2307/1229039

Daoud, A. (2015). "Quality of governance, corruption and absolute child poverty in India," *Journal of South Asian Development*, 10(2), pp. 148–167.

Deyshappriya, N. R. R. (2018). *Examining Poverty Trends in South Asian Countries: Where Is Sri Lanka among Its South Asian Counterparts?* London: School of Economics and Political Science.

Goldstone, J. A. (2001). "Demography, environment, and security," in Diehl, P. (ed.) *Environmental Conflict: An Anthology*. London: Routledge, pp. 84–108.

Government of Maharashtra (2014). *Maharashtra Human Development Report 2012*. New Delhi: Sage Publications.

Hall, J. (2019). *New Data Challenges Traditional Notions of 'Rich' and 'Poor'*. Online at https://policycommons.net/artifacts/2102070/new-data-challenges-traditional-notions-of-rich-and-poor/2857368/ (accessed March 29th 2023).

Howaldt, J. and Hochgerner, J. (2019). "Desperately seeking: A shared understanding of social innovation," in Howaldt, J., Kaletka, C., Schroder, A. and Zirngiebl, M. (eds.) *Atlas of Social Innovation: New Practices for a Better Future*. Dortmund: Sozialforschungsstelle, TU Dortmund University, pp. 18–21.

Huynh, C. M. and Nguyen, T. L. (2019). "Shadow economy and income inequality: New empirical evidence from Asian developing countries," *Journal of the Asia Pacific Economy*, pp. 1–18.

Jha, S. and Arao, R. M. (2018). *Infrastructure Financing in South Asia* (South Asia Working Paper Series No. 59). Manila: Asian Development Bank. http://dx.doi.org/10.22617/WPS189514-2

Kabadurmus, F. N. K. (2021). "Innovation challenges in South Asia: Evidence from Bangladesh, Pakistan and India," *Journal of South Asian Development*, 16(1), pp. 100–129. https://doi.org/10.1177/097317412199173.

Khan, R. (2016). "How frugal innovation promotes social sustainability," *Sustainability*, 8(10), p. 1034.

Khan, Z. (2019). "Balancing and stabilizing South Asia: Challenges and opportunities for sustainable peace and stability," *International Journal of Conflict Management*, 30(5), pp. 589–614.

Khilji, S. (2012). "Editor's perspective: Does South Asia matter? Rethinking South Asia as relevant in international business research," *South Asian Journal of Global Business Research*, 1(1), pp. 8–21.

Kumar Mishra, A., Satapathy, S., Patra, B. and Patro, R. P. (2019). "Distributional change, income mobility and pro-poor growth: Evidence from India," *Journal of the Asia Pacific Economy*, 24(2), pp. 252–269.
Lindenber, S. (2014). "Solidarity: Unpacking the social brain," in Laitinen, A. and Pessi, A. B. (eds.) *Solidarity: Theory and Practice*. Lanham: Lexington Books, pp. 30–54.
Naveed, A. (2021). "Overriding social inequality? Educational aspirations versus the material realities of rural families in Pakistan," in Rose, P., Arnot, M., Jeffery, R. and Singal, N. (eds.) *Reforming Education and Challenging Inequalities in Southern Contexts: Research and Policy in International Development*. London: Routledge, pp. 123–143.
Radjou, N., Prabhu, J. and Ahuja, S. (2012). *Jugaad Innovation: Think Frugal, Be Flexible, and Generate Breakthrough Growth*. Chichester: John Wiley & Sons.
Raghuram, S. (2008). *South Asia-Social Development: Country Perspectives and Regional Concerns* (ISAS Working Paper 36). Singapore: National University of Singapore.
Rasul, G. (2016). "Managing the food, water, and energy nexus for achieving the Sustainable Development Goals in South Asia," *Environmental Development*, 18, pp. 14–25.
Saari, J. and Pessi, A. B. (2014). "National social models and helping others in the European Union," in Laitinen, A. and Pessi, A. B. (eds.) *Solidarity: Theory and Practice*. Lanham: Lexington Books, pp. 238–271.
SEWA (2020). *Birth of SEWA, Self Employed Women's Association*. Online at www.sewa.org/history/. Accessed May 27th, 2022.
Shaban, A. (2022). "Spatial development and inequalities in the Global South," *Regional Science Policy and Practice*, 14, pp. 211–214. https://doi.org/10.1111/rsp3.12531
Shaban, A. and Das, B. (2018). *Farmers' Distress and Impacts of Baliraja Chetana Abhiyan, Osmanabad District, Maharashtra*. Report submitted to Collector Officer. Osmanabad: Government of Maharashtra.
Smith, A., Fressoli, M., Abrol, D. and Arond, E. (eds.) (2016). *Grassroots Innovation Movements*. London: Routledge.
Tiwari, R. and Mishra, A. (2019). "Every second ST, every third Dalit & Muslim in India poor, not just financially: UN report," *The Print*, July 12th. Online at https://theprint.in/india/every-second-st-every-third-dalit-muslim-in-india-poor-not-just-financially-un-report/262270 (accessed March 29th 2023).
Tushnet, M. and Khosla, M. (eds.) (2015). *Unstable Constitutionalism: Law and Politics in South Asia*. Cambridge: Cambridge University Press.
UNCTAD (2022). *Statistical Profiles of Least Developed Countries*. Online at https://unctad.org/topic/least-developed-countries/list (accessed March 29th, 2023).
Urama, K. C. and Acheampong, E. N. (2013). "Social innovation creates prosperous societies," *Stanford Social Innovation Review*, 11(3), A9–A11. https://doi.org/10.48558/AP7A-Y587
World Bank (2017). *Global Financial Development Report 2017/2018: Bankers without Borders*. Washington, DC: The World Bank.
Yadav, A. and Iqbal, B. A. (2021). "Socio-economic Scenario of South Asia: An overview of impacts of COVID-19," *South Asian Survey*, 28(1), pp. 20–37. https://doi.org/10.1177/0971523121994441.

9 Economic, institutional and political advocacy tensions in the field of solidarity economy and commons

An ethnographic approach drawing from three case studies

Jesús Sanz Abad, Sara Sama Acedo and Gaël Carrero Gros

9.1 Introduction

In the last two decades, within a situation of ecosocial crisis characterised by dismantling of the welfare state, privatisation of public services and spaces, concentration of wealth and overexploitation of nature (Prats *et al.*, 2016), countless critical initiatives have emerged throughout the world seeking to develop "alternative" and "transformative" forms of production, distribution and consumption, as well as social and environmental relations that differ from those established under the capitalist economic model and neoliberal policies. Broadly speaking, these initiatives have therefore been described as economies that are transformative, social or oriented towards the common good (Tapia, 2017; Calle & Casadevante, 2015; Collado *et al.*, 2017). They propose to resituate the production, management and ownership of resources in the sphere of the commons to focus their objectives and practices on the idea of the "sustainability of life" and to propose (effective) ways of (re)embedding economic events into the socio-political fabric (Orozco, 2017; Sanz Abad, 2019).

In this chapter, we focus on practical initiatives that, in a work or business environment, have been developed on the basis of the principles of the social solidarity economy (SSE) (Laville, 2013; Guridi & Pérez de Mendiguren, 2014; Coraggio, 2011), along with some that, in a communal urban environment, have been developed on the basis of the concept of the commons (Ostrom, 1990; Linebaugh, 2008; De Angelis, 2012) and the idea of the "right to the city" (Harvey, 2012) via processes of production, regulation and management of "urban commons" (Stavrides, 2016; Foster & Iaione, 2019; Sama, 2016). We consider that an analysis that integrates commons, on the one hand, and SSE, on the other, enables us to identify some key aspects of the transformative capacity of these initiatives, as Eynaud and Laville also suggest in their chapter in this volume.

DOI: 10.4324/9781003306344-10

More specifically, we focus on dilemmas, paradoxes and tensions observed in the practical, day-to-day activities of two types of initiatives taking place in Spain. On the one hand, we look at companies that, being based on a cooperative model (in terms of ownership, labour and decision-making), seek to prioritise people over capital and favour the collectivisation and democratisation of economic relations (as understood in the broadest sense). On the other hand, we looked at the green urban commons and, more specifically, neighbourhood community gardens. These initiatives have arisen through collective management and organisation by which participating individuals and groups form communities of practice (Wenger, 1999) and define rights, thus creating their own institutions of control, decision-making and inclusion/exclusion (Colding & Barthel, 2012: 159; Del Viso *et al.*, 2017; Leal, this volume). The dialogue between these two types of initiatives is enriching in that it allows us to focus on how commons are collectively conceived, produced and managed in the cooperative business environment, while at the same time shedding light on the different economic logics and forms of interaction with the market that occur across different spaces of community practice.

To this end, based on the line of work pursued within the ongoing research project "Changing paradigms: practices and discourses of transformative economies in a context of an ecosocial emergency",[1] we propose an ethnographic approach that makes the everyday social dynamics of each initiative visible in a processual and situated manner. With the aim of identifying tensions that arise from interactions with the state, the market and social activism, three cross-cutting themes were chosen for the analysis: 1) tensions resulting from interactions with public institutions; 2) tensions between the characteristic transformative spirit of these initiatives and their sustainability within the capitalist system and 3) tensions that arise between the desire to maintain ideological coherence (usually of a smaller, militant social base) and, at the same time, to reach out to a broader social majority.

It should be noted that, while we consider it analytically useful to differentiate these themes, in practice this does not demarcate isolated domains. Nonetheless, we found it of interest to establish a dialogue among the themes while analysing the different cases (among which existed both differences and points in common) as it allowed us to reach some deeper socio-anthropological reflections on how issues such as work value, productivity, redistribution, the construction of the commons, participation and emancipation can be understood more broadly.

In addition, this approach allowed us to point out issues that are often overlooked in narratives surrounding such initiatives – both from academic and activist perspectives – because they tend to produce an excessively dichotomous characterisation of "transformative" versus "conventional" practices, prone to idealism or romanticism. We thus seek to advance knowledge about the "transformations" that these diverse initiatives can bring about with regard to their peculiarities and the specific contexts in which they develop and operate. Our analysis looks at the different ways in which this idea of transformation takes shape in reality and is operationalised in everyday situations, on the basis of the testimonies of actors involved in the different initiatives studied. We propose case study analysis as a means of focusing more on practices that actually exist rather than on a prescriptive view of how they should be (Reygadas, 2014; Carrero & Sanz, 2019). This enables us to visualise the real impacts and capacities that these proposals for "transformation" may have with respect to their context (Avelino *et al.*, 2019; Pel *et al.*, 2020; Strasser *et al.*, 2020).

In methodological terms, data were produced through in-depth interviews, collection and analysis of documents, and participant observation in various spaces where everyday activities took place for the three chosen case studies:

- Agresta: a workers' cooperative dedicated to forestry management and consultancy, with a current membership of 63 people (located in several different territories). Founded in 2000 by a group of forestry engineering students who decided to create a company in accordance with SSE principles and as defined by Spain's Alternative and Solidarity Economy Network (REAS, according to its Spanish acronym). It currently has an annual turnover of over 2.3 million euros.
- Fiare Banca Etica: a financial savings and credit cooperative operating in Spain since 2005 as Fiare and since 2014 as a merger with *Banca Populare Etica* from Italy. It finances third sector and SSE projects, presenting itself as a tool for social transformation. It currently has 3,400 members in Spain, with total savings of 285 million euros.
- Madrid's Urban Community Gardens (UCGs, or, in Spanish, *Huertos Urbanos Comunitarios de Madrid*): a group of community gardens that is heterogeneous in terms of the interests, composition, processes, manner of functioning and self-management of each project. Each garden is a community that actively defines itself while producing, managing and redistributing resources collectively (soil, seeds, water, networks of sociability and mutual care, knowledge, harvests, tools, etc.). It is currently made up of 60 community gardens, most of which are neighbourhood-based projects.

9.2 Among the challenges of both transforming and functioning

9.2.1 Tensions resulting from interactions with public institutions

The first source of tension has its origin in the relations between each initiative and public institutions. It can result from the implementation of institutionalised channels of action, such as processes of formalisation, institutionalisation or statisation. A key factor is the manner in which dialogues, alliances, negotiations and dependencies on the public institutional sphere take shape. Within these processes, the initiatives act as active and self-reflective agents, producing spaces for internal debate about how to maintain an alignment between their values and practices and how to consistently reproduce themselves without being co-opted by the dominant institutions they seek to transform. They deploy both logics of distancing and conflict and logics of access and collaboration in their relations with the structures of public policy making and implementation. It is important to look at the concrete changes that these processes bring about in the chosen initiatives. That is how they affect resource management, organisation, decision-making dynamics, attribution of work value and remuneration, prioritisation of dialogue with certain actors, the professionalisation of roles and knowledge, the definition of the services they offer and the orientation of political action (dialogue, demands, confrontation, collaboration, etc.) (Coll-Planas & Cruells, 2007; Mahoney & Thelen, 2009; Pel & Bauler, 2014; Pel *et al.*, 2016).

The tension of institutionalisation was most evident in the case of Madrid's Community Urban Gardens (UCGs). In 2010, in tune with the 15M movement, the UCGs formalised their structure as an association (*La Red de Huertos Urbanos de Madrid* or *La Red* for short). Open and assembly-based, it focused on advising and supporting various groups interested in creating or consolidating community urban gardens, as well as liaising with the administration to gradually advance a process of municipalisation of the UCGs. This municipalisation process – which remained anchored in a conflictual form of dialogue – led to the progressive regularisation of public land that had initially been squatted, the opening of spaces for co-participation in public policies for urban sustainability and greater political recognition that materialised in the "Municipal Programme of Urban Community Gardens".

In 2015, the election of a new municipal government translated into a situation of cooperation and political harmony between the UCGs and public institutions. The UCGs received greater support for their growth and consolidation, both by gaining greater access to public land and by contributing, together with other local associations, towards proposals for several municipal plans and projects on spatial planning, composting and recycling, healthcare, care work and professional development in agroecology and urban gardening. These initiatives thus became key agents during that period in the dynamisation and integration of proposals for offering services and improvements to the urban fabric and in the production of policies for the naturalisation of the city. Their participation in forums where the aim was to "make the city different" strained the autonomy of the UCGs and made it difficult for participants to reconcile the intense work involved in association-institutional cooperation (dialogue, management, organisation and communication) with the care requirements of the crops, the people and the relationships that gave life to the gardens. A debate took place over the pros and cons of extending public funding for activities and projects that the UCGs would like to develop and of introducing salaries and professionalisation of certain profiles.

Then in 2019, with the return of a conservative local government, the City Council's ordinance regulating its cooperation with civil society was repealed, although some dynamics of cooperation remained among the umbrella organisation (*La Red*), the gardens themselves and the municipal departments involved in the Municipal Programme. In addition, in line with commitments made under the Milan Urban Food Policy Pact (2015), the City Council began to push for a new type of "productive urban garden", tendering 200 plots (160 hectares in the south-eastern urban periphery) to be awarded to "entrepreneurial" agroecological exploitation initiatives with a more commercial orientation. This established a new context for interactions between the community and associative sphere and the commercial and institutional spheres. The association *La Red* and community gardens belonging to the Municipal Programme found themselves in a dilemma: on the one hand, not wanting to give up their autonomy in community and environmentally sustainable production and management, but, on the other hand, not wanting to lose the opportunity of opening up to the professionalisation and expansion of agroecology in Madrid.

Another form of this tension is found in the interaction of business initiatives with public institutions. The case of the cooperative company Agresta is interesting, as it operates in a sector where about 80% of its turnover comes from public administrations. In 2012, the economic crisis had a significant impact on the cooperative, demonstrating the inevitable influence of, and dependence on, public administrations. On the one hand, the crisis led them to restructure their finances and apply for new public funds from the EU (H2020, ERDF, etc.). As a consequence, at least in its discourse, Agresta put aside its emphasis on its cooperative nature in favour of adopting the rhetoric of R&D&I (innovation, technological development and internationalisation). On the other hand, the crisis demonstrated the limitations imposed on their business sector by insufficient public investment in forest management. Nevertheless, their way of functioning, based on cooperation and redistribution among different regional branches (those that make more profits support those that have losses), enabled them to be resilient and keep afloat, maintaining their capacity to preserve a certain degree of autonomy in the face of such external pressures.

Finally, the case of *Fiare Banca Etica* illustrates an attempt to preserve its autonomy from the institutional sphere. Still recent in the memory of the banking sector in Spain is the bankruptcy of numerous savings banks due to mismanagement by municipal and regional governments. The participation of the administration in the cooperative is restricted to that of any other member of the cooperative (one member, one vote; or by contracting products such as a savings account). The cooperative does fund projects of partner institutions, but it limits the granting of funds to specific sectors and activities, such as for promoting the "right to housing" (e.g. through housing cooperatives), environmental sustainability or the SSE. In addition, it does not finance ongoing running costs such as salaries and utility bills, thus establishing a clear limit in its relationship with public institutions – especially taking into account that these costs usually represent a substantial part of their budgets. It is nonetheless significant that, in its discourse, Fiare presents the inclusion of public administrations among its members as "a guarantee for society", thereby providing social legitimacy to the administration rather than vice versa.

9.2.2 *Tensions between the transformative spirit and the sustainability of initiatives within the capitalist system*

The second source of tension identified concerns the difficulty of maintaining a balance in an initiative's search for its own sustainability – in both economic and social terms – while trying to prioritise and promote values of redistribution and reciprocity within a market economy where capitalist criteria of competitiveness, profitability and productivity prevail (Reygadas, 2014). This type of tension affects decisions about which actors to engage with and the manner of establishing these relationships, about the orientation and shape given to self-organising practices and about the meaning given to the notion of a practice's sustainability, which may call into question the everyday behaviour of people who promote, participate in and integrate these experiences (Fernández *et al.*, 2015).

In the case of Agresta, debates on criteria for determining the value of work and which aspects to reward are a good example of how this tension can occur within an initiative. Agresta applies an equal pay policy, which is facilitated by the fact that most members and employees have a similar level of education. Nevertheless, debates still emerge over how work should be valued and whether or not any wage differentiation should exist. For example some members argue that valuing seniority in the organisation should not justify a possible wage difference, which they believe could discourage people from getting involved in the cooperative or could promote hierarchies. Others contend that such differentiation could favour productivity, strengthen continuity of membership in the organisation (by establishing economic incentives) and encourage the incorporation of new workers (taking into account that in their sector, it is possible to find higher salaries outside the cooperative), which is presented as a way of improving the competitiveness of the company. However, this view is opposed by those who consider that the motivation for belonging to the cooperative should be rooted in the desire to construct a working environment based on cooperation and redistribution, as well as in the effort to improve collective working conditions (e.g. by raising salaries or expanding benefits such as care policies – receiving full salary when on sick leave or paid hours set aside to care for others).

External factors also create tensions between the economic sustainability of these initiatives and their underlying principles, leading to ethical dilemmas. In the case of Agresta, some members of the cooperative find an ideological incongruence when working for certain clients (such as the World Bank) or when doing jobs that could indirectly endorse a socially or environmentally unsustainable course of action. However, the criterion that prevails here is the profitability of such proposals.

The case of Fiare illustrates the difficult balance between being economically viable and competitive in the market, and remaining true to foundational ideals. It is faced with offering a range of services comparable to that of conventional financial institutions (in terms of the products and conditions offered), obtaining a return that guarantees the economic sustainability of the institution and, at the same time, complying with its ethical and social criteria for choosing which activities to finance. For example Fiare's banking services include current accounts and debit and credit cards, but it does not offer an instant payment system such as Bizum, which is increasingly widespread and very popular among young people, due to the complications and expenses the addition of this service would entail for the institution. It also limits the type of loans it offers. For instance it does not grant mortgages for purchasing housing. In addition, the ethical and social criteria established by the institution for its investments result in significantly lower financial returns compared to conventional institutions.

Finally, the tensions stemming from introducing a market logic also affect the UCGs, despite being community projects that fall outside the business sphere. This is illustrated by the fact that since the municipalisation of the UCGs, it became formally forbidden to carry out economic activities in the community garden, including buying or selling products or charging for participation in activities; yet, they received no funding to cover the fixed costs that were at the same time imposed (such as water, liability insurance and maintenance materials). This means that most UCGs seek to self-finance through a system of membership, regular donations and fundraisers, which implies that the associations managing these gardens must strive to expand and maintain participation by offering some form of benefit to financial contributors. This situation places the UCGs in a difficult balance between respecting the formal framework (of the Municipal Programme of Urban Community Gardens) and the expectations of participants who contribute financially to their viability.

For example produce from the gardens, which in most gardens is presented as a common good redistributed on the basis of non-measurable relationships of trust and reciprocity, is increasingly managed by applying various forms of quantification. Many gardens have come to limit access to the harvest on the basis of a form of formal membership involving a fee, although other forms of contextual valuation are informally applied (presence, work and dedication – generally bundled together under the concept of "commitment"). Also, some gardens have reorganised their space and participation on the basis of a mixed collective-individual model, with a communal area (for cultivation and activities) managed by an assembly and another area divided into individual plots that are allocated to groups or families (through a raffle or a waiting list) in exchange for an annual fee. Gardens that establish these flexible forms of participation tend to broaden and stabilise levels of participation compared to other gardens where everything is communal. This in turn seems to improve their sustainability, not only in economic terms but also in social terms, because steering groups are renewed more often, or at least relieved of part of their workload.

9.2.3 Tensions between maintaining ideological coherence and reaching out to a broader social majority

The third and final source of tension stems from dilemmas that arise when initiatives desire to reach out to a broader public or social base without losing the values that make them different and "alternative". Scaling up and/or amplifying the transformative aims of initiatives, either by replicating a model in multiple locations or by adding new participants and partners, represents a challenge that should not be underestimated. To extend an initiative's influence involves finding ways to adapt its own framework, narratives, accumulated knowledge, activities and communication to appeal to the perspectives and values of new and potential participants (Snow *et al.*, 1986; Rucht, 2004). It also involves facing the difficult dilemma of meeting the expectations and needs of people who have not yet developed a sense of community or commitment or who may be sceptical about, or even opposed to, some of the core values and activities of the initiatives. The latter implies the challenge of stimulating and maintaining cooperative and collaborative relationships within initiatives and, at the same time, with other actors in the field. This is often a complex and taxing task for the more militant grassroots, and it often leads to revisiting the boundaries of inclusion and exclusion of these initiatives until a balance is struck (Strasser *et al.*, 2020).

As is made clear by internal debates and reflections in the cases presented, this tension invites questions about how, where and why to grow (whether growth should be a means or an end in itself), as well as about how flexible to become in terms of discourse, objectives and practices in order to reach a wider and more diverse public and thus achieve greater social influence. The rethinking of these issues also leads to a reflection, in general little explored, on how diversity is managed within these initiatives, as well as to a view over the frontiers that are opened or closed and the renunciations thereby implied.

From this perspective, an interesting debate took place within Agresta on how to manage its growth and on the impact that growth could have on its model of cooperative governance. The debate was triggered by the rapid growth the organisation was experiencing as a result of increasing turnover in recent years. This growth had the consequence of disturbing the balance between workers who were members and those who were not members of the organisation. Also, because the projects had a limited lifespan, the organisation could not ensure that the newly recruited workers would be able to remain and become members of the cooperative in the long term. These issues prompted reflection among members on what direction to give to the cooperative's growth in which two positions can be distinguished: those who accept growth as an end in itself and those who highlight the tensions growth adds to the cooperative model of operating. The latter also point out the difficulty of finding professionals who are committed to this form of organisation. In the end, the cooperative opted for growth because of the opportunity it provides for improving working conditions, but on the condition that this growth be accompanied by a commitment from all members to maintain a "productive tension" that would allow the incorporation and stabilisation of new workers as members of the cooperative.

In the case of *Fiare Banca Etica*, this type of tension is illustrated by debates that took place following the announcement of the sale of a "Responsible Investment Fund" in Spain (managed through *Etica SGR*, a company controlled by the Italian *Banca Popolare Etica*). This product was presented as a way of introducing into the stock market the principles on which ethical finance is based (transparency, participation and use of money to generate positive social and environmental impacts) through investments that comply with those principles. The proposal caused an internal debate that highlighted the diversity of opinions among members on whether it was possible to remain consistent with the principles of ethical finance while entering the stock market. Among the opinions against, doubts were raised about the capacity to generate social transformation through these funds; concern was also expressed over financing certain companies that are not aligned with the SSE, giving priority to the sale of this product over others that are more in demand among the social base (such as loans to individuals) and the contradiction between investing in stock markets and promoting ethical finance – since the former implies the promotion of a financialised form of economy. On the other hand, opinions in favour of this product emphasised the opportunity it offered to introduce ethical finance and the SSE into other areas, the possibility of using it as a strategic tool to influence financial markets and the potential it created for attracting savings and ensuring the economic sustainability of the institution.

The diversity of positions was expressed by the head of institutional relations:

> Many of Fiare's member organisations ask us for [this financial product]. Not the militant member of REAS. But the religious organisation of nuns that has funds, this one does. And other large organisations would also use this tool if it were available. So, surprising as it may seem – and at the grassroots level they didn't believe it – there are people who would hire this tool if they could. Some manage large sums, and putting funds into a fixed-term deposit is important for their cash flow. So, we have a part of our social base that is asking us for this tool, as occurred in Italy.

In the case of the UCGs, recurring debates concerning their spatial design – open versus closed – illustrate the challenge of extending participation without losing the sense of commitment to the commons that defines these initiatives. The Municipal Programme provides for the basic fitting out of the plots, which, among other things, includes installing a perimeter fence. The associations that manage the allotments decide themselves whether to leave them open (with a low fence) or closed (with a high fence) with set opening and closing times. This issue generated an intense debate in one particular community garden located on an allotment plot adjacent to a public square, which had been abandoned for several years and was recovered by the neighbours. The younger people who had been involved in the initial occupation of the plot argued that it should be kept open. They saw it as part of the public space of the square and interpreted that it had been "recovered by the neighbours" for communal use, with no restrictions on access. They also felt that keeping the garden open amplified its educational nature, teaching people that there was no need for fences to protect a common space if it was cared for collectively. On the other hand, those who had not participated in the occupation – mainly middle-aged and retired men – argued that if the plot of land had been assigned by the local government for a garden project, then it should be a "real garden" that was "well made and productive" and that the effort put into it would not yield results without a fence. Finally, a perimeter fence was agreed to be built, but to compensate for this, it was established that the garden would only close at night.

This consensual solution managed to bring together two conflicting ways of understanding the commons: commitment to a collective project and how a garden should be. It also introduced some changes. The gardeners, convinced that the fruits of their labour would be protected behind the fence, became more involved in improving the facilities and increasing the area under cultivation. The "tidier", "greener" space attracted new participants who saw the project as being "more serious" and "stable". But most of all, it attracted families willing to spend the afternoon in a space where their children could roam safely (in an enclosed space) while at the same time "learning where tomatoes come from". This type of participants, however, did not commit themselves to the maintenance and management of the garden, thus attributing to the most involved gardeners the roles of trainers, organisers and managers. Thus, although the garden fulfilled the objective of attracting a growing and more diverse number of people, it also presented a new challenge. To transform this influx into commitment to the project represented a considerable investment of time and effort, which the more committed, albeit politically less active, gardeners did not have the strength or willingness to take on. Faced with this tension, this community garden, like many others today, became less open, adjusting access and activities to a rhythm marked by the friction between life circumstances, personal desires and community responsibilities. As a result, participation by gardeners most committed to the objective of a serious and stable community garden was maintained, but it became a less inclusive and dynamic participatory space.

9.3 Conclusions

Based on the ethnographic analysis of three initiatives situated within the framework of the social and solidarity economy (SSE) and the renewed practices of commoning, this chapter explores some of the debates and tensions that arise and are characteristic of initiatives that define themselves as "transformative alternatives".

The SSE and the commons are usually presented in academic literature as two different concepts. However, as Eynaud and Laville point out in this volume, integrating initiatives from both spheres in the same analysis enables a richer reflection on the transformative capacity of these initiatives. Three insights have thus been obtained. First, this integrative approach helps to situate a third social pole of action that opens up new possibilities for analysis beyond state–market dualism. Second, practices associated with the SSE and the commons challenge what is often presented as a naturalised division between the political and economic spheres in mainstream socio-economic analyses. Third, a look from the perspective of these practices provides a glimpse of the plurality of existing economic forms. It also provides insight into the development of ways of thinking, doing and organising that are becoming institutionalised, challenging, altering and/or replacing the dominant institutions in a specific socio-material context (Pel *et al.*, 2020).

However, this picture is incomplete without addressing the ways in which different economic logics and modes of sociability are interconnected in these initiatives. As we have shown, these initiatives are not only internally heterogeneous in social and ideological terms, but, in their contexts of action, they are also inevitably bound to interact with diverse actors who challenge their ethical and moral frameworks, as well as their ways of putting into practice values such as equity, reciprocity or sustainability. In our opinion, it is necessary to focus on the concrete, everyday tensions and dilemmas faced by these initiatives in their experiences of relating to this diversity.

The analysis of the cases presented, the tensions and limits they face and the responses they propose has enabled us to identify some key areas of analysis – granted, others also exist. These findings enable us to delve deeper into attempts to make transformative aspirations a reality. We here have focused on shedding light on some of the tensions that emerge: 1) when initiatives interact with the public institutional sphere, whether in search of financial backing, greater support and/or legitimacy or to preserve their autonomy and self-management (Coll-Planas & Cruells, 2007; Mahoney & Thelen, 2009; Pel & Bauler, 2014; Pel *et al.*, 2016); 2) when operating within the market, under pressure to be competitive and efficient, while at the same time trying to maintain relationships based on a logic of reciprocity and redistribution (Reygadas, 2014) and 3) when attempting to interact with new and more diverse actors, so as to amplify both their capacity and social impact, making their framework and narratives more flexible while maintaining coherence with their political and moral values (Strasser *et al.*, 2020; Snow *et al.*, 1986; Rucht, 2004).

Finally, we would like to draw attention to the potential of ethnographic methodology for studying experiences aimed at social transformation. This processual, relational and situated approach enables the identification of the deeper socio-anthropological debates that lie behind these tensions and proposals for social transformation, as well as of the multiple dimensions of transformation that these experiences seek and can effectively generate.

Note

1. Project ID: I+D+I PID2019–106757GA-I00. Funded by MCIN/AEI/ 10.13039/501100011033. Research group blog: https://ecoembedded.hypotheses.org/sobre-el-blog (accessed October 10, 2022).

References

Avelino, F., Wittmayer, J. M., Pel, B., Weaver, P., Dumitru, A., Haxeltine, A., Kemp, R., Jørgensen, M. S., Bauler, T., Ruijsink, S. and O'Riordan, T. (2019). "Transformative social innovation and (dis) empowerment," *Technological Forecasting and Social Change*, 145, pp. 195–206.

Calle, Á. and Casadevante, J. L. (2015). "Economías sociales y economías para los bienes comunes," *Otra Economía*, 9(16), pp. 44–68.

Carrero, G. and Sanz, J. (2019). "Articulación de lógicas y modos de sociabilidad económicos: Un análisis a partir de cuatro experiencias de Economía social y solidaria en España," *Revista de Antropología Social*, 28(2), pp. 47–273.

Colding, J. and Barthel, S. (2012). "The potential of 'Urban Green Commons' in the resilience building of cities," *Ecological Economics*, 86, pp. 156–166.

Collado, C., Suriñach, R. and Piñeiro, C. (2017). "Comunes y economías para la sostenibilidad de la vida," in *Rebeldías en común: Sobre comunales, nuevos comunes y economías cooperativas*. Madrid: Libros en Acción, pp. 15–45.

Coll-Planas, G. and Cruells, M. (2007). "Revisión crítica del concepto de institucionalización: Propuesta de distinción analítica y aplicación en el estudio de tres movimientos sociales," IX Congreso Español de Sociología, Barcelona.

Coraggio, J. L. (2011). *Economía Social y Solidaria. El trabajo antes que el capital.* Quito: Ediciones Abya-Yala.

De Angelis, M. (2012). "Crises, movements and commons," *Borderlands*, 11. Online at www.researchgate.net/publication/281624473_Crises_Movements_and_Commons (accessed March 30th 2023).

Del Viso, N., Casadevante, J. L. and Morán, N. (2017). "Cultivando relaciones sociales. Lo común y lo 'comunitario' a través de la experiencia de dos huertos urbanos de Madrid," *Revista de Antropología Social*, 26(2), pp. 449–472.

Fernández, M. I., Litman, L. C. and Sorroche, S. (2015). "Contornos (políticos) de la sustentabilidad (económica): Notas etnográficas a partir del estudio de dos organizaciones de la 'economía social'," *Identidades*, 8(5), pp. 26–41.

Foster, S. R. and Iaione, C. (2019). "Ostrom in the city: Design principles for the urban commons," in Hudson, B., Rosenbloom, J. and Cole, D (eds.) *Routledge Handbook of the Study of the Commons*. London: Routledge, pp. 235–255.

Guridi, L. and Pérez de Mendiguren, J. C. (2014). *La dimensión económica del Desarrollo Humano Local: La economía social y solidaria*. Bilbao: HEGOA, Instituto de Estudios sobre Desarrollo y Cooperación Internacional.

Harvey, D. (2012). *Rebel Cities: From the Right to the City to the Urban Revolution*. London: Verso.

Laville, J. L. (2013). "Économie sociale et solidaire, capitalisme et changement démocratique," in, Hiez, D. and Lavillunière, E. (eds.) *Vers une Théorie de l'Économie Sociale et Solidaire*. Paris: Éditions Larcier, pp. 17–32.

Linebaugh, P. (2008). *The Magna Carta Manifesto: Liberties and Commons For All*. Berkeley and Los Angeles: University of California Press.

Mahoney, J. and Thelen, K. (2009). *Explaining Institutional Change: Ambiguity, Agency and Power*. Cambridge: Cambridge University Press.

Orozco, A. (2017). *Subversión feminista de la economía. Aportes para un debate sobre el conflicto capital-vida*. Madrid: Traficantes de sueños.

Ostrom, E. (1990). *Governing the Commons: The Evolution of Institutions for Collective Action*. Cambridge: Cambridge University Press.

Pel, B. and Bauler, T. (eds.) (2014). *The Institutionalization of Social Innovation: Between Transformation and Capture*. TRANSIT Deliverable 2.2, TRANSIT: EU SSH.2013.3.2–1 Grant agreement no: 613169.

Pel, B., Haxeltine, A., Avelino, F., Dumitru, A., Kemp, R., Bauler, T., Kunze, I., Dorland, J., Wittmayer, J. and Jørgensen, M. S. (2020). "Towards a theory of transformative social innovation: A relational framework and 12 propositions." *Research Policy*, 49(8), 104080.

Pel, B., Weaver, P., Cipolla, C., Afonso, R., Jorgensen, M. S., Elle, M., Avelino, F., Backhaus, J., Lema Blanco, I., Kunze, I., Dumitru, A., van Gameren, V. and Bauler, T. (2016). "Institutionalization Dialectics in Transformative Social Innovation: A Comparative Case Study," *Paper session presented at International Sustainability Transitions Conference*, Wuppertal (DE), September 5–7, 2016.

Prats, F., Herrero, Y. and Torrego, A. (2016). *La gran encrucijada. Sobre la crisis ecosocial y el cambio de ciclo histórico*. Madrid: Foro de Transiciones.

Reygadas, L. (2014). "Más acá y más allá de la utopía. Dilemas y potencialidades de las economías alternativas," in Reygadas, L., Pozzio, M., Gracia, M. A., López, Á. and Ramos, T. (eds.) *Economías alternativas: Utopías, desencantos y procesos emergentes*. México: UNAM-Iztapalapa, pp. 11–48.

Rucht, D. (2004). "Movement allies, adversaries, and third parties," in Snow, D. A., Soule, S. A. and Hanspeter, K. (eds.) *The Blackwell Companion to Social Movements*. Oxford: Blackwell Publishing Ltd, pp. 197–216.

Sama, S. (2016). "De la smart city a los huertos comunitarios," in Cruces, F. (Coord.) (ed.) *Cosmópolis. Nuevas maneras de ser urbanos*. Barcelona: Gedisa, pp. 167–200.

Sanz Abad, J. (2019). "Economía social y solidaria, emprendimiento social y economía popular en la sociedad post-crisis," *Revista de Antropología Social*, 28(2), pp. 205–226.

Snow, D. A., Burke Rochford Jr., E., Worden, S. K. and Benford, R. D. (1986). "Frame alignment processes, micromobilization, and movement participation," *American Sociological Review*, 51, pp. 464–481.

Stavrides, S. (2016). *Common Space: The City as Commons*. London: Zed Books.

Strasser, T., de Kraker, J. and Kemp, R. (2020). "Three dimensions of transformative impact and capacity: A conceptual framework applied in social innovation practice," *Sustainability*, 12(11), pp. 4742.

Tapia, A. A. (2017). "Nuevas economías transformadoras," *Revista Vasca de Economía Social*, 14, pp. 7–60.

Wenger, E. (1999). *Communities of Practice: Learning, Meaning, and Identity*. Cambridge: Cambridge University Press.

10 Solidarity economy movement in Colombia

Two regional experiences promoted by popular education for integral change

Miguel Arturo Fajardo Rojas and Noriko Hataya

10.1 Introduction

This chapter examines the role of popular education inspired by liberation theory in the Catholic Church in Colombia, which emerged from the solidarity economy movement by means of a comparative analysis of two regional experiences.

The first emerged in the southern provinces of the department of Santander, located in the Andean region. The second arose in the Medio Atrato region along the Pacific Coast. Beyond the enormous differences with regard to geopolitical, cultural and ethnic conditions, both cases were originally promoted by social action undertaken by activists of the Catholic Church, influenced by liberation theology.

The chapter first describes the Colombian national context since the 1960s, when social movements in search of alternative solutions emerged in connection with the liberation theology reforms of the Catholic Church in Latin American countries. It then reviews the national dimensions of solidarity economy. Finally, analysis of two regional experiences will help us understand the implications of popular education and adapted practices of solidarity economy in different locations and contexts, as alternative solutions for dignified lives.

10.2 Colombian context since the late 1950s and Second Vatican Council

Since the late 1950s, the world has experienced different social processes, including revolutionary movements in Latin America (Almeida & Cordero Ulate, 2017). Conditions of poverty, the inability of nation-states to provide services to their populations and ideological influences coming from Europe created fertile ground for the emergence of popular movements and insurgencies in Latin America (Nickson, 2019).

The dynamics of violence in Colombia, which caused more than 220,000 deaths between 1958 and 2012, has been one of the most complex sociopolitical issues in Latin America (Grupo de Memoria Histórica, 2013). After lengthy talks

DOI: 10.4324/9781003306344-11

between the Colombian government and the FARC[1] guerrilla movement, in 2016, a peace agreement was signed, which is still in the process of implementation.

Meanwhile, in the years preceding the papacy of Pope John XXIII, internal discussions among bishops of the Catholic Church worldwide sought ways to renew the institution. They recognised a very large gap between the people and the Church, which had lost its influence on society. On 25 January 1959, Pope John announced the convocation of the Second Vatican Council (1962–1965).

The Council produced several documents on the nature of the Church and its relations with the world. *Gaudium et Spes* is one of them. The text begins with these inspiring words: the joys and hopes, griefs and anxieties of the poor are the joys and hopes, griefs and anxieties of the Church (Concilio Vaticano II, 1965 (No.1), and advocates the suppression of inequalities.

The Latin American Episcopal Council (CELAM) held a Conference (ECLA)[2] in Medellin (Colombia) in 1968, with the purpose of reflecting on the role of the Church in the South American continent in the light of the Second Vatican Council. In the resulting documents, the Latin American bishops presented the role of the Church in responding to the issue of injustice.

The bishops made a call to the dioceses to create more humane and just conditions for all people, through liberating education towards the organisation of workers, peasants and poor people and promotion of peace and popular communication. Later, in 1980, another ECLA took place in Puebla (Mexico), which called on all Christians, civil society and authorities to work to overcome the conditions of injustice experienced by the majority of Latin Americans.

As the case studies presented in this chapter illustrate, behind the pastoral work undertaken in Colombia by the Diocese of Socorro and San Gil (Department of Santander) and the Diocese of Quibdó (Department of Chocó), and by the Claretians, there emerged a dedication to the liberating role of the Gospel and the responsibility of all Christians to work towards the integral liberation of the diocesan communities.

10.3 The emergence of the solidarity economy in Colombia

Like many other countries, the emergence of solidarity economy organisations in Colombia has its roots in the ancestral communities of the territory and in the influence of European philanthropic practices. Specifically, solidarity economy practices have their roots in ancestral practices such as "*trabajo colectivo*", "*minga*", "*convite*" and "*mano prestada*"[3] (Dávila *et al.*, 2018: 101). Later, mutual associations and cooperatives arrived hand-in-hand with the Catholic Church and social movements initiated by labour unions in Europe.

Currently, Colombian Law 454 of 1998, Article 2, recognises several entrepreneurial forms of solidarity economy.[4] This law defines the solidarity economy as a socioeconomic, cultural and environmental system formed by different associative, democratic and non-profit organisations that work for the integral development of society.

Table 10.1 Types of solidarity organisations in Colombia

Economic cooperation organisations	*Philanthropic organisations*
Cooperative organisations	Foundations
Mutual associations	Volunteer organisations
Employee funds	Civil defence
Producer and service associations	Red Cross
	Social benefit associations and corporations

Source: Based on the classification of solidarity organisations established under Colombian Law 454 of 1998[5]

Table 10.2 Cooperatives, mutual associations and employee funds in Colombia 2018

Type of solidarity organisations	*Total number in Colombia*	*Total number of associates*
Mutual associations	250	252,477
Cooperative organisations	3,205	6,290,927
Employee funds	1,365	1,155,257

Source: CONFECOOP (2018) and Superintendencia de Economía Solidaria (2020)

Thus, the national solidarity economy is complex and includes different organisational forms. They can be broadly divided into philanthropic organisations and economic cooperation organisations (Table 10.1).

There are no data available about other forms of solidarity economy (such as associations, corporations, foundations and other solidarity enterprises) due to their lack of legal status. However, regarding cooperatives and employee funds, which are the most representative solidarity enterprises, we can rely upon data from the Superintendence of Solidarity Economy and the Confederation of Cooperatives of Colombia (CONFECOOP,[6] 2018) (see Table 10.2).

Up to this point, we have presented a general overview of the institutionalisation process and historical evolution of the solidarity economy in Colombia. The regional cases in the following sections will show how far the solidarity economy has contributed to the sustainable human development of the country.

10.4 The experience of the solidarity territory in the provinces of southern Santander

10.4.1 Local context and background process

The provinces of San Gil, Socorro and Vélez are located in the south of the department of Santander, which is in the north central part of the country. These three provinces cover an area of 10,954 square kilometres and comprise nearly 450,000 inhabitants.

Before the Spanish invasion, the territory was inhabited by indigenous ethnic groups such as the Guane, Yariguíes, Carares and Agataes. The conquest and colonisation periods are inseparable from the evangelisation process by the Catholic Church: it was a conquest of arms, legitimised – as the expression goes – by the Church. During the colonial period, insurgencies by indigenous people occurred for emancipation from any colonial rule, while the Catholic Church maintained its *raison d'être* through social action.

The origins of present-day social institutions in the provinces of southern Santander undoubtedly lie in actions by the Catholic Church. In the 19th and 20th centuries, the Catholic Church played an important role in the organisation of education and health systems. At the end of the 1940s, the Diocese of Socorro and San Gil were influenced by the papal encyclical *Quadragesimo Anno*,[7] which in effect became a set of guidelines for the social action of the Catholic Church (Buchelli, 2006: 43). Likewise, in the early 1960s, some cooperatives in the region were formed under the direction of the Catholic Church, following the same guidelines (Fajardo Rojas *et al.*, 2018: 50).

The Second Vatican Council (1962–1965)[8] proposed to transform the nature and mission of the Church. From 1963, the priest in charge of the social pastoral of the Diocese of Socorro and San Gil, Ramón González Parra, encouraged the acceptance of the social pastoral as a basis for action promoting the liberation of people and society. Cooperative principles and values were especially embraced in the creation of cooperatives and in the other processes promoted by the social pastoral (Secretariado Diocesano de Pastoral Social, SEPAS, 1977).

Table 10.3 summarises the principal strategies elaborated by the activists of SEPAS (Secretariado Diocesano de Pastoral Social). First, they established the province as a space for their intervention, popular education as the method to generate farmer leadership and community-based economic organisations as units of practice of the solidarity economy.

10.4.2 Main results and further exploration

Over the years, different forms of solidarity organisation have been created, forming a very important source of social capital for the human development of the three provinces of southern Santander. Lately, the communities, in a spontaneous way, have sought to organise themselves to solve common problems: water, housing, production, commercialisation of products, transportation and so on. Table 10.4 shows the numbers of organisations active in the territory in 2019.

As shown in Table 10.3, education, economic activity and social communication (local media) are the three main fields of solidarity economy, which have developed in this territory. Networking and multi-tier organisation have been another source of expansion and enforcement of solidarity economy in the territory. For example Coopcentral was founded in 1964 as a network of saving and credit cooperatives. Resander (Red cooperativa de medios de comunicación) is

Table 10.3 Strategies of the development process in the southern provinces of Santander

Master strategies	*Objectives*	*Responsible institution or team*
The province as a unit of human development	To promote the integral development of the territorial communities, based on their own needs and capacities.	Provincial development corporations, cooperative of municipalities.
Education of leaders and communities	To form and train the leadership necessary to promote social change in the provinces.	Mobile education team; institutes of social leadership, University of San Gil.
Economic and social organisation	To create economic, social and cultural organisations that articulately and autonomously work for social change in the provinces.	El Común: network of farmers' organisations, Coopcentral: network of cooperatives.
Social communication and citizen mobilisation	Promote solidarity and cooperative culture on the basis of the experiences of organisations in the territory.	A monthly community paper, community radio stations, community media network (RESANDER).
Strategic alliances	To create synergies among different social actors who have an impact on the integral development of the provinces.	Regional corporations, establishment of agreements and joint plans

Source: Author's own elaboration based on experiences as a member of SEPAS since 1976

Table 10.4 Solidarity organisations in the provinces of southern Santander in (2019)

Solidarity organisations	*Areas of activity*	*Province of Guanentá*	*Province of Comunera*	*Province of Vélez*	*Total*
Cooperatives	Savings and loans, housing, transportation, health, education, associated labour, etc.	75	30	33	138
Other forms of solidarity organisations	Common benefit associations, social corporations, foundations, employee funds, clubs with social work.	651	380	252	1,283
Total		726	410	285	1,421

Source: Author's calculation based on the database from the Bucaramanga Chamber of Commerce and the Superintendence of Solidarity Economy of Colombia, updated through his own field research. See also Fajardo Rojas *et al.* (2018); Corzo Gutiérrez *et al.* (2020)

a second-tier cooperative made up of 37 community media organisations (radio and TV stations) in the region. ACUEDUCTS links more than 150 rural aqueducts in 13 municipalities. El Común is a network of associations of peasant producers of different local agricultural products, which also serve youth and women's organisations campaigning for their rights. In the education sector, UniSangil is a higher education institution created through a joint initiative of Catholic Church in collaboration with cooperatives and social organisations in the territory.[9]

10.5 Medio Atrato of Chocó: marginalised territories of emancipation

10.5.1 Local context and the change brought by CEBs

The second regional experience is the community organisation process and solidarity economy practices promoted by the *Seglares Claretianos*,[10] together with the black community organisation, COCOMACIA *(Consejo Comunitario Mayor de la Asociación Campesina Integral del Atrato)*. The region of Medio Atrato is located in the western part of the country, alongside the Atrato River, between four other municipalities of the Chocó Department and three of the Antioquia Department on the Pacific Coast. Notwithstanding its strategic location and its rich biodiversity, Medio Atrato is one of the poorest regions in Colombia in terms of gross regional product and availability of basic public services. Since the late 1990s, due to an increase in violent incidents, forced displacement has intensified.

From the beginning of colonisation by the Spaniards in the early 18th Century, the Chocó territory was targeted for its potential to become an enclave economy because of its natural resources – gold in particular. Most enslaved black people in the Virreinato de Nueva Granada (today Colombia) were sent to the Pacific region of the Chocó to work for the royal mines. The majority of the present-day communities surrounding the Atrato River were founded following independence and the abolition of slavery in the 19th Century by free afro-descendants who moved away from the mines searching for alternative modes of life (González Escobar, 2003: 61–62). Since then, people have lived at subsistence levels by combining artisanal mining, forestry, self-provisioning agriculture, fishing and hunting.

Father Gonzalo De la Torre, appointed as provincial of the Occidental Region of the Congregation of Claretian Missionary in 1970, who was inspired by the philosophy of liberation theology, decided to get involved in the region of Medio Atrato. His aim was to change the conventional mentality of priests who used to view black communities as barbarians. Settling in the community of Beté, a hamlet in Medio Atrato, in 1979, De la Torre started evangelising, while sharing the daily lives of local people. A secular group called *Seglares Claretianos* had always worked with him. At that time, basic infrastructure and public services were scarce, and the communities' basic human needs were far from being satisfied.

The first mission of the Seglares Claretianos was to promote economic activities so that people could overcome their suffering. The process started with a participative diagnosis so that the afro-descendant people could articulate their own needs and problems. The survey soon revealed abandonment by the Colombian state in the areas of education, health, transportation and logistics, job creation, technical assistance to peasant producers and all areas of social and family welfare, especially childcare. Based on this diagnosis, they built a cafeteria for school children, coordinated along with the ICBF (Colombian Institute for Family Welfare). With guidance from Dancoop (the National Department for the promotion of cooperatives), they built a community shop as their first attempt to create a cooperative.

The Seglares Claretianos also organised a small group of adults, especially aged persons, for Bible reading, which was the origin of the CEB (Base Ecclesial Community) in Medio Atrato. Starting with Beté, CEB undertook social action in an expanding area of intervention among communities in the Medio Atrato. In each community, they built a kindergarten, a house for missionaries and a chapel and places to develop community-based productive activities. Their commitment was indispensable in supporting black community organisations to defend their collective territories and ethnic and cultural identity and to activate the consciousness of women and of youth in order to help create new forms of leadership.

10.5.2 Solidarity economy adapted to the Afro-Atrato situation

To promote endogenous economic activity, the first step was to create a community shop in Beté in the form of a multi-functional cooperative. This experience was very successful and persisted until 1987. However, another community shop in Tagachí had a shorter life. It started as a pre-cooperative in 1981, but friction with local merchants meant that it was dissolved in four years. Following this, the communities abandoned cooperatives as an organisational model for developing their community-based economic activities because they did not have the material conditions necessary to establish more cooperatives.[11]

After this experience, the people and Seglares Claretianos shifted to promoting "community enterprises" via different types of community-based economic organisations, such as sugar mills for sugar cane, threshing machines for rice, tailoring workshops, carpenter's workshop and community shops (see Table 10.5). "Community Enterprise" was an alternative framing, adapted to the people's realities, culture and customs. Within this framing, ownership of the enterprise belongs to the organised community, profits contribute to the services for the whole community and all important decisions should be taken collectively by the general assembly. These principles of community enterprise identify as solidarity economy (Seglares Claretianas, 2005: 37–42). Furthermore, it seeks to promote an alternative way of living in three main

Table 10.5 Principal "community enterprises" created during the 1980s and 1990s

Solidarity economy activities	*Origin*	*Significant aspects*	*Obstacles to sustainability*
Community shops	Difficulties in commercialising regional products and obtaining basic and essential goods.	Due to the intensified armed conflict, the community started to run the shop with humanitarian aid.	Purchase by credit. Poor administration due to a lack of technical training of the people.
Mills for sugar cane	The sugar mills built for the local liquor industry were suspended for years. The community decided to work with sugar mills as their own community enterprise.	Due to the suspension of the departmental program for the sugar mill industry, the sugar cane crop decreased in production.	Purchase by credit. Damage of machinery and equipment, without subsequent repair. Lack of technical knowledge about processing. Due to higher profit from local alcohol, motivation to process sugar cane for honey declined.
Threshing machines for rice	Strategic location to benefit various communities.	The decision taken about location was a consequence of agreement among the different communities who identify themselves as living in the same geographical "zone".	Damage to machinery and theft of rice and equipment. Tendency to purchase with credit.
Carpenter's workshop	For the land characteristic of being mainly tropical forest.	Isolation of the community due to the intensified armed conflict.	Displacement of the community gave the opportunity for theft of machinery and equipment. No repair to damaged machinery.
Tailoring workshops, art and craft workshops.	The Baha'i Church motivated some local women to organise a tailoring group, without success. COCOMACIA took over the initiative and made another proposal for ICBF.	Women work for the benefit of the community and help the functioning of CEMA (Centro Etnoeducativo del Medio Atrato)	Damage to machinery due to disuse. The decline of the women's motivation to continue.

Source: Seglares Claretianas (2005)

ways. First, the community enterprise should be run "with the communities", and its self-administration seeks to achieve a more autonomous society. Second, community enterprises seek alternative models of economy that differ from capitalism. Third, these productive activities follow the concept of ethnodevelopment.

10.5.3 Fight for the collective territory and community organisation

The process of promoting a solidarity economy occurred together with the fight for the right to collective territory in the black community. The Afro-Colombian social movement had made progress in claiming collective ancestral rights since the 1980s, which became legalised through the new Constitution in 1991 and related laws established in the early 1990s. Decreto 1745/1995 stipulates concrete procedures for recognising collective property rights to "Black Communities' Land". This regulation obliges the black community to set up a common council (*consejo comunitario*), a legal entity of the highest authority that internally administers black communities' land. In the Medio Atrato region, the communities first organised themselves as ACIA, which was transformed into COCOMACIA in 1982 (De La Torre, 2002).

The two processes – popular education by CEBs and community organisation through COCOMACIA – have been essential to communities' protection of their own territory in the face of the armed conflict and violence associated with the growing scale of extractivist development, which has intensified since the 1990s. From the mid-1990s, guerrilla groups were forced to advance their front line from more central areas of the country towards the Pacific Coast. Fumigation of coca crops in the central and southern regions of the country also pushed the frontier of coca cultivation towards the western and Pacific regions (Hataya, 2011). Since 2000, illegal mining and oil palm plantations have greatly affected the river ecosystem of the region. Mining equipment and teams are usually escorted by armed groups, most of them presumed to be paramilitary groups. This overall picture suggests a linkage between armed warfare and the aggressive development model employed by global and national interests in pursuit of natural resources. Escalating violence and the threat of displacement caused by armed conflict and aggressive development are the main reasons why alternative economic activities backed by popular education need to be mobilised in defence of the territory. One positive outcome of this situation has been formation of the movement for environmental protection, leading to a formal declaration of the legal right of the Atrato River to conservation and protection in 2016.[12]

10.5.4 Challenges of ASPRODEMA as the new exploration of community enterprise

Under these circumstances, ASPRODEMA (Association of Producers of Medio Atrato) was established through a constitutional assembly of COCOMACIA in 2008. ASPRODEMA is a non-profit organisation aiming to improve the living conditions of peasants in the Medio Atrato. In April 2022, the associations represented 435 people (ASPRODEMA, 2022).

ASPRODEMA promotes agricultural production, processing and commercialisation without the intermediation of a third party. Under the framework of a "circular economy", its associates build solidarity networks and alliances with consumers, thus providing services and products of quality. Their promotion of responsible production and consumption is also consistent with the ethical principles of the solidarity economy.

ASPRODEMA is an autonomous organisation that took over the mission and philosophy of the community enterprises promoted by Seglares Claretianos. Most community enterprises are now working as members of ASPRODEMA in a more autonomous way. They have gained the capacity to approach external organisations and to obtain financial and technical support. This is one of the most significant consequences of the long history of resistance by afro-descendant communities, which has converged upon their fundamental strategy of defending collective territory and natural resources, thereby guaranteeing the capacity for food sovereignty through self-provisioning and solidarity economy.

10.6 Comparative analysis of the two regional experiences

The practices and organisational units of solidarity economy offer enormous variety in terms of characteristics and historical processes according to country, region and locality. In the case of Colombia, as explained earlier in this chapter, the institutional framework has been vague. As Dávila pointed out, in Colombia "the solidarity economy is just emerging as an incipient social movement, as it does not yet have a sufficient identity to give it meaning, given the heterogeneity and diversity of practices that could be classified as solidarity economies" (Dávila *et al.*, 2018: 108–109).

Illustrating this statement, we have described two different regional experiences, which are similar in that they were originally promoted by the social action of the Catholic Church. The southern Santander case was one of the pioneering cooperative movements in Colombia, while the experience of afro-community enterprise in Medio Atrato has been part of a fight to defend their territory. The Medio Atrato solidarity economy movement initially failed in its attempts to create cooperatives, but finally invented its own form of community enterprise as a hybrid unit of solidarity economy by building a circular economy within a very adverse local context.

A number of important implications arise from comparing these two experiences. We have identified six key features that together demonstrate the meaning, scope and further lessons of the solidarity economy movement backed by popular education.

The first is *in relation to the geographical, ethnic and cultural characteristics*. Southern provinces of Santander have easy access to transportation linkages with major cities. In contrast, the Medio Atrato region, including its capital city Quibdó, has poor access to neighbouring departments inland and has consequently been isolated from urban centres, which has helped the region to conserve its rich biodiversity in the Pacific basin. The population of the southern provinces of Santander is mainly mestizo, while the major part of Medio Atrato's population was made up of afro-descendent and indigenous people, who had been exploited by economic extractivism, including the extraction of gold and timber. The two regions show enormous differences in terms of geography, ethnicity, history and cultural conditions. Their circumstances in the particular historical moment, which coincided with the most severe violence in their territories, were also different.

The two regions are similar in terms of *their socioeconomic conditions in the initial stage of settlement*, characterised by high levels of poverty, challenging employment conditions due to the low levels of job creation, lack of association among workers[13] and scarcity of public services resulting from neglect by the state. Both regions also suffered from the presence of illegal armed organisations such as guerrilla groups, paramilitary groups and drug-traffickers. However, this similarity was relative, as shown by Santander's greater success in developing the cooperative movement due to the presence of a basic financial sector and local commerce in the towns. The Santander provinces as a whole had better conditions for promoting entrepreneurship, while in Medio Atrato, communities tried to develop cooperatives, but logistic conditions and high levels of violence prevented them from doing so.

Third, curiously enough, both regional practices were originally inspired by social action oriented by the liberation theology of the Catholic Church and other religious groups. The trigger *to inspire people to overcome their situation and transform their society* in both regions came through the message of emancipation (liberalisation) preached by the missionaries and based in the social doctrines of the Catholic Church. The Diocese of Socorro and San Gil (in the southern province of Santander) promoted the creation of cooperatives and other forms of solidarity economy organisations, while the Diocese of Quibdó focused on the evangelisation of liberalisation and cultural integration and establishment of community-based organisations. In this process, the main objective they had in common was to develop in tandem with their communities to bring about social transformation and in the process to create a more just and fraternal society.

Fourth, with regard to *intervention strategies on the part of agents of evangelisation and social action within the Catholic Church*, both regions had a similar axis and philosophy, but each used different methods. The principal areas of intervention in both regions were formation of working groups, integral evangelisation through small community groups (CEB), development of popular education, promotion of community-based local broadcasting and the establishment of community-based production sectors. Popular education, formation of autonomous community organisations, management of financial resources and active participation of secular actors are the most common strategies of integral evangelisation. In the case of the southern province of Santander, the strategy chosen was to promote different types of cooperatives in order to resolve community problems. The first cooperatives founded had multiple functions but were soon obliged to become specialised due to government regulations. In the Medio Atrato region, attempts were also made to create community shops in the form of cooperatives. However, this organisational type had to be abandoned when local conditions did not meet the requirements of institutional and legal frameworks for their regulation. Instead, "community enterprises" were created as an alternative unit of community-based solidarity economy, applicable to local conditions.

There were two other major factors that distinguished the key actors in the two cases: relations with the State and access to international financial support.

In both cases, the local community was the main actor in the solidarity economy movement, along with SEPAS and Seglares Claretianos, who were the respective facilitators of the processes. However, multiple further actors in the two territories were involved, including youth and women's groups, community organisations (e.g. the communal action committee, JAC, in each neighbourhood, along with village and parish organisations), the secondary or national-level organisation of Pastoral Social and others.

In the case of Santander, labour unions and municipal government officials also participated. In the case of the Medio Atrato, indigenous organisations were included, with CES working together with indigenous communities within the same locality. It is worth mentioning that the philosophy of Seglares Claretianos was based on the concept of cultural integration, which respected the authentic culture of the black and indigenous communities.

The local solidarity economy movements had close relationships with social movements for the right to adequate public services, as well as for the defence of territory and peace. Demand for public services and state assistance for production was the origin of the peasant labour union in Santander. Claim for the collective rights for their territory by the afro-community organisation in the Medio Atrato, especially for human rights after the intensification of armed conflict, was paramount. In both regions, advocacy action often provoked tension with the State, which caused them to be stigmatised. Nevertheless, their activity has been sustained thanks to international financial and moral support, which have come from international Christian organisations and organisations for human rights, including Misereor, the Inter-American Foundation and Adveniat, among others.

Table 10.6 summarises how the two experiences compare along these dimensions.

Reflecting on the implications for theoretical discussion of the Latin American solidarity economy (see for example, Coraggio, 2015a; Guerra, 2002, 2007; Marañón-Pimentel, 2011; Quijano, 2008; Razeto Migliaro, 1995; and Singer & Schiochet, 2015), both cases successfully advanced along their path in search

Table 10.6 Comparison of the two regional cases

Region as the solidarity territory		*Provinces of the southern Santander*	*Medio Atrato Region of Chocó*
Leading educator		Fr. Ramón González (priest and director of SEPAS)	Fr. Gonzalo De la Torre (Claretian missionary)
Ideological position		The Gospel, the social thought of the Catholic Church, particularly the Second Vatican Council and the documents of the Episcopal Conference of Bishops of Latin America.	
Support group		SEPAS	Seglares Claretianas
International financial support		Misereor, Pan para el Mundo, Adveniat, Cevemo, Catholic Relief Services, Inter-American Foundation	Misereor, Pan para el Mundo, Adveniat, Cevemo
Fields of activity to promote solidarity economy	Recovery of their own land	Mobilisation of peasant organisations for the recovery of land for cultivation	Mobilisation of community organisations of Afro-Colombians for legal rights to recover their collective territories
	Promotion of community-based peasant organisations	"*El Común*" as integral organisation of small producers and peasant organisations	ACIA (later COCOMASIA), motivated by defence of collective territories; in Atrato following the same principles as in Santander; the principles of the Claretian missionaries have special influence
	Popular education for integral change of the society	Popular education to create peasant leaders, using mobile classrooms and teaching equipment	EBCs (Ecclesiastic Base Communities) and its social action for adult education for literacy.
	Organisations to help endogenous local development	Foundation of multifunctional cooperatives, later mainly converted into loans and savings cooperatives	Foundation of health attention centre and kindergarten (nursery).

(*Continued*)

Table 10.6 (Continued)

Region as the solidarity territory		*Provinces of the southern Santander*	*Medio Atrato Region of Chocó*
	Promotion of alternative productive organisations (practices of solidarity economy)	Cooperatives of producers (of local products: fique, coffee, cacao, tobacco, etc.), cooperatives for transport, healthcare, food processing and distribution	Community enterprises for processing of local products (community sugar mill of sugar cane, community carpentry shop-woodworking, rice processing and distribution with the aim of food security and sovereignty)
	Recovery and diffusion of local people's own culture, knowledge and tradition	Community broadcasting for the dissemination of local information (Resander)	Recovery and reactivation of the authentic culture (dancing, music and art) (Centro Cultural Mama Ú); community broadcasting (COCOMACIA Stereo)
	Construction of autonomous educational institutions	UniSangil, IDEAR (Instituto Técnico para el Desarrollo Rural), Instituto COOMULDESA, Colegio Cooperativo	UniClaretiana
	Attention to women and youths	Formation of women's groups and youth groups	Formation of women's and youth groups for art, crafts, dancing, music and theatre
	Ecological protection	Construction of rural water pipes, ecological tourism	Protection of the rights of the River Atrato (through legal framework)

of alternative modes of economy and life, despite their peaceful struggle for justice in the face of armed conflict and scarcity of state support. Solidarity economy practices have been promoted by local leaders, with the goal of liberation through popular education.

Considering debates on the institutionalisation of solidarity economy in Latin America, both regional cases in Colombia are set within the mixed economy, as described by Coraggio (2015b: 141–147). However, relationships among the solidarity economy, state and market have not been fully developed. As a result, conflict frequently arises in these two relationships because of the legal framework that, ironically, is supposed to promote the solidarity economy.

The nature of solidarity economy in real life keeps changing according to the local context. This produces the hybridity shown by the case of the community enterprises that became successful alternatives as a result of their experience with failed cooperatives. The hybrid strategy was employed by local communities to sustain their own mode of economy in a way that reflected the realities of their lives, as well as to achieve autonomous and endogenous governance and management. Thus, the support of external actors has been crucial to local communities who have raised consciousness about their right and capacity to solve their own problems, while at the same time risking dependencies that could impede local autonomy. Autonomy and self-administration of the practices of solidarity economy are, after all, the keys to determining the sustainability of local practices of a solidarity economy.

10.7 Conclusion

As shown by the two regional experiences, mainstream history has attempted to legitimise the repression and aggression imposed by the state and global capital under the guise of an inclusive development policy.[14] In contrast, marginalised communities have struggled to gain visibility in public eyes for their legitimate strategies to defend their territories and ways of life.

The two communities have some features in common: they have experienced a long history of deprivation since the Spanish conquest, which continued as a consequence of a policy of extraction of natural resources for the global market. Their ongoing condition of misery and abandonment by the state are derived from an essentially unchanging internal colonialism. Violence and injustice have been critical problems since the 1960s, even though the solidarity economy movement was promoted by liberation theology and popular education. Although the strategies of these two regions were characterised by their respective particularities, according to socio-political circumstances, ethnic identities and involved external actors, they have a shared aspiration for endogenous development and consciousness of sustainability in terms of ecological conservation. Their social strategies to achieve the dignity of life in both territories have been inspired by the liberating messages of the Gospel of Jesus of Nazareth, who proposed a new commandment of love that calls one to work in favour of human rights, education, organisation, communication and the protection of nature as conditions for a human life with dignity.

The long-term results have differed, mainly due to environmental, cultural and political conditions in the territories. The consolidation of peace, the establishment of a sustainable development model, the honest administration of public resources, the recognition of the rights of nature and the collaboration of the state with the territories continue to be the main challenges for the country and the communities that inhabit the case study territories.

Looking at the current situation in 2023, selective assassinations targeting community leaders are desperately cruel and might devastate their motivation to continue what they have been doing for communities in search of a life with dignity. Their activism and advocacy regarding a life with dignity, collective rights and the rights of nature should be heard and recognised, especially by the international community, since the appreciation of what they intend to do for the whole community and its surroundings will undoubtedly help us to learn the path to save our lives and the planet.

Notes

1. Fuerzas Armadas Revolucionarias de Colombia.
2. The Episcopal Conference of Latin America (ECLA).
3. These four expressions refer to the different forms of collaborative work among local people in the same community.
4. Law 454/1998 is derived from the new 1991 Constitution, which recognises the importance of solidarity economy in several articles.
5. Congreso de la República. (1998, 6 de agosto). Ley 454 de 1998. Diario Oficial N.° 43.357. www.secretariasenado.gov.co/senado/basedoc/ley_0454_1998.html
6. Confederación de Cooperativas de Colombia.
7. Pope Pius XI, 40 years after *Rerum Novarum*, sent the encyclical *Quadragesimo Anno* to the Universal Church.
8. The Second Vatican Council consisted of a Universal Assembly of bishops of the Catholic Church held between 1962 and 1965. As a product of the deliberations made over the years, several documents were published to bring about changes in ecclesial organisation.
9. For the institutional structure, see the website of each network: Coopcentral (www.coopcentral.com.co/), Resander (www.resander.com/), UniSangil (www.unisangil.edu.co/), El Común, (www.elcomun.org/). For the network of community aqueducts, see www.facebook.com/Red-Regional-de-Acueductos-Comunitarios-Agua-para-la-Vida-691964474637398/
10. The secular group of the missionary and apostolic Congregation of Claretians, who are dedicated to the social action of the Catholic Church (Diocesan church) in the Medio Atrato region. In that period, Diocesan Church in Quibdó, capital city of Chocó Department, coordinated its social action *(pastral social)* with the secular group of the Claretian congregation.
11. For example it requires that a cooperative should have a certified public accountant, or some agent should take learning courses offered by DANCOOP and community

leaders should therefore commute to the urban centre from the communities, but they could not afford to pay the costs of transportation.
12. The Constitutional Court of Colombia recognised through *Sentencia T-622/2016* that the Atrato River is subject to rights to guarantee its conservation and protection (www.corteconstitucional.gov.co/relatoria/2016/t-622-16.htm).
13. Association is the name of the unit of social organisation of workers in search of the common good, recognised by the state (and different from a labour union) – for example *Asociación Nacional de Usuarios Campesinos*.
14. In the National Development Plan (2018–2022) of the Duque presidency, the main slogan "Pact for Colombia, pact for the equity" was explained within the discourse of social and productive inclusion. In the same way, international organisations such as OECD have recently used "inclusive growth". The World Economic Forum has published the Inclusive Development Index (IDI) since 2017.

References

Almeida, P. and Cordero Ulate, A. (eds.). (2017). *Movimientos sociales en América Latina*. Buenos Aires: Clacso.

ASPRODEMA (Asociación de Productores del Medio Atrato). (2022). "Informe de gestión ASPRODEMA," (internal document, April 7th, 2022).

Buchelli, M. (2006). *Curas Campesinos y Laicos como gerentes del desarrollo. La construcción de un modelo de desarrollo emergente en Colombia*. San Gil: Edisocial.

Concilio Vaticano II. (1965). *Gaudium Et Spes*. Vaticano. Online at www.vatican.va/archive/hist_councils/ii_vatican_council/documents/vat-ii_const_19651207_gaudium-et-spes_po.html (accessed March 30th 2023).

Confederación de Cooperativas de Colombia (CONFECOOP). (2018). *El valor de la solidaridad. Informe de Desempeño 2017*. Bogotá: CONFECOOP. Online at https://confecoop.coop/wp-content/uploads/2018/11/INFORME-2017.pdf (accessed March 30th 2023).

Coraggio, J. L. (ed.). (2015a). *Economía social y solidaria en movimiento*. Quito: Instituto de Altos Estudios Nacionales (IAEN), Centro de Gobierno y Administración Pública.

Coraggio, J. L. (2015b). "Institutionalising the social and solidarity economy in Latin America," in Utting, P. (ed.) *Social and Solidarity Economy Beyond the Fringe*. London: Zed Books, pp. 130–149.

Corzo Gutiérrez, N., Sarmiento Blanco, U. and Fajardo Rojas, M. A. (2020). "Organizaciones solidarias en las provincias de Guanentá departamento de Santander, Colombia," *Cooperativismo & Desarrollo*, 28(118), pp. 1–29. https://doi.org/10.16925/2382-4220.2020.03.01

Dávila, R., Vargas Prieto, A., Blanco, L., Roa, E., Cáceres, L. E. and Vargas, L. A. (2018). "Características de la economía solidaria colombiana. Aproximaciones a las corrientes influyentes en Colombia," *CIRIEC España, Revista de Economía Pública, Social y Cooperativa*, 93, pp. 85–113.

De la Torre, L. M. (2002). *Medio Arato: Territorio de vida, Historia de la Asociación Campesina Integral del Atrato-ACIA*. Quibdó: Consejo Comunitario Mayor del Medio Atrato.

Fajardo Rojas, M. A., González Parra, S. and Tolosa Suárez, B. (2018). *El Padre Ramón: Un líder que inspira el desarrollo regional*. San Gil: Unisangil Editora.

González Escobar, L. F. (2003). *Quibdó: Contexto Histórico Desarrollo Urbano y Patrimonio Arquitectónico*. Medellín: Universidad Nacional de Colombia, Sede Medellín.

Grupo de Memoria Histórica. (2013). *¡Basta Ya! Colombia: Memorias de guerra y dignidad*. Bogotá: Imprenta Nacional de Colombia.

Guerra, P. A. (2002). *Socioeconomía de la Solidaridad; una teoría para dar cuenta de las experiencias sociales y económicas alternativas*. Montevideo: Editorial Nordan Comunidad.

Guerra, P. A. (2007). La Socioeconomía solidaria como estrategia de desarrollo humano. Conferencia de apertura del II Encuentro Sudamericano de Investigadores en Cooperativismo: "Los aportes de la economía social y solidaria a los retos del Milenio," Bogotá, Colombia.

Hataya, N. (2011). "Integración nacional vs. resistencia local en las comunidades afrocolombianas: El Código de Minas y sus contradicciones," in Javeriana, D. V. D. (ed.) *Las memorias del VII Seminario Internacional de Desarrollo Rural: Mundos rurales y transformaciones globales: Desafíos y estrategias de respuesta*. Bogotá: Pontificia Universidad Javeriana.

Marañón-Pimentel, B. (2011). "Elementos comunes en los Movimientos de economía solidaria y sustentabilidad ambiental en México", Paper presented at the 8th Congress of the Asociación Mexicana de Estudios Rurales Campesinos y Procesos Rurales (Diversidad, Disputas y Alternativas Puebla), Puebla, México, May 24–27, 2011.

Nickson, A. (2019). Movimientos insurgentes en América Latina después de la guerra fría: El caso del Ejército Popular Paraguayo. *Nova Polis*, (15), pp. 62–84. Online at http://pyglobal.com/ojs/index.php/novapolis/article/view/104 (accessed March 30th 2023).

Quijano, A. (2008). "Solidaridad y capitalismo colonial/moderno," *Otra Economía*, 2(2), pp. 12–16.

Razeto Migliaro, L. (1995). *Los caminos de la economía de la solidaridad*. Santiago de Chile: Impresos.

Seglares Claretianas. (2005). *Economía Solidaria Afro-Atrato: Sistematización de Experiencias*. Quibdó: Editorial Códice.

Singer, P. y V. Schiochet. (2015). "La construcción de la economía solidaria como alternativa al capitalismo," in Coraggio, J. L. (ed.) *Economía Social y Solidaria en Movimiento*. Quito: Instituto de Altos Estudios Nacionales (IAEN), Centro de Gobierno y Administración Pública., pp. 97–124.

SEPAS. (1977). *Hacia el Cambio integral: Plan de pastoral social diócesis de Socorro y San Gil*. Bogotá: Editorial Carrera Séptima.

Superintendencia de Economía Solidaria. (2020). *Entidades Vigiladas*. Online at www.supersolidaria.gov.co/es/content/entidades-vigiladas-que-reportan-informacion-2020 (accessed March 30th 2023).

11 Democratic governance and financial commons

Leonardo Leal

11.1 Introduction

The aim of this chapter is to analyse the democratic governance of commons in experiences of solidarity finance. Fundamentally, it seeks to answer the following question: how do social movement organisations sustain internal democracy within their organisations? In doing so, it seeks to contribute to the knowledge of democratic governance in social movement organisations.

In this work, the analysis of democratic governance in social movement organisations is carried out through the selection of a typical case (Gerring, 2006), aiming to represent the reality of the solidarity finance movement in general and community banks in particular. The empirical phenomenon in question is that of the Ilhamar Community Development Bank (Ilhamar Bank), a community organisation created in August 2007, located in the fishing and shellfish harvesting community of Matarandiba in the municipality of Vera Cruz on Itaparica Island in Bahia, Brazil. This chapter presents the findings of a qualitative study, analysing the factors that influence the practice of democratic governance in social movement organisations of solidarity finance and community banks.

The argument presented is based on studies of the governance of common goods, particularly those of Elinor Ostrom and collaborators (Ostrom & Ostrom, 1979; Ostrom, 2000; Hess & Ostrom, 2007). Commons studies emphasise the construction of alternative governance models for access to goods and services, recognising different modalities of democratic governance, agreements and rule-making. These studies also suggest a set of principles that provide the support and infrastructure for democratic governance of commons, such as: definition of users, type of resource, rules of use, monitoring, penalties and conflict resolution. These categories are therefore used in the present analysis of Ilhamar Bank, in order to understand the factors that constitute the basis of democratic governance of solidarity financial services.

Ilhamar Bank was studied through different techniques and at different times. First, long-term participant observation between 2008 and 2014. Second, semi-structured interviews with 12 key informants between 2019 and 2020. Third,

DOI: 10.4324/9781003306344-12

analysis of available secondary data, including accountability reports and other documents.

This chapter is organised into five subsequent sections. Section 11.2 introduces a literature review on solidarity finance organisations and interpretative perspectives. Section 11.3 concerns the theme of democratic governance of commons as a transversal paradigm for understanding the practices of the solidarity finance movement and community banks. Section 11.4 focuses on presenting the experience of the Ilhamar Community Bank, its origin, evolution and research results. Section 11.5 analyses Ilhamar Bank in light of the categories of democratic governance of commons. Finally, Section 11.6 presents some conclusions and reflections.

The main results of this research indicate that democratic governance in social movement organisations, especially in solidarity finance and community banks, is sustained by an infrastructure that combines practices of collective self-organisation, emphasising the adoption of agreements, creation of rules that define limits and respect for the diversity of actors involved in a logic of polycentric governance.

11.2 Solidarity finance organisations: understanding perspectives

Solidarity finance organisations operate on ethical, democratic and solidarity principles that condition the creation and maintenance of social ties (Servet & Guérin, 2002; Artis, 2012). At the same time, they provide a range of financial services (microcredit, social currency, etc.) that can invigorate political and economic relations in the territory (Sanchis, 2016). These organisations also put forward a political proposal for financial services that reinvents the conception of wealth within the framework of struggles against domination and inequality (Guérin, 2015) and which constitutes an instrument for democratising economic and market relations (Razeto, 1990).

The most evident manifestation of solidarity finance organisations is the associative and cooperative practices of community banks, ethical banks and financial service cooperatives (Muñoz, 2009; França Filho *et al.*, 2012; Rigo *et al.*, 2015). Mendell and Nogales (2012) and Muñoz (2017) point out that this alternative or parallel form of social finance has grown significantly, complementing the long history of mutualist organisations, credit unions, associations and cooperatives. It has also contributed to a more recent history of social innovation in the field of financial relations, practised by social movements, civil society organisations and communities in different parts of the world.

The last two decades have seen an expansion of studies in the field of social and solidarity finance. Analyses mainly focus on four perspectives of solidarity finance: 1) access to credit and financing, 2) democratisation of the financial system, 3) local development and 4) governance of the commons.

The first perspective concerns solidarity finance as a means of facilitating access to credit for those who create, develop or assume an income-generating activity, especially those who are often excluded from conventional banking channels (Artis, 2012, 2017; Silva & Pereira, 2023).

The second perspective, as presented by Block (2014; also see Dowbor, 2008; Wright, 2010; Mendell, 2015), understands solidarity finance as a potential contribution to reorganising or democratising the financial system, in opposition to the prevailing model of finance that has reinforced global socioeconomic stratification and the unequal distribution of income and power in society.

The third perspective emphasises the role of solidarity finance in poverty reduction (França Filho *et al.*, 2012), allowing groups of people in their respective territories to manage economic resources on the basis of principles of solidarity, trust and mutual aid, creating efficient mechanisms to overcome disadvantages arising from poverty and inequality (França Filho, 2013).

Finally, the fourth perspective frames the governance of solidarity finance organisations in the context of commons, providing financial services under the regime of decisions democratically formulated by social movement organisations, communities and collectives (Leal, 2013; Leal & Santos Almeida, 2016; Hudon & Meyer, 2016; Périlleux & Nyssens, 2017). This idea is connected to governance models beyond market and state relationships (Ostrom, 2000, 2005) and seeks to promote alternatives for re-socialising and re-politicising the economy (De Angelis, 2007; De Angelis & Harvie, 2013). Community banks are seen by these authors as expressive experiences of a new type of commons, which articulates economic and political action (cf. Laville & Eynaud, this volume; Della Porta, this volume).

From this last understanding, it can be inferred that solidarity finance constitutes a genre of financial commons, referring to experiences that decommodify finance, money and debt by placing the principles, rules, regulation and purpose of financial intermediation under democratic governance. To achieve this, they use ethical, fair and solidarity-based principles in creating and operating financial instruments and services.

Recognising the value of each perspective identified in the specialised literature, this chapter relies on the concept of commons to understand democratic governance in organisations of the solidarity finance movement and community banks, directing contestation to the centres of economic power and political power by claiming the democratisation of the economy and the deepening of democracy.

11.3 Commons: a framework for the analysis of democratic governance in solidarity finance organisations

This chapter argues that organisations within the solidarity finance movement and community banks follow strategies of democratic governance that can be better understood through an Ostromian approach. This approach considers trust mechanisms, collective rules and a sense of community all to be important for achieving success and sustainability in the governance of financial commons.

This argument is based on the contributions of different authors to the idea of democratic governance of commons, highlighting the construction of alternative governance models to promote access to goods and services (Ostrom, 2000; Hess & Ostrom, 2007; Laville, 2015; Mattei, 2013). The concept of commons has become central in critical discourse, acquiring political meaning as a challenge to the economic establishment (De Angelis, 2003; Linebaugh, 2008; Federici & Caffentzis, 2013; Bianchi, 2018). Commons have become a prominent feature of many social movements, such as open-source computing, environmentalism, climate action, feminism, solidarity economy and others (Bollier & Helfrich, 2019; also see Della Porta, this volume).

Democratic governance refers to an organisational form in which decision-making is decentralised, non-hierarchical and consensus-based, animated by a prefigurative impulse that seeks to create a society marked by values of radical equality, freedom and community (Polletta, 2013). Although challenging, democratic governance functions as a type of shared belief and a means of maintaining commitment among members (Della Porta, 2013).

The notion of commons, in turn, refers to collective forms of organisation of the production and distribution of wealth and value that aim to displace market forces and capital accumulation (Harvey, 2010, 2012). Furthermore, it can be conceived as a mode of collective production and reproduction, a possibility of governing goods and services that are not subject to the market and State (Federici, 2018; De Angelis, 2017).

Political scientist Elinor Ostrom (2000, 2005) brought the category of commons back to the heart of academic debate with her book *Governing the Commons*. She demonstrated the ability of individuals to self-organise in collective institutional systems through which they are able to share resources without having to privatise or nationalise in order to avoid the so-called "tragedy of the commons" (Hardin, 1968).

Distrustful of the belief that problems of allocation of economic and environmental resources can only be solved by governmental action or through market competence, Ostrom (2000) formulated the concept of collective management of common goods, demonstrating that people are capable of self-organising and creating cooperative initiatives that can survive for long periods. It is therefore necessary to understand the viability of self-organised systems, and instead of relying entirely on governments and businesses to protect and govern resources, to make room for self-management by local populations. Thus, Ostrom (2000) demonstrates that individuals involved in the use of a resource are capable of self-organisation, creating cooperation initiatives to solve scarcity and allocation problems (Ostrom *et al.*, 1992). In these cases, participants design basic operational rules, create organisations to manage shared resources and modify the rules in use over time in light of past experience, according to their own social norms and collective choices (McGinnis & Ostrom, 1996).

Eynaud and Laville (2021) thus understand the practices of democratic governance in the field of solidarity economy as a perspective that seeks to deepen democracy and humanise the economy. This entails taking into account associationalism and forms of self-governance implemented through the collective action of people who choose freely and voluntarily how to govern material and/or immaterial goods through agreements of democratic governance (cf. Eynaud & Laville, this volume). In this sense, collective action for the governance of commons relates to the political action of associated actors, signifying a political act to put goods and services under a regime of democratic governance and common use, aligning with a logic of prefigurative politics (de Tocqueville, 2000; Leach, 2013).

Ostrom's work originally focused on natural resources, such as forests and groundwater (Ostrom, 2000). It subsequently extended its range of application to other common goods (Hess & Ostrom, 2007; Hess, 2008) in areas such as cultural heritage, knowledge, urban planning and others. Recently, new research trends have emerged that address the politicisation of commons (e.g. Bollier & Helfrich, 2013, 2015; Henfrey & Kenrick, 2017). In light of this, some authors associated with social and solidarity economy studies have begun to refer to financial commons, on the basis of findings from research on solidarity finance organisations, namely community banks (Leal, 2013; Hudon & Meyer, 2016; Périlleux & Nyssens, 2017; Dissaux, 2019).

Ostrom's empirical research (2000) revealed that under certain conditions, people can cooperatively appropriate a resource. She identified a number of fundamental principles for the longevity of these initiatives, which are communication among users of a resource, user-defined rules for use of a resource, agreement on levels of resource utilisation and defined penalties for non-compliance with established rules. Thus, different communities have relied on institutions that do not resemble either the State or the market to regulate commons, with significant levels of success over long periods of time (Ostrom, 2000). Based on these principles, Ostrom proposes a theoretical framework identifying explanatory factors concerning under what conditions it is most likely that common resource users will self-organise and effectively govern their own resources.

Therefore, a group of people involved in a concrete situation can solve the problem of institutional provision through mechanisms of trust and a sense of community (Ostrom, 2000). This trust, in turn, results from a set of principles and rules agreed upon and shared by those involved in the collective management of a good. These principles and rules include:

a) Establish a set of authorised users who are permitted to utilise resources in a manner that includes usage limits.
b) Ensure congruence between the characteristics of the resource and territory and the governance rules.

c) Create and define rules with the direct participation of resource users.
d) Implement monitoring mechanisms that are controlled by the resource users themselves.
e) Establish gradual sanctions that are defined and used by the users themselves to discourage non-compliance.

When a group or community of individuals establish principles and rules that satisfy these criteria, they can establish a secure, mutually advantageous and viable commitment. The commitment among users is maintained whenever: 1) individuals placed in similar situations adopt the same commitment and 2) the long-term outcomes are more beneficial than those of individuals who follow short-term strategies (Ostrom, 2000).

Study of a practical case of democratic governance in the context of solidarity finance – that of Ilhamar Community Bank – confirms the relevance and applicability of this set of principles and rules. Based on the Ostromian model of democratic governance of the commons, the following section seeks to demonstrate how such a process was effectively implemented in the experience of Ilhamar Bank.

11.4 The Ilhamar community bank: an emblematic experience

A community development bank is an organisation whose main objective is to promote the development of the local community. The first initiative of this type emerged in 1998 with Banco Palmas in the city of Fortaleza, Ceará. Currently, there are more than 150 community banks that are part of the Brazilian Network of Community Development Banks. These banks aim to invest in territorial capacity for production, service generation and consumption. To achieve this goal, they provide financing and guidance for the development of socio-productive initiatives, local services and consumption. In addition to providing microcredit for different purposes, the main mission of these banks is to promote the construction of local solidarity economy networks, encouraging collaboration among local producers, service providers and consumers (França Filho *et al.*, 2012).

The Community Development Bank (hereinafter Ilhamar Bank) presents a set of characteristics that evidence the conditions for sustainability and longevity of democratic governance in the allocation of financial services. Ilhamar Bank is located in the village of Matarandiba in the municipality of Vera Cruz, Bahia (Brazil). It is a member of the Matarandiba Solidarity Culture and Economy Network, which is supported by a university outreach project that began in 2007 under the coordination of the Solidarity Economy Technological Incubator and Territorial Development Management at the Federal University of Bahia (ITES/UFBA). The bank benefits from democratic governance structures created in the Matarandiba Network, such as the social participation of users in community organisations, the provision of solidarity financial services, the participation and management bodies of the bank and its integration into the local network (Souza, 2019).

Ilhamar Bank was founded on April 27, 2008, by a collective of young people who are part of the Matarandiba Community Association (ASCOMA). The collective had two objectives – to provide access to financial services (such as microcredit and social currency) for investments in socioeconomic activities generating work and income and to promote social participation of the community in activities carried out by the association and the community bank (Projeto Ecosmar, 2008).

The village of Matarandiba is a traditional community of fishermen and shellfish gatherers, whose population, of approximately 1200 families, lives on income generated by tourism, artisanal fishing and mangrove extraction (Projeto Ecosmar, 2008). Like many other traditional and extractive communities in Brazil, Matarandiba suffers numerous deficits in the educational, economic and social spheres and displays significant poverty indicators. Statistics reported in 2020 by the Brazilian Institute of Geography and Statistics for the municipality of Vera Cruz, where Matarandiba is located, show that only 10% of residents have formal employment, 72% live in conditions of poverty and extreme poverty and only 15% have completed high school. In Vera Cruz, the Human Development Index of 0.645 is below the national average, while the average family income is half the minimum wage.

Ilhamar Bank focuses its actions on two main activities: solidarity microcredit and the social currency Concha. Solidarity microcredit is the main strategy used to finance production, service provision and consumption activities. In general, financing for productive activities is carried out in national currency (i.e. in Real, or R$), while supply for consumption (basic food items) takes place almost entirely in social currency. Based on management reports from Ilhamar Bank, it was possible to systematically record the provision of microcredit between April 2008 and December 2021. A total of 2,650 credits were released, distributed in credit lines for Family Consumption (1,340), Production and Services (900), Reform and Housing (350) and Youth Credit (160). 50.6 percent of credit requests are thus intended for household consumption and are entirely made with the Concha social currency, demonstrating widespread use of this payment method in the village of Matarandiba. Of all the credit released, only 4.5% was not repaid (Projeto Ecosmar, 2021).

The governance structure of Ilhamar Bank consists of four levels: in addition to the ASCOMA association as the managing entity, there are the bank's management council and credit evaluation committee (CAC), along with an operational team. Furthermore, Ilhamar Bank is organised into two networks, one local (the Matarandiba Network) and one national (the Brazilian Community Banks Network).

ASCOMA is the managing entity responsible for legal and administrative representation of Ilhamar Bank. It also convenes the local network articulator, organising forums, creating new socioeconomic ventures and representing the community politically in relation to the government.

The governing council is composed of a group of local organisations and community leaders. It has the function of governing the bank, defining its policy and operational strategy. The representativeness of the organisations and leaders is quite diverse, including cultural groups, churches and schools, as well as young leaders and fishermen.

Regarding the credit evaluation committee, its responsibilities relate to the decision-making process regarding issuing credit. The decisions of this committee are based on ethical, social and economic criteria and may result in the approval, revision or denial of credit requests made by users. In this sense, evaluations and decisions consider the social utility and economic viability of microcredit beneficiaries' ventures.

The bank's operational team, finally, fulfils daily administrative and user relationship functions, which are also considered of great relevance in mediating and resolving conflicts.

The networks in which Ilhamar Bank is integrated are instances of participation at the local and national levels, as well as spaces for creating internal and external agreements. In these spaces, network cooperation strategies are discussed, relating to action both within and outside the community. The Brazilian network of community banks, for example, defines a set of principles and methodologies for the operation of community banks associated with the network. It is also a type of social movement in the field of solidarity economy that seeks to influence the formulation of public policies for the solidarity finance sector. The Matarandiba Network of Culture and Solidarity Economy, in turn, brings together community organisations working in the domains of culture, economy and environmental sustainability, aiming at generating work, income and social participation. Both contribute to a characteristic of multi-level governance of Ilhamar Bank regarding rules and decision-making.

Regarding the control of defaults, such situations are treated as a type of conflict resolution, conducted by the CAC and operational team. Thus, insolvency cases are also addressed through democratic governance in a process that can be called debt decommodification: criteria that are eminently technical and financial are avoided in favour of considerations of social utility.

These structures provide the necessary political and organisational support for the exercise of democratic governance at Ilhamar Bank, enabling greater participation of community members in strategic and daily decisions.

11.5 Analysis of democratic governance and financial commons at Ilhamar community bank

This section aims to elucidate the underlying mechanisms and structures of democratic governance in Ilhamar Bank. It therefore describes an analysis of research results in the light of categories of commons governance, highlighting five dimensions: resource users, type of resource, definition of usage rules, monitoring of rules and resources and sanctions in case of non-compliance.

The first step is to consider the Ilhamar Bank's definition of authorised resource users and usage limits. Defining the limits of resource use at Ilhamar Bank is a central concern, as bank members are committed to the longevity of resources and providing access to the largest possible number of users. Thus, the Matarandiba community, through meetings and assemblies, decided that Ilhamar Bank's financial services should be directed exclusively to residents of the territory. The use of financial services imposes certain conditions, such as being of legal age (18 years), participating in local solidarity economy community activities and adhering to the Concha social currency system.

Only one criterion was used for determining who can access Ilhamar Bank's services: being a resident of the Matarandiba Village. However, some requirements were specified: 1) length of residency in the community – people who have lived there for less than a year cannot use the services, except in exceptional situations approved by the credit evaluation committee; 2) temporary residents are not eligible for credit, in order to prevent access by seasonal inhabitants; 3) the user must have a history of good neighbourly relations – residents persistently involved in conflicts and of poor reputation in the community are provided access on an incremental basis and under various conditions, so as not to represent a financial risk or compromise the organisation's credibility; neighbourhood approval may also be required.

According to data collected from documents and interviews, the limits on the use of resources refer to two issues: the value of credit and the number of times a user can request credit during a given time period. Limits for the value that can be requested under each credit line – Consumer Credit, Production and Services, Home Improvement and Housing, Youth Credit – as well as the interest rates and payment terms, are collectively defined by the management council of Ilhamar Bank. Regarding the number of times credit can be requested, the rule is to prohibit any user or member of their family from making a new credit request unless previously issued credit has been repaid. It is important to note that these criteria regarding limits on access to resources, defined by the users themselves, aim to promote equitable distribution and greater control over the longevity of financial resources. Their existence has enabled uninterrupted operation of Ilhamar Bank and provision of services for over 13 years.

The second dimension of commons governance considered here concerns the type of resource, taking into account the congruence between the characteristics of the resource and territory and the operating rules. Note that the rules developed for the operation of Ilhamar Bank reflect the specificities of managing financial services from a solidarity perspective, particularly the conditions for provision of bank funds for the operation of microcredit and the credit lines associated with the characteristics and opportunities of a fishing and tourism territory.

At Ilhamar Bank, users who utilise the services seek to carry out socio-economic activities that are congruent with the work culture and natural resources available in the community. The bank's services allow for basic consumption by families, but above all, investment in fishing and tourism activities, as well as in small commercial enterprises that enable the generation of work and income for the local population.

Use of the Concha social currency also reveals an important symbolic element in the use of financial resources. According to the results of this research, Concha is widely used by the Matarandiba community as a means of payment. Users have access to Conchas through microcredit. The ease of circulation of Conchas is due to the simplicity of access rules, their acceptance in the local economy and the symbolic representation that the Concha iconography brings to the community. It can be said that the social currency has become part of the local identity and culture, serving as a symbol of recognition.

Another relevant point concerns the conditions under which Ilhamar Bank raises funds for the microcredit service and circulation of Concha. The financial resources, about R$60,000, come from Dow Brasil, as a philanthropic donation. However, this type of contribution creates an adverse effect for the community bank, as some users perceive it as money from a multinational corporation. For this reason, some residents feel they are not obliged to repay it to Ilhamar Bank. To overcome this view, Ilhamar Bank undertakes strategies to decommodify the funding by proposing that users participate in the democratic governance of financial resources. Additionally, the bank mobilises other sources of funding, for example by participating in public policy contests to support the solidarity economy. These processes seem to represent a type of boundary commoning (De Angelis, 2017) in which the operation of a financial commons can partly modify the nature of a resource by putting it under democratic governance.

The third dimension of commons governance pertains to defining rules for resource usage with direct participation from local users. At Ilhamar Bank, there are certain principles that translate into collectively decided operating rules. Governance rules constitute mechanisms that guide, discipline and direct the daily workings of the bank. Here, we refer to the work of the management board, credit assessment committee (CAC) and credit agents, along with the rules governing the circulation of the Concha social currency.

The management board is the primary decision-making body at Ilhamar Bank. It includes members of the ASCOMA board and representatives from different segments of the community. In addition to representing users, the board is responsible for debating, developing and updating the operating rules of the community bank while also ensuring its financial sustainability.

The CAC sits at an intermediate level of decision-making, as it has the responsibility of analysing and deciding on credit requests from users and may also act as a mediator in conflict resolution. The operating rules of the CAC take into account economic and financial criteria (adoption of the Concha social currency, loan value and capacity to repay) as well as social criteria (trust relationships, socio-environmental objectives, need and usefulness of credit for users).

The work of credit agents, mainly carried out by women, is based on the rules and procedures created by the management board and CAC, involving tasks such as user support and guidance, request registration and monitoring throughout the microcredit cycle. Agents also provide guidance to users on the use and application of credit, as well as in mediating conflicts and finding solutions to situations of default or insolvency.

Regarding the Concha social currency, the system involves a close relationship among three main actors: Ilhamar Bank, users and local merchants, with each participant having specific responsibilities for the functioning of the system. Ilhamar Bank is responsible for issuing the Concha social currency, offering microcredit in Concha, creating the network of merchant adoption and the agreement for Concha use. Merchants must adopt the social currency system, offer discounts for purchases made in Concha and comply with exchange deadlines and limits for conversion of Concha to Real, permission for which is only granted to merchants who need to purchase stock from the external market. All these procedures give meaning and security to the circulation of the social currency, with the aim of strengthening the local economy, financing production and consumption and ensuring the functioning and continuity of the system.

The rules also serve as a support for the democratic governance structure of Ilhamar Bank, contributing to sustaining the bank's principles and meeting user interests. The definition and periodic revision of operating rules are based on transparency and user participation in Ilhamar's Bank governance. Note that these rules, particularly their updates, are a response to internal and external environmental contingencies, adapting them to conditions better over time.

The fourth dimension refers to the implementation of monitoring under the control and responsibility of the users themselves. This dimension concerns the oversight actions carried out by users directly involved in the governance of Ilhamar Bank, aimed at maintaining system balance, preventing deviations from purpose and ensuring proper use of resources.

We can observe that monitoring of resources, the use of microcredit and operation of a social currency all play fundamental roles in achieving the goals intended by the bank and are directly related to the longevity of Ilhamar's Bank operation over the duration of research.

It is also clear that the use of financial services (microcredit and Concha social currency) requires counter-performance from users, that is repayment, in instalments, of the contracted loan. In this situation, paradoxically, obligated and unobligated relationships are simultaneously established. In the case of credit requests, repayment occurs voluntarily, given that users, in most situations, prefer to comply with collectively agreed rules. Those who do not comply are exposed to moral pressure from neighbours, family and credit agents. Thus, users mostly prefer to pay credits because of the trust placed in them, generating a relationship of reciprocity and avoiding the use of moral pressure. The result is a significantly reduced default rate, with less than 5% of the total credits released not being repaid. It is also evident that there is a type of co-monitoring among users themselves. By noticing that other users comply with established agreements, a virtuous circle is established, so that others also choose to comply. These monitoring mechanisms are perceived as being an integral part of the democratic governance processes of financial commons, allowing them to function sustainably.

It is worth noting that the control of default often results in conflicts and therefore requires social mediation between the bank (CAC and operational team) and users, using social utility criteria to deal with cases of non-compliance. This process, called debt decommodification, is put into practice through a series of measures such as debt suspension for a period, renegotiation of debt terms and provision of services in lieu of repayment. These measures are intended to protect the social and political relationships among community people and Ilhamar Bank.

The fifth and final dimension to be considered here concerns the set of gradual sanctions used by the users themselves against rule-breaking. This refers to certain types of sanctions that were created to curb non-payment of credit and to control the circulation of the social currency Concha.

Default on scheduled repayments of a loan, following attempts at negotiation, results in the prohibition of new requests, which may also be applicable to other family members. Ultimately, the person who took out the loan may be penalised with exclusion from initiatives of the Matarandiba Network, such as services provided by the community association. It should be noted that there are numerous possibilities for negotiation, such as payment on more favourable terms or repayment by providing services or donating goods approved by the management council and CAC.

In cases of improper use of the Concha social currency, a sanction is applied that prevents the user and merchant, for a period stipulated by the management council and CAC, from using the bank's services. During interviews, there was a report of a case that is a good illustration of what can be understood as "improper use." A community merchant was exchanging Concha for Brazilian Real in their establishment, contrary to the established rules, since merchants can only convert Conchas into Real at the Ilhamar Bank headquarters. Once the social currency is acquired, it must be used for the consumption of goods and services in the community and cannot be converted back into Real.

Despite the existence of sanctions, application of penalties is not a routine practice and is not exercised in an authoritarian manner. Penalties occur in specific situations when attempts to negotiate with users are exhausted. However, they are perceived as being important in maintaining a high level of trust among users in the system and discouraging opportunistic behaviour.

Finally, based on Ostrom (2000), it is worth considering that there are other equally important elements for the governance of commons that should be taken into account in future research on financial commons. Among them, we highlight: mechanisms for conflict resolution, levels of institutional recognition by the State and network organisation strategies. These points deserve greater theoretical reflection and empirical research, providing additional elements for understanding the democratic governance of financial commons.

11.6 Conclusions

In order to understand and explain the democratic governance of financial commons in solidarity finance organisations and community banks, the case of Ilhamar Bank was analysed using five analytical categories. Each dimension of analysis is supported by the published literature on commons, forming a theoretical model, as well as using a typical case to represent solidarity finance and community banks.

The analyses carried out in this study suggest four important clues to understanding how social movement organisations of solidarity finance, and community banks, can self-organise for democratic governance of financial commons.

First, it became clear that the existence of rules that delimit the set of authorised users of the resource is a necessary condition for democratic governance to occur. Second, it is observed that the type of resource – solidarity financial services, which is the main focus of democratic governance in Ilhamar Bank – was developed in congruence with the socioeconomic and environmental characteristics of the village of Matarandiba. Third, it is noted that active participation in the definition of the operating rules of Ilhamar Bank is elaborated through participatory processes mediated by the local association and the management council, demonstrating that cooperation among users in defining and updating rules is a necessary condition for effective democratic governance. Fourth, it became evident that monitoring and sanction mechanisms constitute necessary conditions for the balance of the bank system. It was demonstrated that users engage in forms of co-monitoring among themselves. Additionally, there is a set of sanctions that can be applied by the management council to ensure a balance between rights and obligations for the maintenance of democratic governance. Finally, despite there being no institutional recognition of the practice of community banks and solidarity finance, the success of these initiatives can be explained by the dynamism of democratic governance and the participation of communities that mobilise around community bank experiences.

Thus, it is the combination of all the analysed factors that can best explain the democratic governance of financial commons. It is therefore possible to theorise this relationship as follows: application of rules related to authorised users of resources; congruence between resources and community characteristics and participation in defining usage rules, monitoring and penalties. These are the factors that, once combined, can allow us to understand democratic governance in solidarity finance organisations.

References

Artis, A. (2012). *La finance solidaire: Analyse socio-économique d'un système de financement*. Paris: Michel Houdiard éditeur.

Artis, A. (2017). "Social and solidarity finance: A conceptual approach," *Research in International Business and Finance*, 39, pp. 737–749.

Bianchi, I. (2018). "The post-political meaning of the concept of commons: The regulation of the urban commons in Bologna," *Space and Polity*, 22(3), pp. 1–20.

Block, F. (2014). "Democratizing finance," *Politics and Society*, 42(1), pp. 3–28.

Bollier, D. and Helfrich, S. (2013). "Introduction: The commons as a transformative vision," in Bollier, D. and Helfrich, S. (eds.) *The Wealth of the Commons: A World Beyond Market and State*. Amherst: Levellers Press, pp. 8–19.

Bollier, D. and Helfrich, S. (eds.). (2015). *Patterns of Commoning*. Amherst: Commons Strategy Group.

Bollier. D. and Helfrich, S. (2019). *Free, Fair and Alive: The Insurgent Power of the Commons*. Gabriola Island: New Society Publishers.

De Angelis, M. (2003). "Reflections on alternatives, commons and communities or building a new world from the bottom up," *The Commoner*, 6, pp. 1–14.

De Angelis, M. (2007). *The Beginning of History: Value Struggles and Global Capital*. London: Pluto Press.

De Angelis, M. (2017). *Omnia Sunt Communia: On the Commons and Transformation to Postcapitalism*. London: Zed Books.

De Angelis, M. and Harvie, D. (2013). "The Commons," in Parker, M., Cheney, G., Fournier, V. and Land, C. (eds.) *The Routledge Companion to Alternative Organisation*. London: Routledge, pp. 280–94.

De Tocqueville, A. (2000). *Democracy in America*. Translated by H. C. Mansfield and D. Winthrop. Chicago: University of Chicago Press.

Della Porta, D. (2013). "Democracy inside social movements," in Snow, D. A., Della Porta, D. B., Klandermans, B. and McAdam, D. (eds.) *The Wiley-Blackwell Encyclopedia of Social and Political Movements*. Oxford: Wiley-Blackwell, pp. 1–5. https://doi.org/10.1002/9780470674871.wbespm067.pub2

Dissaux, T. (2019). "Inclusion financière et liens sociaux: La monnaie entre marchandisation et mise en commun au Kenya," *Mondes en Développement*, 185(1), pp. 83–108.

Dowbor, L. (2008). *Democracia Econômica*. São Paulo: Vozes.

Eynaud, P. and Laville, J. L. (2021). "How nonprofit governance studies can be enriched by the commons framework: Towards a cross-fertilization agenda of research," in Donnelly-Cox, G., Meyer, M. and Wijkström, F. (eds.) *Research Handbook on Nonprofit Governance*. Cheltenham: Edward Elgar, pp. 220–234. https://doi.org/10.4337/9781788114912.00021

Federici, S. (2018). *Re-Enchanting the World: Feminism and the Politics of the Commons*. Oakland, CA: PM Press.

Federici, S. and Caffentzis, G. (2013)."Commons against and beyond capitalism," *Upping the Anti: A Journal of Theory and Action*, 15, pp. 83–97.

França Filho, G. C. (2013). *Bancos Comunitários de Desenvolvimento (BCDs) como Expressão de Finanças Solidárias: Por uma outra abordagem da inclusão financeira*. Fortaleza: Arte Visual.

França Filho, G. C., Júnior, J. T. S. and Rigo, A. S. (2012). "Solidarity finance through community development banks as a strategy for reshaping local economies: Lessons from Banco Palmas," *Revista de Administração*, 47(3), pp. 500–515.
Gerring, J. (2006). *Case Study Research: Principles and Practices*. Cambridge: Cambridge University Press.
Guérin, I. (2015). *La Microfinance et ses Dérives. Émanciper, Discipliner ou Exploiter?* Paris: Demopolis.
Hardin, G. (1968). "The Tragedy of the Commons," *Science*, 162(3859), pp. 1243–1248.
Harvey, D. (2010). *The Enigma of Capital and the Crisis of Capitalism*. London: Profile Books.
Harvey, D. (2012). *Rebel Cities*. London: Verso.
Henfrey, T. and Kenrick, J. (2017). "Climate, commons and hope: The transition movement in global perspective," in Henfrey, T., Maschkowski, G. and Penha-Lopes, G. (eds.) *Resilience, Community Action and Societal Transformation*. East Meon: Permanent Publications, pp. 161–190.
Hess, C. and Ostrom, E. (2007). *Understanding Knowledge as a Commons: From Theory to Practice*. Cambridge, MA: MIT Press.
Hess, Charlotte. (2008). Mapping the new commons. SSRN. http://dx.doi.org/10.2139/ssrn.1356835
Hudon, M. and Meyer, C. (2016). "A case study of microfinance and community development banks in Brazil: Private or common goods?" *Nonprofit and Voluntary Sector Quarterly*, 45(4_suppl.), pp. 116S–133S.
Laville, J. L. (2015). *Asociarse para el bien común: Tercer sector, economía social y economía solidaria*. Vilassar de Dalt: Icaria.
Leach, D. (2013). "Prefigurative Politics," in Snow, D. A., Della Porta, D. B., Klandermans, B. and McAdam, D. (eds.) *The Wiley-Blackwell Encyclopedia of Social and Political Movements*. Oxford: Wiley-Blackwell. https://doi.org/10.1002/9780470674871.wbespm167.pub2
Leal, L. P. (2013). *Gestão coletiva dos bens comuns na experiência dos Bancos Comunitários de Desenvolvimento: o caso de Matarandiba*. Masters Dissertation, Escola de Administração da Universidade Federal da Bahia.
Leal, L. P. and Santos Almeida, S. C., (2016). "Incubação de iniciativas de finanças solidárias: Perspectivas da gestão coletiva dos bens comuns no Banco comunitário Olhos d'Água em Igaci, Alagoas," *Revista NAU Social*, 7(12), pp. 143–162.
Linebaugh, P. (2008). *The Magna Carta Manifesto: Liberties and Commons for All*. Berkley: University of California Press.
Mattei, U. (2013). *Bienes comunes: Un manifiesto*. Madrid: Ed. Trotta.
McGinnis, M. and Ostrom, E. (1996). "Design principles for local and global commons," *The International Political Economy and International Institutions*, 2, pp. 465–493.
Mendell, M. (2015). "Democratizing capital: Social and solidarity finance in Quebec," in Pun, N., Hok-bun Ku, B., Yan, H. and Koo, A. (eds.) *Social Economy in China and the World*. London: Routledge, pp. 94–114.
Mendell, M. and Nogales, R. (2012). "Solidarity finance: An evolving landscape," *Universitas Forum*, 3(2).
Muñoz, R. E. (2009). "Finanças solidárias," in Cattani, A. D. (ed.) *Dicionário Internacional da Outra Economia*. Coimbra: Edições Almedina, pp. 208–212.

Muñoz, R. E. (2017). "De la perplejidad a una acción monetario – financiera contra-hegemónica. Contexto y desafíos ante la especulación financiera global," *Ciencias Económicas*, 1(14), 123–139.

Ostrom, E. (2000). *El Gobierno de los Comunes. La evolución de las instituciones de acción colectiva*. Mexico: Editorial Fondo de Cultura Económica.

Ostrom, E. (2005). *Understanding Institutional Diversity*. Princeton, NJ: Princeton University Press.

Ostrom, E., Walker, J. and Gardner, R. (1992). "Covenants with and without a sword: Self-governance is possible," *American Political Science Review*, 86(2), pp. 404–417.

Ostrom, V. and Ostrom, E. (1979). "Public goods and public choices," in Savas, E. S. (ed.) *Alternatives for Delivering Public Services*. London: Routledge. pp. 7–49.

Périlleux, A. and Nyssens, M. (2017). "Understanding cooperative finance as a new common," *Annals of Public and Cooperative Economics*, 88(2), pp. 155–177.

Polletta, F. (2013). "Participatory democracy in social movements," in Snow, D. A., Della Porta, D. B., Klandermans, B. and McAdam, D. (eds.) *The Wiley-Blackwell Encyclopedia of Social and Political Movements*. Oxford: Wiley-Blackwell. https://doi.org/10.1002/9780470674871.wbespm442.pub2

Projeto Ecosmar. (2008). *Texto Base*. Escola de Administração da Universidade Federal da Bahia. UFBA, Bahia – Brasil.

Projeto Ecosmar. (2021). *Relatório Final: 2008–2020*. Escola de Administração da Universidade Federal da Bahia. UFBA, Bahia – Brasil.

Razeto, L. (1990). *Economía Popular de Solidaridad: Identidad y proyecto en una visión integradora*. Santiago: Área Pastoral Social de la Conferencia Episcopal de Chile.

Rigo, A. S., de França Filho, G. C. and Leal, L. P. (2015). "Bancos Comunitários de Desenvolvimento na Política Pública de Finanças Solidárias. Apresentando a Realidade do Nordeste e Discutindo Proposições," *Desenvolvimento em Questão*, 13(31), pp. 70–107.

Sanchis, J. R. (2016). "A Revolução das Finanças Éticas e Solidárias," *Oikonomics. Revista d'Economia, Empresa i Societat*, 6, pp. 28–34.

Servet, J. M. and Guérin, I. (2002). *Exclusion et liens financiers: Rapport du Centre Walras*. Paris: Editions Economica.

Silva, S. P. and Pereira, C. A. (2023). *Bancos comunitários, moedas sociais e políticas públicas: Da experiência pioneira do banco Palmas (Fortaleza-CE) ao modelo difusor do banco Mumbuca (Maricá-RJ)*. Brasilia: IPEA.

Souza, E. B. (2019). *Políticas Públicas de Finanças Solidárias no Brasil e as Experiências de Bancos Comunitários de Desenvolvimento: um estudo sobre o Banco Comunitário de Matarandiba – BCD Ilhamar-BA*. Masters Dissertation, Universidade Federal da Bahia.

Wright, E. O. (2010). *Envisioning real utopias*. London: Verso.

12 Policies of social and solidarity economy from the local in Argentina

Subjects, power and markets in San Martín and Moreno[1]

Ruth Muñoz

12.1 Introduction: Argentine social policy of social/popular economy still at the margins

This chapter analyses experiences of promotion of SSE carried out by the 24 municipalities in the Conurbano Bonaerense (CB). It is based on fieldwork carried out with a comparative approach, described more fully in Muñoz (2022). Part of this research was carried out in a UNGS[2] (National University of General Sarmiento) research project, which was the first attempt to establish a baseline understanding of local policies in the CB, based on insights from several academic fields.

Within the categories used in the field that refer to economies oriented mostly towards "life reproduction" in the sense of Coraggio (2011a), rather than reproduction of capital, we adopt that of SSE (Social and Solidarity Economy). We have chosen the SSE category because it is the broadest expression available in our field, building bridges among different types of hybrid experiences. It is also used by well-known networks in our region, such as RIPESS,[3] and increasingly gaining wider recognition, for example in the recent ILO Resolution concerning decent work and SSE.[4] We agree with Hintze that the discussion of denominations "has conceptual, ideological and evaluative components, and even geographical origin, referring to a field under construction that began to take shape in Latin America at the end of the last decade" (Hintze, 2010: 17). Hintze refers to SSE as:

> [A] comprehensive denomination of what has usually and in a restrictive way been called the traditional social economy – cooperative and mutual experiences – joined with the new associative forms and worker-recovered enterprises – emerged in recent years – that are assumed as a solidarity economy. Among the most noticeable are community enterprises, associative enterprises (mercantile and non-mercantile) supported by the State or by civil society, barter networks and bankrupt enterprises recovered by its workers. In general, they are based on collective property, values of solidarity and cooperation. Likewise, they are primarily oriented towards reproduction of

DOI: 10.4324/9781003306344-13

> life, while reproduction of capital is a means to achieve that goal and not an end in itself.
>
> (Hintze, 2010: 17–18)

We also consider the sense of challenging economic practices that Coraggio attributes to SSE as:

> [A] way of doing economy based on consciously building, from society and the State, which organises in an associated and cooperative manner the production, distribution, circulation and consumption of goods and services, not based on the motive of private profit but rather towards the resolution of needs, seeking high quality living conditions for all those who participate in it, their families and communities, in collaboration with other communities, to resolve material needs while establishing fraternal social ties and solidarity, responsibly assuming the management of natural resources and respect for future generations, consolidating harmonious and lasting social ties among communities, without exploiting the work of others.
>
> (Coraggio, 2020: 12–13)

Corragio describes the SSE developing in a mixed economy as an imbrication of three sectors: private capitalist, public state and popular economy (PE), all of them organised by the criterion of socioeconomic rationality. While the private capitalist economy is oriented towards profits and the public state economy is guided by a combination of contradictory systemic needs such as common good (whose definition is a matter of social struggle), capital governance or perpetuity in power, SSE is at the centre, oriented towards the expanded reproduction of the life of all living entities (human and natural). Corragio sees PE as the immediate site of reproduction of human life and the main basis on which to develop SSE in Latin America (but not the only one). By PE, Corragio refers to the economy of the workers, that is, of those members of society who depend on the realisation of their capacity for labour to obtain their sustenance. Coraggio (2020) describes transitions from PE to solidarity PE and its relations with SSE, it being important to distinguish the solidarity component of PE since "It should be noted that the really existing PE is the PE of the peripheral capitalist system and that, rather than solidarity, it can be highly competitive among its members" (Coraggio, 2018: 9). For this reason, we give specific attention in our research to policies of the democratic State, co-constructed with actors in the SSE sector.

As we point out in Muñoz (2022), existing research on SSE policies predominantly focuses on the national rather than sub-national scale. At the local level, previous empirical studies have had limited geographical scope, typically one or two municipalities. In this sense, our research helps address a significant gap in academic treatments of SSE, as well as improving understanding of the largest urban agglomeration in Argentina, one of the most important in Latin America.

Located around the city of Buenos Aires, the CB is composed of 24 municipalities and is home to approximately 30% of the country's inhabitants, in less than 0.1% of its land area, a remarkably uneven spatial development (Muñoz & Coraggio, 2018).

It is worth recognizing the differences between the SSE policies implemented by governments between 2003–2015 and 2016–2019. From the beginning of the 2000s, SSE policies operated mostly in the margins, lacking specific normative frameworks (such as a national SSE law would provide). During both periods, policies were designed through a mono-productive[5] process: the input of SSE actors was limited to occasional consultation sessions, whose outcomes were treated as advisory rather than binding.

During the period from 2003 to 2015, a group of policies emerged, particularly in the social realm, with the National Ministry of Social Development as the leading actor. These policies promoted what was officially referred to as the "Social Economy," with a common thread: inclusion in conventional markets of a very specific and delimited range of vulnerable socio-economic actors. These policies mostly targeted family-based or very small-scale mercantile associative entrepreneurship, along with workers' cooperatives created within the framework of these policies. Although these policies opened a whole new field of collective experimentation, they also left a narrow and sinuous trail, full of precarity and uncertainty that would often end up being resolved by the market. At the same time, opportunities to assess other possible expressions of SSE (such as worker-recovered enterprises) were lost.[6] This is the period that Coraggio characterised as "social policy of Social Economy" (Coraggio, 2014, 2015).

The national government that took office towards the end of 2015 laid out a series of transformational policies. Among them, an emphasis was set on entrepreneurship for the upper classes, while family-based agriculture and workers' cooperatives were assigned lower priority. According to statistics from the National Institute of Associativism (collectivism) and Social Economy (INAES), cooperative entities declined to half in this period, which ended in 2019 (INAES, 2019), leading the president of INAES at the time, Cafiero, to call it a "cooperativicide."[7]

It is also worth noting the increasing use of the term Popular Economy (PE), rather than Social Economy, during this later period. A national law incorporated this expression for the very first time in 2016: the Social Emergency Law (N°27.345/2016), which talks about "the workers of the Popular Economy." This wording reflects the perspective of the Popular Economy Workers' Confederation (CTEP),[8] created in 2011 by several federations, movements and organisations representing those working "without a boss" in the PE, along with those whom the law was designed. Among other things, it instituted a Council and Registry of PE, together with a Complementary Social Salary payable to PE workers, usually set at half of the minimum wage. We agree with Hopp (2018) that the scope of this law and the instruments derived from it amount to a form of individual compensation for imbalances and lack of alternatives in the labour market, while the salary allocation undermines collectivism and self-management as key strategies of PE. Nonetheless, it was an important step towards recognising a particular PE subject and providing a level of income security in adverse and worsening circumstances.

In this later national context, many sub-national governments became environments of resistance, operating as buffers and enacting innovative propositional strategies. In the specific case of the municipalities in the CB, we find a much richer and more varied panorama than at national level.

12.2 The municipalities of the Conurbano Bonaerense as territories of policy innovation in relation to social and solidarity economy

In Muñoz (2022), we identified and comparatively analysed the SSE policies carried out in the CB from 2012 to 2018, with special attention to the microeconomic premises on which they were based. Considering the range of SSE policy measures during 2016–2018, as identified in interviews with municipal agents,[9] we documented 14 municipalities (of 24 municipalities in the territory) who implemented a total of 121 SSE policies. These policy measures were mostly developed by the municipalities themselves: 80 were developed at this level, while 41 were supra-local policies. As previously mentioned, the SSE policy panorama in the CB was more varied and rich than at national level. Within the 80 reported municipal-level policies, we identified instances of co-construction and co-production: an indication of more diverse policy subjects than the institutions targeted at national level (with more associative expressions). Although the Social Economy category predominates, PE and SSE were also used by interviewees.

In relation to the three currents of SSE thought and action identified by Coraggio (2013) for Latin America, we find local policies to have had significant results. The first current seeks market integration, acts at the microeconomic level and focuses on poverty alleviation and self-employment. The second proposes the creation of an organic SSE sector, operating more at an meso level with networks that are not merely economic, but also based on social and political reciprocities and solidarities, accompanied by the strengthening of collective subjects. Finally, a third current thinks and acts at a systemic level and seeks to build what Corragio refers to as the "Other Economy"[10] by overcoming the capitalist cultural system.

In a previous study, we described how Argentine national policies left their imprint, in the form of mercantile PE, in 7 of 14 municipalities with SSE policies (Muñoz, 2021). Of the other seven, we classified three as SSE, while the other four showed clear tendencies in that direction. Avellaneda, Moreno and San Martín were the three districts classified as SSE. The latter two were the most developed cases in the analysed period, both in terms of the quantity and complexity of policies, and in terms of having become institutionalised and achieved sustainability over the course of several years.

In order to give a brief panorama of our territorial case studies, we have selected some socioeconomic indicators. Unfortunately, recent municipal-level demographic and economic information are not easily available in Argentina.[11] Table 12.1 compares a number of key socioeconomic statistics.

As we can see, proximity to Buenos Aires city correlates with better socioeconomic indicators for San Martín, with the exception of the percentage of households in shantytowns and precarious settlements (due to San Martín's population density). Moreno, on the other hand, is a typical suburban district with expansive green areas. In terms of the Gross Geographic Product (GGP), the differences are remarkable. The GGP per capita of San Martín is more than triple that of Moreno, with the former dominated by (basic) industry and the latter by (precarious) services. In several interviews, the expression used by interviewees to refer to San Martín was "the hardware shop of the CB," reflecting the idea of low-complexity production circuits, especially of textiles, while Moreno was more commonly described as a "dormitory town."

Table 12.1 Socioeconomic characterisation of San Martín and Moreno

	San Martín	*Moreno*
Distance from Buenos Aires (km)	24	42
Main characteristic of the territory	Urban	Periurban
Surface (km^2)	55.7	186.1
Population (2010)	414.196	452.505
Population density	7.4362	2.4315
Per capita GGP (Equivalent in €, 2003)	3.785	1.109
% goods	69.3	18.8
% services	30.7	81.2
Households with at least one indicator of UBN (%, 2010)	6.7	12.9
Population without health coverage (%, 2010)	33.9	48.5
Households without running water (%, 2010)	4.5	21.6
Households in shanty towns and precarious settlements (%, 2015)	14.7	11.7
Ratio of municipal income to total public income (national, provincial and municipal) (2017)	62.4	38.3
Number of cooperatives (2018)	334	359
Number of worker-recovered enterprises (2018)	14	2

Source: Author's elaboration based on various official sources[12]

While the numbers of cooperatives in the two territories are quite similar, more worker-recovered enterprises are found in San Martín owing to its industrial character, while Moreno has more cooperatives dedicated to agriculture and provision by the community of housing and utilities. In San Martín, housing and habitation needs are predominantly resolved by the market and by family-based PE strategies such as self-building and waste picking. However, some cooperatives and community-based actors have also started to gain recognition for their roles in local economic development.

In relation to the ratio of municipal income to total income, in a country where the local level does not have many political instruments to promote its economy, we find, once again, remarkable differences between the cases. San Martín is much less vulnerable to extra-local political cycles than Moreno and so has better conditions for the development of SSE policy when the context at supralocal levels is not favourable.

In the following two sections, we analyse each of these two cases. Moreno's SSE policies were in line with those of the national government between 2003 and 2015, to the extent that some of these policies scaled up from local to national level (i.e. microcredit, collective brands, family-based agriculture). San Martín was more aligned with the policy orientation of the national government that took office in 2019 (i.e. promotion by INAES of public procurement from cooperatives). However, we have not yet analysed this last period in a systematic manner.

12.3 Moreno: an innovative case of "social policy of social economy"

The introduction of SSE policies in Moreno began with the first term in office of a mayor elected in 1995 and gained momentum in the aftermath of the 2001 crisis. Some of the main features of the institutionalisation process of SSE in this municipality that we have identified are: creation of the Bonaerense Institute of Business Development (IDEB), a hybrid institution promoted by a policy of the Province of Buenos Aires, which was very productive at local level and overcame a narrow vision of small/medium-sized enterprises through the incorporation of individual and family-based entrepreneurship that could be part of PE and, on some occasions, also SSE; the Municipal Institute of Local Development (IMDEL), which opened the space for SSE policies in many other areas of municipal activity; the Moreno Social Bank, co-managed with IDEB, the first case in Argentina of provision of microcredit with central involvement of municipal agents (which later gained recognition as a pioneering experience towards the making of the national law for microcredit promotion for the development of Social Economy) and the Entrepreneurship of Social Economy ordinance, which focuses on the granting of vending permits.

The municipality benefited from political support at the national level, especially between 2003 and 2012. In 2015, although the same political party continued to govern at local level, it changed its leadership and orientation, which we see reflected in a recurrent phrase in our fieldwork, "20 years of social economy policies," as if they had been interrupted. This coincided with changes of government at provincial and national levels, with different levels of dependency on supra-local funds, meaning negative impacts were stronger in some districts than in others. Between 2016 and 2018, innovation was scarce; approximately half of previously existing SSE policies managed to remain in force, although with significantly reduced reach. There were no further significant changes of political perspective, but SSE lost its central position in the local policy agenda.

In terms of the main perceived targets of SSE policy since its genesis, our interpretation is that although innovations were produced and Moreno was the first municipality to legitimise previously invisible PE practices, an image persisted that underestimated the potential of these economies, especially that of the more powerful community-based actors. We can highlight numerous illustrations of this point: 1) in the mid-1990s, the newly elected mayor was put under pressure to corporatise a community-based transport initiative (El Colmenar) immediately upon taking office,[13] which established a conflictive relationship with the organisations of Cuartel V, a territory of Moreno with one of the strongest levels of presence of associative action related to the right to the city and SSE (Muñoz, 2015); 2) workers' cooperatives were promoted as part of a paternalistic approach; 3) the only ordinance produced defines subjects as individuals and working poor on the basis of economic indicators such as expanded or simple reproduction of capital rather than "life reproduction" in the sense of Coraggio (2011a); 4) Moreno's financing policies, with focus on microcredit (Muñoz, 2007), are particularly illustrative of this restrictive vision of the so-called "Social Economy."

The final dimension we will consider here is the destinations of PE and SSE production. In our fieldwork, we found the reach of both to extend beyond conventional markets alone. Moreno was particularly active in helping PE and SSE gain better access to several markets. The first "Itinerant Popular Market" was set up at the main square and several other public parks in order to promote direct connection between producers and consumers in the district. PE and SSE producers were also granted access to specific fairs predominantly related to producers' primary sector of activity. Among these initiatives, it is worth highlighting the creation of the associative brand "Made in Moreno," which adapts and applies several of the main principles of fair trade in the context of local exchange, in collaboration with two workers' cooperatives (one gastronomic, the other in clothes' manufacturing) that used the brand. Finally, the promotion of self-consumption was also important, particularly in relation to food and provision of housing and infrastructure. An initiative that stood out was the creation of a poultry production centre, which still is the sole source of protein for many families.

12.4 San Martín: a social and solidarity economy policies' co-construction laboratory

The case of San Martín unfolds in a context of continuity in local government. The administration that took office in 2011 has developed an original institutional approach, on the basis of categories and practices that are unique in the CB. It does, however, focus predominantly on the General Directorate for SSE, rather than taking the transversal approach recommended in the literature (e.g. Hintze, 2014; Sánchez, 2014).

We consider San Martín to be a true SSE policy co-construction laboratory, whose main policymaker aims to develop it as part of an international SSE ecosystem and so to "emancipate the PE and SSE actors that belong to it" (Minteguía, 2017). Concretely, this resulted in the co-construction of several SSE policies, along with three specific co-constructed ordinances: the "Solidarity Finance Fund," the "Register System for Social Enterprises and Cooperatives" and the "Municipal Procurement from Social Enterprises and Cooperatives."[14] Of all the participatory processes, the "Co-managed Table" between the Municipality of San Martín and all the worker-recovered enterprises of the city, created in 2012, has probably been the most effective.

In terms of the main targets of SSE policy, we find worker-recovered enterprises (which is remarkable not only within CB but also at the national level), cooperatives (mostly workers', but also of other kinds), associations and community-based organisations. We can also find individual and family-based entrepreneurships, along with some clubs and social enterprises. We could talk of diverse expressions of PE and SSE committed to developing a SSE ecosystem (Lévesque, 2016) in a way that includes PE and strives for a mutually beneficial relationship between the two, an approach that is not well developed in the rest of the region. At the same time, this ecosystem is not limited to what exists at the local level, but it is spread regionally, nationally and throughout Latin-American, particularly Brazil. They also manage to employ a non-colonised use of the social enterprise category (Lucas dos Santos & Banerjee, 2019). Although not the most commonly used expression in general discourse, Social Enterprise operates as an umbrella including conventional entities within the SSE field (especially workers' cooperatives, housing cooperatives and associations) along with those that do not have any legal constitution. This was how the municipality managed to channel resources under a specific legal framework (particularly for state purchases) without obliging promoted subjects to constitute themselves as cooperatives, unless they chose to do so.

Finally, in terms of product destination, we find diverse policy instruments. These include the creation of fairs that promote direct encounters between producers and consumers under certain principles (but do not use the fair trade term) (similar to those described by Esteves, this volume), a solidarity store co-managed with self-managed workers, product and service catalogues of the PE and SSE, as well as self-provisioning of food and renewable energy.

However, the most significant aspect of this dimension is that San Martín is the only municipality in the entire CB that has developed a systematic policy of public procurement from PE and SSE in the territory, along with gradual substitution of conventional suppliers by solidarity suppliers beyond San Martín. Some

Table 12.2 Municipalities of Moreno and San Martín's social and solidarity intervention profile

	Moreno (1995–2018)	*San Martín (2011–2018)*
Institutionalisation processes	• IDEB Moreno (1997) • IMDEL (2000) • Moreno Social Bank (2001) • "Entrepreneurship of Social Economy" Ordinance (2004) • 13 local SSE policies implemented by 2018	• SSE General Direction (2011) • "Solidarity Finance Fund" Ordinance (2012) • "Register of Social enterprises and Cooperatives" Ordinance (2012) • "Municipal Procurement from Social Enterprises and Cooperatives" Ordinance (2015) • 14 local SSE policies implemented by 2018
Main targets	Between informal economy and PE: • Individual and family-based entrepreneurship • Workers' cooperatives created with the support of SSE policies	Embryonic ecosystem of PE and SSE *from the* local: • Individual and family-based entrepreneurship • Social enterprises • Cooperatives (especially workers') • Worker-recovered enterprises • Associations, community-based organisations and some clubs • Several networks, federations and movements of PE and SSE
Destinations of products	• Access to markets: Itinerant Popular Market and accompanied attendance at pre-existing fairs (Luján, Álvarez) and specialised fairs ("Moreno Flourish", "Moreno Produces") • Made in Moreno (HEM) with two co-managed stores and fair trade practices • Self-consumption: poultry development	• Hands of San Martín Fair and specific fairs (green fair and agroecology) • Solidarity store (co-managed) • Public procurement • Specific catalogues • Self-production of food and renewable energies

Source: Synthesis based on Muñoz (2022)

noteworthy examples of the latter are a worker-recovered enterprise from La Matanza in the CB, yerba mate purchased from cooperatives in the province of Misiones and rice from cooperatives in the province of Entre Rios. This policy has escalated to national level through the INAES, making it possible for more municipalities and provinces to help strengthen the national SSE ecosystem through their procurement practices. In fact, in the first-year review of INAES policies conducted in 2020, this was considered one of five key strategic policies in support of SSE at national level (Muñoz & Zamora, 2021).

12.5 Conclusion

The analysis of the case studies developed in this chapter took place within the context of a national process of restoration of neo-conservative hegemony (2016–2019). As a matter of fact, after years of reducing its public debt, Argentina became indebted with the IMF once again.

We find Fraser's (2014) global-scale post-Polanyian reflections particularly instructive for understanding this period in Argentina. Fraser focuses on the systematic domination of some States over others, especially when international organisations such as the IMF use debt as a weapon to reduce the capacity of postcolonial states to provide social protection, forcing them to drastically reduce social expenditure. She asserts that the viability of the national social protection that Polanyi proposed is not universal but has, in the Global North, always depended on the extraction of wealth from the Global South.

In contrast, at the local level, the two municipalities analysed illustrate Harvey's spaces of hope (2003). In these cases, capitalist firms are not the only producers (since PE and SSE are recognised as socioeconomic subjects worthy of promotion by municipal governments), and conventional markets are only one possible destination of products (among others such as fair trade, public procurement and self-consumption). Both have sustained SSE policies over more than two decades, and San Martín has actually co-constructed a number of these policies. This is a very significant finding for our national research field, considering it was the first such case in the CB and probably in Argentina. It also has international significance because Argentina is not yet recognised for these local level practices, which could contribute to building platforms with a positive view of Latin American cities, enlarging existing evidence bases such as that of the UNRISD research programme on the promotion of SSE through local public policies.[15]

In terms of the conception of the territory, they are quite different. Rather than using a spatial designation, in this chapter, we find it more useful to consider territories in relation to alternative economies (Coraggio, 2010), emphasising the social spatialities (Coraggio, 1987). In that sense, we are interested in problematising the relationship between multi-scalarity and the promotion of SSE from the territories. In the same sense, Santos (2012) calls for greater ambition in terms of scale, moving on from the idea of community as a closed and static collectivity (fortress community) to a concept of community as a living and dynamic entity. As we described in previous pages, in terms of the subjects promoted and the policies delivered, Moreno focuses on its own district and has difficulties including all the actors who influence the trajectory of the SSE in its territory. While San Martín has sought another type of development, opening connections and attempting to strengthen solidarity with SSE actors from other communities, regions and provinces in Argentina, and even from other countries in Latin America (especially from Brazil), consolidating articulations of the local state and the PE and SSE ecosystem through several instruments, including even public procurement at the regional level.

On the other hand, the deeper analysis developed by Muñoz (2022) allowed us to identify not only the anticipated novelty in the promotion of PE and SSE in the documented cases, but also certain continuities with neoclassical microeconomics. We are particularly interested in such apparently inconsistent practices. Findings of this kind common to both cases (San Martín and Moreno) include a bias, during some periods, towards commercial reinsertion rather than promotion, at the same level of resourcing, of cooperative housing or collective care; a persistent assumption of conventional markets as the main destination of products; a neoclassical orientation and capitalist approach to marketing in training activities and a preeminence of quantitative indicators over those focusing on quality and processes, among others. We perceive that these kinds of practices are rather the rule than the exception and that they are also present in the academic field.

We conclude with a focus on our social and political responsibility when it comes to creating better conditions for the institutionalisation of SSE. In this sense, it could be useful to recognise microeconomic operationalisations exposed in pedagogical papers oriented towards the promotion of various SSE practices, which allow us to see the formal conception of the economy more clearly.

We have designed a final analytical exercise to do with students in the postgraduate module in Social Microeconomics with Coraggio, part of the Social Economy Masters at UNGS since 2011, in order to identify breakups and continuities (and to propose more coherent instruments with SSE practices where continuities with neoclassical microeconomics are identified). We have extended this practice to the Masters in Social and Solidarity Economy at the Institute of Higher National Studies in Ecuador since 2015. Overall, we have applied this exercise to approximately 35 publications. For example a publication widely used in Argentina illustrates the point about inconsistency (La Yunta, 2007). At the start, it claims to oppose the supply and demand model, but it then proposes as a marketing strategy for the SSE the "4P" Model: Product, Place, Promotion and Price, developed by McCarthy (1968), which is a basic and old-fashioned tool of capitalist marketing. This 4P approach was specifically analysed with the students, with the result that the most important P for the substantive perspective was missing – the Person (Acosta *et al.*, 2017); here, we could also add the P of Planet.

These analyses allow us to assume that sustaining a theoretical and practical approach consistent with SSE, in our cases from a substantive perspective, makes the critical reading of neoclassical microeconomics by heterodoxies necessary but insufficient. Furthermore, we find a fundamental inconsistency in the promotion of PE and SSE with neoclassical microeconomic premises, which were designed for capitalist practices. So, it is crucial for our academic work also to contribute to the formulation of instrumental proposals for such alternatives, in co-construction with actors in the PE and SSE ecosystem.

Notes

1. Many thanks for the feedback on previous versions of this chapter to José Luis Coraggio, Omar Cura and Sebastián Valdecantos.
2. Oriented Research Project CONICET-ICO/UNGS: "Políticas sociales y económicas en los municipios del Conurbano Bonaerense" (2015–2021). www.ungs.edu.ar/
3. www.ripess.org
4. www.ilo.org/wcmsp5/groups/public/-ed_norm/-relconf/documents/meetingdocument/wcms_848633.pdf
5. Vaillancourt distinguishes three policy development scenarios: (1) There is neither co-production nor co-construction, but monoproduction. The policy is funded from the public purse; it is administered by organisations from the state public sector; services are delivered by public sector employees. (2) There is co-production that gives rise to a form of public–private partnership through the implementation of public policies. (3) There is co-construction, with participation ongoing from the initial conception of the policies. "Thus, co-construction takes place before the adoption of public policies, while co-production comes later, at the time of their application" (Vaillancourt, 2011: 2).
6. With the exception of the Self-managed Work Programme, dependent on the National Ministry of Labour, created in 2004 and still current. See: www.argentina.gob.ar/trabajo/autogestionado
7. The argument can be heard in the following radio interview: https://ar.radiocut.fm/audiocut/cooperativicidio-durante-macrismo-dieron-baja-mitad-cooperativas-del-pais/
8. https://ctepargentina.org/
9. To identify SSE policies during interviews, we used the following key categories and their possible combinations: social economy, solidarity economy, popular economy, cooperativism, collectivism, self-management, worker-recovered enterprises. For the next iteration, we plan to add several key categories and hold workshops with SSE and other related socioeconomic and political actors to define them.
10. For a full definition, see https://ediciones.ungs.edu.ar/wp-content/uploads/2020/04/9789876301534-completo.pdf
11. The last economic census was in 2003, so we are forced to work with outdated results. The last population census for which data were available at the time of writing was in 2010, with the release of the 2022 census results pending. In this situation regarding public statistics, such important information as unemployment rate is missing from the chart because of its particularities. The average of the CB exhibited by the Permanent Household Survey exceeded two digits in 2016, 2017 and 2018 (10.6; 10.3 and 11%, respectively).
12. Censo Nacional de Población, Hogares y Vivienda (2010), Instituto Nacional de Estadísticas y Censos; Dirección de Estadística de la provincia de Buenos Aires; Informe de Gestión de la Subsecretaría Social de Tierras, Urbanismo y Vivienda;

Programa Buenos Aires Abierta del Honorable Tribunal de Cuentas de la provincia de Buenos Aires; Instituto Nacional de Asociativismo y Economía Social; Guía de Empresas y Fábricas Recuperadas del Ministerio de Trabajo, Empleo y Seguridad Social, Programa Facultad Abierta de la Facultad de Filosofía y Letras (Universidad de Buenos Aires (www.recuperadasdoc.com.ar).

13. The Colmenar mutual, from Cuartel V (about 1 hour by bus from the centre of Moreno), met the transportation needs of the district between 1990 and 2005 and was part of an SSE movement. See: https://vimeo.com/7676727. An interesting video of the history of Cuartel V is available in: www.youtube.com/watch?v=nRTAc9tLrtM
14. http://observatorioconurbano.ungs.edu.ar/?page_id=7254
15. www.unrisd.org/en/research/projects/promoting-sse-through-public-policies-guidelines-for-local-governments

References

Acosta, V., Barrientos, N., Barrios, O., Basterrechea, M. and Mantel, E. (2017). *Rompiendo las (4)P con los mercados de proximidad.* Los Polvorines: Maestría en Economía Social, UNGS.

Coraggio, J. L. (1987). "Sobre la espacialidad social y el concepto de región," in *Territorios en Transición.* Quito: CIUDAD.

Coraggio, J. L. (2010). "Territorio y economías alternativas," *Revista de Ciencias Sociales, Segunda Época*, 7(18), pp. 7–30.

Coraggio, J. L. (2011a). "Principios, instituciones y prácticas de la economía social y solidaria," in *Economía social y solidaria: El trabajo antes que el capital.* Quito: Ediciones Abya Ayala, pp. 1–25.

Coraggio, J. L. (2013). "Las tres corrientes de pensamiento y acción dentro del campo de la economía social y solidaria," *Revista brasileira de estudos urbanos e regionais (RBEUR)*, 15(2). https://doi.org/10.22296/2317-1529.2013v15n2p11

Coraggio, J. L. (2014). *La presencia de la economía social y solidaria y su institucionalización en América Latina* (UNRISD Occasional Paper No. 7, Geneva). Potential and Limits of Social and Solidarity Economy.

Coraggio, J. L. (2015). "Institutionalising the social and solidarity economy in Latin America" in Utting, P. (ed) *Social and Solidarity Economy: Beyond the Fringe.* London: Zed Books, pp. 130–149.

Coraggio, J. L. (2018). "Potenciar la Economía Popular Solidaria: Una respuesta al Neoliberalismo," *Otra Economía*, 11(20), pp. 4–18.

Coraggio, J. L. (2020). *Economía social y economía popular: Conceptos básicos.* Serie Contribuciones de Consejeres N° 1. Documentos del Consejo Consultivo del Instituto Nacional de Asociativismo y Economía Social. Online at www.argentina.gob.ar/sites/default/files/coraggio.pdf (accessed March 30th 2023).

Fraser, N. (2014). "¿Puede la sociedad transformarse en una commodity? Reflexiones pospolanyianas sobre la crisis capitalista," En Coraggio, J. L. y Laville, J. L. (eds.) *Reinventar la izquierda en el siglo XXI. Hacia un diálogo Norte-Sur.* Quito: Editorial IAEN, pp. 523–537.

Harvey, D. (2003). *Espacios de Esperanza.* Serie Cuestiones de Antagonismo. Madrid: Akal.

Hintze, S. (2010). *La política es un arma cargada de futuro: Economía social y solidaria en Brasil y Venezuela.* Buenos Aires: Consejo Latinoamericano de Ciencias Sociales – CLACSO, CICCUS.

Hintze, S. (2014). "Alcances y desafíos de las políticas públicas para la economía popular solidaria," in Instituto Nacional de Economía Popular y Solidaria (IEPS) (ed.) *La economía popular y solidaria. El ser humano sobre el capital*. Quito: IEPS-MIES.

Hopp, M. (2018) "De la promoción del trabajo cooperativo al salario social complementario. Transformaciones en la transferencia de ingresos por trabajo en la Argentina". Ciudadanías N° 2.

INAES. (2019). *Actualización nacional de datos de cooperativas y mutuales*. Instituto Nacional de Asociativismo y Economía Social (INAES), Ministerio de Salud y Desarrollo Social. Buenos Aires. Online at www.argentina.gob.ar/sites/default/files/informe_2019.pdf (accessed March 30th 2023).

La Yunta. (2007). *Economía social solidaria*. Programa de Capacitación y Fortalecimiento para Organizaciones Sociales y Comunitarias. FSOC, UBA. Online at http://programadecapacitacion.sociales.uba.ar/wp-content/uploads/sites/95/2011/08/Economia-Social-Solidaria.pdf (accessed March 30th 2023).

Lévesque, B. (2016). "Économie sociale et solidaire et entrepreneur social: Vers quels nouveaux écosystèmes?," *Revue Interventions Économiques*, 54. https://doi.org/10.4000/interventionseconomiques.2802

Lucas dos Santos, L. and Banerjee, S. (2019). "Social Enterprise: Is it possible to decolonise this concept?," in Eynaud, P., Laville, J. L., Lucas dos Santos, L., Banerjee, S., Avelino, F. and Hulgard, L. (eds.) *Theory of Social Enterprise and Pluralism: Social Movements, Solidarity Economy and the Global South*. New York: Routledge, pp. 3–17.

McCarthy, E. J. (1968) [1960]. *Basic Marketing: A Managerial Approach*. Homewood, IL: Richard D. Irwin.

Minteguía, O. (2017). *Políticas de economía social y solidaria para emancipar a los actores*. Interview by R. Muñoz. Instituto de Conurbano, Universidad Nacional de General Sarmento. Online at http://observatorioconurbano.ungs.edu.ar/wp-content/uploads/Entrevista-Oscar-Minteguia-versionfinal-29.08.pdf (accessed March 30th 2023).

Muñoz, R. (2007). "Alcance de las microfinanzas para el desarrollo local. Microcrédito en el Conurbano Bonaerense: El Banco Social Moreno y Horizonte," in Muñoz, R., Verbeke, G., Carbonetti, C. and Ozomek, S. (eds.) *Las finanzas y la economía social. Experiencias argentinas*. Buenos Aires: Editorial Altamira, pp. 271–413.

Muñoz, R. (2015). "L'ESS produisant la ville à la périphérie de la périphérie: Deux expériences brésilienne et argentine," *Revue Internationale de l'Économie Sociale*, 337, pp. 72–83. https://doi.org/10.7202/1032524ar

Muñoz, R. (2021). "La promoción estatal de la economía social y solidaria desde lo local," *Otra Economía*, 14(26), pp. 31–48. Online at www.revistaotraeconomia.org/index.php/otraeconomia/article/view/14957 (accessed March 30th 2023).

Muñoz, R. (2022). *La promoción estatal de la economía social y solidaria desde lo local. Aprendizajes y desafíos en los municipios del Conurbano Bonaerense en perspectiva comparada*. PhD Dissertation, Faculty of Social Sciences, University of Buenos Aires.

Muñoz, R. and Coraggio, J. L. (2018). "Actualizando la economía de las ciudades como objeto de estudio y plataforma de acción. Una aproximación desde la economía sustantiva en América Latina," in Coraggio, J. L. and Muñoz, R. (eds.) *Economía de las ciudades de América Latina hoy. Vol. I: Enfoques multidisciplinarios*. Los Polvorines: Ediciones UNGS, pp. 19–84.

Muñoz, R. and Zamora, A. (2021). "Políticas públicas de economía social y solidaria en la Argentina durante la pandemia de la COVID-19. Reflexiones preliminares desde el caso de INAES," *SabereS*, 13(1), pp. 1–30. https://doi.org/10.35305/s.v13i1.247

Sánchez, J. (2014). "La necesaria integralidad de las políticas públicas para la economía social y solidaria," in Instituto Nacional de Economía Popular y Solidaria (IEPS) (ed.) *La economía popular y solidaria. El ser humano sobre el capital*. Quito: IEPS-MIES, pp. 5–19.

Santos, B. de Souza (2012). *De las dualidades a las ecologías*. La Paz: Editora Red Boliviana de Mujeres Transformando la Economía (REMTE).

Vaillancourt, Y. (2011). "La economía social en la co-producción y la co-construcción de las políticas públicas," *Revista del Centro de Estudios de Sociología del Trabajo*, 3, pp. 31–68.

13 Community groups in Lisbon

"Common" paths to democratic co-management in the city

Rogério Roque Amaro and Bárbara Marques Ferreira

13.1 Introduction

This chapter describes processes of Participatory Action Research undertaken in collaboration with Community Groups (CGs) in Lisbon, Portugal, since 1993. Its main purpose is to present the authors' experiences with the CGs, along with new conceptions and practices of transformation of the city and its spatialities emerging from this.

Following a presentation of the theoretical and methodological orientation in Section 13.2, in Section 13.3, we characterise the 16 CGs involved in our action and research, also making some reference to 9 further CGs in the Lisbon Metropolitan Area that we have also followed. In Section 13.4, we reflect on the experiences of the CGs as expressions of the concept of Community or Local Development, along with the theoretical proposal of Shared and Participatory Local Governance, one of the main outcomes. Building on this concept, Section 13.5 presents an analysis of CGs as new urban commons, an innovative model of co-regulation and co-activity for the management of the city's problems and challenges. Finally, Section 13.6 presents some closing reflections, conclusions and challenges for both research and action.

13.2 Methodology

Embracing our own reflexivity, subjectivity and positionality (Haraway, 1988) – as citizens (foremost) and researchers – we followed the methodology of Critical Participatory Action Research (PAR), a "practise-changing practise" whose goal is to propel transformative action upon reality (Kemmis *et al.*, 2014: 26). Action Research is based on the co-construction of knowledge by all its participants and thus challenges researchers' supposed capacity for pure and disinterested objectivity (*ibid.*: 5–6, also cf. Laville & Eynaud, this volume), as well as the enmeshed power relations associated with typical research processes.

The PAR process used research and facilitation techniques drawn from several qualitative traditions, including ethnographic and participatory

DOI: 10.4324/9781003306344-14

methodologies. These techniques include interviews, focus groups, direct and participant observation, photography and video workshops (with children and teenagers from a CG), radio shows, thematic workshops, world café, participatory assemblies and others. The choice of techniques was determined by the diversity of participants, contexts and objectives, involving the action researchers and other actors, in order to minimise asymmetries of power and privilege between participants (cf. Fals Borda & Rahman, 1991: 8–10; Kemmis *et al.*, 2014: 85–87).

The resulting PAR process has so far taken place in a total of 25 CGs, and in particular in 7 CGs where we acted as facilitators. As transversal action research experiences initiated by ourselves, they aimed to create alternative spaces of collective reflection and sociopolitical action. The authors and CG participants have actively collaborated in public dissemination, especially in a radio show called "Utopias in Action" (since 2018) and also in public encounters and conferences promoted by several Universities, local NGOs and other private and public institutions.

Some of the outcomes of this co-creation process are:

1) the creation of the PIC (Inter-Communitary Platform), involving residents of all social housing neighbourhoods in Lisbon that have CGs, where various issues are discussed and transformed from below (e.g. urban waste management, ecological transition, security beyond pathological and/or securitarian approaches, integration of minorities and underrepresented groups);
2) the promotion of regular meetings of CGs (to induce symbiosis and cooperation among distinct experiences), which have assembled, for the first time, more than 100 participants from the metropolitan area of Lisbon, discussing and proposing ways to improve and deepen democracy at the local level;
3) initialisation of a *Shared and Participatory Local Governance* (SPLG) process, bringing elected political representatives together with residents and professionals delegated by their own CGs to represent them in co-production processes in the city of Lisbon, concerning issues relating to their "right to the city" (cf. LeFebvre, 1968; Harvey, 2008) and mutual cooperation strategies to face social challenges amplified by COVID-19;
4) the creation of a "Community Pluriversity" in order to democratise the production of knowledge (epistemologically and cognitively), with a strong intersectional orientation, explicitly focusing on "ecology of knowledges" to construct just cities and societies.

We assume the perspective of Grounded Theory (Glaser & Strauss, 1967) in which researchers and collaborators develop inductive theory on the basis of observation and data collection, with the aim of transforming reality. In this sense, the perspective of Grounded Theory is coherent with our approach and an outcome of PAR.

Based on our experiences,[1] we thus define CGs as informal platforms and dynamics that combine the following concepts and practices:

- *Participation*: Active involvement of communities (residents, as individual and/or collectively, through both informal and formal groups) (Nunes *et al.*, 2017: 70–75);
- *Partnership*: Genuine cooperation between services and institutions, public and/or private, active in the territory (*ibid.*);
- in order to share, in a participative and integrated way, the *diagnosis* of the problems and needs of the Community;
- to claim and/or build together the *responses* and *dreams* to face them;
- and thus achieve the *development, welfare and well-living of the community*.

13.3 History and achievements of Lisbon community groups[2]

The first four CGs were set up as part of an anti-poverty project in 1993 and 1994, all in social housing estates, with disadvantaged and often racialised communities (Nunes *et al.*, 2017: 70–75). All four still exist, in some cases with territorial reconfigurations due to re-housing processes. Replication during the next few years led to the creation of three more CGs, followed by a hiatus until 14 years ago, since when 18 further CGs or Inter-institutional Networks (INs: partnerships among formal institutions with an interest in a particular neighbourhood, not necessarily involving direct participation of community members) have been created in the metropolitan area of Lisbon, 12 of them in Lisbon Municipality. The five most recently created CGs began between 2017 and 2021.

As of 2023, there are 26 CGs and INs in the metropolitan area of Lisbon, 19 of them in Lisbon Municipality (see Table 13.1). Twenty-one are in neighbourhoods that include social housing, with communities in situations of poverty, along with social and political exclusion (including from public policies and interventions), with a strong presence of racialised groups such as Roma families and people of African descent. Some CGs have been inactive in recent years, some due to limitations imposed by COVID-19 and having many residents without internet access and others for longer-standing reasons.

In general, CGs were created to respond better to social problems (in the areas of poverty and social exclusion, housing, employment and mental health) or to promote intercultural dynamics and gender equality, along with participatory citizenship processes. Many were created on the initiative of technicians of various backgrounds and in different combinations. Public technicians were involved in the initiation of 19 CGs, action researchers in 7,[3] NGO technicians in 5, local councillors in 2 and nuns and the community in 1.

Our overall evaluation of the CGs, based on direct participation in CG meetings and gauged along with other participants, is that not all contain all the elements listed in our earlier definition (for further details, see Ferreira & Amaro,

Table 13.1 List of community groups (GGs) and interinstitutional networks (INs) of the Lisbon Metropolitan Area by periods of creation and areas

Time Period	*Designation*	*Neighbourhood/s*	*Municipality*	*Parish*
1–1993–1996	Community Group of Bairro do Padre Cruz (CGPC)	Padre Cruz	Lisbon	Carnide
	Community Group of Horta Nova (CGHN)	Horta Nova	Lisbon	Carnide
	Community Group of Quinta Grande – with some links to Community Group of Alta de Lisboa (CGAL)	Quinta Grande (plus Quinta da Pailepa and Quinta do Louro) – now Alto do Lumiar	Lisbon	Charneca – now Lumiar and Santa Clara
	Community Group of Galinheiras – now Community Group of Galinheiras – Ameixoeira (CGGA)	Galinheiras and Ameixoeira	Lisbon	Ameixoeira – now Santa Clara
	Community Group of Lóios (CGL)	Lóios	Lisbon	Marvila
2–1997–2008	Community Group of Bairro da Flamenga (CGF)*	Flamenga	Lisbon	Marvila
	Community Group of Condado (GCC)*	Condado	Lisbon	Marvila
3–2009–2021	Community Group 4 Crescent (CG4C)	Alfinetes, Marquês de Abrantes, Quinta do Chalé and Salgadas	Lisbon	Marvila
	Community Group Alfredo Bensaúde (CGAB)	Alfredo Bensaúde	Lisbon	Olivais
	Community Group of Bairro do Armador (CGA)**	Armador	Lisbon	Marvila
	(Community Group of Condado – CGC)*	(Condado)	(Lisbon)	(Marvila)
	(Community Group of Bairro da Flamenga – CGF)*	(Flamenga)	(Lisbon)	(Marvila)
	Community Group of Bairro das Fonsecas e Calçada (CGFC)	Fonsecas and Calçada	Lisbon	Alvalade
	Community Group of Liberdade – Serafina (CGL-S)	Liberdade and Serafina	Lisbon	Campolide
	Community Group of Olaias – Portugal Novo (CGO-PN)	Olaias and Portugal Novo	Lisbon	Areeiro

(*Continued*)

Table 13.1 (Continued)

Time Period	*Designation*	*Neighbourhood/s*	*Municipality*	*Parish*
	Community Assembly of Vale de Chelas (CAVC)	Quinta do Lavrado, Carlos Botelho Street, João Nascimento Costa Street and Sarmento Rodrigues Street	Lisbon	Beato and Penha de França
	L & M Network	Quinta das Laranjeiras and Casal dos Machados	Lisbon	Parque das Nações
	Community Group of Marvila Antiga (CGMA)	Marvila Antiga	Lisbon	Marvila
	Community Group of Campo de Ourique (CGCO)	Parish of Campo de Ourique	Lisbon	Campo de Ourique
	Community Group of Santo António (GCSA)***	Parish of Santo António	Lisbon	Santo António
	Telheiras Partnership (TP)	Telheiras	Lisbon	Lumiar
	Community Group of Caparica – Pragal (CGC-P)	Former parishes of Caparica and Pragal	Almada	Parish Councils of Caparica and Trafaria and Parish Councils of Almada, Cova da Piedade, Pragal and Cacilhas
	Network of Development Organisations of Alcabideche (RODA)	Adroana, Alcoitão and Cruz Vermelha	Cascais	Alcabideche
	Institutional Network of Bairro da Galiza (RIG)	Galiza	Cascais	Parish Councils of Cascais and Estoril
	Institutional Network of Bairro da Torre (RIT)	Torre	Cascais	Parish Councils of Cascais and Estoril
(3–2009–2021)	Community Group of Apelação – Quinta da Fonte (CGA-QF)***	Apelação and Quinta da Fonte	Loures	Parish Councils of Camarate, Unhos and Apelação
	Community Group of Pendão (CGP)	Pendão	Sintra	Parish Councils of Queluz and Belas

Notes:

* Interrupted and resumed during period 3.

** Had an ephemeral existence in 2006–2007 before attaining continuity in this period.

*** Inactive.

2021: 81–86; Amaro, 2022: 254–258). Of the 25 analysed, only 11 are what we would call "true Community Groups", meaning that participation is open to the whole community. Of these 11, only 5 have always been so. The other six were created on the initiative of technicians, initially within an institutional and technocratic logic, and only later opened up to the presence of the community. Of these 11, only 8 combine full community participation with a high level of institutional partnership (PI): 4 Crescente, Armador, Condado, Flamenga, Fonsecas e Calçada, Liberdade-Serafina, Galinheiras-Ameixoeira and Padre Cruz and thus can be considered "full or near-full Community Groups" (Amaro, 2018: 73–74).[4] At the opposite extreme are six instances of what we would term "full Interinstitutional Networks", based only on cooperation among municipalities, public services and private institutions, without provision for community participation: Alta de Lisboa, Galiza, Torre, Alcabideche, Alfredo Bensaúde and L&M Network. In some such cases, the absence of the community is deliberate – a way to simplify the work of technicians. In others, the intention is to evolve into a CG through community participation. Other cases lie between these extremes, with different potential to become full CGs.

From 2018, we began to attend all CG and IN meetings. At the time, we noticed a marked absence of communication and collaboration even between CGs in adjoining neighbourhoods. This was despite sharing many similar concerns (such as rubbish collection and safety), and in some cases preparing to take initiatives (such as requesting meetings with political leaders), whose potential impact would be greater if collective and coordinated. We therefore decided to propose a number of joint strategies and actions.

The first and main such action was to create an Inter-Community Platform (PIC) for the 15 Social Housing neighbourhoods of Lisbon, with one or two residents representing each community. The initial focus of the PIC was behaviours concerning rubbish, along with the provision of waste collection facilities. The creation of the PIC was also a way to pressure those CGs that lacked community participation to open up to the involvement of residents, as several did, in some cases thus becoming full CGs (according to our definition earlier).

The PIC had its first meeting on December 28, 2018 and subsequently held 21 meetings in 14 months before restrictions associated with the COVID-19 pandemic came into place. Largely thanks to the commitment and dedication of one of its technicians, it was well-received by the Municipal Directorate of Urban Hygiene and Solid Waste, which accepted community participation, via Community Groups, in co-management of waste issues.

Subsequently, encouraged by a technician from the Aga Khan Foundation, we proposed and held a series of meetings of CGs in the metropolitan area of Lisbon, beginning with four zonal meetings involving 15 CGs from Lisbon social housing neighbourhoods. Following this, the first meeting of CGs (and INs) of the Lisbon Metropolitan Area took place on December 7, 2019, attended by 81 people associated with 21 CGs and INs. The interaction, mutual knowledge, reflection, sharing and collective conviviality among attending CGs resulted in the foundation of a Working Group to create a common website for CGs and INs of the Lisbon Metropolitan Area. Following interruptions due to the COVID-19 pandemic, a second such meeting is scheduled for 25 March 2023.

Another important result was the involvement of the Councillor for Housing and Local Development of the Lisbon City Council, who committed to building, with the CGs, a co-management process for the City of Lisbon. This process aimed to promote local development by discussing and addressing problems faced by the communities of the social housing neighbourhoods. To this end, in May and July 2020, three virtual meetings were held, at which each of the 15 CGs of the social housing neighbourhoods (plus Marvila Antiga) had at least two representatives (one a resident and a technician) attending. The result was the approval of a document outlining an innovative model of *Shared and Participatory Local Governance (SPLG)* for the City of Lisbon (Grupo de Trabalho dos Grupos Comunitários para a GLPP, 2020; also see Ferreira & Amaro, 2021: 94–95).

The SPLG proposal document describes SPLG to be based on the recognition that identifying and addressing the problems and needs of communities are a joint responsibility of all the protagonists of Society. SPLG therefore implies co-responsibility and co-management, involving equal levels of commitment and responsibility on the part of the community, public authorities, private institutions and all companies present in the locality. It emphasises *governance* rather than governing, replacing the presumed monopoly of the state with collective action. It is *local* because it begins with a focus on neighbourhoods, as parts of parishes, which in turn are parts of the municipality (in this case, the City of Lisbon), as the basis for a fairer, more democratic and sustainable city. It is *shared* because it seeks to create partnership among public institutions, civil society (including Social and Solidarity Economy actors) and private entities (companies), collectively mobilising towards community well-being. Finally, and most importantly, it is *participatory*, based on active involvement of community members, both as individuals and as organised groups, thus promoting responsibility and empowerment of all citizens (Grupo de Trabalho dos Grupos Comunitários para a GLPP, 2020).

More recently, in December 2021, joint action of the CGs allowed the birth of the *Community Pluriversity* (CP), an informal structure for knowledge sharing and mutual learning that:

- Intends to value and share a *plurality* of knowledge, with different origins and orientations.
- Starts from the knowledge of *communities* themselves and seeks to address their problems and needs.
- Has neither teachers nor students, only learners.
- Has knowledge-sharing sessions rather than classes.

The CP operates under the support and certification of a Committee of Systematisers and Inductors composed mainly of people from the CGs themselves: 11 residents, 5 technicians and 6 academics. Of these committee members, half have postgraduate academic qualifications and the other half do not (and are not required even to have completed the fourth year of schooling). Half of the committee members are women and half men.

Overall, our assessment is that the CGs and INs have contributed, sometimes in a decisive way, to solving or alleviating many of the issues they seek to address (also see Ferreira & Amaro, 2021: 91–96). Specific achievements include:

- Construction of shared and participatory community diagnosis in ten CGs, giving a voice, in an unconditional and (in some cases) deliberative manner, to the community.
- Instigation of co-management of selected public spaces by six CGs, including local authority halls, outdoor public spaces and three cases of vacant land earmarked for real estate purposes but instead transformed into two community gardens and an urban park.
- Community requisition of equipment in municipal buildings, public gardens and social urban gardens, evident in three CGs.
- Redefining and reinforcing positive, solidarity-based identities in at least 15 social housing neighbourhoods previously marked by a sense of stigmatisation and of negative and aggressive identities and consequent emergence of a new methodology of community participation in these neighbourhoods.
- Support during the COVID-19 pandemic of infected people, families in confinement or who had lost their jobs and children requiring distance learning, including psychological support. In an unprecedented and remarkable process of SPLG (described further in Lima *et al.*, 2021), one CG, in Galinheiras-Ameixoeira, was delegated by the Ministry of Health to survey risk situations, organise tests for local populations and monitor and support infected people and their families.

Increased collective action through mechanisms such as the PIC and SPLG has led to further significant results[5]:

- Recurring participation of staff of the Lisbon Municipal Council Local Development Department (CML-DDL), including the Councillor herself, in meetings of CGs in social housing neighbourhoods, and a commitment of a representative of CML-DDL being present at all CG meetings and the Councillor attending at least once per year;
- Co-responsibility of the CGs for issuing opinions (and, in the future, decisions) on the allocation of municipal non-residential and commercial spaces;
- The creation of a Working Group on Occupations and Evictions, constituted by representatives of Community Groups of neighbourhoods with higher

incidences of illegal occupation of municipal housing to discuss proposals for the just, dignified, equitable and legal resolution of these situations and present them to the democratic structures of the CML;

- Provision to each CG by the CML-DDL of a dedicated space to anchor their community activities, under very favourable financial conditions and managed on behalf of the community as an urban commons (or urban *baldio*)

A side effect of this work has been the initiation of a project, delivered collaboratively by CML-DDL and the Santa Casa da Misericórdia de Lisboa, called *Mudar de Vida* (changing life). The project involves 13 ethnic Roma families evicted in January--March 2020 and aims to achieve a number of social integration and well-being goals, negotiated with them, in several areas – education, employment and entrepreneurship, housing, gender equality, health and autonomy – supported by the CGs of the associated territories. This partnership between the CG and CML-LLD, which gives substance to the SPLG, was preceded by the remarkable joint work between the PIC and the CML-Urban Hygiene Department already described.

13.4 CGs as experiences of community development and Shared and Participatory Local Governance

13.4.1 CGs as experiences of community development

We here employ the concepts of Community Development and Local Development as equivalent. However, their understanding may vary depending on factors such as the historical moment, their recognition (or not) and scientific validation, geographic and cultural context, institutional frameworks and the relative status of protagonists.[6]

Again following the logic of Grounded Theory, our experiences and analysis led us to the following definition[7]: a process of change; centred in a community (of human scale and proximity); it aims, by responding to unmet basic needs, to increase well-being and well-living, starting from endogenous capacities and resources. This implies a methodology and pedagogy of participation and empowerment, with exogenous resources fertilising endogenous ones, in an integrated and multidimensional perspective. It also requires a logic of partnership, that is articulation among institutions and services, with a tendency to impact on the whole community. Finally, it accommodates diverse rhythms, logics, processes and results, reflecting the specific characteristics of each community.

Another interesting link relates to the promotion of economic activities following the principles of Solidarity Economy.[8] We found this in several CGs, including those in 4 Crescente, Alta de Lisboa, Flamenga, Fonsecas e Calçada, Galinheiras-Ameixoeira, Lóios and Pendão.

13.4.2 CGs as Shared and Participatory Local Governance

During the last four years, the Lisbon CGs have developed an innovative process of cooperation with municipal departments to co-manage issues relating to urban hygiene and domestic waste management, housing policy, management of municipal housing and other spaces, management of public and common spaces, and responses to crises such as COVID-19 (Lima *et al.*, 2021). The main goal is to create a new model of political regulation through active cooperation between communities and institutions, based on four key principles:

- Neighbourhood-scale or *local*: effective proximity, life and identity;
- *Shared:* committed partnership of institutions (public and private, including companies) and public services active in the neighbourhood;
- *Participatory:* participation and active involvement of local communities;
- *Governance:* Co-responsibility for management of social problems and challenges, and therefore of the common good.

This combination leads us to name this model and concept *Shared and Participatory Local Governance* (SPLG). Initiated in Lisbon and involving a number of local communities, SPLG has already been replicated in at least two municipalities – Arouca and Santa Maria da Feira in the metropolitan area of Porto. It has a territorial basis of proximity, combines partnerships with participation and proposes a new way of approaching and regulating public action, until now either monopolised by the State or denied/devalued and replaced by the Market.

SPLG is innovative in six main respects:

(i) a new type of cooperation between local communities and local services and institutions, called a Community Group;
(ii) a definition assumed and defined collectively – commoning the knowledge (see Grupo de Trabalho dos Grupos Comunitários para a GLPP, 2020);
(iii) involving local communities in making local policy – commoning the political;
(iv) a new type of community involvement in policy making – politicising communities;
(v) a new designation containing the four essential components listed before;
(vi) unprecedented application to public policy in Lisbon, already replicated by other municipalities.

The concept raises at least four points for reflection.

First, its four central components make clear why its (practical and theoretical) basis is the CGs, since it was them who proposed and initiated the process through the PIC (Section 13.3). Political and technical leaders joined later.

Second, its most fundamental, decisive and innovative element is the (participatory) involvement of the community, and indeed its very presence, which through the CGs is recovered and revalued. This crucial element links SPLG with the concept of empowered participatory governance proposed by Fung (2003: 3–45, also see Amaro, 2018).

Third, the concept of SPLG is also based on institutional partnerships (public and private). In the face of the insufficiency of State-led public action and counterproductive nature of market-led private action (Fung, 2003: 3–6), there is a need for collective mobilisation involving partnership among all major protagonists of society, including local communities. The importance of these institutional partnerships is understated in the empowered participatory governance model, which is based, above all, on the role of the community and its participatory and deliberative processes. However, in our research, we found that the most successful CGs, in terms of results, were those in which community involvement was matched by the involvement of the institutions′ technical staff. In this way, participatory democracy benefits from technical knowledge, provided the latter submits to the logic of the community. This broadening of the role of the SPLG brings it (dangerously) close to essentially neoliberal proposals such Tony Blair's "Third Way" and David Cameron's "Big Society". However, SPLG differs in that it recognises the essential role of the State and aims to reinforce it with a new concept of public action, more independent of the State and enriched by the important role played by the community.

Finally, as we explore further in Section 13.5, the return of "community"[9] as an important societal protagonist, and key participant in the regulation of its own problems and challenges, resonates with the revaluation and resurgence of the concept of commons (also see Laville and Eynaud, this volume).

13.5 CGs as new urban commons

The so-called "return" of the Commons has an interesting and rather wide expression in the scientific literature, following the foundational work of Elinor Ostrom (1990). We can, for example, consider the so-called "New Commons" (Bollier, 2014), relationships with "alternative economic practices" and "alternative spaces" (Gibson-Graham, 2008) or "solidarity economies" (Vathakou, 2015; Eynaud & Laville, 2017; Laville & Eynaud, this volume), with the politics of solidarity (Healy *et al.*, 2018), as co-activities (Dardot & Laval, 2014), relationships with the city and urban spatialities (Harvey, 2000, 2008, 2012; Hollender, 2016; Özkan & Büyüksaraç, 2020) and even view practices as "*commoning projects*" (Varvarousis & Kallis, 2017). As the following five points indicate, CGs can be considered in many of these perspectives.[10]

First of all, CGs are knowledge-sharing experiences, foreshadowing what we earlier referred to as "commoning knowledge". Co-production of knowledge, through Shared and Participatory Diagnostics, allows dialogical exchange among different epistemologies, combining community perspectives with institutional and technical perspectives, popular knowledge with academic knowledge, inductive knowledge with deductive knowledge and practical knowledge with theoretical systematisation. We can relate this to Boaventura de Sousa Santos' (2007) concept of an "ecology of knowledges".

Second, some CGs reflect the conquest of deliberative processes by those most affected by them, which we might call "commoning the decision-making process". Such processes of co-decision within a communitarian approach (territorially based), as well as the inclusion of marginalised groups in previously opaque spheres of urban governance, promote the broadening and deepening of democracy.

Third, some CGs have explicit processes of co-construction of interventions and solutions to the problems and challenges of community life, along with corresponding "co-activities" (Dardot & Laval, 2014). By carrying out these aspects of the commons, CGs, rather than "acting in common" ("*agir en commun*"), propose and achieve processes of "common action" ("*agir commun*") *(ibid.:* 137–188, 276–284): "commoning the action".

Fourth, CGs have put in place effective practices of co-management of public and community spaces in which the community claims and achieves an active role in defining the rules and criteria for their use. In this sense, a CG is a Common (Dardot & Laval, 2014; Healy *et al.*, 2018) as it constitutes an informal collective entity of undefined collective ownership (in fact, the question of ownership does not arise), organised and managed in common with the community's participation, to identify and help solve local problems by carrying out joint activities, or "co-activities", for community use and benefit. At the same time, CGs contribute to making politics a common project (by *commoning* the political) in a transformative way (Ferreira & Amaro, 2021: 95; Hollender, 2016: 3, 6–11).

Finally, CGs have allowed the development and strengthening of a common identity (more visible in the older CGs), essential for building up collective action and mobilisation. The collective exercise of imagining alternative futures, centred around the principles of community development and ideals of common good, promotes the (re)construction of a collective identity, frequently erased (both spatially and psychosocially) by the technocratic policies of rehousing in the Lisbon Metropolitan Area: "commoning the identity".

These are the fundamental characteristics which consubstantiate CGs as Commons, since collective management and use (through co-activities) play a more important role in *commoning* processes than the formal issue of ownership (cf. Dardot & Laval, 2014: 233–284; Healy *et al.*, 2018; Amaro, 2018: 28–30; Ferreira & Amaro, 2021: 91–96). In fact, we here consider commons as "all activities that are fundamental for a Sustainable Life, whose private appropriation (use and management) may jeopardise and/or public management may be insufficient or inadequate, thus being better managed and used autonomously by (or jointly with) the Community" (Amaro, 2018: 29). Two interesting ideas to develop further are those concerning the concepts of "liminal commons" and "rhizomatic movement" (Varvarousis & Kallis, 2017: 131–133), applied to the specific qualities of CGs.

Moreover, CGs can be situated in the same logic as *Baldios*, the Portuguese designation for community lands, with an ancient presence in many regions of the country. Their ownership, management and use are communal through the constitution of *Assembleias de Aldeia* (Village Assemblies). Historically, especially from the 19th Century on, they were subject to private appropriation (under the affirmation of capitalism in Portugal) and public repression (especially in the 20th Century, during the Salazar dictatorship), but in many instances resisted. Several of these traditional commons still exist in Portugal (one of the few countries in Europe where they persist), recognised by special legislation (Ferreira & Amaro, 2021: 86). In a way, CGs have characteristics similar to Baldios, but are urban and intangible.

13.6 Conclusion

The CGs are a very distinctive and specific experience of Portugal and, in particular, of Lisbon, without previous influences or inspirations from other countries. They demonstrate great variety of arrangements and rationales. The (five) oldest are almost 30 years old, which allows for an analysis that is already quite substantive and well-founded. However, it should be noted that, of the 25 CGs that currently exist in the Lisbon Metropolitan Area, 20 were created in the last 14 years (2 of which resumed after a hiatus of many years).

In the CGs with the highest levels of citizen engagement and community participation, we find practices of local participatory and deliberative democracy; histories that are coherent and which pave the way to Community Development; processes of SPLG, with some departments of Lisbon City Council, which express an innovative model of regulation and co-management of the city's (and society's) problems and challenges; an expression and example of a new commons, in reference to their ethos and framework and improvements to the welfare, dignity and sustainability of some local communities. These results, effects or characteristics of the CGs constitute, simultaneously, a potential for sociopolitical innovation and transformation, which may yet be extended to more CGs and strengthened, opening new pathways for change in the near future.

By involving the community and catalysing its active participation, the CGs represent one of the most fruitful ways of returning the raison d'être of the *Polis* and the *Civitas* back to their central protagonists – the citizens – in the process of making and remaking the city and, thus, themselves (cf., e.g. Harvey, 2012). Bringing communities back to the task of identifying and solving the problems and challenges of present-day society undertakes the legitimation of a previously overlooked and undervalued *situated knowledge* (Haraway, 1988), bringing forth new perspectives and priorities, as well as new arrangements of self-organisation and co-management in hitherto fragmented communities.

One of the most important effects of CGs is undoubtedly their actual and potential impacts on urban spatialities. First of all is in the reconfiguration and management of the public spaces of their neighbourhoods, redefining, through their action, some of the uses and decision models concerning these uses – commoning and democratising their spatialities. We can speak of a partial community appropriation of neighbourhood spatialities. The examples given of two CGs impeding real estate interests and instead creating spaces of community interest (urban gardens and an urban park) clearly illustrate this effect.

Another effect that is more difficult to concretise immediately refers to spatialities in the city of Lisbon. The SPLG process under construction may open perspectives in this sense but implies an aggregation of interests and actions, involving the CGs as a whole, which is not evident, and depends on acceptance by the municipality's new political leaders (who are from right-wing parties).

Another important question concerns possibilities for dissemination and replication of this model of local governance. The answer to this question already exists: two municipalities in the metropolitan area of Porto are applying a model inspired by the CGs in 26 of their parishes; another municipality in the centre region has requested support to implement this model in urban neighbourhoods with wicked social problems and a new CG is about to be started in another social neighbourhood in Lisbon. The main precondition has been to combine political and/or technical interest with community mobilisation and interest, as the cases described here demonstrate.

Finally, it should be noted that the model illustrated by the CGs can play an important role in reconfiguring local public policies, especially in the current context of decentralisation of social policies. It can inspire the shift from a logic of governing to one of governance, the assumption of shared regulation with other institutional players and, above all, their democratisation, with the effective participation of citizens, individually and collectively.

Notes

1. See Amaro (2018: 18), Ferreira & Amaro (2021: 69–73), cf. Marchioni (1999: 8–12, 2002: 2–19).
2. For a further discussion of this point, see Amaro (2022: 234–238).
3. The authors of this text.
4. On the decisive importance of this interaction, see, for example Marchioni (1999: 9, 2002: 2–4), Amaro (2018: 18, 69–73) and Ferreira & Amaro (2021: 81–86).
5. Meanwhile, since the first version of this text, local elections have taken place, changing the party in charge of the CML to one more to the right, but the CGs have been pressing for this process not to be lost and to continue in the essential points conquered.
6. See Amaro (2022: 196–208) and references therein.
7. Cf. for example Amaro (2009a: 111; 2018: 21–22).
8. Cf., for example Amaro (2009b); Laville (2018).
9. For discussion of the meaning of "community", see, for example Amaro (2018: 20–21).
10. Cf. also Ferreira and Amaro (2021: 91–96).

References

Amaro, R. R. (2009a). "Desenvolvimento Local," in Cattani, A., Laville, J. L., Gaiger, L. I. and Hespanha, P. (eds.) *Dicionário Internacional da Outra Economia*. Coimbra: CES/Almedina, pp. 108–113.

Amaro, R. R. (2009b). "A Economia Solidária da Macaronésia – Um novo conceito," *Revista de Economia Solidária*, 1, pp. 11–28.

Amaro, R. R. (2018). *Manual de Práticas e Métodos sobre Grupos Comunitários*. Lisboa: Leigos para o Desenvolvimento.

Amaro, R. R. (2022). "Desenvolvimento Comunitário em Portugal: Caminhos para o Aprofundamento da Democracia (Uma Governança Local Partilhada e Participativa em contexto de crises)," in Estivill, J. and Balsa, C. (eds.) *Economia local, comunitária e solidária: O desenvolvimento visto de baixo*. Vila Nova de Famalicão: Editora Húmus, pp. 192–282.

Bollier, D. (2014). *The Commons as a Template for Transformation*. Online at http://greattransition.org/publication/the-commons-as-a-template-for-transformation (accessed March 30th 2023).

Dardot, P. and Laval, C. (2014). *Commun: Essai sur la révolution au XXIe siècle*. Paris: La Découverte.

Eynaud, P. and Laville, J. L. (2017). "Joining the commons with social and solidarity economy research: Towards the renewal of critical thinking and emancipation," *Revista de Economia Solidária*, 11, pp. 12–29.

Fals Borda, O. and Rahman, M. (1991). *Action and Knowledge: Breaking the Monopoly with Participatory Action-Research*. New York: The Apex Press.

Ferreira, B. and Amaro, R. R. (2021). "The Community Groups of Lisboa as 'Commons'," *Revista de Economia Solidária*, 14, pp. 66–101.

Fung, A. (2003). "Thinking about Empowered Participatory Governance," in Fung, A. and Wright, E. O. (eds.) *Deepening Democracy: Institutional Innovations in Empowered Participatory Governance*. London and New York: Verso, pp. 3–44.

Gibson-Graham, J. K. (2008). "Diverse economies: Performative practices for 'other worlds'," *Progress in Human Geography*, 32(5), pp. 613–632.

Glaser, B. and Strauss, A. (1967). *The Discovery of Grounded Theory: Strategies for Qualitative Research*. Chicago: Aldine.

Grupo de Trabalho dos Grupos Comunitários para a GLPP. (2020). *Uma Proposta de Governança Local Partilhada e Participativa para a Cidade de Lisboa, com o envolvimento dos Grupos Comunitários*. Lisboa: documento de trabalho não editado.

Haraway, D. (1988). "Situated knowledges: The science question in feminism and the privilege of partial perspective," *Feminist Studies*, 14(3), pp. 575–599.

Harvey, D. (2000). *Spaces of Hope*. Edinburgh: Edinburgh University Press.

Harvey, D. (2008). "The right to the city," *New Left Review*, 53, pp. 23–40.

Harvey, D. (2012). *Rebel Cities: From the Right to the City to the Urban Revolution*. London: Verso.

Healy, S., Borowiak, C. Pavlovskaya, M. and Safri, M. (2018). "Commoning and the politics of solidarity: Transformational responses to poverty," *Geoforum*, 127, pp. 306–315.

Hollender, R. (2016). "A politics of the commons or commoning the political? Distinct possibilities for post-capitalist transformation," *Spectra*, 5(1), pp. 1–15.

Kemmis, S., McTaggart, R. and Nixon, R. (2014). *The Action Research Planner: Doing Critical Participatory Action Research*. Singapore: Springer.

Laville, J. L. (2018). *A Economia Social e Solidária: Práticas, Teorias e Debates*. Coimbra: CES/Almedina.

LeFebvre, H. (1968). *Le Droit à la Ville*. Paris: Anthropos.

Lima, M., Amaro, R. R. and Ferreira, B. (2021). "An experience of shared and participatory local governance," *Practice Insights*, 17, pp. 34–37. Online at www.iacdglobal.org/wp-content/uploads/2020/12/IACD_033_PI_Issue-17_V1_High-Res.pdf (accessed March 30th 2023).

Marchioni, M. (1999). *Comunidad, participación y desarrollo: Teoría y metodología de la intervención comunitaria*. Madrid: Editorial Popular.

Marchioni, M. (2002). "Organización y desarrollo de la comunidad: La intervención comunitaria en las nuevas condiciones sociales," in Sarrate Capdevila, M. L. (ed.) *Programas de Animación Sociocultural*. Madrid: UNED, pp. 455–482.

Nunes, N., Viana, A. M., Serra, N. and Amaro, R. R. (2017). *Intervenção Comunitária: Conhecimentos e Práticas da Santa Casa da Misericórdia de Lisboa*. Lisbon: Centro Editorial da SCML.

Ostrom, E. (1990). *Governing the Commons: The Evolution of Institutions for Collective Action*. Cambridge: Cambridge University Press.

Özkan, D. and Büyüksaraç, G. B. (eds.) (2020). *Commoning the City: Empirical Perspectives on Urban Ecology, Economics and Ethics*. New York: Routledge.

Santos, B. S. (2007). "Para além do Pensamento Abissal: Das linhas globais a uma ecologia de saberes," *Novos Estudos – CEBRAP*, 79, pp. 71–94.

Varvarousis, A. and Kallis, G. (2017). "Commoning against the crisis," in Castells, M. et al. (ed.) *Another Economy Is Possible: Culture and Economy in a Time of Crisis*. Cambridge: Polity, pp. 128–159.

Vathakou, E. (2015). "Citizens´solidarity initiatives in Greece during the financial crisis," in Huliaras, A. and Clark, J. (eds.) *Austerity and the Third Sector in Greece: Civil Society at the European Front Line*. Farnham: Ashgate, pp. 167–192.

14 The role of Social and Solidarity Economy in the inclusive urban regeneration power of nature-based solutions

What can we learn from the Nadezhda district in Sofia?

Beatriz Caitana, Milena Tasheva-Petrova and Nathalie Vallet

14.1 Introduction

The intertwining of urban space and Social and Solidarity Economy (SSE) has been relevant in different ways. The new forms of sociability derived from the diversified use of the urban spaces, the socio-political engagement in community and the socio-economic adaptive capacity of NBS are among them. By reaffirming nature as a key ingredient of current urban regeneration models (Wilk et al., 2021), this article aims to explore connections between the social, the economic and the environmental dimensions. It is part of the outputs derived from the URBiNAT[1] – Urban inclusive and innovative Nature – a European Union-funded project focusing on innovative urban regeneration through co-creation of *Healthy Corridors* (HCs) in disadvantaged urban areas, with clusters of nature-based solutions (NBS). Differentiation between the NBS and HC concepts is largely a matter of scale: the HC is on a macro-scale (i.e. urban, with links between urban neighbourhoods) and consists of various NBS positioned at a lower or micro-scale (i.e. NBS clustering).

NBS are the building blocks of HC, using wider holistic and innovative perspectives to go beyond the conventional definition of NBS. The macro-scale HC can be characterised by four particular features: (1) specific actions in urban space, customised to respond to the current needs of the community; (2) a focus on the co-creation by citizens, technicians and researchers of material, social and cultural infrastructure based on nature; (3) for the purpose of regenerating the urban place in a deprived (consisting of social housing) urban area and (4) in order to improve the socio-political, physical, mental and/or socio-economic well-being and health of residents, people who are working and visiting, and other stakeholder communities and users of the area. Since 2018, an HC has been implemented in each of three front-runner cities (Porto, Nantes and Sofia) and four follower cities (Siena, Nova Gorica, Brussels and Høje-Taastrup), including the activation of Local Living Labs, the catalogue of NBS and the community of practice.

DOI: 10.4324/9781003306344-15

The central objective of this chapter is to explore how SSE practices within the HC of the Nadezhda District in Sofia support NBS initiatives in public spaces, becoming more than just a "green solution," as well as facilitating the inclusive regeneration of urban neighbourhoods. The chapter is divided into nine sections. Section 14.2 seeks to substantiate the relationship between NBS and SSE on the basis of a literature review. This includes defining the NBS concept, identifying how the SSE concept can be related to inclusive urban regeneration and emphasising how the consequences and effects of NBS can thus be upgraded. Section 14.3 seeks to frame the context-sensitive key concept of Section 14.2, being SSE, in view of our case study of the Nadezhda district in Sofia. This case study examines a Bulgarian reality using three lenses: the political, the investigative and the social. In Sections 14.4 to 14.8, we investigate empirically how the SSE and particular practices in the Nadezhda District reinforce the local NBS and the HC and thus support inclusive urban regeneration within this district. Section 14.9, in conclusion, highlights the relevance of the HC as an alternative space containing practices, epistemologies and pedagogies that support the socio-economic adaptation of communities.

14.2 Moving beyond nature-based solutions

It is widely agreed that systematic actions for mitigating the effects of climate change are need.[2] The European Commission (EC) has been intensively using the term NBS[3] since 2015, defining it as solutions that are "inspired and supported by nature, which are cost-effective, simultaneously provide environmental, social and economic benefits and help build resilience" (European Commission, 2015: 5). Since then, funds, resolutions and policies, initiatives and research (Davies *et al.*, 2021) have been adopted to strengthen NBS worldwide.[4] More recently, a UNEP resolution[5] recognised the roles of NBS in supporting sustainable development, and, innovatively, it includes safeguarding the rights of communities and indigenous peoples.

Although there is general agreement as to their relevance, NBS can be implemented in a variety of ways. Some focus on innovating with nature, privileged investment models (Droste *et al.*, 2017) and institutional governance solutions (Ferreira *et al.*, 2020; Lupp & Zingraff-Hamed, 2021). Others focus on strategic investment in climate mitigation and adaptation (Seddon *et al.*, 2020) and on impact assessment (European Commission, 2021). Unfortunately, only a few focus on the socio-political and socio-economic impacts of NBS (Dumitru *et al.*, 2020). As such, there exists, for instance, the nature-based economy (McQuaid *et al.*, 2021), which focuses on new methods of valuing natural capital and enabling its incorporation into the economic system, although this currently lacks critical position concerning business outputs and the retrogressive effects of their conventional models. Additionally, the Marseille Manifesto (from 2020)[6] explicitly encourages all economic sectors to make investments in nature that advance social justice and inclusion, given pre-existing inequalities.

These broad embedded NBS approaches and foci are scarce, and there is great need for further development. After all, considering NBS as part of a complex set of concepts, solutions and benefits in socio-ecological systems, their main role is to operationalise the concept of ecosystem services in real-world situations (Faivre *et al.*, 2017). Moving beyond conventional definitions of NBS towards broader conceptualisations, this operationalisation occurs through innovative governance, namely amplifying opportunities within their structure, as well as intense participatory, co-creative, community-driven processes. This includes, for instance, NBS that: (1) reinforce human–nature relationships; (2) bring greater diversity of nature into cities, which thus become more resilient; (3) strive for sustainable consumption and production, with particular concern for local communities and indigenous peoples and (4) angle job creation strategies towards (more) social inclusion and equitable distribution.

Thus, following the central objective of this chapter, we can ask ourselves the following questions. Is explicit engagement of SSE in NBS an opportunity to expand the economic and socio-political impact of NBS? Can NBS engagement also facilitate the distribution of justice and equity, as well as enable inclusive regeneration of urban neighbourhoods? Can other overlooked intangible values and benefits be considered and made visible with an SSE perspective? There are indeed several ways to move beyond NBS, starting with a virtuous relationship between SSE and inclusive urban regeneration. This must be considered when looking at urban neighbourhoods as part of a relational dynamic within a set of complex cultural, socio-political, socio-economic and emotional links, rather than merely as spaces for circulation and living. Accordingly, Section 14.3 looks for answers in the existing literature, while Section 14.4 highlights lessons learned from an empirical study in the district of Nadezhda in Sofia.

14.3 The potential of Social and Solidarity Economy in making urban regeneration inclusive

An "inclusive" urban regeneration underlines its people-centred goal (Welden *et al.*, 2021) and benefits from active involvement of residents/users in urban transformation, thus prioritising those in disadvantaged situations. Stijnen (2021) points out the failure to prioritise equity and social inclusion issues in implementing NBS, despite them being considered contributors to urban regeneration (Andreucci, 2022). Accordingly, could SSE help to more closely reconcile the use of NBS with a more "inclusive" urban regeneration?

To answer this question, let us explore the essence of SSE. As a principle, SSE is based on a different economic logic, where profit and accumulation are not the ultimate goals, but consumption and production are instead adapted to the public interest (Laville, 2018; Singer, 2018; Hespanha & Lucas dos Santos,

2016). As a practice, it assumes a double dynamic of democracy and solidarity (Laville, 2018), through associativism and cooperativism, creating spaces for a non-monetary economy, democratic management and political participation.

Therefore, in certain cases, SSE offers sustainable goods and services and takes explicit care of the ecological balance within the immediate environment. For this reason, specific attention is paid by SSE to shortening economic circuits using local materials (e.g. crops from local urban gardening and agriculture), focusing on affordability and local needs. Inclusive production implies that SSE guarantees equal access to the economic resources needed (e.g. through solidarity finance, complementary currencies, microcredit, mutualism, commons). Inclusive consumption, in turn, implies equal access for all consumer profiles, including the deprived and cultural and demographic minorities (e.g. through solidarity markets, consumer groups, exchange clubs). SSE also pays specific attention to local waste and pollution challenges (e.g. clean water, pesticide use, energy production, food waste). Additionally, SSE prioritises small-scale economic activities that promote "sufficiency" over global activities that boost efficiency. Finally, SSE activities are explicitly based on social relations of cooperativism and reciprocity, in contrast to mainstream economic thought based on self-interest and competitiveness.

When investigating how SSE can practically and actually reinforce the capacity of NBS to promote socio-economic inclusion in urban regeneration, we identify four key approaches in existing literature (reinforced by our own empirical research). We consider these approaches as "dimensions" of SSE, crucial to the development of the Nadezhda case study. The following subsections describe each of these four approaches in turn.

14.3.1 Impacts of nature-based solutions on local economic fabric and equity benefits

Involvement of SSE in NBS renders the local and regional economic fabric of production and consumption more empowered, interconnected, resilient and equitable. This occurs through: (1) use of local/regional natural resources to promote economic development, (2) connecting economically developed communities, fostering well-being in a complementary rather than competitive fashion, (3) pluralistic approaches promoting mutual help, which can build resilience, and (4) spreading benefits by ensuring straightforward and unencumbered access for each citizen to production and consumption opportunities.

SSE offers greater guarantees of long-term regeneration, making the local economy more resilient: when profitability declines in the neighbourhood (e.g. due to monetary crises or opportunities in other regions), profit-led entrepreneurs may leave or cease operations, but SSE enterprises will not (c.f. Šimleša, this volume). SSE enterprises also reinforce the skills of their employees and promote other kinds of associative labour (e.g. recovered companies, cooperatives) in a more long-term and sustainable manner. A neighbourhood can thus become a cradle or hub for broader economic regeneration throughout the entire city (cf. Muñoz, this volume). For local inhabitants, unemployment may decrease, and income distribution become more equitable.

Moreover, SSE regenerates the territorial-level interconnectedness of economic activities and their immediate environments. Wealth generated by the community is thus more likely to remain in the territory. SSE reinvests profit in the geographic areas in which it is created, mobilises local actors and resources, creates a cooperative culture, links activities to local needs and maintains activities at risk of disappearing due to a lack of profit. These are all important to the inclusion impacts of NBS.

14.3.2 Impacts of nature-based solutions on respecting public space and human–nature interdependencies

Public space is not merely a background for solidarity actions; it is a strategic priority, as a source of identification and construction of common frames of reference (Martin, 2003), as a focus of struggle (Castells, 1983) and as a location of contestation or meeting point (Oosterlynck *et al.*, 2017). SSE is grounded in territoriality, including public space, and so stimulates the construction of production and consumption subsystems. That, in turn, influences the way a public space is perceived by urban citizens and reinforces the relationships with the pre-existing urban space, which shape a differentiated space (Lefebvre, 1991), through diverse sociocultural practices and new types of conviviality.

There is an understanding of the economy that sees it as including all phenomena related to the interdependencies between humans and nature (Polanyi, 1944; Hillenkamp, 2013). For many years, the commodification of nature due to extractivist capitalism has enriched private interest groups and broken down human–nature relationships. Although not explicit, there is a linkage between SSE and ecological economics, as both seek a just society and democratic transformation of the economy (Šimleša, 2023; also see Umantseva, Hulgård & Hauggaard-Nielsen, this volume).

SSE, through its strong focus on societal aspects of economic activities, engenders a high degree of respect for public space and contributes to more equal power relationships and harmonised human interdependencies in any specific such space (e.g. see Šimleša, this volume; Sanz, Sama & Carrero, this volume). This can be done directly when SSE is also involved in the building, construction and maintenance of the NBS public space. It can also be done indirectly by creating economic activities within the NBS public space, which support and reinforce the overall public nature of the regenerated neighbourhood. In this way, the functionality of green public space is expanded, reducing the public monopoly and diversifying the ways citizens use it. The perception of security increases, as does social cohesion.

14.3.3 Impacts of nature-based solutions on community empowerment and democratic management

SSE is grounded in democratic management; it means the use of shared decision rules, collective work and democratic solidarity. Rather than a perception of solidarity based on a benevolent attitude, democratic solidarity is a principle of the democratisation of society itself, from which collective actions of social reproduction emerge that attempt to reduce inequalities (Laville, 2018). It includes information-sharing, shared decision-making and co-governance. These elements enhance the autonomy of communities when the actions implemented do not depend on the support of third-party organisations but on the commitment and ability to create solutions of the community itself.

The focus of SSE on democratic management and democratic solidarity reinforces democratic skills (listening, communicating, negotiating), as well as self-management skills (cooperation, sharing, reciprocity). Thanks to such skills development, SSE also can shift power relationships towards greater equality. When SSE is involved in NBS, it may not only provide extra support for the co-creation or ambition of the NBS, but may also improve relevant skills and levels of commitment.

14.3.4 Impacts of nature-based solutions on culture and political traditions

Culture, as one of the four main functions of ecosystem services (Croci & Lucchitta, 2021), creates strong connection to a place and contributes to the shaping of particular community identities in organic and fluid processes. SSE influences this spatial connectivity and shapes associated identities. This is done, for instance, by bringing together the social demands of various actors linked by a shared and explicit desire for social change (Vaillancourt & Favreau, 2001; CIRIEC, 2016). Therefore, when SSE is closely involved in NBS, the beneficial impact of the NBS on the culture of the associated space and neighbourhood will increase accordingly.

The connection between economy and society may affect societal power relationships and as such provoke political reforms (Polanyi, 1944). This is certainly also the case with the outspoken ideas of SSE concerning redistributive economic justice, deep sustainability and active citizenship aiming to tackle exclusion, inequality and unsustainability (UNRISD, 2016; Utting, 2016). SSE has further been referred to as "the only new way of thinking about and envisaging effective and profound transformative processes" (Razeto, 1999) capable of addressing a broader civilisational crisis by involving a wide coalition of actors. Thus, SSE is at the heart of cultural change in lifestyles, consumption patterns, patterns of human interaction in harmony with others and nature and collective well-being (Gudynas, 2011; Utting, 2016). Close involvement of SSE with NBS thus increases the impacts of those NBS on political change and, accordingly, on the potential likelihood of political reform.

14.4 Methodological approach of the case study

The goal of our case study research was to explore, on the basis of empirical findings in a real-life setting, if and how SSE initiatives in the district of Nadezhda reinforce and expand the capacity of NBS to contribute to inclusive urban regeneration. To answer this overall question, we consider the following specific research questions (RQs):

- What are the socio-political bases and consequences of SSE activity in the Sofia context? (RQ1);
- How does this SSE activity affect the co-governance of public space, socio-economic priorities in Sofia and the future HC in the District of Nadezhda? (RQ2);
- What action is required and what is the realistic timeframe for achieving synergies among SSE, NBS and the HC in Nadezhda District? (RQ3).

In order to answer the RQs, our account here will address both the context (URBiNAT and the HC and the historical development of SSE practices in Bulgaria) and the case study itself (SSE practices identified from the Living Lab in Sofia and the SSE NBS to be implemented in the HC). Our analysis of SSE practices will use the four dimensions described in Section 14.3 and systematised in Figure 14.1.

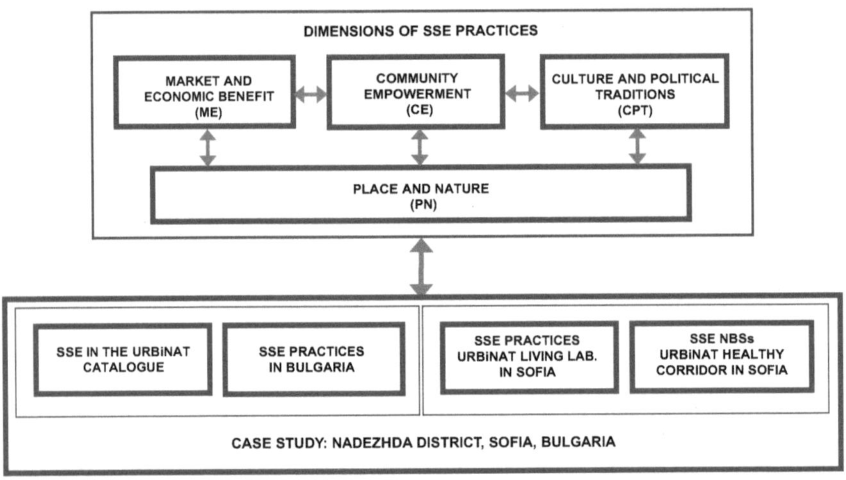

Figure 14.1 Methodological approach to studying SSE in Nadezhda district, Sofia, in the framework of the URBiNAT project

Context-setting is based on desktop research and literature review. The case study itself is based on findings from research conducted within URBiNAT and using several methods. Interviews, conducted in 2019, with 10 for-profit and 15 non-profit organisations, helped fine-tune the contextualisation of SSE case studies in Sofia. Co-design workshops with citizens provided insights into community empowerment, socio-political bases and consequences of SSEs and promoted co-governance by activating local advisory board committees. The URBiNAT HC plan, designed in 2021, provided a better understanding of the concept of SSE among participants, who selected a set of customised SSE solutions. Finally, the URBiNAT catalogue evaluated combined SSE NBS proposals, along with existing technological, territorial and participatory solutions (see Table 14.1).

14.5 SSE practices in Bulgaria and Sofia: historical traditions and the current governance framework

The SSE in Bulgaria was born in response to the increasingly diversified needs of many vulnerable groups, combined with a significant collapse in state-provided social services (European Commission, 2019 and cf. Šimleša, this volume). Historically, the SSE sector was represented by cooperatives and *chitalishta (community cultural centres)* as the earliest form of what were later called social enterprises (Jeliazkova, 2004). Other initiatives such as housing cooperatives and popular banks also emerged at the beginning of the 20th Century, as well as post-1945 enterprises that provided sheltered employment for people with disabilities, cooperative movements and rural agricultural cooperatives (European Commission, 2019; Marinova & Yoneva, 2021).

Since Bulgaria's accession to the EU, social enterprises have developed under different legal forms, including associations and foundations, cultural community centres, specialised enterprises for helping people with disabilities, cooperatives for people with disabilities and women's home-based cooperatives. With the amendment of the Social Assistance Law in 2003, the deinstitutionalisation[7] of major social services began, creating opportunities for non-governmental organisations and private enterprises to provide social services, especially community-based services (Zaimova, 2011).

The characterisation of civil society in Bulgaria in 2011 is valid for the SSE, which was then, and still remains, part of the third sector, characterised by low levels of engagement, a problematic public image, limited internal consolidation and a lack of sustainable influence on policy making. Despite these deficiencies, in this phase of civil society institutionalisation, a new phenomenon was observed – the generation of social energy under informal civic initiatives, through which civil society managed to influence public debate and societal change. At that time, it was assumed that many civil society organisations managed to build capacity, thus developing stronger organisational cultures by taking part in various international and EU projects and programmes (OSI, 2011).

Until 2018, public policy took a fragmentary approach to SSE (Ilcheva, 2019), with researchers pointing out that it is still an untapped business model (Terziev *et al.*, 2019). The recently adopted law on Social and Solidarity-based enterprises[8] (Bulgaria, 2018; European Commission, 2019) reflects a political decision of the Bulgarian government to improve recognition of this economy as a form of business activity (Stoyanov, 2020). The purposes of the Bulgarian SSE Law are reduction of social inequality, sustainable territorial development and creation of conditions for supporting social inclusion. Despite the positive impact of this recognition, a great many informal initiatives could not easily be categorised according to legal parameters.[9] These include urban community gardens, community ovens and threshing floors, producer/consumer associations, solidarity fairs and others.

14.6 SSE practices in Sofia and the Nadezhda district through the lens of the URBiNAT project

The URBiNAT catalogue is a living document collating technological, territorial, participatory and SSE solutions. The goal was to create opportunities for the citizens to co-select and co-create these solutions according to their needs and aspirations, and local environmental conditions. The main achievement was the embedding of conventional NBS solutions with participatory solutions and SSE within the same catalogue. Various evaluation criteria were employed in terms of innovation and up-scaling potential: equity and local economy (ELE), potential for community empowerment (CE), culture and political traditions (CPT) and impact on place and nature (PN), as described in Table 14.1.

Tables 14.2 and 14.3 illustrate the diversity of SSE practices and agents consolidated in Sofia and mapped during the URBiNAT co-diagnostic stage and provide evaluations along the main analytical dimensions referred to in Table 14.1.

Most SSE practices prioritise the strengthening of the local economy and just distribution through economic inclusion and distribution of resources, especially for excluded groups, and socially oriented job creation. The cooperatives (Hrankoop, and the parent cooperatives) integrate all the dimensions of the SSE, while the Baba residence is the only one that is unclear about the existence of economic activities as part of their core goals.

The territorial impacts stimulated by SSE actors assume multiple scales, from international (Bread Houses) to regional, reinforcing urban–rural connections (Baba residence, Bioselena Foundation). Most of the practices demonstrate significant territorial impact. However, few of them are locally rooted, and many come from outside, being part of international networks: Bread House, Food Not Bombs, Bon Appétit at Maria's World Foundation and Network for social economy development in South Eastern Europe. The intergenerational initiatives (Baba residence, tasty gardens of learning implemented by Zaedno Foundations) are cultural practices that contribute directly to human health through recreational activities and cognitive development. Inclusion can be considered as a transversal dimension for almost all initiatives that

Table 14.1 Evaluation of SSE solutions in the URBiNAT NBS Catalogue

SSE NBS	*Innovation*	*Upscaling*	*ELE*	*CE*	*CPT*	*PN*
Local currencies for a nature-based circular economy	Enhance the transition towards nature-based local ecosystems through the involvement of local stakeholders.	Through digital resources and/or applications.	++	++	+	+
Time bank	Promote intergenerational relationships based on attitudes of reciprocity and solidarity.	International networks, digital enablers.	+	++	+	+
Solidarity markets and fairs	Shared management, collective consumption and production practices, space for debate and political articulation, awareness raising and facing community social problems.	Increase in the demand for products, number and diversity of stakeholders.	++	++	++	+++
Farmers' market network	Build social networks of farmers and consumers. Shorten food supply chains.	Depends on local capacities and ability to organise.	+++	++	++	+++
Community social currencies	Expand access to goods and services. Create bonds of mutual trust.	Can be expanded into local commerce and solidarity markets.	++	++	+	++
Bread house	Collective preparation and sharing of food. Facilitate building of community.	Building local, regional, national and international networks.	++	++	++	+++

Source: Adapted from URBiNAT (2021a)

Note: + (low-impact), ++ (medium-impact) and +++ (high-impact)

promote integration of unprivileged groups, such as the disabled and other people with special needs, in two different ways: top down (as a consequence of legislation) or bottom up, for instance through parents' cooperatives (i.e. co-production of services).

Table 14.2 Evaluation of SSE solutions identified in Sofia

SSE practices identified	*Innovation*	*ELE*	*CE*	*CPT*	*PN*
Bon Appétit at Maria's World Foundation	Inclusion of people with intellectual disabilities by providing access to high-quality services, training and possibilities for employment that suits their needs.	+++	+++		+++
Baba residence, project initiated by IDEAS Factory	Connects and builds solidarity between urban youth and elderly from villages across Bulgaria in a socially entrepreneurial model that combines design thinking, ethnographic fieldwork skills and the wisdom of a rural lifestyle with a granny (baba).	+	+++	++	+++
Social enterprise "Rozhdestvo Hristovo"	Provides a supportive environment and gives disadvantaged women the opportunity to be included in manufacturing of souvenirs, thus helping them to build, develop and restore work skills and receive financial support for the work done.	+++	+++		+++
Network for social economy development in South Eastern Europe	Relies on high-quality materials, unique ideas and good workmanship, performed by the young people with disabilities who attend the centre, but also deliver products resulting from the home-based work supported by their parents.	+++	+++		+
Hippocampus project	Offers an attractive touristic service by creating jobs for sightless people who undertake training as part of a mixed crew with capable-to-see captains.	+++	+++		++
Hrankoop – solidarity food cooperative	Creates and sustains direct contact between producers of organic, bio and locally grown food and their potential customers.	+++	+++	+++	+++
"NadEzhko bakery," part of Bread House Network	A social franchise that employs and trains low-income people, orphans and others with special needs as bakers.	+++	+++	+	+++
Parent co-operatives	Parents come up with an initiative of creating coops as an alternative to public kindergartens when private kindergartens are expensive, and public childcare centres are not enough.	+++	+++	+++	+++

Source: URBiNAT (2019); Yotova (2016)

Note: + (low-impact), ++ (medium-impact) and +++ (high-impact)

The Bulgarian state's provision for co-production of services fosters solutions provided by the beneficiaries themselves. Nevertheless, the establishment and operation of parents' cooperatives are subject to diverse laws and ordinances not only regulating the quality of the service (education) and staff management but also stipulating specific requirements on the size of the property, environment health and quality, scope of the amenities and the food offered to children. These require organisations to have a robust administrative and operational structure, but in practice they lack adequate funding to cover such demands.

There are several organisations that, despite not directly enacting SSE practices, nonetheless promote the theme locally. Table 14.3 maps actors who have a strong connection with or interest in activity in the Nadezhda district who were involved in URBiNAT during the local diagnostic phase. This exploratory analysis takes into account formal organisations recognised as NGOs, along with social enterprises and informal grassroots initiatives underpinned by citizen engagement. It is based on interviews conducted within URBiNAT during 2019 with 10 for-profit and 15 non-profit organisations. The same analytical dimensions used in Tables 14.1 and 14.2 will be considered.

Table 14.3 Evaluation of agents of SSE solutions identified in Sofia

SSE agents	*Innovation and actions*	*ELE*	*CE*	*CPT*	*PN*
Food Not Bombs	International network of non-profit organisations that helps the underprivileged with the production of organic food.	++	+	++	+++
Bioselena Foundation	Develops and supports sustainable, organic agriculture, aids in the preservation of biodiversity and protection of the environment. Promotes organic markets as a way of strengthening the connection between the urban and the rural.	+	+	++	+++
Together Foundation (Zaedno)	Implements organic gardens of learning in the kindergartens. Mission – to teach skills and to promote community assets.	+	+++	++	+++
Centre for Art Education and Culture	An art school for music in Nadezhda for dancing and Fine Arts, part of the non-formal education for children from Sofia.	+	+	+++	+++

(*Continued*)

Table 14.3 (Continued)

SSE agents	*Innovation and actions*	*ELE*	*CE*	*CPT*	*PN*
Meshtra organisation	Creates and develops alternative forms of education in order to facilitate the transmission of traditional knowledge and to protect cultural and natural heritage.	++	+++	++	+++
ATD Fourth World	Organisation of citizens architects and other professional activists who aim to plant new trees in Sofia.		++	++	+++
Green School Village	Works from a holistic and interdisciplinary perspective in favour of personal development and sustainable community life.		+++	++	+++
Habitat for Humanity	Focuses on improving the well-being of citizens by making housing accessible and affordable for all.	++	+	++	+++
Za zemiata	Organises public campaigns that aim to achieve sustainable lifestyles. Encourages personal and political responsibility in decision-making; fights the exploitation of people and nature.			+++	++

Source: URBiNAT (2021b)

Note: + (low-impact), ++ (medium-impact) and +++ (high-impact)

According to findings from URBiNAT (2021b), the majority of these organisations and companies are financially supported by donations and voluntary work. In almost all cases, their work involves the creation of non-commercial value. Many of the SSE organisations are educational in nature, provide learning activities and focus particularly on children. All of the organisations and grassroots initiatives studied act directly or indirectly on impacts of climate change, looking at how lifestyles can be improved to enable better solutions for housing and more balanced approaches between consumption and environment protection.

14.7 SSE practices within the Nadezhda Healthy Corridor

Located to the northwest of Sofia city centre, the Nadezhda Administrative District mainly comprises housing estates. A high proportion of the population lives in multifamily mid- and high-rise apartment buildings built in the 1960s to 1980s (URBiNAT, 2019). Originally designed as a hierarchical system, urban open space in the Nadezhda District combined different types in terms of functions, space and size. Large but shrinking public space is subject to competition among users with competing needs and aspirations, enclosure due to privatisation,

Figure 14.2 Co-design activities in Nadezhda – NBS Healthy Corridor

Source: Photo credits: a. Boris Aftanski; b. Bozhidar Petrov; c. Milena Tasheva-Petrova

decline and loss of pedestrian connections, and distorted connectedness and limited access to public space due to the imposition of barriers such as fences or new buildings on restituted land (Tasheva-Petrova *et al.*, 2021).

Some of the middle-class housing estates in the district are considered "deprived areas" due the socio-economic and physical characteristics of the housing stock (URBiNAT, 2019). The district, compared to other districts of Sofia Municipality, is characterised by higher unemployment rates and crime levels, along with lower average monthly income and a lower proportion of the population with tertiary education.

The two-stage process of the HC local diagnostic gave a good baseline for identifying possible solutions that fit local natural and social needs. In the course of the local diagnostic, the suitability of certain territorial (and some technological) NBS was then presented for discussion among inhabitants and experts – technical staff at Sofia municipality and Nadezhda district, along with the research team.

During the first stage of the HC co-design (2019–2020), the following SSE solutions were proposed: solidarity markets, farmers' markets, time banks, repair cafés, Bread House network activities, intergenerational workshops and exhibitions. Although classified as a territorial NBS, tasty gardens of learning and experimental urban agriculture were also often selected. Activities related to shortening of food supply chains were also proposed. The criteria prioritised for selecting NBS were the availability of public space, cultural traditions, inhabitants' appropriation and political support to implement the NBS, potential for clustering and synergistic results and availability of agents (URBiNAT, 2021a).

Nevertheless, viewing the URBiNAT Catalogue as a living document, under an intensive participatory process, the initial SSE proposals were adjusted and a group of new NBS identified onsite as proposed elements of the HC, namely: "Grow a bench" (co-creation of meeting places for neighbours), fruit trees kept by residents and urban agriculture. The opportunity to combine the attractive structure of the pavilion and the educational component of the tasty garden was recognised by the managers of 15 high schools as suitable NBS for integration into the educational environment. In relation to gender, differences between women's and men's choices were identified.

Furthermore, during the preparation of the urban plan, priority was given to territorial and technological NBS. SSE NBS were considered as measures that will fit in the physical HC infrastructure. The spaces with a potential to shelter and act as stages for SSE are described in Table 14.4. The evaluation dimensions considered previously also underline the equity and local economy (ELE), potential for community empowerment (CE), culture and political traditions (CPT) and impact on place and nature (PN).

An online survey[10] customised for the context of Nadezhda (residents and workers)[11] provided information on the potential of the different SSE NBS (URBiNAT, 2021b). The conclusion is that activities of most interest are mainly non-commercial, apart from interest in buying vegetables at a small shop, often mentioned at the local farmers' market. The results will support further strategies following opening of the HC, in particular the opportunity to include an SSE fair or organise a farmers' market at the green amphitheatre in one of the places of intervention. The farmers' market and the events organised and led by the Bread House network might help activate the corridor and may be periodically included in the Nadezhda District's cultural calendar.

Table 14.4 Evaluation of SSE solutions co-designed for Sofia Healthy Corridor

Proposed NBS related to SSE	*Description*	*ELE*	*CE*	*CPT*	*PN*
Green amphitheatre	A flexible outdoor space that will function as an informal social area and gathering spot for citizens, and venue for events (e.g. solidarity fairs).	++	+++	+++	+++
Open green classroom – school greenhouse	A combination of two NBS – leisure pavilion and the tasty garden and using the existing mineral water. A place to organise school activities; classroom using the pavilion as a nursery for shrubs and flowers.	++	+++	++	+++
Tasty garden of learning	Vegetable and herb gardens (in the yard of the Kindergarten N90) integrated with different educational activities. Encouraging physical activity, providing healthy eating lifestyles, and encouraging children and families to work in the garden with direct contact with living nature.	+	+++	+++	+++
"Make a game yourself" – a place for expression of master skills	Space for family outdoor games. This space can accommodate campaign events for the collection and recovery of recyclable items.		+++	++	+++
Two-part place for open-air family games	Space for outdoor activities that will foster transition from sedentary lifestyles of children and adults.				+++
Thermal mineral water swimming pool	Based on the cultural tradition of living in close contact with mineral water. Relies on the use of mineral water to provide a healthy environment for physical education, training and recreational activities of school children. A new functional and business model for cooperation among citizens, municipality and business.	++		+++	+++

Source: URBiNAT (2021c)

Note: + (low-impact), ++ (medium-impact) and +++ (high-impact).

14.8 Discussion of the Nadezhda case study results

In our case study, the HC in the Nadezhda District was the empirical context to examine the potential of SSE to help make urban regeneration more inclusive through the implementation of NBS. The results cover three scales of SSE practices: Sofia city, Nadezhda district and NBS in an HC urban area. Based on mapping and analysis of practices, we have formulated the following nuanced and critical answers to our three research questions.

As far as RQ1 is concerned, we are convinced that historically, the SSE in Sofia-Nadezhda has occupied an important role in providing social and cultural services. As discussed, the cooperatives and *chitalishta* were crucial for social protection, cultural activities and the emergence of social enterprises. Nowadays, we identify high diversity of SSE initiatives in the territory in terms of target groups (women, youth and elderly people) and social problems addressed (economic issues, conviviality, community empowerment, capacity building, healthy food and environmental education).

Regarding RQ2, SSE affects governance and is expected to be impacted by the HC in three ways. First, social and environmental problems are integrated, as demonstrated by the topics addressed by SSE actors. The economy cannot exist as an isolated sphere but must be concerned with environmental conditions (Laville, 2018; Šimleša, 2023). In addition, the inclusion of SSE solutions in the same catalogue as conventional NBS proves the interweaving of environmental and sociopolitical elements. In a catalogue with 40 solutions, 6 are SSE practices, and new local SSE solutions were stimulated during the co-design phase. Second, democratic solidarity improves co-governance structures and can contribute to institutional change. Even with the implementation of the Sofia Advisory Board within the HC, SSE is not explicitly integrated into their broader agenda. Moreover, current SSE legislation makes local actors relevant but does not provide mechanisms for participation in public governance. The influence of citizens on the policymaking process requires future attention. Third, linkage of SSE and NBS for inclusive regeneration should follow existing social engagement patterns. The SSE actors mapped in the context of Nadezhda District provide resources, capacity building, political influence (advocacy) and promote SSE. Otherwise, the results of the local analysis were mostly based on information that represents the communities according to the problems that affect them, rather than their potential. The synergies of SSE and NBS can support the diversification of the HC's diagnostic parameters.

In relation to RQ3, it appears that SSE in the HC in Nadezhda District offers three main opportunities: to adopt democratic management of open public space (e.g. NBS clusters and meeting points), to upscale the benefits of combining activities and fostering synergies and to enhance sustainability through formalisation and recognition of certain key practices within the HC. However, some uncertainties remain concerning the reduction of competition among different activities and SSE practices, and the risk of privatisation of urban spaces. In this respect, the timeframe of the project is too short to allow all necessary social demands to be addressed. Furthermore, the time horizons of affected communities are very different from the timescales of institutions and projects.

A close observation of complex local configurations where public, private, associative and cooperative actors and issues are deeply entangled enables one to achieve a nuanced understanding of the territorial dynamics of SSE. It is clear that due to socio-economic conditions in the city of Sofia over the years, the SSE sector performs an important role. In this sense, the HC can strengthen local organisations, just as an SSE organisation can enhance its impact. Appropriate institutional actions from the HC could support SSE organisations to achieve greater autonomy, build capacity, create an enabling environment at the local level of government, improve dialogue with local authorities for incentives for companies and projects, build a network and promote research into territorial dynamics.

14.9 Conclusions

The main findings of the literature study demonstrate the potential of SSE to contribute to the socio-economic adaptive capacity of NBS. Four dimensions were outlined through the lens of the pluralist notion of economy and NBS. The main findings of the Nadezhda case study confirmed on the one hand the existence of a historical tradition in Bulgarian society that supported the development of SSE practices deeply rooted in the territory or/and connected to spatial transformations. On the other hand, a closer and more sustainable relationship between SSE and the HC needs to be consolidated. It can be achieved with the insertion of SSE into the municipal agenda for urban regeneration, including more investment, strategic plans and community-driven participation.

Further research into the context of SSE and NBS is needed. This promising area may generate interesting solutions that tackle various challenges simultaneously and should take into account the complexity of historical, socio-political and cultural aspects of the urban contexts. SSE for inclusive urban regeneration goes far beyond formally established institutional rules and remains based on the notions of self-organisation. As illustrated, its principles and practices might be used to reconfigure public space, transforming NBS into more than a "green solution." In this way, the HC model can be considered as alternative spaces that contain practices, epistemologies and pedagogies that constitute what has been called in this book "everyday politics."

Notes

1. Research was conducted as part of the project "URBiNAT – Healthy corridors as drivers of social housing neighbourhoods for the co-creation of social, environmental and marketable NBS' implementation," funded by the European Union's Horizon 2020. Research and Innovation Programme under Grant Agreement No. 776783. https://urbinat.eu
2. For example IPCC Sixth Assessment Report – Mitigation of Climate Change. Accessed on 26 January 2022. www.ipcc.ch/report/ar6/wg2/

3. Several initiatives have been promoted by the EC, namely Green Infrastructure, Ecosystem-based Disaster Risk Reduction and Natural Water Retention Measures (Faivre *et al.*, 2017).
4. Green Deal, IUCN Standard for NBS, EU Action Plan for Disaster Risk Reduction, EU Biodiversity Strategy.
5. The resolution UNEA-5 (2022) defines NBS as being focused on actions in different ecosystems in order to address social, economic and environmental challenges effectively and adaptively, while simultaneously providing human well-being, ecosystem services and resilience and biodiversity benefits.

   Accessed on September 10, 2022. Retrieved from www.unep.org/environmentassembly/unea-5.2/proceedings-report-ministerial-declaration-resolutions-and-decisions-unea-5.2?%2Fproceedings-report-ministerial-declaration-resolutions-and-decisions-unea-5_2=
6. The Marseille Manifesto, created during the 2020 IUCN Congress, encourages investment in nature to create sustainable jobs and accelerate the just transition and additionally to respect and engage communities, especially indigenous peoples and youth. It also advocates reform of the financial, economic and regulatory systems and for the circular economy approach to be adopted as a solution for the preservation of the global commons. Accessed on September 10, 2022: www.iucncongress2020.org/programme/marseille-manifesto
7. Beyond the partnership with social economy organisations, the local public authorities, under the Municipal Property Act, can also establish municipal social enterprises. They have a high level of autonomy in the formulation of local policies and in provision of support to the social economy (Ilcheva, 2019).
8. The objectives of this law are: (1) to regulate public actions related to SSE, (2) to define the types of social enterprise involved and measures for their support and (3) to describe the conditions and requirements regulating the activities of social enterprises (Bulgaria, 2018). Results from mapping undertaken within the European Commission (2019) reveal that social enterprises comprise around 1% of all businesses in the country, employing about 2% of the working population.
9. The legislation by default classifies all social enterprises as coming under "class A" (Stoyanov, 2020). Nevertheless, the entities need to comply with certain conditions, such as social added value, social activities, employees from vulnerable social groups.
10. The survey aimed to identify the market potential of different NBS on the basis of criteria for shortlisting in each of the three frontrunner cities. Questionnaires were completed between March 15 and April 3, 2021. The research design and implementation were conducted by City Facilitators company (URBiNAT, 2021b).
11. In total, 47 positive responses were received during this exploratory study, despite many changes faced during its implementation, including those caused by the effects of COVID-19.

References

Andreucci, M. B. (2022). "The role of nature in urban regeneration," in Croci, E. and Lucchitta, B. (eds.) *Nature-Based Solutions for More Sustainable Cities: A Framework Approach for Planning and Evaluation.* Bingley: Emerald Publishing, pp. 111–124.

Bulgaria. (2018). *Social and Solidarity-Based Enterprises: ACT. Decree No. 240.* Online at www.ilo.org/dyn/natlex/docs/ELECTRONIC/112803/141077/F385589937/BGR-112803.pdf (accessed March 30th 2023).

Castells, M. (1983). *The City and the Grassroots: A Cross-Cultural Theory of Urban Social Movements*. Berkeley: University of California Press.

CIRIEC. (2016). *Recent Evolutions of the Social Economy in the European Union*. Brussels: EESC. Online at www.eesc.europa.eu/sites/default/files/files/qe-04-17-875-en-n.pdf (accessed March 30th 2023).

Croci, E. and Lucchitta, B. (eds.) (2021). *Nature-Based Solutions for More Sustainable Cities: A Framework Approach for Planning and Evaluation*. Bingley: Emerald Publishing Limited.

Davies, C., Chen, W. Y., Sanesi, G. and Lafortezza, R. (2021). "The European Union roadmap for implementing nature-based solutions: A review," *Environmental Science and Policy*, 121, pp. 49–67. https://doi.org/10.1016/j.envsci.2021.03.018

Droste, N., Schröter-Schlaack, C., Hansjürgens, B. and Zimmermann, H. (2017). "Implementing nature-based solutions in urban areas: Financing and governance aspects," in Kabisch, N., Korn, H., Stadler, J. and Bonn, A. (eds.) *Nature-Based Solutions to Climate Change Adaptation in Urban Areas. Theory and Practice of Urban Sustainability Transitions*. Cham.: Springer, pp. 307–321. https://doi.org/10.1007/978-3-319-56091-5_18

Dumitru, A., Frantzeskaki, N. and Collier, M. (2020). "Identifying principles for the design of robust impact evaluation frameworks for nature-based solutions in cities," *Environmental Science and Policy*, 112, pp. 107–116.

European Commission, Directorate-General for Research and Innovation. (2015). *Towards an EU Research and Innovation Policy Agenda for Nature-Based Solutions & Re-Naturing Cities: Final Report of the Horizon 2020 Expert Group on Nature-Based Solutions and Re-Naturing Cities*. Brussels: Publications Office of the European Union. Online at https://data.europa.eu/doi/10.2777/479582 (accessed March 30th 2023).

European Commission (2019) *Social enterprises and their ecosystems in Europe. Updated country report: Bulgaria*. Author: Maria Jeliazkova. Luxembourg: Publications Office of the European Union. Online at https://europa.eu/!Qq64ny

European Commission, Directorate-General for Research and Innovation. (2021). *Evaluating the Impact of Nature-Based Solutions: A Handbook for Practitioners*. Brussels: Publications Office of the European Union. Online at https://data.europa.eu/doi/10.2777/244577 (accessed March 30th 2023).

Faivre, N., Fritz, M., Freitas, T., Boissezon, B. and Vandewoestijne, S. (2017). "Nature-based solutions in the EU: Innovating with nature to address social, economic and environmental challenges," *Environmental Research*, 159, pp. 509–518. https://doi.org/10.1016/j.envres.2017.08.032

Ferreira, V., Barreira, A. P., Loures, L., Antunes, D. and Panagopoulos, T. (2020). "Stakeholders' engagement on nature-based solutions: A systematic literature review," *Sustainability*, *12*(640), pp. 1–27. https://doi.org/10.3390/su12020640

Gudynas, E. (2011). "Buen vivir: Today's tomorrow," *Development*, 54(4), pp. 441–447.

Hespanha, P. and Lucas dos Santos, L. (2016). "O nome e a coisa. Sobre a invisibilidade e a ausência de reconhecimento institucional da Economia Solidária em Portugal," *Revista de Economia Solidária*, 9, pp. 22–63.

Hillenkamp, I. (2013). "Le principe de householding aujourd'hui. Discussion théorique et approche empirique par l'économie populaire," in Hillenkamp, I. and Laville, J. L. (eds.) *Socioéconomie et démocratie. L'actualité de Karl Polanyi*. Toulouse: Érès, pp. 215–239.

Ilcheva, M. (2019). "New policy and legislation for social economy in Bulgaria," *Knowledge: International Journal*, 30(1), pp. 65–72. https://doi.org/10.35120/kij300165i

Jeliazkova, M. (2004). "The co-operative model in Bulgaria: Prospects and problems of the social economy," in Borzaga, C. and Spear, R. (eds.) *Trends and Challenges for Co-Operatives and Social Enterprises*. Trento: Edizione 31, pp. 229–246.

Laville, J. L. (2018). *A Economia Social e Solidária: Práticas, Teorias e Debates*. Coimbra: CES/Almedina.

Lefebvre, H. (1991). *The Production of Space*. Malden: Blackwell Publishing.

Lupp, G. and Zingraff-Hamed, A. (2021). "Nature-based solutions – Concept, evaluation, and governance," *Sustainability*, 13(6), 3012, pp. 2–5. https://doi.org/10.3390/su13063012

Marinova, T. and Yoneva, E. (2021). "Social enterprises in Bulgaria: Historical and institutional perspective," in Defourny, J. and Nyssens, M. (eds.) *Social Enterprise in Central and Eastern Europe*. New York: Routledge, pp. 23–39.

Martin, D. G. (2003). "Place-framing as place-making: Constituting a neighborhood for organizing and activism," *Annals of the Association of American Geographers*, 93, pp. 730–750.

McQuaid, S., Rhodes, M. L., Andersson, T., Croci, E., Feichtinger-Hofer, M., Grosjean, M., Lueck, A. E., Kooijman, E., Lucchitta, B., Rizzi, D., Reil, A. and Schante, J. (2021). *From Nature-Based Solutions to the Nature-Based Economy: Delivering the Green Deal for Europe: Draft White Paper for Consultation: Nature-Based Economy Working Group of EC Task Force III on Nature Based Solutions*. Online at https://networknature.eu/Nature-Based-Economy-White-Paper-Consultation (accessed March 30th 2023).

Oosterlynck, S., Schuermans, N. and Loopmans, M. (2017). *Place, Diversity and Solidarity*. New York: Routledge.

OSI. (2001). *Open Society Institute Sofia 2011 Annual Report*. Online at http://osis.bg/wp-content/uploads/2018/04/Annual_Report_2011_BG_Ed.pdf (accessed March 30th 2023).

Polanyi, K. (1944). *The Great Transformation: The Political and Economic Origins of Our Time*. 2nd edition. Boston: Beacon.

Razeto, M. L. (1999). "La economía de solidaridad: Concepto, realidad y proyecto," *Persona y Sociedad*, 13(12), pp. 1–19.

Seddon, N., Chausson, A., Berry, P., Girardin, C. A. J., Smith, A. and Turner, B. (2020). "Understanding the value and limits of nature-based solutions to climate change and other global challenges," *Philosophical Transactions of the Royal Society B*, 375: 20190120. http://dx.doi.org/10.1098/rstb.2019.0120

Šimleša, D. (2023). "Ecological economics and the social and solidarity economy," in Yi, I. et al. (eds) *Encyclopedia of the Social and Solidarity Economy*. Cheltenham: Edward Elgar.

Singer, P. (2018). *Ensaios Sobre Economia Solidária*. Coimbra: Almedina.

Stijnen, C. A. E. (2021). *Co-Creating Socially Inclusive Urban Nature-Based Solutions: Towards a Framework for Socially Inclusive Co-Creation Processes*. Master's Thesis, Utrecht University Faculty of Geosciences. Online at https://studenttheses.uu.nl/handle/20.500.12932/39931 (accessed March 30th 2023).

Stoyanov, K. (2020). "Applicability of business models in the social and solidarity economy among social enterprises in Bulgaria," *Trakia Journal of Sciences*, 18(1), pp. 350–353.

Tasheva-Petrova, M., Dimitrova, E., Burov, A. and Mutafchiiska, I. (2021). "Re-claiming space for public life: Messages from the north-west periphery of Sofia," *Urbani izziv*, 32, supplement, pp. 91–105. DOI: 10.5379/urbani-izziv-en-2021–32-supplement-6

Terziev, V., Nichev, N. and Georgiev, M. (2019). "Social enterprises and their impact in Bulgaria," *Knowledge: International Journal*, 30(6). Retrieved from https://ssrn.com/abstract=3371857 (accessed March 30th 2023).

UNRISD. (2016). *Policy Innovations for Transformative Change: Implementing the 2030 Agenda for Sustainable Development*. Geneva: UNRISD. Online at www.un-ilibrary.org/content/books/9789210601023 (accessed March 30th 2023).

URBiNAT. (2019). *Local Diagnostic*. URBiNAT Project Deliverable 2.1. Milan: IULM University.

URBiNAT. (2021a). *New NBS Co-Creation of URBiNAT NBS (live) Catalogue and Toolkit for Healthy Corridor*. URBiNAT Project Deliverable 4.1. Barcelona: IAAC.

URBiNAT. (2021b). *Market Potential for NBS*. URBiNAT Project Deliverable 4.2. Copenhagen: City Facilitators.

URBiNAT. (2021c). *Sofia URBiNAT Healthy Corridor*. URBiNAT Project Deliverable 4.2. Coimbra: Centre for Social Studies.

Utting, P. (2016). *Mainstreaming Social and Solidarity Economy: Opportunities and Risks for Policy Change*. UN Inter-Agency Task Force on Social and Solidarity Economy. Online at https://base.socioeco.org/docs/paper-mainstreaming-sse-12-november-2016-edit-untfsse.pdf (accessed March 30th 2023).

Vaillancourt, Y. and Favreau, L. (2001). Le modèle québécois d'économie sociale et solidaire. Revue internationale de l'économie sociale, (281), pp. 69–83. https://doi.org/10.7202/1024022ar

Welden, E. A., Chausson, A. and Melanidis, M. S. (2021). "Leveraging nature-based solutions for transformation: Reconnecting people and nature," *People and Nature*, 3, pp. 966–977. https://doi.org/10.1002/pan3.10212

Wilk, B., Vetter, A. and Schröder, A. (2021). *Tackling the Climate and Biodiversity Crises in Europe through Urban Greening Plans: Recommendations for Avoiding the Implementation Gap*. Dessau-Roßlau: Umweltbundesamt. Online at www.umweltbundesamt.de/sites/default/files/medien/380/dokumente/2021-10-18_scientific_opinion_paper_urban_greening_plans_0.pdf (accessed March 30th 2023).

Yotova, A. (2016). "Collaborative networks changing the face of the educational system. Three case studies in the pre-school and elementary education." *Годишник на Стопанския факултет на СУ „Св. Климент Охридски "*, 13(1), pp. 101–121.

Zaimova, D. (2011). "Emergence and development perspectives of the third sector in Bulgaria," *Review of Applied Socio-Economic Research*, 2, pp. 198–205.

Index

Note: Page numbers in *italics* indicate figures and in **bold** indicate tables on the corresponding pages.

Techno-economics and Life Cycle Assessment of Bioreactors

Techno-economics and Life Cycle Assessment of Bioreactors

Post-Covid19 Waste Management Approach

Edited by

PURANJAN MISHRA
Faculty of Civil Engineering Technology, Universiti Malaysia Pahang (UMP), Gambang, Pahang, Malaysia

LAKHVEER SINGH
Department of Environment Science, SRM-University-AP, Amaravati, India

POOJA GHOSH
Centre for Rural Development and Technology, Indian Institute of Technology Delhi, New Delhi, India

ELSEVIER

Elsevier
Radarweg 29, PO Box 211, 1000 AE Amsterdam, Netherlands
The Boulevard, Langford Lane, Kidlington, Oxford OX5 1GB, United Kingdom
50 Hampshire Street, 5th Floor, Cambridge, MA 02139, United States

ISBN: 978-0-323-89848-5

For Information on all Elsevier publications
visit our website at https://www.elsevier.com/books-and-journals

Publisher: Susan Dennis
Editorial Project Manager: Lena Sparks
Production Project Manager: Bharatwaj Varatharajan
Cover Designer: Mark Rogers

Typeset by MPS Limited, Chennai, India

Contents

Part 2 Techno-economic assessment of bioreactors 93

List of contributors

Norhayati Abdullah
Malaysia-Japan International Institute of Technology (MJIIT), Universiti Teknologi Malaysia, Kuala Lumpur, Malaysia

Abiola John Adeyi
Department of Mechanical Engineering, Ladoke Akintola University of Technology, Ogbomoso, Oyo State, Nigeria

Oladayo Adeyi
Department of Chemical Engineering, Michael Okpara University of Agriculture, Umudike, Abia State, Nigeria

Imran Ahmad
Malaysia-Japan International Institute of Technology (MJIIT), Universiti Teknologi Malaysia, Kuala Lumpur, Malaysia

Hamoud Alenezi
Process Systems Engineering Centre (PROSPECT), Research Institute for Sustainable Environment, School of Chemical and Energy Engineering, Universiti Teknologi, Kuala Lumpur, Malaysia

Tarnima Warda Andalib
BRAC Business School, BRAC University, Dhaka, Bangladesh

Shreeshivadasan Chelliapan
Razak Faculty of Technology and Informatics, Universiti Teknologi Malaysia, Kuala Lumpur, Malaysia

Mohd Fadhil Bin Md Din
Department of Water and Environmental, Centre for Environmental Sustainability and Water Security (IPASA), Research Institute of Sustainable Environment (RISE), School of Civil Engineering, Faculty of Engineering, Universiti Teknologi Malaysia (UTM), Skudai, Malaysia; Department of Water and Environmental Engineering, School of Civil Engineering, Faculty of Engineering, Universiti Teknologi Malaysia (UTM), Skudai, Malaysia

Chee-Yuen Gan
Analytical Biochemistry Research Center(ABrC), Universiti Sains Malaysia, University Innovation Incubator Building, Sains@USM, Bayan Lepas, Penang, Malaysia

Lalit Goswami
Centre for Environment, Indian Institute of Technology, Guwahati, Assam, India

Norahim bin Ibrahim
Department of Biosciences and Health Sciences, Faculty of Biosciences and Medical Engineering, Universiti Teknologi Malaysia (UTM), Skudai, Malaysia

Pramod Jadhav
Faculty of Civil Engineering Technology, Universiti Malaysia Pahang (UMP), Pahang, Malaysia

Monika Jain
Department of Natural Resource Management, College of Forestry, Banda University of Agriculture & Technology, Banda, Uttar Pradesh, India

Aida Batrisyia Jasni
School of Engineering, Faculty of Engineering, Universiti Teknologi Malaysia, Skudai, Johor, Malaysia

Santosh Kumar Jha
Department of Bio-Engineering and Biotechnology, Birla Institute of Technology, Ranchi, Jharkhand, India

Abudukeremu Kadier
Laboratory of Environmental Science and Technology, The Xinjiang Technical Institute of Physics and Chemistry, Key Laboratory of Functional Materials and Devices for Special Environments, Chinese Academy of Sciences, Urumqi, PR China

Bishwajit Singh Kapoor
Department of Biotechnology, National Institute of Technology, Durgapur, West Bengal, India

Ahasanul Karim
Department of Soil Sciences and Agri-food Engineering, Université Laval, Quebec, QC, Canada

Zaied Bin Khalid
Faculty of Civil Engineering Technology, Universiti Malaysia Pahang (UMP), Pahang, Malaysia

Iwamoto Koji
Malaysia-Japan International Institute of Technology (MJIIT), Universiti Teknologi Malaysia, Kuala Lumpur, Malaysia

Santhana Krishnan
Department of Water and Environmental, Centre for Environmental Sustainability and Water Security (IPASA), Research Institute of Sustainable Environment (RISE), School of Civil Engineering, Faculty of Engineering, Universiti Teknologi Malaysia (UTM), Skudai, Malaysia; PSU Energy Systems Research Institute, Department of Environmental Engineering, Faculty of Engineering, Prince of Songkla University, Songkhla, Thailand; Center of Environmental Sustainability and Water Security (IPASA), Research Institute of Sustainable Environment (RISE), Faculty of Engineering, Universiti Teknologi Malaysia, Johor Bahru, Malaysia; PSU Energy Systems Research Institute (PERIN), Department of Environmental Engineering, Faculty of Engineering, Prince of Songkla University, Hat Yai, Thailand

Saurabh Kulshrestha
Faculty of Applied Sciences and Biotechnology, Shoolini University of Biotechnology and Management Sciences, Solan, Himachal Pradesh, India; Center for Omics and Biodiversity Research, Shoolini University of Biotechnology and Management Sciences, Solan, Himachal Pradesh, India

Smita S. Kumar
Department of Environmental Sciences, J.C. Bose University of Science & Technology, YMCA, Faridabad, Haryana, India

Puranjan Mishra
Faculty of Civil Engineering Technology, Universiti Malaysia Pahang (UMP), Pahang, Malaysia; Institute of Bioresource and Agriculture, Hong Kong Baptist University, Kowloon Tong, Hong Kong

Mohd Nasrullah
Faculty of Civil Engineering Technology, Universiti Malaysia Pahang (UMP), Pahang, Malaysia

Vinod Kumar Nigam
Department of Bioengineering & Biotechnology, Birla Institute of Technology, Ranchi, Jharkhand, India

Olusegun Abayomi Olalere
Analytical Biochemistry Research Center(ABrC), Universiti Sains Malaysia, University Innovation Incubator Building, Sains@USM, Bayan Lepas, Penang, Malaysia

Supriya Pandey
Department of Biotechnology, Manipal Institute of Technology, Manipal Academy of Higher Education (MAHE), Udupi, Karnataka, India

Pragya Prakash
Department of Bio-Engineering and Biotechnology, Birla Institute of Technology, Ranchi, Jharkhand, India; Centre for Biopharmaceutical Technology, Department of Chemical Engineering, Indian Institute of Technology, New Delhi, India

Mohd Hafiz Bin Puteh
Department of Environmental Engineering, Faculty of Civil Engineering, Universiti Teknologi Malaysia (UTM), Skudai, Malaysia

Renu
Department of Chemical Engineering, Malaviya National Institute of Technology, Jaipur, Rajasthan, India

Nurfarhain Md Rusli
Department of Water and Environmental, Centre for Environmental Sustainability and Water Security (IPASA), Research Institute of Sustainable Environment (RISE), School of Civil Engineering, Faculty of Engineering, Universiti Teknologi Malaysia (UTM), Skudai, Malaysia; Department of Water and Environmental Engineering, School of Civil Engineering, Faculty of Engineering, Universiti Teknologi Malaysia (UTM), Skudai, Malaysia

Fadzlin Md Sairan
Department of Water and Environmental, Centre for Environmental Sustainability and Water Security (IPASA), Research Institute of Sustainable Environment (RISE), School of Civil Engineering, Faculty of Engineering, Universiti Teknologi Malaysia (UTM), Skudai, Malaysia; Department of Water and Environmental Engineering, School of Civil Engineering, Faculty of Engineering, Universiti Teknologi Malaysia (UTM), Skudai, Malaysia

Nur Shahidah
Department of Water and Environmental, Centre for Environmental Sustainability and Water Security (IPASA), Research Institute of Sustainable Environment (RISE), School of Civil Engineering, Faculty of Engineering, Universiti Teknologi Malaysia (UTM), Skudai, Malaysia; Department of Water and Environmental Engineering, School of Civil Engineering, Faculty of Engineering, Universiti Teknologi Malaysia (UTM), Skudai, Malaysia

Mamta Devi Sharma
Faculty of Applied Sciences and Biotechnology, Shoolini University of Biotechnology and Management Sciences, Solan, Himachal Pradesh, India; Center for Omics and Biodiversity Research, Shoolini University of Biotechnology and Management Sciences, Solan, Himachal Pradesh, India

Shubha Rani Sharma
Department of Bioengineering & Biotechnology, Birla Institute of Technology, Ranchi, Jharkhand, India

Swati Sharma
Shoolini Institute of Life Sciences and Business Management, Solan, Himachal Pradesh, India

Hare Ram Singh
Department of Bio-Engineering and Biotechnology, Birla Institute of Technology, Ranchi, Jharkhand, India

Lakhveer Singh
Department of Environmental Science, SRM University-AP, Amaravati, Andhra Pradesh, India

Snehi Soy
Department of Bioengineering & Biotechnology, Birla Institute of Technology, Ranchi, Jharkhand, India

Shazwin Mat Taib
Department of Water and Environmental, Centre for Environmental Sustainability and Water Security (IPASA), Research Institute of Sustainable Environment (RISE), School of Civil Engineering, Faculty of Engineering, Universiti Teknologi Malaysia (UTM), Skudai, Malaysia; Department of Water and Environmental Engineering, School of Civil Engineering, Faculty of Engineering, Universiti Teknologi Malaysia (UTM), Skudai, Malaysia

Abiola Ezekiel Taiwo
Department of Chemical Engineering, Landmark University, Omu-Aran, Kwara State, Nigeria

Vikram Thakur
Department of Virology, Postgraduate Institute of Medical Education and Research, PGIMER, Chandigarh, India

Zularisam Bin Abd Wahid
Faculty of Civil Engineering Technology, Universiti Malaysia Pahang (UMP), Pahang, Malaysia

Ali Yuzir
Malaysia-Japan International Institute of Technology (MJIIT), Universiti Teknologi Malaysia, Kuala Lumpur, Malaysia

PART 1

Bioreactors: Current status, recent trends and challenges

CHAPTER 1

Impact of COVID-19 on waste and resource management practices

Vikram Thakur
Department of Virology, Postgraduate Institute of Medical Education and Research, PGIMER, Chandigarh, India

1.1 Introduction

As of October 4, 2021, there have been more than 234 million confirmed cases of COVID-19, including 4,800,375 deaths reported globally to the World Health Organization (WHO Coronavirus., 2021). Pandemic not only affected the socioeconomic poor countries, but middle and higher-income countries like United States, Brazil, Russia, and the United Kingdom were are also worse affected. The effect of the second wave and the suspicion of the emergence of third-wave with new SARS-CoV-2 deadly variants in coming months is a matter of great concern not only in terms of loss of life but also in terms of the economic structure, geopolitical relations, change in social behavior and personal habits, and the attitude toward life and environment.

Even the 5 sustainable development goals (SDSs) like clean water and sanitation (World Health Organization, 2018), climate action (Van Fan et al., 2021), life below water [Waste management an essential public service in the fight to beat COVID-19., 2021], and life on land (Liang et al., 2021) are facing challenges to sustain due to the COVID-19 pandemic (THE 17 GOALS, 2021). These are essential for the sustenance of the human race in close association with nature and biodiversity. Already the world is facing devastating issues like global climate change, air, and marine pollution, plastic and microplastics as a pollutant, exploding population creating enormous biodegradable and nonbiodegradable waste. Due to the emergence of the COVID-19 pandemic, a huge increase in a medical and hazardous waste generation has put a burden on the existing remedial resources. Additionally, ensuring the safe handling and proper disposal of hazardous COVID-19 associated waste is vital for protecting human health and the environment for future generations.

Techno-economics and Life Cycle Assessment of Bioreactors
DOI: https://doi.org/10.1016/B978-0-323-89848-5.00010-X

During the initial nationwide lockdown to curtail COVID-19, the world had witnessed the rejuvenating impact on the environment and ecosystem such as low pollution, clearer skies, and cleaner rivers (National Geographic., 2020). But simultaneously COVID-19 preventive measures generated and altered the dynamics of solid and medical waste generated, creating woes among policymakers.

1.2 Types of waste

With the rise in living standards and urbanization, there is a hike in the complexity and volume of the waste generated. Industrialization and advancements in medical facilities have added substantial quantities of infectious waste into the environment which have adverse human health consequences. Usually, there are 6 types of waste generated in the environment, that is, municipal waste (household), industrial waste, agricultural waste, biomedical waste (BMW), e-waste, and hazardous waste.

1.2.1 Waste generation during COVID-19 pandemic

Municipal waste, that is, solid waste is generated from households and other commercial or residential spaces where food waste, plastic, etc., are the main component. During the worldwide lockdown, there is a surge in the generation of common packing plastic waste for groceries purposes adding the pool of already existing nonbiodegradable waste (The Amount Of Plastic Waste Is Surging Because Of The Coronavirus Pandemic., 2020). This menace is further enhanced by the use of single-use plastic (SUP). The main concern is the survival of the virus for a prolonged time on these materials. However, the change in the behavioral pattern and lifestyle during COVID-19 certainly forced the consumers to prefer plastic packaging for hygiene reasons dominating the plastic waste's environmental impacts (Grodzińska-Jurczak et al., 2020).

BMW, that is, waste generated by hospitals, medical laboratories, and research institutions includes wastes of sharps, infectious, pathological, chemical, and radioactive nature (World Health Organization). Broadly categorized as infectious waste, hazardous chemical waste, radioactive waste, and pharmaceutical waste. It is composed of nonhazardous waste (85%) and hazardous waste (15%) of which infectious waste is 10% and chemical waste is 5%.

Amid the COVID-19 pandemic, medical waste includes infected masks, gloves, and protective equipment generated due to a sudden surge in the demand and mandatory use of protective items. As per WHO, 89 million masks and 76 million gloves are the monthly requirements to deal with this virus (Shortage of personal protective equipment endangering health workers worldwide., 2020). In addition to the infected masks and gloves, the virus can survive on cardboard, plastic, and metals for hours to days, endangering the lives of waste management workers while collecting or managing such waste (Kampf et al., 2020). Safe handling and disposal of such waste are important to avoid contamination of municipal solid waste with the virus, soil, and underground water contamination which could pose a risk of transmission (Datta et al., 2018).

1.3 Impact of COVID-19 on waste management

In the pre-COVID era, approximately 3 billion people worldwide are devoid of controlled waste collection and waste disposal facilities (Global Waste Management Outlook, 2015). Additionally, lack of technical and scientific knowledge is the contributing factor worsening waste management in the low socioeconomic developing countries. Inadequate medical waste management can be very detrimental to the humans and ecosystem. However, with the emergence of the COVID-19, the quantity, composition, disposal frequency and timing (temporal), and distribution (spatial) of waste changes. The problem of BMW and wastewater disposal has caused widespread public concern (International Water, 2020). The presence of SARS-CoV-2 in sewage waste indicates the potential risk of waterborne transmission of the coronavirus (Quilliam et al., 2020) (Fig. 1.1).

Marine plastic pollution has increased due to the rapid use and improper disposal of face masks. Approximately 0.15 million tons to 0.39 million tons of plastic debris could end up in global oceans within a year. The documentation of "more masks than jellyfish" along the French Mediterranean coast is an alarming concern for river and marine pollution. As a source of microplastic, face masks contribute negative impacts on the ecosystem due to the breakup of their constituents like polypropylene and polyethylene. The healthcare waste generation during the COVID-19 pandemic is increased to 3.4 kg/person/day. Such change in the waste dynamics fortifies the need for special attention as evidenced by Basel, Rotterdam, and Stockholm Convention (BRS) where treatment of medical, household, as well as hazardous waste, is evaluated as an essential public service during with COVID-19 [Waste management an essential public service in the fight to beat COVID-19., 2021]. Therefore the

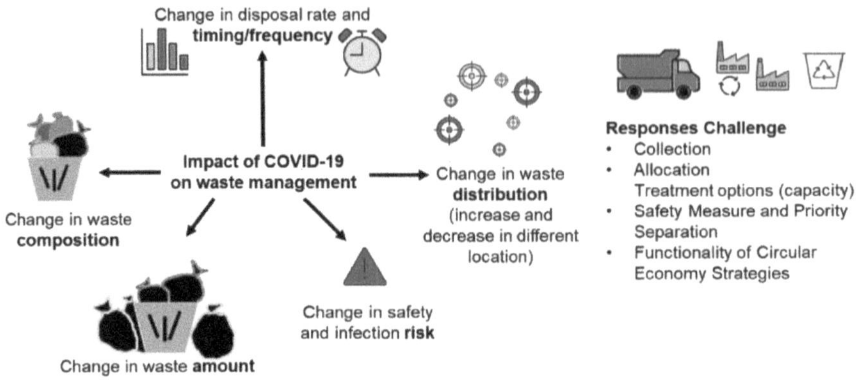

Figure 1.1 Impacts and challenges of COVID-19 on waste management (Van Fan et al., 2021).

foremost criteria should be an accurate assessment and statistical prediction of COVID-19 waste flow through governmental or public agencies. However, multisectorial efforts including local, and NGOs are also required to cope with such pandemic challenges (Liang et al., 2021).

1.4 The unique challenge with SARS CoV-2 and waste management

During this pandemic, the major challenges are collecting and treating wastes effectively. The quantity of solid waste has increased whereas the recycling of waste has reduced (Zambrano-Monserrate et al., 2020). Virus-contaminated wastes are also generated by infected people quarantined at home, therefore may be responsible for the further spreading of the virus.

The SARS-CoV-2 remains viable and infectious for up to 72 h on plastic and metal surfaces and for more than 9 days on inanimate surfaces. Evidence suggested shedding of virus in the stool of COVID-19 patients that can lead to contamination of drinking water along with other environmental implications. Solid waste when contaminated with body fluids and secretions of COVID-19 patients is considered infectious and can be disinfected with 0.5% hypochlorite, 0.5% hydrogen peroxide, and 2% glutaraldehyde. However, the fate of coronavirus in wastewater treatment plants or the water environment is yet to be elucidated (Nghiem et al., 2020).

1.4.1 Waste management strategies

The waste management strategy depends on the quantity, characteristics, and seasonal variations of waste generation. Identification, collection, separation, storage, transportation, treatment, and disposal are the crucial steps involved in the effective management of BMW (Fig. 1.2).

Storage and collection: Waste segregation is very important before proceeding to waste treatment. Different categories of wastes are collected in separate color-coded bags as infectious and noninfectious wastes are separated. While collecting waste, the management staff should be equipped with proper PPE to avoid contact with coronavirus (Cohen, 2020). Efforts should be done to transport the waste as earliest as possible to the treatment site.

Waste transport: The contaminated waste material should be transported in a properly bar-coded sealed container. Dedicated trolleys carrying the infected waste material should be disinfected with 1% sodium hypochlorite. Separate vehicles with trained drivers should be arranged for transportation of waste through the less crowded or nonresidential area. The vehicle container should be closed to avoid any accident or transport glitch (Central, 2021).

Waste treatment: The COVID-19 wastes are usually treated by chemical methods, autoclaving, and incineration. Highly infectious waste cannot be

Figure 1.2 Schematic representation of different stages of waste management.

landfilled, reused, or recycled, therefore should be incinerated at high temperatures. However European countries preferred chemical treatment and autoclaving over incineration to dispose of COVID-19 waste to avoid furans and dioxins toxic effects (Mattiello et al., 2013). Additionally, high-temperature pyrolysis (540°C–830°C) and medium-temperature microwave technique are proved to be very helpful for on-site disinfection of COVID-19 waste (Wang et al., 2020).

Recycle and reuse: Ideally, recycling and reusing the waste for alternative applications is the best practice. The contaminated or used face masks containing different types of plastics are difficult to recycle. Face masks such as N95, and surgical masks, contain a considerable portion of nonrecyclable plastic material. Additionally, it is not economical to collect, separate and recycle PPE, in addition to confounding concerns of infections and contamination in the recycled products. The waste recycling program halted during the COVID-19, fearing the risk of contaminated waste in recycling centers. In hospital setups, collection, segregation, and safe disposal procedures for gloves and PPE restricted the entry of these in the open environment. Sustainable packaging, guidelines for optimum packaging size, and using environmentally friendly materials for packaging needs to be developed. Lightweight and strong plastic containers for sanitizers, etc., are manufactured with less energy-intensive procedures; however, PET and PP-based bottles should be prioritized due to their recyclability.

Waste incineration: This practice is best for infectious BMW. But the associated concerns are aerosol emissions from grinding/shredding of the wastes which can be dealt with care to prevent further infections. Basic infrastructures with autoclaving, incineration, chemical disinfection are to be installed and need to be tightly regulated. Medical waste management systems are based on waste incineration plants and thermal decontamination facilities at low temperatures as treatment and disposal options for hazardous fractions under current legislation.

Landfill disposal: Postincineration the generated ash and treated waste are disposed of in landfills. Installing decontamination and other facilities like thermal sterilization, shredding, chopping, grinding, and compacting at the hospital level may tackle the problem of increasing medical waste.

COVID-19 pandemic-related healthcare waste largely contributed by SUPs including gloves, masks, gowns, and protective equipment infected with the virus. Such waste adds to the plastic pollution problem and had a direct devastating impact on the environment, including climate change.

If not managed properly, and subject to dumping or open burning, this leads to the release of toxins in the environment causing loss of biodiversity.

1.5 Policy and regulatory approaches

A national medical waste management plan and policies with an approved strategy needs to be implemented by the national, and municipal governments in their response to COVID-19 waste. Factors such as good governance, communication, and accountability also played a constructive role.

Governance: Waste management is a complex and multidimensional governance issue that includes governance at individual and multijurisdictional levels. When an individual is responsible for waste generation and change in the individual behavior and actions dictates the remedial approach, is known as self-governance (Waste., 2019). On the jurisdictional level, city administrative structure and local government are the main players. Only efficient waste management counteracts the strain on the economy, health, local and global environment by reducing the expenses and improving the quality of life. On a small scale, local authorities, and on the larger scale settings, metropolitan waste management are accountable for all the operations and logistics for effective waste management (Abdel-Shafy & Mansour, 2018). Imposing restrictions on disposal and framing laws for violators can also be effective. Therefore clear and factual communication between the different stakeholders is required for the successful management of solid waste.

Communication: For hassle-free management of waste, communication is the most important approach among generators, collectors, disposers, and recyclers of the waste (Paul & Bussemaker, 2020). Further, community participation can play a pivotal role in the effective and safe disposal of waste (Dalton et al., 2018).

Accountability: For successful and reliable waste management accountability holds a prominent place therefore, proper documentation of the generated waste in terms of the amount and type, its collection and disposal along with environmental clearance are crucial. Mixing up waste and improper transport may increase the risk of spreading the COVID-19 virus (Di Maria et al., 2020).

Recommendations to avoid COVID-19 plastic waste: Prioritizing sustainable packing by developing guidelines for optimum packaging size and using environmentally friendly materials which can be recycled and reused

(PharmTech, 2020). The concept of a plastic circular economy deals with the recycling of plastic which had faced challenges during the COVID-19 pandemic. Breakthrough innovations must be developed to use recycled plastic in high-value products. Consumer green behavior can be promoted by prioritizing paper-based recyclable boxes for food packaging, promoting green civic culture, restricting the use of plastic bags, and branding green products (Cohen, 2020).

Technological intervention: Advancements in nanotechnology lead to the creation of self-cleaning and antiviral masks. Innovative textile engineering and design created sustainable materials which can be re-used to avoid the menace of SUP. However, considering the SARS-CoV-2 associated severity and prime focus toward immediate pandemic management, ambitious targets to ban SUPs faced setbacks.

1.6 WHO guidelines on waste management

WHO had released guidelines for proper collection, labeling, safe handling, and treatment of COVID-19 waste and recommended it to be done by professionally trained manpower. Onsite treatment should be preferred to reduce mishaps however, for offsite waste treatment care should be taken for its proper disposal. Waste handlers are advised to use proper safety equipment of high quality like heavy-duty boots, goggles, masks, and face shields while handling waste.

Waste generated during home quarantine, admission in isolation wards, ICUs, and care centers are potentially infectious and require proper and safe disposal. COVID-19 infected dead bodies need to be safely buried or cremated as per the protocol. Real-time supervision along with the implementation of existing guidelines is of paramount importance (United Nations Environment Programme. SBC World Health Organization, 2021).

1.7 Conclusion and future perspective

According to the prevalent situation, this pandemic will remain for the coming few years as evidenced by the emergence of the SARS-CoV-2 variants and COVID-19 waves. Therefore long-term plans are mandatory for waste management. Latest technology intervention must be employed for the collection and disposal of waste. Working staff needs to be equipped with all modern protective kits and equipment. Attempts will be done to reduce plastic waste footprints. Citizens need to be vigilant and concerned about environmental health to deal with a situation of such magnitude in the future.

References

Abdel-Shafy, H. I., & Mansour, M. S. M. (2018). Solid waste issue: Sources, composition, disposal, recycling, and valorization. *Egyptian Journal of Petroleum, 27*(4), 1275–1290.

Cohen, M. J. (2020). Does the COVID-19 outbreak mark the onset of a sustainable consumption transition? *Sustainability, 16*(1), 1–3. Available from https://doi.org/10.1080/15487733202017404 72. Available from https://www.tandfonline.com/doi/abs/10.1080/15487733.2020.1740472.

CPCB. Central Pollution Control Board (2021). Available from: <https://cpcb.nic.in/covid-waste-management/>.

Dalton, H. R., Kamar, N., Baylis, S. A., Moradpour, D., Wedemeyer, H., & Negro, F. (2018). EASL clinical practice guidelines on hepatitis E virus infection. *Journal of Hepatology, 68*(6), 1256–1271.

Datta, P., Mohi, G. K., & Chander, J. (2018). Biomedical waste management in India: Critical appraisal. *Journal of Laboratory Physicians, 10*(1), 006–014. Available from https://pubmed.ncbi.nlm.nih.gov/29403196/.

Di Maria, F., Beccaloni, E., Bonadonna, L., Cini, C., Confalonieri, E., La Rosa, G., et al. (2020). Minimization of spreading of SARS-CoV-2 via household waste produced by subjects affected by COVID-19 or in quarantine. *The Science of the Total Environment, 743*. Available from https://pubmed.ncbi.nlm.nih.gov/32653701/.

Global Waste Management Outlook (2015). | UNEP - UN Environment Programme Available from: https://www.unep.org/resources/report/global-waste-management-outlook. Accessed: 2022-03-23

Grodzińska-Jurczak, M., Krawczyk, A., Jurczak, A., Strzelecka, M., Rechciński, M., & Boćkowski, M. (2020). Environmental choices vs. Covid-19 pandemic fear – Plastic governance re-assessment. *Society Register, 4*(2), 49–66. Available from https://pressto.amu.edu.pl/index.php/sr/article/view/22507.

International Water Association. COVID-19 and safe water treatment – Utilities are in the focus – International Water Association (2020). Available from: <https://iwa-network.org/covid-19-and-safe-water-treatment-utilities-are-in-the-focus/>.

Kampf, G., Todt, D., Pfaender, S., & Steinmann, E. (2020). Persistence of coronaviruses on inanimate surfaces and their inactivation with biocidal agents. *The Journal of Hospital Infection, 104*(3), 246–251. Available from https://pubmed.ncbi.nlm.nih.gov/32035997/.

Liang, Y., Song, Q., Wu, N., Li, J., Zhong, Y., & Zeng, W. (2021). Repercussions of COVID-19 pandemic on solid waste generation and management strategies. *Frontiers of Environmental Science & Engineering, 15*(6), 1–18. Available from https://link.springer.com/article/10.1007/s11783-021-1407-5.

Mattiello, A., Chiodini, P., Bianco, E., Forgione, N., Flammia, I., Gallo, C., et al. (2013). Health effects associated with the disposal of solid waste in landfills and incinerators in populations living in surrounding areas: A systematic review. *International Journal of Public Health, 58*(5), 725–735. Available from https://pubmed.ncbi.nlm.nih.gov/23887611/.

National Geographic (2020). Pollution made the pandemic worse, but lockdowns clean the sky. Available from: <https://www.nationalgeographic.com/science/article/pollution-made-the-pandemic-worse-but-lockdowns-clean-the-sky>.

Nghiem, L. D., Morgan, B., Donner, E., & Short, M. D. (2020). The COVID-19 pandemic: Considerations for the waste and wastewater services sector. *Case Studies in Chemical and Environmental Engineering*, *1*, 100006.

Paul, M., & Bussemaker, M. J. (2020). A web-based geographic interface system to support decision making for municipal solid waste management in England. *Journal of Cleaner Production*, *263*.

PharmTech. Prioritizing sustainable packaging (2020). Available from: <https://www.pharmtech.com/view/prioritizing-sustainable-packaging>.

Quilliam, R. S., Weidmann, M., Moresco, V., Purshouse, H., O'Hara, Z., & Oliver, D. M. (2020). COVID-19: The environmental implications of shedding SARS-CoV-2 in human faeces. *Environment International*, *140*, 105790.

Shortage of personal protective equipment endangering health workers worldwide (2020). Available from: <https://www.who.int/news/item/03-03-2020-shortage-of-personal-protective-equipment-endangering-health-workers-worldwide>.

THE 17 GOALS. Sustainable Development (2021). [cited 2021 Jul 7]. Available from: <https://sdgs.un.org/goals>.

The Amount Of Plastic Waste Is Surging Because Of The Coronavirus Pandemic (2020). [cited 2021 Aug 5]. Available from: <https://www.forbes.com/sites/lauratenenbaum/2020/04/25/plastic-waste-during-the-time-of-covid-19/?sh = 8d46ef07e484>.

United Nations Environment Programme. SBC World Health Organization National Health-Care Waste Management Plan • Guidance Manual • Fundamentals of health-care waste management (2021). [cited 2021 Oct 10]; Available from: <http://www.who.int/mediacentre/factsheets/fs231/en/>.

Van Fan, Y., Jiang, P., Hemzal, M., & Klemeš, J. J. (2021). An update of COVID-19 influence on waste management. *The Science of the Total Environment*, *754*, 142014.

Wang, J., Shen, J., Ye, D., Yan, X., Zhang, Y., Yang, W., et al. (2020). Disinfection technology of hospital wastes and wastewater: Suggestions for disinfection strategy during coronavirus Disease 2019 (COVID-19) pandemic in China. *Environmental Pollution (Barking, Essex: 1987)*, *262*, 114665.

Waste – 2nd Edition (2019). Available from: <https://www.elsevier.com/books/waste/letcher/978-0-12-815060-3>.

Waste management an essential public service in the fight to beat COVID-19 (2021). Available from: https://www.unep.org/news-and-stories/press-release/waste-management-essential-public-service-fight-beat-covid-19. Accessed: 2022-03-23

WHO Coronavirus (COVID-19) Dashboard | WHO Coronavirus (COVID-19) Dashboard With Vaccination Data [Internet]. [cited 2021 Oct 5]. Available from: https://covid19.who.int/

World Health Organization. Health-care waste (2018). Available from: <https://www.who.int/news-room/fact-sheets/detail/health-care-waste>.

Zambrano-Monserrate, M. A., Ruano, M. A., & Sanchez-Alcalde, L. (2020). Indirect effects of COVID-19 on the environment. *The Science of the Total Environment*, *728*. Available from https://pubmed.ncbi.nlm.nih.gov/32334159/.

CHAPTER 2

Aerobic and anaerobic bioreactor systems for wastewater treatment

Monika Jain[1], Smita S. Kumar[2] and Lalit Goswami[3]
[1]Department of Natural Resource Management, College of Forestry, Banda University of Agriculture & Technology, Banda, Uttar Pradesh, India
[2]Department of Environmental Sciences, J.C. Bose University of Science & Technology, YMCA, Faridabad, Haryana, India
[3]Centre for Environment, Indian Institute of Technology, Guwahati, Assam, India

2.1 Introduction

The wastewater management technologies should involve two things, first remove the contaminants efficiently and secondly be able to recover useful resources from the wastewater. This can be achieved effectively with the help of bioreactors. A bioreactor is a vessel in which a chemical process is carried out which involves organisms or biochemically active substances derived from such organisms or a bioreactor is a manufactured device or system that supports a biologically active environment. Bioreactors can be aerobic or anaerobic. These bioreactors are commonly cylindrical, ranging in size from liters to cubic meters, and are often made of stainless steel. The organisms (yeast, bacteria, or animal cells) are grown under controlled conditions. They supply a homogeneous environment by constantly stirring the contents and giving the cells a controlled environment by ensuring the same temperature, pH, and oxygen levels. Organisms growing in bioreactors could be free-floating, submerged in a liquid medium, or may be attached to the surface of a solid medium. The environmental conditions inside the bioreactor such as temperature, nutrient concentrations, pH, and dissolved gases (especially oxygen for aerobic fermentation) affect the growth and productivity of the organisms. Fouling can harm the overall efficiency of the bioreactor. To avoid it, the bioreactor must be cleaned and for this, the interior surfaces are made of stainless steel for easy cleaning and sanitation. The bioreactors must be cleaned between batches, in order to reduce the fouling as much as possible when operated continuously.

Techno-economics and Life Cycle Assessment of Bioreactors
DOI: https://doi.org/10.1016/B978-0-323-89848-5.00008-1

Bioreactors are used in industrial processes to produce pharmaceuticals, vaccines, or antibodies (Mishra et al., 2019). They are also used to convert raw materials into useful by-products such as bioconversion of corn into ethanol. Bioreactor usage in the course of wastewater treatment has moved from an exotic, new technology to a standard process. The aerobic treatment utilizes oxygen and bacterial biomass to collect organic matter and other pollutants like nitrogen and phosphorus that are converted into carbon dioxide, water, and other biomass (Ranade & Bhandari, 2014). Whereas, anaerobic treatment, breaks down the organic impurities in the absence of oxygen, producing methane, carbon dioxide, and other biomass (Youcai, 2018). The low-strength wastewater with chemical oxygen demand (COD) < 1000 mg/L and wastewater containing nitrogen and phosphorus are treated aerobically in the presence of oxygen. Whereas, high strength wastewater having COD > 4000 mg/L are treated anaerobically in the absence of oxygen (Sandra et al., 2017).

The wastewater treated aerobically has some advantages over the anaerobic treatment process (Mishra et al., 2021). These include (Ranade & Bhandari, 2014): (1) Low odor due to no production of methane or hydrogen sulfide (2) good nutrient removal efficiency thus enabling the direct discharge of water into surface waters or disinfection, etc. Besides, there are certain disadvantages also of aerobic treatment: (1) Requirement of oxygen is an energy-consuming process that increases the overall cost of the process. (2) Solid wastes that cannot be decomposed by microorganisms settle down as bio-solids that need to be disposed of carefully. Whereas, the anaerobic treatment process has a number of advantages over aerobic treatment (Youcai, 2018). They are:

(1) Biogas produced during the anaerobic process can be used as a source of natural gas/methane that can be used as an energy resource. (2) Production of sludge is very less that is stable and safe for use as an agricultural fertilizer making the process economic and simple. It's just that the anaerobic treatment process produces unpleasant odors, that need to be managed in some or the other way. Sometimes, in order to treat the wastewater containing high concentrations of organic contaminants efficiently, both the aerobic and anaerobic systems are clubbed together. Consequently, anaerobic treatment leads to the reduction of organic contaminants, and aerobic treatment leads to a further reduction in biochemical oxygen demand (BOD) and total suspended solids (TSS). Sometimes, the secondary aerobic treatment leads to the oxidation of ammonia to nitrate. So, in nutshell, clubbing both technologies is more beneficial for

the treatment of wastewater than the individual process. The integration of these technologies in the paired form can substantially lower the operational and waste discharge cost but will increase the capital cost. The following section throws light on some of the most popular configurations of bioreactors used in wastewater treatment. Bioreactors operate in three modes that are batch process, bed-batch, and continuous process: *Batch process:* It is a partially closed system in which the materials are added into the bioreactor aseptically and are removed at the end of the operation. In Batch process, the bioreactor consists of a tank with an agitator and an integral heating/cooling system. The vessels vary in size from less than 1 litre to more than 15,000 litres. The vessels are made of steel, glass or alloy. The materials that could be added or removed during the operation are air/gas exchange, antifoam, and pH controlling agents (Spier et al., 2016). Plants producing fine chemicals, pharmaceuticals, semiconductors, and foods employ batch processes, because they have to produce small amounts of a variety of specialized products, which may vary from month to month or even day to day. In continuous process, there is a continuous stream of feed into the bioreactor and the product is continuously taken out of the bioreactor. Continuous bioprocessing is currently in the early stages of development; however, the process has the potential to go indefinitely, manufacturing the product at a constant rate. A continuous process is beneficial as there is no downtime between batches, there are no expensive and laborious cleaning tasks, and there is no batch-to-batch variability in your product.

2.2 Bioreactor and different configurations

There are various types of bioreactors that have been used for the treatment of diverse wastewaters. In these bioreactors, polluted water is allowed to agitate in aerobic or anaerobic tanks where free suspended microbes or immobilized cells on a matrix are added to metabolize organic matter, resulting in the formation of sludge that is recycled or discharged.

2.3 Continuous stirred tank bioreactor

As the name suggests, in such a configuration, the biomaterial is continuously stirred in the bioreactor with the help of impellers mechanically. The impellers are normally in the center and suspended in the superior part of the tank (Spier et al., 2016). Continuous stirred tank bioreactors (CSTRs) can be used in series with more than one bioreactor with different conditions in each one (Spier et al., 2016). CSTRs consist of a constant volume tank equipped with an agitation system to mix all the components together. They are also equipped with influent and effluent ports for the inflow of reactants and harvest of products, respectively (Mekawy et al., 2016). The CSTR is frequently used in research due to its simplicity in design and operation. There are two types of CSTR based on the operational strategies: (1) Chemostat (chemical environment is static): A bioreactor in which fresh medium or nutrients are added continuously in excess, while the liquid volume is continuously removed to keep the culture volume constant by setting the inlet and outlet flow rates equal (Spier et al., 2016). (2) Turbidostat: In Turbidostat, the cell concentration is maintained constant by the monitoring optical density of the culture and the liquid volume is kept constant by setting the outlet flow rate equal to the inlet flow rate (Spier et al., 2016).

2.4 Airlift bioreactors

Airlift bioreactors (ALRs) get the name because some parts of the bioreactors are connected by a draft tube filled with some kind of air or gas. There is no mechanical stirring for the mixing of liquid in ALRs. So, the mixing of liquid is done by turbulence of the gas flow. The inner draft tube is present in the center of the reactor. The effluent (liquid) and the air (gas) are introduced from the bottom which moves upwards and results in circulatory flow in the entire reactor (Doble & Kumar, 2005) There are two main basic configurations of the ALRs: External loop reactors and internal loop reactors. In the first one, the circulation of the fluids follow distinct channels and in the second one, there is only a barrier that is positioned in a vessel, which creates some channels for the circulation or concentric tubes that leads to a central and a peripheral channel (Spier et al., 2016).

2.5 Anaerobic fluidized bed bioreactors

In anaerobic fluidized bed (AFB) reactors, a mixed culture of bacteria in the form of a film is made to grow on the surface of some inert carrier particle. These particles are then fluidized using the energy of the influent stream. The linear velocity of the effluent is kept higher than the minimum fluidization velocity so that the film-covered particles are always in motion but lower than the terminal free settling velocity of each particle-biofilm aggregate (Narayanan & Narayan, 2019). The effluent substrate diffuses into the "biofilm" and gets converted into volatile fatty acids and ultimately to methane, which diffuses out through the biofilm into the bulk liquid. The mixing and mass transfer attained in these reactors is excellent, so the resulting conversions are comparable or even superior to those obtained with UASB (upflow anaerobic sludge blanket) reactors. These reactors have typical loading rates of 25 kg COD/m^3 day. However, as the biofilm grows, the film-covered particles increase in size, and hence their composite density decreases. This causes the particle to move up in the bed, ultimately resulting in its leaving the reactor, thereby leading to a reduction in the carrier particle concentration inside the reactor. This problem is overcome by removing the biofilm from the carrier particle that has exited the reactor and then recycling it back into the reactor. Another drawback of AFB reactors is the high energy requirement resulting from the large recycle rates employed in these systems (Forster & Wase, 1987). These bioreactors can be operated at much higher fluid velocities or flow rates.

2.6 Packed bed (fixed bed) bioreactors

A bed of solid particles (attached biofilms which is immobilized in nature employing attached growth of microbes), with biocatalysts on or within the matrix of solids, is packed in a column that constitutes the bed of the reactor. The fixed-film reactors are so named because the biomass grows on a fixed supporting material such as poly vinyl chloride (PVC), silica granules, wood, polymer beads, carbon, rock, activated carbon particles, etc. In these bioreactors, waste effluent is pumped from the top of the reactor which flows down through the packed bed, and the air is pumped from the bottom. The microorganisms in the aerated packed bed grow and degrade organic matter present in the wastewater (Doble & Kumar, 2005). A trickle bed biofilm reactor is an example of a packed (fixed) bed bioreactor. It is the oldest process used for aerobic wastewater treatment. In this bioreactor, the feed water flows downward (under gravity) through the bed of particle-biofilm aggregates at low velocities. The reactor is kept open so that atmospheric air could diffuse into the substrate solution and no air compressors are used (Narayanan & Narayan, 2019). Besides, there some disadvantages of packed beds are: the pores of the bed get filled with the passage of time and the bed becomes compact. As a result of this, the pressure drops across the bed, and secondly, a large portion of the reactor volume is occupied by the media. If aerobic and anaerobic processes are compared in terms of efficiency, then the anaerobic process is considered to be a better option because of low-energy requirements and small amounts of sludge production. Therefore, the anaerobic process is catching the attention for the treatment of complex industrial wastewater, which contains toxic materials, and low concentrations of domestic wastewater (Abdelgadir et al., 2014). In this consideration, Najafpour et al. (2009) investigated the performance of upflow anaerobic packed bed bioreactor for the treatment of cheese whey. The authors revealed that the removal of COD and lactose were 94.5 and 99% at a Hydraulic Retention Time (HRT) of 16 h. The methane gas was produced at the rate of 6.57 and 3.25 L/h at an HRT of 6 and 24 h, respectively (Najafpour et al., 2009).

2.7 Membrane bioreactors

Membrane bioreactors (MBRs) are a combination of a bioreactor and a membrane filtration unit. In MBR, the biological degradation of organic matter is done in the bioreactor with the help of microorganisms, and separation of microorganisms from the treated wastewater is done by the membrane (Marrot et al., 2004). The MBR process retains the biomass in the bioreactor, that is, bacteria and viruses. There is no need to disinfect the treated effluents after going through an MBR (Baek & Pagilla, 2006). MBRs are used to treat municipal and industrial wastewater. The main disadvantages associated with the MBR are that they are quite expensive as compared to conventional technology and another one is fouling of membrane (Achilli et al., 2011). Two types of MBR have been classified based on their configuration; (1) Aerobic MBR (AMBR): The AMBR is a combination of a membrane filtration unit and aerobic bioreactor (Baek & Pagilla, 2006). They are mostly submerged systems. The operating costs in these systems are high because of the cost of aeration. (2) Anaerobic (AnMBR): The AnMBR is a combination of a membrane unit and an anaerobic reactor.

AnMBR systems treat high strength, organic industrial wastewater, such as alcohol-distillery wastewater, pulp, and paper, food processing wastewater, municipal wastewater, brewery wastewater, palm oil wastewater, landfill leachate, etc. having high loading rates such as 5–30 kg COD/m^3/day as compared to less than 1 kg COD/m^3/day for aerobic systems. AnMBR has certain advantages over aerobic systems, like aeration-energy savings, low sludge production, methane gas generation but still, their use is limited, because of the high membrane fouling as compared to AMBR systems (Achilli et al., 2011). The disadvantage of AnMBR is negligible or no removal of ammonia, total nitrogen, and phosphorus. In AnMBRs, biomass could be effectively retained inside the reactor that provides optimum conditions for degradation of organic matter without any carry-over of suspended solids. A high-quality effluent could be obtained in terms of suspended solids, COD, and pathogen counts by incorporating membranes to anaerobic municipal wastewater treatment as compared to conventional anaerobic processes (Ozgun et al., 2013). AnMBRs can achieve around 90% or higher COD removal and methane production of 0.25 to 0.35 m^3 CH_4/kg COD (Chang, 2014). In these prospects, Yurtsever et al. (2015) have studied the treatment of textile wastewater containing azo dye in anaerobic (AnMBR) and aerobic (AeMBR) MBRs at 35°C. The authors found that the color of contaminated wastewater was almost completely removed in AnMBR at 9.0 L/(m^2 h) while it was only 30%–50% in AeMBR at 50 L/(m^2 h). The fouling in both the MBRs was completely removed using sodium Hypochlorite (NaOCl) and sulfuric acid (Yurtsever et al., 2015). Membrane fouling is the most common problem that affects the performance of the system. Membrane fouling is due to the interaction between the membrane and the components of the activated sludge liquor, biological flocs formed by the number of living and dead microorganisms along with colloidal and soluble compounds (Meng et al., 2008). Due to this problem, cleaning or replacement of membrane is required regularly and this increases the operating costs of the system because of the use of cleaning agents. In a study conducted by Lew et al. (2009), the authors used AnMBR for the treatment of domestic wastewater. The authors found that COD was removed up to 88% and the accumulation of inert particulate matter was 350 mg TSS/L/day. The authors also tried the backwash for reducing the fouling and particulate matter settling on the membrane. The frequency at which the fouling could be reduced and energy could be saved were between 30 and 60 min (Lew et al., 2009).

2.8 Upflow anaerobic sludge blanket reactor

In UASB reactor system, sludge granules are put in the bioreactor, which are minute colonies of several classes of microbes that lead to bioconversion. No support particles are used here. The reactor column consists of a sludge bed at the bottom and a sludge blanket of larger height above it. These bioreactors provide a large degree of BOD removal (more than 95%) even with high-strength feedstocks (Narayanan & Narayan, 2019). Here, the biomass layer is submerged below the treated effluent that flows upward towards the surface of the tank as the name suggests. The anaerobic bacteria, especially methanogens are employed in UASB. The effluent flows up the bioreactor through a sludge blanket which is composed of gas bubbles formed during the anaerobic process (Doble & Kumar, 2005). The effluent diffuses into the sludge granules and is degraded anaerobically. In UASB, the effluent is fed from the bottom and leaves from the top through an internal baffle system thus, separating the gas, sludge, and liquid phases. The granular sludge and biogas are separated using this device. A COD loading of 30 kg/m^3 day can be treated with a COD separation efficiency of 85%–95% at optimum conditions. The methane level of the produced biogas ranges from 80% to 90% (v/v). Hydraulic retention time (HRTs) of as low as 4 h are practical, with superior settling sludge and solid retention time of greater than 100 days (Goli et al., 2019). UASB has several advantages like; (1) no supporting medium is required for the attachment of the biomass, therefore the cost is decreased. (2) There is no mechanical mixing, recirculation of sludge, or effluent within the reactor hence, the requirement of energy is less. (3) Reduced odor problems, increased sludge quality, less land requirement, mechanical simplicity, easy movement and control, less venture and operational cost, and low maintenance. The disadvantages of UASB include: (1) long start-up time, because sludge granules formation is a very slow biological process, (2) the need of skilled personnel, (3) they are economically not feasible at low temperature, (4) subtle towards noxious substances, etc. The UASB can be used for treating the effluents from various industries like tanneries, distilleries, food processing, breweries, and pulp and paper industries. Through UASB, pollutants in wastewater are degraded by microbes that produce 75%–80% CH_4 by volume, 15%–25% CO_2, and minor amounts of N_2, H_2, and other gases. This system, therefore, is feasible and efficient for the waste containing a high level of BOD (Goli et al., 2019).

2.9 Conclusion

It has been observed that various kinds of bioreactors with different characteristics have been developed for the treatment of both domestic and industrial wastewater. The bioreactors are cost-effective, reliable, efficient, and lead to the removal of a wide range of pollutants. Whereas, the already established bioreactor types such as Continuous Stirred Tank Reactor, Upflow Anaerobic Sludge Bioreactor, and Packed bed bioreactor, etc. continue to function at a large scale globally for treatment of wastewater having different compositions, the newly emergent ones such as MBR are also making their presence felt. Also, it has become imperative to upgrade the already existing bioreactors so that they can tune-up with new types of emerging pollutants which are recalcitrant in nature. It is also important to improve the performance of bioreactor technologies during operations.

Acknowledgment

The corresponding author would like to thank the Department of Science & Technology for providing financial aid in the form of the project under the ECRA scheme (grant number ECR/2018/001158, 15 March 2019) for writing this book chapter.

References

Abdelgadir, A., Chen, X., Liu, J., Xie, X., Zhang, J., Zhang, K., Wang, H., & Na, L. (2014). Characteristics, process parameters, and inner components of anaerobic bioreactors. *BioMed Research International, 1-11.*

Achilli, A., Marchand, E. A., & Childress, A. E. (2011). A performance evaluation of three membrane bioreactor systems: Aerobic, anaerobic, and attached-growth. *Water Science and Technology, 63*(12), 2999–3005.

Baek, S. H., & Pagilla, K. R. (2006). Aerobic and anaerobic membrane bioreactors for municipal wastewater treatment. *Water Environment Research, 78*(2), 133–140.

Chang, S. (2014). Anaerobic membrane bioreactors (AnMBR) for wastewater treatment. *Advances in Chemical Engineering and Science, 4*, 56–61.

Doble, M., & Kumar, A. (2005). Aerobic and anaerobic bioreactors CHAPTER 3. In *Biotreatment of industrial effluents*, (pp. 19–38). Burlington: Butterworth-Heinemann.

Forster, C. F., & Wase, D. A. J. (1987). *Environmental biotechnology* (p. 453) Chichester: Ellis Horwood Ltd.

Goli, A., Shamiri, A., Khosroyar, S., Talaiekhozani, A., Sanaye, R., & Azizi, K. (2019). A Review on different aerobic and anaerobic treatment methods in dairy industry wastewater. *Journal of Environmental Treatment Techniques, 6*(1), 113–141.

Lew, B., Tarre, S., Beliavski, M., Dosoretz, C., & Green, M. (2009). Anaerobic membrane bioreactor (AnMBR) for domestic wastewater treatment. *Desalination, 243*, 251–257.

Marrot, B., Barrios-Martinez, A., Moulin, P., & Roche, N. (2004). Industrial wastewater treatment in a membrane bioreactor: A Review. *Environmental Progress, 23*(1), 59–68.

Meng, F., Yang, F., Shi, B., & Zhang, H. (2008). A comprehensive study on membrane fouling in submerged membrane bioreactors operated under different aeration intensities. *Separation and Purification Technology, 59*(1), 91–100.

Mekawy, A., Mohanakrishna, G., Srikanth, S., & Pant, D. (2016). The role of bioreactors in industrial wastewater treatment. In R. Chandra (Ed.), *Environmental waste management* (pp. 157–184). CRC Press, Taylor & Francis Group.

Mishra, P., Krishnan, S., Rana, S., Singh, L., Sakinah, M., & Ab Wahid, Z. (2019). Outlook of fermentative hydrogen production techniques: An overview of dark, photo and integrated dark-photo fermentative approach to biomass. *Energy Strategy Reviews*, *24*, 27–37. Available from https://doi.org/10.1016/j.esr.2019.01.001.

Mishra, P., Wahid, Z. A., Karim, A., Pant, K. K., Ghosh, P., Kumar, D., & Singh, L. (2021). Chronological perspective on fermentative-hydrogen from hypothesis in early nineteenth century to recent developments: A review. *Biomass Conversion and Biorefinery*. Available from https://doi.org/10.1007/s13399-020-01180-4.

Najafpour, G. D., Tajallipour, M., Komeili, M., & Mohammadi, M. (2009). Kinetic model for an up-flow anaerobic packed bed bioreactor: Dairy wastewater treatment. *African Journal of Biotechnology*, *8*, 3590–3596.

Narayanan, C. M., & Narayan, V. (2019). Biological wastewater treatment and bioreactor design: A review. *Sustainable Environment Research*, *29*(33), 1–17.

Ozgun, H., Dereli, R. K., Ersahin, M. E., Kinaci, C., Spanjers, H., & van Lier, J. B. (2013). A review of anaerobic membrane bioreactors for municipal wastewater treatment: Integration options, limitations and expectations. *Separation and Purification Technology*, *118*, 89–104.

Sandra, C. A., Jamil, N. A. M., Jabbar, S., Sakyat, S., & Gomes, C. (2017). Aerobic and anaerobic sewage biodegradable processes: The gap analysis. *International Journal of Research in Environmental Science*, *3*, 9–19.

Spier, M.R., de Souza Vandenberghe, L.P., Medeiros, A.B.P., Soccol, C.R. (2016). Application of different types of bioreactors in bioprocesses. In P.G. Antolli & Z. Liu (Eds.), *Bioreactors: Design, properties and applications* (Chapter 2, pp. 55-90).

Youcai, Z. (2018). *Pollution control technology for leachate from municipal solid waste* (pp. 361–522). Cambridge: Elsevier Inc.

Yurtsever, A., Sahinkaya, E., Aktaş, Ö., Uçar, D., Çınar, Ö., & Wang, Z. (2015). Performances of anaerobic and aerobic membrane bioreactors for the treatment of synthetic textile wastewater. *Bioresource Technology*, *192*, 564–573.

Ranade, V.V., Bhandari, V.M. (2014). *Industrial wastewater treatment, recycling and reuse* (Chapter 9, pp. 369-397). Oxford: Elsevier Science & Technology.

CHAPTER 3

Emerging trends in bioreactor systems for an improved wastes valorization

Olusegun Abayomi Olalere[1], Chee-Yuen Gan[1], Abiola Ezekiel Taiwo[2], Hamoud Alenezi[3], Oladayo Adeyi[4] and Abiola John Adeyi[5]
[1]Analytical Biochemistry Research Center(ABrC), Universiti Sains Malaysia, University Innovation Incubator Building, Sains@USM, Bayan Lepas, Penang, Malaysia
[2]Department of Chemical Engineering, Landmark University, Omu-Aran, Kwara State, Nigeria
[3]Process Systems Engineering Centre (PROSPECT), Research Institute for Sustainable Environment, School of Chemical and Energy Engineering, Universiti Teknologi, Kuala Lumpur, Malaysia
[4]Department of Chemical Engineering, Michael Okpara University of Agriculture, Umudike, Abia State, Nigeria
[5]Department of Mechanical Engineering, Ladoke Akintola University of Technology, Ogbomoso, Oyo State, Nigeria

3.1 Introduction

Bioreactors are closed systems that allow for the regulated execution of biological processes. It consists of a bioreactor, sensors and actuators, a control system, and algorithms for monitoring and controlling the bioreactor's parameters (Keijzer et al., 2011). Mechanical, electrical, and bioprocess design are all included in the design of a bioreactor system. Given the versatility of conventional bioreactors, the schematic design should indeed be coordinated in such a manner that devices may be utilized in compliance with the most stringent standards. It is reported that many investigators have constructed different types of bioreactors with desirable features, and their industrial adaption is highly suggested. Bioreactors come in a variety of configurations, including stirred tank, fluidized bed, and packed-bed biofilm bioreactors.

3.1.1 Stirred tank system

The stirred tank bioreactor is by far the most frequently used bioreactor model with the capacity to manage both aerobic and anaerobic waste. The aerobic treatment of industrial effluents in stirred tank bioreactors is one of the oldest industrial biotechnological processes (Meena et al., 2021). Despite its obvious limitations, this method continues to remain prevalent. It is also the procedure that has been modified and varied the

Techno-economics and Life Cycle Assessment of Bioreactors
DOI: https://doi.org/10.1016/B978-0-323-89848-5.00006-8

most. The traditional activated sludge method uses a stirred aerobic tank (stirred tank bioreactor) loaded with microbial sludge, with the halting of the growth (Narayanan & Narayan, 2019). For oxygen levels, high-pressure air is sprayed from the base. Due to the enormous capacity of the aerobic tank and the poor water solubility of atmospheric oxygen in water or aqueous solutions, massive air compressors would be required to sparge in considerable amounts of air to meet the microorganisms' and the aerobic process' oxygen requirements (Verma et al., 2021). However, the high running costs of air compressors restrict the process's economic viability, despite its ease of design and installation. As previously mentioned, several studies have suggested changes to the activated sludge system with Rao and Subrahmanyam (2004) reporting a comprehensive overview. Regardless, all use stirred tank bioreactors. This method uses two bioreactors (stirred tanks) in succession, one aerobic for organic matter breakdown and nitrification. The second bioreactor functions for anoxic denitrification. A sedimentation tank clarifies the denitrification discharge; treated wastewater exits and the thickest base sludge is returned to the aerobic tank. The quantity of microbiological sludge regenerated must be adjusted to reduce endogenous microbe degradation while increasing Biological oxygen demand (BOD) reduction.

Rather than a single stirred tank bioreactor, a succession of miniaturized stirred tanks should therefore be used, with the overall capacity of the cascade maintaining the same. In the activated sludge system, stepwise aeration is used to accomplish this design and enhances the overall operation of the bioreactor (Metcalf & Eddy Inc.) The aerobic tank is split into sections, each receiving a distinct compressed air surge. The raw wastewater enters the first chamber, and the partly treated current drains to the next, with the treated water exiting the last. The method improves BOD reduction but raises total running costs. Because each container contained a small volume and aerated independently; the performance of each chamber may reach optimum performance with hundred percent back-mixing.

As with aerobic waste processing, stirred tank bioreactors were the first and remain a good choice for anaerobic waste removal of various pollutants, residential, and urban trash. The fundamental grounds for this decision are the high capacity and simplicity of assembly. Anaerobic bioremediation of sludges, especially when a heterogeneous culture of acidogenic, acetogenic, and methanogenic microorganisms is used, offers the added benefit of converting organic matter into useful materials such as biofuels containing a mixture of mainly carbon (IV) oxide and methane gas.

The anaerobic digestion may also be carried out at elevated temperatures utilizing thermophilic microorganisms. This aids in the quicker elimination of germs, but there will be extra costs associated with the construction of heating pipes and the delivery of heat externally. Typically, the cost of higher input energy outweighs the advantage of quicker microbial elimination and greater methane output. Additionally, thermophilic microorganisms develop at a slightly slower pace than mesophilic germs. Whenever waste heat is accessible, as in integrated power and heat systems, thermophilic biological treatment is not an appealing or advantageous proposal. Nonetheless, a thermophilic preparation of the feeder slurry may be used if microbial elimination is a significant issue (Momoh & Nwaogazie, 2008). The majority of research on anaerobic digestion utilizing mesophilic microorganisms published in the research concern the use of alternative, heterogeneous feedstock (Costa et al., 2012; Samson & LeDuy, 1983). The majority of them used labs stirred tanks known as chemo-stats to perform their studies, and almost all of them relate to dispersed microbe growth (Yuan et al., 2012). While these studies show the possibility of biogas production through anaerobic digestion of a variety of substrates, they do not emphasize the actual performance attributes of commercial bioreactors in this context (Krustok & Nehrenheim, 2012).

3.1.2 Fluidized-bed reactor

Fluidized bed biofilm reactors are better suitable for large-scale applications, as they can run at significantly greater velocities (Shieh & Keenan, 1986). Industry waste is allowed at a rate significantly greater than that of the flow speed but less than the terminal free velocity gradient of each particulate aggregation. As a result, all aggregates stay suspended in the rising flow of fluidized flow mixture. Since each aggregate is completely encircled by the substrate, the interaction between the two is more intense, which enhances bioreactor effectiveness. Additionally, when the bed widens, the reactor's total active volume rises. Another intriguing characteristic of these bioreactors is that after the bed is completely fluidized, the pressure loss throughout the bed stays relatively constant and therefore does not rise in proportion to the rate of flowing fluid. As a result, the running costs of the bioreactor remain constant as the feeding flow rate increases.

Narayanan and Biswas (2015) explored the treatment of aerobic effluent in multiple fluidized bed bioreactors. The research includes robust mathematically modeling and simulation of bioreactor functionality, followed by confirmation of the simulation findings via comparison to extensive experimental data gathered on laboratory level pilot plants scales. The difference between model predictions and observed data is a little below 10%.

Mowla and Ahmadi (2007) presented a quantitative study of treating wastewater in a multiple fluidized bioreactor system. It was nevertheless, maintained first order anaerobic decomposition kinetics and therefore obtained an exact solution to the effectiveness formula. That, within itself, is a significant restriction of their investigation, since the findings presented can be extended to the very few particular situations in which first-order kinetics for biomass conversion may be postulated. Numerous scientists have published laboratory research on fluidized bed bioreactors. Gonzalez et al. (2001) investigated dephenolization of effluent in a lab fluidized bed column consisting of immobilized Pseudomonas cells, whereas Deckwer et al. (2004) describe laboratory studies on microbiological mercury reduction in multiple fluidizations. Additional research on pilot plant scale-up resulting in the development of commercial bioreactors would undoubtedly be beneficial.

Additionally, efforts have been attempted to enhance the construction of fluidized bed bioreactors. For instance, Narayanan et al. (2014) demonstrated enhanced use of a widely divergent fluidized bed bioreactor to synthesize lactic acid from cheese whey and molasses utilizing the microbial species referenced and identified that a bioreactor of this design converts lactose/sucrose 20%–25% more efficiently than a traditional bioreactor at the very same feeding rate. Simultaneously, the total pressure loss and therefore the running cost of the bioreactor are only increased slightly.

3.1.3 Fixed bed bioreactor

Packed-bed biofilm bioreactors are heterogeneous multistage reactors that rely on microorganisms adhering to the reactor walls to develop (Iliuta & Iliuta, 2022). Support particles including silica grains, polymeric pellets, activated charcoal bits, and others are used in these bioreactors (except for DSFF bioreactors, which will be addressed later) (Xie et al., 2021). A tiny biofilm forms around each particle, which is bordered by microbial cells. The way biofilm reactors handle particle-biofilm aggregates distinguishes them (Xie et al., 2021). A packed (fixed) bed is one of the easiest (and oldest) methods of handling these aggregates (Swain et al., 2021). One such method is the trickling bed biofilm bioreactor, which is among the first aerobic wastewater treatment technologies. Due to their low running cost, the p article-biofilm aggregates are used as a bed in this bioreactor, with feedwater flowing down (by gravitation) across them.

Nonetheless, the reactor's capacity is limited unless otherwise built with enormous dimensions since the feed solution is trickling down the bed at low speeds (De Vela & Gostomski, 2021). The reactor is left open to allow ambient air to permeate into the substrate solution, but no air compressors are employed in the procedure (Molaei et al., 2022). Notwithstanding, useful products can be recovered from organic effluents using aerobic biological processes, such as the synthesizing of Xanthan gum from milk and cheese wastes (Narayanan & Narayan, 2021). In these instances, the bioreactor cannot be kept closed, and compact sterilized air must be sparged from the lowest part. Aerobic wastewater treatment uses trickle bed bioreactors, which are mostly based on experimental test data (Zimba et al., 2021). In addition to being overly empirical, this method limits the reactor's adaptability.

The packed (fixed) bioreactors were designed and analyzed by Narayanan (2005) on the basis that they are the same as plugging for a flow reactor. One such supposition, however, does lead to some representation of the true situation. Modeling the bioreactor as a plug flow dispersion reactor and solving the controlling efficiency equation numerically might have been a more efficient solution (Zarei et al., 2021). Anaerobic fixed bed biofilm reactors with up-flow may also be studied in a comparable pattern. Whenever the process involves gas evolution, the bioreactor transforms into a multiple-phase system, and its three-phased nature must be properly addressed. Some believe that gas is distributed in the form of extremely small bubbles and therefore does not interfere with substrate migration into the biofilm. It's still important to assess the proportionate gas and liquid holdup in the bed based on the current number of experimental findings (Xie et al., 2021).

3.2 The theory of bioreactor and its geometry

Bioreactors are often depicted in a variety of forms, generally cylindrical and spherical in the top and bottom portions, with capacities ranging from 1 to 100 L and constructed of stainless steel or glass. The majority of bioreactors contain an agitator or stirrers that revolve around the vessel's center. In different studies, the geometrical ratios of various bioreactor vessels have been published (Narayanan & Narayan, 2019). The system geometry of a bioreactor is shown in Fig. 3.1. A glass vessel with a heating or cooling blanket, a driving motor to drive the fermentation, and sensors to monitor the amount of foam, dissolved oxygen concentration, and pH are all typical components of a bioreactor. The exhaust condenser includes a thermowell, a sample tube, a cooling coil, a six-blade Rushton impeller (depending on the kind of bioreactor), and a baffle (Narayanan & Narayan, 2019). The shaft, baffle, and impeller, which are made up of impeller disc and blade, make up the agitator system (Martens et al., 2014). During fermentation broth mixing, the agitator system created an interface between the bulk fluid and the gas phase, allowing for air dispersion, oxygenation, and heat transmission. The agitation vessel allows gases or air to enter the fermentation tank more easily (Kim et al., 2021). Up to four gases, comprising air, nitrogen, carbon dioxide, and oxygen, may be injected into the medium through the sparge ring or supplementary microsparger. The sparger draws pressured gas into the vessel through a ring or tube with a single aperture. The medium may be injected with air, nitrogen, carbon dioxide, or oxygen through the sparge ring or supplementary microsparger. The sparger injects pressured gas into the vessel through a single hole in the shape of a ring or tube.

In a bioreactor, the mixing is accomplished via the use of an impeller placed on the vessel. The literature has standard impeller specifications for

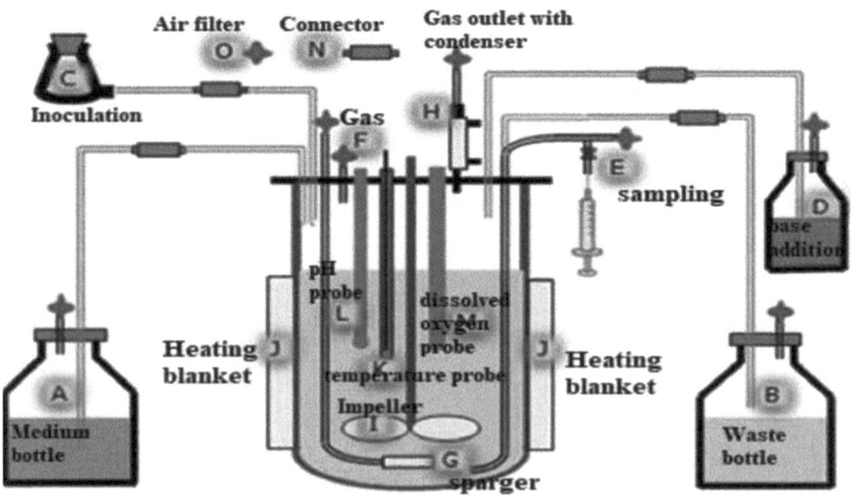

Figure 3.1 A diagram of a laboratory-scale bioreactor arrangement (Martens et al., 2014).

the different vessels of a bioreactor. The Rushton turbine is the most often used impeller in fermentation, with its six flat blades mounted on a disc (Doran, 2012). Within the fermentation vessel, baffles are attached to improve gas movement and diffusion. These baffles are used to increase the effectiveness of aeration in agitated containers of different sizes. Baffles are metal strips about one-tenth the diameter of the vessel that is radially connected to the wall of the bioreactor. Bioreactor dimension (V_T) varies based on type or classes while other metrics depend on the vessel's diameter (D_T). Literature provides information about the bioreactor geometric ratio (Doran, 2012). For a bioreactor, the height-to-diameter ratio is crucial. While a ratio of two to three is preferable, when the tank contents are not stratified or when a mixer is utilized, a higher ratio may be used. Eq. (3.1) can be used to calculate the volume of a bioreactor vessel of cylindrical shape.

$$V_T = \pi \left(\frac{D^2{}_T}{4} \right) H_T \tag{3.1}$$

With the height to diameter ratio (aspect ratio) of 2.0, vessel capacity., vessel diameter $D_T = 0.15$ m. Additional vessel geometric characteristics include the vessel's height, the liquid's height, the baffle's breadth, and the impeller's height (Alade & Betiku, 2010).

3.3 Bioreactor development for improved waste valorization

The research of Rodríguez et al. (2020) focused on generating additional value from biogas produced during waste treatment. The authors demonstrate the viability of using biogas as a substrate in a bubble column bioreactor with gas recirculation, and they analyze a polyhydroxybutyrate (PH)-producing strain. Tetteh and Rathilal (2021) created a five-unit bioreactor system for wastewater treatment and biogas upgrading to natural quality. The study used wastewater and sludge from a wastewater treatment plant to test a lab-scale biomethane potential system. The impact of adding biomagnetic nanoparticles to improve anaerobic digestion of wastewater into bioenergy was considered a very promising and sustainable organic waste management strategy. Sarlaki et al. (2021) built a mechanically agitated tank reactor and used it to evaluate the optimal generation of humic acid from lignite processing wastes. The laboratory bioreactor was utilized to improve the extraction efficiency of humic acid from lignite processing wastes. By constructing a helix around the inner reactor tank, the heating system was intended to deliver heat to the materials inside the reactor. After flowing between the tank's two walls, hot fluid entered the inlet at the top and exited through the outlet at the bottom. To avoid overheating and maintain temperature control, a cold-water chamber was used. Food waste was valorized as a value-added commodity by Svensson et al. (2021) The authors offer a method for valuing bread waste by creating a protein- and fatty-acid-rich fungal biomass that also serves as a source of microfibers. A bench and pilot-scale bubble column bioreactor were used to conduct a scale-up investigation. The study concludes that employing filamentous fungi for the valorization of food waste is a long-term solution for reducing food waste's environmental impact while also producing value-added products. According to Vu et al. (2020), wastewater is not frequently regarded as waste in recycling and reuse but rather a source of water, energy, and nutrients. They developed a hybrid system consisting of an anaerobic membrane bioreactor and a microalgal membrane reactor to harvest energy, nutrients, and microalgal biomass from food and agri-business industry waste. Pio et al. (2020) demonstrated on a small scale the direct (air) co-gasification of waste generated fuel and biomass utilizing a bubbling fluidized bed reactor. The potential for valorizing wastes as an energy resource was shown via co-gasification of refuse-derived fuel and biomass. The report provides an update that can be used as a supplement to help make decisions about co-gasification initiatives, such as scaling up the process to industrial size and building co-gasification facilities (Pio et al., 2020) (Table 3.1).

3.4 Current trends in the bioreactor system

In recent times numerous trends in bioreactor design have been discovered. Consequently, the last few years have been driven by advancements in single-use bioreactor innovation. This has mostly been targeted on small- and large-scale capacity utilization bioprocesses, to lower the upfront investment costs of new manufacturing plants. Some other trend emphasizes the research and development component of biotechnology, which is primarily cost-reflective; this involves scaling down bioreactors to smaller capacities, with the primary objective of shortening the time required to bring new products to light (Wasewar, 2021). Recent advancements in sensing and actuation technology have made it possible for bioreactors to be scaled

Table 3.1 Recent cases of biotransformation processes targeting different value-added products (Alade & Betiku, 2010).

Biosystem	Bioreactor type	Operating conditions	Value-added targeted end product	References
Methylocystis hirsuta produces bioplastic from biogas waste valorization	Bubble column	Working volume; 2.5 L; temperature; 25°C; speed; 500 rpm; time; 30–120 min	Polyhydroxyalkanoates	Rodríguez et al. (2020)
Biogas production from wastewater treatment with biostimulation	Improvised reactor	Working volume; 800 mL bioreactors at a mesophilic temperature; 35°C; time; 30 days	Water and biogas	Tetteh and Rathilal (2021)
Lignite waste valorization	Mechanically agitated tank	Total volume; 10 L; time; 4 h, speed; 850 rpm; temperature; 70°C	Humic acids	Sarlaki et al. (2021)
Bread waste valorization	Bubble column	Working volume; 3.5, 4.5, and 26 L	Fungal biomass	Svensson et al. (2021)
Wastewater with high organic and nutritional content in the food system	Anaerobic and microalgal membrane	Working volume of 2 L; temperature; 35°C; time; 24 h	Biogas and microalgal biomass production	Vu et al. (2020)
Co-gasification of Biomass and refuse-derived fuel	Bubbling fluidized bed	Superficial gas velocity; 0.27 and 0.30 m/s; ratio. between 0.21 and 0.36 and the bed temperature between 785 and 829°C	Refused derived fuel	Pio et al. (2020)

down whilst also retaining the necessary adaptability to piloting and production quantities (Mitra & Murthy, 2021). This system emphasizes the collection of additional data at an initial phase of the design process, allowing for better decision-making when choosing particular strains or mediums for future design processes or assembly (Keijzer et al., 2011). This design necessitates the simultaneous operation of a significant range of cultures within uniform and regulated production settings.

It is important to know that the process development of bioreactor systems must be at the optimal condition to maintain a feasible time-efficient system throughout the following course of operational scale-up (Wasewar, 2021). Essentially, this requires running a huge proportion of cultures simultaneously under a range of conditions to determine the optimum growth and production parameters for the chosen strains. The majority of small stirred tank bioreactors are agitated using a magnetic stirring rod. This is suitable for animal cell culture when blending with low oxygen requiring a more intense method of mixing for microbial cultures. Recent advancements have shown that a tiny direct drive can run smoothly at around two thousand revolutions per minute, thereby ensuring appropriate mixing and mass transfer on a miniature basis (Keijzer et al., 2011).

3.5 Conclusion

Bioreactor development is important for waste management and achieving the United Nations' sustainable development goals and targets. Managing waste and tackling numerous issues of sustainability are currently among the most significant difficulties facing any civilization. As a result, while promoting the concepts of a circular economy, bioreactor development should be improved for waste valorization management, integration with the environment, and human health protection. In the last few years, advances in the bioreactor design process have mostly concentrated on the programming and controlling features of such systems, while the single-use innovation has altered the structure of the pilot-scale and industrial bioreactors for waste treatment. A major area of improvement is the downsizing of the bioreactor system, and new sensing and actuation technologies are now accessible. This cumulates in the generation of data in a shorter period, the time required to valorize the wastes will be significantly decreased.

References

Alade, E., & Betiku, O. (2010). Design of a continuous bioreactor for laboratory scale production of ethanol from cassava starch hydrolysate using *Saccharomyces cerevisiae*. *IFE Journal of Technology*, *19*, 15–20.

Costa, J. C., Goncalves, P. R., Nobrel, A. M., & Alves, M. S. (2012). Biomethanation potential of macroalgae *Ulva* spp. and *Gracilaria* spp. and in co-digestion with waste activated sludge. *Bioresource Technology*, *114*, 320–326.

Deckwer, W.-D., Becker, F. U., Ledakowicz, S., & Wagner-Döbler, I. (2004). Microbial removal of ionic mercury in a three-phase fluidized bed reactor. *Environmental Science & Technology*, *38*, 1858–1865.

De Vela, P. A., & Gostomski, R. J. L. (2021). Design and performance of a toluene-degrading differential biotrickling filter as an alternative research tool to column reactors. *Journal of Environmental Engineering*, *147*(3), 04020159.

Doran, P. M. (2012). *Bioprocess engineering principles*.

Gonzalez, P. M., Herrera, M. G., & Garcia, M. T. (2001). Biodegradation of phenol in a continuous process: Comparative study of stirred tank and fluidized-bed bioreactors. *Bioresource Technology*, *76*, 245–251.

Iliuta, M. C., & Iliuta, I. (2022). Intensified phenol and p-cresol biodegradation for wastewater treatment in countercurrent packed-bed column bioreactors. *Chemosphere*, *286*, 131716.

Keijzer, T., Kakes, E., & van Halsema, E. (2011). Advances in the design of bioreactor systems. *Innovations in Pharmaceutical Technology*, *4*, 60–64.

Kim, T. M., Behrens, T., & LaPara, S. (2021). Direct evidence for deterministic assembly of bacterial communities in full-scale municipal wastewater treatment facilities. *Applied and Environmental Microbiology*, *87*, e01086–21, p. AEM-01086.

Krustok, O. M. I., & Nehrenheim, E. (2012). *Cultivation of microalgae for potential heavy metal reduction in a wastewater treatment plant.*

Martens, M., Van Den End, D. E., & Streefland, E. J. (2014). Configuration of bioreactors. In R. Pörtner (Ed.), *Animal cell biotechnology, in Methods in molecular biology (methods and protocols)* (p. 100). Totowa, NJ: Humana Press.

Meena, M. P., Yadav, M., Sonigra, G., & Shah, P. (2021). A comprehensive review on application of bioreactor for industrial wastewater treatment. *Letters in Applied Microbiology*, 13557. [Online]. Available: https://doi.org/10.1111/lam.13557.

Metcalf & Eddy Inc. *Wastewater engineering: Treatment, disposal and reuse* (2nd ed.). New Delhi: Tata McGraw-Hill.

Mitra, G. S., & Murthy, S. (2021). Bioreactor control systems in the biopharmaceutical industry: A critical perspective. *Systems Microbiology and Biomanufacturing*, 1–22.

Molaei, S., Moussavi, S., Talebbeydokhti, G., & Shekoohiyan, N. (2022). Biodegradation of the petroleum hydrocarbons using an anoxic packed-bed biofilm reactor with in-situ biosurfactant-producing bacteria. *Journal of Hazardous Materials*, *421*, 126699.

Momoh, Y. O. L., & Nwaogazie, I. L. (2008). Effect of waste paper on biogas production from co-digestion of cow dung and water hyacinth in batch reactors. *Journal of Applied Sciences and Environmental Management*, *12*, 95–98.

Mowla, D., & Ahmadi, S. M. (2007). Theoretical and experimental investigation of biodegradation of hydrocarbon polluted water in a three phase fluidized bed bioreactor with PVC biofilm support. *Biochemical Engineering Journal*, *36*, 147–156.

Narayanan, C. M. (2005). *Trickle bed reactors for biological wastewater treatment – Multi parameter simulation and software development. International conference on advances in industrial wastewater treatment* (p. 236) New Delhi: Allied Publishers.

Narayanan, C. M., Basak, A., Saha, A., & Jha, S. (2014). Studies on performance characteristics of diverging – Converging fluidized bed biofilm reactor with special reference to lactic acid synthesis from molasses and cheese whey. *International Review of Chemical Engineering*, *6*, 142–152.

Narayanan, C. M., & Biswas, S. (2015). Computer aided design and analysis of three phase fluidized bed biofilm reactors for waste water treatment. *Asian Journal of Biochemical and Pharmaceutical Research*, *5*, 224–249.

Narayanan, C. M., & Narayan, V. (2019). Biological wastewater treatment and bioreactor design: A review. *Sustainable Environment Research*, *1*(1), 1–17. Available from https://doi.org/10.1186/s42834-019-0036-1.

Narayanan, V., & Narayan, C. M. (2021). Studies on synthesis of lactic acid and xanthan gum from cheese whey permeate in two phase and three phase moving bed biofilm reactors. *Korean Journal of Chemical Engineering*, 1–15.

Pio, V., Tarelho, D., Tavares, L., Matos, A., & Silva, M. (2020). Co-gasification of refused derived fuel and biomass in a pilot-scale bubbling fluidized bed reactor. *Energy Conversion and Management*, *206*, 112476.

Rao, K. R., & Subrahmanyam, N. (2004). Process variations in activated sludge process – A review. *Indian Chemical Engineering*, *46*, 48–55.

Rodríguez, R., Firmino, Y., Pérez, P. I. M., Lebrero, V., & Muñoz, R. (2020). Biogas valorization via continuous polyhydroxybutyrate production by *Methylocystis hirsuta* in a bubble column bioreactor. *Waste Management (New York, N.Y.)*, *113*, 395–403.

Samson, R., & LeDuy, A. (1983). Improved performance of anaerobic digestion of *Spirulina maxima* algal biomass by addition of carbon-rich wastes. *Biotechnology Letters*, *5*, 677–682.

Sarlaki, K. A., Paghaleh, E., Kianmehr, A. S., & Vakilian, M. H. (2021). Valorization of lignite wastes into humic acids: Process optimization, energy efficiency and structural features analysis. *Renewable Energy*, *163*, 105–122.

Shieh, W. K., & Keenan, J. D. (1986). Fluidized bed biofilm reactor for wastewater treatment. *Advances in Biochemical Engineering/Biotechnology*, 131–169.

Svensson, A., Bucuricova, S. E., Ferreira, L., Souza Filho, J. A., Taherzadeh, P. F., & Zamani, M. J. (2021). Valorization of bread waste to a fiber-and protein-rich fungal biomass. *Fermentation*, *7*, 91.

Swain, B. N., Sonwani, G., Singh, R. K., Jaiswal, R. S., & Rai, R. P. (2021). A comparative study of 4-chlorophenol biodegradation in a packed bed and moving bed bioreactor: Performance evaluation and toxicity analysis. *Environmental Technology & Innovation*, *24*, 101820.

Tetteh, S., & Rathilal, E. K. (2021). Application of biomagnetic nanoparticles for biostimulation of biogas production from wastewater treatment. *Materials Today: Proceedings*, *45*, 5214–5220.

Verma, R. S., Singh, R., Savitha, P., Singh, H. S., Srivastava, P., & Jagadish, A. (2021). "Bioremediation of distillery wastewater by sequential anaerobic and aerobic treatment in pilot scale bioreactor. *International Journal of Lakes and Rivers*, *14*(1), 33–42.

Vu, L. D., Vu, M. T., Nguyen, H. P., Semblante, L. N., Johir, G. U., & Nghiem, M. A. H. (2020). A hybrid anaerobic and microalgal membrane reactor for energy and microalgal biomass production from wastewater. *Environmental Technology & Innovation*, *19*, 100834.

Wasewar, K. L. (2021). Process intensification in wastewater treatments. Health risk assessment and treatment strategies. *Contamination of Water* (pp. 303–311). United Kingdom: Academic Press.

Xie, C., Zhu, L., Ramírez, J., & Jiang, M. (2021). CFD-single particle modeling and simulation of the removal of H2S in a packed-bed bioreactor. *Journal of Environmental Chemical Engineering*, *9*(4), 105692.

Yuan, E. S. X., Wang, M., Park, C., & Sahu, A. K. (2012). Microalgae growth using highstrength wastewater followed by anaerobic co-digestion. *Water Environment Research*, *84*, 396–404.
Zarei, A., Mousavi, S., Amani, S. M., Khamforoush, T., & Jafari, M. (2021). Three-dimensional CFD simulation of anaerobic reactions in a continuous packed-bed bioreactor. *Renewable Energy*, *169*, 461–472.
Zimba, P. H., Kumar, S., Mohan, T. S., & Rao, N. (2021). Evaluation of various waste substrates for biofilm formation and subsequent use in aerobic packed-bed reactor for secondary treatment of domestic wastewater. *World Journal of Microbiology and Biotechnology*, *37*(2), 1–8.

CHAPTER 4

Development of bioreactors: current scenario and future challenges

Pragya Prakash[1,2], Supriya Pandey[3], Santosh Kumar Jha[1] and Hare Ram Singh[1]

[1]Department of Bio-Engineering and Biotechnology, Birla Institute of Technology, Ranchi, Jharkhand, India

[2]Centre for Biopharmaceutical Technology, Department of Chemical Engineering, Indian Institute of Technology, New Delhi, India

[3]Department of Biotechnology, Manipal Institute of Technology, Manipal Academy of Higher Education (MAHE), Udupi, Karnataka, India

4.1 Introduction

Bioreactors have been an integral part of the downstream processing of biologics. The production of secondary metabolites, primary metabolites, microbial products, and mammalian cell culture are industrially carried out using bioreactors. The optimum procedures are achieved at a very small scale in laboratories but the industrial processes are to be carried out at a large scale in huge capacity reactors. The application of large-capacity reactors does lead to the generation of a lot of waste which is then disposed of using proper sustainable practices. Care is always taken to minimize waste which has always played an important role in the designing of bioreactors. With the emerging risk of novel SARS-CoV-2, there is a need to develop bioreactors that can handle more efficiently as the waste from bioreactors involved in the production of the vaccines could be of higher potential threat to the environment. The bioreactors have emerged from their basic types of stirred tanks to advanced forms like airlift, bubble column, membrane bioreactors (MBRs), and photobioreactors. Development and design of bioreactors depend upon a number of factors such as application, microorganism to be cultured, its potential risk, maintenance of sterility. The upcoming sections will discuss the current form of bioreactors in use and the need for the advanced form of bioreactors for the sustainability of the environment.

Techno-economics and Life Cycle Assessment of Bioreactors
DOI: https://doi.org/10.1016/B978-0-323-89848-5.00012-3

4.2 Stirred tank bioreactors

It is the most common type of bioreactor which is in use, it is easy to operate, low at maintenance, good for the applications needing higher agitation and aerobic conditions. However, this is not suited for culturing anaerobic bacteria. The development of foam and high agitation may cause contamination and other issues which are to be handled carefully (Khan et al., 2018). Stirred tank bioreactors are usually designed for the unsteady state bioprocess. Since most of the systems are used for batch or fed-batch culture it leads to the generation of a lot of biomass and hence causes an unsteady state. The stirred tank bioreactors take into consideration the working volume and the headspace volume. The headspace volume is 33% of the total volume of the bioreactor. The headspace volume is left for the agitation and aeration to work well and to properly handle the probable rise in volume due to microbial growth and associated phenomena such as foaming. It is generally used for aerobic cultures and consists of a sparger at the bottom for the air to dissipate in the medium. The mixing of medium and dissipation of the air is ensured by the impellers which and designed for the purpose. However, these types of reactors are less used in waste management systems.

4.2.1 Stirred tank bioreactors in waste management

Stirred tank bioreactors have been used for a long time for waste treatment despite their limitations. These types of bioreactors have been upgraded from time to time trying to address their limitations. Depending upon the applications they have been divided into a number of types. Some of which will be discussed here.

The aerobic treatment of industrial effluents is done by an activated sludge process. This process requires the inoculation of waste material with microbes leading to the growth of suspended microbial colonies in the reactor. The procedure basically works on the system of biological oxygen demand. Here oxygen is needed to treat the waste effluent by microbes. Since a large amount of oxygen is required to the system as in the effluent oxygen solubility is really low hence the requirements make it an expansive procedure to carry out (Narayanan & Narayan, 2019).

In the case of anaerobic treatment of waste, the advantage is that the by-products formed are utilized in one or the other industrial process. One such example is the treatment of dung and cattle waste in an anaerobic digester which leads to the formation of simpler molecules of methane which is utilized as fuel, chiefly in rural areas (Narayanan, 2012). Anaerobic sludge can also be used as nitrogenous fertilizer, one more advantage of such reactors is that thermophilic bacteria can be used for treatment and the process can be carried out at high temperatures but this advantage has a limitation associated with itself that the development of complete setup becomes expansive also some bacteria involved in the anaerobic digestion are sensitive to pH and temperatures leading to a reduction inefficiency of the system in terms of availability of useful products at the end (Salahaldin et al., 2020). The associated limitations have led to the development of advanced bioreactors such as bubble column bioreactors and MBRs.

4.3 Bubble column reactors

A bubble column reactor is an advanced form of bioreactor minimizing the waste generated. It is used for cultures requiring aeration. This type of bioreactor is mostly used for the treatment of wastewater. In this type of bioreactor, the mass transfer is decided on the size of the bubbles causing hydrodynamics. It is used for the production of Baker's yeast, beer, and other malt-based beverages (Dasan et al., 2020).

The bubble column-based reactors are supplied with compressed air which is used for mixing as these reactors do not have any moving parts to mix. These are designed with great heights to provide a good aspect ratio to the system and it plays a very crucial role as the designing is being done on the basis of its application (Jaibiba et al., 2020). Since the bubble column reactors do not have moving parts their maintenance cost is really low making them appropriate for industrial applications. These are widely used for the treatment of wastes, production of proteins, enzymes, antibiotics. However, despite several advantages, they are complex to design and the scale-up processes are tough to maintain Fig. 4.1.

4.3.1 Advances in bubble column bioreactors

4.3.1.1 Development of miniature bubble column bioreactors

Since its initial discovery, there have been numerous modifications to the bubble column reactors, as discussed for stirred tanks the modifications in the stirred tank bioreactors were done keeping in mind the related applications and reduction in cost.

Soheila and co-workers reported the development of miniature bubble column bioreactors. The concept originated from the available microtiter plates which serve as small-scale bioreactors in themselves allowing the complete reaction with multiple components to get carried out in very low

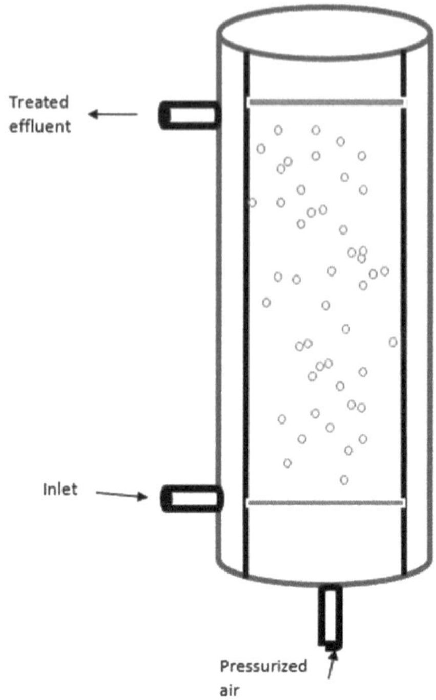

Figure 4.1 Basic structure of a bubble column bioreactor.

volume increases the sensitivity of the system. The need for a miniature bubble column arises because the available lab-scale system which is commonly used for initial studies leads to the utilization of consumables in significant volume making the process inefficient. The shake flask method which serves for preliminary studies also lacks support as there is no scope of controlling the pH, micro-environment inside the flask which many times leads to non-reproducibility of the results once the scale-up process is done .

Soheila and researchers developed miniature bubble column reactors of 20 mL volume. The miniature setup comprised of a small size column, a gas diffuser of 20–30 μM pore size. Sterilization of air was done using 0.2 μM. Dissolved oxygen was measured using an attached optical sensor and pH was measured using a small size pH probe. Growth kinetic studies of *Escherichia coli* can be and optimization studies were carried out of various factors of microbial growth.

4.3.1.2 Development of in-situ product recovery technologies

Bioreactors allow us the production of the desired product from small to large scale but to achieve the desired product in its usable form, a systematic procedure has to be followed which is termed as downstream processing. Once downstream processing is complete, we get our desired product in its usable form. The additional process after the production causes the cost of the products to rise significantly. How about a technology that leads to recovery of the product in its usable form directly from the bioreactor? which means integration of downstream processing with the upstream to develop a technology that is in-situ product recovery technology. Scientists have been working in this direction and the reports suggest the development of in-situ recovery technology by the use of organic liquid to the bubble column reactor which will add to their hydrodynamics and will lead to the development of droplets. The formation of these droplets largely depends upon the type of organic phase added and the oil loading. The use of organic chemicals such as hexadecane led to the formation of aqueous organic interfacial areas, as the molecules of hexadecane disperse throughout the bubble column. Organic compounds which form a distinct separate layer are easy to separate, an excellent recovery percentage of 65%–95% has been observed in such systems. One more aspect is to using such systems is that even if they don't yield purified compounds, they allow the concentration of the desired product by many folds which ultimately simplifies the downstream processing (McClure et al., 2020).

4.3.2 Bubble column reactor in waste management: recent advances

Apart from the traditional waste management approach using the bubble column bioreactors, multiple modifications in the reactor have taken place to enhance its suitability for waste treatment. One such development is the use of bubble column bioreactors with immobilized cells or enzymes.

Food wastes containing amylase, starch are being catalyzed to form other useful products using the reactor operations. Researchers have developed a bioleaching-based approach for the separation of copper, nickel, and iron from e-wastes (Arshadi et al., 2021). The approach was developed with a lower microbial load which gave concrete evidence of bioleaching for metals such as copper with high aeration and initial low microbial load. The procedure resulted in achieving 100% of the metals and reducing the load of PCBs by 64%. The emission of methane has been a serious issue in the industries as it shows abundant greenhouse effect. However, Perez and co-workers have worked upon recycling methane into polyhydroxybutyrate (PHB) using continuous operations of bubble column reactor. Another aspect of this research has been the use of *Mairia hirsuta* which is a small methanotrophic plant in Langeberg between Swallendem, Suurbraak, and warm Waterberg. The plant converts methane as it uses the compound as a nitrogenous source for its growth and nutrition provided there are nitrogen deficit conditions in the growth medium. The researchers used the minimal salt medium using nitrogen sources as the limiting source inducing *M. hirsuta* to use methane in the medium as a source of nitrogen. Additional conditions such as a deficit of potassium and manganese with an excess iron led to the accumulation of PHB in the medium post utilization of methane (Perez et al., 2018).

Process development for the availability of lipid-rich biomass has been done by Paul and researchers. The lipid-rich biomass of *Rhodococcus opacus* was obtained using refinery wastewater and its components ammonium chloride, potassium di-hydrogen phosphate, and di-sodium hydrogen phosphate. *R. opacus* was found to be highly efficient in the removal of chemical oxygen demand (COD) which when subjected to hydrothermal liquefaction led to the production of bio-oil with 26.5% of yield (Paul et al., 2020). Even the by-product obtained after the production of bio-oil is of tremendous industrial potential, the carbon left as a by-product can be used as activated carbon making the whole process highly efficient (Liu et al., 2017).

Chunye and co-workers successfully enhanced the biomass production of algae *Chlorella sorokiniana* in cocoon wastewater. The studies related to the subject were well documented but the biomass level attained (0.49 g/L) was the highest achieved by the researchers. Apart from that excellent values of aluminum removal, copper removal, and COD was achieved (Xue et al., 2021).

4.4 Membrane bioreactors

MBRs are the reactors in which a membrane is used to separate cells from the cellular products and feed. A dual membrane system is applied to the reactors where cell debris is removed from the feed and the by-products are removed from the desired product Fig. 4.2. This type of bioreactor is utilized in the development of biosimilars, biopharmaceutical products, treatment of industrial wastes. A membrane-based bioreactor may comprise a multi-walled layer system made up of immobilized materials such as enzymes, nano-materials, and an embedded pore system. As it works on a combination of biological and physical treatment hence it poses as an ideal choice for the treatment of waste products. These are highly efficient

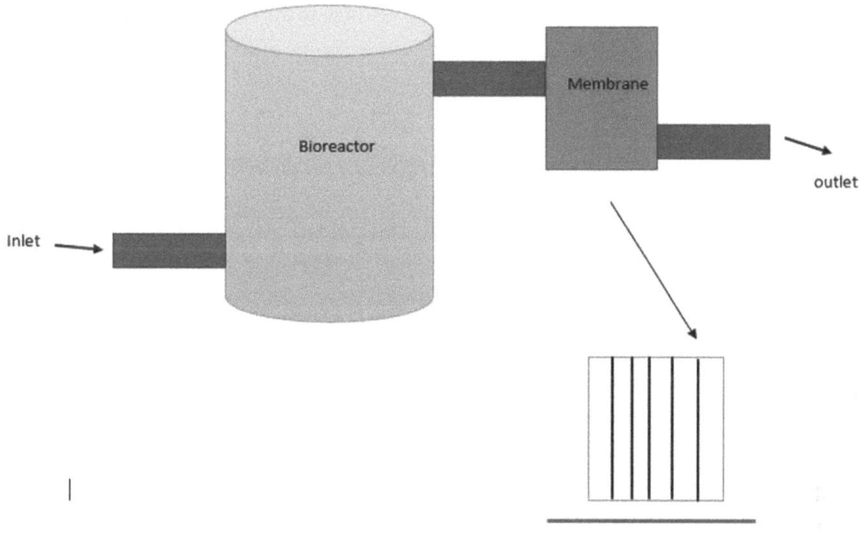

Figure 4.2 Schematic arrangement of a membrane bioreactor.

in the removal of micro-contaminants such as trace metals, antibiotics, organic compounds such as phenols. Depending upon the application several types of MBRs are being developed for large-scale level industrial purposes. These are also used for the hydrolysis of macromolecules, peptide synthesis, growth, and production of bio-transformed micro-organisms (Galinha et al., 2018).

4.4.1 Anaerobic membrane bioreactor

Anaerobic biological treatment processes are largely being used as they consume low energy, produce low sludge, and generate biogas. The anaerobic systems are now clubbed with membrane separation technique that helps to retain the anaerobic microbial biomass, thus overcoming the issue of holding on to slow-growing anaerobic microbes with a short hydraulic retention time (HRT) (Haandel & Lettinga, 1994). Added to this, they produce solid free effluents and stop unintended sludge wasting. In a bioreactor, membrane for solid-liquid separation can also be used for obtaining high biomass concentration by coupling short HRT with long solids retention time (SRT). Anaerobic MBRs (AnMBRs) working at longer SRT by decoupling HRT and SRT can effectively work towards the treatment of high organic loads and give rise to high-quality effluents compliant to reuse. Apart from this, the use of membrane prevents fouling that can use up to 50% of the total energy required and increase the chemical consumption. Its usage for treatment of low strength wastewater has increased as AnMBR allows the production of high-quality effluents at the same time recovering the majority of resources present in the wastewater, in the form of both nutrients and energy as biogas. Methane recovery in the form of biogas is easily recovered whereas dissolved methane is more difficult to obtain. In order to overcome this, anaerobic technologies like psychrophilic temperature operation lead to a significant amount of the total methane that remains dissolved in the membrane permeate. To remove dissolved methane, sulfide, nitrogen, and phosphorus from AnMBR that treats domestic wastewater, an additional process is required such as the use of pilot-scale gas sparged AnMBR.

The fundamental principle operating in a submerged anaerobic bioreactor (SAnMBR) is similar to that operating in aerobic submerged MBR. The system could hold on to sulfate-reducing bacteria with a slow growth rate and thereby attain an increased sulfate reduction rate. It is reported that at 3 h HRT, more than 90% soluble COD removal efficiency could be achieved, with an inlet concentration of 460 mg/L. This finding helped to demonstrate that SAnMBR for over a given time period of 3 months can effectively treat low-strength wastewater without biomass being washed out. Using SAnMBR it was also reported that Both Mitsubishi Rayon hollow-fiber and Kubota flat sheet membranes having a pore size of 0.4 m lead to the same level of COD removal. Here are some features of membrane-based anaerobic bioreactor reported by Liu et al. (2019) Table 4.1.

Table 4.1 Features of some membrane-based bioreactors.

Gas sparged anaerobic bioreactor	Recovery of dissolved methane	Through membrane contractor	Lim et al. (2019)
Gas sparged anaerobic bioreactor	Recovery of—(a) sulfide and (b) phosphorus	Through—(a) coagulation, (b) flocculation, and (c) sedimentation	
Gas sparged anaerobic bioreactor	Capturing ammonia	Through clinoptilolite (IX column)	
Submerged anaerobic bioreactor	High sulfate reduction rate	Retain sulfate-reducing bacteria	Marais et al. (2020)

4.4.2 Membrane fouling

Membrane fouling is the major issue related to AnMBR and refers to biofouling of the membrane which is deposition or building up of biofilm (microbial consortium) on the membrane surface. It is controlled mostly by membrane pore size, membrane flux, materials, operation temperature, pressure, sludge characteristics, and hydrodynamics (Liao et al., 2006). In SAnMBR membrane fouling is also affected by the HRT and SRT which influences different treatment operations and biomass features (Haandel & Lettinga, 1994; Liao et al., 2006). Increased level of mixed liquor suspended solids (MLSS) concentration greatly affect the membrane fouling and it is present mainly in either aerobic MBR with long SRT (Ng & Hermanowicz, 2005) Or AnMBR that treats high strength wastewater at long SRT (Jeison & Van Lier, 2006a, 2006b). Still, the reason for membrane fouling and the effect of HRT and SRT on treatment performance in SAnMBR with low-strength wastewater remains unexplored. It has been observed that:

1. As the organic load or methanogenesis increases biogas production also increases at short HRT or longer SRT.
2. Membrane fouling gets aggravated at decreased HRT as the biomass increases leading to the accumulation of soluble microbial products (SMP).
3. Fouling is inversely affected by a decrease in carbohydrate to protein ratio.
4. In the case of a high carbohydrate to protein ratio in SMP, at longer SRT the membrane fouling rate is also very high.
5. Reduced extracellular polymeric substances (EPS) contribute to decreased flocculation of particulates at longer SRT. Further, the particle size accelerates the membrane fouling process.

Biofouling is a consequence of biofilm formation that consists of bacterial consortium and EPS constantly secreted from them. Based on this information, it is believed that the steps involved in the early stages of biofilm development might act as a key factor in controlling or preventing biofouling. The first step of biofilm formation is affected by the following:

1. Cell transfer coefficient affected by hydrodynamic shear and membrane surface energy.
2. The anaerobic suspension consists mainly of bacteria and archaea that remain the same under all conditions.
3. The ratio of the bacteria and archaea under various conditions.

In order to control membrane fouling various methods have been studied such as periodic physical cleaning, sub-critical flux operation, periodic chemical cleaning, and interval operation (Chang et al., 2002; Jeison & Van Lier, 2006a, 2006b; Liao et al., 2006). One of the recently explored methods is quorum quenching (QQ) AnMBR (QQAnMBR) that used a bead entrapped facultative QQ (FQQ) consortium that helps to treat the domestic wastewater. It has been reported that FQQ shows extended membrane filtration by an average of 75%. QQ could help to alter fluorescent microbial products and further contribute to reduced cake layer formation. QQ depends on quorum sensing (QS) which is cell-to-cell communication within the bacterial colony. This cell-to-cell communication is promoted by *N*-acyl-homoserine lactones (AHLs) which act as a QS signal (Huang et al., 2020; Lv et al., 2018). QS is important for anaerobic treatment procedures as the QS is responsible for biofilm development (Kim et al., 2013) it could help to manipulate membrane fouling. QQ is basically based on disruption of QS through FQQ consortium and it was reported using FQQ bacterium—*Mycobacterium* sp. Where it was found to reduce membrane fouling on lab-scale QQAnMBR designed to treat synthetic wastewater (Liu et al., 2019). The following table provides a summary of the recent developments in AnMBRs with application to waste management Table 4.2.

4.5 Some modern types of bioreactors and their applications

4.5.1 Fixed bed bioreactors

Fixed bed bioreactors are used for the production of viral vaccines using Vero cells which are popular adherent cell lines. The process requires large-scale manpower, space, and numerous resources. Berrie et al. (2020) developed a single-use carbo bioreactor. The novel feature of the system is that it provided the integrated downstream and concentration feature. The researchers developed a live stomatitis virus vaccine with viral proteins. Since the reactor features an integrated system of production and concentration hence the waste is minimized compared to the traditional bioreactors.

4.5.2 Integrated membrane and hanging sponge bioreactor

Choerudin and co-workers developed an integrated bioreactor with a combination of an AnMBR and a downflow hanging sponge reactor. The reactor was used to treat synthetic textile wastewater containing azo dye. The combined bioreactor works on the principle that integration

Table 4.2 Anaerobic membrane bioreactor in waste management: recent advances.

Bioreactor type	Description	Advantages	References
Anaerobic MBR	• Biofouling is observed more in hydrophobic membranes as compared to hydrophilic membranes • Bacterial and archeal communities developed show dissimilarity due to shear rate and membrane surface properties	Treatment of low strength wastewater	Huang et al. (2011) and Yang et al. (2020)
Anaerobic membrane bioreactor	The bacterial population could be acclimatized for the treatment of landfill leachates	COD can be reduced from leachates and synthetic wastewater mixture	Bohdziewicz et al. (2008)
Submerged AnMBR	• COD removal efficiency achieved up to more than 90% • It can treat wastewater without the biomass being washed out	• Efficiently treats diluted wastewater	Hu and Stackey (2006)
Pilot-scale gas sparged AnMBR	• Methane obtained in the form of biogas • 42% dissolved methane in the permeate was also obtained • Nutrient recovery of ammonia, phosphorus, and sulfide	• Holistic wastewater treatment • Reduces the risk of global warming as dissolved methane easily escapes and acts as a greenhouse gas • Contributes towards energy neutrality	Lim et al. (2019)
Quorum quenching AnMBR	• Disruption of quorum signal using FQQ consortium • Decreased biopolymer yield in EPS • Reduced organic contents in colloids • Decreases membrane fouling	• Used for the treatment of domestic wastewater • Reduces the organic load in the wastewater	Xu et al. (2020)

AnMBRs, Anaerobic membrane bioreactors; *COD*, chemical oxygen demand; *EPS*, extracellular polymeric substances; *FQQ*, facultative quorum quenching; *MBR*, membrane bioreactor.

reduces the biological oxygen demand. *Euryarchaeota*, *Caldiserica*, and *Proteobacteria* are the microbial components of the bioreactor which reduce the azo dyes and sulfonated aromatic amines (Choerudin et al., 2021).

4.5.3 Disposable bioreactors

Disposable bioreactors have been the need of the current hour, they are well used as both seed and production bioreactors both. These offer advantages over traditionally used bioreactors in terms of design, instrumentation, scale, power input, flexibility, and ease of use. Various types of bioreactors such as orbital shaking stirred tanks and wave mixed bioreactors have been developed. The initially used bioreactors (disposable) can be referred to as the polymer-based one-time used Petri-dishes and shake flasks. The advancement led to the development of hollow fiber-based disposable reactors which further progressed into wave mixed bag, stirred tank disposable bioreactors (Eibl et al., 2010).

4.5.4 Denitrification bioreactors

Denitrification bioreactors are used for the removal of nitrates from water. Nitrates are responsible for soil and water contamination; nitrates are a major contaminant not only in wastewater but also in the drinking water. Zhao and researchers developed a woodchip-packed bioreactor with gradient filling for the treatment of nitrate-containing water. The gradient filling improved the nitrate removal rate and led to low nitrite accumulation. Apart from woodchip solid-phase denitrification bioreactors, denitrification has been developed by the integration of biodegradable polymers, natural extracts while woodchip-based bioreactors are developed using pine woodchips and sawdust. The additional nitrogen and carbon material concentrations are varied based on the application. The capability of the reactor majorly depends upon the concentration of carbon dosage (Zhao et al., 2020).

4.6 COVID waste management in the pandemic times

Towards the end of the year 2019, a novel strain of the coronavirus family was discovered in humans causing a life-threatening infection. It was established that the viral particles travel in droplets released into the environment by the sneeze of an infected individual. However other than a sneeze or oral fluids it was later found that the infected individuals may release the virus in the environment through their feces also which has posed a bigger threat in the front of the globe (Quilliam et al., 2020). Not only the patients of novel coronavirus but also healthy people who are asymptomatic are at the risk of viral load shedding in an open environment. It can cause a bigger threat if the waste management of the hospitals and even households is not done properly. The world has faced a serious situation earlier when the SARS epidemic occurred back (Golan et al., 2021). These risks indicate there is a need for better management of waste especially related to the frontline workers and patients admitted or in isolation centers. Additional waste load is added by the protective gears against COVID (PPE kits, gloves, masks, shields). However, there is little evidence on the viral load release by mild or asymptomatic patients but the future is uncertain.

Italy was once struggling with the large no. of deaths due to COVID-19, bioreactor-based air purifiers were installed at places to tackle SARS-CoV2 viral particles. Even for the detection of the virus, a bioreactor-based detection system was installed using the rapid biomonitoring system. The bioreactors were installed at various spots in public places which helped in the early detection and destruction of the virus. The AIRcel air purifiers installed for the detection of viral particles work on the mechanism that attracts the pollutants by the formation of concentration gradients. The gradients capture the pollutants, including the viral particles, and transfer them to the water tank. The particles which become charged are removed by electrical grounding, the organic compounds in the pollutants are removed via oxidation. The water present in the tank attached to the AIRcel systems is to be replaced on a weekly basis and the blend of micro-organisms that are responsible for the digestion of contaminants and to be recharged on a monthly basis (Marchetti et al., 2020).

Since managing COVID-19 waste is a big challenge hence the natural resources can play a big role in managing pandemics. *Nicotiana benthamiana* plant tissues have been utilized for the production of COVID viral proteins which are easy to cultivate as the plants act as a natural bioreactor for the speedy production of viral proteins. The plants can easily be dealt with in regard to waste management. The transient expression approach is used in plants to make them work as natural and green bioreactors. After the plants indicate the production of viral proteins, they are harvested for plant biomass. It takes less than ten days to get the purified viral protein, that is, it takes such a short span to achieve the purified protein. However, talking about the large-scale production in kiloliters, it takes a month time apart from its downstream processing (McDonald & Holtz, 2020). However, there are a no. of challenges that are to be dealt with the plant-based systems

Field-grown plants have been used for medico-applications, however, it is quite tough to achieve a good expression level. However, process optimization can be done to achieve high productivity. McDonald and Holtz proposed the production of COVID antigen with their past results of different recombinant proteins with transient expression in plants, sunflower (Jung & McDonald, 2016). The production has been performed at the laboratory scale; a lot of research is still needed to take the production at an industrial scale. One of the important processes involved in the handling of the waste produced from the plant-based system. There is a need to develop a biological production and management system in which optimized conditions are achieved for the viral antigens to produce. Post-harvest technologies, downstream processing, and waste management approach, a lot of equipment modifications are needed to be done to get an integrated system performing and managing the tasks.

4.6.1 Membrane bio-reactors in the removal of COVID viral load

As an alternative approach to the conventional anaerobic digestion process and the ability to retain and remove the viral load, MBRs could be of potential use for the treatment of COVID waste in wastewaters. Studies have been performed to report the efficiency of removal of viral loads as well as the recovery and regeneration of the membranes. Apart from the COVID-19 viral load, the membranes have been reported to be efficient in the removal of microbial load of other pathogens as well (Foladori et al., 2020). The reactors have been efficient in the removal of viral loads of really low concentrations of 2 copies/mL.

Higher disinfection viability is accomplished in MBR at a lower dose of disinfectant with fewer disinfection by-products (Vickers et al., 2019). In the past, MBR was considered inappropriate in WWTP due to its high operating cost; however, decreasing cost and stringent standards are making the use of MBR systems more economically viable (Lesimple et al., 2020). For instance, when the limit of MBR plants is increased up to five folds their operating cost is projected to reduce sharply (Liu et al., 2010).

4.7 Conclusion

The chapter has discussed the most recent trends and possible future developments in the field of bioreactors for waste management. The ongoing scenario, that is, the need for a clean environment, treatment, and management of COVID wastes are the things that are to be addressed with a more practical approach. The development of integrated bioreactor systems, miniature bubble column bioreactors could be the future of reactor systems. Bioreactor-based air purifiers, integrated bioreactors for vaccine development are some aspects that mark their importance in COVID management; not only in COVID waste management but also in its detection. Conversion of the initial by-products to some useful products is another aspect that needs to be looked up in-depth for better and more efficient waste management. The need is to bring up the developments from the lab scale to the industrial scale so that they can be utilized for their real-life applications. For those who are already in the market making people aware of their features becomes important to increase their utility at a mass scale.

References

Arshadi, M., Pourhossein, F., Mousavi, S. M., & Yaghmaei, S. (2021). Green recovery of Cu-Ni-Fe from a mixture of spent PCBs using adapted *A. ferrooxidans* in a bubble column bioreactor. *Separation and Purification Technology*, 118701.

Berrie, D. M., Waters, R. C., Montoya, C., Chatel, A., & Vela, E. M. (2020). Development of a high-yield live-virus vaccine production platform using a novel fixed-bed bioreactor. *Vaccine*, *38*(20), 3639–3645.

Bohdziewicz, J., Neczaj, E., & Kwarciak, A. (2008). Landfill leachate treatment by means of anaerobic membrane bioreactor. *Desalination*, *221*(1–3), 559–565.

Chang, I. S., Le Clech, P., Jefferson, B., & Judd, S. (2002). Membrane fouling in membrane bioreactors for wastewater treatment. *Journal of Environmental Engineering*, *128* (11), 1018–1029.

Choerudin, C., Arrahmah, F. I., Daniel, J. K., Watari, T., Yamaguchi, T., & Setiadi, T. (2021). Evaluation of combined anaerobic membrane bioreactor and downflow hanging sponge reactor for treatment of synthetic textile wastewater. *Journal of Environmental Chemical Engineering*, *9*(4)105276.

Dasan, Y. K., Lam, M. K., Yusup, S., Lim, J. W., Show, P. L., Tan, I. S., & Lee, K. T. (2020). Cultivation of Chlorella vulgaris using sequential-flow bubble column photobioreactor: A stress-inducing strategy for lipid accumulation and carbon dioxide fixation. *Journal of CO_2 Utilization*, *41*101226.

Eibl, R., Kaiser, S., Lombriser, R., & Eibl, D. (2010). Disposable bioreactors: The current state-of-the-art and recommended applications in biotechnology. *Applied Microbiology and Biotechnology*, *86*(1), 41–49.

Foladori, P., Cutrupi, F., Segata, N., Manara, S., Pinto, F., Malpei, F., Bruni, L., & La Rosa, G. (2020). SARS-CoV-2 from faeces to wastewater treatment: What do we know? A review. *Sci Total Environ*, *743*, 140444. Available from https://doi.org/10.1016/j.scitotenv.2020.140444.

Galinha, C. F., Sanches, S., & Crespo, J. G. (2018). *Membrane bioreactors. Fundamental modelling of membrane systems* (pp. 209–249). Elsevier.

Haandel, A. C. V., & Lettinga, G. (1994). (Eds.) *Anaerobic sewage treatment: A practical guide for regions with a hot climate*. Chichester, New York: J. Wiley.

Huang, S., Zhang, H., Ng, T. C. A., Xu, B., Shi, X., & Ng, H. Y. (2020). Analysis of N-Acy-L-homoserine lactones (AHLs) in wastewater treatment systems using SPE-LLE with LC-MS/MS. *Water Research*, *177*115756.

Hu, A. Y, & Stuckey, D. C. (2006). Treatment of Dilute Wastewaters Using a Novel Submerged Anaerobic Membrane Bioreactor. *JOURNAL OF ENVIRONMENTAL ENGINEERING*, *132*(2), 190–198. Available from 10.1061/(ASCE)0733-9372 (2006)132:2(190), In this issue.

Huang, Z., Ong, S. L., & Ng, H. Y. (2011). Submerged anaerobic membrane bioreactor for low-strength wastewater treatment: Effect of HRT and SRT on treatment performance and membrane fouling. *Water Research*, *45*(2), 705–713.

Jaibiba, P., Vignesh, S. N., & Hariharan, S. (2020). *Working principle of typical bioreactors. Bioreactors* (pp. 145–173). Elsevier.

Jeison, D., & Van Lier, J. B. (2006a). Cake layer formation in anaerobic submerged membrane bioreactors (AnSMBR) for wastewater treatment. *Journal of Membrane Science*, *284*(1–2), 227–236.

Jeison, D., & Van Lier, J. B. (2006b). On-line cake-layer management by trans-membrane pressure steady state assessment in anaerobic membrane bioreactors for wastewater treatment. *Biochemical Engineering Journal*, *29*(3), 204–209.

Jung, S. K., & McDonald, K. A. (2016). Improved transient production of a cellulase enzyme in detached sunflower leaves using plant hormones. *Biotechnology and Bioprocess Engineering*, *21*(6), 726–732.

Khan, S. A., Siddiqui, M. H., & Osama, K. (2018). Bioreactors for hairy roots culture: A review. *Current Biotechnology*, 7(6), 417–427.

Kim, S. R., Oh, H. S., Jo, S. J., Yeon, K. M., Lee, C. H., Lim, D. J., Lee, C. H., & Lee, J. K. (2013). Biofouling control with bead-entrapped quorum quenching bacteria in membrane bioreactors: physical and biological effects. *Environmental Science & Technology*, *47*(2), 836–842.

Lesimple, A., Jasim, S. Y., Johnson, D. J., & Hilal, N. (2020). The role of wastewater treatment plants as tools for SARS-CoV-2 early detection and removal. *Journal of Water Process Engineering*101544.

Liao, B. Q., Kraemer, J. T., & Bagley, D. M. (2006). Anaerobic membrane bioreactors: Applications and research directions. *Critical Reviews in Environmental Science and Technology*, *36*(6), 489–530.

Lim, K., Evans, P. J., & Parameswaran, P. (2019). Long-term performance of a pilot-scale gas-sparged anaerobic membrane bioreactor under ambient temperatures for holistic wastewater treatment. *Environmental Science & Technology*, *53*(13), 7347–7354.

Liu, J., Eng, C. Y., Ho, J. S., Chong, T. H., Wang, L., Zhang, P., & Zhou, Y. (2019). Quorum quenching in anaerobic membrane bioreactor for fouling control. *Water Res*, *156*, 159–167. Available from 10.1016/j.watres.2019.03.029.

Liu, H., Ma, M., & Xie, X. A. (2017). New materials from solid residues for investigation the mechanism of biomass hydrothermal liquefaction. *Industrial Crops and Products*, *108*, 63–71.

Liu, Q., Zhou, Y., Chen, L., & Zheng, X. (2010). Application of MBR for hospital wastewater treatment in China. *Desalination*, *250*(2), 605–608.

Lv, L., Li, W., Zheng, Z., Li, D., & Zhang, N. (2018). Exogenous acyl-homoserine lactones adjust community structures of bacteria and methanogens to ameliorate the performance of anaerobic granular sludge. *Journal of Hazardous Materials*, *354*, 72–80.

Marais, T. S., Huddy, R. J., Harrison, S. T. L., & van Hille, R. P. (2020). Demonstration of simultaneous biological sulphate reduction and partial sulphide oxidation in a hybrid linear flow channel reactor. *Journal of Water Process Engineering*, *34*101143.

Golan, M. S., Trump, B. D., Cegan, J. C., & Linkov, I. (2021). *The vaccine supply chain: A call for resilience analytics to support COVID-19 vaccine production and distribution*. arXiv preprint arXiv:2011.14231.

Marchetti, R., Stella, M., Talukdar, D., & Pileci, R. E. (2020). *Rapid environmental monitoring, capture, and destruction activities of SARS-CoV-2 during the COVID-19 health emergency*. medRxiv.

McClure, D. D., Zheng, Z., Hu, G., & Kavanagh, J. M. (2020). Towards in situ product recovery for bubble column bioreactors. *Chemical Engineering Journal, 393*124745.

McDonald, K. A., & Holtz, R. B. (2020). From farm to finger prick—A perspective on how plants can help in the fight against COVID-19. *Frontiers in Bioengineering and Biotechnology, 8*, 782.

Narayanan, C. M., & Narayan, V. (2019). Biological wastewater treatment and bioreactor design: A review. *Sustainable Environment Research, 29*(1), 1–17.

Narayanan, C. M. (2012). *Production of phosphate-rich biofertiliser using vermicompost and anaerobic digestor sludge—A case study.*

Ng, H. Y., & Hermanowicz, S. W. (2005). Membrane bioreactor operation at short solids retention times: Performance and biomass characteristics. *Water Research, 39*(6), 981–992.

Paul, T., Sinharoy, A., Pakshirajan, K., & Pugazhenthi, G. (2020). Lipid-rich bacterial biomass production using refinery wastewater in a bubble column bioreactor for bio-oil conversion by hydrothermal liquefaction. *Journal of Water Process Engineering, 37*101462.

Quilliam, R. S., Weidmann, M., Moresco, V., Purshouse, H., O'Hara, Z., & Oliver, D. M. (2020). COVID-19: The environmental implications of shedding SARS-CoV-2 in human faeces. In: *Environment international.*

Salahaldin, S. M. A., et al. (2020). A review of anaerobic membrane bioreactors (AnMBR) for the treatment of highly contaminated landfill leachate and biogas production: Effectiveness, limitations and future perspectives. *Journal of Cleaner Production, 255*(120215), 1–12. Available from https://doi.org/10.1016/j.jclepro.2020.120215, In this issue.

Vickers, J. C., Dummer, M., Le, T., & Zoba, J. B. (2019). Removal of MS-2 coliphage in full-scale reverse osmosis systems. *AWWA Water Science, 1*(6), e1158.

Xu, B., Ng, T. C. A., Huang, S., & Ng, H. Y. (2020). Effect of quorum quenching on EPS and size-fractioned particles and organics in anaerobic membrane bioreactor for domestic wastewater treatment. *Water Research, 179*115850.

Xue, C., Gao, K., Qian, P., Dong, J., Gao, Z., Liu, Q., Chen, B., & Deng, X. (2021). Cultivation of *Chlorella sorokiniana* in a bubble-column bioreactor coupled with cooking cocoon wastewater treatment: effects of initial cell density and aeration rate. *Water Science and Technology.*

Yang, Y., Bogler, A., Ronen, Z., Oron, G., Herzberg, M., & Bernstein, R. (2020). Initial deposition and pioneering colonization on polymeric membranes of anaerobes isolated from an anaerobic membrane bioreactor (AnMBR). *Environmental Science & Technology, 54*(9), 5832–5842.

Zhao, J., He, Q., Chen, N., Peng, T., & Feng, C. (2020). Denitrification behavior in a woodchip-packed bioreactor with gradient filling for nitrate-contaminated water treatment. *Biochemical Engineering Journal, 154*107454.

Further reading

Abuabdou, S. M., Ahmad, W., Aun, N. C., & Bashir, M. J. (2020). A review of anaerobic membrane bioreactors (AnMBR) for the treatment of highly contaminated landfill leachate and biogas production: effectiveness, limitations and future perspectives. *Journal of Cleaner Production, 255*120215.

Chaudhry, A. K., & Sachdeva, P. (2020). Coronavirus disease 2019 (COVID-19): a new challenge in untreated wastewater. *Canadian Journal of Civil Engineering, 47*(8), 1005–1009.

García-Pérez, T., López, J. C., Passos, F., Lebrero, R., Revah, S., & Muñoz, R. (2018). Simultaneous methane abatement and PHB production by *Methylocystis hirsuta* in a novel gas-recycling bubble column bioreactor. *Chemical Engineering Journal, 334*, 691–697.

Kheradmandnia, S., Hashemi-Najafabadi, S., Shojaosadati, S. A., Mousavi, S. M., & Malek Khosravi, K. (2015). Development of parallel miniature bubble column bioreactors for fermentation process. *Journal of Chemical Technology & Biotechnology*, *90*(6), 1051–1061.

Kiani, S., Kujala, K., Pulkkinen, J. T., Aalto, S. L., Suurnäkki, S., Kiuru, T., Tiirola, M., Kløve, B., & Ronkanen, A. K. (2020). Enhanced nitrogen removal of low carbon wastewater in denitrification bioreactors by utilizing industrial waste toward circular economy. *Journal of Cleaner Production*, *254*119973.

Kweinor Tetteh, E., Opoku Amankwa, M., Armah, E. K., & Rathilal, S. (2020). Fate of COVID-19 occurrences in wastewater systems: Emerging detection and treatment technologies—A review. *Water*, *12*(10), 2680.

CHAPTER 5

Economic aspects of bioreactors: current trends and future perspective

Mamta Devi Sharma[1,2], Swati Sharma[3], Puranjan Mishra[4] and Saurabh Kulshrestha[1,2]

[1]Faculty of Applied Sciences and Biotechnology, Shoolini University of Biotechnology and Management Sciences, Solan, Himachal Pradesh, India

[2]Center for Omics and Biodiversity Research, Shoolini University of Biotechnology and Management Sciences, Solan, Himachal Pradesh, India

[3]Shoolini Institute of Life Sciences and Business Management, Solan, India

[4]Institute of Bioresource and Agriculture, Hong Kong Baptist University, Kowloon Tong, Hong Kong

5.1 Introduction

An economic analysis is an important aspect and plays a critical role at every level of plant design, project, and control. A thorough economic analysis should consider all stages of manufacturing, including research, process design, development, product, and bioproduct marketing. It is required to introduce the most important principles and criteria that should be followed, whether for new processes or for the development of consolidated processes and plants, in order to execute such an analysis. The entire process flow chart should be examined, considering process equipment sizing, materials, utility requirements, operating, plant expenses, and profit estimation as a requisition (Calabr Ò & Iorio, 2013). The fermenter should be designed to produce a high-quality product at a cheap cost, while also increasing productivity and ensuring that the desired parameters are verified. Microorganism production, product value, conditions required for desired product development, and production size, all influence the fermenter's design and mode of operation (Gaikwad et al., 2018). Because the goal of industrial fermentation is to produce high yields from low-cost raw materials with minimal capital expenditures, cost analysis may be a useful tool for deciding on a culture method that is achieved through various methods. It has been suggested that replacing batch procedures with continuous processes could be a natural way to cut costs and boost efficiency. Other

Techno-economics and Life Cycle Assessment of Bioreactors
DOI: https://doi.org/10.1016/B978-0-323-89848-5.00003-2

research has focused on the simulation of innovative biopharmaceutical plant layouts and payoff time predictions (Cardoso et al., 2020).

5.2 Directives of economic analysis

The cost of new technology in comparison to competing technologies is an important consideration. The cost-effectiveness of a project is frequently the deciding factor in the successful implementation of a process design (Lin et al., 2011). From the inception of a product idea, through a preliminary evaluation of the economics and market, to taking into account all design details, raw materials, products and finally an economic evaluation of engineering costs, such as the location of building and equipment, economic analysis is required at every stage of the process for the design of a plant devoted to product marketing. Raw materials are received, stored, and processed in the upstream section, while final product preparation, such as packaging and shipment, is done in the downstream section. Each section's economic analysis is based on an assessment of utility expenses, process effluent disposal, maintenance, capital, and operating costs, which allows the cost analysis to be performed in the following manner (Table 5.1).

5.3 Cost analysis

The Cost studies are normally done on four cost bases: capital, production, materials, and utilities, with a profitability analysis at the end. The parameters that make up a cost analysis are as follows.

Table 5.1 Economic analysis depends on the following stages (Cardoso et al., 2020).

1. Plant design project
2. Foundation
3. Preliminary assessment of economics and market
4. Development of data necessary for final design
5. Final economic evaluation
6. Detailed engineering design
7. Procurement
8. Construction
9. Start-up and trial runs
10. Production

5.3.1 Capital costs

The expenditure is done on basic equipment. These costs keep evolving with time and vary according to the countries where they are manufactured and sized.

The basic features of a bioreactor are:

1. The headspace volume—It is the total volume of the bioreactor minus the working volume. The working volumes are the space taken up by the medium, microorganism, and gas bubbles. It is around 70%–80%, however, this value may change depending on foam formation during fermentation.
2. Agitator system—This is the system used for proper mixing and comprises impeller and baffles that consume power.
3. Aeration system—This comprises compressor, air sparser, and air sterilization systems.
4. Temperature and pH control systems—These comprise probes, heating jackets or coils, coolants such as ammonia, neutralizing agents like sodium carbonate to control pH.
5. Foam control system—This system is used to prevent excessive foam formation that may block air circulation or build pressure.
6. Sterilization system—This system checks contamination. Sterilization may be carried out by steam (thermal sterilization), chemical substances, or radiations.
7. Sampling ports—These facilitate the injection of nutrients and collection of samples.
8. Separation Devices—These are the apparatus, membrane systems, etc. required for product recovery and pretreatment of feed (Gaikwad et al., 2018).

All the above equipment contributes to the capital costs. Appropriate cost indices can be used to update the cost estimate of this equipment with the passage of time. When it comes to size, the costs can be scaled up according to different criteria for each of these—capacity of fermenters—the surface area of the membranes used for separation, etc. (Figs. 5.1 and 5.2).

5.3.2 Production costs

These include different costs related to running of a bioreactor and include the expenditure on supplies, payments and salaries of administrative, technical and engineering staff, direct and indirect labor in quality control, material handling, sanitation, taxes and insurance, telecommunication services, legal and medical services, etc.

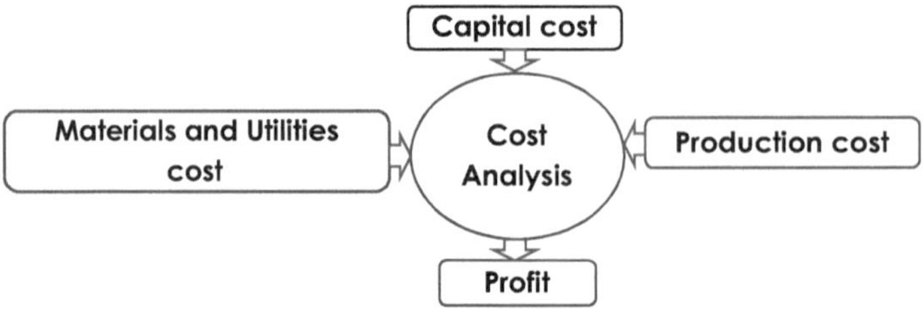

Figure 5.1 Depicting the different aspects affecting the cost analysis.

Figure 5.2 Classification of bioreactor system performance expenditure.

5.3.3 Materials and utilities

Materials costs are the costs of obtaining all of the raw materials, as well as all of the chemicals and biochemicals required for the manufacturing process. Utility companies, particularly electrical and thermal power, should take a similar strategy. The system's mass and energy balance allow the quality and number of materials, as well as the electrical and thermal supply necessary for the whole process, to be determined. A detailed stage-by-stage examination can be carried out with the goal of lowering the cost.

Profit analysis: Last, however one of the most important steps in cost analysis is the estimation of profits. Once the capital, production, material, and utility cost is available, an estimation can be made as to how much return of investment is expected in a fermentation process (Calabr Ò & Iorio, 2013).

5.4 Cost analysis for bioreactors applied for waste management

Cost analysis of membrane bioreactors used for wastewater treatment: Membrane bioreactors and reactors can be analyzed as full plants and process units, with the membranes serving as catalyst support, biocatalyst, and separation unit all at the same time. In this situation, the system must be analyzed, and all costs must be associated with it. When membranes are used as a separating unit, such as in pretreatment or downstream processes, the flow sheet of the process is separated into multiple stages: pretreatment, (bio) reaction, product recovery, and downstream. Cost Analysis for small or immersed membrane bioreactor (iMBR): iMBR systems can be custom-designed or delivered as a containerized technology that requires very minor site changes. All major municipal facilities are custom-built, and the costs are classified as either operating expenses (OPEX), cost per treated product volume, or capital expenses (CAPEX). Other factors besides energy can considerably contribute to overall cost when considering TOTEX (total expenditure) for installation and operation during the whole life cycle of a facility. In such circumstances, the net present value (NPV) should be calculated to account for changes in base utility and service costs, asset value, and the value of money itself over the plant's lifetime. The limited reports of TOTEX and/or NPV in peer-reviewed literature have tended to support the role of energy consumption in determining OPEX. For a large (19–48 MLD, or megalitres/day, flow capacity) municipal MBR, energy appears to account for 27%–34% of overall OPEX (Lo et al., 2015).

Specifications for the classified components (tanks, pumps, blowers, mixers, screen, membrane, and diffuser) were utilized to acquire itemized pricing from regional suppliers in each country. The costs within each category were then added together for a more in-depth look at CAPEX trends. The combined cost of energy demand, essential component replacement, chemical use, waste management/disposal, and labor determines the OPEX in \$ per m^3 permeate

$$\mathrm{OPEX} = L_E E_{\mathrm{tot}} + 365 L_M / \left(\mathrm{Jt}_{\mathrm{mem}}\right) + L_C + L_W + L_L \tag{5.1}$$

where L_E is the cost of electrical energy in dollars per kilowatt-hour, L_M is the membrane cost per square meter of membrane area, J is the flux in meters per second, and t_{mem} is the membrane life in years. Chemical consumption, waste disposal, and labor costs per m^3 treated water are represented by L_C, L_W, and L_L, with everything but waste disposal included in the current analysis. The sum of each component's power consumption rating W in kW, the (estimated) fractional operating duration (hours per day of operation divided by 24), and the permeate flow QP in m^3/day provides the overall specific energy demand E_{tot} in kWh/m^3:

$$E_{\text{tot}} = \frac{24W\tau}{\text{Qp}} \tag{5.2}$$

Averaged NPV is estimated by combining CAPEX and OPEX according to the simplified relationship:

$$\text{NPV} = -\text{OPEX } 1 - (1+i)^t/i - \text{CAPEX} \tag{5.3}$$

where t is the amortization term (or plant life) in years and i is the annual discount rate. The above equation accounts for inflation and assumes that the plant will have no residual value at the end of its life. Based on annual retail price index data, all expenses for the literature data are converted to US$ (Lo et al., 2015).

5.5 Cost evaluation of submerged anaerobic membrane bioreactor for municipal secondary wastewater treatment

The total capital and operational costs are the overall costs of the SAnMBR system. Because the prices were estimated in different currencies, they were all translated to US dollars. The SAnMBR system's entire life cycle costs are calculated using the NPV method. The strategy presented in the following equation was based on a 30-year plant lifespan, a long-term nominal interest rate of 6%, and a 3% inflation rate in this study.

$$\text{NPV} = (\text{Capex})_t + (\text{Opex})_t/(1+i)^t \tag{5.4}$$

Where i is the real interest rate, calculated by subtracting the inflation rate from a nominal interest rate (Lin et al., 2011).

Previously, the performance of both aerobic and anaerobic MBR systems was investigated in theoretical scenarios using various scale systems [0.05–10 million gallons per day (MGD)] serving various population densities (2000–100,000 people per square mile), land area combinations, operating temperature (20°C and 35°C), climate conditions (ambient temperature 6°C and 26°C), and various population density (2000–100,000 people per square mile) (flared, converted to electricity and combined heat and power) (Morelli et al., 2019) (Tables 5.2 and 5.3).

Table 5.2 Annual expenditure for aerobic membrane bioreactor facility by scale used for wastewater treatment.

Volume of wastewater (MGD)	Cost estimate by scale ($)	Volume of wastewater (MGD)	Cost estimate by scale per m^3 ($)
0.05	1,000,000	0.05	7.00–8.00
0.1	1,000,000	0.1	4.00–5.00
1	1,000,000–2,000,000	1	1.00
5	4,000,000–5,000,000	5	0.00–1.00
10	7,000,000	10	0.00–1.00

Table 5.3 Annual expenditure for anaerobic membrane bioreactor facility by scale operating at 35°C and 20°C used for wastewater treatment.

Volume of wastewater (MGD)	Cost estimate by scale at 35°C ($)	Volume of wastewater (MGD)	Cost estimate by scale at 20°C ($)
0.05	0–1,000,000	0.05	0–1,000,000
0.1	0–2,000,000	0.1	0–2,000,000
1	0–4,000,000	1	0–4,000,000
5	10,000,000–12,000,000	5	10,000,000–12,000,000
10	20,000,000–22,000,000	10	15,000,000–20,000,000

5.6 Monte Carlo cost estimation method for wastewater treatment membrane bioreactors

A well-known method for evaluating costs is the Monte Carlo method. Based on the distribution of input parameters, it predicts a statistical distribution of outputs. The method is used in a variety of mathematical models in which analytic prediction of output statistics is impossible due to system complexity. In the water and wastewater sector, there are several instances of how to use the Monte Carlo approach. Monte Carlo analysis can give decision-makers more information about the likelihood of failure and alternate therapies. The danger of surpassing chemical concentrations in the WWTP effluent was also assessed using Monte Carlo simulations. In the concrete simulated case, a 21% reduction in biological reactor dimensioning was assessed as an arguable risk, resulting in a 43% investment cost savings. When the cost of MBRs in relation to aeration intensity, filtering time, and backwash time was analyzed, it was examined that if the aeration rate was lowered, the biggest cost savings of up to 20% of operational costs were discovered (Verhuelsdonk et al., 2021).

The first occurrence of the Monte Carlo simulation method dates from 1944. This approach has undergone a lengthy evolution and development process. The Monte Carlo approach uses a random uniformly distributed number generator in the [0,1] interval to generate artificial values for a probabilistic variable, as well as the cumulative distribution function associated with these stochastic variables. Economic decision simulation can be used to solve a variety of problems including operational rules, policies, and procedures, such as decision adaptation, decision control, and price policy. The simulation technique's activity is not, in fact, a decision-making process. In order to reach the goal, solving problems using simulation approaches necessitates the employment of interactive algorithms and the existence of well-defined steps. Random variables created by a random number generator are commonly used as input data. The approach algorithm is demonstrated in five interactive steps:

Step 1: Make a parametric model with $y = f(X_1, X_2, \ldots, X_q)$

Step 2: Create a random data input set, $X_{i1}, X_{i2}, \ldots, X_{iq}$

Step 3: As y_i perform effective calculations and memorize the findings.

Step 4: Repeat steps 2 and 3 for $i = 1$ to n ($n \geq 5000$)

Step 5: Analyze the data using histograms, confidence intervals, and other statistical indicators generated by the simulation, among other things.

Figs. 5.3 and 5.4 depict the key distinction between deterministic and stochastic models. The two models, deterministic and stochastic, are depicted in this diagram. A parametric deterministic model creates a collection of input variables that are then reported to a set of output variables. The input variables are randomized (represented by a random

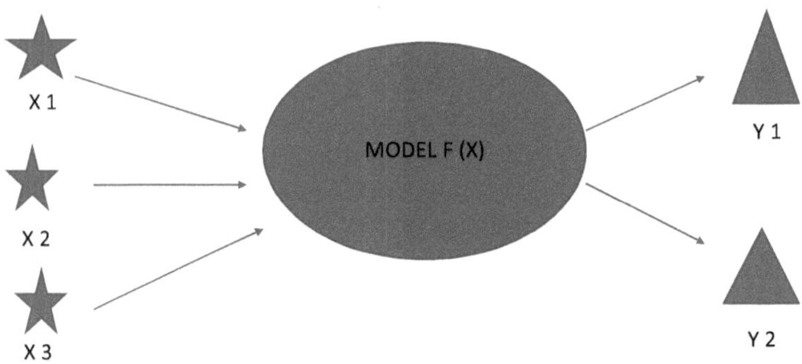

Figure 5.3 Deterministic model described by Platon and Constantinescu (2014) (Where, Here X1, X2, and X3 are input varia les and Y1 and Y2 are output variables).

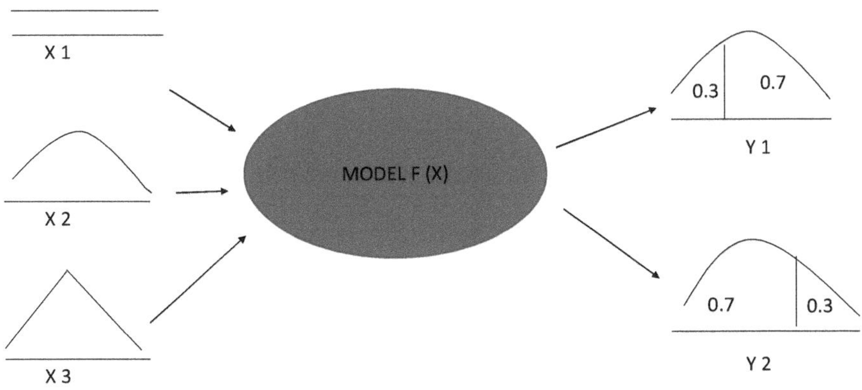

Figure 5.4 Stochastic Model described by Platon and Constantinescu (2014) (In stochastic model X1, X2 and X3 are random input variables and Y1 and Y2 are random output variables following a normal distribution).

distribution) in the stochastic model of uncertainty propagation, and the result is also random, usually following the Normal Distribution. Monte Carlo simulation is based on this premise (Platon & Constantinescu, 2014).

5.7 Cost analysis for aerobic fermenters

Aerobic fermentation is a crucial step in a wide range of processes such as the conversion of lignocellulosic sugars to hydrocarbons, cellulosic biofuel production, etc. The design of aerobic fermenters and their economy play a crucial role in large aerobic processes being a primary cost contributor. Further, the compressors and agitators used also contribute greatly to the power demand for making fuel range hydrocarbons or their precursors. Fermentations like making fuel range hydrocarbons on low margins and hence require as much possible cost minimization. According to the Techno-economic analysis (TEA) report, in the aerobic conversion of lignocellulosic sugars to hydrocarbons, the aerobic fermentation steps were the greatest cost contributors. Even in the case of the biorefinery process, the power demand of compressors and agitators is the largest. Two important bioreactors used for aerobic fermentation processes are Stirred tank reactor (STR) and bubble column reactor (BCR) (Humbird et al., 2017).

Stirred tank bioreactor (STR) is the most frequently used fermenter. They are cylindrical in design and have motor-driven shafts to mix the contents in the vessel. Further, the stirrer or agitator may be top-driven or bottom-driven. Other variable characteristics are -size, type, impellers, size of sparger, etc. STR enables functions like aeration, suspension of solids, mixing, heat exchange, and gas-liquid mixture dispersion.

BCR is comparatively simple in design. It is a cylindrical vessel with a gas sparger. Aeration and mixing functions are both carried out by gas bubbles that push their way through the liquid or liquid–solid suspension. In the case of semisolid phases, the reactor is termed a slurry BCR. Shear forces created due to bubbles are less in comparison to mechanical agitators used in STR (Singh et al., 2014).

5.7.1 Stirred tank reactor and bubble column reactor cost analysis

One of the methods for rapid comparative analysis of capital costs of bioreactors is developed using Aspen Capital Cost Estimator (ACCE). This method estimates the costs of material and labor involved in making equipment based on its specified volume models. For equipment that is too heavy to be transported as one unit, the ACCE method will take into consideration the costs of each transportable piece and their final assembly into the cost of basic equipment. Metallurgy and design contribute to the thickness and weight of a fermentation vessel and hence are important aspects of this method. The given table gives the ACCE cost estimates for medium to large-scale STR and BCRs and one anaerobic fermenter. The costs are of bare vessels without agitators (Tables 5.4 and 5.5) (Cashman et al., 2016).

The air delivery power for STR is nearly constant due to optimized agitation and aeration powers. In addition, the oxygen transfer rate

Table 5.4 Annual expenditure for anaerobic membrane bioreactor facility by scale per m^3 operating at 35°C and 20°C used for wastewater treatment.

Volume of wastewater	Cost estimate by scale at 35°C	Volume of wastewater	Cost estimate by scale at 20°C
0.05	8.00–10.00	0.05	8.00–9.00
0.1	4.00–6.00	0.1	5.00–6.00
1	2.00–3.00	1	2.00–3.00
5	0.00–2.00	5	1.00–2.00
10	0.00–2.00	10	1.00–2.00

Data from Cashman, S., Mosley, J., Ma, X., & Garland, J. (2016). Life cycle assessment and cost analysis of water and wastewater treatment options for sustainability: Influence of scale on membrane bioreactor systems. EPA/600/R-16/243.

Table 5.5 Aspen Capital Cost Estimator cost estimates for medium to large scale STRs and bubble column reactors (BCRs).

Equipment	Aspen capital cost estimator (ACCE) specification guidelines	ACCE cost
MMgal anaerobic fermentor (bare vessel)	Storage tank, cone roof 304SS shell 55 ¢ diam. X 53 ¢ height 5 psig	$911,000
200 m^3 STR (bare vessel)	Vertical process vessel 304SS shell 15 ¢ diam. X 40 ¢ height Vacuum to 45 psig	$383,000
300 m^3 STR (Bare vessel)	Vertical process vessel 316SS shell 17 ¢ diam. X 45.5 ¢ height 0–45 psig +20% allowance for internals	$440,000
670 m^3 BCR	Vertical process vessel 316SS shell 17 ¢ diam. X 100 ¢ height Vacuum to 45 psig Half-pipe jacket in A204C	$2,040,000

(OTR) also changes little with vessel size. A change in volume from 500 to 1000 m^3 the increase in power is less than 5%. However as in BCR oxygen transfer is controlled by aeration rate, the gassing power input required for air circulation in larger volumes will be more. At higher OTR, the difference in power required for 500 and 1000 m^3 vessels is around 10%. For both types, in large volume reactors, the power required for efficient aeration varies approximately linearly with the volume of liquid suggesting that for large-sized vessels economic benefit is largely a result of reduced capital costs of equipment in comparison to reduced operative costs (Humbird et al., 2017)

5.8 Future perspectives

For decades, bioreactors have been employed to make a variety of medicinal biomolecules and other high-value goods. They allow for constant monitoring and control of environmental variables during the culture/reaction period, as well as the benefit of keeping a closed system. They play a crucial role in the creation of many novel processes. The economic viability of a bioprocess and its accompanying capital investment is determined by the right selection and design of a bioreactor that addresses high process efficiencies. To gain a quantitative understanding of mass transfer, suitable process engineering calculation methods should be devised.

Process engineering requires innovative approaches for gas transport, pH management, temperature sensors and actuators, optimal feeding, and cell quantification, among other things. Because temperature control is so important in bioreactors, it's critical to choose the right temperature control device based on the individual needs of each application by determining the heat load. The type of bioreactor would be determined by the morphology of the cells, their shear tolerance, and the culture's growth and production behavior. In the Indian context, creating various bioprocesses with extensive studies on reaction kinetics, mass transfer, and other factors is crucial, particularly when it comes to scaling up the process by designing and building appropriate bioreactors. Postgraduate biotechnology engineering programs that specialize in process and mechanical design and manufacturing of bioprocessing equipment would go a long way toward developing the country's indigenous potential (Singh et al., 2014). Despite the fact that the AnMBR process modeling area is still in its infancy, it has the potential to significantly improve the design, operation, and control of complex systems. It will improve system performance, lower costs, and broaden the technology's usefulness. Membrane fouling in heterogeneous settings varies substantially depending on the type of the foulant substance. By depicting critical connections between biology and fouling dynamics, a better knowledge of individual and collective foulant behavior is necessary to better anticipate treatment efficiency. Due to a lack of mechanistic knowledge of fouling in AnMBRs, more research into open and closed-loop control systems is needed to optimize AnMBRs on an industrial scale (Robles et al., 2018).

Improved membrane characteristics, novel membrane materials, and process optimization using new modeling methodologies will allow for higher performances, and as a result, the costs of processes that utilize membrane systems should be decreased, with considerable savings for process innovations. Landfilling and illegal trash disposal have become more common in response to COVID-19 potentially infectious waste, particularly in poor nations, aggravating plastic pollution and posing inherent health risks to humans and animals. In the first year, an estimated 3.5 million metric tonnes of masks (equivalent to 601 TIR containers) were landfilled globally, with the potential to increase global plastic municipal solid waste by 3.5 percent, change biogas composition, and release 2.3 1021 microplastics into leachates or adjacent environments in the coming years. COVID-19 will pass, but unless immediate action is taken to implement effective plastic policies, replace plastics with sustainable alternatives (e.g., biobased plastics), improve waste management streams (prioritizing flexible and decentralized approaches), and increase public awareness and responsibility, we will soon reach a tipping point (Silva et al., 2021). There is a need for proper maintenance of particular construction facilities for safe shear wall openings at building infrastructures that exist close to sanitary landfill bioreactors. The relative guidelines should be followed properly during the surveillance services by stakeholders after high earthquake magnitudes events or other combinations of dynamic loads for the right decision making at associated construction designs in terms of health – safety and public health protection. Physical experiments, in combination with computer simulations of shear walls in particular dynamic loads, are required in order to reach useful conclusions in the operational management of specific land uses within efficient sustainable development construction designs, appropriate manufacturing with opportunities in the exploitation of clean technologies related to landfill emissions, and sustainable tourism infrastructure (Koliopoulos et al., 1985).

References

Calabr Ò, V., & Iorio, G. (2013). *Economic aspects of membrane bioreactors*. Italy: University of Calabria. Available from http://doi.org/10.1533/9780857097347.4.888.

Cardoso, V. M., Campani, G., Santos, M. P., Silva, G. G., Pires, M. C., Gonçalves, V. M., Giordano, R. D. C., Sargo, C. R., Horta, A. C., & Zangirolami, T. C. (2020). Cost analysis based on bioreactor cultivation conditions: Production of a soluble recombinant protein using Escherichia coli BL21 (DE3). *Biotechnology Reports*, *26*, e00441. Available from https://doi.org/10.1016/j.btre.2020.e00441.

Cashman, S., Mosley, J., Ma, X., & Garland, J. (2016). *Life cycle assessment and cost analysis of water and wastewater treatment options for sustainability: Influence of scale on membrane bioreactor systems*. EPA/600/R-16/243.

Gaikwad, V., Panghal, A., Jadhav, S., Sharma, P., Bagal, A., Jadhav, A., Chhikara, N., (2018). Designing of fermenter and its utilization in food industries. Preprints, 2018080433 <http://doi:10.20944/preprints201808.0433.v1>.

Humbird, D., Davis, R., & McMillan, J. D. (2017). Aeration costs in stirred-tank and bubble column bioreactors. *Biochemical Engineering Journal*, *127*, 161–166. Available from https://doi.org/10.1016/j.bej.2017.08.006, 1369-703/© 2017.

Koliopoulos, T. K., Kouloumbis, P., Papakonstantinou, D., & Hilcenko, S. (1985). *Mitigation of environmental health risks within safe openings at buildings close to sanitary bioreactors*. vol. 3 2020 ISSN 2623–4874, e-ISSN 2623–4882.

Lin, H., Chen, J., Wang, F., Ding, L., & Hong, H. (2011). Feasibility evaluation of submerged anaerobic membrane bioreactor for municipal secondary wastewater treatment. *Desalination*, *280*(1–3), 120–126. Available from https://doi.org/10.1016/j.desal.2011.06.058.

Lo, C. H., McAdam, E., & Judd, S. (2015). The cost of a small membrane bioreactor. *Water Science and Technology: A Journal of the International Association on Water Pollution Research*, *72*(10), 1739–1746. Available from https://doi.org/10.2166/wst.2015.394.

Morelli, B., Cashman, S., Ma, C., Garland, J., Bless, D., & Jahne, M. (2019). *Life cycle assessment and cost analysis of distributed mixed wastewater and graywater treatment for water recycling in the context of an urban case study* (p. 162). EPA/600/R-18/280.

Platon, V., & Constantinescu, A. (2014). Monte Carlo method in risk analysis for investment projects. *Procedia Economics and Finance*, *15*, 393–400. Available from https://doi.org/10.1016/S2212-5671(14)00463-8.

Robles, Á., Ruano, M. V., Charfi, A., Lesage, G., Heran, M., Harmand, J., Seco, A., Steyer, J. P., Batstone, D. J., Kim, J., & Ferrer, J. (2018). A review on anaerobic membrane bioreactors (AnMBRs) focused on modelling and control aspects. *Bioresource Technology*, *270*, 612–626. Available from https://doi.org/10.1016/j.biortech.2018.09.049.

Silva, A. L. P., Prata, J. C., Duarte, A. C., Barcelò, D., & Rocha-Santos, T. (2021). An urgent call to think globally and act locally on landfill disposable plastics under and after covid-19 pandemic: Pollution prevention and technological (Bio) remediation solutions. *Chemical Engineering Journal*, 131201. Available from https://doi.org/10.1016/j.cej.2021.131201.

Singh, J., Kaushik, N., & Biswas, S. (2014). Bioreactors—technology & design analysis. *The Scitech Journal*, *1*(6), 28–36.

Verhuelsdonk, M., Glas, K., & Parlar, H. (2021). Economic evaluation of the reuse of brewery wastewater. *Journal of Environmental Management*, *281*, 111804. Available from https://doi.org/10.1016/j.jenvman.2020.111804.

Further reading

Cashman, S., Ma, X., Mosley, J., Garland, J., Crone, B., & Xue, X. (2018). Energy and greenhouse gas life cycle assessment and cost analysis of aerobic and anaerobic membrane bioreactor systems: Influence of scale, population density, climate, and methane recovery. *Bioresource Technology*, *254*, 56–66. Available from https://doi.org/10.1016/j.biortech.2018.01.060.

Shimizu, K., Takada, S., Minekawa, K., & Kawase, Y. (2000). Phenomenological model for bubble column reactors: Prediction of gas hold-ups and volumetric mass transfer coefficients. *Chemical Engineering Journal*, *78*(1), 21–28. Available from https://doi.org/10.1016/S1385-8947(99)00165-5.

CHAPTER 6

Landfill management and efficacy of anaerobic reactors in the treatment of landfill leachate

Imran Ahmad[1], Aida Batrisyia Jasni[2], Norhayati Abdullah[1], Santhana Krishnan[3,4], Iwamoto Koji[1], Shreeshivadasan Chelliapan[5], Ali Yuzir[1] and Mohd Nasrullah[6]

[1]Malaysia-Japan International Institute of Technology (MJIIT), Universiti Teknologi Malaysia, Kuala Lumpur, Malaysia
[2]School of Engineering, Faculty of Engineering, Universiti Teknologi Malaysia, Skudai, Johor, Malaysia
[3]Center of Environmental Sustainability and Water Security (IPASA), Research Institute of Sustainable Environment (RISE), Faculty of Engineering, Universiti Teknologi Malaysia, Johor Bahru, Malaysia
[4]PSU Energy Systems Research Institute (PERIN), Department of Environmental Engineering, Faculty of Engineering, Prince of Songkla University, Hat Yai, Thailand
[5]Razak Faculty of Technology and Informatics, Universiti Teknologi Malaysia, Kuala Lumpur, Malaysia
[6]Faculty of Civil Engineering Technology, Universiti Malaysia Pahang (UMP), Pahang, Malaysia

6.1 Introduction

Increasing thrust on technological advancement around the globe has led to a drastic increase in the consumption of various products or raw materials consequently leading to an enormous amount of solid waste generation. The ever-increasing generation of solid waste has become a great concern for society because of the relentless economic and environmental issues associated with its disposal. Solid waste is too heterogeneous and can be classified as kitchen waste, yard waste, paper, and cardboard waste, plastic and rubber waste, metallic waste, glass waste, and miscellaneous/others (electronic waste, construction and demolition waste, medical waste) waste and it is shown in Fig. 6.1. The world generates 2.01 billion tons of municipal solid waste annually, with at least 33% of that is not managed in an environmentally safe manner. Approximately, an average of 0.74 kg of waste is generated per capita per day but it is having a wide range from 0.11 to 4.54 kg/capita/day. Due to increasing urbanization and economic developments, global waste generation is expected to reach 3.4 billion tons by 2050 which is double the growth rate of the population (Atlas, 2018). This employs that the variation in income also plays a crucial role in the generation of solid waste.

Techno-economics and Life Cycle Assessment of Bioreactors
DOI: https://doi.org/10.1016/B978-0-323-89848-5.00005-6

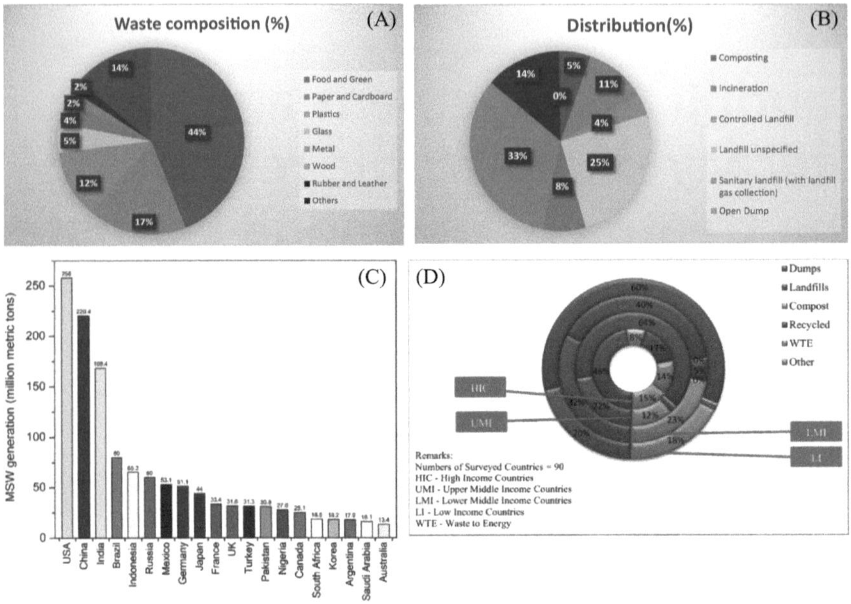

Figure 6.1 Solid waste management: (A) global waste composition (Kaza, Yao, Bhada-Tata, et al., 2018) (B) solid waste disposal proportioning (Kaza & Yao, 2018) (C) solid waste generation (Nanda & Berruti, 2020) and (D) solid waste disposal as per income (Show et al., 2019). Source: *From Kaza, S. & Yao, L. (2018).* At a glance: A global picture of solid waste management.

Solid waste management (SWM) is considered a major social, environmental, and economic problem globally mainly because of its huge volumes and variable characteristics. SWM depends on the infrastructure and technological advancement of the respective countries. In developed countries, SWM already attained an advanced stage, and the solid waste is converted to energy using WtE technologies, conversion to fuels, heat, and power is well established. In developing countries SWM is in a dilemmatic situation as most of the solid waste is carried for disposal at the landfills. Landfilling is adopted because it is a relatively inexpensive and expedient method of solid waste disposal. By conducting an explicit survey in about 90 countries, it has been reported that the dominating practice among these countries was landfilling of solid waste (Fig. 6.1D).

Broadly landfills can be classified into three categories (Jayasinghe et al., 2014): (1) open dump landfill-In this type of landfill solid waste is arbitrarily disposed of in low-lying areas open to the environment where they are poorly managed hence becoming the breeding site for the scavengers. (2) Semi-controlled landfills in this type of landfill the solid waste is sorted, shredded before being disposed of, and then it is covered with a layer of soil thus preventing the site from scavenging. Sanitary landfill is the improvised and Hi-tech type of semi-controlled landfill having the leachate management system as well as the gas collection system. Sanitary landfills are engineered landfills designed for sustainable SWM thus reducing the environmental footprint (Shehzad et al., 2015).

Modern landfills are highly engineered facilities yet they pose a serious threat to the environment due to the generation of highly polluted and recalcitrant landfill leachate. Landfill leachate if not managed and treated with suitable and efficient methods can be a severe problem for soil and water bodies (Luo et al., 2019). It was reported in previous studies that about 200 hazardous compounds have been found so far in landfill leachates (Clarke et al., 2015; Hamid et al., 2018). Landfill leachate can be defined as the liquid effluent produced by the percolation of rainwater in the disposed waste with the simultaneous decomposition of the waste. The decomposition of waste generally follows the pathway: (1) Starting aerobic phase, (2) Anaerobic acidogenic phase, (3) methanogenic phase, and (4) Stabilization phase. Therefore depending on the stages, the composition is extremely variable and heterogeneous (Naveen et al., 2017). Characteristics and quality of landfill leachate depend on various factors such as climatic conditions, Site hydrogeology, water movement through the landfill, age of landfill, design of landfill, the composition of the waste disposed of, degree of decomposition taking place, and the category of the landfill (Luo et al., 2020; Oulego et al., 2016).

The parameters of the landfill leachate can be classified among young, intermediate, and stabilized leachate and are shown in Table 6.1. After the collection of landfill leachate in the leachate ponds, the criteria which mainly govern the characteristics of landfill leachate is the age of landfills (Nor Nazrieza et al., 2015). Pollutants in leachate can be classified into four groups: (1) dissolved organic matter (volatile fatty acids, and refractory organic compounds like humic and fulvic acids) (2) macro inorganic fraction including ammonia ($NH_4^+{-}N$), sodium (Na^+), potassium (K^+), calcium (Ca^{2+}), magnesium (Mg^{2+}), manganese (Mn^{2+}), iron (Fe^{2+}), chloride (Cl^-), sulfate (SO_4^{2-}), and hydrogen carbonate (HCO_3^-); (3) heavy metals such as chromium (Cr^{3+}), nickel (Ni^{2+}), copper (Cu^{2+}), zinc (Zn^{2+}), cadmium (Cd^{2+}), mercury (Hg^{2+}), and lead (Pb^{2+}) (Robinson, 2017), and (4) xenobiotic organic compounds (pesticides, and plasticizers, aromatic hydrocarbons, phenols) (Luo et al.,

Table 6.1 Composition of landfill leachate according to its age (Ahmad et al., 2020; Nanda & Berruti, 2020).

Parameters	Young	Intermediate	Stabilized
Age of landfill (years)	<5	5–10	>10
pH	<6.5	6.5–7.5	>7.5
BOD/COD	0.5–1.0	0.1–0.5	<0.1
Biodegradability	High	Medium	Low
COD (mg/L)	>15,000	3000–15,000	<3000
Organic materials	VFA (80%)	VFA (5%–30%), humic	Humic and fulvic
NH_3–N (mg/L)	<400	NA	>400
TOC/COD	<0.3	0.3–0.5	>0.5
Kjeldahl nitrogen (mg/L)	100–2000	NA	NA
Heavy metals (mg/L)	>2	<2	<2

COD, Chemical oxygen demand; *BOD*, biological oxygen demand; *VFA*, volatile fatty acids; *TOC*, total organic carbon.
Source: From Nanda, S. & Berruti, F. (2020). Municipal solid waste management and landfilling technologies: a review. *Environmental Chemistry Letters*. https://doi.org/10.1007/s10311-020-01100-y.

2019). Pollutants incorporated above have alarming and threatening consequences for ecology, aquatic organisms, and food chains, and cause detrimental effects on public health and the environment (Budi et al., 2016).

This chapter will provide an insight into the various treatment technologies including biological, physical, and chemical but more emphasis is given to elaborate on the anaerobic technologies utilized in the treatment of landfill leachate because of their advantages over aerobic technologies. The study will also discuss some hybrid technologies used recently in the treatment of landfill leachate. Therefore to acquiesce to the stringent discharge standards for the landfill leachate various types of treatment methods are studied and implemented in different countries. Physical–chemical and biological treatment methods are commonly used for the treatment of landfill leachate, to overcome the limitations of these processes recently researchers are using hybrid technologies or the combination of two or more technologies for the treatment too (Torretta et al., 2017). Microorganisms help to degrade the organic substances to CO_2 in anaerobic while biogas ($CO_2 + CH_4$) are in the anaerobic biological process. Physical–chemical methods assist in the treatment of refractory compounds from the old leachate as well as they also work as post-treatment for the biological process to increase the efficiency (Aftab et al., 2019).

6.2 Advantages of biological treatment over physical and chemical treatment

Usual landfill leachate treatment methods can be classified into three major methods: biological, physical, and chemical. The biological method further branches out into aerobic and anaerobic treatments. The chemical treatments include flotation and coagulation-flocculation, while physical treatment includes adsorption and membrane filtration. Aerobic and anaerobic treatment involves suspended growth systems and attached growth systems. Within the subset of chemical treatments, flotation involves air oxidation to break down pollutants and coagulation involves the use of chemical coagulants to sink the pollutants. Adsorption, on the other hand, involves the use of an adsorbent to absorb pollutants, and membrane filtration involves the passage of wastewater through a filter membrane.

Electrochemical treatment is one of the most common methods in the treatment of landfill leachate (Mandal et al., 2017). Electrochemical treatment efficiently reduces two of the most concerning pollutants in landfill leachate which are organic matter and ammonium nitrogen. However, this method uses high energy consumption and is relatively expensive to operate. Besides electrochemical treatment, coagulation-flocculation is also favored by the industry. Though it effectively removes the nonbiodegradable matters in leachate, at the end of the coagulation-flocculation process, a high volume of concentrated sludge will be formed. Thus, this method is highly recommended as a pretreatment system to achieve maximum COD and total suspended solids (TSS) removal via combination with another treatment system such as membranes and adsorption (Shu et al., 2016; Zolfaghari et al., 2016). Apart from these methods, there are other emerging removal processes such as ion exchange, chemical precipitation, ultrafiltration, nanofiltration, and reverse osmosis (Dolar et al., 2016; Fudala-Ksiazek et al., 2018; Simonič, 2017). Although effective, the operational and frequent maintenance costs of these processes are relatively high due to the cost of chemicals and materials used. The generation of chemical sludge and residues which need to be carefully managed and disposed of are among other drawbacks for some of these processes.

Lately, the trends in the leachate treatment industry are a combination of the different treatment systems to enhance the treatment performance by overcoming the limitation of a single conventional treatment system (Liu et al., 2017; Nivya & Pieus, 2016; Rasool et al., 2016). The advantages and disadvantages of current methods for treating landfill leachate are summarized in Table 6.2. From Table 6.2, it could be deduced that

Table 6.2 Overview of treatment processes in the treatment of landfill leachate.

Process	Reactor type	Advantages	Disadvantages	Reference
Biological	Aerobic lagoons	Very effective in removing pathogens from leachate A cost-effective method	Does not completely satisfy the treatment requirement as the requirement is stricter. High dependency on temperature	Huang et al. (2014), Bolyard and Reinhart (2016), Raghab et al. (2013)
	Sequencing batch reactor	Ideal for nitrification-denitrification process Good process flexibility	Sludge bulking or inadequate separability Poor quality effluent	Chen et al. (2017)
	Trickling filter	Effective biological nitrogen lowering from landfill leachate Low-cost filter media Does not depend on temperature (5°C–25°C)	Not recommended for leachate with a high concentration of suspended solid Requires primary settling Growth of algae or fungi decreases the efficiency	Renou et al. (2008), Bove et al. (2015)
	Moving-bed biofilm reactor	Higher biomass concentration Short sludge settling period Low sensitivity of toxic compounds High removal of both organic and ammonia in a single process	Resistant to toxic substances	Xie et al. (2014)
	Anaerobic sequencing batch reactors	Able to achieve solid capture and organic removal in one vessel, removing the need for a clarifier	Requires a pre-treatment	Mukherjee et al. (2015)
	Upflow anaerobic sludge blanket	High treatment efficiency, Short hydraulic retention time (HRT), Capable of high volumetric organic loading, Does not depend on temperature	High sensitivity to toxic substances	Bharathiraja et al. (2016)
	Upflow anaerobic filter	Enhances solid's retention without causing channeling and short-circuiting	An additional cost of support media	Rajagopal et al. (2013)

Chemical	Flotation	Effective in removing colloids, ions, macromolecules, microorganisms, and fibers	Must be combined with another treatment which increases the cost	Majlesi et al. (2015)
	Coagulation/ flocculation	Effective in removing nonbiodegradable organic matter. Enhance floc-settling rate	High consistent sludge volume Increase on the concentration of aluminum or iron	Amor et al. (2015)
	Chemical precipitation	Effective in removing high-strength of ammonium-nitrogen in leachate Short reaction time	Generates large volume of sludge which needs further treatment	Huang et al. (2014)
	Adsorption	Effective in removing toxic heavy metals and organics	Cannot operate for a large quantity of wastewater Carbon fouling Costly	Kumar et al. (2013)
Physical	Ammonium stripping	Efficient in removing ammonium-nitrogen in leachate	Operating in high pH value Release of ammonia into atmosphere Scaling of calcium carbonate when lime is used for pH adjustment Foaming problem	Raboni and Viotti (2017)
	Chemical oxidation	Used for treatment of wastewater containing soluble organic nonbiodegradable and toxic substance	Costly High dosage of oxidants needed for complete treatment Some oxidation products can increase the toxicity of wastewater	Mojiri et al. (2013)

(Continued)

Table 6.2 (Continued)

Process	Reactor type	Advantages	Disadvantages	Reference
	Ion exchange	Effectively remove traces of metal impurities in leachate	High operational cost Requires an appropriate pre-treatment	Fudala-Ksiazek et al. (2018)
	Electrochemical treatment	Effectively breakdown recalcitrant organic compounds in landfill leachate	High energy consumption Relatively expensive	Fudala-Ksiazek et al. (2018)
	Ultrafiltration	Effective in eliminating the macromolecules and the particles	Strongly dependant on the type of material constituting the membrane Must combine with another treatment for complete pollutant removal	Dolar et al. (2016)
	Nanofiltration	Successfully removed recalcitrant organic compounds and heavy metals from landfill leachate	Requires efficient control of membrane fouling	Simonič (2017)
	Reverse osmosis	Energy-efficient technique for purifying wastewater	Costly Requires extensive pre-treatment Membrane fouling	Kumar et al. (2013)

physical and chemical treatment are generally uneconomical and possess drawbacks such as a large amount of sludge generated during the treatment, resistance to certain inorganic pollutants, and increasing the toxicity of residual water at the end of the treatment process. Nevertheless, less sludge generation, cost-effectiveness, and environmental-friendly aspects of biological treatment had made it to be an appropriate treatment system (Bove et al., 2015).

6.3 Advantages of anaerobic process over aerobic process

A rich organic substance such as landfill leachate is usually treated using biological treatment as it is a simple, reliable, and low-cost solution. It is mainly divided into two which are aerobic and anaerobic treatment. Aerobic treatment is domineering the current treatment of landfill leachate compared to anaerobic treatment (Xiao & Roberts, 2010). Though it is often considered effective, the main by-product of the treatment, which is a high amount of sludge, is a nuisance as it requires further treatment, thus slightly increasing the cost (Luo et al., 2020). Hence, the focus has shifted to anaerobic treatment of landfill leachate as of late.

Anaerobic treatment of landfill leachate is primarily the process of converting the pollutants in the leachate into carbon dioxide and methane under oxygen-deprived conditions. Fig. 6.2 shows a general overview of the anaerobic process. The organic compounds undergo two stages; acidogenesis and methanogenesis. In the acidogenesis stage, the complex organics consist of carbohydrates, proteins, and lipids are broken down into simpler organics such as monosaccharides, amino acids, and fatty acids. The acidogens will further degrade the organics into acids mainly acetic, propionic, and butyric. The main by-products of this process are produced in the methanogenesis stage where the acids are degraded into methane and carbon dioxide (Neba et al., 2019). This approach of anaerobic treatment has a longer start-up period and is more sensitive to the changes in the surrounding, making it a bit difficult to control. Nevertheless, anaerobic treatment has more advantages than aerobic treatment. This includes the lower amount of sludge, smaller reactor footprints, methane production for energy conversion, and the ability to degrade the recalcitrant compounds that are aerobically non-degradable (Huang et al., 2020). The anaerobic treatment has also been shown to reduce greenhouse gas emissions and is able to cater to a higher loading rate than aerobic treatment (Huang et al., 2014).

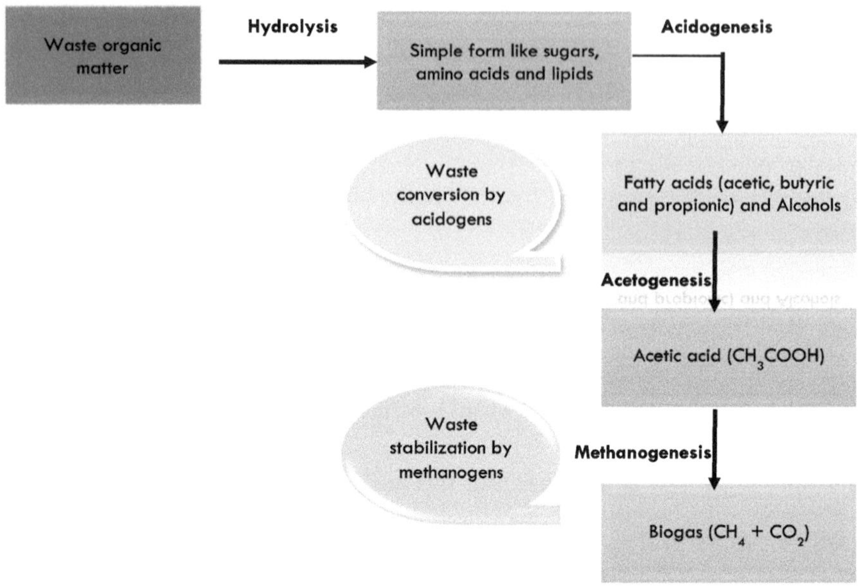

Figure 6.2 Simplified anaerobic process (Neba et al., 2019). Source: *From Neba, F. A., Asiedu, N. Y., Addo, A., Morken, J., Østerhus, S. W. & Seidu, R. (2019). Use of attainable regions for synthesis and optimization of multistage anaerobic digesters.* Applied Energy, 242, *334–350. https://doi.org/10.1016/j.apenergy.2019.03.095.*

6.4 Latest development of anaerobic reactors treating landfill leachate

The basic anaerobic processes apply in any design of an anaerobic reactor if it meets the main living condition of the oxygen-deprived microorganisms. In the beginning, the simple anaerobic reactor is used to treat wastewater. As modernization kicks in, the wastewater becomes more and more difficult to treat due to the more complex inorganic compounds, especially in landfill leachate. Thus, the designs of the anaerobic reactors had been modified to cater to the intended feed and increase its' performance efficiency. Other parameters must also be taken into account such as the climate, demographic of the area, and limitations of the treatment plant. Several designs of anaerobic reactors are widely studied in the treatment of landfill leachates such as anaerobic membrane bioreactor (AnMBR), upflow anaerobic sludge blanket (UASB) reactor, anaerobic fixed bed reactor (AFBR), anaerobic contact reactor (ACR), anaerobic baffled reactor (ABR), and stage anaerobic reactor. The following segment briefly reviews a few latest developments of anaerobic reactors treating landfill leachate (Shreeshivadasan et al., 2020).

6.4.1 Anaerobic membrane bioreactor

Membrane bioreactors had been extensively used in biological treatments. However, the use of a membrane in the anaerobic treatment proves to be more advantageous because it does not require aeration, produces methane for energy conversion, and has a considerably low amount of sludge (Burman & Sinha, 2020). The coupling of an anaerobic reactor with a membrane eliminates the need for a sedimentation unit in a landfill leachate treatment. Basically, an external membrane is placed before or after the anaerobic reactor which permits the sludge to be trapped and returned to the reactor. This approach however often resulted in membrane fouling due to the accumulation of the microbes. In a study by Burman and Sinha (2020), a ceramic micro-filter membrane is attached to an anaerobic reactor used to treat synthetic landfill leachate. The organic loading rate (OLR) is gradually increased from 1.6 to 13.9 kg COD/(m^3 d) in a period of 250 days. The average chemical oxygen demand (COD) removal was above 88% at 100% raw leachate. An almost similar result was obtained by Trzcinski and Stuckey (2016) using a submerged AnMBR (SAMBR) treating an organic fraction of municipal solid waste whereby more than 90% COD removal was observed (Trzcinski & Stuckey, 2016). Mnif et al. (2012) also recorded a maximum of 93% COD removal at a steady-state condition (Mnif et al., 2012). Another AnMBR is used in a study treating landfill leachate. High treatment efficiency was recorded both in COD removal and biogas yield, with 90% and 0.46 L/$gCOD_{remove}$, respectively (Zayen et al., 2010). These studies show that AnMBR is a highly efficient method of treatment for landfill leachate.

6.4.2 Upflow anaerobic sludge blanket reactor

Conventionally, UASB allows the influent to move upward and pass through two sludge blankets with different biomass concentrations. The schematic of the UASB is shown in Fig. 6.3. The influent will then go through a three-phase separator, located above the sludge blankets. The separator will then separate the influent into gas, liquid, and solid whereby the gas and liquid be leaving the reactor, while the solid remains (Bastiani et al., 2020). UASB is used to treat young leachate and was investigated in a mesophilic condition using raw leachate at an OLR of 12.5 kgCOD/m^3.d (Ye et al., 2011). The COD removal efficiency was approximately 82.4%. Another study of landfill leachate treatment by Selvam et al. (2017) achieved a 79.04% COD removal under mesophilic conditions

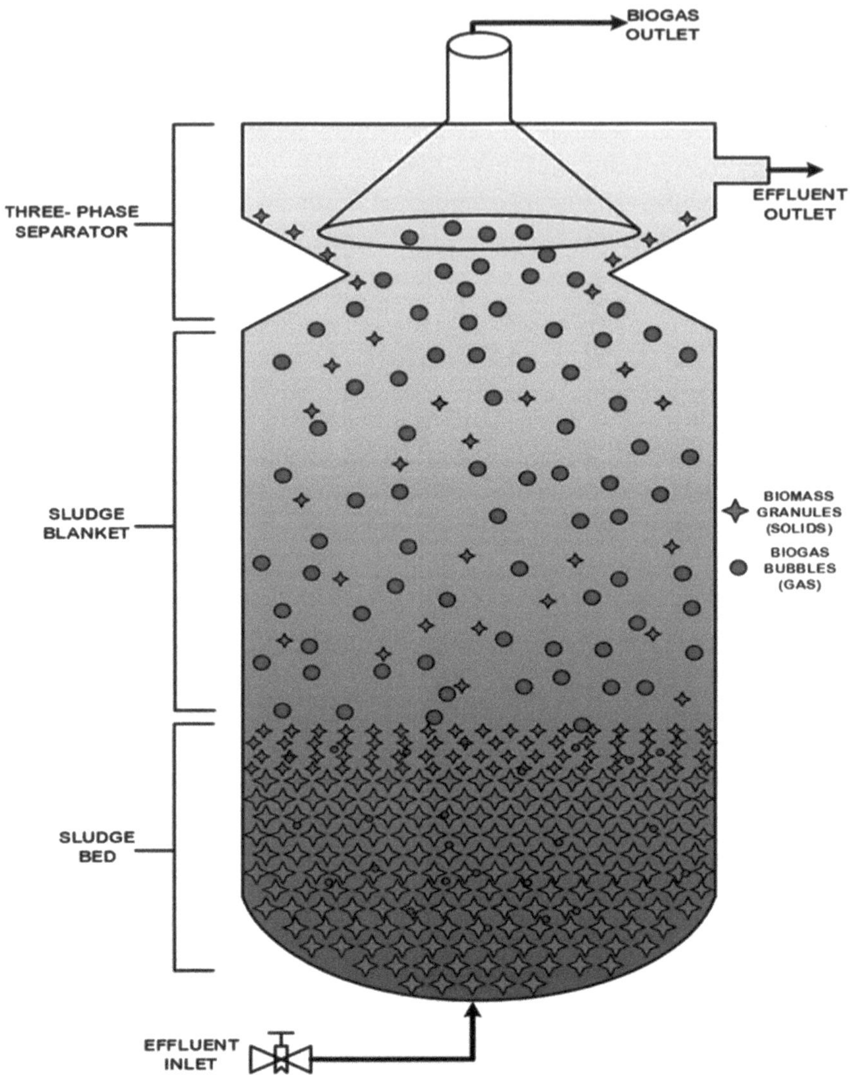

Figure 6.3 Schematic diagram of UASB (D'Bastiani et al., 2020). *UASB*, Upflow anaerobic sludge blanket. Source: *From Bastiani, C. D., Alba, J. L., Mazzarotto, G. T., de Farias Neto, S. R., Reynolds, A., Kennedy, D. & Beal, L. L. (2020). Three-phase hydrodynamic simulation and experimental validation of an upflow anaerobic sludge blanket reactor.* Computers and Mathematics with Applications. *https://doi.org/10.1016/j.camwa.2020.02.017.*

using a conventional UASB (Selvam et al., 2017). Jasni et al. (2020) used a granular multistage anaerobic reactor (GMSAR) whereby four UASB were arranged in series with a constant height difference between each one (Jasni et al., 2020). The average result of 71.9% COD removal and 65.9 mL/day of biogas yield was projected by response surface methodology (RSM) under the optimum condition. On the other hand, a COD removal of 81% is recorded by a hybrid upflow anaerobic sludge semi-fixed filter (UASSF) at an OLR of 9 kgCOD/(m m^3 day) (Hua et al., 2017a, 2017b).

6.4.3 Anaerobic fixed bed reactor

A fixed bed reactor is a wastewater treatment approach where an inert medium is employed to the bottom of the reactor to promote microbial growth on the media. A large amount of biomass retains on the media to prolong the solid retention time despite a short hydraulic retention time. The simplicity of the construction, stability at higher OLR, and the ability to withstand shock loading are among the advantage of AFBR. The main disadvantage of this reactor is the possibility of clogging due to the non-uniform growth of the microbes (Bolyard & Reinhart, 2016; Reinhart, Amini, & Bolyard, 2012). A study by Sudibyo et al. (2017) uses zeolite as the growth media for the AFBR, treating landfill leachate. The different volumes of zeolite (0, 150, 240, and 350 g/g sCOD) were investigated to determine the optimum zeolite volume for the treatment of leachate The removal of sCOD is up to 62% with the highest methane produced and ammonia reduced at 350 g zolite/g sCOD (Sudibyo et al., 2017). de Castro et al. (2021) investigated the efficiency of an anaerobic bioreactor with a fixed-structure bed (ABFSB) in treating landfill leachate. Polyurethane (PU) foam is used as the support media. Different OLR (2, 3.5, 7.1, and 11.6 gCOD/(L day)) is evaluated to study the effect on treatment efficiency. Under the mesophilic condition, the maximum result is obtained at OLR 7.1 gCOD/(L day), in which the COD removal is above 90% and methane yield is 0.3 L/$gCOD_{removed}$ (de Castro et al., 2020).

6.4.4 Anaerobic contact reactor

This reactor is designed to minimize the measure of the reactor and to withstand high OLRs. The reactor works like a high-rate anaerobic reactor, yet it has an extra component, which is a settling tank. The effluent is released to a gushing tank where solids readily settle down and after some

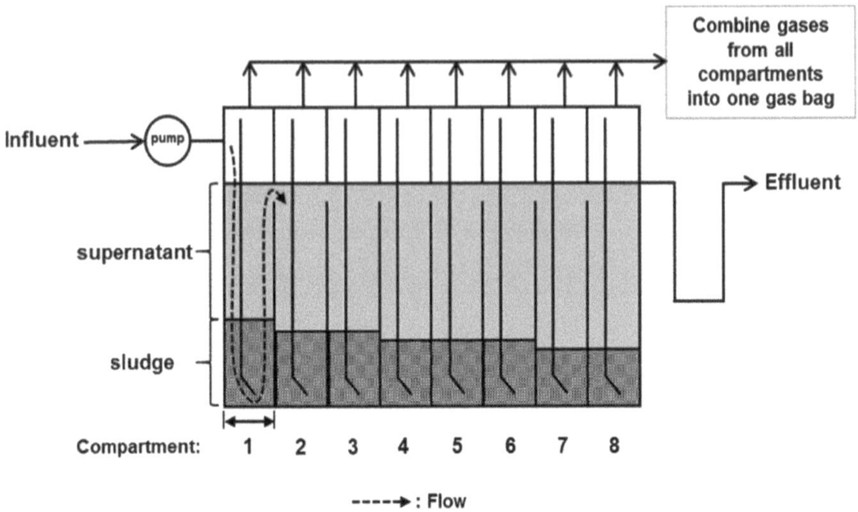

Figure 6.4 Schematic diagram of an ABR (Soh et al., 2020). *ABR*, Anaerobic baffled reactor. Source: *From Soh, Y. N. A., Kunacheva, C., Webster, R. D. & Stuckey, D. C. (2020). Composition and biotransformational changes in soluble microbial products (SMPs) along an anaerobic baffled reactor (ABR).* Chemosphere, *254. https://doi.org/10.1016/j.chemosphere.2020.126775.*

time the slime gathered in the settling tank is returned once again into the anaerobic reactor (Renou et al., 2008). The downside of this reactor is the development of gas in the settling tank, which upsets the solid settlement process. Another downside is that the reactor is more useful in treating wastewaters that are rich in solids. According to Şentürk et al. (2013), ACRs can remove up to 80% COD and produce 60% methane. In a previous study, Şentürk et al. (2010) found COD removal efficiencies to be 78%–92% and the methane percentage of the biogas produced to be 80 to 89% (Elif et al., 2013; Şentürk et al., 2010). El-Gohary and Kamel (2016) recently found that an ACR was able to remove 37.5 and 40.5% COD and BOD, respectively, from young leachate (El-Gohary & Kamel, 2016).

6.4.5 Anaerobic baffled reactor

ABR is predominantly two or more UASB reactors in a series of arrays. Fig. 6.4 shows the basic schematic of an ABR. The influent will flow over and under the baffle in each chamber before flowing into the next chamber. This ensures the sludge to retain in each chamber, bringing over additional sludge to the next chamber, thus reducing the solid washout in the reactor. The successful separation in the chamber guarantees the phase division of acidogenesis and methanogenesis stages (Renou et al., 2008). A recent study by Ahmad et al. (2020) using a modified ABR (MABR) recorded an average of 79.3% COD removal during a stable condition with an OLR of 1.40 kgCOD/(m^3 day). The MABR also successfully removed heavy metals such as arsenic (As), chromium (Cr), and iron (Fe) at an efficiency of 87.5%, 88.8%, and 87.8%, respectively (Ahmad et al., 2020). According to Rongrong et al. (2011), an ABR demonstrated COD and Polyvinyl alcohol (in leachate) removal efficiencies around 42.0% and 18.0% respectively (Rongrong et al., 2011).

6.4.6 Anaerobic ammonium qxidation (anammox)

Anammox is mainly a nitrogen removal method, which uses ammonia as the electron donor and nitrite as the receptor, thus removing the nitrogen in the landfill leachate. As it requires nitrate as the energy source, hence eliminating carbon as the main energy source, reducing the carbon dioxide and sludge emissions (Luo et al., 2020; Wang et al., 2018). A study by Wang et al. (2016), deduced that COD from mature leachate does not inhibit the process of anammox. The TN in the anammox was gradually increased from 0.5 to 1.2 kg/(m^3 day). The observed TN and COD removal efficiencies were 94% and 62% respectively under the high loading rate (Wang et al., 2016). A similar result was obtained by Phan et al. (2017) using an internal circulation (IC) anammox reactor treating landfill leachate. The nitrite removal efficiencies maintain at a high removal efficiency (76%-93%) despite a shock loading of TN concentration of 1290 mg N/L. These studies show the potential of anammox as the treatment of nitrogen-rich landfill leachate (Phan et al., 2017).

6.5 Combined anaerobic technologies

In recent years, hybrid/combined anaerobic reactors are widely researched to increase the efficiency of landfill leachate treatment. Kheradmand et al., (2010) used an anaerobic-aerobic reactor to treat landfill leachate in Barmshour, Iran. Two anaerobic reactors were operated continuously in mesophilic conditions and connected to an activated sludge unit. The OLR was increased stepwise from 0.07 to 3.37 g/(L day) and the COD removal efficiencies were around 83%−94%. An average of 60%−63% of the methane yield was recorded. This combined reactor had also successfully removed heavy metals such as Fe, Cu, Mn, and Ni in the range of 88.8%−99.9%.

A combination of an ABR-aerobic reactor with effluent recirculation treatment of fresh landfill leachate was explored by (Yin et al., 2017). Fig. 6.5 demonstrates the schematic diagram of the combined reactor. The fresh leachate was first treated using ABR before the effluent is fed into the aerobic reactor. The nitrified effluent from the aerobic reactor is recirculated into the third compartment of the ABR for denitrification purposes. The recirculation not only increases the total sCOD removal but also the total nitrogen (TN) removal. The total sCOD removal is in the range between 92.9% and 97% while the TN removal increases from 12.7% to 67.4% with recirculation ratios of 0.25, 0.5, and 2.

Research carried out by Ismail et al. (2020) investigated the use of a combined UASB-self aerated sponge (SAS) for the treatment of landfill leachate focusing on the polychlorinated biphenyls (PCBs) and heavy metals. The schematic of the combined treatment is shown in Fig. 6.6. The landfill leachate flowed upwards through the UASB and goes into the SAS in a downward direction before being discharged. The combined system was operated continuously at three different HRTs, that is, 40, 20, and 10 h. The total COD removal was 34.5%–59.2% while the total ammoniacal nitrogen removed was 72.3%–92.8%. The considerably low total COD removal was

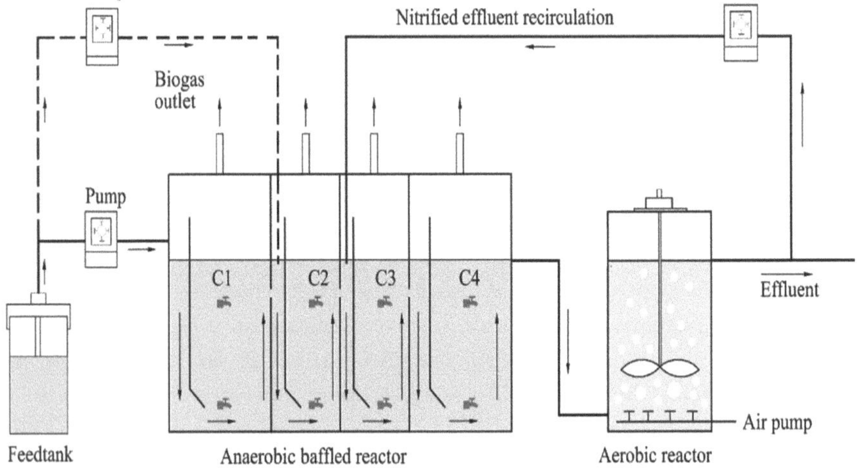

Figure 6.5 Schematic diagram of ABR with aerobic reactor (Yin et al., 2017). *ABR*, Anaerobic baffled reactor. Source*: From Yin, Z., Xie, L., Cui, X. & Zhou, Q. (2017). Effective carbon and nitrogen removal with reduced sulfur oxidation in an anaerobic baffled reactor for fresh leachate treatment.* Journal of Bioscience and Bioengineering, 123*(1), 84–90. https://doi.org/10.1016/j.jbiosc.2016.07.004.*

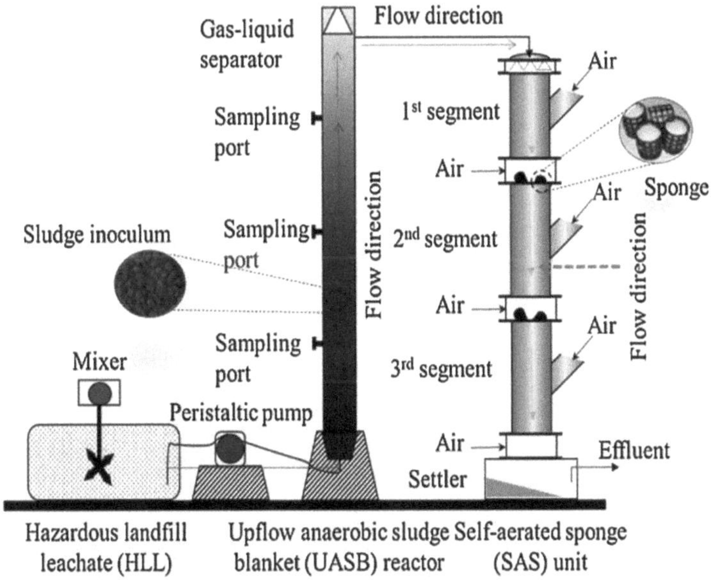

Figure 6.6 Schematic diagram of UASB-SAS reactor (Ismail et al., 2020). *SAS*, Self aerated sponge; *UASB*, upflow anaerobic sludge blanket. Source: *From Ismail, S., Nasr, M., Abdelrazek, E., Awad, H. M., Zhaof, S., Meng, F. & Tawfik, A. (2020). Techno-economic feasibility of energy-saving self-aerated sponge tower combined with up-flow anaerobic sludge blanket reactor for the treatment of hazardous landfill leachate.* Journal of Water Process Engineering, 37. *https://doi.org/10.1016/j.jwpe.2020.101415.*

probably due to the abundant presence of heavy metals. On the other hand, the removal of different types of PCBs was considerably high which is between 87.2% and 95.7%. The heavy metals i.e., Fe, Zn, Cu, Ni, Cd, Pb, Cr and Mn removal efficiencies were 85.6 ± 4.8%, 73.6 ± 5.4%, 87.6 ± 6.2%, 76.5 ± 3.8%, 77.8 ± 4.0%, 42.9 ± 1.9%, 59.3 ± 4.5%, and 80.6 ± 4.5%, respectively (Ismail et al., 2020).

The latest combined anaerobic-aerobic treatment of landfill leachate was investigated using completely stirred tank reactors. The study involved a series of two anaerobic completely stirred tank reactors (CSTR) and an anaerobic reactor. The reactors were arranged such that the effluent of the first CSTR was the influent for the second CSTR. The effluent of the second CSTR was then fed to the sedimentation tank for solid retention purposes before going into the aeration tank. OLR was increased gradually in five steps from 0.55 to 2.65 kg COD/m^3. The COD removal efficiencies reported were between 89.4% and 95.6% while the average biogas production rate was between 1.04–16.88 and

1.9–8 L/day for the first and second CSTR, respectively. The higher biogas production rate was observed in the first CSTR due to the plenty of degradable organic matter for the microbes to digest (Ghanbari Azad Pashaki et al., 2020).

Apart from the anaerobic-aerobic combination of leachate treatment, anaerobic-electrochemical combined reactors were also studied in the past years. One of the electrochemical methods used in treating landfill leachate is microbial fuel cell (MFC). MFC utilizes the microbes as catalysts for electron generation to convert the energy-rich organics in anaerobic oxidation into electrical energy (Gupta et al., 2020). The main goal for the anaerobic-MFC combination is to generate electricity using the anaerobic microbes. Tugtas et al. (2013) use a UASB and a two-chamber MFC to treat landfill leachate. The study was conducted in two operating conditions which are batch and continuous-flow operation (Tugtas et al., 2013).

In the batch MFC study, the effluent of UASB was fed once to the anode chamber while in the continuous flow study, the effluent was fed to the anode chamber continuously at HRT 1d and 5d. The batch anaerobic-MFC recorded a total of 90% VFA removal with a maximum current and power densities of 712 mA/m^2 and 109 mW/m^2, respectively. In the continuous anaerobic-MFC, the highest current and power densities observed were 525 mA/m^2 and 158 mW/m^2 at HRT of 5d. The long HRT increases the inhibitory effects of free ammonia and possibly causes the occurrence of partial nitrification thus reducing the maximum current observed. On the other hand, Mahmoud et al. (2014) combined an anaerobic digester and microbial electrolysis cell (MEC) for the treatment of recalcitrant landfill leachate. The study concluded that the combined anaerobic MEC increased the performance of the treatment of landfill leachate compared to the standalone MEC. An 83% BOD_5 removal and a maximum current of 16 mA/m^2 were achieved by the combined treatment compared to 5.6% BOD_5 removal and 1.7 mA/m^2 of maximum current for the standalone MEC (Mahmoud et al., 2014).

6.6 Conclusion

Landfill leachate is a recognized and common environmental burden that poses a considerable danger to surface water, groundwater, and soil because of the presence of harmful substances such as heavy metals and xenobiotic compounds. To meet stringent wastewater discharge standards for direct discharge into water bodies or sewer systems, various sustainable methods and technologies have been studied and implemented for the treatment of landfill leachates. Selection of the most appropriate treatment technology for landfill leachate depends mainly on the leachate characteristics (landfill age, COD, etc.), the legal requirements of effluent concentrations of pollutants, the efficiency of the treatment process, reliability, and resilience of technology, and the economic aspects. This chapter encompasses an overview of different treatment processes like biological, chemical, and physical processes with their advantages and disadvantages. More emphasis is given to various anaerobic reactor technologies utilized in the treatment of landfill leachate because of their superiority in terms of less sludge production and the production of biogas.

Acknowledgement

Authors would like to acknowledge the grants FRGS R.J130000.7801.5F221, PDRU Grant- Vot No. Q.J130000.21A2.04E53, Hitachi Global Foundation 2019, and MRUN R.J130000.7805.4L886, and also Universiti Teknologi Malaysia for providing us the platform for the study.

Conflict of interest

Authors does not find any conflict of interest.

References

Aftab, B., Ok, Y. S., Cho, J., & Hur, J. (2019). Targeted removal of organic foulants in landfill leachate in forward osmosis system integrated with biochar/activated carbon treatment. *Water Research*, *160*, 217–227. Available from https://doi.org/10.1016/j.watres.2019.05.076.

Ahmad, I., Abdullah, N., Chelliapan, S., Yuzir, A., Koji, I., Al-Dailami, A., & Arumugham, T. (2020). *Effectiveness of anaerobic technologies in the treatment of landfill leachate. Solid Waste Management*. IntechOpen.

Amor, C., De Torres-Socías, E., Peres, J. A., Maldonado, M. I., Oller, I., Malato, S., & Lucas, M. S. (2015). Mature landfill leachate treatment by coagulation/flocculation combined with Fenton and solar photo-Fenton processes. *Journal of Hazardous Materials*, *286*, 261–268.

Atlas, W., Nanda, S., & Berruti, F. (2021). Municipal solid waste management and landfilling technologies: a review. *Environmental Chemistry Letters*, *19*(2), 1433–1456.

Bastiani, C. D., Alba, J. L., Mazzarotto, G. T., de Farias Neto, S. R., Reynolds, A., Kennedy, D., & Beal, L. L. (2020). Three-phase hydrodynamic simulation and experimental validation of an upflow anaerobic sludge blanket reactor. *Computers and Mathematics with Applications*. Available from https://doi.org/10.1016/j.camwa.2020.02.017.

Bharathiraja, B., Sudharsanaa, T., Bharghavi, A., Jayamuthunagai, J., & Praveenkumar, R. (2016). Biohydrogen and biogas—An overview on feedstocks and enhancement process. *Fuel*, *185*, 810–828.

Bolyard, S. C., & Reinhart, D. R. (2016). Application of landfill treatment approaches for stabilization of municipal solid waste. *Waste Management, 55*, 22–30. Available from https://doi.org/10.1016/j.wasman.2016.01.024.

Bove, D., Merello, S., Frumento, D., Arni, S. A., Aliakbarian, B., & Converti, A. (2015). A critical review of biological processes and technologies for landfill leachate treatment. *Chemical Engineering and Technology, 38*(12), 2115–2126. Available from https://doi.org/10.1002/ceat.201500257.

Budi, S., Suliasih, B. A., Othman, M. S., Heng, L. Y., & Surif, S. (2016). Toxicity identification evaluation of landfill leachate using fish, prawn and seed plant. *Waste Management, 55*, 231–237. Available from https://doi.org/10.1016/j.wasman.2015.09.022.

Burman, I., & Sinha, A. (2020). Anaerobic hybrid membrane bioreactor for treatment of synthetic leachate: Impact of organic loading rate and sludge fractions on membrane fouling. *Waste Management, 108*, 41–50. Available from https://doi.org/10.1016/j.wasman.2020.04.031.

Chen, L., Yang, X., Tian, X., Yao, S., Li, J., Wang, A., Yao, Q., & Peng, D. (2017). Partial nitritation of stored source-separated urine by granular activated sludge in a sequencing batch reactor. *AMB Express*, 7, 1–10.

Clarke, B. O., Anumol, T., Barlaz, M., & Snyder, S. A. (2015). Investigating landfill leachate as a source of trace organic pollutants. *Chemosphere, 127*, 269–275. Available from https://doi.org/10.1016/j.chemosphere.2015.02.030.

D'Bastiani, C., Alba, J. L., Mazzarotto, G. T., de Farias Neto, S. R., Reynolds, A., Kennedy, D., & Beal, L. L. (2020). Three-phase hydrodynamic simulation and experimental validation of an upflow anaerobic sludge blanket reactor. *Computers & Mathematics with Applications*.

de Castro, T. M., Torres, D. G. B., Arantes, E. J., de Carvalho, K. Q., Passig, F. H., Christ, D., Gotardo, J. T., & Gomes, S. D. (2020). Anaerobic co-digestion of industrial landfill leachate and glycerin: methanogenic potential, organic matter removal and process optimization. *Environmental Technology (United Kingdom), 41*(20), 2583–2593. Available from https://doi.org/10.1080/09593330.2019.1575915.

de Castro, T. M., Arantes, E. J., de Mendonça Costa, M. S. S., Gotardo, J. T., Passig, F. H., de Carvalho, K. Q., & Gomes, S. D. (2021). Anaerobic co-digestion of industrial waste landfill leachate and glycerin in a continuous anaerobic bioreactor with a fixed-structured bed (ABFSB): Effects of volumetric organic loading rate and alkaline supplementation. *Renewable Energy, 164*, 1436–1446.

Dolar, D., Košutić, K., & Strmecky, T. (2016). Hybrid processes for treatment of landfill leachate: Coagulation/UF/NF-RO and adsorption/UF/NF-RO. *Separation and Purification Technology, 168*, 39–46. Available from https://doi.org/10.1016/j.seppur.2016.05.016.

El-Gohary, F. A., & Kamel, G. (2016). Characterization and biological treatment of pretreated landfill leachate. *Ecological Engineering, 94*, 268–274. Available from https://doi.org/10.1016/j.ecoleng.2016.05.074.

Elif, Ş., Mahir, İ., & Onkal, E. G. (2013). The effect of transient loading on the performance of a mesophilic anaerobic contact reactor at constant feed strength. *Journal of Biotechnology*, 232–237. Available from https://doi.org/10.1016/j.jbiotec.2012.08.016.

Fudala-Ksiazek, S., Sobaszek, M., Luczkiewicz, A., Pieczynska, A., Ofiarska, A., Fiszka-Borzyszkowska, A., Sawczak, M., Ficek, M., Bogdanowicz, R., & Siedlecka, E. M. (2018). Influence of the boron doping level on the electrochemical oxidation of raw landfill leachates: Advanced pre-treatment prior to the biological nitrogen removal. *Chemical Engineering Journal, 334*, 1074–1084. Available from https://doi.org/10.1016/j.cej.2017.09.196.

Ghanbari Azad Pashaki, S., Khojastehpour, M., Ebrahimi-Nik, M., & Rohani, A. (2020). Treatment of municipal landfill leachate: Optimization of organic loading rate in a two-stage CSTR followed by aerobic degradation. *Renewable Energy*.

Gupta, S., Srivastava, P., Patil, S. A., & Yadav, A. K. (2020). A comprehensive review on emerging constructed wetland coupled microbial fuel cell technology: potential applications and challenges. *Bioresource Technology*, *320*, 124376.

Hamid, H., Li, L. Y., & Grace, J. R. (2018). Review of the fate and transformation of per- and polyfluoroalkyl substances (PFASs) in landfills. *Environmental Pollution*, *235*, 74–84. Available from https://doi.org/10.1016/j.envpol.2017.12.030.

Hua, J., Bai, S., Li, Z. & Zhou, H. (2017a). Treatment of landfill leachate using an up-flow anaerobic sludge semi-fixed filter. In: *Proceedings of 3rd international conference on water resource and environment (WRE 2017)*. 26–29.

Hua, J., Bai, S. Y., Li, Z. Y., & Zhou, H. C. (2017b). *Treatment of landfill leachate using an up-flow anaerobic sludge semi-fixed filter*. *IOP Conference Series: Earth and Environmental Science* (Vol. 82). Institute of Physics Publishing Issue 1. Available from https://doi.org/10.1088/1755-1315/82/1/012066.

Huang, H., Xiao, D., Zhang, Q., & Ding, L. (2014). Removal of ammonia from landfill leachate by struvite precipitation with the use of low-cost phosphate and magnesium sources. *Journal of Environmental Management*, *145*, 191–198. Available from https://doi.org/10.1016/j.jenvman.2014.06.021.

Huang, Z., He, X., Nye, C., Bagley, D., Urynowicz, M., & Fan, M. (2020). Effective anaerobic treatment of produced water from petroleum production using an anaerobic digestion inoculum from a brewery wastewater treatment facility. *Journal of Hazardous Materials*. Available from https://doi.org/10.1016/j.jhazmat.2020.124348.

Ismail, S., Nasr, M., Abdelrazek, E., Awad, H. M., Zhaof, S., Meng, F., & Tawfik, A. (2020). Techno-economic feasibility of energy-saving self-aerated sponge tower combined with up-flow anaerobic sludge blanket reactor for treatment of hazardous landfill leachate. *Journal of Water Process Engineering*, 37. Available from https://doi.org/10.1016/j.jwpe.2020.101415.

Jasni, A. B., Chelliapan, S., Din, M. F. M., & Arumugam, N. (2020). Treatment of landfill leachate using granular multi-stage anaerobic reactor: Optimisation through response surface methodology. *Journal of Environmental Treatment Techniques*, *8*(2), 567–572. Available from http://www.jett.dormaj.com/docs/Volume8/Issue%202/Treatment%20of%20Landfill%20Leachate%20using%20Granular%20Multi-Stage%20Anaerobic%20Reactor%20Optimisation%20through%20Response%20Surface%20Methodology.pdf.

Jayasinghe, P. A., Hettiaratchi, J. P. A., Mehrotra, A. K., & Kumar, S. (2014). Reaction mechanisms and rate constants of waste degradation in landfill bioreactor systems with enzymatic-enhancement. *Bioresource Technology*, *162*, 279–282. Available from https://doi.org/10.1016/j.biortech.2014.03.147.

Kaza, S. & Yao, L. (2018). *At a glance: A global picture of solid waste management.*

Kaza, S., Yao, L., Bhada-Tata, P., & Van Woerden, F. (2018). *What a waste 2.0: a global snapshot of solid waste management to 2050*. The World Bank.

Kheradmand, S., Karimi-Jashni, A., & Sartaj, M. (2010). Treatment of municipal landfill leachate using a combined anaerobic digester and activated sludge system. *Waste Management*, *30*(6), 1025–1031.

Kumar, S., Katoria, D., & Singh, G. (2013). Leachate Treatment Technologies. *International Journal of Environmental Engineering and Management*, *4*, 439–444.

Liu, J., Zhang, H., Zhang, P., Wu, Y., Gou, X., Song, Y., Tian, Z., & Zeng, G. (2017). Two-stage anoxic/oxic combined membrane bioreactor system for landfill leachate treatment: Pollutant removal performances and microbial community. *Bioresource Technology*, *243*, 738–746. Available from https://doi.org/10.1016/j.biortech.2017.07.002.

Luo, H., Cheng, Y., He, D., & Yang, E. H. (2019). Review of leaching behavior of municipal solid waste incineration (MSWI) ash. *Science of the Total Environment*, *668*, 90–103. Available from https://doi.org/10.1016/j.scitotenv.2019.03.004.

Luo, H., Zeng, Y., Cheng, Y., He, D., & Pan, X. (2020). Recent advances in municipal landfill leachate: A review focusing on its characteristics, treatment, and toxicity assessment. *Science of The Total Environment*, *703*, 135468.
Mahmoud, M., Parameswaran, P., Torres, C. I., & Rittmann, B. E. (2014). Fermentation pre-treatment of landfill leachate for enhanced electron recovery in a microbial electrolysis cell. *Bioresource Technology*, *151*, 151–158. Available from https://doi.org/10.1016/j.biortech.2013.10.053.
Majlesi, M., Yazdanbakhsh, A. R., Jabbari, V., & Sheikhmohammadi, A. (2015). Landfill leachate treatment using electro-coagulation-flotation process. *Advances in Environmental Biology*, *9*, 167–173.
Mandal, P., Dubey, B. K., & Gupta, A. K. (2017). Review on landfill leachate treatment by electrochemical oxidation: Drawbacks, challenges and future scope. *Waste Management*, *69*, 250–273. Available from https://doi.org/10.1016/j.wasman.2017.08.034.
Mnif, S., Zayen, A., Karray, F., Bru-Adan, V., Loukil, S., Godon, J. J., Chamkha, M., & Sayadi, S. (2012). Microbial population changes in anaerobic membrane bioreactor treating landfill leachate monitored by single-strand conformation polymorphism analysis of 16S rDNA gene fragments. *International Biodeterioration and Biodegradation*, *73*, 50–59. Available from https://doi.org/10.1016/j.ibiod.2012.04.014.
Mojiri, A., Aziz, H. A., & Aziz, S. Q. (2013). Trends in physical-chemical methods for landfill leachate treatment. *International Journal of Scientific Research in Environmental Sciences*, *1*, 16–25.
Mukherjee, S., Mukhopadhyay, S., Hashim, M. A., & Sen Gupta, B. (2015). Contemporary environmental issues of landfill leachate: Assessment and remedies. *Critical reviews in environmental science and technology*, *45*, 472–590.
Nanda, S., & Berruti, F. (2020). Municipal solid waste management and landfilling technologies: A review. *Environmental Chemistry Letters*, 1–24.
Naveen, B. P., Mahapatra, D. M., Sitharam, T. G., Sivapullaiah, P. V., & Ramachandra, T. V. (2017). Physico-chemical and biological characterization of urban municipal landfill leachate. *Environmental Pollution*, *220*, 1–12. Available from https://doi.org/10.1016/j.envpol.2016.09.002.
Neba, F. A., Asiedu, N. Y., Addo, A., Morken, J., Østerhus, S. W., & Seidu, R. (2019). Use of attainable regions for synthesis and optimization of multistage anaerobic digesters. *Applied Energy*, *242*, 334–350.
Nivya, T., & Pieus, T. M. (2016). Comparison of photo electrofenton process (PEF) and combination of PEF process and membrane bioreactor in the treatment of landfill leachate. *Procedia Technology*, *24*, 224–231.
Nor Nazrieza, M. S., Siti Rohana, M. Y., Subramaniam, K., Hazilia, H., & Amir Herberd, A. (2015). Characterization of leachate from Panchang bedena landfill, batang padang landfill and matang landfill: A comparative study. *Malaysian Journal of Science*, *34*(1), 69–77. Available from https://doi.org/10.22452/mjs.vol34no1.7.
Oulego, P., Collado, S., Laca, A., & Díaz, M. (2016). Impact of leachate composition on the advanced oxidation treatment. *Water Research*, *88*, 389–402. Available from https://doi.org/10.1016/j.watres.2015.09.048.
Phan, T. N., Van Truong, T. T., Ha, N. B., Nguyen, P. D., Bui, X. T., Dang, B. T., Doan, V. T., Park, J., Guo, W., & Ngo, H. H. (2017). High rate nitrogen removal by ANAMMOX internal circulation reactor (IC) for old landfill leachate treatment. *Bioresource Technology*, *234*, 281–288. Available from https://doi.org/10.1016/j.biortech.2017.02.117.
Raboni, M., & Viotti, P. (2017). Predictive model of limestone scaling in ammonia stripping towers and its experimental validation on a treatment plant fed by MSW leachate-polluted groundwater. *Waste Management*, *59*, 537–544.
Raghab, S. M., Abd El Meguid, A. M., & Hegazi, H. A. (2013). Treatment of leachate from municipal solid waste landfill. *HBRC Journal*, *9*, 187–192.

Rajagopal, R., Torrijos, M., Kumar, P., & Mehrotra, I. (2013). Substrate removal kinetics in high-rate upflow anaerobic filters packed with low-density polyethylene media treating high-strength agro-food wastewaters. *Journal of Environmental Management, 116*, 101–106.

Rasool, M. A., Tavakoli, B., Chaibakhsh, N., Pendashteh, A. R., & Mirroshandel, A. S. (2016). Use of a plant-based coagulant in coagulation-ozonation combined treatment of leachate from a waste dumping site. *Ecological Engineering, 90*, 431–437. Available from https://doi.org/10.1016/j.ecoleng.2016.01.057.

Reinhart, D. R., Amini, H., & Bolyard, S. C. (2012). The role of landfills in us sustainable waste management. *Environmental Engineer: Applied Research and Practice, American Academy of Environmental Engineers and Scientists, 15*, 1–6.

Renou, S., Givaudan, J. G., Poulain, S., Dirassouyan, F., & Moulin, P. (2008). Landfill leachate treatment: Review and opportunity. *Journal of Hazardous Materials, 150*(3), 468–493. Available from https://doi.org/10.1016/j.jhazmat.2007.09.077.

Robinson, T. (2017). Removal of toxic metals during biological treatment of landfill leachates. *Waste Management, 63*, 299–309. Available from https://doi.org/10.1016/j.wasman.2016.12.032.

Rongrong, L., Xujie, L., Qing, T., Bo, Y., & Jihua, C. (2011). The performance evaluation of hybrid anaerobic baffled reactor for treatment of PVA-containing desizing wastewater. *Desalination, 271*(1–3), 287–294. Available from https://doi.org/10.1016/j.desal.2010.12.044.

Selvam, S. B., Chelliapan, S., Din, M. F. M., Nasri, N. S., Abdullah, N., & Yuzir, A. (2017). Performance of an up-flow anaerobic sludge bed (UASB) reactor for treating landfill leachate containing heavy metals and formaldehyde. *Desalination and Water Treatment, 86*, 51–58. Available from https://doi.org/10.5004/dwt.2017.21406.

Şentürk, E., İnce, M., & Engin, G. O. (2013). The effect of transient loading on the performance of a mesophilic anaerobic contact reactor at constant feed strength. *Journal of Biotechnology, 164*, 232–237.

Şentürk, E., Ince, M., & Onkal Engin, G. (2010). Kinetic evaluation and performance of a mesophilic anaerobic contact reactor treating medium-strength food-processing wastewater. *Bioresource Technology, 101*(11), 3970–3977. Available from https://doi.org/10.1016/j.biortech.2010.01.034.

Shehzad, A., Bashir, M. J. K., Sethupathi, S., & Lim, J. W. (2015). An overview of heavily polluted landfill leachate treatment using food waste as an alternative and renewable source of activated carbon. *Process Safety and Environmental Protection, 98*, 309–318. Available from https://doi.org/10.1016/j.psep.2015.09.005.

Show, P. L., Pal, P., Leong, H. Y., Juan, J. C., & Ling, T. C. (2019). A review on the advanced leachate treatment technologies and their performance comparison: An opportunity to keep the environment safe. *Environmental Monitoring and Assessment, 191*, 227.

Shreeshivadasan, C., Nithiya, A., Mohd. Fadhil, M. D., Hesam, K., & Shafiei, E. S. (2020). *Anaerobic treatment of municipal solid waste landfill leachate* (pp. 175–193). Elsevier BV. Available from https://doi.org/10.1016/b978-0-12–821264-6.00011-5.

Shu, Z., Lü, Y., Huang, J., & Zhang, W. (2016). Treatment of compost leachate by the combination of coagulation and membrane process. *Chinese Journal of Chemical Engineering, 24*(10), 1369–1374. Available from https://doi.org/10.1016/j.cjche.2016.05.022.

Simonič, M. (2017). Compost leachate treatment using polyaluminium chloride and nanofiltration. *Open Chemistry, 15*(1), 123–128. Available from https://doi.org/10.1515/chem-2017-0015.

Soh, Y. N. A., Kunacheva, C., Webster, R. D., & Stuckey, D. C. (2020). Composition and biotransformational changes in soluble microbial products (SMPs) along an anaerobic baffled reactor (ABR). *Chemosphere, 254*, 126775.

Sudibyo, H., Shabrina, Z. L., Halim, L., & Budhijanto, W. (2017). *Mathematical modelling and statistical approach to assess the performance of anaerobic fixed bed reactor for biogas production from piyungan sanitary landfill leachate. Energy procedia* (Vol. 105, pp. 256–262). Elsevier Ltd. Available from https://doi.org/10.1016/j.egypro.2017.03.311.

Torretta, V., Ferronato, N., Katsoyiannis, I. A., Tolkou, A. K., & Airoldi, M. (2017). Novel and conventional technologies for landfill leachates treatment: A review. *Sustainability (Switzerland)*, *9*(1). Available from https://doi.org/10.3390/su9010009.

Trzcinski, A. P., & Stuckey, D. C. (2016). Effect of sparging rate on permeate quality in a submerged anaerobic membrane bioreactor (SAMBR) treating leachate from the organic fraction of municipal solid waste (OFMSW). *Journal of Environmental Management*, *168*, 67–73. Available from https://doi.org/10.1016/j.jenvman.2015.11.055.

Tugtas, A. E., Cavdar, P., & Calli, B. (2013). Bio-electrochemical post-treatment of anaerobically treated landfill leachate. *Bioresource Technology*, *128*, 266–272. Available from https://doi.org/10.1016/j.biortech.2012.10.035.

Wang, K., Li, L., Tan, F., & Wu, D. (2018). Treatment of landfill leachate using activated sludge technology: A review. *Archaea (Vancouver, BC)*. Available from https://doi.org/10.1155/2018/1039453, 2018.

Wang, Z., Peng, Y., Miao, L., Cao, T., Zhang, F., Wang, S., & Han, J. (2016). Continuous-flow combined process of nitritation and ANAMMOX for treatment of landfill leachate. *Bioresource Technology*, *214*, 514–519.

Xiao, Y., & Roberts, D. J. (2010). A review of anaerobic treatment of saline wastewater. *Environmental Technology*, *31*(8–9), 1025–1043. Available from https://doi.org/10.1080/09593331003734202.

Xie, Z., Wang, Z., Wang, Q., Zhu, C., & Wu, Z. (2014). An anaerobic dynamic membrane bioreactor (AnDMBR) for landfill leachate treatment: performance and microbial community identification. *Bioresource Technology*, *161*, 29–39.

Ye, J., Mu, Y., Cheng, X., & Sun, D. (2011). Treatment of fresh leachate with high-strength organics and calcium from municipal solid waste incineration plant using UASB reactor. *Bioresource Technology*, *102*(9), 5498–5503. Available from https://doi.org/10.1016/j.biortech.2011.01.001.

Yin, Z., Xie, L., Cui, X., & Zhou, Q. (2017). Effective carbon and nitrogen removal with reduced sulfur oxidation in an anaerobic baffled reactor for fresh leachate treatment. *Journal of Bioscience and Bioengineering*, *123*(1), 84–90. Available from https://doi.org/10.1016/j.jbiosc.2016.07.004.

Zayen, A., Mnif, S., Aloui, F., Fki, F., Loukil, S., Bouaziz, M., & Sayadi, S. (2010). Anaerobic membrane bioreactor for the treatment of leachates from Jebel Chakir discharge in Tunisia. *Journal of Hazardous Materials*, *177*(1–3), 918–923. Available from https://doi.org/10.1016/j.jhazmat.2010.01.004.

Zolfaghari, M., Jardak, K., Drogui, P., Brar, S. K., Buelna, G., & Dubé, R. (2016). Landfill leachate treatment by sequential membrane bioreactor and electro-oxidation processes. *Journal of Environmental Management*, *184*, 318–326. Available from https://doi.org/10.1016/j.jenvman.2016.10.010.

PART 2

Techno-economic assessment of bioreactors

CHAPTER 7

Technoeconomics and lifecycle assessment of bioreactors: wastewater treatment plant management

Tarnima Warda Andalib[1], Zaied Bin Khalid[2] and Puranjan Mishra[2,3]
[1]BRAC Business School, BRAC University, Dhaka, Bangladesh
[2]Faculty of Civil Engineering Technology, Universiti Malaysia Pahang (UMP), Pahang, Malaysia
[3]Institute of Bioresource and Agriculture, Hong Kong Baptist University, Kowloon Tong, Hong Kong

7.1 Introduction

Contemporary capitalism has been increasingly techno-scientifically and thus techno-economic analysis (TEA) is increasingly becoming a decision and norm. The escalated aspiration for techno-economic experts in the field of the decision-making process, for example, the economists having specialization and knowledge base about technological innovation is indeed a social uprising necessity. Besides, as per Harvie (2014) and Fuller (2016), the continuing transformation of social institutions and non-profit organizations like manufacturing Small and Medium enterprises (SMEs) into techno-scientific producers through academic publications showcases the consistent need for techno-economic concepts. Therefore, techno-economic knowledge drives towards the quality of life and has become significantly necessary in today's organizational structures, governance, political solutions, and crises-handling projects (Fuller, 2016; Harvie, 2014; Keen, 2015; Morozov, 2013). Techno-economic assumptions act along with technological frameworks in various sectors like in the pharmaceutical production area, universities, entrepreneurial technological or manufacturing organizations either in large scale or in small scale, high-end multiple production companies, etc. (Andalib, 2018; Fuller, 2016; Harvie, 2014). Furthermore, growing techno-economic optimism besides innovation modeling also inflects famous concepts around the relationship between capitalism and technoscience as well as put great impacts on the industrial relationships and connections between the leaders, managers,

Techno-economics and Life Cycle Assessment of Bioreactors
DOI: https://doi.org/10.1016/B978-0-323-89848-5.00009-3

and employees of these manufacturing companies (Keen, 2015; Morozov, 2013; Andalib & Halim, 2019).

Techno-economic assumptions include the vast span of "adept" and "lay" judgments regarding the value, purpose, and solution mechanism of "technoscience". Therefore, these assumptions frequently remain implicit, however, meaning that they are unaccountable, despite the powerful influence they have on an array of decisions, strategies, policies, media representations, public engagements, professional claims, and so on. Examples of these assumptions are ubiquitous. Standards of living and livelihoods are frequently equated with rising GDP; human behavior and decision-making are frequently related to naturalized notions of competitive individualism; government policies are frequently assessed against conceptions of efficiency based on financial cost—benefit analysis; capital-intensive technologies are frequently normalized as innovation, and, in contrast, their opposites are denigrated as stagnation; technology is frequently promised as the solution to societal challenges, as well as the significant source of financial returns; and successful product development is frequently considered following public acceptance (Birch, 2017; Muniesa, 2014a, 2014b; Roy and King, 2016). For all such issues, the underlying assumptions are normative and constitutive, even if claiming to be merely descriptive.

According to Welsh and Wynne (2013), the continual resistance to economic assumptions and their embedding of a particular attitude to technoscience, namely as an unambiguous driver or source of "national economic progress" (see de Saille, 2015; de Saille and Medvecky, 2016; Hess, 2010). Given that technoscience and economics are immensely entangled as ontological and epistemic objects, as bits of knowledge, and as practices, more research is needed to unpack the economic assumptions underpinning technoscience. The emergence and ascendancy of techno-scientific *capitalism*, as Rajan (2006) and others call it (e.g., Lyotard, 1984), represents a critical moment for science and technology studies (STS) to engage with this task. In light of these concerns, it makes conceptual and normative sense for STS scholars to analyze economic assumptions, and to unpack the economic black boxes that are often left unopened when we dig into the *other* assumptions underlying technoscience (Wynne, 1988).

On the other hand, connections between the bio-molecules and technological integrations have always been an interesting discussion area in the field of Biotechnology. In this chapter, the overall tactics of impactful bioreactors including techno-analysis have been observed to reveal the compliance with the Post-Covid situation. In general, the fermentation procedures that are under the biotechnological arena, produce hugely diversified molecules from biologics, whereas compact grouped-atom curatives are processed to specialty, bulk, commodity chemicals, and even biofuels. Therefore, knowledge regarding reaction kinetics is hugely necessary to comprehend the processes of biological reactors' procedures. Furthermore, knowledge regarding bioprocess engineering is extremely necessary as well, where mass and energy balances, mixing, mass transfer, and heat transfer are observed and scrutinized. Usually, the bioreactor is the core of discrete biochemical procedures where specific items like enzymes, plant cells, microbial or mammalian are brought together and utilized to manufacture different ranges of useful biological products. Therefore, bioreactors' performances depend on several functions like Biomass concentration, Nutrient supply, Sterile conditions, Product removal, Effective agitations, Product inhibition, Heat removal, Aeration, Correct shear conditions, Metabolisms/microbial activities, etc.

In this chapter, this illustration will be revealed through a dissection of economic assumptions to view the percentage of probability of expertise by analyzing their task responsibilities in science, technology, and innovation. Also, TEA at step-by-step stages of conversion can be observed to comprehend the impact on the bioreactors especially while dealing with waste management during Covid. Techno-analysts work to create the balance and sustainability between the techno-environment and economics. Therefore, while dealing with long term agenda they also have to keep the "Green environmental concepts" in their minds for a healthier and safer working place (Abdul-Halim, et al., 2020; Kaman et al., 2016)

7.2 Concepts of techno-economy analyses

Techno-economy is the technique that discusses the technical and economic aspects of the process, product, and service of any company. Callon proposed his idea about the Techno-Economic Network (TEN) in 1991 and 1992 to discrete particular cases as a distinct approach, where organizational provisions and innovations are happening no matter if these applicabilities are becoming failures or successes or radical or incremental ones. Callon also procures composed write-up related to economics related to the motion of *arbitrators* like sociological phenomenons with notions, finances, contracts, etc. to view the entirety of connected and working actors. TENs, therefore, involve the scrutiny and depiction of the active connections and flows of the mandatory intermediaries for the evolvement of an explicit modernization. This TEA will be based on the results of the application of a combination of tools and methods on the provided scenarios. TEN is established by exponents of the actor-network procedure by portraying the type of organizational configuration stemming from conductivities among multifarious heterogeneous actors such as university laboratories, technical research hearts, financial organizations, users, public authorities, etc. Since the early 1980s a variety of disciplinary perspectives, from economics to management and policy studies and sociology, have utilized forms of network analysis to study the formal and informal linkages, alliances, and connections between and within private and public institutions (Coombs and Holladay, 2002; Thompson et al., 1991).

Previously designed network analyzes are pretty different from the concept of Callon's actor-network perspective because Callon's actor-network suggests a combination of agency and structure, where neither exists independently; as a result neither the networks nor the actors can exist independently in addition both have interconnections with other humans and non-humans to define them and elaborate their functions. Here, the word "network" originally means "the work of making a net," and the actor-network perspective places great emphasis on the work of constructing and maintaining the network. Discrete individuals with diverse curiosity are thus all able to perceive their separate focus that leads to achieving a common goal, where the detailed enlistment procedure is named as *intéressement* in actor-network writings. Meanwhile, the concept of *translation* reveals the relationship between two actors or intermediaries representing particular interests, plans, desires, strategies, reflexes, or afterthoughts. Callon's (1998) Banana peeling experiments to produce biogas has experimented in two ways, where firstly biogas production method works, and secondly, the bio-refinery module gets applied. Interestingly, in both of the events, production scales' impact on process economy has been analyzed and feasibility has been found. Therefore, the software Aspen Plus along with kinetic models were applied to establish the mass and energy balances (Callon, 1998). Based on Colombian economic conditions, the operational procedures of economic and environmental analysis got formed.

Outcomes showed that distinct procedures and scales have a tremendous amount of potentiality to produce biogas along with wastewater treatment plants (WWTPs), where plants with higher capacity generate higher economic benefits and plants with lower capabilities do minuscule economic benefit generation. However, this benefit directs to high-energy consumption with a huge impact on the environment, and there come to innovation tactics to convert the negative impact to positive ones (Hull et al., 1999). Hull et al. (1999) mentioned that Techno-economic assessment/ analysis (TEA) is a method-oriented framework to analyze the technical-economical performances of the processes, products, and services. TEA normally combines the three layers, which are process modeling, engineering designs, and economic assessment; as a result, TEA firstly, forecasts the options of innovated technological deployment on any scale based on economic assessment; secondly, integrates process-modeling and engineering design through economic viability; thirdly provides direction to research, development, investment, and policymaking; fourthly, eliminates bottlenecks and optimizes processes (Hull et al., 1999). The tool, Aspen Plus does the integration processes by detailed process modeling and simulation (Table 7.1).

7.3 Methodology of techno-economic analysis

Methodology of TEA is complicated but useful that obtains various objectives, which include a cost estimate, income estimate, risk estimate, depreciation, etc. (Ahuja & Walsh, 1983). As per Ahuja and Walsh (1983), TEA has five methods in the industrial production scenario, which are static cost—benefit assessment, annuity method, net cash flow table, net present value (NPV), and internal rate of return (IRR).

7.3.1 Static cost—benefit assessment

Static cost—benefit assessment is an easy and convenient method to do a comparison of cost and profit in one average year (Pearce, 1994). The weakness of this method is the lack of precision, which ignores the effect of interest rates and inflation rates. The more deviation to the real value is reflected on the conditions of high-interest rates or a huge difference between interest rate and inflation rate (Wills, 1993). Generally, this method is utilized in the preliminary check to explore the feasibility of a project.

7.3.2 Annuity method

Similar to static cost—benefit assessment in principle, the annuity method is another convenient method to simple TEA, whereas Perimenis et al.

Table 7.1 Techno-economic analysis (TEA) steps.

Steps of TEA	Description/points
Process design	(1) Entails ideas, (2) combines collaboration with R&D, finance, engineering teams
Engineering design (mass and energy balance)	(1) Mass balance obtained, (2) energy balance pursued, (3) applied mass yields besides energy consumption, (4) incorporate mass and energy through engineering design and commercial feasibility
Cost estimations and profitability analysis	(1) Scale-up data provides an opportunity to identify commercial-scale equipment through TEA. (2) Aspen Plus and SuperPro both provide options of equipment models closest to the utilized equipment specifications. (3) TEA model provides an estimation of CAPEX, OPEX, and capital and its depreciation. (4) Additional barriers help to refocus in significant segments. (5) Profitability analysis is done through several factors like annual production, unit production cost, revenues, gross margin, profit, return on investment, payback time, and capital investment.
Sensitivity analysis	(1) Sensitivity analyses deal with bottlenecks, identify target yields and production scales. (2) It anticipates restrictions. (3) After the development of the entire process, it assists to select design variables.

Source: Knoope, M. M. J., Ramírez, A., & Faaij, A. P. C. (2013). A state-of-the-art review of techno-economic models predicting the costs of CO_2 pipeline transport. *International Journal of Greenhouse Gas Control, 16*, 241–270. https://doi.org/10.1016/j.ijggc.2013.01.005 (Knoope et al., 2013).

(2004) mentioned that interests added as per the rate to the capital are measured through the calculation of the annuity (Perimenis et al., 2004). The main content of annuity is composed of the capital payback and the interest, which holds a fixed and constant annual payment during the whole project's lifetime. By utilizing a hypothesized interest rate to extend the initial investment pricing about the whole project, the annuity method regards the net benefit of project operation annually as the static method does (Perimenis et al., 2004). At a normal inflation and interest rate, this method easily shows economic results and rapidly compares different projects. The limitation of this method is that it is hard to explore the variations in costs and benefits within a year unit, which is caused by setting the 6 same net benefits every year. Another weakness of this method is it has a blind spot between the investment and early period regular operations.

7.3.3 Net cash flow

A net cash flow table is an efficient method to illustrate the development of profits and the cash flow over the development stage and technical lifetime of a project. The advantages of this method include an expectation of how long it takes a project to get positive cash flow, an indication on questions of financing and presents the overall situation of a project. While disadvantages are also evident, this method can only work efficiently on a project with detailed, available information on all benefits and cost issues. In addition, this method is not sensitive enough for comparative technology assessment and is difficult to investigate the economic viability of a technology application, which requires the calculation of the NPV of the cash flows over the years (West & Riggs, 1986). Compared with profit or loss that only emphasizes income and expenses at a certain point in time, the net cash flow table is more dynamic, where it is vital to consider the movement of liquidity and its timing in and out of a project.

7.3.4 Net present value

The NPV is another method utilized in TEA, which presents an indication of how the project will change in current money value over a certain period. This method is widely used for all engineering projects, especially long project phases, high inflation rates, and non-linear developments in prices (Zimmermann, 2018). The NPV should contain the value of zero; and all investment costs should be exact 7 recoups over the lifetime of a project, such as utilizing the hypothesized discount rate. If the NPV is positive, the investor's property will continuously grow by this value over the whole investment process (Lier & Grünewald, 2011). But for a negative value of NPV, the project is hard to realize without suffering losses, considering the hypothesized discount rate. Similar to the net cash flow table, NPV works efficiently when evaluating very specific projects with all simulation data available, and has a better performance when used to compare different projects.

7.3.5 Internal rate of return

Different from the method above, the IRR is a graphic method to evaluate the economic quality of a project (Magni, 2013). If several potential projects need to be compared to each other at the same time, this method judges independent factors (project size and technology) and indicates the optimal project with the highest profit. The structure of this method utilizes a number of judgments of the efficacy of the project. If the IRR is lower than the rate of bank cash deposits, it is dangerous to open investment on a project where the capital is unsafe and the payback is doubtful to recoup the rate of return. After considering the degrees of risk associated with the investment, investors can conveniently explore an attractive project, where the IRR is higher than other options.

7.4 Techno-economic analysis models

TEA integrates certain units like Feedstock handling, Biomass Deconstruction, Fermentation, Product Recovery, Wastewater treatment and settles the model with produced and recognizes the most expensive processes and material handling steps. Furthermore, also finds the geographical location-oriented restrictions that can sway the economic analysis. The Conceptually developed TEA models can compare and benchmark the end-to-end technology pathways through economic assessment Table 7.2.

7.5 Techno-economic paradigm

The techno-economic paradigm (TEP) is at the core of the innovation-based theory of economic growth and social development conceived by Chris Freeman and Carlota Perez. It claims that technology plays the most important role in economic development and focuses on the economic process of technological change. Its basic idea is that technology and economy co-evolve. Perez in 1983 and Freeman in 1987 discussed the notion regarding TEP that deals with sustainable long-term standard technologies, which works with the economic fluctuations in the long run as well as technical change. During the course of these long-term fluctuations, periods of match and mismatch occur between major innovative generic technologies and the organizational alignments; sometimes, boom periods occur when there is mutual reinforcement between the

Table 7.2 Techno-economic assessment-models as per literature.

Model type	Objective	Onshore/offshore	Terrain factor	Corridor factor	Cost issues	Ref.
Linear	To construct a large-scale CO_2/waste water infrastructure by 2050	Onshore and offshore	Yes	Yes	Material, construction, insurance, licenses, engineering	van den Broek et al. (2010)
Linear	To assess CO_2 economics regarding transport and storage	Different equations for onshore, offshore	No	No	Material, labor, Right-of-way (ROW), miscellaneous	Heddle et al. (2003)
Linear	To optimize worldwide source and sink connections for 2030 and 2050	Onshore and offshore	Yes	No	Material, labor, ROW, contingencies, and owners cost	
Weight-based model	To estimate the cost for different modes of CO_2 transport (ships, pipeline, and train) for a given case study	Only onshore	No	No	Material, labor, ROW, miscellaneous	Gao et al. (2011)
Weight-based model	To build a projection tool for Carbon Capture and Sequestration (CCS) in Belgium till 2050	Only onshore	Yes	No	Material, labor, ROW, miscellaneous	Piessens et al. (2008)
Quadratic	To do an initial assessment about the costs of CO_2 transport.	Different equations for onshore, offshore	Yes	No	Material, equipment, and installation costs	IEA GHG (2002)
Quadratic	To estimate H_2 costs	Only onshore	No	No	Material, labor, ROW, miscellaneous	Parker (2004)
Engineering-Economic model	To estimate CO_2 pipeline costs over a range of distances for different regions	Only onshore	No	No	Material, labor, ROW, miscellaneous	McCoy and Rubin (2008)

(Continued)

Table 7.2 (Continued)

Model type	Objective	Onshore/offshore	Terrain factor	Corridor factor	Cost issues	Ref.
Flow-based	To construct cost curves for CO_2 transport and storage in the US	Only onshore	Avg.	No	Material, labor, ROW, miscellaneous	Dahowski et al. (2004)
Flow-based	To construct cost curves for CO_2 transport and storage in China	Only onshore			Material, labor, ROW, miscellaneous	Dahowski et al. (2009)
Flow-based	To minimize costs of H_2 with CCS delivered to fuel station.	Only onshore	No	No	Material and labor of pipeline and compressor (initial + intermediate)	Ogden et al. (2004)
Flow-based	To estimate the average, maximum and minimum costs of a CO_2 pipeline	Only onshore	No	No	Not specified	McCollum and Ogden (2006)
Flow-based	To analyze the economies of scale which can be realized by building a CO_2 trunkline	Only onshore	No	No	Material, labor, ROW, miscellaneous, pumping costs during and at the end of the transport	Chandel et al. (2010)
Flow-based	To develop an accurate cost equation for CO_2 pipelines, which can be used in a linear optimization prog	Onshore and offshore	Yes	No	Material, equipment, installation	Chandel et al. (2010)

technological and institutional changes, and stability occurs in social, economic, institutional and technological settings, where these changes labeled "Techno-Economic Paradigms." (Freeman, 1991). Freeman (1991) mentioned that TEN focuses more on the emergence and continuous innovation with economic analysis, whereas TEP focuses more on stabilized perspectives. Aydin and Takay (2012) discussed that even though the TEN and TEP approaches are different, both have sociological validity and policy relevance, both suggest the adoption of a particular style of the analytic framework which is neither micro nor case-study based nor macro and policy-oriented. Nevertheless, there is a meso-level techno-economic method that might be suitable for both TEN and TEP if there is a situation of reconciliation. The validity of sociological macro analyses or policy-relevant microanalyses is focused.

7.6 Techno-economic innovations

For the last two decades not just computers but various converged communication technologies are widely innovated, recognized, and even appreciated in regular life, let it be at home or the officer. Freeman in 1994 and 1996 observed a series of patterns regarding the macro analytical situation regarding Information and Communication Technologies, over a long time-scale at various parts of the world and also comprehended that several indicators like patents, productivity, and numbers of microprocessors play a significant role. He also suggested the matched policies with the innovative technologies in the social and economic context, such as education and training, the regulation of telecoms, and finally firm strategies. As per Andalib et al. (2020), the innovative entrepreneurial activities in manufacturing large companies and SMEs are key issues to change.

On the other hand, Orlikowski et al. (1996) and Bloomfield et al. (2010) have revealed the complex scenario of detailed case studies while developing and implementing specific ICTs in the bottom-up or microanalyses context. For instance, a set of flexible and locally established arrangements, formal plans, and policies were not intended but the result of analysis (ŽSuchman, 1987). ŽSuchman (1987) also observed that the arrangements and outcomes are more dependent on the specific actors involved in each case and how those actors interact with each other. As per Halim et al. (2020), the external environment affects the emerging economic analysis as well as technological innovations. Therefore, it has been revealed that micro analyses lead to useful corrective to the top-down analyses, which make broad assumptions regarding the policies' applications. Nevertheless, microanalyses do not provide a smooth comparison mechanism between particular cases, rather these analyses have limitations in ICTs technologies from environmental, social as well as economic aspects.

Nevertheless, scientific activities, entrepreneurial bricolage, and technological innovations are driven by environmental factors to develop sustainable and meaningful inventions as well as to protect the outside environment. Other than ICTs, manufacturing firms have few generic sets of technologies, but it seems that development has increased. For instance, the explicit creation of a new market mechanism for carbon dioxide emission control and monitoring technologies, with the Kyoto Agreement has allowed the market transactions of carbon dioxide emission. This inevitably shows new technologies based on TEA monitor and controls the carbon-dioxide emission in the socio-economic context. As per DeLaat (1996), intense negotiations occurs between the parameter and boundaries regarding risk assessment, where the macro view of the necessary intertwining between technological, economic, and social factors is again in contrast to microanalyses. Furthermore, a distinct form of looking ahead and foresight is in the future negotiation planning and scripts (DeLaat, 1996), where government-sponsored R&D programs are designed beside the engineering deployment for the environment. Therefore, cost analysis and negotiations provide outcomes regarding formulated plans, policies, and statements that are to be implemented.

7.7 Environmental impact assessment

Environmental impact assessment (EIA) is an activity designed to assess and forecast the impact of an industrial project on the environment and human health. It is recommended that decision-makers make appropriate measures and operational procedures to minimize the impact (Hung et al., 2012). Hung et al. (2012) also mentioned that EIA is quite similar to TEA but related to multidisciplinary fields and background that engages researchers to utilize synthesis applications to receive results of complicated assessments. As per Morgan (1998), EIA has been mentioned in the USA in 1970, where about fifty years it has been developed to various phases in the developed countries and some developing countries as well. Holder (2004) discussed that EIA usually monitors, identifies, and measures the probabilities of negative impacts on the environment from the proposed project based on various public and detailed research studies. Moreover, EIA also designs simulation mechanisms to identify as well as to reduce potential risks, uncertainty, and any negative impacts of the proposed project by minimizing the environmental degradation level (Holder, 2004). Therefore, EIA has three basic steps, which are identification, prediction, and evaluation those are related to biological, physio-chemical, ecological, social, health, economic, and other correlative subjects (Glasson et al., 2013). As per Glasson et al. (2013), at first, the identification step provides detailed descriptions of the project's components and the environmental system. Secondly, the prediction step works on the changes, both regarding quality and quantity, and forecasts with estimated impacts on a time scale. Thirdly, the evaluation step significantly affected factors due to uncertainty, and risks are finalized. Successful EIA occurs when the depth of analysis and alternative comparisons are counted for the sake of users and the public. EIA concentrates more on the process itself and becomes less time-consuming than complicated life cycle assessment (LCA).

7.8 Environmental impact assessment methodology

There are near about fourteen EIA methods to measure the industrial production's efficiency and impact and these are the ad hoc method, checklists method, matrices method, networks method, overlays method, environmental index using factor analysis, benefits analysis, and predictive simulation methods (Canter et al., 1997; Fischer & Bührer, 2013; Bell & Johnson, 1975; Lohani et al., 1997; Wathern, 2013; Westman, 1990). Among these, the most prominent applied ones are the ad-hoc method, the checklist method, and the overlay method.

The ad hoc method focuses on each environmental aspect separately depending on the subjective and broad impacts with composite characteristics. Whenever there are time constraints and a lack of expertise regarding the resources, this becomes a useful method, but it is quite weak while handling a comprehensive set of all relevant environmental factors and lacks consistency in analysis, which requires a continuing effort to modify and collect an appropriate panel for each assessment (Bell & Johnson, 1975). The checklists' method is strong on impact identification, which is a very significant fundamental function of EIA. This method ranges from listing environmental aspects according to their importance weighting of various factors that smoothens the site prioritizing and selecting process; nevertheless, it is quite weak while distinguishing between the direct and the indirect impacts as well as difficult to find the connectivity between the action and the impact (Fischer & Bührer, 2013). The overlay method involves a set of transparent maps with various environmental characteristics, which include biological, ecological, social, health, economic and other relevant aspects. These maps are overlaid to produce a composite so critical environmental features are reflected at the same scale and also easier to perceive, prioritize settings of the site selection (15 composite mapping done on sensitive and ecological areas) but quite difficult to comprehend the impact duration and probability due to a limited number of overlaid transparencies (Lohani et al., 1997). Excluding the three methods listed above, there are still other methods commonly used in EIA, including the matrice's method, networks method, and benefits analysis. In a complicated EIA project, different assessment stages require various methods and techniques to be utilized cooperatively so final assessments are accurate and convincing.

7.9 Bioreactors, categorization, and sustainable factors

The bioreactor is elucidated as a hollow container carrying out any biological reaction that also cultures aerobic cells to perform cellular or enzymatic immobilization. A bioreactor provides a controllable environment enabling the biological, biochemical, and biomechanical demands to construct the engineered products (Abdul Syukor et al., 2021; Islam et al., 2019, 2020). As the bioreactor aims to create a desired biological product, it is mandatory to monitor the reaction variables as fluid velocity, absorption of heat, internal and external mass transfer, pressure, etc. Researchers have inscribed these reaction variables' impacts on biological cultures as well as analyzed the disparate parameters such as oxygen, carbon dioxide, nutrient, and metabolism waste material transports. A sophisticated and secure bioreactor plan with unique performance characteristics is essential to assemble useful biotechnological products both generate naturally or produced from genetically modified cell systems. Understanding the mass transfer behavior in bioreactors would result in improved reactor designs, reactor functioning, and modeling tools, which are important for maximizing reaction rates, optimizing throughput rates, and minimizing cost. The paper discusses the bioreactor design and various types of bioreactors, which are useful and sustainable for industrial operations, especially for WWTPs.

7.10 Types of bioreactor

There are mainly three types of reactions involved in the fermentation process, that is, batch, continuous, and semi-constant or fed-batch conditionally based on the sustainable culture scheme and the methods applied into the bioreactor (McNeil & Harvey, 2008). Traditional batch stirred tank reactors (STRs) and continuously STRs (CSTRs) have been applied in the industry for the last many decades as well as have been adopted widely in the recent chemical and bioprocessing industry due to their simple usage formula (McNeil & Harvey, 2008). Other bioreactors, which have special design and operational attributes are photo-bioreactors, rotary drum reactors, mist bioreactor, membrane bioreactor, packed bioreactors, bubble column & airlift bioreactors, etc. These have been developed to cater to application-specific processes. Batch Process: in the batch process, after sterilization, the sterile culture medium is inoculated with microorganisms. During this reaction period, cells, substrates including the nutrient salts, vitamins, and concentrations of the products vary with time. The fermentation is allowed to run for a predetermined time and the product is harvested at the end (Smith & Carberry, 1976). To promote aerobic cultivation, the medium is aerated to provide a continuous flow of oxygen. Gaseous by-products such as CO_2 are removed; aeration and gas removal processes take place semi-continuously (Williams, 2002). Lag-phase: growth of microbial population when it is inoculated The with a fresh medium starts after a certain period of time called lag phase. Vapors and gases also discharge through connections in the top. Usually, liquids are removed from the bottom. STRs are generally jacketed for steam heating or cooling requirements and are equipped with baffles and round spargers for aeration. The impeller in STRs is connected to an external motor, which drives the stirrer system. The agitator assembly, including the seal, is a route of contamination and hence the shaft has to pass into the bioreactor through a set of aseptic seals (Abbott et al., 2013). The impellers contribute to the mixing and dissolution of the essential atmospheric oxygen into the aqueous phase and maximize the interfacial space by separating the gaseous and aqueous phases (Garcia-Ochoa & Gomez, 2009; Martin et al., 2008). The design of the impeller blades, speed of agitation, and the depth of liquid determine the effectiveness of agitation. The important variables, which affect mixing and mass transfer rates are the number and types of the stirrer, speed of stirrer, and the flow rate of gas used.

7.10.1 Osmotic membrane bioreactors

The osmotic membrane bioreactor (OMBR) is a novel process that produces more bioenergy, eliminates pollutants, and has a low fouling trend. The principal disadvantage of this procedure is the salinity build-up. The process of producing bioenergy and treating contaminants can be improved by recognizing the microbial community. Overall, the OMBR procedure has a lot of prospects for producing bioenergy while also treating wastewater (Hosseinzadeh et al., 2021). The driving force for purified water from a low salinity feed solution into the draw solution (DS) through a forwarding osmosis (FO) semipermeable membrane in the OMBR procedure is the difference in osmotic pressures between two sides of the membrane. Following that, other desalination procedures such as distillation and reverse osmosis (RO) may be used to regenerate clean water from DS for various applications such as irrigation and fertilizer production (Alturki et al., 2012; Cai & Hu, 2016; Hosseinzadeh et al., 2020). For this process, two separate modes, FO and pressure retarded osmosis (PRO), are proposed for membrane orientation. When DS is applied to the selective thin and support layers, the procedure is referred to as FO and PRO, respectively (Ge et al., 2013). OMBRs have a number of advantages over traditional MBRs, including low energy consumption, low fouling proclivity, and superior performance in the removal of contaminants, particularly emerging contaminants such as endocrine-disrupting chemicals, steroid hormones, pesticides, and pharmaceutically active compounds, which are currently of the greatest concern (Luo et al., 2018).

7.10.2 Integrated two-phase fixed-film baffled bioreactor

Biofilm-based reactors, which are called attached growth processes, are promising alternatives for avoiding the aforementioned drawbacks and improving the performance of both anaerobic and aerobic bioreactors. The use of immobilized cells on the media (carrier) has a number of benefits over suspended growth, including the ability to overcome the limits described earlier (Ahmadi et al., 2020; Mishra et al., 2020). Other benefits of these biofilm cells include increased operational stability, greater resistance to environmental shocks such as toxic compounds, pH, and temperature, higher substrate utilization rate, high biomass concentration even under brief hydraulic retention times (HRTs), and no need for active biomass recycling (Ahmadi et al., 2017; Yousefzadeh et al., 2017). Baffles in the design of bioreactors may also provide advantages such as phase separation (such as the separation of acidogenic and methanogen biomass) (Yu et al., 2014), simple design (Sarathai et al., 2010), reducing biomass washout and dead space, easy bioreactor recovery from hydraulic and organic shocks, and eliminating the need for gas and sludge separation equipment (Mara & Horan, 2003). Despite the benefits of baffles and attached growth carriers listed above, according to the literature review, no research has been done from the perspective of designing an anaerobic-aerobic bioreactor that incorporates the benefits of baffles and carriers for a series of both phases. As a result, the current research looked into the performance of an integrated two-phase fixed-film baffled bioreactor as a novel wastewater treatment procedure. However, traditional analysis of biochemical oxygen demand (BOD5) and COD tests, which require continuous and time-consuming sampling and analyzing, or investigations of microbial structures, such as polymerase chain reaction (PCR) methods, cannot provide a complete picture of microbial activity and environmental conditions in bioreactors (Sepehri et al., 2020). Meanwhile, mathematical modeling and kinetic studies, which are promising tools for suggesting microbial activity and can be easily used by a wide range of engineers and policymakers, are critical in the design, prediction, and assessment of bioreactors. However, there is little or no information about the kinetic and mathematical modeling of integrated two-phase bioreactors, and most previous research has focused on single-phase bioreactor modeling and kinetics (AlSayed et al., 2018).

7.10.3 High-solid anaerobic membrane bioreactor

The best solution is an anaerobic membrane bioreactor (AnMBR), which can sustain solids such as slow-growing microbes and undigested substrates (Karim et al., 2021; Mishra et al., 2019a, 2019b). Organic waste can be degraded more quickly and carefully in this manner, resulting in increased biogas production and improved effluent quality (Abdelrahman, 2020; Cheng et al., 2018). Furthermore, in the AnMBR, sludge retention time (SRT) and HRT can be decoupled, which is not possible in traditional digesters. Not only does a proper prolonged SRT promote the growth of anaerobic microbes, but it also promotes the growth of aerobic microbes (Wang et al., 2020), however, since the total solids are concentrated, the footprint is considerably reduced. Membrane fouling and flux decline, however, remain significant barriers to the widespread use of AnMBRs, particularly in the treatment of OFMSW with a high solid content (Cheng et al., 2020). Various techniques have been used to reduce membrane fouling. Biogas sparging is the most widely used of these methods. Biogas sparging, on the other hand, can dramatically increase the energy consumption of the treatment process. In pilot-scale AnMBRs for sewage treatment, fouling control with different biogas sparging rates was responsible for 77%–80% of the total energy demand (heating is not included; Shin & Bae, 2018). Energy return on investment (EROI) analysis is a useful method for reviewing the drawbacks and benefits of various fuels, as well as the ability to look into the future in ways that markets do not appear to be capable of (Hall et al., 2009).

7.10.4 Solar assisted bioreactor

Solar energy is used to power anaerobic reactors, which are less expensive. The bioreactor's anaerobic solar heating system is linked to a higher bioenergy yield. Rather than using electric or diesel heating systems for bioreactors, solar-powered reactors generate more bioenergy, lowering the cost of bioenergy generation in the future (Zaied et al., 2020). A solar thermal energy accumulator, a temperature controller, a reactor, and a delivered biogas collector make up the solar-assisted bioreactor (SABr) (Ahmad et al., 2003). Solar radioactivity collected by solar panels is converted to electricity, which provides the necessary temperature for biological waste degradation while still maintaining the reactor's temperature balance (Zaied et al., 2020b). The main reactor then emits biogas and methane at the optimum reaction temperature, maximizing net energy efficiency (Siedlecka & Stepnowski, 2005). According to prior research, mesophilic (308K) and thermophilic (328K) temperatures are the stable operating temperatures for the ACOD method of bioenergy production. The bioreactor heating system can easily be powered by a solar energy storage system, and it produces bioenergy all year (Zaied et al., 2020a).

7.10.5 Anaerobic landfill bioreactors

Due to the slow degradation caused by MSW heterogeneity, sole disposal of MSW in landfill bioreactors yields limited energy recovery (Chakma and Mathur, 2013; Rana et al., 2020). Colandfilling of organic sludge with MSW in landfill bioreactors, on the other hand, maybe an intriguing alternative for enhancing mixed waste bio-efficiency by increasing energy yield from co-waste mass while also improving leachate quality (Ağdağ & Sponza, 2007). Furthermore, landfilling industrial organic waste could be a cost–effective alternative to more expensive bioconversion processes. It is widely recognized that pursuing anaerobic digestion (AD) of such concentrated waste is advantageous for its efficient treatment and removal of organic pollutants (Li et al., 2020). There are some other benefits to disposing of two or more substrates together: (1) improved digestion rate and hygienic stabilization (Salehiyoun et al., 2020), (2) dilution of toxic complexes (Latifi et al., 2019), (3) Synergistic action of microorganisms degrades increased organic loading (Mu et al., 2020) and a higher biomethane yield with a shorter digestion time These considerations support the use of co-disposal in landfilling scenarios.

Over the years, research on MSW treatment and disposal in bioreactor landfills has predominantly focused on single-stream MSW disposal. There have been several studies that have attempted to enhance MSW biostabilization (Bartholameuz et al., 2016), leachate and landfill gas monitoring (Cossu et al., 2016), settlement behavior of degrading waste (Chakma & Mathur, 2013), ammonia management (Sri Shalini & Joseph, 2018) in bioreactor landfills are available. Nonetheless, the lack of literature on the co-disposal of industrial waste with MSW limits our understanding of waste co-treatment in anaerobic landfilling (Ağdağ & Sponza, 2005) looked at dumping mixed industrial waste alongside MSW in an anaerobic landfill bioreactor. However, no research on leachate and biomethane tracking of co-disposed industrial organic waste and MSW in simulated anaerobic landfill bioreactors is currently available.

7.10.6 Microbial fuel cells

The microbial fuel cell (MFC) is a bio-electrochemical technology that generates electricity from organic materials using anaerobic bacteria (e.g., carbohydrate, protein, and glycerol). Through the degradation of organic compounds, anaerobic bacteria growing on anode surfaces emit electrons and protons (Abdul Syukor et al., 2021; Islam et al., 2019, 2020). The electrons make their way to the cathode surface through the external circuit, where they interact with oxygen and protons to form water. To minimize internal resistance and increase power densities, different MFC configurations such as single-chamber MFC (SCMFC) have been designed (Liu & Logan, 2004; Tartakovsky et al., 2008). However, simple organic compounds (e.g., volatile fatty acids, alcohols, and acetate) have been used in MFC experiments to generate electricity (Chen & Yang, 2003; Liu & Logan, 2004; Niessen et al., 2004; Sharma & Li, 2010). MFC uses bacteria and a high-energy oxidant such as O2 to generate an electric current (Schmidt-Rohr, 2020), replicating natural bacterial interactions MFCs can be classified into two types: mediated and unmediated. The first MFCs, which were demonstrated in the early twentieth century, used a mediator, which is a chemical that transfers electrons from the cell's bacteria to the anode. Unmediated MFCs first appeared in the 1970s; in this type of MFC, bacteria have electrochemically active redox proteins on their outer membranes, such as cytochromes, which can transfer electrons directly to the anode (Badwal et al., 2014; Min et al., 2005). MFCs have begun to be used commercially in wastewater treatment in the twenty-first century.

7.11 Technological impact assessment of bioreactors on WWTP

According to Puyol et al. (2017), during the waster water pollutants removal and cleansing phase physical, chemical, and/or biological processes are applied in various treatment technological levels known as preliminary, primary, secondary (with or without nutrient removal), and tertiary treatment. There are various treatment plans based on differences in secondary treatment types. These treatment plans are termed activated sludge (AS), aerated lagoon (AL), trickling filter (TF), and rotating biological contactor or bio disk (BD). Each of the technologies that are discussed here is briefly described below; including

In general, the preliminary treatment technique removes gross solids and grit from the wastewater that sometimes may damage equipment, whereas in primary treatment, a physical operation, sedimentation technique gets applied that removes the floating and settleable materials found in wastewater; nevertheless, in secondary treatment, biological processes remove organic matter and nutrients and in conventional secondary treatments, only nutrients associated with the growth of micro-organisms responsible for the degradation of organic matter are removed. In comparison, in secondary treatments that involve nutrient removal, the operating conditions of reactors are modified to include the removal of nitrogen and/or phosphorus. In tertiary treatment, high-quality effluent is obtained by removing pathogens and substances that were not previously eliminated. The applied technologies that are discussed here, are briefly described below; including

WWTPs based on the conventional AS (CAS) process have been imprudent to meet the environmental and economic necessities of the circular biobased economy since they are designed to remove resources rather than recover them (Guest et al., 2009). According to Puyol et al. (2017), WWTPs technologies and processes have been configured with the risen issues where resources harvesting and transition supports can be provided towards wastewater resource recovery facilities (WRRF) as well, therefore the societal, economical, legal, and ethical modifications are evident both in a short-term and long-term manner.

7.12 Economical impact assessment of bioreactors on WWTP

The economic impact is significant and feasible since the combination of FO, RO and anaerobic membrane bioreactor (AnMBR) technologies for municipal wastewater treatment with energy and water production is greatly possible. FO was used to pre-concentrate the AnMBR influent, RO for DS regeneration and water production, and AnMBR for wastewater treatment and energy production. The minimum wastewater treatment cost was estimated at 0.81 €/m^3, achieved when limiting the FO recovery to 50% in a closed-loop scheme. However, the cost increased to 1.01 and 1.27 €/m^3 for FO recoveries of 80% and 90%, respectively. The freshwater production cost was estimated at 0.80 and 1.16 €/m^3 for an open-loop scheme maximizing water production and a closed-loop scheme, respectively. The low FO membrane fluxes were identified as a limiting factor and a sensitivity analysis revealed that FO membrane fluxes of 10 LMH would significantly improve the competitiveness of FO-RO + AnMBR technology. To comprehend the best practice and alternate treatment plan for recovering energy & cleansing waste-water TEA done through computer simulation tool from an environmental perspective has been scrutinized. Therefore, the economic impact generated due to bioreactors processing different types of organic wastes is scrutinized.

7.13 Challenges in dealing with waste water treatment plant

Wastewater treatment technologies could be categorized into three major groups: physical, chemical, or biological operations; examples of unit operations from each category are illustrated in Fig. 7.1. A typical WWTP

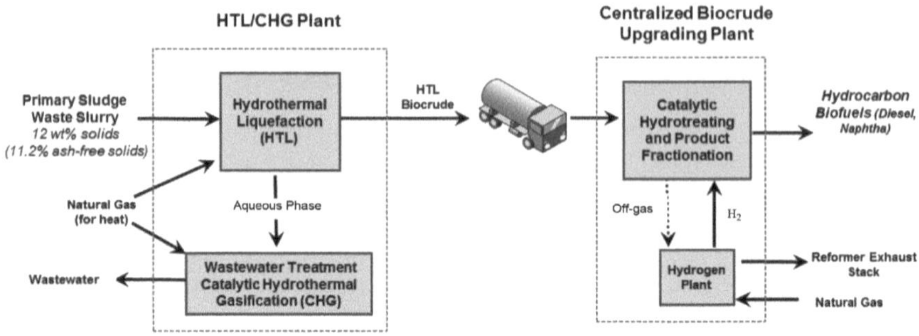

Figure 7.1 A simplified block diagram of the overall HTL and crude upgrading process configuration is shown in Fig. 7.1. The HTL facility is co-located with the WWTP and produces crude and an aqueous stream containing about 1.25% carbon. CHG is used to treat the aqueous phase and recover energy from this stream before discharge. *CHG*, Catalytic hydrothermal gasification; *HTL*, hydrothermal liquefaction; *WWTP*, wastewater treatment plant. *Reproduced with permission from: Snowden-Swan, L., Zhu, Y., Jones, S., Elliott, D., Schmidt, A., Hallen, R., Billing, J., Hart, T., Fox, S., & Maupin, G. (2016). Pacific Northwest National Laboratory (1st (ed.), Vol. 25464). https://doi.org/pnnl.gov/main/publications/external/technical_reports/PNNL-25464.pdf.*

consists of a combination of physical, chemical, and biological unit operations for removing pollutants. Physical operation units mean physically removing the pollutants from wastewater without causing any change in the chemical or biological characteristics of the treated water (Moussa et al., 2017). Moussa and colleagues also mentioned that chemical operation units are referred to as additive processes since additional chemicals are applied to react and remove the contaminants. Biological operation units utilize microorganisms for the biodegradation of contaminants in wastewater, as a result the organic content and nutrients in the wastewater are reduced; meanwhile, biological units are generally classified into aerobic, anaerobic, or facultative depending on the availability of dissolved oxygen in wastewater (Asia, 2003).

The WWTP's primary and secondary treatment processes generate sludge (wet solids) as a surplus. EPA (2016) agreed and mentioned that also Clean Watershed Needs Survey (CWNS) revealed that approximately 84% of municipal WWTP facilities include both primary and secondary treatment levels. WWTP's mostly applied treatment levels are sludge management including stabilization/treatment with AD, landfill disposal, and incineration. The AD process produces biogas, which is used for onsite heat, and bio-solids, which can be used as fertilizer on agricultural land. As per SCAP, 2013, even though the utilization of biosolids might be good for some crops but if it gets into the waste stream, public health issues become risky. Nevertheless, sludge management is expensive whereas landfilling has no added benefit. Production of fuel via hydrothermal liquefaction (HTL) could provide an economically favorable alternative to AD and other existing sludge management practices. Preliminary techno-economic analyses and assumptions are observed here to comprehend the challenges of WWTP alternatives. These alternative options are process and assumption overview, feedstock and plant scale, HTL, HTL aqueous phase treatment by catalytic HTL/gasification (CHG), and sludge HTL oil upgrading, which also has uncertainties and constraints (Zhu, 2016).

7.13.1 Upgraded biocrude-HTL configuration process and theory

Natural gas is used at the HTL plant and upgrading facilities for process heat and hydrogen, respectively, where crude is transported and used (Sheppard, 2011). According to Jones et al. (2014), the design and cost of the different practices regarding the WWTP (wastewater treatment plan) along with MSWTP (municipal solid waste treatment plan) vary based on HTLbio-crude up-gradation processes. All capital equipment costs for the HTL plant and the upgrading facility are scaled on values used in the algae HTL design case (Jones et al., 2014). The HTL and CHG equipment costs are scaled on costs originally obtained for a much larger plant scale of 2,200 dry tons/day (Knorr, 2013). Future work will include revisiting these estimates and updating with costs more appropriate at this comparatively small scale Fig. 7.1.

7.14 Feedstock and plant scale

The experimental testing of HTL on municipal WWTP sludge waste, CHG of the HTL aqueous phase, and upgrading of the HTL bio-crude produces primary and secondary sludge solids that are then processed in thermophilic anaerobic digesters, resulting in Class A biosolids designated to sewage solids as per US EPA guidelines for land application with no restrictions (EPA, 2015b). Experimental testing of HTL and bio-crude upgrading included primary sludge, secondary sludge, and biosolids resulting from tertiary treatment where thermophilic AD bioreactor is applied. The HTL plant processes 100 dry tons/day (92.4 ton/day dry, ash-free basis) of sludge in a slurry (water + solids) containing 12% total solids (11.2% ash-free solids). As per WWTP Shammas and Wang (2008), WWTP produces 100 dry tons/day of primary and secondary sludge mixture would treat roughly 133 million gal/day of wastewater and would serve an approximate population of 1.7 million, where WWTPs pay to dispose of sludge (EPA, 2015a) and bio-crude product is transported to a centralized upgrading plant from HTL plant (Sheppard, 2011). Sensitivity analysis is conducted to investigate the effect of both scale and sludge credit on the minimum fuel selling price of bio-crude and final fuel (Fig. 7.2).

The upgrading plant receives bio-crude from 10 HTL plants and produces 2020 BPSD of final fuel. The chosen plant scales are based upon initial estimates of sludge generation from EPA CWNS data (EPAm 2015a) and a rough estimate of what the potential sludge availability might be within a 100-mi radius. In addition, we received valuable feedback from the wastewater treatment industry as part of the WERF collaboration that helped form the basis for the selected plant scales, as well as the assumed feedstock credit (current sludge disposal cost). For comparison, the upgrading plant scale is about 40% of other BETO design cases of ~5000 BPSD (Jones et al., 2013, 2014) and only 4% of the average

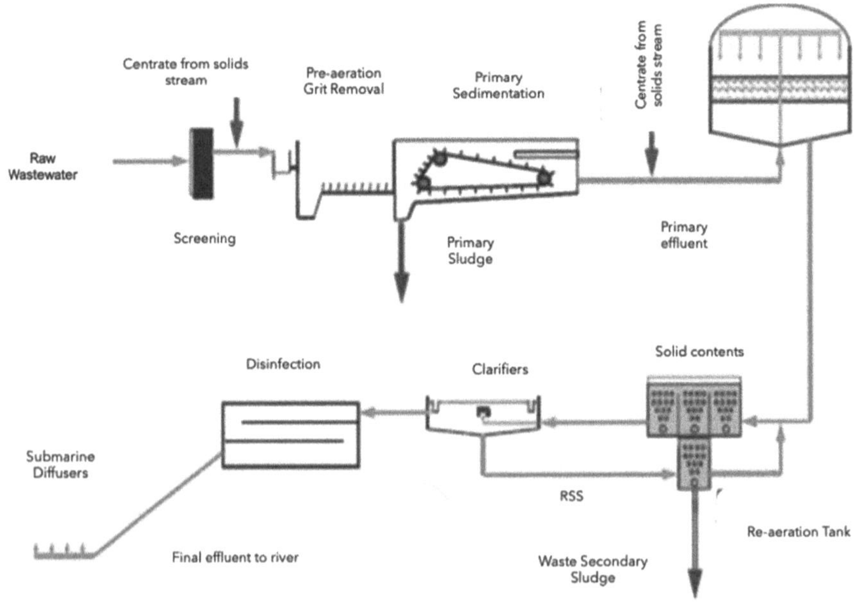

Figure 7.2 Simplified flow diagram of Annacis Island WWTP (Metro Vancouver 2015) showing primary and secondary sludge generation that is then treated with thermophilic anaerobic digestion. *WWTP*, Wastewater treatment plant. *(Reproduced with permission from Snowden-Swan et al., 2016a, 2016b).*

scale for gasoline and diesel production at US refineries of about 50,000 BPSD (EIA, 2015).

7.15 Hydrothermal liquefaction

As described previously for the algae HTL process (Jones et al., 2014), the slurry feed (sludge + water) is pumped and preheated to the reactor conditions of 2926 psi and 622°F (339°C).

The bioreactor effluent is composed of an organic bio-crude phase, a separate aqueous phase, and small amounts of solids and gases. Solids are filtered and the bio-crude, aqueous, and gas phases are cooled and then separated, where bio-crude is then shipped to the upgrading facility, while the aqueous phase is treated by CHG and the off-gas used for process heat additionally, excess natural gas is required to provide enough heat for the HTL and CHG processes. The remaining heat is used to produce steam for a steam driver, where it is assumed that the solids are disposed of in a landfill, however, it may be possible to sell them for beneficial reuse (e.g., fertilizer).

7.16 Hydrothermal liquefaction aqueous phase treatment by catalytic hydrothermal liquefaction/gasification

HTL aqueous phase is treated by CHG (catalytic HTL) to recover energy from the dissolved organics and to reduce the chemical oxygen demand (COD) of the water for subsequent disposal and reuse. The COD in the water is 99.9% converted in the CHG process and the produced gas is used for heat in the HTL and CHG areas. CHG water returns to the headwaters of the WWTP (Fig. 7.3).

7.17 Sludge hydrothermal liquefaction oil upgrading

The HTL bio-crude is transported from the WWTP to a centralized upgrading facility that gets supplied to the plant at 26 psi and 110°F. Afterward, pumped to 1540 psi, mixed with compressed hydrogen, and preheated to the hydrotreater reactor temperature of 752°F (400°C). Hydrogen is produced on-site via steam reforming of the upgrading offgas and purchased natural gas. During the hydrotreating process, bio-crude oxygen is converted to CO_2 and water, nitrogen is converted to ammonia, and sulfur is converted to hydrogen sulfide. The bioreactor effluent is

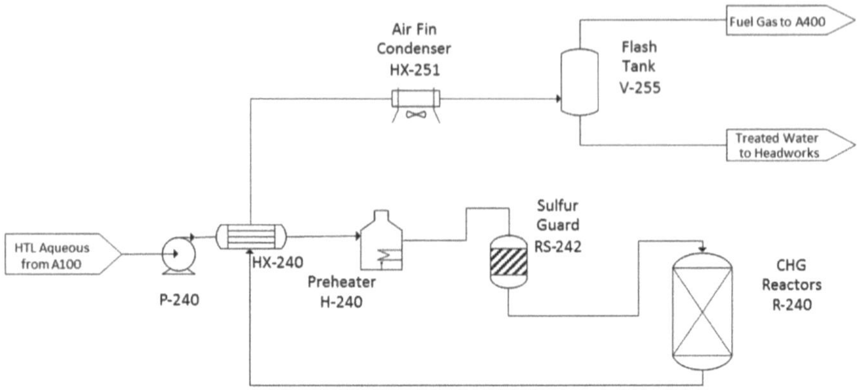

Figure 7.3 CHG process diagram. *CHG,* Catalytic hydrothermal gasification. *Reproduced with permission from Snowden-Swan, L., Zhu, Y., Jones, S., Elliott, D., Schmidt, A., Hallen, R., Billing, J., Hart, T., Fox, S., & Maupin, G. (2016a). Pacific Northwest National Laboratory (1st (ed.), Vol. 25464). https://doi.org/pnnl.gov/main/publications/external/technical_reports/PNNL-25464.pdf; Snowden-Swan, L. J., Zhu, Y., Jones, S. B., Elliott, D. C., Schmidt, A., Hallen, R. T., Billing, Hart, T. R., Fox, S. P., & Maupin, G. (2016b).* Hydrothermal liquefaction and upgrading of municipal wastewater treatment plant sludge: A preliminary techno-economic analysis *(Snowden-Swan et al., 2016a, 2016b).*

cooled to condense the produced water and hydrocarbons, the latter of which is then fractionated into lights, naphtha, diesel, and heavy oil Fig. 7.4.

7.18 Conclusion

Researchers have applied the content analysis and systematic review process in this chapter to comprehend the Techno-economics and LCA of Bioreactors regarding the Waste Water Treatment Plant. The TEM and TEP dimensions are discussed thoroughly along with the bioreactors categorization and its effects on the WWTP situation. Scholars from different countries have analyzed previously and found various impact records in the Pre-Covid era. The findings are discussed in the following table.

Researchers have discussed the concepts of techno analysis concepts (TEN, TEP, TEI), Methodology of TEA, EIA, Methodology of EIA, Bioreactor, its categorization, impact assessment, and sustainability on WWTP has been observed and discussed. The purpose of the paper was to do a content analysis of the scholarly literature to find the logical

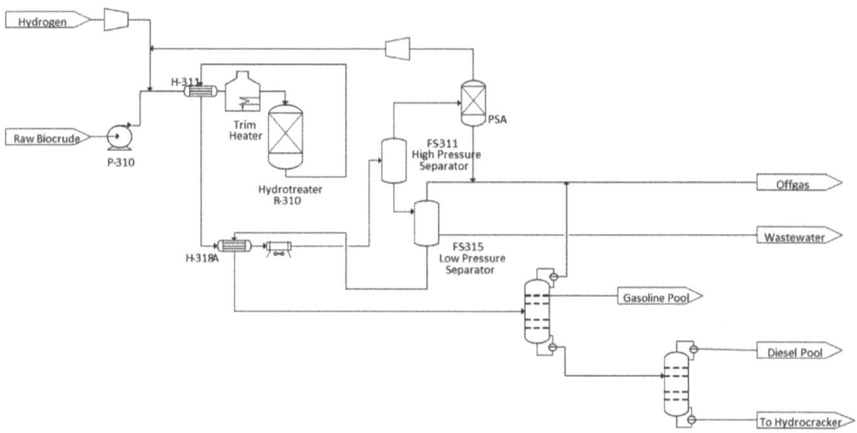

Figure 7.4 HTL biocrude hydrotreating process diagram. *HTL*, Hydrothermal liquefaction. *Reproduced with permission from: Snowden-Swan, L., Zhu, Y., Jones, S., Elliott, D., Schmidt, A., Hallen, R., Billing, J., Hart, T., Fox, S., & Maupin, G. (2016a). Pacific Northwest National Laboratory (1st (ed.), Vol. 25464). https://doi.org/pnnl.gov/main/publications/external/technical_reports/PNNL-25464.pdf; Snowden-Swan, L. J., Zhu, Y., Jones, S. B., Elliott, D. C., Schmidt, A., Hallen, R. T., Billing, Hart, T. R., Fox, S. P., & Maupin, G. (2016b).* Hydrothermal liquefaction and upgrading of municipal wastewater treatment plant sludge: A preliminary techno-economic analysis.

modes, subjectivities, actors, processes, and practices involved with the techno-economic analyses and bioreactors while dealing with WWTPs, which has been discussed thoroughly as well. These scenarios have been difficult in the pre-covid era and during the covid time, some additional challenges have occurred. But, at the same time, technical analyses show that due to Covid's impact on the environment has changed its dimension as well. As per Andalib (2018) Technologies applied have taken a more humane tone and turn as a result of the manufacturing large companies to small companies all have taken a more humane approach while dealing with production and power consumption matters that indicates a sociological atmospheric change as well.

7.19 Contribution of authors

Tarnima Warda Andalib has contributed to the initiation, outline design, concept design, writing draft regarding techno analysis concepts (TEN, TEP, TEI), Methodology of TEA, EIA, Methodology of EIA, waster water treatment plants regarding challenges and bioreactors' usage with sustainability (Technological Impact assessment of Bioreactors, Economical Impact assessment of Bioreactors on WWTP, Challenges in dealing with WWTP) and conclusion writing and editing the final version, fixing references and format as per template mechanism and submitting the chapter as the corresponding author. Zaied Bin Khalid and Puranjan Mishra have contributed to the writing draft regarding Bioreactor and types of bioreactor part, and impacts on WWTP. Puranjan Mishra has contributed to the template and upgrading Elsa's processes.

Acknowledgment

We would like to express our sincere thanks to the editors of this Elsevier book for providing us with this opportunity.

References

Abbott, R., Albach, D., Ansell, S., Arntzen, J. W., Baird, S. J., Bierne, N., ... Zinner, D. (2013). Hybridization and speciation. *Journal of Evolutionary Biology*, *26*(2), 229–246.

Abdelrahman, M. (2020). Personality traits, risk perception, and protective behaviors of Arab residents of Qatar during the COVID-19 pandemic. *International Journal of Mental Health and Addiction*, 1–12.

Abdul Syukor, A. R., Sulaiman, S., Chandrakant, J. P., Mishra, P., Nasrullah, M., Singh, L., & Zularism, A. W. (2021). *Energy generation from fish-processing waste using microbial fuel cells* (pp. 101–121). Elsevier BV. Available from https://doi.org/10.1016/b978-0-12-821841-9.00009-8.

Abdul-Halim, H., Andalib, T. W., Ahmad, N. H., & Ramayah, T. (2020). Leveraging entrepreneurial bricolage and innovation performance among manufacturing SMEs in Malaysia under a resource constrained environment. *International Journal of Supply Chain Management*, *9*(5), 1030–1041.

Ahuja, H. N., & Walsh, M. A. (1983). *Successful methods in cost engineering* (Vol. 35). Wiley.

Ahmad, A. L., Ismail, S., Ibrahim, N., & Bhatia, S. (2003). Removal of suspended solids and residual oil from palm oil mill effluent. *Journal of Chemical Technology and Biotechnology*, *78*(9), 971–978. Available from https://doi.org/10.1002/jctb.892.

Ahmadi, E., Yousefzadeh, S., Mokammel, A., Miri, M., Ansari, M., Arfaeinia, H., Badi, M. Y., Ghaffari, H. R., Rezaei, S., & Mahvi, A. H. (2020). Kinetic study and performance evaluation of an integrated two-phase fixed-film baffled bioreactor for bioenergy recovery from wastewater and bio-wasted sludge. *Renewable and Sustainable Energy Reviews*, *121*. Available from https://doi.org/10.1016/j.rser.2019.109674.

Ahmadi, Ehsan, Yousefzadeh, S., Ansari, M., Ghaffari, H. R., Azari, A., Miri, M., Mesdaghinia, A., Nabizadeh, R., Kakavandi, B., Ahmadi, P., Badi, M. Y., Gholami, M., Sharafi, K., Karimaei, M., Ghoochani, M., Brahmand, M. B., Mohseni, S. M., Sarkhosh, M., Rezaei, S., et al. Taghipour, N. (2017). Performance, kinetic, and biodegradation pathway evaluation of anaerobic fixed film fixed bed reactor in removing phthalic acid esters from wastewater. *Scientific Reports*. Available from https://doi.org/10.1038/srep41020.

AlSayed, A., Fergala, A., Khattab, S., ElSharkawy, A., & Eldyasti, A. (2018). Optimization of methane bio-hydroxylation using waste activated sludge mixed culture of type I methanotrophs as biocatalyst. *Applied Energy*, *211*, 755–763. Available from https://doi.org/10.1016/j.apenergy.2017.11.090.

Alturki, A., McDonald, J., Khan, S. J., Hai, F. I., Price, W. E., & Nghiem, L. D. (2012). Performance of a novel osmotic membrane bioreactor (OMBR) system: Flux stability and removal of trace organics. *Bioresource Technology*, *113*, 201–206. Available from https://doi.org/10.1016/j.biortech.2012.01.082.

Andalib, T., Azizan, A., Halim, H. A., Adresi, M., Darun., Sultana., & US. (2020). Converged entrepreneurial framework integrating block-chain for the SMEs of the emerging economy: Case studies with soft systems analysis. *Test, Engineering and Management Journal*, *83*.

Andalib, T. W. (2018). *A study on convergence of international employee rights within human resources management practices in Bangladesh* (Doctoral Dissertation).

Andalib, T. W., & Halim, H. A. (2019). Convergence of conceptual innovation model to reduce challenges faced by the small and medium sized enterprises' (SMEs) in Bangladesh. *Journal of Open Innovation: Technology, Market, and Complexity*, *5*(3). Available from https://doi.org/10.3390/joitmc5030063.

Aydin, D. G., & Takay, B. A. (2012). The role of competition in the technoeconomic paradigm on the market. *Economic Annals*, *57*(193), 137–150. Available from https://doi.org/10.2298/EKA1293137A.

Ağdağ, O. N., & Sponza, D. T. (2005). Co-digestion of industrial sludge with municipal solid wastes in anaerobic simulated landfilling reactors. *Process Biochemistry*, *40*(5), 1871–1879. Available from https://doi.org/10.1016/j.procbio.2004.06.057.

Ağdağ, O. N., & Sponza, D. T. (2007). Co-digestion of mixed industrial sludge with municipal solid wastes in anaerobic simulated landfilling bioreactors. *Journal of Hazardous Materials*, *140*(1–2), 75–85. Available from https://doi.org/10.1016/j.jhazmat.2006.06.059.

Asia, W. (2003). Enhancing Agricultural Productivity Through On-Farm Water-Use Efficiency: An Empirical Case Study Of Wheat Producton in Iraq. [*online*] http://www.econbiz.de/en/search/detailed-view/doc/all/enhancing-agricultural-productivity-through-on-farm-wateruse-efficiency-an-empirical-case-study-of-wheat-production-iniraq/10001953647.

Badwal, S. P. S., Giddey, S. S., Munnings, C., Bhatt, A. I., & Hollenkamp, A. F. (2014). Emerging electrochemical energy conversion and storage technologies. *Frontiers in Chemistry*, *2*. Available from https://doi.org/10.3389/fchem.2014.00079.

Bartholameuz, E. M., Hettiaratchi, J. P. A., & Kumar, S. (2016). Enhanced performance of the aerobic landfill reactor by augmentation of manganese peroxidase. *Bioresource Technology*, *218*, 46–52. Available from https://doi.org/10.1016/j.biortech.2016.06.048.

Bell, D. T., & Johnson, F. L. (1975). Phenological patterns in the trees of the streamside forest. *Bulletin of the Torrey Botanical Club*, 187–193.

Birch, K. (2017). Techno-economic assumptions. *Science as Culture*, *26*(4), 433–444.

Bloomfield, B. P., Latham, Y., & Vurdubakis, T. (2010). Bodies, technologies and action possibilities: When is an affordance? *Sociology*, *44*(3), 415–433.

Cai, Y., & Hu, X. M. (2016). A critical review on draw solutes development for forward osmosis. *Desalination*, *391*, 16–29. Available from https://doi.org/10.1016/j.desal.2016.03.021.

Callon, M. (Ed.), (1998). *The Laws of the Markets*. Oxford: Blackwell.

Canter, C., Naftel, D., Caldwell, R., Chinnock, R., Pahl, E., Frazier, E., ... Morrow, R. (1997). Survival and risk factors for death after cardiac transplantation in infants: a multi-institutional study. *Circulation*, *96*(1), 227–231.

Chakma, S., & Mathur, S. (2013). Postclosure long-term settlement for MSW landfills. *Journal of Hazardous, Toxic, and Radioactive Waste*, *17*(2), 81–88. Available from https://doi.org/10.1061/(ASCE)HZ.2153-5515.0000164.

Chandel, M. K., Pratson, L. F., & Williams, E. (2010). Potential economies of scale in CO_2 transport through use of a trunk pipeline. *Energy Conversion and Management, 51* (12), 2825–2834. Available from https://doi.org/10.1016/j.enconman.2010.06.020.

Chen, C. Y., & Yang, P. (2003). Performance of an air-breathing direct methanol fuel cell. *Journal of Power Sources, 123*(1), 37–42. Available from https://doi.org/10.1016/S0378-7753(03)00434-8.

Cheng, H., Hiro, Y., Hojo, T., & Li, Y. Y. (2018). Upgrading methane fermentation of food waste by using a hollow fiber type anaerobic membrane bioreactor. *Bioresource Technology, 267*, 386–394. Available from https://doi.org/10.1016/j.biortech.2018.07.045.

Cheng, H., Li, Y., Li, L., Chen, R., & Li, Y. Y. (2020). Long-term operation performance and fouling behavior of a high-solid anaerobic membrane bioreactor in treating food waste. *Chemical Engineering Journal*, 394. Available from https://doi.org/10.1016/j.cej.2020.124918.

Coombs, W. T., & Holladay, S. J. (2002). Helping crisis managers protect reputational assets: Initial tests of the situational crisis communication theory. *Management Communication Quarterly, 16*(2), 165–186.

Cossu, R., Morello, L., Raga, R., & Cerminara, G. (2016). Biogas production enhancement using semi-aerobic pre-aeration in a hybrid bioreactor landfill. *Waste Management, 55*, 83–92. Available from https://doi.org/10.1016/j.wasman.2015.10.025.

Dahowski, R. T., Dooley, J. J., Davidson, C. L., Bachu, S., & Gupta, N. (2004). A CO_2 storage supply curve for North America. *PNWD, 3471*, 1–92.

Dahowski, R. T., Li, X., Davidson, C. L., Wei, N., & Dooley, J. J. (2009). Regional opportunities for carbon dioxide capture and storage in China. A comprehensive CO2 storage cost curve and analysis of the potential for large scale carbon dioxide capture and storage in the people's Republic of China.

DeLaat, J., Southwick, R., & Gallops, G. (1996). High stability engine control (HISTEC). In *32nd Joint Propulsion Conference and Exhibit* (p. 2586).

De Saille, S. (2015). Innovating innovation policy: the emergence of 'Responsible Research and Innovation'. *Journal of Responsible Innovation, 2*(2), 152–168.

de Saille, S., & Medvecky, F. (2016). Innovation for a steady state: a case for responsible stagnation. *Economy and Society, 45*(1), 1–23.

EPA (2015a). EPA (Energy and Environment Guide to Action), State Policies and Best Practices for Advancing Energy Efficiency, Renewable Energy, and Combined Heat and Power, 2015a Edition, U.S. Environmental Protection Agency, US.

EPA (2015b). EPA (Energy and Environment Guide to Action), State, UST System Compatibility with Petroleum-Biofuel Blends: A Brief Guide to the 2015 Federal UST Regulations for Owners and Operators of USTs Located on Tribal Lands. 2015b Edition, U.S. Environmental Protection Agency, US.

EPA (2016). EPA (Energy and Environment Guide to Action), Federal Register/Vol. 81, No. 167/Monday, August 29, 2016/Rules and Regulations. Environmental Protection Agency, US.

Fischer, H. S., & Bührer, C. (2013). Avoiding endotracheal ventilation to prevent bronchopulmonary dysplasia: a meta-analysis. *Pediatrics, 132*(5), e1351–e1360.

Freeman, C. (1991). Innovation, changes of techno-economic paradigm and biological analogies in economics. *Revue Économique*, 211–232. Available from https://doi.org/10.3406/reco.1991.409276.

Fuller, D. B. (2016). *Paper tigers, hidden dragons: Firms and the political economy of China's technological development*. Oxford University Press.

Gao, L., Fang, M., Li, H., & Hetland, J. (2011). *Cost analysis of CO_2 transportation: Case study in China, . Energy Procedia* (4, pp. 5974–5981). Elsevier Ltd. Available from https://doi.org/10.1016/j.egypro.2011.02.600.

Garcia-Ochoa, F., & Gomez, E. (2009). Bioreactor scale-up and oxygen transfer rate in microbial processes: an overview. *Biotechnology Advances*, *27*(2), 153–176.
Ge, Q., Ling, M., & Chung, T. S. (2013). Draw solutions for forward osmosis processes: Developments, challenges, and prospects for the future. *Journal of Membrane Science*, *442*, 225–237. Available from https://doi.org/10.1016/j.memsci.2013.03.046.
GHG, I. (2002). *Pipeline transmission of CO_2 and energy, . Transmission study report, PH4/* (6, pp. 1–140).
Glasson, C., Chapman, K., Wilson, T., Gander, K., Hughes, C., Hudson, N., & James, E. (2013). Increased exposure to community-based education and 'below the line'social marketing results in increased fruit and vegetable consumption. *Public Health Nutrition*, *16*(11), 1961–1970.
Guest, J. S., Skerlos, S. J., Barnard, J. L., Beck, M. B., Daigger, G. T., Hilger, H., ... & Love, N. G. (2009). A new planning and design paradigm to achieve sustainable resource recovery from wastewater.
Halim, H. A., Andalib, T. W., Ahmad, N. A., & Ramayah, T. (2020). The effects of external barriers on entrepreneurial bricolage among SMEs in an emerging economy. *Test, Engineering and Management Journal*, *83*, 15493–15507.
Hall, C. A. S., Balogh, S., & Murphy, D. J. R. (2009). What is the minimum EROI that a sustainable society must have? *Energies*, *2*(1), 25–47. Available from https://doi.org/10.3390/en20100025.
Harvie, M. (2014). Nutritional supplements and cancer: potential benefits and proven harms. *American Society of Clinical Oncology Educational Book*, *34*(1), e478–e486.
Heddle, G., Herzog, H., & Klett, M. (2003). *The economics of CO_2 storage. MIT LFEE 2003-003 RP* (pp. 1–115).
Hess, S. (2010). *News & Newsmaking: Essays by Stephen Hess*. Brookings Institution Press.
Holder, C. D. (2004). Rainfall interception and fog precipitation in a tropical montane cloud forest of Guatemala. *Forest Ecology and Management*, *190*(2-3), 373–384.
Hosseinzadeh, A., Zhou, J. L., Altaee, A., Baziar, M., & Li, X. (2020). Modeling water flux in osmotic membrane bioreactor by adaptive network-based fuzzy inference system and artificial neural network. *Bioresource Technology*, 310. Available from https://doi.org/10.1016/j.biortech.2020.123391.
Hosseinzadeh, A., Zhou, J. L., Navidpour, A. H., & Altaee, A. (2021). Progress in osmotic membrane bioreactors research: Contaminant removal, microbial community and bioenergy production in wastewater. *Bioresource Technology*, 330. Available from https://doi.org/10.1016/j.biortech.2021.124998.
Hull, R., Walsh, V., Green, K., & McMeekin, A. (1999). The techno-economic: Perspectives for analysis and intervention. *Journal of Technology Transfer*, *24*(2–3), 185–195. Available from https://doi.org/10.1023/A:1007803405567.
Hung, C. M., Hwang, G. J., & Huang, I. (2012). A project-based digital storytelling approach for improving students' learning motivation, problem-solving competence and learning achievement. *Journal of Educational Technology & Society*, *15* (4), 368–379.
Islam, M. A., Karim, A., Mishra, P., Dubowski, J. J., Yousuf, A., Sarmin, S., & Khan, M. M. R. (2020). Microbial synergistic interactions enhanced power generation in co-culture driven microbial fuel cell. *Science of the Total Environment*, 738. Available from https://doi.org/10.1016/j.scitotenv.2020.140138.
Islam, M. Amirul, Karim, A., Mishra, P., Faizal, C. K. M., Khan, M. R., & Yousuf, A. (2019). *Role of biocatalyst in microbial fuel cell performance* (pp. 85–105). Informa UK Limited. Available from https://doi.org/10.1201/9780429448799-6.
Jones, C., Boxenbaum, E., & Anthony, C. (2013). *The immateriality of material practices in institutional logics. Institutional logics in action, Part A*. Emerald Group Publishing Limited.

Jones, A. L., Jennings, D. E., Hooks, C. R., & Shrewsbury, P. M. (2014). Sentinel eggs underestimate rates of parasitism of the exotic brown marmorated stink bug, Halyomorpha halys. *Biological Control*, *78*, 61–66.

Kaman, Z. K., Ibrahim, A., Othman, Z., & Andalib, T. W. (2016). A green practice on environmental protection: A case of multinational company. *Advanced Science Letters*, *22*(5–6), 1749–1755. Available from https://doi.org/10.1166/asl.2016.6758.

Karim, A., Islam, M. A., Mishra, P., Muzahid, A. J. M., Yousuf, A., Khan, M. M. R., & Faizal, C. K. M. (2021). Yeast and bacteria co-culture-based lipid production through bioremediation of palm oil mill effluent: a statistical optimization. *Biomass Conversion and Biorefinery*. Available from https://doi.org/10.1007/s13399-021-01275-6.

Keen, A. (2015). *The Internet is not the answer*. Open Road + Grove/Atlantic.

Knoope, M. M. J., Ramírez, A., & Faaij, A. P. C. (2013). A state-of-the-art review of techno-economic models predicting the costs of CO_2 pipeline transport. *International Journal of Greenhouse Gas Control*, *16*, 241–270. Available from https://doi.org/10.1016/j.ijggc.2013.01.005.

Knorr, K. H. (2013). DOC-dynamics in a small headwater catchment as driven by redox fluctuations and hydrological flow paths–are DOC exports mediated by iron reduction/oxidation cycles? *Biogeosciences*, *10*(2), 891–904.

Latifi, P., Karrabi, M., & Danesh, S. (2019). Anaerobic co-digestion of poultry slaughterhouse wastes with sewage sludge in batch-mode bioreactors (effect of inoculum-substrate ratio and total solids). *Renewable and Sustainable Energy Reviews*, *107*, 288–296. Available from https://doi.org/10.1016/j.rser.2019.03.015.

Li, G., Zhang, J., Li, H., Hu, R., Yao, X., Liu, Y., Zhou, Y., & Lyu, T. (2020). Towards high-quality biodiesel production from microalgae using original and anaerobically-digested livestock wastewater. *Chemosphere*, 128578.

Lier, S., & Grünewald, M. (2011). Net present value analysis of modular chemical production plants. *Chemical Engineering & Technology*, *34*(5), 809–816.

Liu, H., & Logan, B. E. (2004). Electricity generation using an air-cathode single chamber microbial fuel cell in the presence and absence of a proton exchange membrane. *Environmental Science and Technology*, *38*(14), 4040–4046. Available from https://doi.org/10.1021/es0499344.

Lohani, B. N., Evans, J. W., Everitt, R. R., Ludwig, H., Carpenter, R. A., & Tu, S. L. (1997). Environmental impact assessment for developing countries in Asia: Volume 1-overview.

Luo, W., Xie, M., Song, X., Guo, W., Ngo, H. H., Zhou, J. L., & Nghiem, L. D. (2018). Biomimetic aquaporin membranes for osmotic membrane bioreactors: Membrane performance and contaminant removal. *Bioresource Technology*, *249*, 62–68. Available from https://doi.org/10.1016/j.biortech.2017.09.170.

Lyotard, J. F. (1984). *The postmodern condition: A report on knowledge* (Vol. 10). U of Minnesota Press.

Magni, C. A. (2013). The internal rate of return approach and the AIRR paradigm: a refutation and a corroboration. *The Engineering Economist*, *58*(2), 73–111.

Mara, D., & Horan, N. J. (2003). Handbook of water and wastewater microbiology.

Martin, L. W., Crane, S. P., Chu, Y. H., Holcomb, M. B., Gajek, M., Huijben, M., … Ramesh, R. (2008). Multiferroics and magnetoelectrics: thin films and nanostructures. *Journal of Physics: Condensed Matter*, *20*(43), 434220.

McCollum, D. L., & Ogden, J. M. (2006). Techno-economic models for carbon dioxide compression, transport, and storage & correlations for estimating carbon dioxide density and viscosity (. 1–87).

McCoy, S. T., & Rubin, E. S. (2008). An engineering-economic model of pipeline transport of CO2 with application to carbon capture and storage. *International Journal of Greenhouse Gas Control*, *2*(2), 219–229. Available from https://doi.org/10.1016/S1750-5836(07)00119-3.

Min, B., Cheng, S., & Logan, B. E. (2005). Electricity generation using membrane and salt bridge microbial fuel cells. *Water Research, 39*(9), 1675–1686. Available from https://doi.org/10.1016/j.watres.2005.02.002.

Mishra, P., Ameen, F., Zaid, R. M., Singh, L., Wahid, Z. A., Islam, M. A., Gupta, A., & Al Nadhari, S. (2019a). Relative effectiveness of substrate-inoculum ratio and initial pH on hydrogen production from palm oil mill effluent: Kinetics and statistical optimization. *Journal of Cleaner Production, 228*, 276–283. Available from https://doi.org/10.1016/j.jclepro.2019.04.317.

Mishra, P., Krishnan, S., Rana, S., Singh, L., Sakinah, M., & Ab Wahid, Z. (2019b). Outlook of fermentative hydrogen production techniques: An overview of dark, photo and integrated dark-photo fermentative approach to biomass. *Energy Strategy Reviews, 24*, 27–37. Available from https://doi.org/10.1016/j.esr.2019.01.001.

Mishra, P., Wahid, Z. A., Zaid, R. M., Rana, S., Tabassum, S., Karim, A., Singh, L., Islam, M. A., Jaing, X., & Sakinah, M. (2020). Kinetics and statistical optimization study of bio-hydrogen production using the immobilized photo-bacterium. *Biomass Conversion and Biorefinery*. Available from https://doi.org/10.1007/s13399-020-00835-6.

Morgan, D. L. (1998). Practical strategies for combining qualitative and quantitative methods: Applications to health research. *Qualitative Health Research, 8*(3), 362–376.

Morozov, E. (2013). *To Save Everything, Click Here: The Folly of Technological Solutionism.* New York: PublicAffairs.

Moussa, D. T., El-Naas, M. H., Nasser, M., & Al-Marri, M. J. (2017). A comprehensive review of electrocoagulation for water treatment: Potentials and challenges. *Journal of Environmental Management, 186*, 24–41. Available from https://doi.org/10.1016/j.jenvman.2016.10.032.

Mu, L., Zhang, L., Zhu, K., Ma, J., Ifran, M., & Li, A. (2020). Anaerobic co-digestion of sewage sludge, food waste and yard waste: Synergistic enhancement on process stability and biogas production. *Science of The Total Environment, 704*, 135429. Available from https://doi.org/10.1016/j.scitotenv.2019.135429.

Muniesa, F. (2014a). *The Provoked Economy*. London: Routledge.

Muniesa, F. (2014b). *The provoked economy: Economic reality and the performative turn.* Routledge.

Niessen, J., Schröder, U., & Scholz, F. (2004). Exploiting complex carbohydrates for microbial electricity generation - A bacterial fuel cell operating on starch. *Electrochemistry Communications, 6*(9), 955–958. Available from https://doi.org/10.1016/j.elecom.2004.07.010.

Ogden, J. M., Yang, C., Johnson, N., Ni, J., & Johnson, J. (2004). *Conceptual design of optimized fossil energy systems with capture and sequestration of carbon dioxide. Final report* (pp. 1–191). , DE-FC26-02NT41623.

Orlikowski, W. J., Walsham, G., Jones, M. R., & DeGross, J. I. (Eds.), (1996). *Information technology and changes in organizational work.* Springer Science & Business Media.

Parker, N. (2004). *Using natural gas transmission pipeline costs to estimate hydrogen pipeline costs* (pp. 1–85).

Pearce, J. M. (1994). Similarity and discrimination: a selective review and a connectionist model. *Psychological Review, 101*(4), 587.

Perimenis, P., Markou, S., Gyftopoulos, K., Giannitsas, K., Athanasopoulos, A., Liatsikos, E., & Barbalias, G. (2004). Efficacy of apomorphine and sildenafil in men with nonarteriogenic erectile dysfunction. A comparative crossover study. *Andrologia, 36*(3), 106–110. Available from https://doi.org/10.1111/j.1439-0272.2004.00614.x.

Piessens, K., Laenen, B., Nijs, W., Mathieu, P., Baele, J. M., Hendriks, C., ... & Welkenhuysen, K. (2008). Policy support system for carbon capture and storage. *Relatório final para a Science for a Sustainable Development (SSD).*

Puyol, D., Batstone, D. J., Hülsen, T., Astals, S., Peces, M., & Krömer, J. O. (2017). Resource recovery from wastewater by biological technologies: opportunities, challenges, and prospects. *Frontiers in Microbiology*, 7, 2106.

Rajan, R. G. (2006). Has finance made the world riskier? *European Financial Management*, *12*(4), 499–533.

Rana, S., Mishra, P., Gupta, R., ab bin Wahid, Z., & Singh, L. (2020). *Circular economy* (pp. 223–240). Elsevier BV. Available from https://doi.org/10.1016/b978-0-444-64309-4.00010-6.

Roy, V., & King, L. (2016). Betting on hepatitis C: how financial speculation in drug development influences access to medicines. *Bmj*, *354*.

Salehiyoun, A. R., Di Maria, F., Sharifi, M., Norouzi, O., Zilouei, H., & Aghbashlo, M. (2020). Anaerobic co-digestion of sewage sludge and slaughterhouse waste in existing wastewater digesters. *Renewable Energy*, *145*, 2503–2509. Available from https://doi.org/10.1016/j.renene.2019.08.001.

Sarathai, Y., Koottatep, T., & Morel, A. (2010). Hydraulic characteristics of an anaerobic baffled reactor as onsite wastewater treatment system. *Journal of Environmental Sciences*, *22*(9), 1319–1326. Available from https://doi.org/10.1016/S1001-0742(09)60257-6.

Schmidt-Rohr, K. (2020). Oxygen is the high-energy molecule powering complex multicellular life: Fundamental corrections to traditional bioenergetics. *ACS Omega*, *5*(5), 2221–2233. Available from https://doi.org/10.1021/acsomega.9b03352.

Sepehri, A., Sarrafzadeh, M.-H., & Avateffazeli, M. (2020). Interaction between *Chlorella vulgaris* and nitrifying-enriched activated sludge in the treatment of wastewater with low C/N ratio. *Journal of Cleaner Production*, *247*, 119164. Available from https://doi.org/10.1016/j.jclepro.2019.119164.

Shammas, N. K., & Wang, L. K. (2008). *Transport and pumping of sewage sludge and biosolids. Biosolids Engineering and Management* (pp. 1–64). Humana Press.

Sharma, Y., & Li, B. (2010). The variation of power generation with organic substrates in single-chamber microbial fuel cells (SCMFCs). *Bioresource Technology*, *101*(6), 1844–1850. Available from https://doi.org/10.1016/j.biortech.2009.10.040.

Sheppard, E. (2011). Geographical political economy. *Journal of Economic Geography*, *11*(2), 319–331.

Shin, C., & Bae, J. (2018). Current status of the pilot-scale anaerobic membrane bioreactor treatments of domestic wastewaters: A critical review. *Bioresource Technology*, *247*, 1038–1046. Available from https://doi.org/10.1016/j.biortech.2017.09.002.

Siedlecka, E. M., & Stepnowski, P. (2005). Phenols degradation by Fenton reaction in the presence of chlorides and sulfates. *Polish Journal of Environmental Studies*, *14*(6), 823–828.

Smith, T. G., & Carberry, J. J. (1976). Dynamics of a tube-wall reactor. *Chemical Engineering Science*, *31*(11), 1071–1076.

Snowden-Swan, L., Zhu, Y., Jones, S., Elliott, D., Schmidt, A., Hallen, R., Billing, J., Hart, T., Fox, S., & Maupin, G. (2016a). Pacific Northwest National Laboratory. (1st (ed.), Vol. 25464). https://pnnl.gov/main/publications/external/technical_reports/PNNL-25464.pdf

Snowden-Swan, L. J., Zhu, Y., Jones, S. B., Elliott, D. C., Schmidt, A., Hallen, R. T., Billing., Hart, T. R., Fox, S. P., & Maupin, G. (2016b). *Hydrothermal liquefaction and upgrading of municipal wastewater treatment plant sludge: A preliminary techno-economic analysis*.

Sri Shalini, S., & Joseph, K. (2018). Combined SHARON and ANAMMOX processes for ammoniacal nitrogen stabilisation in landfill bioreactors. *Bioresource Technology*, *250*, 723–732. Available from https://doi.org/10.1016/j.biortech.2017.10.077.

Tartakovsky, B., Manuel, M. F., Neburchilov, V., Wang, H., & Guiot, S. R. (2008). Biocatalyzed hydrogen production in a continuous flow microbial fuel cell with a gas phase cathode. *Journal of Power Sources*, *182*(1), 291–297. Available from https://doi.org/10.1016/j.jpowsour.2008.03.062.

Thompson, R. L., Higgins, C. A., & Howell, J. M. (1991). Personal computing: Toward a conceptual model of utilization. *MIS Quarterly*, 125–143.

van den Broek, M., Ramírez, A., Groenenberg, H., Neele, F., Viebahn, P., Turkenburg, W., & Faaij, A. (2010). Feasibility of storing CO_2 in the Utsira formation as part of a long term Dutch CCS strategy. An evaluation based on a GIS/MARKAL toolbox. *International Journal of Greenhouse Gas Control*, *4*(2), 351–366. Available from https://doi.org/10.1016/j.ijggc.2009.09.002.

Wang, C., Wang, Y., Wang, Y., Cheung, K. k, Ju, F., Xia, Y., & Zhang, T. (2020). Genome-centric microbiome analysis reveals solid retention time (SRT)-shaped species interactions and niche differentiation in food waste and sludge co-digesters. *Water Research*, 181. Available from https://doi.org/10.1016/j.watres.2020.115858.

Wathern, P. (2013). Environmental impact assessment and bilateral development aid: an overview WV KENNEDY. *Environmental Impact Assessment*, 281–294.

Welsh, I., & Wynne, B. (2013). Science, scientism and imaginaries of publics in the UK: Passive objects, incipient threats. *Science as Culture*, *22*(4), 540–566.

Westman, W. E. (1990). Managing for biodiversity. *BioScience*, *40*(1), 26–33.

Williams, P. (2002). The competent boundary spanner. *Public administration*, *80*(1), 103–124.

Wills Jr, J. E. (1993). Maritime Asia, 1500-1800: The Interactive Emergence of European Domination.

Wynne, B. (1988). Unruly technology: Practical rules, impractical discourses and public understanding. *Social Studies of Science*, *18*(1), 147–167.

Yousefzadeh, S., Ahmadi, E., Gholami, M., Ghaffari, H. R., Azari, A., Ansari, M., Miri, M., Sharafi, K., & Rezaei, S. (2017). A comparative study of anaerobic fixed film baffled reactor and up-flow anaerobic fixed film fixed bed reactor for biological removal of diethyl phthalate from wastewater: A performance, kinetic, biogas, and metabolic pathway study. *Biotechnology for Biofuels*, *10*(1). Available from https://doi.org/10.1186/s13068-017-0826-9.

Yu, Y., Lu, X., & Wu, Y. (2014). Performance of an anaerobic baffled filter reactor in the treatment of algae-laden water and the contribution of granular sludge. *Water*, *6*(1), 122–138. Available from https://doi.org/10.3390/w6010122.

Zaied, B., Nasrullah, M., Siddique, M. N. I., Zularisam, A., Singh, L., & Krishnan, S. (2020). Enhanced bioenergy production from palm oil mill effluent by co-digestion in solar assisted bioreactor: Effects of hydrogen peroxide pretreatment. *Journal of Environmental Chemical Engineering*, *8*(2).

Zaied, B. K., Nasrullah, M., Siddique, M. N. I., Zularisam, A. W., Singh, L., & Krishnan, S. (2020). Co-digestion of palm oil mill effluent for enhanced biogas production in a solar assisted bioreactor: Supplementation with ammonium bicarbonate. *Science of the Total Environment*, 706. Available from https://doi.org/10.1016/j.scitotenv.2019.136095.

Zhu, J. K. (2016). Abiotic stress signaling and responses in plants. *Cell*, *167*(2), 313–324.

Zimmermann, A. W. (2018). Guidelines for techno-economic assessment of carbon capture and utilization technologies. In *AIChE 2018 annual meeting*.

ŽSuchman, L. A. (1987). *Plans and situated actions: The problem of human-machine communication*. Cambridge university press.

CHAPTER 8

Strategies toward sustainable management of organic waste

Renu[1] and Puranjan Mishra[2]
[1]Department of Chemical Engineering, Malaviya National Institute of Technology, Jaipur, Rajasthan, India
[2]Institute of Bioresource and Agriculture, Hong Kong Baptist University, Kowloon Tong, Hong Kong

8.1 Introduction

The generation of waste shows the evolution of society and it also arises the problems related to its disposal (Abdel-Shafy & Mansour, 2018). These wastes can be solid, liquid, and gas (Misra & Pandey, 2005). These useless wastes are generated by various human activities, and they are discarded in the environment (Ye et al., 2019). These discarded wastes cause various problems to human health and the environment either directly or indirectly mode. In the indirect method the waste comes in direct contact with the human being however in the indirect method it passes through the use of soil, food, or water (Sharma et al., 2021). It necessitates the requirement of proper waste management. Waste management includes the activities which are involved in handling waste materials. Sustainable management of waste is required for the reduction of the effect of waste on the environment and also on human health (Awasthi et al., 2019). However, waste management is a costly process that includes 20%−50% of municipal budgets. The waste comes out from various sources such as commercial, residential, institutional, municipal services, construction and demolition, treatment plant sites, industrial, and agricultural (Ayilara et al., 2020). These wastes can be categorized as organic wastes and inorganic wastes (Fig. 8.1). Organic wastes are also called biodegradable waste, and they come out from animals and plants. Further, organic waste can be subcategorized as agricultural waste, clinical waste, domestic waste, green waste, municipal solid waste (MSW), human waste, paper waste, food waste, slaughterhouse waste, etc. Inorganic wastes are the wastes that do not contain organic compounds and are hard to decompose by microorganisms and can be categorized as chemical, commercial, composite, electronic waste, etc. (Kiddee et al., 2013) (Table 8.1).

Techno-economics and Life Cycle Assessment of Bioreactors
DOI: https://doi.org/10.1016/B978-0-323-89848-5.00007-X

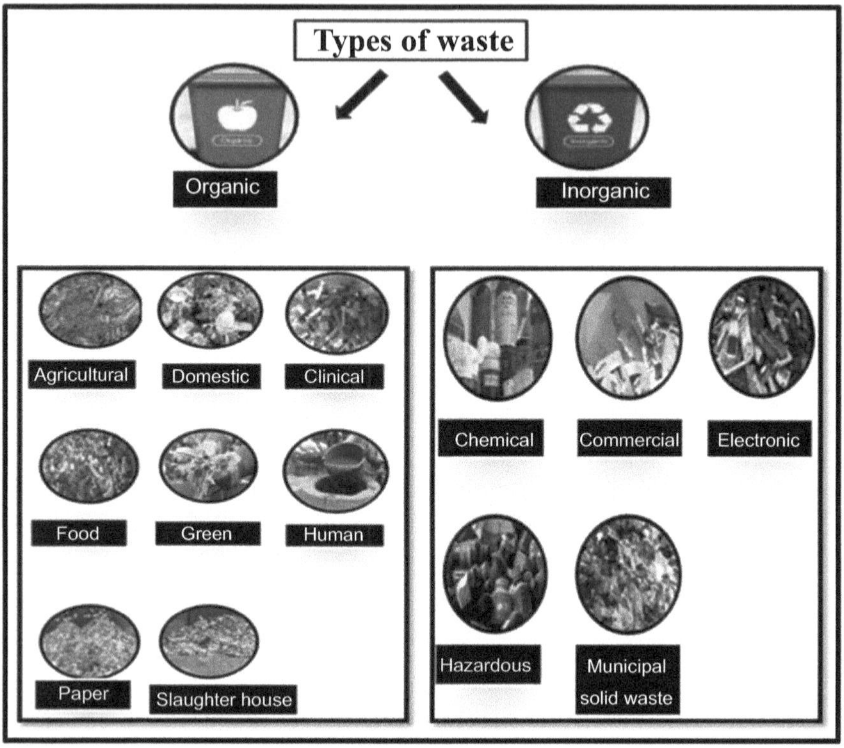

Figure 8.1 Pictorial diagram of types of wastes.

Table 8.1 Difference between organic and inorganic waste.

Organic waste	Inorganic waste
Organic waste is biodegradable waste and comes from either a plant or an animal	Organic waste is nonbiodegradable and includes glass, dust, metal, etc.
Organic wastes are produced from living organisms	Inorganic wastes are produced by nonliving organisms
This waste get affected by heat	This waste does not get affected by heat
Organic waste contains carbon and hydrogen	This waste does not contain carbon at all
The reaction of organic matter is slower than inorganic matter	Inorganic waste forms salts and is readily soluble in water

Organic wastes can be categorized into the following criteria which include; (1) Agricultural waste: Agricultural waste is organic waste. Agricultural waste is manure, wastes from poultry houses, slaughterhouses, and farms. This waste generates due to various agricultural operations. (2) Domestic waste: Domestic waste is also organic waste and this waste is generated due to several household activities such as cleaning, cooking, packaging, and use of plastic bags, etc. (3) Green waste: This waste is also named as "biological waste." The waste which contains a high amount of nitrogen is considered green waste. Leaves, grass clippings, industrial kitchen waste is green waste. Green waste is utilized in the soil to increase its nutrients. (4) Clinical waste: Wastes that come out from hospitals, and clinics is called clinical waste. This type of waste is capable of causing infections (Tabasi & Marthandan, 2013). The cause of infection is swabs dressings, bandages, tissue (animal or human). (5) Human waste: Human waste includes the waste products of the human digestive system such as menses, feces, urine, etc. It is a bio-waste and it is the cause of viral diseases. This human waste can enter drinking water and cause many health problems. Wastewater which contains human waste is used for irrigation of fields. (6) Paper waste: This is the waste that comes out from many industries and offices. It includes papers because of billings, packaging, and junk mails. (7) Food waste: This is food that we do not eat. The loss of this food is in the entire food system. Food loss takes place during production, processing, distribution, retail, and consumption. The food loss amount is one-third or one-half of all the food produced. In developed countries, food is wasted at the time of consumption however in developing countries most loss occurs during production and (8) Slaughterhouse waste: This is the waste that is produced due to slaughtering and comes out from the slaughterhouse.

Whereas inorganic wastes can be categorized as follows. (1) Chemical waste: Chemical waste comes out from various factories, this is the unused chemical and is harmful. It includes pesticides, batteries, paints, solvents, etc. (2) Commercial waste: Commercial waste is inorganic waste and it comes out from various activities of catering establishments, wholesalers, shops, and offices. (3) Electronic waste *or* e-waste: Electronic wastes are discarded electrical or electronic devices. Electronic scrap components, such as CPUs, contain harmful materials such as cadmium, lead, beryllium, or brominated flame retardants. (4) Hazardous waste: It is the wastes that impose threats on people and the environment. Hazardous wastes have characteristics such as reactivity, toxicity, corrosivity, and ignitability and (5) MSW: MSW includes organic wastes such as cardboard, paper, food, and plastics, and inorganic wastes such as metal and glass.

Due to various human activities, waste management is one of the areas which requires sustainable development. Due to population and industrial growth, there is unsustainable production of waste. The waste management practices are not sustainable. For sustainable waste management, there is a requirement for waste prevention and a circular economy to manufacturing products from wastes (Brunner & Rechberger, 2015). Waste affects negatively economic development and also human health. Therefore there is a requirement to develop strategies that give sustainable development to protect the environment with economic and social benefits (Wan et al., 2019). Waste management is a process that is complex and it also includes many technologies. These technologies include handling, storage, collection, transfer, transportation, processing, and disposal of solid wastes (Abdel-Shafy & Mansour, 2018). There is a necessity to reduce the toxicity of generated waste. As people are raising their standard of living, at the same time they are consuming more goods and creating more waste in the environment. Therefore it is mandatory to search for new ways for improving waste management. This chapter has focused on strategies toward sustainable management of organic waste (Fig. 8.1).

8.2 Activities for solid waste management

Different activities are involved in the management of solid. These activities are waste generation, waste handling, sorting, storage and processing, collection, transfer and transport, Processing and recovery, disposal (Fig. 8.2).

1. Waste generation: In this activity, any material which has completed its life has no value, thrown away is generated. This activity is not controllable.
2. Waste handling, sorting, storage, and processing: Waste handling includes the activity which takes place before placing the waste into storage. Another important step is sorting. Sorting of waste takes place at the source of waste generation (Yadav, 2015). Households are being aware of separating sorting bottles, kitchen waste, ferrous and nonferrous materials. Further storage is made and waste processing takes place (Zhuang et al., 2008).
3. Collection: This included the process where waste is collected from specific locations. It also includes the transport of solid waste to the location where vehicles are emptied.

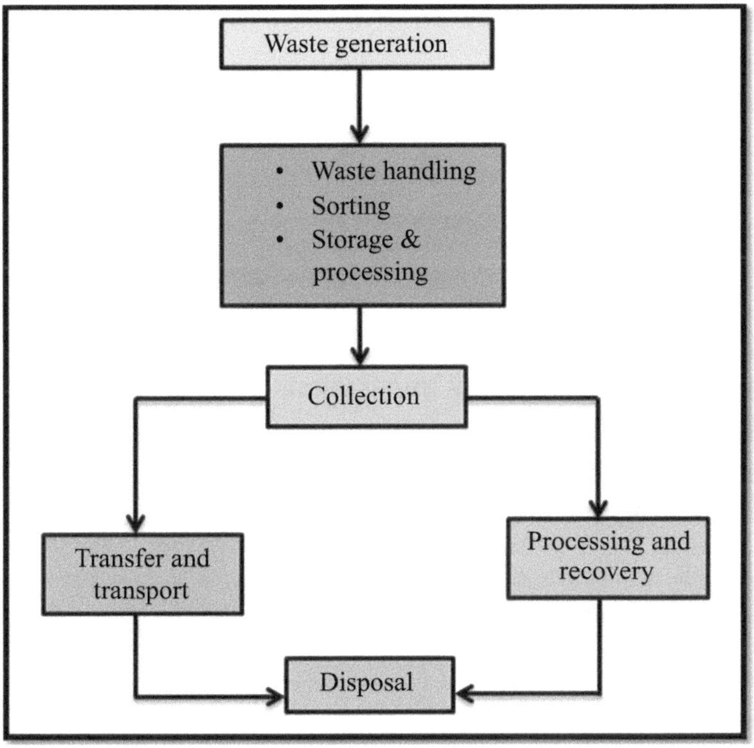

Figure 8.2 Activities involved in solid waste management.

4. Transfer and transport: In this activity, waste is transferred from collection sites to the vehicles and then further transported to the disposal site. It includes the transfer of waste from smaller collection vehicles to large transport equipment and then further transport of waste on long distances.
5. Processing and recovery: In this activity waste is processed by various methods and recovered for recycling purposes.
6. Disposal: In this step, waste is disposed of at the landfill site. This is the final activity in solid waste management.

8.3 Strategies for waste management

The hierarchy of waste management consists of prevention, minimization, recycling, reuse, biological treatment, incineration, and landfill disposal (Fig. 8.3). This can be described as follows.

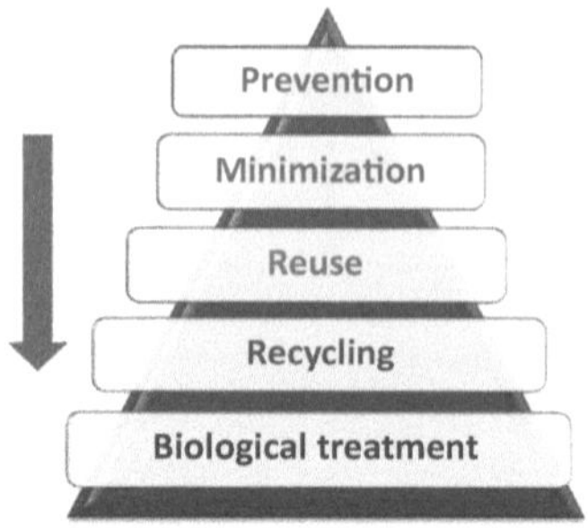

Figure 8.3 Waste management hierarchy.

8.3.1 Prevention of waste generation

Prevention of waste is at top of the hierarchy. It aims to reduce the generated waste and its toxicity (Cheremisinoff, 2003). The prevention of waste is important because it protects the environment and also protects the economy. To prevent waste management, we can stop generating waste-creating products. Many public campaigns can be organized to educate the people about the monetary benefits and environmental benefits of the prevention of waste generation. Also, people can be encouraged to live with greener and minimal lifestyle (Papargyropoulou et al., 2016). The policymakers also play an important role in waste management. Use of second-hand/refabricated items should be encouraged. The best example of this is the use of reusable products and packaging bottles. Similarly, there is food waste, people should be made aware of this food because food security is a global concern therefore we should encourage zero food waste. In this respect there are many NGOs, these NGOs collect food from different restaurants and distribute them to needy people (Chaaban, 2001). Source reduction is the responsibility of every individual and it requires a change in the behavior of each individual.

8.3.2 Minimization

Waste minimization includes source reduction and environmentally sound recycling methods. This technique provides successful revenue growth, market share and saves cost. This includes a set of processes that reduce the amount of waste produced. Waste minimization encourages a most sustainable society and changes patterns of consumption and production (McGrath, 2001). Manufacturers can minimize the amount of packaging required for a product, and they can use packaging that is recyclable and also degradable. In many processes, less hazardous chemicals can be used in place of toxic chemicals (Guthrie & Mallett, 1995). Such as detergent-based cleaners in place of corrosive cleaners, pump sprays in place of aerosol cans, citrus-based solvents in place of chlorinated solvents. In dry cleaners, tetrachloroethylene is used as a dry cleaning solvent which is a toxic compound. Therefore petroleum-based products are less toxic replacements.

8.3.3 Reuse

The reuse method has one advantage in that it delays the need for producing a new product. Reuse is considered as the best method than recycling because in reuse there is no requirement of energy, machinery for the process. The reuse method is prioritized because it produces no waste and also increases the life span of a product. For reuse, it is important to establish an exchange center on campuses, promotional programs, setting up quality-assurance schemes to provide information about the quality of reused materials and change the perspective of people and accommodate according to the environment (Kabirifar et al., 2020).

8.3.4 Recycling

The recycling process collects reusable products from the waste stream and will return raw materials to the market (Kabirifar et al., 2020). Recycled building materials such as mortar, bricks, concrete, glasses, metal, clay, and wood can be utilized in other industries. After smelting, scraps of metals can be recycled and reused by metallurgical industries. Further, they can be utilized in manufacturing automobiles, electric, plumbing appliances, containers. Glass wastes that come out from various industries can be utilized. There are two types of solid waste recycling one is product recycling another is material recycling. Product recycling is an alternative to producing new products. In material recycling, recyclable materials come from home and industry. It includes paper, aluminum, iron, textiles, plastics, and also food waste. In this, materials are recycled either by remanufacturing or by producing raw materials.

The environmental benefits of recycling are as follows,

- It reduces the waste generated by raw material extraction.
- It reduces the requirement for raw materials.
- It reduces the cost of transportation for raw materials and pollution.
- The economic benefits of recycling are as follows,
- It reduces the cost of waste disposal.
- It creates jobs in the market.

Organic waste, that is, paper waste is recycled into new products. It has many benefits such as a lot of waste paper occupying the homes of people (Villanueva & Wenzel, 2007). The recycling process keeps the carbon locked up inside the paper. This recycling process mixes old paper with chemicals and water to break them down. Then it is chopped up and heated and broken into cellulose. It is called the pulp. Then it is passed through the screen and makes new recycled paper (Ozola et al., 2019).

8.3.5 Biological treatment

Biological treatment includes processes that include the decomposition of organic waste (Mishra et al., 2019). Therefore it includes composting and anaerobic digestion. Composting is an old process. In composting, there are biological processes that convert organic waste into soil conditioner in the presence of microbes and air by controlling waste decomposition rates (Cerda et al., 2018). This process also detoxifies industrial waste to produce manure. Anaerobic digestion includes processes that decompose organic waste in presence of bacteria only with no oxygen (Mishra et al., 2021). This process also converts animal waste into biogas and biofertilizers. Another biological process is vermicomposting, this process uses earthworms for the conversion of organic waste into vermicompost (Garg et al., 2006). Vermicompost is used as the best fertilizer and also as a soil conditioner.

Following are the benefits of using compost/vermicompost.

- They improve the structure of soil and also control soil erosion.
- Reduction in greenhouse gas causes climate change mitigation.
- There is a reduction in the volume of waste.

For an instance, Food waste contains high moisture. Food waste produces odor and a large amount of leachate. These odors can be prevented by using well-aerated piles and for the prevention of leachate, aeration and bulking agents are used (Jaafar, 2010). There are both environmental and agricultural benefits of biological treatment. Composting has environmental and agricultural benefits.

Following are the environmental benefits of compost,

- It conserves soil and water
- It stops the formation of methane and leachate formation
- The need for fertilizers and pesticides is reduced
- It conserves the quality of groundwater

- It will bind heavy metals which will stop their transportation to the water resources or among humans.

However, agricultural benefits are can be described in the following points,

- Reduces requirement of water and irrigation
- It increases the nutrient content of soil also their water holding capacity
- It also increases earthworms in the soil
- Reduces odors from agricultural areas

8.3.6 Incineration

It is a thermal waste treatment technique that has the purpose of volume reduction and energy recovery from the waste stream (Crowley, 2003). It is one of the popular waste treatment techniques. In this process combustion of waste takes place under controlled conditions. This process reduces the volume of waste and also kills pathogens and organics. However, it releases ashes and gas in the environment which has serious effects on the environment. To overcome these drawbacks new technologies such as immobilization or stabilization of these toxic ashes to recyclable products will be followed. In incineration, a combustion reaction takes place between any combustible substance present in the waste and oxygen at high temperature and anaerobic conditions where heat is released (Lombardi et al., 2013). In incineration, the toxic and harmful chemicals and pathogens are oxidatively decomposed & destroyed. The incineration process has three phases, that is, dying phase, the Combustion phase, and the Burnout phase (Allsopp et al., 2001). In the drying phase, the solid waste which contains water is dried out utilizing a large amount of heat. Whereas, in the combustion phase, solid waste is burnt at high temperatures, and in the burnout phase concentration of solid waste is reduced. According to National Research Council 2000, for incinerators, three factors play an important role, that is, time, temperature, and turbulence. For any incinerator, the residence time is the time for flue gases, temperature plays a vital role in the combustion of organic matter, turbulence is agitation in chambers and it affects combustion efficiency (Li et al., 2014).

8.3.7 Landfill disposal

Landfill disposal is also known as a garbage dump, rubbish dump. Landfills are the oldest way of waste disposal (Butt et al., 2008). However, Landfills are not considered a sustainable way for waste management because of their cost. These landfills are opposed by the people. Landfill produces a large number of greenhouse gases, landfill gases, and large consumption of energy. There are two types of waste disposal that are used for waste disposal.

8.3.8 Sanitary landfill

In a sanitary landfill, there is a pit with a bottom and to isolate the trash from the environment clay liners are used. The garbage is buried in landfills in layers and also compressed to make it solid (Qasim & Chiang, 2017). To avoid the risk of disposal safety measures were also integrated with the landfill. Sanitary landfills are also called secure landfills and this landfill also accepts toxic waste (Fig. 8.4).

8.3.9 Municipal solid waste landfills

In these landfills, solid is collected from commercial, institutional, residential sources. They have isolated lands that collect waste (Fig. 8.5).

8.3.10 Construction and demolition waste landfills

In these landfills, waste is collected which has been generated due to construction, demolitions, and renovations. They do not collect hazardous waste until they meet certain standards. It collects concrete, metals, plastics, glass, trees, doors, windows, and building components (Garrido et al., 2005).

8.3.11 Industrial waste landfills

Industrial waste is that which we cannot be sent to the MSW landfill that is dumped in the industrial waste landfills. Industrial waste landfills do not accept any hazardous waste (Benfenati et al., 2003).

Figure 8.4 Sanitary landfill.

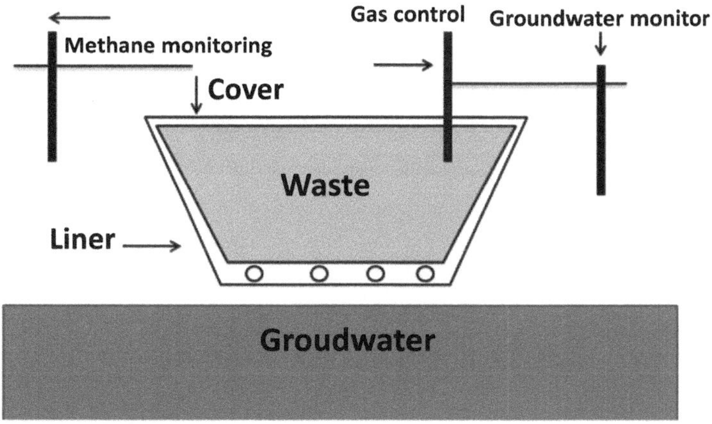

Figure 8.5 Municipal solid waste landfills.

8.3.12 Hazardous waste landfills

Hazardous waste is waste that is harmful to human health and also to the environment (Li et al., 2014). Hazardous waste can be solid, liquid, gas, or a combination of them. This landfill is used for the collection of hazardous waste. These landfills are made underground to store hazardous waste for many decades. These landfills require strict regulation and contain double liners and technology for leak detection. These liners prevent hazardous waste from entering the soil. They are kept under strict inspection to protect the environment (Ravina et al., 2020). Hazardous waste contains different types of fractions that can be separated based on their nature. For hazardous waste, landfills are selected based on topography and geohydrology. If hazardous waste is well planned then it imposes little threat on humans however risk to human health is either due to exposure to contaminated dust and leaks (Fig. 8.6)

8.4 Conclusion

This chapter summarizes various approaches used for the sustainable management of organic waste. These approaches help in the reduction of greenhouse gases, conserve land, and also act as a chemical fertilizer. Various activities such as waste generation, waste handling, sorting, storage and processing, collection, transfer and transport, Processing and recovery, disposal are implemented in sustainable management of waste. Further, to achieve the goal of sustainable waste management, citizens and the

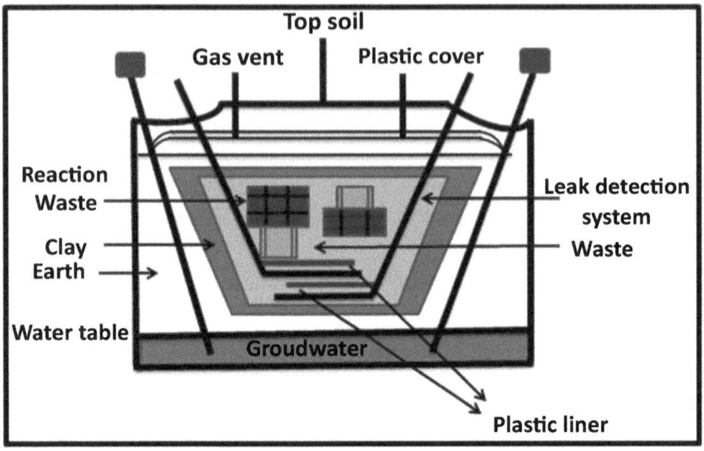

Figure 8.6 Hazardous waste landfill.

government need to work in harmony. It also covers various effective strategies for waste management such as prevention, minimization, recycling and reuse, biological treatment, incineration, and landfill disposal. They are beneficial from an economic and environmental point of view. Further, there is a requirement to take moral responsibility for less waste generation. Also, the adoption of a green lifestyle and following the proper guidelines for waste management can help us to manage sustainable waste disposal.

Acknowledgment

The authors wish to thank the Department of Chemical Engineering, MNIT Jaipur for providing the financial support to carry out my research work. The authors declare that there are no conflicts of interest regarding the publication of this chapter.

References

Abdel-Shafy, H. I., & Mansour, M. S. M. (2018). Solid waste issue: Sources, composition, disposal, recycling, and valorization. *Egyptian Journal of Petroleum*, *27*(4), 1275–1290. Available from https://doi.org/10.1016/j.ejpe.2018.07.003.

Allsopp, M., Costner, P., & Johnston, P. (2001). Incineration and human health. *Environmental Science and Pollution Research*, *8*(2), 141–145. Available from https://doi.org/10.1007/bf02987308.

Awasthi, M. K., Zhao, J., Soundari, P. G., Kumar, S., Chen, H., Awasthi, S. K., & Zhang, Z. (2019). Sustainable management of solid waste. *Sustainable Resource Recovery and Zero Waste Approaches*, 79–99. Available from https://doi.org/10.1016/B978-0-444-64200-4.00006-2.

Ayilara, M. S., Olanrewaju, O. S., Babalola, O. O., & Odeyemi, O. (2020). Waste management through composting: Challenges and potentials. *Sustainability*, *12*, 1–23. Available from https://doi.org/10.3390/su12114456.

Benfenati, E., Barcelò, D., Johnson, I., Galassi, S., & Levsen, K. (2003). Emerging organic contaminants in leachates from industrial waste landfills and industrial effluent. *TrAC – Trends in Analytical Chemistry*, *22*(10), 757–765. Available from https://doi.org/10.1016/S0165-9936(03)01004-5.

Brunner, P. H., & Rechberger, H. (2015). Waste to energy – Key element for sustainable waste management. *Waste Management*, *37*, 3–12. Available from https://doi.org/10.1016/j.wasman.2014.02.003.

Butt, T. E., Lockley, E., & Oduyemi, K. O. K. (2008). Risk assessment of landfill disposal sites – State of the art. *Waste Management*, *28*(6), 952–964. Available from https://doi.org/10.1016/j.wasman.2007.05.012.

Cerda, A., Artola, A., Font, X., Barrena, R., Gea, T., & Sánchez, A. (2018). Composting of food wastes: Status and challenges. *Bioresource Technology*, *248*, 57–67. Available from https://doi.org/10.1016/j.biortech.2017.06.133.

Chaaban, M. A. (2001). Hazardous waste source reduction in materials and processing technologies. *Journal of Materials Processing Technology*, *119*(1–3), 336–343. Available from https://doi.org/10.1016/S0924-0136(01)00920-7.

Cheremisinoff, N. P. (2003). Handbook of solid waste management and waste minimization technologies. *Chemical Engineer*, *744*, 48. Available from http://www.tcetoday.com.

Crowley, D. (2003). *Health and environmental effects of landfilling and incineration of waste: A literature review*.

Garg, P., Gupta, A., & Satya, S. (2006). Vermicomposting of different types of waste using *Eisenia foetida*: A comparative study. *Bioresource Technology*, *97*(3), 391–395. Available from https://doi.org/10.1016/j.biortech.2005.03.009.

Garrido, E., Calvo, F., Ramos, A. F., & Zamorano, M. (2005). Methodology of environmental diagnosis for construction and demolition waste landfills: A tool for planning and making decisions. *Environmental Technology*, *26*(11), 1231–1242. Available from https://doi.org/10.1080/09593332608618601.

Guthrie, P., & Mallett, H. (1995). *Waste minimisation and recycling in construction—A review*.

Jaafar, N. b. (2010). *Study on performance of aerobic composting of oil sludge contaminated soil using different bulking agents* (Doctoral dissertation, UNIVERSITI TEKNOLOGI PETRONAS).

Kabirifar, K., Mojtahedi, M., Wang, C., & Tam, V. W. Y. (2020). Construction and demolition waste management contributing factors coupled with reduce, reuse, and recycle strategies for effective waste management: A review. *Journal of Cleaner Production*, *263*121265. Available from https://doi.org/10.1016/j.jclepro.2020.121265.

Kiddee, P., Naidu, R., & Wong, M. H. (2013). Electronic waste management approaches: An overview. *Waste management*, *33*, 1237–1250. Available from https://doi.org/10.1016/j.wasman.2013.01.006.

Li, B., Wang, F., Chi, Y., & Yan, J. H. (2014). Study on optimal energy efficiency of a sludge drying-incineration combined system. *Journal of Material Cycles and Waste Management*, *16*(4), 684–692. Available from https://doi.org/10.1007/s10163-014-0293-3.

Lombardi, F., Lategano, E., Cordiner, S., & Torretta, V. (2013). Waste incineration in rotary kilns: A new simulation combustion tool to support design and technical change. *Waste Management & Research*, *31*(7), 739–750. Available from https://doi.org/10.1177/0734242X13484187.

McGrath, C. (2001). Waste minimisation in practice. *Resources, Conservation and Recycling*, *32*(3–4), 227–238. Available from https://doi.org/10.1016/S0921-3449(01)00063-5.

Mishra, P., Krishnan, S., Rana, S., Singh, L., Sakinah, M., & Ab Wahid, Z. (2019). Outlook of fermentative hydrogen production techniques: An overview of dark, photo and integrated dark-photo fermentative approach to biomass. *Energy Strategy Reviews*, *24*, 27–37. Available from https://doi.org/10.1016/j.esr.2019.01.001.

Mishra, P., Wahid, Z. a, Singh, L., Zaid, R. M., Tabassum, S., Sakinah, M., & Jiang, X. (2021). Synergistic effect of ultrasonic and microwave pretreatment on improved bio-hydrogen generation from palm oil mill effluent. *Biomass Conversion and Biorefinery*. Available from https://doi.org/10.1007/s13399-021-01285-4.

Misra, V., & Pandey, S. D. (2005). Hazardous waste, impact on health and environment for development of better waste management strategies in future in India. *Environment international*, *31*, 417–431. Available from https://doi.org/10.1016/j.envint.2004.08.005.

Ozola, Z. U., Vesere, R., Kalnins, S. N., & Blumberga, D. (2019). Paper waste recycling. Circular economy aspects. *Environmental & Climate Technologies*, *3*, 260–273.

Papargyropoulou, E., Wright, N., Lozano, R., Steinberger, J., Padfield, R., & Ujang, Z. (2016). Conceptual framework for the study of food waste generation and prevention in the hospitality sector. *Waste Management*, *49*, 326–336. Available from https://doi.org/10.1016/j.wasman.2016.01.017.

Qasim, S. R., & Chiang, W. (2017). *Sanitary landfill leachate: Generation, control and treatment. Sanitary landfill leachate: Generation, control and treatment* (pp. 1–339). CRC Press. Available from https://doi.org/10.1201/9780203740217.

Ravina, M., Facelli, A., & Zanetti, M. (2020). Halocarbon emissions from hazardous waste landfills: Analysis of sources and risks. *Atmosphere*, *11*(4). Available from https://doi.org/10.3390/ATMOS11040375.

Sharma, H. B., Venna, S., & Dubey, B. K. (2021). Resource recovery and circular economy approach in organic waste management using hydrothermal carbonization. *Clean Energy and Resources Recovery*, 313–326. Available from https://doi.org/10.1016/B978-0-323-85223-4.00003-8.

Tabasi, R., & Marthandan, G. (2013). Clinical waste management: A review on important factors in clinical waste generation rate. *International Journal of Science and Technology*, *3*, 194–200.

Villanueva, A., & Wenzel, H. (2007). Paper waste—recycling, incineration or landfilling? A review of existing life cycle assessments. *Waste Management*, *27*(8), S29–S46.

Wan, C., Shen, G. Q., & Choi, S. (2019). *Waste management strategies for sustainable development*.

Yadav, R. (2015). Solid waste management. *Pollution Research*, *34*(1), 93–102. Available from http://www.envirobiotechjournals.com/journal_details.php?jid = 4.

Ye, G., Lin, Y., Kuzyakov, Y., Liu, D., Luo, J., Lindsey, S., & Ding, W. (2019). Manure over crop residues increases soil organic matter but decreases microbial necromass relative contribution in upland Ultisols: Results of a 27-year field experiment. *Soil Biology and Biochemistry*, *134*, 15–24. Available from https://doi.org/10.1016/j.soilbio.2019.03.018.

Zhuang, Y., Wu, S. W., Wang, Y. L., Wu, W. X., & Chen, Y. X. (2008). Source separation of household waste: A case study in China. *Waste Management*, *28*(10), 2022–2030. Available from https://doi.org/10.1016/j.wasman.2007.08.012.

CHAPTER 9

Application of matrices for the development of next-gen bioreactors from COVID-19 waste management prospects

Snehi Soy[1], Bishwajit Singh Kapoor[2], Shubha Rani Sharma[1] and Vinod Kumar Nigam[1]
[1]Department of Bioengineering & Biotechnology, Birla Institute of Technology, Ranchi, Jharkhand, India
[2]Department of Biotechnology, National Institute of Technology, Durgapur, West Bengal, India

9.1 Introduction

Bioreactors are vessels providing a feasible environment for cell growth resulting in desired biological activity. Since its inception, bioreactor has helped to resolve cultivation bottlenecks and has been successfully utilized for the cultivation of stem cells, algal cells, microbial cells, mammalian cells, insect cells, and plant cells in numerous bioprocess applications. Bioreactors form the core of the biotechnological process where constant improvisation for enhanced cultivation efficiency, reproducibility of growth, product formation, and quality is a prime requirement. Designing an efficient bioreactor needs important criteria to be met to mimic the actual biological process. Providing optimal biological, biochemical, and biomechanical requirements is critical to ensure maximum productivity and sustainable processivity on an industrial scale. Some essential parameters for consideration are maintenance of optimal temperature, pH, O_2 transfer, CO_2, metabolite concentration, redox potential, nutrient uptake, etc. Other bioprocessing parameters include fluid velocity, viscosity, shear, stress, mass, and heat transfer (Mustafa et al., 2018). The matrix plays a very important role in the creation of an optimal environment within the bioreactor. Matrix is generally synthesized from polymeric biomaterials due to its low toxicity, safe and simple disposal procedure, innate inheritance and acceptance of cells, mechanical stability, and durability. The advancement in instrumentation design and miniaturization technologies has further augmented matrices design for the development of flexible and modular

Techno-economics and Life Cycle Assessment of Bioreactors
DOI: https://doi.org/10.1016/B978-0-323-89848-5.00011-1

bioreactors and has heavily accelerated the biomaterial market (Tripathi & Melo, 2019). Different types of bioreactors are available for diverse applications such as wastewater treatment (WWT) and solid waste management in the environmental sector, production of high-value pharmaceuticals, biologics and bulk chemicals in pharma and industrial biotechnology, cell culture and tissue engineering in healthcare, algae cultivation for biofuel and oxygen generation in space exploration, etc (Wang, Wang, et al., 2020; Zhuo et al., 2018; Christoffersson & Mandenius, 2019). Analyzing the sustainable applications and demands of the bioreactor, further augmentation, and technological advancements have stimulated improvement in bioreactor design such as anaerobic membrane bioreactors for WWT and single-use bioreactors (SUBs) for small-scale pharmaceuticals production (Metze et al., 2020; Zhuo et al., 2018). Also, the extensive and efficient application of hybrid bioreactor technology in waste management has propelled the expansion of the bioreactor market.

The recent onset of pandemic (2019–ongoing) has observed elevated usage of bioreactors for the production of diagnostic tools, therapeutics, vaccines, etc. Although significant attention is being given to vaccine production for combating viral infection, the prevalence of novel SARS-CoV-2 as a potential contaminant in the environment cannot be overlooked. Therefore, there is an immediate need of fabricating innovative rational technologies that can be incorporated into conventional bioreactors for efficient waste management. The chapter addresses recent advancements in the design of matrix, its integration for the design of hybrid bioreactors, and the up-gradation of conventional bioreactors. Also, the suitability and effectiveness of the approach for sustainable practices are discussed.

9.2 Emerging trends in bioreactors with respect to matrix and applications

Sophisticated bioprocess entails modern interdisciplinary strategies to overcome the challenges offered by conventional methods. Some notable research developments w.r.t. to the matrix in designing next-gen bioreactors are mentioned below along with their applications in several sectors.

9.2.1 Monoclonal antibodies production

As per the biopharma trend survey in March 2019, monoclonal antibodies (mAbs) occupy the top-notch among biopharma products. Despite the mAbs global market flourishing at an unprecedented pace, there are several manufacturing constraints being faced by the industry such as efficiency and robustness of the bioprocess, product reproducibility as well as yield and characterization of therapeutics. The failure in combating the challenges is leading to the rejection of drugs even after getting approval. One such example is Zynbryta (a drug for multiple sclerosis); it had to suffer withdrawal in March 2018 after exhibiting symptoms of brain inflammation.

The increasing demands of mAbs as therapeutics are putting thrust on the manufacturing process for higher yield. In order to achieve desirable upstream processing and production (along with consideration of challenges) of mAbs, preference of advanced technologies to conventional technology is taking over. The following table summarizes the conventional methods and their limitations for the production of mAbs in bioreactors Table 9.1.

Table 9.1 Conventional methods and limitations of traditionally used bioreactors for the production of monoclonal antibodies (mAbs).

Sl no.	Conventional methods for mAbs production	Key limitations	References
1.	small-scale suspension cell culture system using T-flask, Triple flask, Cellstack, Hyper flask, spinner flasks, roller bottles, and shake-flasks	Low cell density resulting in mAbs concentration 10–100 μg/mL	Baron (1990)
2.	Hollow fiber bioreactors	Enhanced oxygen transfer is achieved via increasing the rate of media exchange which leads to an increase in overall costs	Jyothilekshmi and Jayaprakash (2021)
3.	STBR	(1) Few cells lines pose inability to adapt to serum-free media hence low production of mAbs and (2) cell lines sensitive to shear stress due to agitation in suspension media	Strobl et al. (2021)

STBR, Stirred tank bioreactors.

9.2.1.1 High-density cell culture systems

These have been introduced because of the need for maximum production of therapeutics and reduction in production and processing costs. These systems are constantly improvising and are one of the preferred bioreactor systems for mAbs production via in vitro approach. *Hollow fiber bioreactors (HFBR)* work on perfusion mode and provide a large surface area in a small volume for high-density cell culture growth. Perfusion bioreactors are capable of providing continuous nourishment to cells along with continuous removal of waste products being generated which would otherwise inhibit cell growth thus ensuring prolonged stability of cells. A recent development has led to the design of a novel disposable bioreactor, consisting of cryogel as a matrix for cell growth (Jyothilekshmi & Jayaprakash, 2021). Packed bed systems and disposable wave bioreactors are other new additions to the series of high cell density culture bioreactors. These developments have made mAbs production safe, efficient, economically viable, and sustainable. They provide the advantage of working with both serum and serum-free media. Usage of serum-free media in the production of therapeutic proteins is advantageous from the perspective that it cuts the cost of serum. The serum is a naturally occurring substance, its presence not only leads to the inclusion of additional processing/purification steps but it is also crucial to eliminate the compromising factors which would otherwise trigger a fatal immune response.

The need for an efficient *matrix* system for mAbs production with high cell density and cell viability is the call of the hour. Some cell lines are incompetent of growing in suspension; there is a need for the cells to adhere to the surface of a supporting frame or medium; in this case high cell density, low volumetric systems are preferable. Therefore, improvisation in the design of the conventional systems is a necessity such as techniques for immobilizing cells to porous beads via adsorption or entrapment method. Here the matrix plays a pivotal role as an immobilization medium. Matrix is a polymer substance that is either natural or synthetic and based on adsorption requirements can be subjected to chemical modifications. The size, porosity, and surface characteristics of the matrix establish the effectiveness of cell adsorption. The typical bioreactors that harness the immobilization strategy for the cultivation of mammalian cells are packed bed and polymer-based bioreactors. Although the HFBRs and membrane bioreactors have exhibited remarkable performance as high cell density bioreactors; they suffer some limitations like contamination risk, blockage of cells in the membrane; difficulties in monitoring, which furthered the development of matrices for the immobilization of cells.

9.2.1.2 Cryogel bioreactors

Disposable bioreactors are easy to handle, have a low risk of cross-contamination, possess high flexibility, and have a meager running cost. One of the best examples is the cryogel bioreactor which promises economical viability at both lab-scale and industrial levels. It is a disposable, high cell density perfusion bioreactor, which supports a long productive lifetime for cells. Hence, ensures long-term continuous production of therapeutic proteins. It is noteworthy that the productivity of cryogel bioreactors is at par in performance with HFBR. The striking feature of this bioreactor is the cryogel matrix. Cryogels are 3-D polymeric scaffolds formed at subzero temperature by the phenomenon of cryogelation.

The major advantage with cryogels matrices are:

- Cryogels have an interconnected network of macropores and are made of polymers such as *polyacrylamide (PAAm)-gelatin, PAAm-chitosan, etc.*
- The cryogel matrix provides an optimum microenvironment for the diffusion of substrates and metabolites to the cell lines adsorbed onto the inner pore walls of cryogel matrix which is covalently immobilized with gelatin (Verma et al., 2021). Gelatin enhances the adherence of cells to the matrices.
- Can be synthesized of different polymeric blends in different sizes and shapes e.g., sheets or monoliths. It immensely contributes toward high cell density and long-term culture stability (Jain & Kumar, 2013).
- Also, the polymer-based cryogels have ease of synthesis, use aqueous solvent; possess high porosity, high mechanical strength as well as osmotic stability.

Nilsang et al. (2007) have reported a bioreactor with polyacrylamide-based cryogel which operated on continuous mode for 55 days and obtained mAbs productivity of 130 μg/mL on the 36th day. Recent uses of cryogel bioreactors are upscaling of several mAbs, in vitro modeling studies for cancer metastasis, WWT, and industrial production of maltose by immobilizing cryogels with α-amylase for starch hydrolysis (Bray et al., 2018; Guilherme et al., 2017; Zhang, Chen, et al., 2017). In one study cryogels were used for the storage and transportation of mammalian cells. It didn't affect the cell viability; it was approximately 1.5 times higher compared to suspension culture (Jyoti and Kumar, 2017).

9.2.1.3 Cell tank bioreactors

This is another such disposable bioreactor for the perfusion mode of culture. It uses a non-woven polyester matrix caged in a cassette immersed in a reservoir; the whole assembly being used for cell entrapment. It applies to both adherent and non-adherent cell lines at high cell density (Zhang & Veronique, 2015). Zhang, Stobbe, Silvander, et al. (2015) were able to cultivate recombinant Chinese hamster ovary (CHO) cells for mAbs (IgG) production which was 35 times higher compared to batch culture for the same reactor volume and period of production. The novel cell tank reactor integrated the bioreactor and the cell retention function. The cells were harbored in a non-woven polyester matrix and although cells were adapted to suspension; they remained entrapped in the matrix. Due to the efficient circulation of the cell-free medium into- and through the matrix, a homogenous cell environment was maintained resulting in high cell density of CHO cells.

9.2.2 Wastewater treatment

We are already familiar with the inadequate availability of freshwater as well as the crisis issue growing at an alarming rate. 60% of the world population is expected to face a water crisis by 2050 (Boretti & Rosa, 2019). Therefore, taking into consideration the mentioned problems, the impetus is being given toward the implementation of wastewater recycling technologies. It is also noteworthy to mention that wastewater, despite being given secondary treatment needs further treatment or else might become the cause of concern. Espíndola et al. (2019) have designed a promising technique for the removal of oxytetracycline (OTC) which has become a contaminant of emerging concern (CEC). OTC is a pharmaceutical that finds application in veterinary medicine. The concern is its minimal metabolism in the body, hence excreted in its usual state, and has been found in surface water and groundwater (Liu, Yang, et al., 2018). A low-pressure membrane system namely microfiltration (MF) was harnessed for the removal of OTC using a nano-engineered membrane (NEM) as an immobilization medium for photocatalysis. Espíndola et al. (2019) designed a photocatalytic membrane reactor (PMRs) which can be integrated as a tertiary treatment method into advanced WWT plants. The results were quite promising. Integrated hybrid systems, that is, PMR coupled MF with photolysis (UVA-MF) or TiO_2-P25 nanoparticle photocatalysis (UVA/TiO_2-MF) for testing the removal of OTC. NEM plays a critical role by acting as a selectively permeable membrane only allowing water and small molecules to permeate through. It also ensured the separation of photocatalysts from the treated solution, thus promoting the reusability of photocatalysts, a sustainable approach. Thus, the NEMs photocatalytic activity carried out in situ oxidation/reduction of pollutants, enhancing its antifouling properties, as well as releasing high-quality permeate and retentate with low organic load (Szymański et al., 2018). The NEM serving as immobilization matrix, exhibited high efficiency in continuous OTC removal, during 3 consecutive photocatalytic cycles.

TC, a common antibiotic frequently gets discharged into wastewater as a parent compound and is highly toxic to aquatic life. Current WWT strategies rely on the activated sludge process for the removal of TC from wastewater. Activated sludge is a bio-flocculation consisting of indigenous microbial consortia which produce extracellular polymers substances (EPS) for the formation of biofilm. The biofilm matrix consists of functional groups such as hydroxyl, carboxyl, and amino groups which offer adsorption sites for rapid adsorption of TC and biochemical process for its disintegration (Chen et al., 2015). In aerobic/anaerobic moving bed biofilm reactors, TC removal takes place via adsorption under anaerobic conditions whereas degradation occurs under aerobic conditions (Chen et al., 2018). However, the limitation of the activated sludge process is that it cannot efficiently degrade micropollutants as well as it is not effective in disintegrating the parent compound into non-toxic products. Membrane bioreactors can efficiently biodegrade TC and have significantly reduced (in parts-per-billion) the degradation products such as anhydrotetracycline, 4-epi-TC, and epianhydrotetracycline (Taşkan et al., 2019). Membrane bioreactors have long sludge retention times and high biomass (Wang, Ma, et al., 2020). Sludge retention times play an important role in microbial cell proliferation thus maintaining optimum biomass for TC degradation and removal (Liu, Lu, et al., 2018). It was also highly resistant to the toxicity of TC; the presence of TC did not affect the removal of organic compounds and ammonia (Prado et al., 2009). However, it yields degradation products such as anhydrotetracycline and epianhydrotetracycline which are comparatively more toxic. Therefore, complete mineralization of the degraded as well as biotransformed product is a must. It can be achieved by coupling advantages of several technologies like the activated sludge process, advanced oxidation process, and photocatalysis (Bethi et al., 2016; Saadati et al., 2016). Intimately coupled photocatalysis and biodegradation (ICPB) approach uses a high porosity biofilm carrier, it regulates the photoelectron transfer between the microbial cells immobilized in EPS matrix and photocatalysts in membrane matrix (Ding et al., 2018). This not only results in increased degradation but also yields less toxic photocatalytic products. On the other hand, the advanced oxidation (ozone or ultraviolet light) approach causes transformation by chemicals containing oxygen groups (Babu et al., 2019). Oxidation causes rapid degradation of organic compounds releasing primary transformed products, which are eventually mineralized by the consortia in the bioreactor. Table 9.2 summarizes the coupling approach used in different applications of bioreactors.

9.2.3 Application of fixed-film microbial reactors for the treatment of effluents

Bacteria are able to thrive in both planktonic form and fixed-form by means of biofilm via adherence to a solid surface. The phenomenon of biofilm formation by microbes is a process wherein the microbes acquire resistance to environmental stresses by immobilizing on a solid surface. From an engineering perspective, biofilm matrix formation within bioreactors offers several advantages such as augmented biomass concentration, safety against hazardous waste, and intrinsic biomass maintenance (Das et al., 2012). This ability of biofilm formation when utilized for the formation of a biofilm reactor ensures one-time inoculation with sustained performance for several purposes (Saha et al., 2018).

Table 9.2 Coupling approach used for different applications of bioreactors.

Sl no.	Coupling approach	Conclusion	References
1.	ICPB photocatalyst-Ag-doped TiO_2	70% TC removal rate achieved >20% COD removal	Xiong et al. (2017)
2.	ICPB photocatalyst-$BiOCl/Bi_2WO_6/Bi$	Almost complete degradation of TC hydrochloride	Li et al. (2020)
3.	Advanced oxidation (ozonation) and biodegradation	97% TC removal in 2 h with reduced toxicity	Su et al. (2020)

COD, Chemical oxygen demand; *ICPB*, intimately coupled photocatalysis and biodegradation; *TC*, tetracycline.

Effluents consisting of metalworking fluid are hazardous; the presence of inhibitory constituents and the sluggish degradation kinetics of complex organic constituents compromises the viability of the waste treatment process (Thill et al., 2016). Therefore, the utilization of indigenous consortium of wastewater itself for the development of biofilm matrix by optimizing the biostimulation caused by the nutrients available in the media (wastewater) is a feasible approach. The biological process is typically slower compared to other physical and chemical treatments and is, therefore, more practicable for treating metalworking fluid wastewater in bulk (Cheng et al., 2005). When we talk of biostimulation, it means the addition of nutrients to WWT systems to develop a sustainable bioreactor as well as improvisation of the treatment process. A novel approach was undertaken by Singh et al. (2017) for the remediation of waste metalworking fluid. In situ WWT was carried out by testing growth parameters that might affect the biofilm matrix and which might influence reactor performance. NH_4Cl and KH_2PO_4 are common wastewater stimulants added to wastewater systems for enhanced growth of microbial biomass. It was observed that either of them when present in a limiting quantity induces biofilm formation, which severely declines when either completely stripped off or provided in excess. KH_2PO_4 stimulation resulted in enhanced total carbon removal performance of the bioreactor and positively improved the biofilm yield. On the other hand, NH_4Cl stimulation increased the removal of saturated fatty amides and diethylene glycol butyl ether but led to reduced carbon removal, also inhibiting the removal of diisopropylamine.

Nitrogen, phosphorous, and potassium (N, P, K) are three essential macronutrients required for plant growth and are the main components of fertilizers as nitrates and phosphates. However, when the water leaches out and mixes with the freshwater body might lead to eutrophication. Therefore, a sustainable treatment process of wastewater is a necessity. Although we have a number of treatment strategies and technologies in the current scenario they are costly and have not been effective in retaining N and P. Simultaneous nitrate and phosphate removal via bioremediation approach has earlier been reported by several researchers through various systems, namely, two sludge system (Kuba et al., 1996), single sludge sequential batch reactors (Yang et al., 2010) and anoxic laboratory-scale reactor (Jena et al., 2015) using denitrifying phosphate accumulating organisms (DNPAOs). However, the process has the requirement of organic carbon which is one of the limiting substrates. Saha et al. (2018)

developed one strategy for the simultaneous sequestration of nitrate and phosphate from wastewater by using a packed bed biofilm reactor. For the development of biofilm, the columns of the reactor were filled up to 60% with steel mesh, biofilm development, the reactor columns served as a matrix. The system not only generated minimum sludge but also yielded N and P rich biomass from the matrix, generating minimum sludge and which could be used as a fertilizer. Their reduction was achieved up to 68% of phosphate, 73% in total organic carbon (TOC), 93% of chemical oxygen demand (COD), 94% of nitrate, and 97% of biochemical oxygen demand (BOD), and the treated wastewater met the standard criterion to be reused for irrigation, aquaculture process, and recharging of the groundwater.

9.2.4 Abatement of air pollutants

Total reduced sulfur (TRS) compounds are toxic in nature, are highly carcinogenic, and are mostly emitted by cellulose and petrochemical industries. The gaseous emissions contain these compounds at high temperatures (>50°C) in areas like smelting and composting facilities, boiler combustion, petroleum refinery (Valdebenito-Rolack et al., 2017). Also, high temperatures favor rapid biochemical transformations of these compounds (Li et al., 2015) further posing risks. Hence, designing an efficient biofiltration assembly for the bioreactor is a must for its removal. Biofilters inoculated with thermophilic sulfur-oxidizing bacteria (SOB) have been sought after as potential designs for the degradation of TRS. Hyperthermophiles/thermophiles are robust microbes and have exhibited the ability to oxidize the compounds at elevated temperatures (>60°C). The immobilization of desulphurizing microbe on packing support material in a bioreactor for the formation of biofilm is sought after as an efficient degrading setup. The treatment procedure in the thermophilic bioreactor is economical, has high degradation kinetics, and has no requirement of cooling equipment (Li et al., 2015).

9.2.5 Matrix design and development for cell cultivation

Matrices play an indomitable role in the bioprocessing arena but have been least described in the literature, thus narrowing the concepts we need to be familiar with. Several companies in the field of high throughput reactor development are constantly striving to mitigate limiting factors affecting the high performance of bioreactors.

The team of Express Bioreactor has launched a patented next-gen bioreactor for cell cultivation; it is disposable, pre-sterilized, and supports the growth of both suspension and anchorage-dependent cells. Although the striking feature of the reactor is a matrix, the core is where all process occurs. The unique design of the honeycomb structured matrix supports increased oxygen availability and nutrient exchange resulting in high cell density. Since no external agitation facility is required, there are zero shears. The matrix also facilitates the removal of the product as well as waste metabolites from the cells in a synchronous manner. The bee-hive-like spongy matrix is porous and mimics "lung" whereby its large surface area allows gas exchange in a highly effective manner thus supporting a large population of cells grown on its surface where cells are never in a submerged condition but rather bathed by a thin film of media continuously. The inoculation, feeding, and harvesting are all achieved through the simple media exchange process. Thus, the overall process is cost-efficient and environmentally sustainable due to its low carbon footprint.

Fibra-Cel disks provide a growth matrix in several bioreactors but are preferably used in packed-bed bioreactors. These 6-mm diameter disks are made up of polyester and polypropylene meshwork which is pretreated for cell adherence. It contributes toward an increase in total biomass in the bioreactor by offering several advantages to the cell. The disks provide a 3-D growth surface to the cells, have a high surface-to-volume ratio, and act as the protective sheath of cells from damaging shear forces. They have been applied for cell culture cultivation such as Vero cells and the production of recombinant proteins and viruses (Suttle et al., 2019).

9.2.6 Advancement in the development of photobioreactor

Since the past few decades, photobioreactors (PBRs) have emerged as a potential technology; it has combined approach for microalgal/phototrophic bacteria biomass cultivation and wastewater bioremediation, thus paving the way to sustainable processes. A characteristic PBR is a three-phase system comprising of production medium (liquid phase), microalgae/microbial cells (solid phase), and the gas phase (Galinha et al., 2018). Cultivation of microalgae/phototrophic bacteria for H_2 gas production/bioremediation demands specific construction strategies to design a competent PBR and very few attempts have been quite successful in this regard. Among the design constraints, avoidance of H_2 leakage and membrane fouling (membrane bioreactor) is the crucial part, but optimum cell growth and production is the prerequisite. Despite much research on applications for cultivation and production processes, the research in this arena is suffering major setbacks. Some of them are outlined in Table 9.3.

9.2.7 Immobilization and the role of matrices in the improvement of bioreactor function

Phototrophic bioprocess in conjunction with bioremediation is quite promising and for it to be commercially feasible, continuous operation must be ensured. Immobilization of cells in matrices is advantageous in this regard, it offers

Table 9.3 Limitations of conventional type photobioreactors for microalgae/phototrophic bacteria cultivation and hydrogen production.

Sl no.	Types of bioreactor	Disadvantages
1.	Shaking flask	Continuous gas collection impeded
2.	STR	Require the balancing of cell growth with dilution rates to prevent biomass washout low surface-to-volume ratio energy-intensive due to agitation not applicable for outdoor cultivation and upscaling
3.	Horizontal tubular	Temperature control low gas exchange formation of the significant gas gradient along the tubes high energy input accumulation of algal biomass in the tubes
4.	Tubular coiled	Low gas exchange high shear stress accumulation of biomass in the tubes energy-intensive
5.	Vertical tubular (bubble column/ airlift)	Low surface/volume ratio inefficient solar radiation capture during outdoor cultivation inconvenient for hydrogen production due to agitation factor gas addition leads to dilution of the produced hydrogen/gas circulation leading to a higher risk of leakages
6.	Flat-panel	Agitation by sparging results in dilution /recirculation of the hydrogen gas making it prone to an elevated risk of leakages Agitation by stirring (magnetic stirring/ impeller) is energy-intensive

STR, Stirred tank reactor.

Increased mechanical strength thus preventing cell lysis in prolonged operating conditions

- Minimum diffusional resistance to substrates
- Maintenance of stability and viability of entrapped cells for an expanded period
- Phase separation between cells and liquid medium thus allowing optimal hydraulic and solid retention time and no biomass washout
- Protection from shear stress, pH, temperature fluctuations
- Improved resistance to chemical and enzymatic degradation within the system
- Production of biohydrogen is independent of cell growth; thus, the cells in the stationary phase can be immobilized and utilized as biocatalysts for optimum continuous production (Canbay et al., 2018; du Toit & Pott, 2020; Zhang, Song, et al., 2017).

To date, a number of immobilization matrices have been developed for immobilization of cells such as alginate beads, alginate films, biofilm on solid surfaces, robust hydrogel/cryogel, etc. (See et al., 2015; Skjånes et al., 2016). Laurinavichene et al. (2006) demonstrated for the first time hydrogen production from immobilized microalgae on a glass fiber matrix. Laurinavichene et al. (2008) in another study performed immobilization of algal cells in alginate films (a protective matrix) where the continuous H_2 production was achieved for a protracted period, that is, 90 days by supplying a limiting concentration of sulfur. Developing films consisting of a very thin layer of cells not only provide excellent surface-to-volume ratio and high cell density but also has a requirement of a very short light path. Additionally, the absence of shear stress keeps cells intact within the gel, and the cells can also be easily harvested. Also, the nutrient availability can be efficiently altered and tailored according to the H_2 production process which gives an upper hand to this method. In one study, the presence of a carboxyl functional group in alginate gels facilitated the removal of ammonium via ionic interaction in immobilized algal cells (Mujtaba et al., 2018). O_2 is another bottleneck in H_2 production as its presence inactivates the production. Its mitigation was achieved by encapsulating algal cells in alginate films. The system exhibited higher tolerance against O_2 perhaps due to slower diffusion of O_2 through the matrix (Kosourov & Seibert, 2009). Algae immobilized in alginate films also displayed increased production of hydrogen during different light/dark periods by varying different C-sources and pH (Rashid et al., 2011, 2013). Since then, significant research works have been done on the development of matrices for integrated hybrid systems and promising approaches and are listed in Table 9.4.

9.2.8 Other applications

Apart from the aforementioned applications, matrices development and applications in several other sectors are also noteworthy and have been documented in Table 9.5.

9.3 Application of matrices-based bioreactors in COVID-19 waste management

The emergence of the SARS-CoV-2 pandemic has changed the course of the research world. Researchers have focused majorly on viral treatments and their waste management around the world. A number of approaches in designing bioreactors and development of application-based strategies have been done keeping in mind the treatment of viral load in biowaste. Different forms of bio-composites have been developed for the treatment of biological solutions, biological wastes (Prakash et al., 2020). Matrices-based sensors have also been developed for the detection of viral loads (Yousefi et al., 2021). Numerous types of polymeric materials, nanomaterials, nanoparticles have been used for the development of matrices for the entrapment of viral particles. Microbial products which are considered as contaminants can be used for the development of viral entrapment matrices. Lipopolysaccharides (endotoxins), exopolysaccharides are microbial products that can entrap viral particles (Bhatt et al., 2020). Apart from matrices, a number of devices have been developed which act as a filter for the removal of viral particles (specifically SARS-CoV-2) (Marchetti et al., 2020). Although, research is ongoing for the development of matrices-based bioreactors these may prove to be highly effective in the removal of viral load in the coming future, keeping in mind that the future is unseen and viral epidemics may hit the world in near future.

9.4 Conclusion

In this chapter, major emphasis has been placed on the design of matrices w.r.t. their utility and applications as well as recent trends unlocking their potential as future developments. The ongoing COVID-19 pandemic has stimulated the need for early detection and understanding of the fate of SARS-CoV-2 in the environment. Application of novel matrices in

Table 9.4 Recent developments in photobioreactors (PBRs) and their applications.

Sl no.	System	Applications	Advantages	References
1.	*Rhodopseudomonas palustris* immobilized in PVA cryogel matrix for fluidized bed PBR operation	H_2 production and WWT	Can be integrated into WWT plants enhanced H_2 production rate of 16 mL/g/h 43% substrate (glycerol) conversion efficiency to H_2 achieved	Ross and Pott (2021)
2.	Integrated bacterial-microalgal consortium coupled with microalgae immobilization	ADE treatment	Increased resistance to high nutrient loading 93% of NH_4^+–N and complete PO_4^{3-}–P removal was achieved	Gong et al. (2019)
3.	PBR coupled with UF system constituting *C. vulgaris* immobilized in beads matrix + PAC	Algae cultivation and ADE purification	Membrane fouling mitigated efficient nutrient removal from ADE Immobilization promoted high algal biomass due to decreased algal cell lysis	Xie et al. (2018)
4.	Agar immobilized *Rhodobacter capsulatus* in a sequential batch PBR	bioH_2 production	Immobilization increased the stability of the system facilitates long-term operation and H_2 production	Elkahlout et al. (2017)
5.	Photocatalytic membrane made up of nanocomposite consisting of TiO_2 nanoparticles in PVDF membrane matrix	Nitrate removal	High-efficiency microalgal-bacterial MPBR up to 99% nitrate removal efficiency	Sobhanipour et al. (2021)
6.	Panel PBR consisting of agar immobilized *R. capsulatus* YO3	bioH_2 production	Promising technology production can be carried out under large-scale natural conditions	Sagir et al. (2018)
7.	Immobilized photosynthetic bacteria integration with GO/PSF composite membrane matrix in membrane bioreactor	Textile WWT	The higher removal efficiency of color, ammonia–nitrogen, and COD increased membrane permeability reduced membrane fouling	Cheng et al. (2021)

ADE, Anaerobic digestion effluent; *GO*, graphene oxide; *MPBR*, membrane PBR; *PAC*, powdered activated carbon; *PSF*, polysulfone; *PVA*, Polyvinyl alcohol; *PVDF*, Polyvinylidene fluoride; *UF*, ultrafiltration; *WWT*, wastewater treatment.

Table 9.5 Other applications of matrices-based bioreactors.

Sl no.	System	Application	Advantages	References
1.	Immobilized yeast cells in PVA cryogel matrix	Ethanol production (Biofuel production)	90% yield of ethanol High efficacy of multiple reusing under batch conditions withstand long-term storage in frozen form (2 years) retaining high metabolic activity	Stepanov and Efremenko (2017)
2.	Membrane bioreactor consisting of ceramic UF-MBR. Nanoporous biopolymeric membrane synthesized using iron oxide nanoparticles and chitosan as matrix	Pesticide remediation from WWT	Resulted in 96% removal of atrazine reduced membrane fouling complete biomass separation in a synthetic system provided a high quality of treated wastewater for reuse	Mukherjee et al. (2018)
3.	Ultrafiltration membrane fabricated of nanocomposite MMT and Ag-TiO_2 NPs into the CA polymer matrix	Hazardous textile WWT	Can be benchmarked to the commercial membrane's superior antifouling and mechanically stable	Abdel-Karim et al. (2021)

CA, Cellulose-acetate; *MMT*, montmorillonite; *NP*, Nanoparticles; *PVA*, Polyvinyl alcohol; *UF-MBR*, ultrafiltration membrane; *WWT*, wastewater treatment.

membrane bioreactors and use of thermophilic strains are some promising aspects that can give a new dimension to this research thus facilitating complete removal of viruses from wastewater. The advent of novel technologies and new application-oriented research can propel the new interdisciplinary research on polymers, biomaterials, and processes to put the novel knowledge into real-life biological applications Moreover, extensive research and evaluation are required to establish the economic feasibility on a commercial scale.

References

Abdel-Karim, A., El-Naggar, M. E., Radwan, E. K., Mohamed, I. M., Azaam, M., & Kenawy, E. R. (2021). High-performance mixed-matrix membranes enabled by organically/inorganic modified montmorillonite for the treatment of hazardous textile wastewater. *Chemical Engineering Journal, 405*, 126964.

Babu, D. S., Srivastava, V., Nidheesh, P. V., & Kumar, M. S. (2019). Detoxification of water and wastewater by advanced oxidation processes. *Science of the Total Environment, 696*, 133961.

Baron, D. (1990). Industrial production of monoclonal antibodies. *Die Naturwissenschaften*, 77(10), 465–471.

Bethi, B., Sonawane, S. H., Bhanvase, B. A., & Gumfekar, S. P. (2016). Nanomaterials-based advanced oxidation processes for wastewater treatment: A review. *Chemical Engineering and Processing-Process Intensification, 109*, 178–189.

Bhatt, A., Arora, P., & Prajapati, S. K. (2020). Occurrence, fates and potential treatment approaches for removal of viruses from wastewater: A review with emphasis on SARS-CoV-2. *Journal of Environmental Chemical Engineering*, 104429.

Boretti, A., & Rosa, L. (2019). Reassessing the projections of the world water development report. *NPJ Clean Water, 2*(1), 1–6.

Bray, L. J., Secker, C., Murekatete, B., Sievers, J., Binner, M., Welzel, P. B., & Werner, C. (2018). Three-dimensional in vitro hydro-and cryogel-based cell-culture models for the study of breast-cancer metastasis to bone. *Cancers, 10*(9), 292.

Canbay, E., Kose, A., & Oncel, S. S. (2018). Photobiological hydrogen production via immobilization: understanding the nature of the immobilization and investigation on various conventional photobioreactors. *3 Biotech, 8*(5), 1–8.

Chen, A., Chen, Y., Ding, C., Liang, H., & Yang, B. (2015). Effects of tetracycline on simultaneous biological wastewater nitrogen and phosphorus removal. *RSC advances, 5*(73), 59326–59334.

Chen, H. Y., Liu, Y. D., & Dong, B. (2018). Biodegradation of tetracycline antibiotics in A/O moving-bed biofilm reactor systems. *Bioprocess and Biosystems Engineering, 41*(1), 47–56.

Cheng, C., Phipps, D., & Alkhaddar, R. M. (2005). Treatment of spent metalworking fluids. *Water Research, 39*, 4051–4063.

Cheng, J., Wu, X., Jin, B., Zhang, C., Zheng, R., & Qin, L. (2021). Coupling of immobilized photosynthetic bacteria with a graphene oxides/PSF composite membrane for textile wastewater treatment: Biodegradation performance and membrane anti-fouling behavior. *Membranes, 11*(3), 226.

Christoffersson, J., & Mandenius, C. F. (2019). *Using a microfluidic device for culture and drug toxicity testing of 3D cells. Cell-based assays using iPSCs for drug development and testing* (pp. 235–241). New York, NY: Humana.

Das, N., Basak, L. G., Salam, J. A., & Abigail, M. E. A. (2012). Application of biofilms on remediation of pollutants—An overview. *J Microbiol Biotechnol Res*, *2*, 783–790.

Ding, R., Yan, W., Wu, Y., Xiao, Y., Gang, H., Wang, S., Chen, L., & Zhao, F. (2018). Light-excited photoelectrons coupled with bio-photocatalysis enhanced the degradation efficiency of oxytetracycline. *Water Research*, *143*, 589–598.

du Toit, J. P., & Pott, R. W. (2020). Transparent polyvinyl-alcohol cryogel as immobilisation matrix for continuous biohydrogen production by phototrophic bacteria. *Biotechnology for Biofuels*, *13*(1), 1–16.

Elkahlout, K., Alipour, S., Eroglu, I., Gunduz, U., & Yucel, M. (2017). Long-term biological hydrogen production by agar immobilized *Rhodobacter capsulatus* in a sequential batch photobioreactor. *Bioprocess and Biosystems Engineering*, *40*(4), 589–599.

Espíndola, J. C., et al. (2019). Photocatalytic membrane reactor performance towards oxytetracycline removal from synthetic and real matrices: Suspended vs immobilized TiO_2-P25. *Chemical Engineering Journal*, *378*, 122114. Available from https://doi.org/10.1016/j.cej.2019.122114.

Galinha, C. F., Sanches, S., & Crespo, J. G. (2018). *Membrane bioreactors. Fundamental modelling of membrane systems* (pp. 209–249). Elsevier.

Gong, W., Xie, B., Deng, S., Fan, Y., Tang, X., & Liang, H. (2019). Enhancement of anaerobic digestion effluent treatment by microalgae immobilization: characterized by fluorescence excitation-emission matrix coupled with parallel factor analysis in the photobioreactor. *Science of the Total Environment*, *678*, 105–113.

Guilherme, E. P. X., de Carvalho, L. M., Brandi, I. V., Santos, S. H. S., de Carvalho, G. G. P., Cota, J., & Mara Aparecida de Carvalho, B. (2017). Synthesis of supermacroporous cryogel for bioreactors continuous starch hydrolysis. *Electrophoresis*, *38*(22–23), 2940–2946. Available from https://doi.org/10.1002/elps.201700208.

Jain, E., & Kumar, A. (2013). Disposable polymeric cryogel bioreactor matrix for therapeutic protein production. *Nature Protocols*, *8*(5), 821–835.

Jena, J., Kumar, R., Dixit, A., Pandey, S., & Das, T. (2015). Evaluation of simultaneous nutrient and COD removal with polyhydroxybutyrate (PHB) accumulation using mixed microbial consortia under anoxic condition and their bioinformatics analysis. *PLoS One*, *10*(2), e0116230.

Jyothilekshmi, I., & Jayaprakash, N. S. (2021). Trends in monoclonal antibody production using various bioreactor systems. *Journal of Microbiology and Biotechnology*, *31*(3), 349–357.

Kosourov, S. N., & Seibert, M. (2009). Hydrogen photoproduction by nutrient-deprived *Chlamydomonas reinhardtii* cells immobilized within thin alginate films under aerobic and anaerobic conditions. *Biotechnology and Bioengineering*, *102*(1), 50–58.

Kuba, T. M. C. M., Van Loosdrecht, M. C. M., & Heijnen, J. J. (1996). Phosphorus and nitrogen removal with minimal COD requirement by integration of denitrifying dephosphatation and nitrification in a two-sludge system. *Water Research*, *30*(7), 1702–1710.

Laurinavichene, T. V., Fedorov, A. S., Ghirardi, M. L., Seibert, M., & Tsygankov, A. A. (2006). Demonstration of sustained hydrogen photoproduction by immobilized, sulfur-deprived *Chlamydomonas reinhardtii* cells. *International Journal of Hydrogen Energy*, *31*(5), 659–667.

Laurinavichene, T. V., Kosourov, S. N., Ghirardi, M. L., Seibert, M., & Tsygankov, A. A. (2008). Prolongation of H2 photoproduction by immobilized, sulfur-limited *Chlamydomonas reinhardtii* cultures. *Journal of Biotechnology*, *134*(3–4), 275–277.

Li, F., Lan, X., Wang, L., Kong, X., Xu, P., Tai, Y., Liu, G., & Shi, J. (2020). An efficient photocatalyst coating strategy for intimately coupled photocatalysis and biodegradation (ICPB): Powder spraying method. *Chemical Engineering Journal, 383*, 123092.

Li, L., Zhang, J., Lin, J., & Liu, J. (2015). Biological technologies for the removal of sulfur containing compounds from waste streams: bioreactors and microbial characteristics. *World Journal of Microbiology and Biotechnology, 31*(10), 1501–1515.

Liu, H., Yang, Y., Sun, H., Zhao, L., & Liu, Y. (2018). Fate of tetracycline in enhanced biological nutrient removal process. *Chemosphere, 193*, 998–1003.

Liu, X., Lu, S., Guo, W., Xi, B., & Wang, W. (2018). Antibiotics in the aquatic environments: A review of lakes, China. *Science of the total environment, 627*, 1195–1208.

Marchetti, R., Stella, M., Talukdar, D., & Pileci, R. E. (2020). *Rapid environmental monitoring, capture, and destruction activities of SARS-CoV-2 during the Covid-19 health emergency*. medRxiv.

Metze, S., Ruhl, S., Greller, G., Grimm, C., & Scholz, J. (2020). Monitoring online biomass with a capacitance sensor during scale-up of industrially relevant CHO cell culture fed-batch processes in single-use bioreactors. *Bioprocess and Biosystems Engineering, 43*(2), 193–205.

Mujtaba, G., Rizwan, M., Kim, G., & Lee, K. (2018). Removal of nutrients and COD through co-culturing activated sludge and immobilized Chlorella vulgaris. *Chemical Engineering Journal, 343*, 155–162.

Mukherjee, D., Bhattacharya, P., Jana, A., Bhattacharya, S., Sarkar, S., Ghosh, S., Majumdar, S., & Swarnakar, S. (2018). Synthesis of ceramic ultrafiltration membrane and application in membrane bioreactor process for pesticide remediation from wastewater. *Process Safety and Environmental Protection, 116*, 22–33.

Mustafa, M. G., Khan, M. G. M., Nguyen, D., & Iqbal, S. (2018). *Techniques in biotechnology: Essential for industry. Omics technologies and bio-engineering* (pp. 233–249). Academic Press.

Nilsang, S., Nandakumar, K. S., Galaev, I. Y., Rakshit, S. K., Holmdahl, R., Mattiason, B., et al. (2007). Monoclonal antibody production using a new supermacroporous cryogel perfusion reactor. *Biotechnology Progress, 23*, 932–939.

Prado, N., Ochoa, J., & Amrane, A. (2009). Biodegradation by activated sludge and toxicity of tetracycline into a semi-industrial membrane bioreactor. *Bioresource Technology, 100*(15), 3769–3774.

Prakash, P., Singh, H. R., & Jha, S. K. (2020). Preparation, characterization and application of curcumin based polymeric bio-composite for efficient removal of endotoxins and bacterial cells from therapeutic preparations. *Journal of Biomaterials Science, Polymer Edition*, 1–18.

Rashid, N., Lee, K., Han, J. I., & Gross, M. (2013). Hydrogen production by immobilized *Chlorella vulgaris*: optimizing pH, carbon source and light. *Bioprocess and Biosystems Engineering, 36*(7), 867–872.

Rashid, N., Lee, K., & Mahmood, Q. (2011). Bio-hydrogen production by *Chlorella vulgaris* under diverse photoperiods. *Bioresource Technology, 102*(2), 2101–2104.

Ross, B. S., & Pott, R. W. (2021). Hydrogen production by immobilized *Rhodopseudomonas palustris* in packed or fluidized bed photobioreactor systems. *International Journal of Hydrogen Energy, 46*(2), 1715–1727.

Saadati, F., Keramati, N., & Ghazi, M. M. (2016). Influence of parameters on the photocatalytic degradation of tetracycline in wastewater: a review. *Critical Reviews in Environmental Science and Technology, 46*(8), 757–782.

Sagir, E., Alipour, S., Elkahlout, K., Koku, H., Gunduz, U., Eroglu, I., & Yucel, M. (2018). Biological hydrogen production from sugar beet molasses by agar immobilized *R. capsulatus* in a panel photobioreactor. *International Journal of Hydrogen Energy, 43*(32), 14987–14995.

Saha, A., Bhushan, S., Mukherjee, P., Chanda, C., Bhaumik, M., Ghosh, M., Sharmin, J., Datta, P., Banerjee, S., Barat, P., & Thakur, A. R. (2018). Simultaneous sequestration of nitrate and phosphate from wastewater using a tailor-made bacterial consortium in biofilm bioreactor. *Journal of Chemical Technology & Biotechnology*, *93*(5), 1279–1289.

See, S., Lim, P., Lim, J., Seng, C., & Adnan, R. (2015). Evaluation of o-cresol removal using PVA-cryogel-immobilised biomass enhanced by PAC. *Water SA*, *41*(1), 55–60.

Singh, S., Adapa, L. M., & Hankins, N. (2017). Influences of ammonium and phosphate stimulation on metalworking fluid biofilm reactor development and performance. *New Biotechnology*, *39*, 240–246.

Skjånes, K., Andersen, U., Heidorn, T., & Borgvang, S. A. (2016). Design and construction of a photobioreactor for hydrogen production, including status in the field. *Journal of Applied Phycology*, *28*(4), 2205–2223.

Sobhanipour, A. R., Khodabakhshi, M. R., Karimian, R., & Alizadeh, M. (2021). Removal of nitrate from water using TiO_2/PVDF membrane photobioreactor. *Iranian Journal of Chemistry and Chemical Engineering, Vol, 40*(1), 167–183.

Stepanov, N., & Efremenko, E. (2017). Immobilised cells of *Pachysolen tannophilus* yeast for ethanol production from crude glycerol. *New Biotechnology*, *34*, 54–58.

Strobl, F., Duerkop, M., Palmberger, D., & Striedner, G. (2021). High shear resistance of insect cells: The basis for substantial improvements in cell culture process design. *Scientific Reports*, *11*(1), 1–11.

Su, Y., Wang, X., Dong, S., Fu, S., Zhou, D., & Rittmann, B. E. (2020). Towards a simultaneous combination of ozonation and biodegradation for enhancing tetracycline decomposition and toxicity elimination. *Bioresource Technology*, *304*, 123009.

Suttle, A., Rasche, U., & Sha, M. (2019). Cell culture bioprocessing in perfusion. *BioProcess International*, *17*(5), si, 2019.

Szymański, K., Morawski, A. W., & Mozia, S. (2018). Effectiveness of treatment of secondary effluent from a municipal wastewater treatment plant in a photocatalytic membrane reactor and hybrid UV/H2O2–ultrafiltration system. *Chemical Engineering and Processing-Process Intensification*, *125*, 318–324.

Taşkan, B., Casey, E., & Hasar, H. (2019). Simultaneous oxidation of ammonium and tetracycline in a membrane aerated biofilm reactor. *Science of the Total Environment*, *682*, 553–560.

Thill, P. G., Ager, D. K., Vojnovic, B., Tesh, S. J., Scott, T. B., & Thompson, I. P. (2016). Hybrid biological, electron beam and zero-valent nano iron treatment of recalcitrant metalworking fluids. *Water Research*, *93*, 214–221.

Tripathi, A., & Melo, J. S. (2019). Cryostructurization of polymeric systems for developing macroporous cryogel as a foundational framework in bioengineering applications. *Journal of Chemical Sciences*, *131*(9), 1–11.

Valdebenito-Rolack, E., Ruiz-Tagle, N., Abarzúa, L., Aroca, G., & Urrutia, H. (2017). Characterization of a hyperthermophilic sulphur-oxidizing biofilm produced by archaea isolated from a hot spring. *Electronic Journal of Biotechnology*, *25*, 58–63.

Verma, S. K., Modi, A., & Bellare, J. (2021). Hollow fibre membrane bioreactor functionalized with GO-cryogel 3D matrix promotes liver cell anchoring and their functional maintenance. *Medical Devices & Sensors*, *4*(1), e10128.

Wang, B., Wang, Z., Chen, T., & Zhao, X. (2020). Development of novel bioreactor control systems based on smart sensors and actuators. *Frontiers in Bioengineering and Biotechnology*, *8*, 7.

Wang, S., Ma, X., Liu, Y., Yi, X., Du, G., & Li, J. (2020). Fate of antibiotics, antibiotic-resistant bacteria, and cell-free antibiotic-resistant genes in full-scale membrane bioreactor wastewater treatment plants. *Bioresource Technology*, *302*, 122825.

Xie, B., Gong, W., Yu, H., Tang, X., Yan, Z., Luo, X., Gan, Z., Wang, T., Li, G., & Liang, H. (2018). Immobilized microalgae for anaerobic digestion effluent treatment in a photobioreactor-ultrafiltration system: Algal harvest and membrane fouling control. *Bioresource Technology*, *268*, 139–148.

Xiong, H., Zou, D., Zhou, D., Dong, S., Wang, J., & Rittmann, B. E. (2017). Enhancing degradation and mineralization of tetracycline using intimately coupled photocatalysis and biodegradation (ICPB). *Chemical Engineering Journal*, *316*, 7–14.

Yang, Q., Luo, K., Li, X. M., Wang, D. B., Zheng, W., Zeng, G. M., & Liu, J. J. (2010). Enhanced efficiency of biological excess sludge hydrolysis under anaerobic digestion by additional enzymes. *Bioresource Technology*, *101*(9), 2924–2930.

Yousefi, H., Mahmud, A., Chang, D., Das, J., Gomis, S., Chen, J. B., Wang, H., Been, T., Yip, L., Coomes, E., & Li, Z. (2021). Detection of SARS-CoV-2 viral particles using direct, reagent-free electrochemical sensing. *Journal of the American Chemical Society*, *143*(4), 1722–1727.

Zhang, G., Song, X., Mei, J., Ye, G., Wang, L., Yu, L., Xing, M. M., & Qiu, X. (2017). A simple 3D cryogel co-culture system used to study the role of CAFs in EMT of MDA-MB-231 cells. *RSC Advances*, 7(28), 17208–17216.

Zhang, H., Chen, G., Zhang, Q., Lee, D. J., Zhang, Z., Li, Y., Li, P., Hu, J., & Yan, B. (2017). Photosynthetic hydrogen production by alginate immobilized bacterial consortium. *Bioresource Technology*, *236*, 44–48.

Zhang, Y., Stobbe, P., Silvander, C. O., & Chotteau, V. (2015). Very high cell density perfusion of CHO cells anchored in a non-woven matrix-based bioreactor. *Journal of Biotechnology*, *213*, 28–41.

Zhang, Y., & Veronique, C. (2015). Observation of Chinese hamster ovary cells retained inside the non-woven fiber matrix of the CellTank bioreactor. *Data Brief*, *5*, 586–588.

Zhuo, M., Abass, O. K., & Zhang, K. (2018). New insights into the treatment of real *N*, *N*-dimethylacetamide contaminated wastewater using a membrane bioreactor and its membrane fouling implications. *RSC Advances*, *8*(23), 12799–12807.

Further reading

Kumari, J., & Kumar, A. (2017). Development of polymer based cryogel matrix for transportation and storage of mammalian cells. *Scientific Reports*, 7(1), 1–13.

Top trends in biomanufacturing (Texere Publishing). Trends in Biopharma manufacturing survey report, 2019. Available from https://www.nibrt.ie/wp-content/uploads/2019/03/Biopharma_Trends_Survey_Mar19.pdf. Accessed June 13, 2021.

CHAPTER 10

Sustainable engineering of food waste into high-quality animal feed using a drying technology

Santhana Krishnan[1,2], Nur Shahidah[1,5], Mohd Fadhil Bin Md Din[1,5], Puranjan Mishra[3], Mohd Nasrullah[3], Abudukeremu Kadier[4], Shazwin Mat Taib[1,5], Mohd Hafiz Bin Puteh[6], Norahim bin Ibrahim[7], Nurfarhain Md Rusli[1,5], Fadzlin Md Sairan[1,5] and Lakhveer Singh[8]

[1]Department of Water and Environmental, Centre for Environmental Sustainability and Water Security (IPASA), Research Institute of Sustainable Environment (RISE), School of Civil Engineering, Faculty of Engineering, Universiti Teknologi Malaysia (UTM), Skudai, Malaysia
[2]PSU Energy Systems Research Institute, Department of Environmental Engineering, Faculty of Engineering, Prince of Songkla University, Songkhla, Thailand
[3]Faculty of Civil Engineering Technology, Universiti Malaysia Pahang (UMP), Pahang, Malaysia
[4]Laboratory of Environmental Science and Technology, The Xinjiang Technical Institute of Physics and Chemistry, Key Laboratory of Functional Materials and Devices for Special Environments, Chinese Academy of Sciences, Urumqi, PR China
[5]Department of Water and Environmental Engineering, School of Civil Engineering, Faculty of Engineering, Universiti Teknologi Malaysia (UTM), Skudai, Malaysia
[6]Department of Environmental Engineering, Faculty of Civil Engineering, Universiti Teknologi Malaysia (UTM), Skudai, Malaysia
[7]Department of Biosciences and Health Sciences, Faculty of Biosciences and Medical Engineering, Universiti Teknologi Malaysia (UTM), Skudai, Malaysia
[8]Department of Environmental Science, SRM University-AP, Amaravati, Andhra Pradesh, India

10.1 Introduction

Management of solid waste has become a serious concern as well as a major challenge for developing and developed countries throughout the world. The rate of waste generation is increasing every day due to the significant growth of the world population (Woon & Lo, 2013). Moreover, the increasing rate of waste generation may also be influenced by higher economic development and the rate of urbanization. It is estimated that by 2100, the amount of waste generation will be three times greater than the current amount (Villalba et al., 2002). In Malaysia, total estimated municipal solid waste (MSW) generation had increased from 1998 to 2010 which is 8 million tons per year and the amount is estimated to be nearly 10 million tons per year by 2020 (Johari et al., 2012). Due to the amount of waste that produces increases, it causes the capacity of solid waste to be disposed of increases and the space and lifespan of the landfill will be decreased

Techno-economics and Life Cycle Assessment of Bioreactors
DOI: https://doi.org/10.1016/B978-0-323-89848-5.00001-9

(Abd Hamid et al., 2015). Currently, in Malaysia, food waste is the most generated waste that takes up landfill space instead of paper and plastics. The composition of waste dumped at the Malaysian landfills consists of 47% food waste, 20% plastics, 17% paper, 4% metals, 3% glass, and the rest 9% is another waste (Abd Kadir et al., 2013). The high amount of food waste generated might cause the space of the landfill to decrease as well as cause odor and gas emission problems. However, there are many preventive actions have been taken to decrease the capacity of food waste that needs to be disposed of in the landfill. For instance, via composting, anaerobic digestion, disposed of through incinerator and recycling food waste to animal feeds (Komakech, 2014). The food waste issue can be solved by recycling them as fertilizer and animal feeds that can give more benefit (Ting et al., 2015). To transform food waste into valuable products, an effective method and process are required to obtain high-quality end products. Food waste contains a high nutritive value and high moisture content. Food waste with high moisture content will cause the quality of the waste to deteriorate easily and rapid development of pathogens (Hamid et al., 2012). The presence of pathogens such as *Escherichia coli* in the food waste will cause the food to be contaminated and these pathogens could be potentially transferred to animals through the ingested feed and cause infectious diseases that might be transferred to human beings (Kelley & Walker, 1999). South Korea and Japan are examples of developed countries that recycled food waste into animal feeds which the percentage is increased up to 42.5% and 35.9%, respectively (Salemdeeb et al., 2017). However, adverse management practice in Malaysia due to lack of awareness and mostly, people would only tend to recycle food waste via composting (Microbial Pathogen Data Sheets: Escherichia Coli O157, 2001). European Union (EU) guidelines state that food waste should be used as animal feed even though this practice is currently illegal due to disease control concerns (Salemdeeb et al., 2017). The action of using food waste to feed animals has been banned in some developed countries due to lack of safety. In the European Union (UK), pig feeding was banned in 2002 due to the spread of Foot-and-Mouth Disease (Jones & Pushton, 2013). There are some reasons that may lead to the lack of safety such as the inefficient method of food waste process as it is unable to inactivate the presence of bacteria until it leads to a foot-and-mouth disease that may affect humans and animals. Meanwhile, some developed countries still practice the recycling of food waste to animal feeds since this is one of the methods to reduce the amount of waste that needs to be disposed of in the landfill (Kim & Kim, 2010).

Universiti Teknologi Malaysia (UTM) is one of the institutes in Malaysia that facilitates the initiative from food waste to animal feedstock. The process of food waste into animal feed has been carried out inside UTM's Waste Hub, named as Bio-Recycling Waste. Food waste will be processed every day to feed the animals inside the UTM's orchard. In addition, the main source of the food waste is from the food court in UTM which is called Arked Meranti (rebranding as Kafe Lestari). The bins which contain raw food waste is collected every day and sent to the UTM orchard for processing purpose. However, the safety of animal feeds is in doubt due to the presence of bacteria during the processes such as *E. coli*. Hence, this research will describe the effective method to reduce the presence of pathogens in food waste during the process of recycling. The outcomes of the chapter will provide an idea to reduce the pathogens present in food waste as well as increase the safety of using food waste to feed the animals.

UTM is one of the institutes in Malaysia that facilitates the initiative from food waste to animal feedstock. The process of food waste into animal feed has been carried out inside UTM's Waste Hub, named as Bio-Recycling Waste. Food waste will be processed every day to feed the animals inside the UTM's orchard. In addition, the main source of food waste is from the food court in UTM which is called Arked Meranti (rebranding as Kafe Lestari). The bins which contain raw food waste is collected every day and sent to the UTM orchard for processing purpose. However, the safety of animal feeds is in doubt due to the presence of bacteria during the processes such as *E. coli*. Hence, this research will describe the effective method to reduce the presence of pathogens in food waste during the process of recycling. The outcomes of the study will help to reduce the pathogens as well as increase the safety of using food waste to feed the animals. The specific objectives are to investigate the effectiveness of conventional fan drying method of food waste at the UTM processing site based on the quality of its end product, to evaluate the quality of end product by alternative drying method of heat treatment by the oven and solar, and to compare the number of bacteria present in the end product of fan and heat treatment which is solar and oven.

10.2 Applied processing for food waste into animal feed

The processing site of the production of animal feeds was located at "UTM Bio-Recycling Waste Hub." Firstly, this process used food waste is collected from Kafe Lestari, one of the student food courts in UTM.

Every day, the bins full of raw food wastes at Kafe Lestari were collected and sent to the Bio-Recycling Waste Hub for the food waste-animal feeds processing. The waste generated was in wet conditions since it is raw waste mixed with other waste like plastics, straws, toothpicks, and so on. Then, wastes from the bins were poured on a dripping table for segregation purposes. Food waste was segregated manually from the other waste. This is because food waste is the only source that can be used as raw materials in the preparation of animal feeds. In addition, a dripping table is used to collect the leachate from the wastes. After the segregation process, the wet food waste was left for a day on a dripping table for natural drying purposes. Further, food wastes were mixed with coconut husk as it helps to smoothen the grinding process due to food wastes containing objects which hard to have grinned like chicken bones. Coconut husks also help to provide the additional protein content in the food waste. During the process, food wastes were sprayed 5–6 times a day by using in-house effective microorganism (EM) products. This is to avoid odor problems and prevent the flies from alighted on the food wastes as it might be the cause of the development and presence of pathogens. This process might take up several days to reduce the moisture content in the food waste by removing any leftover water content. The targeted maximum percentage of moisture content during the process is 20% which is anticipated to be more effective for further processing.

The mixture of coconut husk with food waste was further grounded using the grinder machine. The longest time taken for the grinding process is 1 h. After that, the ground food wastes were undergone for the drying process. The drying method is used to reduce again the moisture content and presence of bacteria as drying is considered as one of the simplest processes to remove excess water from the food waste (2015). Further, the grounded food wastes were dried for 2 days by using a modulated fan. A drying table was used to carry out this process. However, the drying process might cause nutrient losses in food waste. Finally, after 2 days of drying, the end products are ready to be used as animal feedstock. Fig. 10.1 shows the pictorial chart of food waste-animal feeds conversion.

10.2.1 Drying technology

The drying method was used in the process of recycling food waste into animal feeds at the UTM farm to reduce moisture content and the presence of pathogens in the animal feeds. Regulated fan, oven, and solar

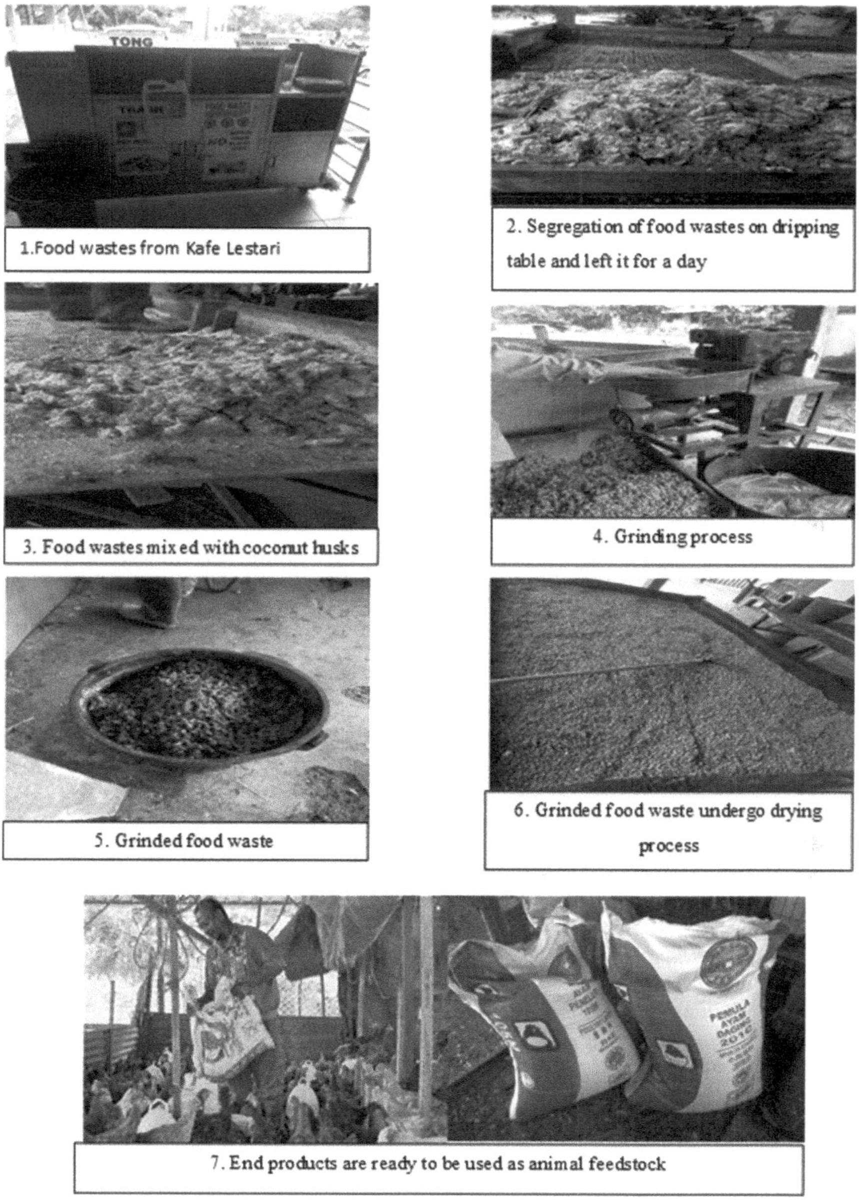

Figure 10.1 Pictorial representation of food waste-animal feeds conversion. *No permission required.*

drying (all fabricated from recyclable materials) were selected as drying methods in the process of drying the food waste. This study was focused on the effectiveness of using the selected method which is based on the quality of end products after the food waste undergoes the drying process.

10.2.1.1 Conventional fan

The modulated electric fan from the homemade fume hood was used to dry the food waste as it helps to circulate the air to the food waste as well as to reduce moisture content in the food waste. Firstly, 2 kg of food waste was weighed by using the weighing machine. Food wastes collection was randomly from the bins that arrived from Kafe Lestari. Further, food wastes were poured on the dripping table to remove leachate as well as to decrease the moisture content. Further, it has undergone for mixing process where it is mixed with the coconut husk. The mixtures were grounded using a grinder machine. After being ground, the mixtures had undergone a drying process. By using a fan, the drying process might take up to 2 days to dry the ground food waste. The time taken for food waste to dry depends on the speed of the fan. After it is dried, triplet samples of the end product were sent to the laboratory for further analysis.

10.2.2 Solar drying

The solar drying method in this study was performed in the fabricated form of the cabinet dryer. The drying cabinet was constructed from a 1 cm-thick plywood and wooden frame and fully insulated by the transparent glass at the sides and top of the walls. On top of the cabinet, the slanted front wall was covered with transparent glass to allow the sunlight to pass through. There are air holes in the cabinet to allow air to enter and exit the chamber. The cabinet was painted black to absorb and trap heat from the sunlight. Two kilograms of ground food wastes were placed on a tray inside the cabinet. The solar dryer was located at a suitable place where the place is able to get direct sunlight. By using a solar dryer, the drying process might take up to 2 days to dry the ground food waste. The length of the drying process is depending on the atmospheric conditions and the surrounding temperature. After it is dried, triplet samples of the end product were sent to the laboratory for further analysis.

10.2.3 Oven

After undergoing segregation and grinding processes, 1 kg of ground food wastes was selected randomly and was weighed using the weighing machine. The ground mixtures were sealed in a sealed bag and sent to the laboratory to dry in the oven. The temperature of the oven is set at 80°C. The drying process might take up to 1 h to dry the ground food waste. The time taken for the food waste to dry depends on the temperature of the oven. After it is dried, triplets samples of the end product were sent to the laboratory for further analysis. The samples were taken from the production of animal feeds using a fan, solar, and ovens which there were three different samples from different methods Environmental Laboratory was used to analyzed moisture content and *E. coli* and for protein analysis (Official Methods of Analysis of AOAC, 1990).

10.3 Results and discussion

10.3.1 Effectiveness of conventional fan

The result suggested that suggested after the food waste was ground, it was poured on the table with a fan to dry it before being completely changed into an end product. The type and speed of the fan determine the effectiveness and the desired quality of food waste as end products. In addition, the higher speed of the fan decreases the time to dry the food waste as well as reduces the high percentage of moisture content. However, based on the observation at the processing site, the conventional fan used was not as effective as the time taken for the food waste to be dried is prolonged as unexpected. Basically, the duration was estimated between 1 and 2 days but after 2 days, the food waste was still not fully dried and it caused the process to be delayed. This was due to the low speed of the fan and sometimes it malfunctioned. The fan was malfunctioned due to it is running continuously for 2 days during the process. So, the process for one batch of food waste was delayed as the fan needs to be repaired and it might cause the food waste to be easily contaminated by flies and dust, increase the growth of bacteria as well as damage the properties of the food waste during the maintenance duration. Fig. 10.2 shows the example of a fan used at the site.

10.3.2 Effectiveness of solar drying

The solar drying cabinet has been set up and placed under the sun for the consecutive 2 days. Food waste weighing 2 kg is placed in the solar dryer cabinet and it was only collected after 2 days. The performance of the solar drying method to dry the food waste was highly dependent on solar radiation and ambient temperature (2015). This is the consequence of UV

Figure 10.2 Conventional fan at UTM farm. *UTM*, Universiti Teknologi Malaysia. *No permission required.*

Figure 10.3 Solar drying cabinet. *No permission required.*

sunlight is essential to use the solar drying method to dry the food waste. It also depends on the location of the cabinet where a position with direct solar radiation be effective as it can reduce the time for the food waste to be dried (Aravindh & Sreekumar, 2015). The position of the solar dryer cabinet needed to be changed to maximize the heat received from the sun. During the processing duration at the UTM farm, it was observed that the end product in batch 3 was completely dried as compared to the end product in batch 1 and batch 2. This may relate to the consistent weather that might affect the temperature and humidity within 2 days of the drying process (Mustayen et al., 2014). Hence, it reduces the moisture content of the food waste. Fig. 10.3 shows the solar drying cabinet used at the UTM farm.

10.3.3 Effectiveness of oven drying

Oven drying was the fastest method to dry the food waste as it only took 1–2 h compared to other methods. Oven-method was able to reduce high water content from food waste. However, the oven was the most expensive method compared to fans and solar dryers. Moreover, the

Figure 10.4 End products after 1 h in the oven. *No permission required.*

amount of food waste to be dried in the oven was limited due to its space, and lots of aluminum dishes (or containers) needed to be used. In addition, using the oven to dry the food waste increased the percentage loss of nutrients and decreased the nutrients contained in the animal feeds. On the other hand, it might slow down the growth rate of animals, especially poultry. Fig. 10.4 shows the end products after 1 h in the oven.

10.3.4 Improvement of the drying process

The result was shown in terms of moisture content, protein, and *E. coli* analysis. End products from the different drying methods which are a conventional fan, solar dryer, and oven are analyzed in the research laboratory. The results of these methods were compared to achieve the objectives of this study which is to find the most effective method to be used at the processing site, UTM Bio-Recycling Centre, and to compare the amount of *E. coli* presence in end products. The most effective methods are compared based on the quality of the end products which contain low moisture content and high protein content. The end products also show less amount of *E. coli* presence in the end products.

10.3.5 Moisture content

Moisture content is defined as the ratio of the weight of water content in the food waste to the total weight of the wet wastes. After the experiment is conducted, the moisture content in the end products was calculated. Then, the results of moisture content from a conventional fan, solar, and

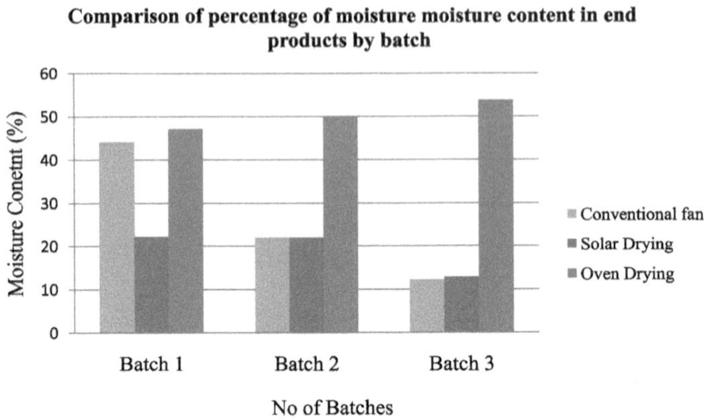

Figure 10.5 Comparison of percentage of moisture content in end products by batch. *No permission required.*

oven drying method were compared. The method with the lowest percentage of moisture content was considered an effective method as it is able to reduce the high amount of excess water from the end products. Low moisture content was able to avoid the growth of the bacteria which vulnerable to moisture. The moisture content of each batch before and after undergoing the drying process has been calculated. Fig. 10.5, shows the percentage of moisture content from different drying methods which are compared by batch.

Fig. 10.5 shows that the end product of solar drying has the lowest percentage of moisture content. This was because this method is highly dependent on solar radiation where the excess water from food waste was able to be easily absorbed by direct UV sunlight (Kumar et al., 2016). Moreover, the location of the cabinet is well-positioned as the sunlight was able to penetrate into it and further dried up naturally. Meanwhile, the conventional fan was highly dependent on the speed of the fan, and oven drying is dependent on the high temperature set in the oven. However, batch 1, shows that there is a slight difference in the percentage of moisture content between conventional fan and oven drying. During the sampling process in batch 1, the fan used at the processing site malfunctioned. It causes the end products were not to be fully dried. Thus, from this result, it can be concluded that the proposed alternative method which is solar drying is effective in reducing moisture content in the end products. Meanwhile, Fig. 10.6 shows the comparison of the percentage of moisture content in end products from different drying methods. The result shows that the oven drying method has had the highest

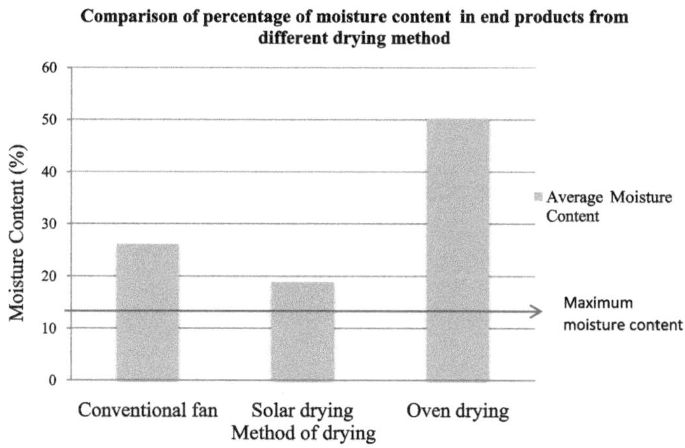

Figure 10.6 Comparison of percentage of moisture content in end products from different drying methods. *No permission required.*

moisture content in the end products compared to the conventional fan and solar drying method. Thus it can be concluded that the proposed alternative method, was not satisfied in the oven drying to reduce moisture content as the percentage of water loss was lowered than a conventional fan and solar. This was likely due to the time taken for the food waste to be dried in the oven being only 1 h. It caused the end products that were not fully dried. There is a difference in terms of drying duration between oven with fan and solar as both of these methods take 2 days to dry the food waste. Hence, from the result obtained, it can be summarized that solar was the most effective method as the end products have the lowest moisture content than a conventional fan and oven drying which the percentage is 18% respectively. Moreover, the lower moisture content is able to decrease the weight of end products as well as avoid the presence and growth of microorganism such as *E. coli*, and *salmonella* that causes deterioration. Even though end products from the solar drying method have the lowest moisture content, it is still unable to achieve the targeted maximum percentage of moisture content in animal feeds which is 12%, respectively.

10.3.6 Analysis of protein content

Protein is one of the important nutrition needed in food waste before processing it to animal feedstock. Adequate nutritive value in end products will help to increase the growth rate of animals and prevent the

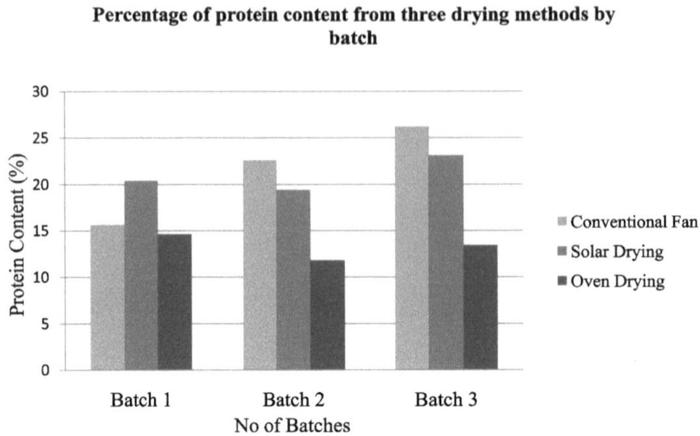

Figure 10.7 Percentage of protein content from three drying methods by batch. *No permission required.*

animals from any disease (Trchounian & Trchounian, 2015). Fig. 10.7 shows the percentage of protein content after undergoing a different drying method.

The oven drying method has the lowest percentage of protein content in end products as shown in Fig. 10.6. This is due to the food waste was being heated by high temperature and it causes a certain loss of nutrients. According to Agoreyo et al. (2011), the removal of water by heat has affected the nutrient content of food waste in various ways. Besides, from the result obtained, it can be seen that the percentage of the protein content of solar drying in batch 2 and 3 were recorded lowered than a conventional fan. This was also due to the application of heat from the temperature that might decrease the protein in food waste. However, the percentage of protein content in the solar drying sample was the highest in batch 1 which is 21.4% compared to the conventional fan and oven drying methods. It was likely affected by the temperature and humidity during the process.

Fig. 10.8 shows the comparison of the percentage of protein content in end products from different drying methods. The obtained result showed that conventional fan has the highest protein content which is 21.5% compared to solar drying and oven drying. The conventional fan was highly dependent on fan speed rather than weather and temperature. In addition, the speed of the fan was controlled by electricity and it helps to ensure the flow of air and circulation. Moreover, it helps to produce a low level of heat. The low heat level is essential to protect the nutritive

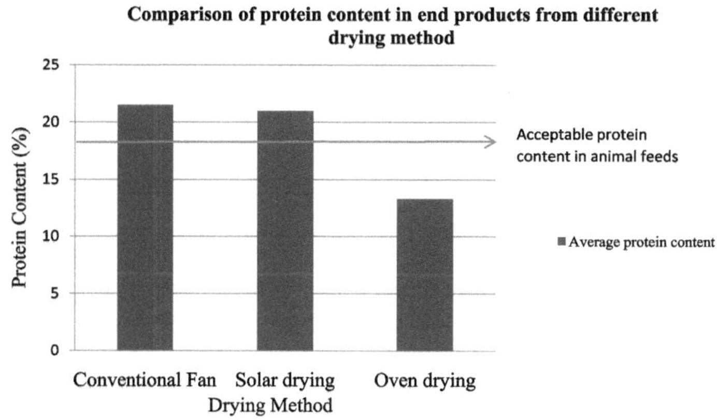

Figure 10.8 Comparison of protein content in end products from different drying methods. *No permission required.*

value of food waste during the drying process. Based on the observation, the application of kinetic energy that controls fan speed is not highly affected by the protein content of end products.

However, oven drying has the lowest protein content in end products which was 13.3% due to the high heat level that might cause the nutritive value to be decreased significantly. Thus the conventional fan was the most effective method as it has high protein content after undergoing the drying process. The alternative method, oven drying was not able to maintain high protein content. Drying of food waste affects the protein quality as different drying methods will have different effects on nutrient composition. In addition, from the comparison, it can be concluded that solar drying is also effective as there was a slight difference in the percentage of protein content between conventional fan and solar which is 21.5% and 21%, respectively. Moreover, the data shows that both methods achieved a high percentage of protein content where it passed the acceptable limit of protein content in animal feeds. Thus the end products from these methods are acceptable to be used as animal feeds as the protein content is high when compared with the minimum percentage of the protein content of animal feeds obtained from the factory which was 18%.

10.3.7 Analysis of *Escherichia coli*

In total, nine samples of end products were tested to determine the amount of *E. coli* presence in the samples. End products that have less amount of *E. coli* are considered safe. However, the amount of *E. coli* obtained must

Table 10.1 Analysis of *Escherichia coli* in end products from different drying methods.

Batch	*Escherichia coli* (CFU/g) $\times 10^2$		
	Conventional fan	Solar drying	Oven drying
1	ND (<10)	ND (<10)	ND (<10)
2	3300	ND (<10) ND (<10)	ND (<10)
3	800	1200	500

ND, Not detected.

not exceed the maximum allowed number of pathogenic microorganisms present in animal feeds, which is 50 CFU/g (Cabarkapa et al., 2009). Food waste that contained a high amount of *E. coli* is unsafe to be produced into animal feeds as it will cause post-weanling diarrhea (PWD) which will slow down the growth rate of animals. Hence, this study is important to know the amount of *E. coli* presence in end products.

The results of laboratory analysis are shown in Table 10.1. As can be seen from Table 10.1, in batch 3, the amount of *E. coli* presence in end products using the oven drying method was lower than the amount of *E. coli* presence using solar and conventional fan methods. It can be concluded that oven drying was the most effective method as it has lower *E. coli* content. The amount of *E. coli* decreases when there was lower moisture content in end products (Trchounian & Trchounian, 2015). However, this study could not able to prove this theory as the amount of *E. coli* in end products by using the solar method is higher when the moisture content is lower. This is might be due to the presence of *E. coli* being inconsistent and causing an error during the experiment. The changes in temperature and humidity of the samples may inhibit the growth of *E. coli*. However, the amount of *E. coli* presence in every method proposed in this study is high as the results exceeded 50 CFU/g, the maximum allowed number of pathogenic microorganisms present in animal feeds. Thus it can be concluded that the end products are unsafe to be used as animal feeds as it contains high *E. coli*.

From Table 10.1, it can be seen that some *E. coli* results are less than 10 CFU/g which is considered as not detected. This was likely due to the targeted organism is not found in the sample at that moment. According to the (American Chemical Society (2010)), sometimes it is difficult to find samples that contain *E. coli* in large samples. At the processing site, there were 20 kg of ground food waste is being poured on the drying table for further dying processes. However, only 50 g of end products is selected as a sample to be sent to the laboratory for *E. coli* testing. The *E. coli* is not detected might due to the targeted bacteria is not present in the samples taken. Hence, improvement in sampling and sensitivity is important. Besides, it also might be due to the samples being contaminated. Contamination can occur when the samples are not handled properly during sample preparation to determine *E. coli* or when the samples are stored in the freezer (Kumar et al., 2016). Contamination is caused by other bacteria that attack the samples and make *E. coli* bacteria disappear from the samples. According to the Environmental Protection Agency, the sampling method can also cause bacteria to spread to food waste and cause contamination (Kumar et al., 2016). For instance, the date and name of the samples were labeled on the sealed bag using a nonwaterproof marker. It caused contamination as it will penetrate the bag and end products. The contamination may also be due to the plastic seal bag. The plastic seal bag might contain chemicals that can kill the bacteria since the sample may pick up the contamination from it. During the preparation of the sample, an unsterile spatula was used to transfer the sample from the food container into the plastic seal bag. Unclean tools could lead to contamination of the sample.

Moreover, cross-contamination could have occurred during the preservation of the sample. All nine samples were placed in the freezer along with other samples. Another sample might have contaminated the end product sample if there is a crack or leakage of the sealed bag used. Next, the laboratory analyst may also contribute to the damages of these samples. The analyst should use disposable gloves, head covers, face masks, etc. when handling samples. In addition, *E. coli* is sensitive to the surrounding. It might be disappeared when the samples are not well handled. The presence of *E. coli* needs to be detected as it will affect the growth and health of animals, especially poultry and it will transfer to humans.

10.4 Conclusions

From the analysis, solar drying was the most effective method when compared with conventional fan and oven as the quality of end products is the highest. This is based on the end product that contains the lowest moisture content which is 18%. Lower moisture content can reduce and avoid the development of bacteria in food waste, especially *E. coli*. Then, it contains high protein content which is acceptable when compared with the value of protein content in animal feeds the product from the factory, where the percentage is 21% which is higher than the minimum value of protein content of animal feeds in the factory, 18%. Hence, it was acceptable to be used as animal feeds due to the end product being enriched with protein that is essential for animal growth. Moreover, this method was cost-effective as it is only depending on the sunlight and humidity to dry the food waste as well as it conserves energy. It is highly dependent on solar energy as it was the only source of energy used to dry the food waste. Moreover, the cost to construct the cabinet dryer was not expensive and can be used for a longer period of time. End products from oven drying have the highest moisture content and the lowest protein content which the percentage was 50% and 13%, respectively. High moisture content might be due to the drying duration being shorter which is 1 h as it is unable for the end products to completely dry. Then, it has the lowest moisture content due to the effect of high temperature that causes the loss of nutrient content in the food waste. Thus the quality of end products using this method was the lowest as it was unable to maintain high nutrient content as well as moisture content. Conventional fan method able to reduce the high amount of moisture content compared to oven drying and achieve high protein content which was 26% and 21.5%, respectively. On the other hand, when it was compared with solar drying, the quality of end products was slightly lower than the solar method. Based on the analysis, it can be seen that moisture content in end products was higher than end products using solar Thus it can be concluded that the solar drying method is the most effective method to be used at the processing site, UTM farm as the quality of end products is the highest compared to another method. Even though this drying treatment induced a loss of nutrients, the residual nutrient content can still satisfy the feeding purposes. In addition, the nutrient content of end products can be increased by adding wheat bran and soybean hull after the drying process. Then, contaminated samples cause the presence of *E. coli* not to be detected. The contamination might occur before or after the analysis. Hence, improvement to avoid contamination is essential.

Acknowledgments

This research is financially supported by FRGS R.J130000.7801.5F221, PDRU Grant-Vot No. Q.J130000.21A2.04E53, Hitachi Global Foundation 2019, and MRUN R. J130000.7805.4L886, which are gratefully acknowledged.

References

2015. In International Journal of Renewable Energy Technology Research. (Vol. 4, Issue 2, pp. 1–9).

Abd Hamid, K. B., Ishak, M. Y., & Abu Samah, M. A. (2015). Analysis of municipal solid waste generation and composition at administrative building café in Universiti Putra Malaysia: A case study. *Polish Journal of Environmental Studies*, *24*(5), 1969–1982. Available from https://doi.org/10.15244/pjoes/39106.

Abd Kadir, S. A. S., Yin, C. Y., Rosli Sulaiman, M., Chen, X., & El-Harbawi, M. (2013). Incineration of municipal solid waste in Malaysia: Salient issues, policies and waste-to-energy initiatives. *Renewable and Sustainable Energy Reviews*, *24*, 181–186. Available from https://doi.org/10.1016/j.rser.2013.03.041.

Agoreyo, B. O., Akpiroroh, O., Orukpe, O. A., Osaweren, O. R., & Owabor, C. N. (2011). The effects of various drying methods on the nutritional composition of *Musa paradisiaca*, *Dioscorea rotundata* and *Colocasia esculenta*. *Asian Journal of Biochemistry*, 458–464. Available from https://doi.org/10.3923/ajb.2011.458.464.

American Chemical Society (ACS). (2010). *News releases. A two-in-one test for detecting E. coli in ground beef and other food Embargoed for release*, March 23. https://www.acs.org/content/acs/en/pressroom/newsreleases/2010/march.

Aravindh, M. A., & Sreekumar, A. (2015). Solar drying—A sustainable way of food processing. *Green Energy and Technology*, *201*, 27–46. Available from https://doi.org/10.1007/978-81-322-2337-5_2.

Cabarkapa, I., Kokic, B., Plavsic, D., Ivanov, D., & Levic, J. (2009). Microbiological safety of animal feed. *Biotechnology in Animal Husbandry*, *25*(5–6–2), 1155–1162.

Hamid, A. A., Ahmad, A., Ibrahim, M. H., & Rahman, N. N. N. A. (2012). Food waste management in Malaysia—Current situation and future management options. *Journal of Industrial Research & Technology*, *2*(1), 36–39, Journal of Industrial Research.

Johari, A., Ahmed, S. I., Hashim, H., Alkali, H., & Ramli, M. (2012). Economic and environmental benefits of landfill gas from municipal solid waste in Malaysia. *Renewable and Sustainable Energy Reviews*, *16*(5), 2907–2912. Available from https://doi.org/10.1016/j.rser.2012.02.005.

Jones, J., & Pushton, J. (2013). The economic impacts of foot-and- mouth disease. *Preventive Veterinary Medicine*, *112*, 161–173.

Kelley, T. R., & Walker, P. M. (1999). Bacterial concentration reduction of food waste amended animal feed using a single-screw dry-extrusion process. *Bioresource Technology*, *67*(3), 247–253. Available from https://doi.org/10.1016/S0960-8524(98)00118-7.

Kim, M. H., & Kim, J. W. (2010). Comparison through a LCA evaluation analysis of food waste disposal options from the perspective of global warming and resource recovery. *Science of the Total Environment*, *408*(19), 3998–4006. Available from https://doi.org/10.1016/j.scitotenv.2010.04.049.

Komakech, A.J. (2014). *Urban waste management and the environmental impact of organic waste treatment systems in Kampala* (pp. 1652–6880).

Kumar, M., Sansaniwal, S. K., & Khatak, P. (2016). Progress in solar dryers for drying various commodities. *Renewable and Sustainable Energy Reviews*, *55*, 346–360. Available from https://doi.org/10.1016/j.rser.2015.10.158.

Microbial Pathogen Data Sheets: Escherichia Coli O157. (2001).

Mustayen, A. G. M. B., Mekhilef, S., & Saidur, R. (2014). Performance study of different solar dryers: A review. *Renewable and Sustainable Energy Reviews*, *34*, 463–470. Available from https://doi.org/10.1016/j.rser.2014.03.020.

Official Methods of Analysis of AOAC. (1990). In *Association of Official Analytical Chemists*.

Salemdeeb, R., zu Ermgassen, E. K. H. J., Kim, M. H., Balmford, A., & Al-Tabbaa, A. (2017). Environmental and health impacts of using food waste as animal feed: A comparative analysis of food waste management options. *Journal of Cleaner Production, 140*, 871–880. Available from https://doi.org/10.1016/j.jclepro.2016.05.049.

Ting, C., Yiying, J., & Dongsheng, S. (2015). A safety analysis of food waste-derived animal feeds from three typical conversion techniques in China. *Waste Management*, 42–50. Available from https://doi.org/10.1016/j.wasman.2015.06.041.

Trchounian, K., & Trchounian, A. (2015). Hydrogen production from glycerol by *Escherichia coli* and other bacteria: An overview and perspectives. *Applied Energy, 156*, 174–184. Available from https://doi.org/10.1016/j.apenergy.2015.07.009.

Villalba, G., Segarra, M., Fernández, A. I., Chimenos, J. M., & Espiell, F. (2002). A proposal for quantifying the recyclability of materials. *Resources, Conservation and Recycling*, 39–53. Available from https://doi.org/10.1016/s0921-3449(02)00056-3.

Woon, K. S., & Lo, I. M. C. (2013). Greenhouse gas accounting of the proposed landfill extension and advanced incineration facility for municipal solid waste management in Hong Kong. *Science of the Total Environment, 458–460*, 499–507. Available from https://doi.org/10.1016/j.scitotenv.2013.04.061.

CHAPTER 11

Environmental and economic life cycle assessment of biochar use in anaerobic digestion for biogas production

Zaied Bin Khalid[1], Ahasanul Karim[2], Pramod Jadhav[1], Puranjan Mishra[1], Zularisam Bin Abd Wahid[1] and Mohd Nasrullah[1]
[1]Faculty of Civil Engineering Technology, Universiti Malaysia Pahang (UMP), Pahang, Malaysia
[2]Department of Soil Sciences and Agri-food Engineering, Université Laval, Quebec, QC, Canada

11.1 Introduction

Because many individuals working in urban society consume energy on a regular basis, it is an important aspect of everyday life. Environmental deterioration, on the other hand, is far worse than previously assumed. Energy scarcity and trash creation are two of the most pressing concerns in modern life. Traditional emission reduction technologies consume a lot of power and produce a lot of CO_2. Recycling materials and generating power from wastewater hold a new trend (Lam et al., 2020). Anaerobic digestion (AD) is a biological treatment that employs microorganisms to convert organic waste into bioenergy. Over the last few decades, AD has been researched in a variety of wastewater treatment applications for real-time wastewater decontamination and bioenergy yield (Wu et al., 2020; Zaied, Siddique, Nasrullah, et al., 2019). While chemical–biological interactions account for the majority of AD's efficacy, there are still substantial limitations to its wider use (Chen et al., 2020; Zaied, Siddique, Zularisam, et al., 2019). Combining a chemical–biological solution with traditional wastewater treatment technologies is presumed to improve the efficiency of natural wastewater treatment. However, a number of unfavorable elements in the AD system constantly disrupt microbial behavior, resulting in inadequate energy recovery. The build-up of free ammonia and volatile fatty acids (VFA) restricted methanogenic archaea activity, limiting the total organic loading rate (OLR) of AD methods, for example, due to intermediate metabolites (Jiang et al., 2019). Industrial wastewaters contained phenol and

Techno-economics and Life Cycle Assessment of Bioreactors
DOI: https://doi.org/10.1016/B978-0-323-89848-5.00002-0

polymeric aromatic hydrocarbons resistant to biodegradation and toxic microbes (Chen et al., 2014). Antibiotic overuse in the livestock business has as well raised the prospect of bacterial deactivation in AD procedures for the treatment of manure waste (Lee et al., 2020). Consequently, designing realistic solutions to these hurdles is crucial for increasing energy production and expanding AD techniques to real-world functions.

Biochar (BC) is a carbon-rich material formed from the pyrolysis of biomass. BC has been a research hot spot in the area of soil improvement, useable substance planning, ecological monitoring, and biowaste reduction because of its unique carbon sequestration role and flexibility (Liu et al., 2019; Palansooriya et al., 2019). Since it is a low-cost component, BC may be employed as an additive to increase AD systems' functioning (Qiu et al., 2019). First, the eco-compatibility of the BC surface, as well as its established porous structures, offer effective locations for the adsorption of gaseous by-products, ammonium, and hazardous pollutants, as well as a haven for bacterial adhesion (Ahmad et al., 2014). BC's alkaline composition and organic functional groups also showed a robust buffering capability, that helped to offset pH drops triggered through VFA aggregation in AD procedures. On the other hand, BC has electrochemical characteristics that allow it to operate as a mediator in syntrophic metabolism, allowing for interspecies electron transfer. Combining the biological and thermochemical conversion systems, which are both promising waste biomass conversion processes, necessitates adding BC to the AD approach in order to increase process productivity and stability (Pecchi & Baratieri, 2019).

However, when considering the process's environmental feasibility, utilizing BC in an anaerobic bioreactor is more cost-effective. In this case, a comprehensive life cycle assessment (LCA) for the entire process is required. From conception to disposal, LCA stands as a comprehensive technique for exploring the potential implications of a product's life cycle (Vondra et al., 2019). LCA presents a complete and new unambiguous image of the genuine ecological benefits in the final stage. The International Organization for Standardization (ISO) created the ISO 14040 sequence as an international standard for LCA (Chan et al., 2016). An LCA analysis that includes upstream, downstream and waste valorization is required to provide a comprehensive and accurate picture of the business. With respect to energy concentration, environmental consequences, and economic repercussions, new advances must be considered (Máša et al., 2013). The economic viability of LCA incorporation is influenced by a number of factors. There are other expenses, such as digested transportation and application, liquid digested dry matter quality, evaporator energy utilization, and so on, in addition to the spending expense.

The completion of method modeling by limited information and understanding, as well as the creation of relevant LCA findings for identifying strategic environmental decisions, are the key difficulties of LCA. LCA has to be used to determine the most ecologically acceptable technical factors and create biomolecules to assure the ecological consequence of this technology from an environmental perspective (Chopra et al., 2020). Some challenges would be solved, such as design concerns caused by stream limits in manufacturing, the necessary molecules, and sensitivity testing of certain parameters at the AD plant size. The output restrictions should be considered while designing the method (nature and quantity of biomolecule). As a result, modeling the entire process with these constraints is unusual in LCA studies of AD facilities, where modeling is often based on the amount of waste handled (Foulet et al., 2019). For sensitivity studies, the selection of principles for each investigated factor is required. This familiarity of performance, however, is still absent in the issue of developing technology.

11.2 Life cycle assessment technology

LCA has been acknowledged as an advanced way to analyze its by-products' cumulative effect across its life cycle considering environmental aspects. LCA is being carried out in a variety of domains in order to provide the most accurate feasible evaluation (Parra-Saldivar et al., 2020). The usage of LCA in waste and wastewater treatment technologies, as well as new breakthroughs in LCA and their effective use to identify the destiny of dangerous compounds, are all important problems that must be addressed. According to the available literature, the production of various pollutants is a hot spot throughout the life cycle of different manufacturing processes. Synergies between various industrial sectors, combined with LCA techniques, result in highly productive, accurate, effective, and long-lasting manufacturing processes with minimal environmental impact. A well-designed LCA protocol often delivers detailed knowledge to manufacturers, customers, regulators, and regulatory bodies, allowing LCA to be used in more realistic ways, mitigate environmental insecurity, and reduce human health risks.

As a result, assessing the environmental impact of many production units that create and release a variety of undesired chemicals into the atmosphere in general and the aquatic system, in particular, is crucial. Furthermore, using an LCA plan, a zero-waste method to resource utilization in the industrial sector should be considered. LCA is a sophisticated tool for reviewing and debating the environmentally friendly consequences of the method or an entire industrial cycle. The LCA is sometimes stated as a "cradle-to-grave" evaluation. Several scientists have compiled literature-based LCA research, underlining the relevance of LCA in present-day areas, including food, water, oil, agriculture, the environment, and medicine (Awad et al., 2019; Gallego-Schmid & Tarpani, 2019; Roy et al., 2009). Some recent developments and deployments of LCA technology, particularly in the water and climate, have yet to be published. With this in mind, the current research is a quick overview of the LCAs technology.

11.2.1 Life cycle assessment–based methodology

The most commonly used LCA approach is focused on four key measures that follow ISO principles and prescribed recommendations. As seen in Fig. 11.1, the first move is to define the objective and scope, followed by the inventory, effect evaluation, and analysis. The inputs and outputs of a basic framework can be compiled using this technique in its current form with no established relations between flows. For complicated and low-TRL schemes, the method must be adjusted. The AD's specification is still under investigation, and there are no industrial procedures in place to

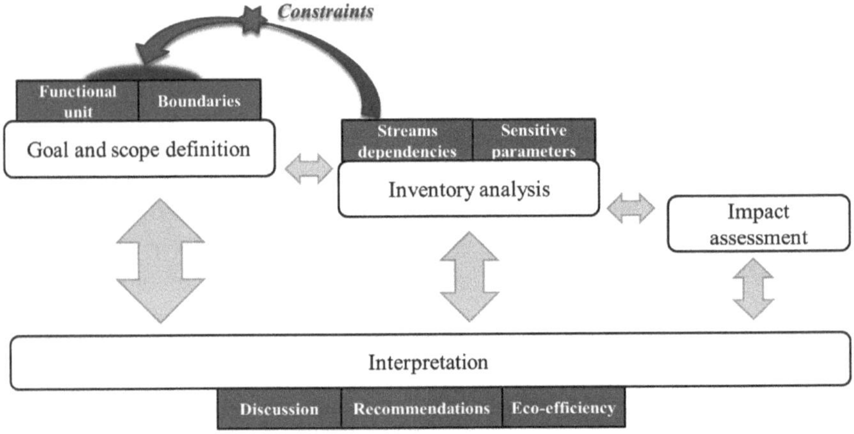

Figure 11.1 Adjusted LCA methodology. *LCA*, Life cycle analysis.

verify the chosen values or the strength of the flow dependencies. The sensitive parameters and dependencies must be defined and analyzed before the process can be designed. Because of the streams' dependencies, the functional unit (FU) is restricted by the inventory phase, as seen in Fig. 11.1. As a result, an LCA protocol that synchronizes the first and second phases of the standard technique must be presented. Finally, the interpretation stage involves an assessment of output performance in terms of environmental and economic variables, as well as the proficiency of the method. The effective objective is to distinguish the selected biomolecules with the ultimate ecological concern, an adjustment between the process's environmental performance and the future market share of the targeted molecules.

11.2.1.1 The goal, scope, and boundaries of the study

The purpose of this report is to find the critical factors that define the procedure and its impact on the environment. Fig. 11.2 depicts the interdependence of the AD mechanism. The waste input is removed from the system's boundary in nearly all LCA studies concentrating on waste recycling since it is assigned no responsibility. The sample materials utilized in the AD process, BC products, and other chemicals must all be included inside the system boundary. Fabrication of materials, on the other hand, could be phased out due to their extended lifespan (for instance, hydrolysis, AD digestion tanks, pyrolysis reactor).

The FU is described as the production of 1000 tons of the desired commodity from the treatment of the comparable quantity of organic waste, which defines the technology's primary goal and enables for comparison. For the

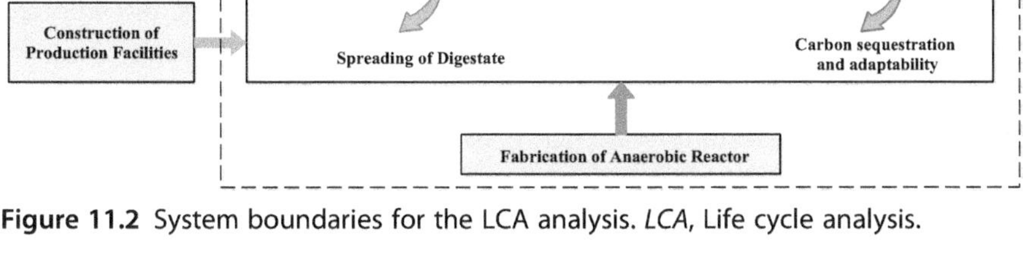

Figure 11.2 System boundaries for the LCA analysis. *LCA*, Life cycle analysis.

output of 1000 tons of BC, the latter has been estimated to be up to 35,000 tons. The project's goal is to finish the concept requirements for the pyrolysis reactor complex. It has yet to be achieved the theoretical and practical integration of such a methodology with an AD facility. The development of a specific and coherent model for the BC device, as well as its integration with an AD plant, are essential concerns, and its implementation would also address sensitivity analyses.

11.2.1.2 Inventory

The GaBi 7.2.1 LCA software package can be used to model any of the life cycle scenarios (Thinkstep, 1992). Experimental studies, informative documentation, and previous work from both authors' respective institutions were accustomed to assembling the foreground life cycle inventory (LCI) details. The inventory of the AD mechanism should be scrutinized closely to ensure that it adhered to current biowaste management guidelines (Manfredi & Pant, 2011). The PE worldwide (previous name of Thinkstep) database and contextual LCI details (e.g., for energy, heat, and other chemicals utilized) must be acquired. Even with solid data, scaling up technology demands precise estimations. The behavior of the BC and its capacity to generate biogas and the requisite operational parameters must be understood to execute the LCA. Given the lack of BC usage in conjunction with AD on a pilot scale, a novel measurement technique must be suggested.

11.2.1.3 Environmental impact assessment

A procedure is desperately needed to evaluate the probable environmentally friendly effect of each consequence outlined. The substance that has been released has a long-term impact on the ecosystem. To evaluate potential effect transfers, ten different impact groups might be employed. Different forms of toxicity include abiotic degradation, eutrophication, acidification, ozone depletion, global warming, photochemical ozone production, human toxicity, and ecotoxicity. Several methods are available to compute considering emissions, waste control and recycling, hazardous chemical treatment, water and land usage (including noise), and air pollution. In most reported LCAs, greenhouse gas (GHG) emissions are the primary indicator of ecological impacts (Cherubini & Strømman, 2011). The pollution may be assessed in terms of global warming potential (GWP), which is defined as the amount of CO_2 emitted into the atmosphere in equal grams. There are several pollution systems of measurement and periods established; a specific system would not be suitable for all uses (Pachauri et al., 2014). BC incorporation in AD is recommended wherever feasible to lessen the total environmental impacts of biogas production.

The environmental effects of the BC yield phase can be assessed using a variety of methods. A systematic (and realistic) LCA analysis considers the bulk of the consequences of the biochemical mechanism and the upstream as well as downstream actions concerned. To perform a credible LCA analysis with practical implications, the importance of different appraisal criteria must be rated and quantified. The LCA result would be subject to random choices by the analyzer without a specific structure dictating at least a minimal degree of method comprehension. Among the alternatives are system limitations, FUs, temporal units, allocation, energy, and environmental measurements. As a result, the LCA of BC modified biogas can vary depending on the amount of understanding (as opposed to the method's practical consequences); without a standard, similar LCA results may be inconclusive.

11.2.1.4 Eco-efficiency of bioenergy production

The World Business Council For Sustainable Development (WBCSD) specifies eco-efficiency as a concept focused on producing more products and services through less usage of energy, waste, and emissions (Helminen, 2000). The eco-efficiency criteria can be used to evaluate two systems that have the same goal but function in various ways while still considering the climate while remaining constrained by economic considerations. Eq. (11.1) may be used to describe the eco-efficiency criteria (Kuosmanen & Kortelainen, 2005):

$$\mathrm{EE} = \frac{\text{Economic Value Added}}{\text{Environmental Damage}} \tag{11.1}$$

This calculation necessitates the knowledge or the ability to quantify the economic benefit added from accessible data. However, since the process is still in its infancy, statistics on spending, manufacturing costs, and retail selling prices are inaccessible. As a result, the eco-efficiency requirement is updated to (Eq. 11.2):

$$\mathrm{EE} = \frac{\%\ \text{Market Share}}{\Delta I} \tag{11.2}$$

The market sharing could assert the process is dependent on existing biogas yield market shares in France and Europe. ΔI is the discrepancy between the impact and comparison situation, separated by the number of all scenarios' impact values. ΔI may be somewhere between -1 and 1. In comparison to the reference case, a pessimistic value signifies ecological burdens, whilst a certain value suggests environmental gains. On the other hand, a favorable benefit suggests that the technology is safer for the community than the comparison case. Bioenergy processing using BC technologies in AD can be compared to an environmental biorefinery. Since organic stock is deterministic and reasonable for mass processing, it is essential to define the biomolecule supply that is part of the appropriate demand and has good environmental efficiency (Gargalo et al., 2017). Biogas production is related to methane content to get to the proper demand since the latter is part of a primary oil market, while biogas is deemed an intermediate commodity.

11.2.2 Life cycle assessment evaluation measures

The LCA technique stands as a useful tool for assessing the environmental effects of a product across its entire life cycle, from fresh substance removal to processing, usage, recycling, and waste disposal (Adesanya et al., 2014). This method would include evidence on the ecological effect of the supply chain (Pant et al., 2011) and might be employed as a decision-making instrument to improve process design while reducing environmentally friendly effects (Lam et al., 2009). The LCA would evaluate the environmental implications of a process across its whole life cycle through analyzing the profit content and energy responses (ISO, 2003; Zabalza Bribián et al., 2011). Furthermore, large-scale industry information may not be accessible during the review. In this situation, mathematical modeling and simulation might be utilized to achieve content and energy ratios for large-scale activities (Collet et al., 2015). The LCA's response data are stored in a database called the LCI. It is described inside the system limits by stating the response constraints for each operation step (Davis et al., 2009). Any deficiencies in the LCI list result in substantial changes (and variances) in the LCA evaluation findings.

11.2.2.1 Functional units

A FU is a unit of measurement for the functioning of a system defined by its inputs and outputs in LCA (Davis et al., 2009). The FU that is chosen has a considerable influence on the LCA findings (Adesanya et al., 2014; Cherubini & Strømman, 2011). In the biogas production situation, there is presently no standard structure for the working units. As a result, in the literature, discrepancies in FU selection (by multiple analysts) have an impact on overall LCA outcomes. The LCA studies of the biogas production method suggest three types of FU:

- Service-oriented
- Energy-oriented
- Material-oriented.

The service-oriented FU refers to the overall transportation distances, for example, yearly vehicle kilometers traveled (VKT) per hectare-year, per VKT, per km of transportation, kg fuel (biodiesel) per 1 km traveled, and the ignition of enough ton (t) of fuel to transport 1 ton of carriage for 1 km. The biogas energy represented in biochemical energy such as generation and ignition per 1 MJ biogas is referred to as the energy-oriented FU. The mass-oriented FU is a proportion of the overall mass of biogas produced throughout the operation.

11.2.2.2 Temporal units

The temporal units in LCA assign a particular time cycle or operating time during the year. The LCA has a significant flaw in ignoring the temporal units (Levasseur et al., 2010). The volume of GHGs emitted throughout a product's life cycle has been limited by the Intergovernmental Panel on Climate Change (IPCC). However, it has been unable to visualize a specific period (Kendall, 2012); this could take the lead to imprecise anticipation of the short-term effects of global warming. Theoretical and realistic predictions of climate change implications increase whatever time is allocated (Kendall & Price, 2012; Levasseur et al., 2010, 2013; Pinsonnault et al., 2014). Since the biogas plant cannot run all year, another consideration that affects environmental and economic factors is the operating period. A strategic management framework can be used to understand these complex variables in the LCA (in policy- and decision-making) (Levasseur et al., 2010).

11.2.2.3 System boundaries

The system boundaries differ not just in terms of the beginning and finish points of method chains, but additionally in terms of space and time. Electricity and environmental costs will be significantly impacted by these developments. A well-to-gate LCA takes into account the complete process from resource extraction to the factory gate. The tool constraints of the LCA have been increased to include well-to-pump biogas transit to the user station. In LCA, feedstock growth, biogas collection, biogas distribution, transport, and ignition in a vehicle are all considered. The car, transportation road, restoring (maintenance), and recycling or reuse are all included in the cradle-to-grave scheme boundary. As a result, a cradle-to-grave framework boundary is chosen for environmental analysis in the LCA since it encompasses the whole operation (van der Voet et al., 2010). By widening the method limits, the data demand in the LCA study rises.

11.2.2.4 Allocation

It may be challenging to distinguish between environmental effects as co-products are made in the same phase as the main product. This is particularly valid when the method is carried out in many plants. In the LCA, allocation can measure individual inputs of the methane and coproduct, carbon dioxide, to the process's total environmental impacts. Because the allocation technique selected influences energy and environmental implications, evaluating several theoretical and functional issues linked with the chosen allotment technique is a crucial task that supports policymaking. There are several different paths for processing AD biogas, each of which yields various by-products. When there are disparities in the mass, market value, or energy content of by-products, evaluating the effect of an allotment method becomes problematic (Zaimes et al., 2013). Where necessary, the ISO 14040 specification recommends avoiding allocation (ISO, 2003; Weidema, 2014). To reduce/remove ambiguities and gaps in distribution, system boundary expansion (SBE), also recognized as the displacement method, could be utilized (Weidema, 2000; Zaimes & Khanna, 2014).

11.2.3 Life cycle cost assessment

The feasibility of applying the mechanism can be calculated using an advanced technical method by estimating capital expenditure with respect to net present value. The expense of 10,000 tons of microbes by 30% biomass is expected to be around \$2.80/L, including conversion, excise, and promotion costs. The cost of biomass is related to the cost of waster as the nutrient from AD is recycled (Davis et al., 2011). Reduced fatty acid concentration will increase biogas supply, and the average cost of biogas is \$4.34 per gallon. When the method is used as an advanced biorefinery, the economic sustainability would be higher. The productions of the energy and mass surplus were utilized to assess operational and investment expenditures to evaluate the entire production cost. The manufacturing values are principal expenditure estimates for biogas output. The direct and indirect costs were factored into the equipment price, and the building cost was determined by the manufacturer. Due to the cost of site design, the average installation cost has increased by 10%. Multiple sources of data were used to calculate the expected equipment costs (Davis et al., 2011; Lundquist et al., 2010). The overhead expense element is used in the calculation of fixed capital spending and gross direct expenditure. According to the study of (Rogers et al., 2014), the expense of pumping conditions on the job site is approximate. Electricity, ventilation, water, minerals, and staffing costs are also included in the maintenance costs (MCs). The cost of labor may be calculated and measured (Davis, Kinchin, et al., 2014). For model validation, economic considerations such as tax rate and depreciation model were taken into account (Davis, Fishman, et al., 2014; Davis, Kinchin, et al., 2014).

Life cycle cost (LCC) may be used to determine the sensitivity and effectiveness of using BC in AD. That is the total cost of electricity, installation, downstream, running, repair, environmental, and decommissioning for the product's whole lifespan (Strazza et al., 2015). The LCC is performed based on operating cost (OC), salvage value (SV), MC, and capital cost (CC). The cost of storage, instrumentation, and piping is considered a capital expenditure. The following calculation is used to measure the gross capital expense of using BC in AD, taking into account various parameters by (Zhu et al., 2014),

$$C_{\text{Total}} = \sum_{n=1}^{20} \frac{x}{(1 + r^n)}$$

where C_{Total} is the total capital expense, x is the annual capital cost, and r is the discount rate of 5% over a 20-year usage period. Fixed and contingent costs, such as labor, repairs, laboratory costs, benefits, factory overheads, and licensing fees, are included when evaluating OCs or commodity costs. The prices of services and raw products may be counted due to a lack of evidence on labor costs (Eggeman & Elander, 2005). The total operational expense of bioenergy yield using net present value is projected as,

$$OC_{\text{biochar/biogas}} = \sum_{i=1}^{n} \frac{\text{AOC}_{\text{biochar/biogas}}}{(1+r)^i}$$

The MC for 20 years using present value is estimated as,

$$\text{MC}_{\text{biochar/biogas}} = \sum_{i=1}^{n} \frac{\text{MR}_{\text{biochar/biogas}} \times \text{CC}_{\text{biochar/biogas}}}{(1+r)^i}$$

The net operating expense is MC, the maintenance rate is MR, and the fixed cost is CC. The net cost comprises the total LCC, benefit, and delivery costs. The profit and transportation costs account for 10% of the biogas production rate.

11.3 Life cycle assessment studies in anaerobic digestion for biogas production

Several BC-based biowaste disposals and management programs have been shown to be unsuccessful. A systematic approach to assess the advantages and risks of different biowaste disposal methods and solutions in terms of goals and a step-by-step methodological structure will significantly assist in making informed decisions. Present industry rules and initiatives have been criticized for ignoring precisely this concept, according to (Nasr et al., 2012). As a consequence, enhancing the interaction between circular economy (CE) and bioeconomy conflicts might be a crucial step in establishing the CE's viability and, as a consequence, particular needs for efficient trade procedures. In this regard, according to a decision standard proposed by (Jones et al., 2017), cost-benefit assessment or multi-standards policymaking tactics are utilized in waste management decision-support procedures, although only a few studies apply LCA tools. The most applicable LCA/CE approaches are mostly qualitative subject analysis, which is comfortable to analyze interaction in a comprehensive, theory-guided approach. Other LCA resources focus on, among other things, waste flow research, waste avoidance and CE valorization capability, and environmental evidence. These methodologies are completely utilized in identifying waste flows in cities with the greatest potential for CE valorization (Zhu et al., 2009). On this aspect, Güereca et al. (2006) used LCA to measure biowaste control, but they just looked at electricity use, water consumption, pollution to the environment, and water and room requirements. Notably, most appraisal methods are solely employed by professionals who concentrate on evaluating and synthesizing current evidence to make judgments. As a result, we can just use the LCA method to test certain biological and thermal biowaste treatments in this paper. The model was defined as a site-specific LCI inventory, a Mechanical Biological Treatment (MBT) technology data inventory, the USLCI database, and technologies as LCA/CE resources. Biowaste makes up the majority of urban waste, but careful control is a significant concern if the bioeconomy is to be sustained in the immediate future (Kung et al., 2013).

The usage of the digestate and the final use of biogas were highlighted as essential aspects of biogas production. Furthermore, certain considerations, such as site-specific circumstances and the realistic deployment of biogas units, may result in significant variations in life cycle impacts. As a result, their research stresses the significance of LCA analysis for consistent effect evaluations. In addition, for the more robust use of the LCA of policy strategy, this report proposes incorporating stakeholder meetings into the study. Ardolino and Arena (2019) evaluated biowaste using various situations (worse-case, pessimistic, realistic, and optimistic). The LCA/CE instruments can measure quantitative assessments based on scenario review, broken down at the county level, and GHGs.

Ardolino and Arena (2019), described the constituted organic portion of municipal solid waste's overall biomethane production sustainability over AD. In this sense, the waste-to-methane scenario's nonrenewable energy and GWPs could increase by 36% and 79%, respectively, compared to the waste-to-energy condition. Starr et al. (2014) utilized LCA to compare two carbon mineralization technologies for biogas upgrade and identify possible improvements. Although (Xu et al., 2015) looked at the environmental and energy impacts of a well-equipped biomethane unit utilizing three different upgrade technologies: monoethanolamide liquid cleansing, strained water cleansing, and ionic cleansing (liquid). Similarly, Mohammadi et al. (2011) used data from the Eco-invent databank to link three different biological treatment procedures for the organic component of MSW: (1) composting; AD with an eventual digestate composting; (2) AD with final digestate composting; (3) pressure swing adsorption to upgrade biogas. Gunamantha and Sarto (2012), compared different energetic valorization alternatives using the standard LCA technique. Climate warming, eutrophication acidification, and photochemical oxidant formation were among the effect groups identified by the inventory. Nizami et al. (2017) have expanded on the socioeconomic evaluation, ecologically-based LCA, life cycle estimates, economic responses of LCA, and life cycle sustainability estimation linked with waste biorefinery LCA. The positiveness includes the recovery of oil and useful materials, as well as potential market opportunities and cost savings from landfills. They have also given environmental advantages by reducing GHG pollution from new disposal methods.

Bueno et al. (2015) conducted a comparative LCA analysis to figure out the cumulative impacts on the environment of two different technologies, due to previously indicated LCA points, alternative methods of straight material recapture or direct energy recovery may be avoided in comparisons. Most individuals utilize the Eco-invent datasets to estimate the environmental efficiency of biowaste treatment, according to the LCA evaluation of the research described earlier. The results obtained from the LCA technique are complicated due to the various system limits and observations created during the calculations. However, the LCA studies looked at similar essential phases. For example, Tufvesson et al. (2013) proposed that if agricultural residues historically used as animal protein are used as a feedstock for processing, alternative protein feed agronomy properties should be considered. Furthermore, when certain of the effect categories are included, such as energy balance and CO_2 pollution, the LCA tool only produces modest amounts of overall impacts. As a result, the effects of the life cycle differ depending on the location. As a result, even site-specific and geographic constraints may be considered using the LCAs method for biogas yield technologies (Börjesson & Berglund, 2006). Diverse configurations, as well as their control in production processes, can have significant differences. In addition, for more straightforward analyses, such as studies on the possible climate mitigating potential of biogas, individual LCAs as well as many integrated LCA functions must be investigated. Myllyviita et al. (2012) suggested an alternative approach may be to conduct life cycle and social impact evaluations. This technique allows for the consideration of additional qualitative indicators in the decision-making process. Furthermore, based on the views of several biogas players, a more thorough integration of a full life cycle plan into the policymaking techniques of both individual firms and municipal governments is required. Although the traditional waste treatment and management approach for producing biogas can result in sub-optimal choices, the additional comprehensive visualization can change the thoughtful in waste management and convert nutrients to fertilizer and energy output, culminating in feature optimization. As a result, it will be important to follow and create common practices in biowaste treatment and management connected to environmental licenses and environmental impact evaluations, as well as to track community impact at regular intervals in any site. Given the need to improve the efficiency and application of LCA, as well as the requirement to analyze sustainability, including diverse stakeholders in the LCA process might be more efficient and beneficial (Apostolakou et al., 2009).

A recent study used LCA to evaluate the environmental efficiency of constructed wetland structures for winery wastewater treatment. LCA was used to analyze the environmental and economic output of two autonomous, small-scale wastewater treatment units coupled to produce wetlands

(Resende et al., 2019). The majority of environmental consequences, according to the research, are produced by pollutants and discharges from the activity process. In addition, the environmental implications of aerated wetlands demonstrated that the activity stage had a substantial influence in all categories evaluated. Finally, the LCC per cubic meter of treated sewage for the aerated technique was 1.8 times lower than the system without aeration after treatment. Awad et al. (2019) evaluate the environmental impacts and costs of four different wastewater treatment system upgrades that include tertiary treatment and anaerobic sludge digestion. This is because wastewater treatment in most contemporary countries is straightforward, involving just basic and secondary treatment with minimal tertiary treatment or sludge disposal. The CML 2000 approach may be used to evaluate the environmental effects of four scenarios: (1) the current/pristine condition of the wastewater plant, (2) the addition of AD sludge, (3) the addition of a tertiary treatment point, and (4) the inclusion of both AD sludge and a tertiary treatment stage. The study profile might show environmental and economic advantages; for example, tertiary treatment might result in financial advantages due to the value of reused treated water.

11.4 Challenges for life cycle assessment technology

Despite recent advances in the LCA research methodology, several issues remain unaddressed or inadequately addressed, especially in developed countries. As part of the 2030 Plan for Sustainable Development, emerging countries can adopt the developed countries' effectively adopted LCA framework (Assembly, 2015). Inadequate studies, a lack of or ignorance of detailed information about the influent, effluent, and sludge generated during the wastewater treatment process, and a lack of in-depth understanding of advanced treatment procedures, as well as the generation and release of environmentally related contaminants, are some of the main challenges that developing countries face.

The good news is that LCA is gaining popularity. LCA is developed and robust enough for decision-making in commercial and governmental bodies after many years of process development, case studies, international standards, database, and software development. The most well-known methodology for measuring a product's environmental performance is LCA, which is utilized by a broad variety of stakeholders throughout the globe, including government, business, nongovernmental organizations (NGOs), and academia. However, just because LCA is the "best possible form" does not imply "perfect." Although the LCA ecosystem has encouraged LCA adoption for a long time, it is now critical not to oversell it. For long-term growth, a balanced understanding and application of LCA are needed. We must stop moving right from the past "LCA-aversion" to a kind of "LCA-hype."

Regarding the method's gaps and obstacles, all international LCA guidelines and research literature are apparent. LCA does not, at this time, provide the "complete environmental truth." The central LCA guidelines (ISO 14040 2006) and (ISO 14044 2006) recognize that every LCA analysis has limitations. As a result, every study's limitations must be recorded in the target and scope specification (ISO 14040, 5.2.1.2). Furthermore, ISO 14040, 5.4 contains a detailed chapter on the shortcomings of life cycle impact assessment (LCIA). LCIA has three drawbacks: "The LCIA addresses only the environmental concerns identified in the target and scope." As a result, LCIA would not include a comprehensive evaluation of all environmental problems related to the product scheme under consideration. LCIA will not often show substantial variations between effect groups and alternate commodity framework predictor outcomes. This may be due to the LCIA process, there was limited production of characterization models, sensitivity analysis, and uncertainty analysis; the LCI phase includes difficulties due to cut-offs and data gaps, such as defining a system threshold that does not cover all feasible unit processes for a commodities system or offer all inputs and outputs of a unit process; constraints of the LCI process, such as low LCI data quality due to uncertainty or differences in allocation and aggregation techniques; and limitations in the compilation of inventory data for an acceptable effect group and representative (ISO 14040 2006).

An early review of drawbacks in the scientific literature is needed. Recent contributions in terms of discrepancies and analysis need revisions. However, based on this recent years' experience, a thorough analysis of gaps and problems is still lacking, especially in light of recent advances in carbon and water footprints, as well as lesser-known aspects such as littering and animal welfare.

11.5 Concluding remarks and recommendations

BC has been widely used in the AD method to improve production in recent years. BC has been shown to enhance and balance hydrolysis, acidogenesis–acetogenesis, and methanogenesis and reduce inhibitor discomfort. By sustaining microbial colonies and reinforcing buffer energy, BC can aid the biomethane process, resulting in a steady electron transfer chain between fermentative bacteria and methanogens. BC's effects on acid buffering, propionic acid reduction, and increasing syntropy between hydrolysis and acidogenesis–acetogenesis should be investigated more in the future. The LCA tool, on the other hand, is useful for evaluating the environmental consequences and effects of different consuming activities within a framework, such as biogas generation. According to the studies examined here, LCA will reduce an environmental load of a process by choosing sophisticated alternate manufacturing, refining, and delivery design. It ensures process safety and environmental quality while also providing additional benefits, including optimum handling, cost-effective ratio, decreased emissions, and water reusability. Consideration and execution of the above problems will significantly improve the efficiency and precision of wastewater-related LCAs in developed countries and their advantages. Although several advances have been made in modern LCA procedures, further international standardization is urgently needed. Regardless of spatial or temporal dissemination problems, such a strategic development will serve as a reference point for everyone. This would also provide precise comparisons of various scenarios, expanding the practical applications of LCAs in biogas production technologies.

LCA may help find ways to enhance a product's environmental sustainability at different stages in its life cycle. It also allows business, government, and nongovernment organizations to make fact-based decisions (e.g., strategic planning, priority setting, product or process design, environmental hot spot analysis, and optimization). Although every actual case study does not suffer from both gaps, methodological limitations and difficulties may significantly impact the outcomes of LCA studies. As a consequence, in most case studies, they do not constitute a serious difficulty. When LCAs are undertaken for plastic goods or livestock processing, however, the lack of proper coverage of "littering" or "animal well-being" excludes potentially major issues. The LCA approach has various problems, such as "allocation," "functional unit," and "uncertainty study." While many of the issues raised above may be resolved by potential research and development, some of the most fundamental problems could necessitate essential choices. These decisions can be based on empirical evidence, but they also merit decisions. On a scientific level, the only thing that can be tested is whether certain value choices are made regularly in a sample, particularly when comparing alternatives.

The study's finding for the research world is somewhat self-explanatory. The issues raised should be used to develop a study plan for LCA. The majority of distance definitions provide detailed study ideas. They are meant to encourage the LCA group to address these issues and create scientifically sound solutions. Many of the difficulties identified have a repeating theme of the need for new, robust, and suitable data. This is a challenge for all those involved, not just scientists. Users and policymakers face a somewhat more complicated circumstance before these strategies are created, as the importance of the holes vary depending on the items examined and the LCA's expected use. As a consequence, each case study should include a check to determine whether and how the differences discovered impact or even limit the conclusions of the LCA research. Some holes may be insignificant, others may be of minor importance, while others will be important. The possibly significant problems can either be documented as a study's reach constraint or addressed using complementary methods such as risk evaluation, environmental impact assessment, content flow analysis, or input-output studies. Decision-makers in both commercial and governmental enterprises must realize the benefits of LCA. A solid, long-term, and trustworthy LCA implementation, on the other hand, demands a thorough examination of its shortcomings and limits. However, as ISO 14044 (2006) explains, "An LCIA must not offer the entire foundation of overall environmental dominance or equivalency, since further information would be required to rectify some of the inherent deficiencies in the LCIA."

11.6 Acknowledgment

The authors wish to express their appreciation to Malaysian Higher Education and Universiti Malaysia Pahang (UMP) for providing financial support (RACER/1/2019/TK10/UMP//1, RDU192614).

11.7 Declaration of competing interest

The authors declare that they have no known competing financial interests or personal relationships that could have influenced the work reported in this paper. All listed authors are qualified for authorship and mutually agree to submit this article for consideration. Each author has participated and contributed sufficiently to take responsibility for every portion of the content.

References

Adesanya, V. O., Cadena, E., Scott, S. A., & Smith, A. G. (2014). Life cycle assessment on microalgal biodiesel production using a hybrid cultivation system. *Bioresource Technology, 163*, 343–355.

Ahmad, M., Rajapaksha, A. U., Lim, J. E., Zhang, M., Bolan, N., Mohan, D., Vithanage, M., Lee, S. S., & Ok, Y. S. (2014). Biochar as a sorbent for contaminant management in soil and water: A review. *Chemosphere, 99*, 19–33.

Apostolakou, A. A., Kookos, I. K., Marazioti, C., & Angelopoulos, K. C. (2009). Techno-economic analysis of a biodiesel production process from vegetable oils. *Fuel Processing Technology, 90*(7), 1023–1031.

Ardolino, F., & Arena, U. (2019). Biowaste-to-Biomethane: An LCA study on biogas and syngas roads. *Waste Management, 87*, 441–453.

Assembly, G. (2015). *Resolution adopted by the General Assembly on 19 September 2016. A/RES/71/1, 3 October 2016 (The New York Declaration).*

Awad, H., Gar Alalm, M., & El-Etriby, H. K. (2019). Environmental and cost life cycle assessment of different alternatives for improvement of wastewater treatment plants in developing countries. *Science of The Total Environment, 660*, 57–68.

Börjesson, P., & Berglund, M. (2006). Environmental systems analysis of biogas systems—Part I: Fuel-cycle emissions. *Biomass and Bioenergy, 30*(5), 469–485.

Bueno, G., Latasa, I., & Lozano, P. J. (2015). Comparative LCA of two approaches with different emphasis on energy or material recovery for a municipal solid waste management system in Gipuzkoa. *Renewable and Sustainable Energy Reviews, 51*, 449–459.

Chan, Y. H., Tan, R. R., Yusup, S., Lam, H. L., & Quitain, A. T. (2016). Comparative life cycle assessment (LCA) of bio-oil production from fast pyrolysis and hydrothermal liquefaction of oil palm empty fruit bunch (EFB). *Clean Technologies and Environmental Policy, 18*(6), 1759–1768.

Chen, J. L., Ortiz, R., Steele, T. W. J., & Stuckey, D. C. (2014). Toxicants inhibiting anaerobic digestion: A review. *Biotechnology Advances, 32*(8), 1523–1534.

Chen, Q., Wu, W., Qi, D., Ding, Y., & Zhao, Z. (2020). Review on microaeration-based anaerobic digestion: State of the art, challenges, and prospectives. *Science of The Total Environment, 710*, 136388.

Cherubini, F., & Strømman, A. H. (2011). Life cycle assessment of bioenergy systems: State of the art and future challenges. *Bioresource Technology, 102*(2), 437–451.

Chopra, J., Tiwari, B. R., Dubey, B. K., & Sen, R. (2020). Environmental impact analysis of oleaginous yeast based biodiesel and bio-crude production by life cycle assessment. *Journal of Cleaner Production, 271*, 122349.

Collet, P., Hélias, A., Lardon, L., Steyer, J.-P., & Bernard, O. (2015). Recommendations for life cycle assessment of algal fuels. *Applied Energy, 154*, 1089–1102.

Davis, R., Aden, A., & Pienkos, P. T. (2011). Techno-economic analysis of autotrophic microalgae for fuel production. *Applied Energy, 88*(10), 3524–3531.

Davis, R., Kinchin, C., Markham, J., Tan, E., Laurens, L., Sexton, D., Knorr, D., Schoen, P., & Lukas, J. (2014). *Process design and economics for the conversion of algal biomass to biofuels: Algal biomass fractionation to lipid- and carbohydrate-derived fuel products.*

Davis, R. E., Fishman, D. B., Frank, E. D., Johnson, M. C., Jones, S. B., Kinchin, C. M., Skaggs, R. L., Venteris, E. R., & Wigmosta, M. S. (2014). Integrated evaluation of cost, emissions, and resource potential for algal biofuels at the national scale. *Environmental Science & Technology, 48*(10), 6035–6042.

Davis, S. C., Anderson-Teixeira, K. J., & DeLucia, E. H. (2009). Life-cycle analysis and the ecology of biofuels. *Trends in Plant Science, 14*(3), 140–146.

Eggeman, T., & Elander, R. T. (2005). Process and economic analysis of pretreatment technologies. *Bioresource Technology, 96*(18), 2019–2025.

Foulet, A., Bouchez, T., Desmond-Le Quéméner, E., Giard, L., Renvoisé, L., & Aissani, L. (2019). Eco-design of microbial electrochemical technologies for the production of waste-based succinic acid thanks to a life cycle assessment. *Journal of Cleaner Production, 225*, 1155–1168.

Gallego-Schmid, A., & Tarpani, R. R. Z. (2019). Life cycle assessment of wastewater treatment in developing countries: A review. *Water Research, 153*, 63–79.

Gargalo, C. L., Carvalho, A., Gernaey, K. V., & Sin, G. (2017). Optimal design and planning of glycerol-based biorefinery supply chains under uncertainty. *Industrial & Engineering Chemistry Research, 56*(41), 11870–11893.

Güereca, L. P., Gassó, S., Baldasano, J. M., & Jiménez-Guerrero, P. (2006). Life cycle assessment of two biowaste management systems for Barcelona, Spain. *Resources, Conservation and Recycling, 49*(1), 32–48.

Gunamantha, M., & Sarto. (2012). Life cycle assessment of municipal solid waste treatment to energy options: Case study of KARTAMANTUL region, Yogyakarta. *Renewable Energy, 41*, 277–284.

Helminen, R.-R. (2000). Developing tangible measures for eco-efficiency: the case of the Finnish and Swedish pulp and paper industry. *Business Strategy and the Environment, 9* (3), 196–210.

ISO, I. (2003). *14040: 1997—Environmental management—Life cycle assessment-principles and framework*. Switzerland: International Organization for Standardization (ISO).

Jiang, Y., McAdam, E., Zhang, Y., Heaven, S., Banks, C., & Longhurst, P. (2019). Ammonia inhibition and toxicity in anaerobic digestion: A critical review. *Journal of Water Process Engineering, 32*, 100899.

Jones, R. J., Massanet-Nicolau, J., Mulder, M. J. J., Premier, G., Dinsdale, R., & Guwy, A. (2017). Increased biohydrogen yields, volatile fatty acid production and substrate utilisation rates via the electrodialysis of a continually fed sucrose fermenter. *Bioresource Technology, 229*, 46–52.

Kendall, A. (2012). Time-adjusted global warming potentials for LCA and carbon footprints. *The International Journal of Life Cycle Assessment, 17*(8), 1042–1049.

Kendall, A., & Price, L. (2012). Incorporating time-corrected life cycle greenhouse gas emissions in vehicle regulations. *Environmental Science & Technology, 46*(5), 2557–2563.

Kung, C.-C., McCarl, B. A., & Cao, X. (2013). Economics of pyrolysis-based energy production and biochar utilization: A case study in Taiwan. *Energy Policy, 60*, 317–323.

Kuosmanen, T., & Kortelainen, M. (2005). Measuring eco-efficiency of production with data envelopment analysis. *Journal of Industrial Ecology, 9*(4), 59–72.

Lam, K. L., Zlatanović, L., & van der Hoek, J. P. (2020). Life cycle assessment of nutrient recycling from wastewater: A critical review. *Water Research, 173*, 115519.

Lam, M. K., Lee, K. T., & Mohamed, A. R. (2009). Life cycle assessment for the production of biodiesel: A case study in Malaysia for palm oil vs jatropha oil. *Biofuels, Bioproducts and Biorefining, 3*(6), 601–612.

Lee, C., Jeong, S., Ju, M., & Kim, J. Y. (2020). Fate of chlortetracycline antibiotics during anaerobic degradation of cattle manure. *Journal of Hazardous Materials, 386*, 121894.

Levasseur, A., Lesage, P., Margni, M., Deschênes, L., & Samson, R. (2010). Considering time in LCA: Dynamic LCA and its application to global warming impact assessments. *Environmental Science & Technology, 44*(8), 3169–3174.

Levasseur, A., Lesage, P., Margni, M., & Samson, R. (2013). Biogenic carbon and temporary storage addressed with dynamic life cycle assessment. *Journal of Industrial Ecology, 17*(1), 117–128.

Liu, W.-J., Jiang, H., & Yu, H.-Q. (2019). Emerging applications of biochar-based materials for energy storage and conversion. *Energy & Environmental Science, 12*(6), 1751–1779.

Lundquist, T. J., Woertz, I. C., Quinn, N., & Benemann, J. R. (2010). A realistic technology and engineering assessment of algae biofuel production. *Energy Biosciences Institute*, 1.

Manfredi, S., & Pant, R. (2011). *Supporting environmentally sound decisions for bio-waste management: A practical guide to life cycle thinking (LCT) and life cycle assessment (LCA).* Publications Office.
Máša, V., Bobák, P., Kuba, P., & Stehlík, P. (2013). Analysis of energy efficient and environmentally friendly technologies in professional laundry service. *Clean Technologies and Environmental Policy, 15*(3), 445–457.
Mohammadi, M., Najafpour, G. D., Younesi, H., Lahijani, P., Uzir, M. H., & Mohamed, A. R. (2011). Bioconversion of synthesis gas to second generation biofuels: A review. *Renewable and Sustainable Energy Reviews, 15*(9), 4255–4273.
Myllyviita, T., Holma, A., Antikainen, R., Lähtinen, K., & Leskinen, P. (2012). Assessing environmental impacts of biomass production chains – Application of life cycle assessment (LCA) and multi-criteria decision analysis (MCDA). *Journal of Cleaner Production, 29–30,* 238–245.
Nasr, N., Elbeshbishy, E., Hafez, H., Nakhla, G., & Hesham El Naggar, M. (2012). Comparative assessment of single-stage and two-stage anaerobic digestion for the treatment of thin stillage. *Bioresource Technology, 111,* 122–126.
Nizami, A. S., Rehan, M., Waqas, M., Naqvi, M., Ouda, O. K. M., Shahzad, K., Miandad, R., Khan, M. Z., Syamsiro, M., Ismail, I. M. I., & Pant, D. (2017). Waste biorefineries: Enabling circular economies in developing countries. *Bioresource Technology, 241,* 1101–1117.
Pachauri, R. K., Allen, M. R., Barros, V. R., Broome, J., Cramer, W., Christ, R., Church, J. A., Clarke, L., Dahe, Q., & Dasgupta, P. (2014). *Climate change 2014: Synthesis report. Contribution of Working Groups I, II and III to the fifth assessment report of the Intergovernmental Panel on Climate Change.* IPCC.
Palansooriya, K. N., Wong, J. T. F., Hashimoto, Y., Huang, L., Rinklebe, J., Chang, S. X., Bolan, N., Wang, H., & Ok, Y. S. (2019). Response of microbial communities to biochar-amended soils: a critical review. *Biochar, 1*(1), 3–22.
Pant, D., Singh, A., Van Bogaert, G., Gallego, Y. A., Diels, L., & Vanbroekhoven, K. (2011). An introduction to the life cycle assessment (LCA) of bioelectrochemical systems (BES) for sustainable energy and product generation: Relevance and key aspects. *Renewable and Sustainable Energy Reviews, 15*(2), 1305–1313.
Parra-Saldivar, R., Bilal, M., & Iqbal, H. M. N. (2020). Life cycle assessment in wastewater treatment technology. *Current Opinion in Environmental Science & Health, 13,* 80–84.
Pecchi, M., & Baratieri, M. (2019). Coupling anaerobic digestion with gasification, pyrolysis or hydrothermal carbonization: A review. *Renewable and Sustainable Energy Reviews, 105,* 462–475.
Pinsonnault, A., Lesage, P., Levasseur, A., & Samson, R. (2014). Temporal differentiation of background systems in LCA: relevance of adding temporal information in LCI databases. *The International Journal of Life Cycle Assessment, 19*(11), 1843–1853.
Qiu, L., Deng, Y. F., Wang, F., Davaritouchaee, M., & Yao, Y. Q. (2019). A review on biochar-mediated anaerobic digestion with enhanced methane recovery. *Renewable and Sustainable Energy Reviews, 115,* 109373.
Resende, J. D., Nolasco, M. A., & Pacca, S. A. (2019). Life cycle assessment and costing of wastewater treatment systems coupled to constructed wetlands. *Resources, Conservation and Recycling, 148,* 170–177.
Rogers, J. N., Rosenberg, J. N., Guzman, B. J., Oh, V. H., Mimbela, L. E., Ghassemi, A., Betenbaugh, M. J., Oyler, G. A., & Donohue, M. D. (2014). A critical analysis of paddlewheel-driven raceway ponds for algal biofuel production at commercial scales. *Algal Research, 4,* 76–88.
Roy, P., Nei, D., Orikasa, T., Xu, Q., Okadome, H., Nakamura, N., & Shiina, T. (2009). A review of life cycle assessment (LCA) on some food products. *Journal of Food Engineering, 90*(1), 1–10.

Starr, K., Talens Peiro, L., Lombardi, L., Gabarrell, X., & Villalba, G. (2014). Optimization of environmental benefits of carbon mineralization technologies for biogas upgrading. *Journal of Cleaner Production*, *76*, 32–41.

Strazza, C., Del Borghi, A., Costamagna, P., Gallo, M., Brignole, E., & Girdinio, P. (2015). Life Cycle Assessment and Life Cycle Costing of a SOFC system for distributed power generation. *Energy Conversion and Management*, *100*, 64–77.

Thinkstep, A. (1992). *GaBi software system and database for life cycle engineering*. Stuttgart, Germany: LBP–University of Stuttgart, 2016.

Tufvesson, L. M., Lantz, M., & Börjesson, P. (2013). Environmental performance of biogas produced from industrial residues including competition with animal feed – life-cycle calculations according to different methodologies and standards. *Journal of Cleaner Production*, *53*, 214–223.

van der Voet, E., Lifset, R. J., & Luo, L. (2010). Life-cycle assessment of biofuels, convergence and divergence. *Biofuels*, *1*(3), 435–449.

Vondra, M., Touš, M., & Teng, S. Y. (2019). Digestate evaporation treatment in biogas plants: A techno-economic assessment by Monte Carlo, neural networks and decision trees. *Journal of Cleaner Production*, *238*, 117870.

Weidema, B. (2000). Avoiding co-product allocation in life-cycle assessment. *Journal of Industrial Ecology*, *4*(3), 11–33.

Weidema, B. (2014). Has ISO 14040/44 failed its role as a standard for life cycle assessment? *Journal of Industrial Ecology*, *18*(3), 324–326.

Wu, Y., Wang, S., Liang, D., & Li, N. (2020). Conductive materials in anaerobic digestion: From mechanism to application. *Bioresource Technology*, *298*, 122403.

Xu, C., Shi, W., Hong, J., Zhang, F., & Chen, W. (2015). Life cycle assessment of food waste-based biogas generation. *Renewable and Sustainable Energy Reviews*, *49*, 169–177.

Zabalza Bribián, I., Valero Capilla, A., & Aranda Usón, A. (2011). Life cycle assessment of building materials: Comparative analysis of energy and environmental impacts and evaluation of the eco-efficiency improvement potential. *Building and Environment*, *46* (5), 1133–1140.

Zaied, B., Siddique, M., Zularisam, A., Ahmad, M., & Salih, Y. (2019). Biomethane production from anaerobic codigestion of palm oil mill effluent with cattle manure: A review. *Asian Journal of Chemistry*, *31*(11), 2413–2424.

Zaied, B. K., Siddique, M. N. I., Nasrullah, M., Singh, L., Wahid, Z. B. A., & Ahmad, M. F. (2019). Application of solar assisted bioreactor for biogas production from palm oil mill effluent co-digested with cattle manure. *Environmental Technology & Innovation*, *16*, 100446.

Zaimes, G., Borkowski, M., & Khanna, V. (2013). Life-cycle environmental impacts of biofuels and co-products. In V. K. Gupta, & M. G. Tuohy (Eds.), *Biofuel technologies: recent developments* (pp. 471–499). Berlin, Heidelberg: Springer Berlin Heidelberg.

Zaimes, G. G., & Khanna, V. (2014). The role of allocation and coproducts in environmental evaluation of microalgal biofuels: How important? *Sustainable Energy Technologies and Assessments*, *7*, 247–256.

Zhu, B., Sun, F., Yang, M., Lu, L., Yang, G., & Pan, K. (2014). Large-scale biodiesel production using flue gas from coal-fired power plants with Nannochloropsis microalgal biomass in open raceway ponds. *Bioresource Technology*, *174*, 53–59.

Zhu, H., Parker, W., Basnar, R., Proracki, A., Falletta, P., Béland, M., & Seto, P. (2009). Buffer requirements for enhanced hydrogen production in acidogenic digestion of food wastes. *Bioresource Technology*, *100*(21), 5097–5102.

CHAPTER 12

Challenges and emerging approaches in life cycle assessment of engineered nanomaterials usage in anaerobic bioreactor

Pramod Jadhav, Zaied Bin Khalid, Puranjan Mishra, Zularisam Bin Abd Wahid and Mohd Nasrullah
Faculty of Civil Engineering Technology, Universiti Malaysia Pahang (UMP), Pahang, Malaysia

12.1 Introduction

Anaerobic digestion (AD) is a natural biochemical practice when the high level of organic waste matter is in the absence of dissolved oxygen (Li et al., 2019). In the multistage AD process, organic waste is converted into biogas (carbon dioxide and methane) and simultaneously reduces environmental pollution. Biogas is the significant component in the AD process apart from this there are other gases (nitrogen, ammonia, hydrogen, and hydrogen sulfide) are generating in the AD process (Lee & Lee, 2019; Lee et al., 2016; Myszograj et al., 2019; Suanon et al., 2016). AD process depends on the microorganism activity in each stage, which helps produce biogas as a final product from waste materials (Cheng & Call, 2016; Luo et al., 2015). C/N, temperature, pH value, volatile substances, biological oxygen demand (BOD), chemical oxygen needs (COD) are the main parameters affecting AD reactions (Amiri et al., 2017). Nowadays, nanoparticles (NPs) provide significant attenuation to enhance biogas yield and purity in the AD process. Different types of NPs (metal NPs, oxides, carbon-based NPs, engineered NPs, etc.) are used in the AD process to boost microbe's activity for increasing biogas production. Artificial materials for AD process as industrial applications are engineered NPs (ENPs)

Techno-economics and Life Cycle Assessment of Bioreactors
DOI: https://doi.org/10.1016/B978-0-323-89848-5.00004-4

and most frequently with 1–100 nm of the dimension (Faisal et al., 2018; Wang et al., 2016). The scientific community recognizes that ENPs have enormous potential to convert industrial processes to shape the functioning of society and the global economy (Besha et al., 2020).

This paper analyses the current ENPs approaches and applications incorporating biogas production in the AD process. With the applications and benefits of various ENPs (Fe, Ni, Zn, etc.), nanotechnology's fundamental principles are introduced. Then, the following section covers the AD process and ENPs role between biomass (Qiang et al., 2012; Wang et al., 2017). Recent developments and techno-economic analysis (TEA) are then presented in the AD process based on ENPs, including nanocatalysts for increased biogas production and advanced AD process for improving fuel blending capacity. In addition, future projects and challenges are emphasized to offer insight into the potential growth of ENPs for biogas production in the AD process. To provide a clear framework for concerned scholars on how ENPs can enhance biogas yield, this study with detailed comparative analysis will help in bioenergy.

12.2 Anaerobic digestion process in the bioreactor

12.2.1 Hydrolysis

The initial step of the AD process is hydrolysis which depends on primary microbes called the anaerobic fermentation process. Throughout this process, extracellular enzymes, such as polysaccharides, fat, and lipids (fat and grade), are decomposed by microbes. They produce mono and oligomers, soluble products such as fatty acids, amino acids, and sugar. These are insignificant molecules transferred throughout the cell membrane at the hydrolysis phase in the AD process (Batstone et al., 2015; Capson-Tojo et al., 2018; Vyrides et al., 2018). The decay rate depends on the substrate characteristics (pH, COD, BOD, TS) of the raw material (Auffan et al., 2009; Parthasarathy & Narayanan, 2014). Cellulose and hemicellulose transformation generally take longer than protein materials to decompose at the first stage of the AD process (Vögeli et al., 2014; Fermoso et al., 2019).

12.2.2 Acidogenesis

During acidogenesis, fermentation of hydrolyzed AD stage biomass by anaerobic oxidation of relatively simple solution compounds forms alcoholics, carbon dioxide, hydrogen, and ammonia (Liu et al., 2012;

Arsova, Themelis, & Chandran, 2010). Fatty acid levels in the AD bioreactor are essential for AD system function because high concentrations of fatty acids can inhibit biological processes. Organic acids (acetic acid, butyric acid, propionic acid, alcohols, carbon dioxide) are the most important products during the acidogenesis phase (Kong et al., 2016; Zhao et al., 2017). Different bacterial species undertake different fermenting activities, that is, Saccharomyces (fermentation of alcoholics), Butyribacterium and Clostridio (fermentation of butyrate), Lactobacillen, and Streptococcus (lactate), Clostridium (fermentation of propionates) (Lee et al., 2012; Liang et al., 2010). The types of acetobacterium, eubacterium, and sporomusa are responsible for producing acetate bacteria that form fermenting bacteria at the acidogenesis stage. Other acidogenesis products are hydrogen sulfide and ammonia, giving this process phase an extremely unpleasant odor (Zou et al., 2020).

12.2.3 Acetogenesis

In the acetogenesis stage, acetogenic microbes alter large compounds from the prior step, such as acetic acid, VFAs and alcohols, carbon dioxide, and hydrogen. Acetogens, *Syntrophobavter wolinii*, and *Smithella proprionica*, have been known as the bacteria accountable for converting butyrate and propionate into acetate, respectively, in the AD process (Akuzawa et al., 2011; Ma et al., 2019). Additional microbial clusters (*Syntrophobacter fumaroxidans, Pelotomaculum thermopropionicum, Syntrophomonas wolfei*, and *Pelotomaculum schinkii*) convert VFAs to H_2 and CO_2 in the AD operation (Shen et al., 2016; Yamada et al., 2015).

12.2.4 Methanogenesis

Methanogenesis stands as the methane (CH_4) formation phase in the AD operation. In this phase, the leading microbes (methanogenic bacteria) convert acetic acid into CH4 and CO_2, and water (Kato et al., 2012). Specifically, 70% of CH_4 produced comes from acetoclastic methanogenesis (the conversion of acetate to methane), whilst the remaining 30% occurs from the decline of CO_2 by H_2 in the methanogenesis stage (Abdelwahab et al., 2020; Vögeli et al., 2014). The methanogenic bacterial groups involved are (1) *Methanothrix soehngenii* and *Methanosaeta concilii* (alteration of acetate to methane and carbon dioxide—acetoclastic methanogenic pathway); (2) *Methanobacterium bryantii, Methanobacterium thermoautotrophicum*, and *Methanobrevibacter arboriphilus* (production of methane from

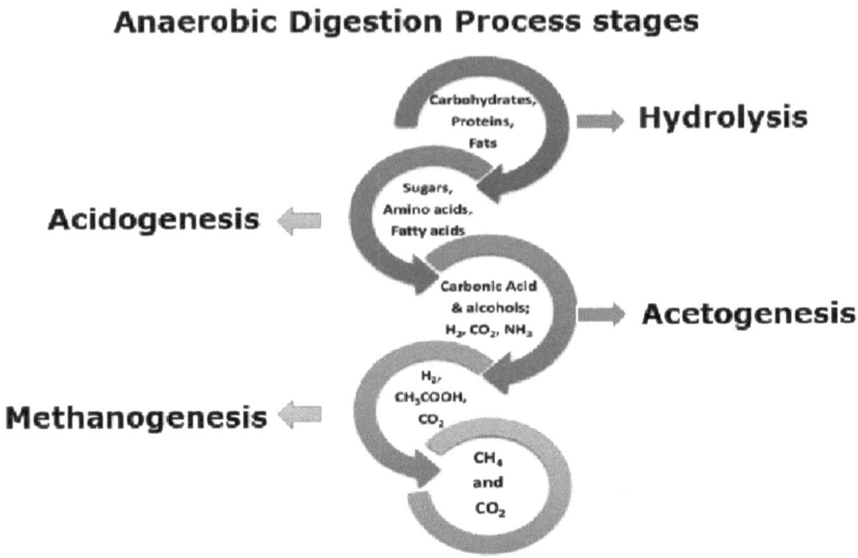

Figure 12.1 Illustrative diagram of AD process stages. *AD*, Anaerobic digestion.

hydrogen and carbon dioxide—hydrogen) (Boone et al., 1989; Lin et al., 2017) (Fig. 12.1).

12.3 Engineered nanoparticles in the anaerobic digestion process

12.3.1 Interaction of nanoparticles in the anaerobic digestion process

Several NPs have positive and negative properties, which play an essential role in biogas production with liquid biomass (Garron et al., 2015; Li et al., 2011). Different metal NPs, carbonaceous nanomaterials, zeolites, and dendrimers are the types of ENPs being studied as functional materials for water biogas production with a bioreactor. NPs are active material for enhancing biogas production (Wang et al., 2016). NPs have a large surface area (surface/volume ratio), which produces better results in the bioreactor for energy production. Adsorption, photocatalysis, membrane processes, disinfection, sensing, microbial control, and monitoring are some of the present and probable functions of nanotechnology in energy production from biomass. However, NPs toxicity is yet in its early stages. Two key considerations determine the antibacterial activity of NPs: (1) the physicochemical

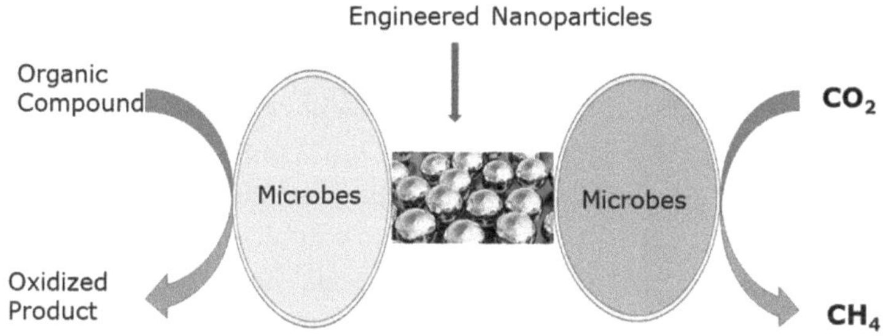

Figure 12.2 ENPs interaction with microbes in the AD process. *AD*, Anaerobic digestion; *ENPs*, engineered nanoparticles.

properties of NPs and (2) types of bacteria (Adams et al., 2006; Liu et al., 2011). Many experiments on NPs indicated that silver (Ag) NPs have a significant antibacterial biofilm activity. The bactericidal effect and Ag-NPs concentrations have positive relation between microbes and antibacterial effect (Adams et al., 2006; Sinha et al., 2011; Slavin et al., 2017). Throbäck et al. (2007) investigated the antimicrobial activity of Ag-NPs compared to *Escherichia coli* and *Staphylococcus aureus*, which results that the *E. coli* being hindered at low intensities, but the repressing impacts on *S. aureus* expansion were less prominent (Chen et al., 2008; Zayed & Winter, 2000). AG-NPs have an adverse impact on filamentous green algae growth and morphology. Fig. 12.2 shows the path of waste-to-energy transformation and the contact of functionalized NPs to demonstrate the importance of nanomaterials in waste-to-bioenergy production. The process of converting biomass-to-biogas could be thermal, chemical, or biological bioprocess in the bioreactor. Organic biomass's molecular size and inorganic contaminants affect the conversion process (Günther et al., 2015; Morgan et al., 2019).

12.3.2 Engineered nanoparticles in bioreactor

There are vast numbers of environmental NPs globally, far beyond the comparatively insignificant deliveries of carbon nanotubes, metal NPs (Fe, Zn, Cu, Co), etc. While the production of pure NPs is intense and less active, several studies on physical characteristics and effects of NPs have been engaged on ENPs (Choi et al., 2017). Because of the quick development of nanotechnology, ENPs are being fabricated and employed extensively in several industrial activities (energy, pharma, catalyst waste conversion, etc.). AD process is an excellent application in waste-to-energy conversion, and ENPs boost material in the AD process

(Chen et al., 2020; Shi et al., 2011). Many types of ENPs are used in the AD process, which helps to enhance biogas yield. For example, the impact of ENPs containing silver oxide (AgO, 20 nm), titanium dioxide (TiO_2, 30−40 nm), and zinc oxide (ZnO, 20 nm) relative to their bulk metal salts was studied in three parallel pilot-scale treatment facilities for biogas production in the AD reactor (Eduok et al., 2013). In the AD bioreactor, many environmental parameters (e.g., light, pH, ionic strength, natural organic matter, etc.) influence the destiny and behavior of ENPs in the environment (Klaine et al., 2008). A variety of factors may influence the physical, chemical, and bioavailable characteristics of ENPs in nature. To evaluate the dangers posed by ENPs, it is necessary to examine their potential movement, transformation, and interaction with other NPs (Farré et al., 2011). The influence of particle size and shape on microbial behavior/reactivity in aquatic and terrestrial media of the AD process may be seen in the particle size and shape of ENPs. For example, ENPs smaller than 30 nm were cytotoxic to *E. coli* and *S. aureus* compared to particle sizes of 80−90 nm (Pelletier et al., 2010). According to, Martínez-Castañón et al. (2008), AgO with particle size more than 30 nm is non-inhibitory to microbial activities, however ENPs with a size smaller than 5 nm in suspension may block nitrification in the AD process. Apart from particle size, the form of ENPs (triangular, spherical, or rod-shaped) has been shown to have a significant impact on biogas generation in the AD process. The truncated triangular form of AgO-NPs was shown to have the highest bactericidal impact on *E. coli* in the AD process when ENPs were compared (Ribeiro et al., 2014). Metallic ENPs such as Zn, Cr, Cu, and Cd interact with microorganisms, and their physicochemical and toxicological impacts affect microbial activity in the AD process (Auffan et al., 2009). CuO ENP concentrations of 10.7 and 129 mg/L in bulk CoO, for example, have been shown to suppress CH4 formation in the AD process. Similarly, NPs were suppressed by 57.4 mg of ZnO ENPs and 101 mg/L of ZnO bulk (Abdelsalam et al., 2016; Eduok et al., 2017). Another study found that in the AD process, ENPs and bulk materials block CH4 by 18.3% and 75.1% at concentrations of 30 and 150 mg ZnO/gTSS, respectively (Mu & Chen, 2011; Mu et al., 2011). Table 12.1 shows the effect of ENPS on biogas production rate.

Table 12.1 Effect of engineered nanomaterials in biogas production.

ENPs	ENPs size	ENPs concentration	Types of biomass and biogas yield
Titanium oxide (TiO_2)	7.5 nm	11,120 mg/L	10% increase in biogas production from wastewater
Cerium oxide (CeO_2)	192 nm	10 mgt/L	11% increase in the production of biogas from Upflow anaerobic sludge blanket (UASB) waste sludge
Ferrous oxide (Sludge.)	7.0 nm	10 ppm concentration	180% increase in biogas production increased by and 234% increase in methane production
NZVI particles	20 nm	Not available	30.4% increase of biogas production and 40.4% methane production
NZVI particles	50 nm	Not available	Methane production increased from 58 to 275 mmol
Metal nano substances encapsulated in porous Silicon dioxide SiO_2	Not available	Not available	Methane production increased 70%, 48%, 7%, and 6% with nanoparticles of nickel, cobalt, iron, and platinum, respectively
MNFA	Not available	Not available	Biogas production was increased by 2.9 times
MNBA	Not available	Not available	Biogas production was increased 3.5 times by using MNBA

ENPs, Engineered nanoparticles; *MNBA*, micro/nano bottom ash; *MNFA*, micro/nano fly ash; *NZVI*, nano zero valence iron.

12.4 Challenges and assessment of engineered nanoparticles in bioreactor

12.4.1 Techno-economic analysis of engineered nanoparticles in the anaerobic digestion process

ENPs will have both beneficial and bad repercussions for people and the environment if used to create biogas. It is critical to conduct a hazard assessment to determine whether the ENPs are hazardous or non-hazardous. Different methods are used to evaluate the toxicity of ENPs using currently available in-vitro methods. However, in-vivo (interaction with living organisms) research will be needed to fully comprehend the significance of these NPs in biogas production in the AD process. By the year 2035, energy demand is expected to increase by more than 30%, making it critical to find reliable and renewable energy sources. It will be much more critical to limit environmental effects (Jaziri et al., 2020). As a consequence of nanotechnological problems, the green-nano industry has gained increasing legislative and scientific attention, which is crucial to the sector's growth and guiding the sector in the direction of ENPs production. ENPs are used for commercial and social purposes in large-scale processes such as the production of biogas from the AD process. Various tools, such as green energy and solar biomass, estimate the commercial value of green nanotechnologies as ENPs. However, to realize the investment, research and production must be undertaken to adopt standards and regulations and monitor the processing system (Basiuk & Basiuk, 2015). The use of private and public capital must be justified based on the factors at hand, such as time, cost-benefit analysis, and the opportunity cost of the AD process to produce biogas. Take into account the benefits that these technologies are likely to have over traditional ones. Supply chains, third parties, and the environment are some of the effects that may arise during the use of ENPs. Nonetheless, because the cost and benefit effects are gradual and long-term, it is impossible to quantify them all. TEA of ENPs is based on the nanosize and activity of the NPs (Serrano et al., 2009). An analysis of ENPs would consider the industry's development and entry costs and the industry's potential profitability in terms of time and perspective. The expenditures have both long and short ENPs sustainability general, and detailed scientific and technical research helps enhance biogas production from the AD process. The investigation of the economic consequences of new technologies, particularly their long-term sustainability of ENPs in the AD process with cost-effectiveness, is challenging, although transition state of ENPs is critical in nanotechnology-based industries (Serrano et al., 2009).

The concept of life cycle assessment (LCA) developed from an economic and social standpoint of ENPs role in the AD process. LCA of ENPs outputs, environmental impacts, and the amount of energy required can all be considered inputs to the AD process. The green energy production process needs to prepare various ENPs with cost-effective and long sustainability in the AD process. ENPs production needs to develop cheaper methods of manufacturing for future energy costs. The "life cycle assessment" or "energy life cycle analysis" method is a rigorous way to study a product's environmental impacts, and it can be done from the cradle to the grave (Aziz et al., 2019). For product design evaluation, empirical testing has gained acceptance as a viable alternative to theoretical approaches. The entire life cycle of LCA includes the following steps: (1) definition of the objective and framework; (2) data collection; (3) impact assessment; and (4) results analysis (Koido et al., 2018; Ruiz et al., 2018). It can also be used to conduct in-depth analyses of techniques, technologies, and products to assess their overall environmental impact. As a result, the LCA method can calculate greenhouse gas (GHG) emissions from a manufacturing process (Aziz et al., 2019). The LCA is a tool for determining the environmental impact of ENPs and the long-term viability of biogas manufacturing processes in the AD process. LCA can be used to calculate GHG emission balances ENPs activity sustainability and microbes interaction in the AD process (Eduok et al., 2017).

12.4.2 Challenges of engineered nanoparticles

The main impediments to workplace creativity are the environment, labor, and human health and safety. ENPs hold the promise of a plethora of new ideas and applications, but it is forced to confront and accept the field's current limitations and challenges (Paul & Dutta, 2018). The unintended consequences of ENPs on human health and the environment must be weighed against the technology once it becomes available. A user of ENPs should try to reduce the risks that NPs will introduce during the design stage, rather than after they have already embedded themselves in the roadbed (i.e., as a by-product of the pavement manufacture or the product itself has been produced). The following are five design principles for safe ENPs, which state that:

Reduction (evaluate the option to use nanosized ENPs product maintain with their functionality).

Encapsulation (enclose a potential hazardous ENPs with material that should be less hazardous).

Functionalization (ENPs molecule bond changes their properties with the functionalization and reduces the hazard).

Innovative alternative materials (identify an alternative material that can be used to replace the hazardous ENPs).

Size, surface, and structure (change the size, surface, or structure to reduce the hazard potential of the ENPs while maintaining its functionality).

Another significant application of ENPs in nanotechnology is the vast scope of research and development. It can be used on a variety of ENPs for energy production. Considering ENPs applying nanotechnology to pavements, it's essential to consider the engineer's unique working environment in dealing with large amounts of material. The overall effects and properties of ENPs on manufacturing capacity, performance, and performance use bulk materials and binders to ensure that the beneficial properties are retained and affordable (Forgács et al., 2012; Mao et al., 2015; Sekoai et al., 2019).

12.5 Conclusion

Several ENP has been mentioned as biogas additives, depending on the method of AD. Various ENPs (metal NPs, zerovalent NPs, and carbon-based NPs) were divided into categories by the AD process. The concentration, types, and size of metal ENPs, as well as the types of NPs in combination, were found to have an impact on biogas production. An increase in the use of ENPs in everyday life increases the waste-to-energy production from biomass or wastewater. ENPs could be potentially active in the biomass and could be reused when present in higher concentrations (mg/L) in the AD process. ENPs impact treatment methods, including lowering the efficacy of microbes in secondary treatment, causing sedimentation, and increasing turbidity in AD sewage treatment. In this present article, a comprehensive study was conducted on the role of ENPs in the AD process. TEA on the synthesis method of highly active, sustainable ENPs and application on AD process for increased biogas production.

Acknowledgment

The authors wish to express their appreciation to Malaysian Higher Education and Universiti Malaysia Pahang (UMP) for providing financial support (RACER/1/2019/TK10/UMP//1, RDU192614).

Declaration of competing interest

The authors declare that they have no known competing financial interests or personal relationships that could have appeared to influence the work reported in this paper. All listed authors are qualified for authorship and mutually agree to submit this article for consideration. Each author has participated and contributed sufficiently to take responsibility for every portion of the content.

References

Abdelsalam, E., Samer, M., Attia, Y. A., Abdel-Hadi, M. A., Hassan, H. E., & Badr, Y. (2016). Comparison of nanoparticles effects on biogas and methane production from anaerobic digestion of cattle dung slurry. *Renewable Energy, 87*, 592–598. Available from https://doi.org/10.1016/j.renene.2015.10.053.

Abdelwahab, T. A. M., Mohanty, M. K., Sahoo, P. K., & Behera, D. (2020). Impact of iron nanoparticles on biogas production and effluent chemical composition from anaerobic digestion of cattle manure. *Biomass Conversion and Biorefinery*. Available from https://doi.org/10.1007/s13399-020-00985-7.

Adams, L. K., Lyon, D. Y., & Alvarez, P. J. J. (2006). Comparative eco-toxicity of nanoscale TiO_2, SiO_2, and ZnO water suspensions. *Water Research, 40*, 3527–3532. Available from https://doi.org/10.1016/j.watres.2006.08.004.

Akuzawa, M., Hori, T., Haruta, S., Ueno, Y., Ishii, M., & Igarashi, Y. (2011). Distinctive responses of metabolically active microbiota to acidification in a thermophilic anaerobic digester. *Microbial Ecology, 61*, 595–605. Available from https://doi.org/10.1007/s00248-010-9788-1.

Amiri, L., Abdoli, M. A., Gitipour, S., & Madadian, E. (2017). The effects of co-substrate and thermal pretreatment on anaerobic digestion performance. *Environmental Technology (United Kingdom), 38*, 2352–2361. Available from https://doi.org/10.1080/09593330.2016.1260643.

Arsova, L., Themelis, N. J., & Chandran, K. (2010). *Anaerobic digestion of food waste: Current status, problems and an alternative product. Thesis*. Available from http://citeseerx.ist.psu.edu/viewdoc/download?doi=10.1.1.462.7158&rep=rep1&type=pdf.

Auffan, M., Rose, J., Wiesner, M. R., & Bottero, J. Y. (2009). Chemical stability of metallic nanoparticles: A parameter controlling their potential cellular toxicity in vitro. *Environmental Pollution*. Available from https://doi.org/10.1016/j.envpol.2008.10.002.

Aziz, N. I. H. A., Hanafiah, M. M., & Gheewala, S. H. (2019). A review on life cycle assessment of biogas production: Challenges and future perspectives in Malaysia. *Biomass and Bioenergy, 122*, 361–374. Available from https://doi.org/10.1016/j.biombioe.2019.01.047.

Basiuk, V. A., & Basiuk, E. V. (2015). Green processes for nanotechnology: From inorganic to bioinspired nanomaterials. *Green Processes for Nanotechnology: From Inorganic to Bioinspired Nanomaterials*, 1–446. Available from https://doi.org/10.1007/978-3-319-15461-9.

Batstone, D. J., Puyol, D., Flores-Alsina, X., & Rodríguez, J. (2015). Mathematical modelling of anaerobic digestion processes: Applications and future needs. *Reviews in Environmental Science and Biotechnology, 14*, 595–613. Available from https://doi.org/10.1007/s11157-015-9376-4.

Besha, A. T., Liu, Y., Bekele, D. N., Dong, Z., Naidu, R., & Gebremariam, G. N. (2020). Sustainability and environmental ethics for the application of engineered nanoparticles. *Environmental Science & Policy, 103*, 85–98. Available from https://doi.org/10.1016/j.envsci.2019.10.013.

Boone, D. R., Johnson, R. L., & Liu, Y. (1989). Diffusion of the interspecies electron carriers H_2 and formate in methanogenic ecosystems and its implications in the measurement of km for H_2 or formate uptake. *Applied and Environmental Microbiology, 55*, 1735–1741. Available from https://doi.org/10.1128/aem.55.7.1735-1741.1989.

Capson-Tojo, G., Moscoviz, R., Ruiz, D., Santa-Catalina, G., Trably, E., Rouez, M., Crest, M., Steyer, J. P., Bernet, N., Delgenès, J. P., & Escudié, R. (2018). Addition of granular activated carbon and trace elements to favor volatile fatty acid consumption during anaerobic digestion of food waste. *Bioresource Technology, 260*, 157–168. Available from https://doi.org/10.1016/j.biortech.2018.03.097.

Chen, Y., Cheng, J. J., & Creamer, K. S. (2008). Inhibition of anaerobic digestion process: A review. *Bioresource Technology*. Available from https://doi.org/10.1016/j.biortech.2007.01.057.

Chen, Y., Yang, Z., Zhang, Y., Xiang, Y., Xu, R., Jia, M., Cao, J., & Xiong, W. (2020). Effects of different conductive nanomaterials on anaerobic digestion process and microbial community of sludge. *Bioresource Technology*, 304. Available from https://doi.org/10.1016/j.biortech.2020.123016.

Cheng, Q., & Call, D. F. (2016). Hardwiring microbes: Via direct interspecies electron transfer: Mechanisms and applications. *Environmental Science: Processes & Impacts*. Available from https://doi.org/10.1039/c6em00219f.

Choi, S., Johnston, M. V., Wang, G. S., & Huang, C. P. (2017). Looking for engineered nanoparticles (ENPs) in wastewater treatment systems: Qualification and quantification aspects. *Science of the Total Environment, 590–591*, 809–817. Available from https://doi.org/10.1016/j.scitotenv.2017.03.061.

Eduok, S., Ferguson, R., Jefferson, B., Villa, R., & Coulon, F. (2017). Aged-engineered nanoparticles effect on sludge anaerobic digestion performance and associated microbial communities. *Science of the Total Environment, 609*, 232–241. Available from https://doi.org/10.1016/j.scitotenv.2017.07.178.

Eduok, S., Martin, B., Villa, R., Nocker, A., Jefferson, B., & Coulon, F. (2013). Evaluation of engineered nanoparticle toxic effect on wastewater microorganisms: Current status and challenges. *Ecotoxicology and Environmental Safety*. Available from https://doi.org/10.1016/j.ecoenv.2013.05.022.

Faisal, S., Yusuf Hafeez, F., Zafar, Y., Majeed, S., Leng, X., Zhao, S., Saif, I., Malik, K., & Li, X. (2018). A review on nanoparticles as boon for biogas producers—Nano fuels and biosensing monitoring. *Applied Sciences, 9*, 59. Available from https://doi.org/10.3390/app9010059.

Farré, M., Sanchís, J., & Barceló, D. (2011). Analysis and assessment of the occurrence, the fate and the behavior of nanomaterials in the environment. *TrAC Trends in Analytical Chemistry, 30*, 517–527. Available from https://doi.org/10.1016/j.trac.2010.11.014.

Forgács, G., Pourbafrani, M., Niklasson, C., Taherzadeh, M. J., & Hováth, I. S. (2012). Methane production from citrus wastes: Process development and cost estimation. *Journal of Chemical Technology & Biotechnology, 87*, 250–255. Available from https://doi.org/10.1002/jctb.2707.

Garron, A., Al Maksoud, W., Larabi, C., Arquillière, P., Szeto, K. C., Walter, J. J., & Santini, C. C. (2015). Direct thermo-catalytic transformation of pine wood into low oxygenated fuel: Influence of the support. *Catalysis Today, 255*, 75–79. Available from https://doi.org/10.1016/j.cattod.2014.10.055.

Günther, A., Huth, V., Jurasinski, G., & Glatzel, S. (2015). The effect of biomass harvesting on greenhouse gas emissions from a rewetted temperate fen. *GCB Bioenergy, 7*, 1092–1106. Available from https://doi.org/10.1111/gcbb.12214.

Jaziri, N., Boughamoura, A., Müller, J., Mezghani, B., Tounsi, F., & Ismail, M. (2020). A comprehensive review of thermoelectric generators: Technologies and common applications. *Energy Reports*, *6*, 264–287. Available from https://doi.org/10.1016/j.egyr.2019.12.011.

Kato, S., Hashimoto, K., & Watanabe, K. (2012). Methanogenesis facilitated by electric syntrophy via (semi)conductive iron-oxide minerals. *Environmental Microbiology*, *14*, 1646–1654. Available from https://doi.org/10.1111/j.1462-2920.2011.02611.x.

Klaine, S. J., Alvarez, P. J. J., Batley, G. E., Fernandes, T. F., Handy, R. D., Lyon, D. Y., Mahendra, S., McLaughlin, M. J., & Lead, J. R. (2008). Nanomaterials in the environment: Behavior, fate, bioavailability, and effects. *Environmental Toxicology and Chemistry*, *27*, 1825–1851. Available from https://doi.org/10.1897/08-090.1.

Koido, K., Takeuchi, H., & Hasegawa, T. (2018). Life cycle environmental and economic analysis of regional-scale food-waste biogas production with digestate nutrient management for fig fertilisation. *Journal of Cleaner Production*, *190*, 552–562. Available from https://doi.org/10.1016/j.jclepro.2018.04.165.

Kong, X., Wei, Y., Xu, S., Liu, J., Li, H., Liu, Y., & Yu, S. (2016). Inhibiting excessive acidification using zero-valent iron in anaerobic digestion of food waste at high organic load rates. *Bioresource Technology*, *211*, 65–71. Available from https://doi.org/10.1016/j.biortech.2016.03.078.

Lee, J. Y., Lee, S. H., & Park, H. D. (2016). Enrichment of specific electro-active microorganisms and enhancement of methane production by adding granular activated carbon in anaerobic reactors. *Bioresource Technology*, *205*, 205–212. Available from https://doi.org/10.1016/j.biortech.2016.01.054.

Lee, S. H., Kang, H. J., Lee, Y. H., Lee, T. J., Han, K., Choi, Y., & Park, H. D. (2012). Monitoring bacterial community structure and variability in time scale in full-scale anaerobic digesters. *Journal of Environmental Monitoring*, *14*, 1893–1905. Available from https://doi.org/10.1039/c2em10958a.

Lee, Y. J., & Lee, D. J. (2019). Impact of adding metal nanoparticles on anaerobic digestion performance – A review. *Bioresource Technology*. Available from https://doi.org/10.1016/j.biortech.2019.121926.

Li, Y., Chen, Y., & Wu, J. (2019). Enhancement of methane production in anaerobic digestion process: A review. *Applied Energy*, *240*, 120–137. Available from https://doi.org/10.1016/j.apenergy.2019.01.243.

Li, Y., Park, S. Y., & Zhu, J. (2011). Solid-state anaerobic digestion for methane production from organic waste. *Renewable and Sustainable Energy Reviews*. Available from https://doi.org/10.1016/j.rser.2010.07.042.

Liang, Z., Das, A., & Hu, Z. (2010). Bacterial response to a shock load of nanosilver in an activated sludge treatment system. *Water Research*, *44*, 5432–5438. Available from https://doi.org/10.1016/j.watres.2010.06.060.

Lin, R., Cheng, J., Zhang, J., Zhou, J., Cen, K., & Murphy, J. D. (2017). Boosting biomethane yield and production rate with graphene: The potential of direct interspecies electron transfer in anaerobic digestion. *Bioresource Technology*, *239*, 345–352. Available from https://doi.org/10.1016/j.biortech.2017.05.017.

Liu, S., Zeng, T. H., Hofmann, M., Burcombe, E., Wei, J., Jiang, R., Kong, J., & Chen, Y. (2011). Antibacterial activity of graphite, graphite oxide, graphene oxide, and reduced graphene oxide: Membrane and oxidative stress. *ACS Nano*, *5*, 6971–6980. Available from https://doi.org/10.1021/nn202451x.

Liu, Y., Zhang, Y., Quan, X., Li, Y., Zhao, Z., Meng, X., & Chen, S. (2012). Optimization of anaerobic acidogenesis by adding Fe0 powder to enhance anaerobic wastewater treatment. *Chemical Engineering Journal*, *192*, 179–185. Available from https://doi.org/10.1016/j.cej.2012.03.044.

Fermoso, F. G., Van Hullebusch, E., Collins, G., Roussel, J., Mucha, A. P., & Esposito, G. (2019). Chapter 3 - Trace element enzymes in reactions essential for anaerobic digestion. *Trace elements in anaerobic biotechnologies*. Available from https://library.oapen.org/bitstream/id/0d1b9b0e-e497-4c41-b931-c0761718e282/wio9781789060225.pdf.

Luo, C., Lü, F., Shao, L., & He, P. (2015). Application of eco-compatible biochar in anaerobic digestion to relieve acid stress and promote the selective colonization of functional microbes. *Water Research*, *68*, 710–718. Available from https://doi.org/10.1016/j.watres.2014.10.052.

Ma, L., Zhou, L., Ruan, M. Y., Gu, J. D., & Mu, B. Z. (2019). Simultaneous methanogenesis and acetogenesis from the greenhouse carbon dioxide by an enrichment culture supplemented with zero-valent iron. *Renewable Energy*, *132*, 861–870. Available from https://doi.org/10.1016/j.renene.2018.08.059.

Mao, C., Feng, Y., Wang, X., & Ren, G. (2015). Review on research achievements of biogas from anaerobic digestion. *Renewable and Sustainable Energy Reviews*, *45*, 540–555. Available from https://doi.org/10.1016/j.rser.2015.02.032.

Martínez-Castañón, G. A., Niño-Martínez, N., Martínez-Gutierrez, F., Martínez-Mendoza, J. R., & Ruiz, F. (2008). Synthesis and antibacterial activity of silver nanoparticles with different sizes. *Journal of Nanoparticle Research*, *10*, 1343–1348. Available from https://doi.org/10.1007/s11051-008-9428-6.

Morgan, T. J., Youkhana, A., Turn, S. Q., Ogoshi, R., & Garcia-Pérez, M. (2019). Review of biomass resources and conversion technologies for alternative jet fuel production in Hawai'i and tropical regions. *Energy and Fuels*, *33*, 2699–2762. Available from https://doi.org/10.1021/acs.energyfuels.8b03001.

Mu, H., & Chen, Y. (2011). Long-term effect of ZnO nanoparticles on waste activated sludge anaerobic digestion. *Water Research*, *45*, 5612–5620. Available from https://doi.org/10.1016/j.watres.2011.08.022.

Mu, H., Chen, Y., & Xiao, N. (2011). Effects of metal oxide nanoparticles (TiO_2, Al_2O_3, SiO_2 and ZnO) on waste activated sludge anaerobic digestion. *Bioresource Technology*, *102*, 10305–10311. Available from https://doi.org/10.1016/j.biortech.2011.08.100.

Myszograj, S., Stadnik, A., & Płuciennik-Koropczuk, E. (2019). The influence of trace elements on anaerobic digestion process. *Civil and Environmental Engineering Reports*, *28*, 105–115. Available from https://doi.org/10.2478/ceer-2018-0054.

Parthasarathy, P., & Narayanan, S. K. (2014). Effect of hydrothermal carbonization reaction parameters on. *Environmental Progress & Sustainable Energy*, *33*, 676–680. Available from https://doi.org/10.1002/ep.

Paul, S., & Dutta, A. (2018). Challenges and opportunities of lignocellulosic biomass for anaerobic digestion. *Resources, Conservation & Recycling*. Available from https://doi.org/10.1016/j.resconrec.2017.12.005.

Pelletier, D. A., Suresh, A. K., Holton, G. A., McKeown, C. K., Wang, W., Gu, B., Mortensen, N. P., Allison, D. P., Joy, D. C., Allison, M. R., Brown, S. D., Phelps, T. J., & Doktycz, M. J. (2010). Effects of engineered cerium oxide nanoparticles on bacterial growth and viability. *Applied and Environmental Microbiology*, *76*, 7981–7989. Available from https://doi.org/10.1128/AEM.00650-10.

Qiang, H., Lang, D. L., & Li, Y. Y. (2012). High-solid mesophilic methane fermentation of food waste with an emphasis on iron, cobalt, and nickel requirements. *Bioresource Technology*, *103*, 21–27. Available from https://doi.org/10.1016/j.biortech.2011.09.036.

Ribeiro, F., Gallego-Urrea, J. A., Jurkschat, K., Crossley, A., Hassellöv, M., Taylor, C., Soares, A. M. V. M., & Loureiro, S. (2014). Silver nanoparticles and silver nitrate induce high toxicity to *Pseudokirchneriella subcapitata, Daphnia magna* and *Danio rerio*. *Science of the Total Environment*, *466–467*, 232–241. Available from https://doi.org/10.1016/j.scitotenv.2013.06.101.

Ruiz, D., San Miguel, G., Corona, B., Gaitero, A., & Domínguez, A. (2018). Environmental and economic analysis of power generation in a thermophilic biogas plant. *Science of the Total Environment, 633*, 1418–1428. Available from https://doi.org/10.1016/j.scitotenv.2018.03.169.

Sekoai, P. T., Ouma, C. N. M., du Preez, S. P., Modisha, P., Engelbrecht, N., Bessarabov, D. G., & Ghimire, A. (2019). Application of nanoparticles in biofuels: An overview. *Fuel, 237*, 380–397. Available from https://doi.org/10.1016/j.fuel.2018.10.030.

Serrano, E., Rus, G., & García-Martínez, J. (2009). Nanotechnology for sustainable energy. *Renewable and Sustainable Energy Reviews, 13*, 2373–2384. Available from https://doi.org/10.1016/j.rser.2009.06.003.

Shen, L., Zhao, Q., Wu, X., Li, X., Li, Q., & Wang, Y. (2016). Interspecies electron transfer in syntrophic methanogenic consortia: From cultures to bioreactors. *Renewable and Sustainable Energy Reviews*. Available from https://doi.org/10.1016/j.rser.2015.10.102.

Shi, Z., Nurmi, J. T., & Tratnyek, P. G. (2011). Effects of nano zero-valent iron on oxidation-reduction potential. *Environmental Science & Technology, 45*, 1586–1592. Available from https://doi.org/10.1021/es103185t.

Sinha, R., Karan, R., Sinha, A., & Khare, S. K. (2011). Interaction and nanotoxic effect of ZnO and Ag nanoparticles on mesophilic and halophilic bacterial cells. *Bioresource Technology, 102*, 1516–1520. Available from https://doi.org/10.1016/j.biortech.2010.07.117.

Slavin, Y. N., Asnis, J., Häfeli, U. O., & Bach, H. (2017). Metal nanoparticles: Understanding the mechanisms behind antibacterial activity. *Journal of Nanobiotechnology*. Available from https://doi.org/10.1186/s12951-017-0308-z.

Suanon, F., Sun, Q., Mama, D., Li, J., Dimon, B., & Yu, C. P. (2016). Effect of nanoscale zero-valent iron and magnetite (Fe3O4) on the fate of metals during anaerobic digestion of sludge. *Water Research, 88*, 897–903. Available from https://doi.org/10.1016/j.watres.2015.11.014.

Throbäck, I. N., Johansson, M., Rosenquist, M., Pell, M., Hansson, M., & Hallin, S. (2007). Silver (Ag^+) reduces denitrification and induces enrichment of novel *nirK* genotypes in soil. *FEMS Microbiology Letters, 270*, 189–194. Available from https://doi.org/10.1111/j.1574-6968.2007.00632.x.

Vögeli, Y., Riu, C., Gallardo, A., Diener, S., & Zurbrügg, C. (2014). Anaerobic digestion of biowaste in developing countries. *Sandec: Department of Water and Sanitation in Developing Countries*. Available from https://doi.org/10.13140/2.1.2663.1045.

Vyrides, I., Andronikou, M., Kyprianou, A., Modic, A., Filippeti, A., Yiakoumis, C., & Samanides, C. G. (2018). CO2 conversion to CH4 using zero valent iron (ZVI) and anaerobic granular sludge: Optimum batch conditions and microbial pathways. *Journal of CO_2 Utilization, 27*, 415–422. Available from https://doi.org/10.1016/j.jcou.2018.08.023.

Wang, C., Zhang, Y., Wang, Y., & Zhao, Y. (2017). Comparative studies of non-noble metal modified mesoporous M-Ni-CaO-ZrO2(M = Fe, Co, Cu) catalysts for simulated biogas dry reforming. *Chinese Journal of Chemistry, 35*, 113–120. Available from https://doi.org/10.1002/cjoc.201600609.

Wang, T., Zhang, D., Dai, L., Chen, Y., & Dai, X. (2016). Effects of metal nanoparticles on methane production from waste-activated sludge and microorganism community shift in anaerobic granular sludge. *Scientific Reports, 6*, 1–10. Available from https://doi.org/10.1038/srep25857.

Yamada, C., Kato, S., Ueno, Y., Ishii, M., & Igarashi, Y. (2015). Conductive iron oxides accelerate thermophilic methanogenesis from acetate and propionate. *Journal of Bioscience and Bioengineering, 119*, 678–682. Available from https://doi.org/10.1016/j.jbiosc.2014.11.001.

Zayed, G., & Winter, J. (2000). Inhibition of methane production from whey by heavy metals – Protective effect of sulfide. *Applied Microbiology and Biotechnology*, *53*, 726–731. Available from https://doi.org/10.1007/s002530000336.

Zhao, Z., Zhang, Y., Li, Y., Dang, Y., Zhu, T., & Quan, X. (2017). Potentially shifting from interspecies hydrogen transfer to direct interspecies electron transfer for syntrophic metabolism to resist acidic impact with conductive carbon cloth. *Chemical Engineering Journal*, *313*, 10–18. Available from https://doi.org/10.1016/j.cej.2016.11.149.

Zou, H., Jiang, Q., Zhu, R., Chen, Y., Sun, T., Li, M., Zhai, J., Shi, D., Ai, H., Gu, L., & He, Q. (2020). Enhanced hydrolysis of lignocellulose in corn cob by using food waste pretreatment to improve anaerobic digestion performance. *Journal of Environmental Management*, *254*, 109830. Available from https://doi.org/10.1016/j.jenvman.2019.109830.

Index

Note: Page numbers followed by "*f*" and "*t*" refer to figures and tables, respectively.

FSC
www.fsc.org
MIX
Papier | Fördert
gute Waldnutzung
FSC® C083411

Kolibri 360 GmbH
Ferdinand-Jühlke-Straße 7
99095 Erfurt, Deutschland
produktsicherheit@kolibri360.de